Endorsements

I congratulate you on writing this timely work. This will promote better mutual understanding between America and Asia.

Tommy Koh, *Singapore Ambassador to the U.N. and U.S.*

Your book covers a broad range of topics that I am sure many…will find very useful. I certainly agree with you on the importance of mutual understanding, which [this] book serves to promote.

Clark T. Randt, Jr., *U.S. Ambassador to China*

I greatly appreciate your efforts in sharing with other people your opinion and experience on the exchanges between different peoples and cultures. It is so important for us to better understand each other while striving to build a better world for all.

Zhou Wenzhong, *China Ambassador to U.S.*

A to Z is by a scholar of globalization. Raised and schooled in India and widely traveled, I believe that discrimination is based on ignorance. [This book] tears at this veil and is as objective as is humanly possible. The message is clear, the text has flow and the language is easy to understand. Readers will find this book useful, no matter which portal they would like to enter from.

Dr. Stephen Gill, *poet, novelist and literary critic*

Misunderstandings often happen needlessly due to ignorance and differences in cultures. I really wish I had read this book when I lived in China in order to learn more about the U.S. Since moving to America and getting my MBA, it is not too late because there is so much to learn from *A to Z*. I highly recommend this book that could change your life!

Lily Lang, *financial analyst, Washington, D.C.*

I found this book refreshingly different from the general run of books in this genre because it shows both Americans and foreigners warts and all!

Mohammad Vazeeruddin, *India journalist; former Associate Editor*, The Tribune

The *A to Z* chapters are nicely written and are very informative. The language is simple and lucid and presented in a nice manner with fine sequence. The writer's efforts of thorough research are praiseworthy. It is, in short, a realistic bible of modern America.

Jay Gajjar, *India language professor, writer of three hundred short stories*

I've lived in America 20 years. I took ESL [English as a Second Language] classes for three years and studied five years with a tutor. Until reading *A to Z*, I never found a book to help me with my grammar, pronunciation, phrasing and other essential speaking skills. It also helped me understand important American culture. So many of the questions I have always had about America and its people are answered in this book. I love this book's generous use of helpful hints. I highly recommend it for anyone who wants to learn more about America like I did.

Sarah Kim, Korean American business owner, Los Angeles

Teachers of English from our schools were selected to attend a unique and extensive course in which Mr. Lance Johnson was our educator. Not only did we want them to improve their command of English grammar and speech, but also to learn about America, its people and its culture. He used his *A to Z* book as a guide for his classes.

We were extremely pleased with the knowledge our teachers gained from this program. Their level of listening, reading, speaking, and writing English increased dramatically. Equally important, they gained confidence in using the English language and understanding Western ways.

His chapters on English grammar and speech identify common problems for foreigners and easy ways to overcome them. His book also summarizes the important aspects of American customs and culture that foreigners should know more about. This combined approach to learning was fun and informative for our teachers.

I strongly recommend Mr. Johnson's book to anyone who wants to learn about America and Western culture, its people, customs and language. It will certainly benefit those going to America or those who have contact with Americans in their homelands.

Tianchi Lu, Director-Suzhou Education Research Institute, Suzhou, China

What Foreigners Need To Know About America From A To Z

How To Understand Crazy American Culture, People,
Government, Business, Language And More

Lance Johnson

A to Z Publishing

Los Angeles, California, USA

Published by A to Z Publishing
COPYRIGHT © 2012 by Lance Johnson

ISBN-13: 978-1468172362
ISBN-10: 1468172360

BISAC: REF015000, SEL027000, SOC007000. (Additional: BUS025000, EDU015000, FOR007000, HIS036000, LAN006000, LAN018000, POL011000, POL040000, REF011000, REF026000)

Printed in the United States of America.

Available worldwide through Amazon.com.
    Austria – amazon.at
    Canada – amazon.ca
    France – amazon.fr
    Germany – amazon.de
    Italy – amazon.it
    Japan – amazon.co.jp
    Spain – amazon.es
    United Kingdom – amazon.co.uk
    United States – amazon.com

Book website: www.AmericaAtoZ.com

(This book is available at a discount when purchased in quantity for premiums, sales promotions, corporate training programs, or by schools or organizations for educational purposes. For information, including permission for excerpts, contact info@AmericaAtoZ.com.)

To increase mutual understanding, we need to understand each other's history and culture. If we do not, we will not understand why we make different choices, or why we do not think and behave in exactly the same way. Increased contacts and greater knowledge will reduce misunderstanding and lead to greater mutual respect.

Tommy Koh, former Singapore Ambassador to the U.N. and U.S.

America–
rather, the United States–
seems to me to be…resourceful,
adaptable,
maligned,
envied,
feared,
imposed upon.
It is warm-hearted,
over-friendly;
quick-witted,
lavish,
colorful;
given to extravagant speech
and gestures;
its people are travelers
and wanderers by nature,
moving,
shifting,
restless;
swarming in Fords,
in oceanliners;
craving entertainment;
volatile.
The chuckle among the nations of the world.

Edna Ferber, American author, 1887-1968

About the Author

Equation of life: Knowledge + Understanding +
Acceptance = A Better World for All. - Lance Johnson

Born and raised in America, Lance Johnson has long been fascinated with the history and culture of America and foreign countries and how they differ. Having visited 49 of the 50 U.S. states and traveled in 81 countries, he's learned among other things that the Black Sea, Red Sea, and the Blue Danube do not reflect those colors, and that Iceland might better be called Greenland and vice versa. He's also learned how America and its people are perceived abroad both correctly and incorrectly. And how America's perception of the rest of the world can vary, too.

A student of cultural differences, his travels also allow him to explore the difficulties foreigners face understanding American ways and language, and how that affects their success in dealing with us. He consults, teaches, and conducts seminars about the subjects in this book. He has an Ivy League graduate business degree and has studied at Oxford University in England.

The author and lecturer was a manager with an international management consulting firm and a corporate president for 26 years before taking up acting and writing. He now volunteers his services to nonprofit organizations and immigrants. He has appeared in movies, stage plays, national

Author at Yunnan Stone Forest outside Kunming, China.

commercials, and TV dramas, including a lead American role in a 28-part China TV production.

As a second-generation American, he shares his love of history and culture with visitors at a leading museum of history where he is a docent. He also golfs and skis, adores his grandchildren, and plays with Malibu Barbie, his third Great Dane, and Max, his Bulldog-Pug mix. He has also mentored underprivileged youth.

His American heroes include American visionary presidents Thomas Jefferson, Abraham Lincoln, and Teddy Roosevelt, and inventor Thomas Edison, all of whom had significant roles in the development of America and its culture as we know it today.

Equally important on his list are those foreigners who came to America and despite overwhelming discrimination, sacrifice, and deprivation contributed to the rich history of the early settlement of America. The legacy of all these immigrants resides throughout America today.

A Personal Note from the Author

I've witnessed my foreign heritage friends in America struggle to adjust to a new culture that's in stark contrast to their own. There is so much for them to learn as they get new jobs, open businesses, enter school, and make friends. Even our rules of etiquette pose difficulties for them.

When I teach overseas and travel the world, I'm always amazed at the interest people have in all things American. Our language, government, people, music, and films. Our behavior. Even our negative image on the world stage. They want to know why the rules for our crazy English language are not more consistent like their languages. They're puzzled why the U.S. feels it must be the policeman of the world. They want to know why Americans feel they are better than the rest of the world. Why we dislike foreigners but like wars. Why we don't share our wealth with the rest of the world. Why we are all fat and drive such big cars and if the two are related. I'm especially amused when they ask me why we say "excuse me" for the slightest of things because I don't think we do that as often as we should.

When we discuss my culture I learn about theirs, too. After years of these exchanges I searched for a book that I could recommend to them that condensed and simplified what America is all about. There wasn't one. So I began thinking about writing one, not quite sure I wanted to tackle such a big undertaking. That soon changed.

I was on a cruise ship in Asia and worried that our itinerary called for two stops in Vietnam. Did they still consider us their enemy? At one stop in Ho Chi Minh City my tour group and our Vietnamese guides ate box lunches in a park. Off in the distance I spotted hundreds of schoolgirls in immaculate white dresses riding rusty bicycles down a dirty street over lorded by dilapidated buildings.

Author at Giza, Egypt.

Because the Vietnamese lived under communism, I assumed these girls would be repressed just like their depressing surroundings. I was wrong. Smiling and chatting, they waved merrily to us as they peddled their way to school. Sitting there, I wondered how many other misconceptions I had about this country fourteen time zones away from home.

One tour guide sat down next to me and had non-stop questions about America. In order to advance in his job, he said he had to improve his knowledge about America and our language. He asked if I knew of a book like the one I had envisioned. His disappointment showed when I shook my head no. He then asked if he could e-mail me more questions about my country. Much to his delight I nodded yes. That was it. His infectious dedication became my dedication to start this book.

I not only wanted my book to enlighten those who merely have a curious interest about the world's last remaining superpower, but also to help further the personal lives of those who have dealings with Americans, either in the U.S. or abroad, like my new friend. Perhaps one day one of the school girls in white.

I learned other lessons from that visit. I assumed the Vietnamese still hated America for the devastation we wrought on their country four decades earlier, as did the French before us. We lost fifty-eight thousand soldiers. They lost millions. People were missing arms and legs. Buildings were still riddled with bullet holes. Twenty percent of the country had unexploded land mines that had killed 40,000 people since the war ended.

Author exploring archeological site in Peru.

In spite all these losses, these same people— even those with missing limbs—were genuinely friendly to us Americans. The tour guide explained, "The war is long over. We have all moved on." How nice it would be, I thought, if we all could follow the example set by these people. Maybe, just maybe, my book would help a little. More reasons for starting the book.

Alone that night in the silence of the ship's wood paneled library as we headed for Bangkok, I listed the objectives for my book that might someday be sitting on a foreigner's bookshelf. Maybe in my tour guide's hand. Here's what I wrote.

To serve the reader, this book must:

- Be an easy-to-read, fun resource for those who want to learn what America is really like, in ways that will increase understanding between peoples, whether they reside in their native countries or come to live, play, work, or study in America.
- Use simple language and sentences because English might be the reader's second language. (I made a note to myself with our slang word "KISS" that means keep it simple, stupid.)
- Use and explain slang words and sayings that foreigners might encounter and actually use themselves.
- Provide some good honest explaining on my part about America *and* about foreigners with no sugar coating. (I made a note to myself using another one of our slang sayings: "Be a straight shooter.")
- Make the reader feel he or she is one-on-one with me, just as my young friend was in the park.

- Provide comparisons of how we do things in the U.S. versus how they are done in other countries. I've learned from acting and teaching culture that comparisons are excellent learning tools.

- Have "From A to Z" in the title to convey the broad scope of the book, yet group and condense the 26 most important aspects about America so they are easily understood.

- Identify the true character and values of the American people. Discuss what's on our minds today and how we compare to people in other countries.

- Explain the underlying forces that helped mold our culture so others can understand the reasons *why* we are the way we are.

- Provide practical tips for enhancing one's daily experiences for those who visit or reside in America.

- Provide additional learning tools such as the names of recommended books, magazines, newspapers, films, and Internet sites.

- Explain how readers can improve their English grammar and speech if they have that need. Their ability to do this will enhance the image they project to Americans and other Westerners and perhaps further their chances for success.

- Provide important information for the millions of foreign students who attend school in the U.S. Explain our admission process and how they can improve their experience once here.

- Discuss our business environment for those who work for an American employer here or abroad, or for those who want to start a business or get a job in the U.S.

- Encourage readers by introducing them to many of America's leaders and achievers who have come from other countries.

- Provide pictures to further illustrate topics and make the reader feel at home.

I also reflected on a discussion I had with an American executive I sat next to on my flight to Asia where I was to board the cruise ship. He was in charge of overseas operations for a major U.S. corporation and lamented the difficulty he had teaching American business concepts to his foreign managers because of differing cultures. I told him I was thinking about writing a book for foreigners that would include a few pages on business matters. He said he would definitely have them read it if I should write it, but he suggested I expand the scope of my discussion

Author in remote Fiji village classroom.

xi

on business. He said this would make the book an even more valuable training aid that he could give to his foreign managers and executives. "Good hard facts," he said, "culture, plus the big picture, plus the details so they understand the how and why of our business culture, something we keep trying and trying to drive home, but because of cultural differences, they just don't get it and revert back to local customs." I took his advice.

When I returned home, I began my *A to Z* book that would take two years to write. Halfway through my writing, research, and consultations with dozens of experts in some fields, a major overseas publisher acquired the book's rights. I finally had the confirmation I wanted: What I was doing was indeed important. Another year and this undertaking would be finished and I knew it would be of help to that young Vietnamese tour guide and hopefully millions of others around the world.

∞

That was the past. Today, this updated version of that book is for everyone around the world who wants to learn more about America. And that includes Americans! Even I learned a lot about America from the research I did.

The importance of understanding our culture *and* the subtleties of our difficult English language cannot be overstressed for those who deal with Americans. As you learn about our culture and language, you will become more comfortable and confident in your relations with us, and that just might lead to further success for you and perhaps indirectly for us, too.

With this better understanding, we will all feel more positive and have mutual respect for one another. It has worked for my students and it will work for you.

With all of our cultural differences though, you'll be surprised to learn how much our countries—and we as human beings—have in

Author in Romanian countryside.

common on this third rock from the sun called Earth. After all, the song played at our Disneyland parks around the world is "It's A Small World After All."

Thanks for coming along on this journey with me. Thank you for allowing me to share my America with you. And thanks to all of you who shared your country with me. Peace. LJ

Note: Your comments about this book are welcome. Would you like to see something added in a later edition? Do you have an experience or knowledge to share that will help foreigners better understand America and succeed in their endeavors with us? Please e-mail your comments to info@AmericaAtoZ.com. Thanks.

Let's Get the Most Out of This Book

As the title suggests, this book is for "foreigners." But what *is* a foreigner? Are you one? Dictionaries say they are people who are not citizens of a country. But that doesn't work for this book. Instead, I simply define them as anyone who is not sufficiently familiar with our culture in the U.S. They may actually be U.S. citizens from foreign countries but don't have a good grasp of our culture as they would like to have. This includes my foreign-born, naturalized friends who have lived here 20 years and still struggle with our ways and language and want to know more.

By my definition, a foreigner could also be a first-generation American whose immigrant parents did not fully expose their children to our culture. They often do this with the best of intentions by sending them to their private native language schools here. They pay the price later when they enter the American mainstream. There are lots of other examples, too. You get the picture.

This book paints a unique, revealing picture of America and its people for foreigners who will benefit from a better understanding of our country. With this knowledge, they will be better informed and will create a nice, informed impression with their American counterparts. For some, this may lead to greater personal success in their dealings with us, including job promotions, schooling, and personal relationships.

Each of the 26 chapters' brush strokes contributes to the final painting of what America is all about and who we are. The chapters are grouped into four sections. (Individual books are also available for each section.)

- **Section I – America's Heritage**. This defines the historical background of *why* America and its people became who and what we are today. To understand complex America, it is important to gain this understanding.
- **Section II – America's Culture**. This describes who we are as a nation and how we conduct our everyday lives, ranging from customs and etiquette, to what's on the minds of Americans, to education, literature, movies, and a whole lot more. Even what we think of foreigners and what they think of us.
- **Section III – America's Business**. This explains our complex business environment, operations, customs, and why American businesses are successful around the world. Information is also provided for dealing with American business personnel, starting and operating a business of your own as many foreigners do, as well as how to increase your chances of being hired by an American employer here or abroad.
- **Section IV – America's Language**. For those with an interest, these chapters discuss practical ways to improve their English grammar, speech, writing, and communication skills, including accent reduction. Common English grammar

and speech errors made by foreigners are identified with simple tips for overcoming them and improving the image they create.

Emphasis throughout the book is on how we do things here in the U.S. and perhaps by Americans living in your country such as employers, co-workers, or teachers. Only you can be the judge of whether or not you adopt any aspect of our culture when dealing with us, either here or in your native country. We do not expect you to change your culture any more than you expect us to change ours when we deal with you. There is a middle ground, however, and an understanding of our differences and some adjustments might further your interests and enhance how we perceive and relate to each other.

Depending on your needs, you may choose to skip over some parts of the book, while others might have keen interest in that same information. Its breadth is designed to serve both of you.

Comparisons – Comparisons are made between America and other countries throughout the book. In no way am I promoting the U.S.—or the other countries for that matter. I do this to illustrate our similarities and to clarify our differences. Comparisons can help us see both cultures more clearly. I am merely painting a picture of the America I know and you may draw your own conclusions.

Please don't be offended if in the interest of brevity I compare how something is done in one country and do not include a comparison with your country. Also, if I compare America and "Asia," "South America," or "Europe," remember it is a general comparison and might not apply to your particular country, region, or family. You be the judge of whether or not my comparisons apply to your particular situation.

The same applies to my discussion of America. As you will learn, we are a country of diversity and change. So when I describe various aspects of our culture in the U.S., it is general in nature and there will always be exceptions, just like in your country.

I have had acting teachers who similarly compare a student's performance in class to a well-known actor in order to better illustrate the teacher's point. Once during rehearsals, a movie director tried to explain to me what he wanted from the complex character I was creating for the screen. I tried and tried for three days but couldn't give him what he wanted. Finally, he told me to be less like James Stewart (a famous American actor) and more like another famous actor. Suddenly I knew exactly what he was after. Comparisons provide a frame of reference for actors just as they do for those learning about a foreign culture.

Knowledge Foundation – This book provides a foundation upon which *you* can add to your knowledge about America on your own, which I hope you will do. I provide different tools to aid you.

- *Sayings and Phrases* – These are popular sayings and phrases we use. Technically they can be defined as aphorisms, slang, colloquialisms, proverbs, and idioms. But to make it easy for you to look them up in the Index, they are listed under "saying/proverb" or "slang/idiom." Sayings and proverbs usually impart advice or knowledge. Slang and idioms can be informal words or expressions that mean something different from what they appear to mean and are somewhat unique to a culture. For example, "honesty is the best policy" is listed under saying/proverb because it provides advice, while "cinch up your belt" is found under slang/idiom because it suggests difficult times are coming and is not necessarily referring to a belt. Also found under saying/proverb are quotations by famous people that you might hear us use and eventually use yourself, such as President Reagan's, "Tear down this wall, Mr. Gorbachev."
- *Books and Publications* – Names of our relevant books, newspapers, and magazines will help you explore a subject matter further.
- *Internet Sites* – Recommended sites are valuable learning tools, but they may change or disappear from time to time.

  Hint: If a recommended website address comes at the end of a sentence in this book, such as "…html." do not include the period at the end of the Internet address.

- *Movies* – Movies will give you added insight about America. They can be purchased, rented, downloaded, and viewed from Internet sites like www.netflix.com.
- *Surveys* – References are made to various studies and surveys of America and its people. Further research into these sites can expand your knowledge.
- *Successful Foreigners in the U.S.* – Some chapters provide information about foreigners who have achieved success in the U.S. Perhaps reading about them will inspire you.
- *Hints* – And finally, you will see "**Hints**:" throughout the book. They are my little helpers that give you personal pointers about how to further discuss or understand a given topic. Page numbers for hints to improve your conversation skills on specific topics are listed in the Index under "conversation Hints:".

I hope you have a good English dictionary. Some are now available for hand-held devices. The Merriam-Webster dictionaries are good ones and can be purchased online at http://amzn.to/GoodDictionary.

To understand how dollar amounts referred to translate to your currency, you can go to a website such as www.xe.com/ucc.

New Words And Phrases – You will learn new words or phrases in this book. Words that might be hard for you to pronounce are shown in brackets *[ ]* to simplify your recognizing and learning their syllables (single sounds in our words). For example, when we discuss the Appalachian Mountains, I give you the simple pronunciation that you see here *[app-ah-LAY-chee-un]*. The capital letters indicate the strongest stress in each word. Emphasis on syllables enhances your spoken English, which we discuss in Chapter Z on speaking better English.

I encourage my students to use 3x5 inch cards. On these cards you write everything from this book that you want to memorize. When you finish the book, you should have two to three hundred cards. A number of these entries can be found in the Index. I recommend a three-step process for what will become your "America File."

- *Step 1 – Record.* When you find words or phrases in **bold typeface**, that is your signal to write them on a 3x5 inch card along with an explanation of what they mean. Each word or topic gets its own card, even topics not in bold that you want to remember. For example, in the chapter on speech, we discuss the saying "tip of the iceberg" and how you can use it in your speech. Make a 3x5 card with a heading titled "tip of the iceberg," a description of what it means, and some sample sentences using it. You might file it under "Slang." Some students use the 3x5 card as a flashcard by writing the term on one side and the explanation on the reverse side so they can test themselves. (Some even transfer their cards to their computer or hand-held digital devices.)

- *Step 2 – Memorize.* Leave new cards on your desk, in your car, taped to your bicycle or scooter, taped to your bathroom mirror, or anywhere you will see them during the day. Do not put a card away in your file until you have used the word or topic in speech or writings and feel comfortable using it.

- *Step 3 – Review.* Occasionally go back through your cards and refresh your memory. You can even make this into a game. Have a friend randomly pull cards from your file and quiz you on them. Or quiz them. It might refresh your memory, too.

Expand your file with information you gather on your own from discussions with Americans or from what you pick up in our media. I have an immigrant friend who carries around a small tablet to record new things she learns each day. She often stops me at the end of my sentence, asks the meaning of the new word, records it, then tells me to continue. I love it! Who knows, you might end up writing your own book about America for people from your country.

Contents

Contents

SECTION II – AMERICA'S CULTURE

Contents

SECTION III – AMERICA'S BUSINESS

Contents

SECTION IV – AMERICA'S LANGUAGE

Importance of Understanding Cultural Differences

We have become not a melting pot but a beautiful mosaic.
Different people, different beliefs, different yearnings, different
hopes, different dreams. - Jimmy Carter, U.S. president 1977–1981

Our world is overflowing with hundreds of cultures and thousands of misconceptions and myths that we have about each other and our countries. America has had an enormous influx of people who brought these cultures and views with them. In fact, the U.S. allows more immigration than all other countries of the world combined. In 1970, one in twenty Americans was from a foreign country; today, one in nine. They might come to the U.S. to seek a better life, work for American employers, open branch offices or factories for their homeland employers, start their own businesses, or go to school. Others might work for American organizations in their homelands or have American teachers or neighbors there. Either way, an understanding of our culture and language can be important for them.

Unfortunately, with accelerating interdependency among our nations today, we simply do not know enough about each other's cultures and, as a result, our relationships suffer. As I have learned, a better understanding of each other will reveal the truth and, in turn, will benefit all.

I took a British visitor to a baseball game and tried to explain the game to him. I was surprised to learn it wasn't the easy task I thought it would be. When a Danish family visited me, we stopped at a McDonald's **drive thru** (where we order from and then eat it in the car) to eat breakfast on the way to a tourist attraction. They had never experienced this and asked why Americans don't slow down and take time to go inside and enjoy their meals as they do in Europe.

Author exploring ancient library ruins in Ephesus, Turkey.

And in Budapest, Hungary, I was shocked that I had to pay for a packet of McDonald's ketchup—something that's free in the U.S.—and how ketchup in Australia is sweeter than ours in the U.S. And how Coca-Cola's taste also varies around the world according to local culture, and how flashing the soles of your feet in Thailand is a big no-no. And the confusing time in Bulgaria when I learned they nod up and down to signify "no" and left to right for "yes," the exact opposite of what Americans do. And in India where drivers ignored stop signs and traffic lights, and in France...well, you get the point. This cultural diversity thing is fascinating.

And back home at a McDonald's restaurant where I eat now and then, most of the counter help are first generation Mexican Americans with limited English skills and familiarity with our slang terms. So when I took my half-empty coffee cup to the counterperson and asked her to "warm it up," she gave me a puzzled look, took the cup and handed it to the cook to put in the oven to heat it up. I informed her that the popular saying I used merely means to pour more hot coffee in it. There have been other similar misunderstandings with other workers there as well thanks to cultural differences.

Author teaching American culture/English in China.

A welcome dinner was held in my honor at the university in China where I was to teach American culture and language. The day before, I learned that the teaching assistant assigned to me had expressed to her boss and the staff that she wanted to someday study and teach in the U.S. for a few months to improve her English, as many foreigners do. Knowing this, I said jokingly at the dinner that I was going to take her back to the U.S. with me. Unfortunately, they thought I had a romantic interest in her. It took a couple of days to clarify the issue. My cultural lesson learned: Something as simple as humor varies in ways we do not expect. (Speaking of romance, even the finger on which we wear our wedding ring varies around the world.)

These cultural differences are enlightening. But they also make me realize how difficult it can be for a foreigner to understand complex America, or, as some foreigners say, crazy America. I also understand the difficulty of learning about America from a book as opposed to learning it firsthand.

Surveys suggest that the world is increasingly uncomfortable with U.S. policy and its dominant economic and political outreach, due in part to the Iraq War that started in 2003. It reveals that the U.S. has problems relating to countries whose *cultures* are very different, much older, and more traditional than our own. Those interviewed who had visited the U.S. or actually had relationships with us in business, education, or other matters had a more positive attitude toward the U.S.

Author on New Zealand sheep ranch.

This tells us that firsthand knowledge helps us better understand each other.

With this decline in overall American attractiveness, surveys show that American *culture* and American *values* have remained appealing. Perhaps our four most important virtues are gratitude, honesty, fairness, and kindness, which are expressed in our actions.

Understanding these factors, all of which are emphasized in this book, will contribute to your better understanding of true America and perhaps aid your advancement in our culture.

Americans realize we are a target of criticism on the world stage. Each year a Gallup Poll (www.gallup.com) asks us how we think America is viewed in the eyes of the rest of the world. When asked in 2012 if we were comfortable with the position of the U.S. in the world, only 53 percent were comfortable, up from 30 percent in 2008 at the end of President Bush's years.

Why do we have this negative image around the world? A frequent complaint from Europeans is that Americans don't know much about anyone but themselves. To a certain extent they are correct because most Americans only speak one language (only eight percent of our college students study a foreign language), have never been to another country (two-thirds of us have no passport), tend to concentrate on news in the U.S. (we are inundated with local and national newscasts), and are work-oriented (we work more hours per week than those in all other countries). Consequently, foreigners believe we don't care about other countries, which, as you will learn, is simply not true for the average American.

Author viewing Copper Canyon, Mexico.

We also live in a huge country with lots going on. Vast oceans separate us from the rest of the world. We have two friendly nations on our borders, one of which speaks English, and our economy is largely self-sufficient, so most of us do not interact with other countries. Consequently, our firsthand knowledge about the rest of the world is somewhat limited. But this is changing slowly as the world becomes more globalized.

At the same time, foreign visitors to the U.S. often comment how nice Americans are, which tends to contradict their earlier *perception* of us. As you will learn in later chapters, this ability to reach out to people of different backgrounds is embedded in our national character, even though it might not show all the time.

With this expanding contact between U.S. and foreign countries comes a need for better understanding of each other's

Author in ancient Ecuador village.

culture and language. This even has economic ramifications. For example, an officer of an outsourcing firm in Asia that handles customer service calls from Americans said, "When foreigners take calls from their respective countries, it helps that they [employees] know the *culture* of the person they are speaking to. That can often be the differentiating factor between a successful outsourcing company and a failure." This book gives those who must communicate with Americans the knowledge they need, and we will both benefit from this better understanding.

Foreign outsourcing firms also need people with a strong command of the English language—another topic of this book. U.S. computer maker Dell dropped an Asian outsourcing firm that answered calls from American customers. Why? U.S. customers complained that the technical support representatives were difficult to deal with because of thick accents and irritating scripted/repeated responses. (I can attest to that!) In fact, because of the broad extent of this communication problem we have with foreign call centers, there is now a law in the U.S. that a customer can ask for, and speak to, a native American if they so choose.

To counter these cultural and English language problems, some countries now have training institutes for call center workers. One instructor in Bangalore said, "We teach

Author learning Tahitian culture.

[our employees] about U.S. culture, the U.S. accent, and U.S. vowels and consonants." These accent-neutralization classes also incorporate geography lessons, regional dialects, and introductions to American culture—including holidays and baseball scores. This book addresses these very same topics and a **train load** (large amount) more to assist foreigners to succeed personally and economically in their dealings with us. Or, in some cases, to just simply understand America better.

CULTURAL MISCONCEPTIONS

Let there be no doubt, foreigners and Americans have misconceptions about each other. Lots of them. Here's a sampling of just a few cultural misunderstandings I have encountered and learned from, ranging from China to Germany to Walmart.

China – Long after World War II ended, I met a man in China who was born after the war. I told him I had relatives who served in the war and witnessed death, disease, monsoons, and enemy attacks to build the famous 1,300-kilometer Burma lifeline into China that saved the lives of millions of Chinese.

I was shocked when he told me the people of China will never forget the help of the U.S. and those Americans who lost their lives to save the Chinese people. Tears came to my eyes. In my mind, given the often-contentious relationship our two governments have had since 1949, I assumed the people of China today would be unaware of this helping hand from America. I was wrong. I learned a valuable lesson about

Author exploring Chinese culture.

cultural misconception. We must learn to differentiate between the people and the governments of our different nations when passing judgments on each other.

Germany – I asked a German couple in my travels if there was something about the U.S. they wanted to know more about or didn't understand, something I always ask foreigners I meet. They wanted to know why we all get along so well here. I was surprised by the question because we *do* have social problems here. A lot of them.

We spent an hour examining why they had this somewhat incorrect perception. First, Germany, like other European nations, now has workers from different cultures, particularly from North Africa or the Middle East, who are disliked by some. But their *perception* is that the U.S. has always welcomed foreigners, thus we get along well. The fact is we do have similar problems with immigrant workers in the U.S., especially illegal immigrants, something my friends were unaware of. Cultural anthropologists say this fear of immigrants is rooted in ignorance and prejudice. Secondly, we had a black president, which suggests that we all get along. And last, they were big fans of U.S. television shows with numerous minority actors. That contributed to their belief that we were accepting of minorities. So, their *perception* of America was slightly skewed, just as my perception of their country and people might be inaccurate because of my limited knowledge. They **turned the tables** (they did the asking) on me and asked if I had questions about Germany. Thinking about their cars, I wanted to know what it was about their culture that makes them such great engineers. They didn't have an answer. Sometimes I don't have answers about America either.

Morocco – In Morocco I became aware of my warped perception of Muslim culture caused by our media's focus on Islamic extremists and terrorism. I asked my Muslim guide why their Islamic mosques had three small metal balls stacked at the top of a pole on the roofs. He said for centuries they signified that Jews, Christians, and Muslims are sisters and brothers and must get along together. In fact, he was angry at the militant Islamic minority that has caused the world to have a negative view of Muslims today. The cultural lesson I learned: The actions of a minority, no matter where they are in the world, do not necessarily define the culture of the majority.

Author in Dubai.

South America – A tour guide asked me why we dare call ourselves "Americans" when all people in North and South *America* were "Americans." He thought we were self-centered for using this name. I explained that the "United States of America" is the only one of the three-dozen countries in North and South America with "America" in its country's name, plus it is snappier to pronounce than "The United States." Besides, it would be ungrammatical to say we are "United Statesians." He then apologized for his negative *perception* of Americans. Reflecting on this, I also realized that the world's common perception of America's large overreach may have **added fuel** (contributed) to his negative attitude about our absconding with this name.

Retailers – Cultural differences even affect businesses operations around the world. Walmart, the U.S. based retail giant, is one of the world's largest public corporations by revenue. Surprisingly, it has struggled in countries like South Korea, Germany, and Japan. It discovered that its formula for success in the U.S.—low prices, precise inventory control, and a vast array of merchandise—does not translate to markets and shoppers in different cultures. After nearly a decade of trying, Walmart **closed up shop** (ceased operating) in Germany (its first entry into Europe) in 2006 because it failed to become the one-stop shopping destination for Germans that it is for millions of Americans and shoppers in 15 other countries with its 8500 stores.

Trying to fix their problems there, they changed practices that are used successfully in other countries. They stopped requiring sales clerks to smile at customers—a practice that some male shoppers interpreted as flirting—and scrapped the morning employee group chant. Customers and employees found these and other things strange because Germans don't behave that way. Moreover, Walmart never established comfortable relations with its German labor unions and did not understand that companies and unions are closely connected there. This is unlike Walmart's stores in North America that are not unionized, but are today in other countries. Cultural lesson: The culture in one nation is not necessarily transferable to another nation, and it is important we understand our differences.

Walmart is still learning, as is Tesco, the British retail giant that recently closed numerous underperforming Fresh & Easy stores in California. They were hampered by cultural norms imported from Britain that proved mystifying to U.S. shoppers. Some of the stores' private-label products, for example, were more expensive than brand-name competition, a **no-no** (not acceptable) in American retailing. And much of the fresh produce was tightly wrapped in cellophane for freshness, something Americans view as lower quality than those in bulk. Further, their faulty computerized ordering system had stores running out of stock on everyday items; another big no-no in U.S. retailing.

Author studying ancient Greek stadium.

These factors would be **no big deal** (unimportant) in the U.K., but they did not translate well in the U.S. My grandfather had a whimsical motto he stressed to me growing up: As you go through life, whatever be your goal, keep your eye upon the donut, not upon the hole. In other words, first learn about and then keep focused on the important things in the culture in which you are dealing.

WHY WE HAVE MISCONCEPTIONS

Sign in a Delta Airline ramp to an airplane I was boarding overseas: *Understanding peoples' different values enables us to better serve our 100 million customers around the world.*

Why do we have these different values and misconceptions about each other? Putting aside the media, politics, longstanding myths and beliefs, and other man-controlled factors, some psychologists suggest that people in different parts of the world simply think differently. Consequently we view situations and each other differently, just as Walmart and Tesco are learning. For example:

- *Main Object* – Studies show that Westerners focus on a main object, while some cultures tend to see overall surroundings and the relationships between the main object and other things. So, when viewing a situation, Westerners typically categorize (such as animal types) while some cultures tend to see relationships (monkeys eat bananas). Such differences in thinking can disturb our social, political, and business relationships. As an example, foreigners will sometimes ask that a contract be modified as changing circumstances dictate. To most Westerners, **a deal is a deal** and is to be honored.

Author posing on award stand at Olympic Stadium, Athens.

- *Inferences* – We also draw inferences differently. In one study, a line graph was drawn that showed a rate of growth that was accelerating (the line got steeper to the right). Researchers then asked college students in the U.S. and Beijing whether they thought the growth rate would go up, go down, or stay the same. The Americans were more likely to predict a continued rise, based on trends, than were the Chinese who saw trends as likely to reverse. We all have these cultural experiences upon which we draw our own conclusions and let them enter into our perceptions of, and dealings with, others.

- *Principles* – Westerners guide their actions by generally accepted universal principles while some nationalities apply rules that are more appropriate to a specific situation. For instance, when asked what they would do about an employee whose work had been substandard for a year after 15 years of exemplary service, more than 75 percent of Americans and Canadians said they would let her go, but only 20 percent of Singaporeans and Koreans would part ways with her.

- *Basic Values* – Basic values about life in general vary between countries. The American Dream emphasizes autonomy, national pride, and material wealth, all of which affect how we conduct ourselves each day. In contrast, Europe's vision of the future emphasizes community and quality of life. While Americas value hard work, property ownership, and a somewhat unilateral foreign policy (which is slowly changing), Europeans champion fun and free time and multilateral foreign policy. So, it is easy to see how these cultural differences in everyday life affect how we behave and view each other.

Vietnam War – There is not a better example of the tragic consequences of cultural misconceptions than the Vietnam War in the late 1960s and early 70s that bitterly divided Americans. The American movie, *The Fog of War* (2003), won an Academy Award for Best Documentary. In the film, Robert McNamara, the U.S. Secretary of Defense during the war and the architect of its buildup, meets with his North Vietnamese counterpart and they admit they misinterpreted each other's motives. They concluded that the U.S. mistakenly viewed the North's invasion of South Vietnam as a communist move to conquer all of Southeast Asia. We called this the **Domino Theory** in which country after country would fall like tumbling dominos to the communists. His counterpart said it was nothing but a civil war, something the U.S. had gone through a hundred

Author in Sydney, Australia.

years prior. The war is yet another painful reminder of the consequences of not understanding each other's culture. Perhaps your country has reminders of its misunderstandings, too.

Are We Different? – Are we really that much different from the rest of the world? Or, are our differences cultural misconceptions? Or myths? A survey was recently taken to answer this question. Overall, it found that differences of opinion between Americans and others on a range of topics (happiness, religious conviction, and individualism, among others) are somewhat different but not shocking. Americans, it found, are less out of step with the global mainstream than we were a century ago. But because of our differences, we can be misinterpreted and not understood by the rest of the world whose cultures differ from ours. This is the same problem noted above that *we* have relating to cultures different than ours.

The survey also found that the most significant difference had to do with *individualism*. Americans tend to be more optimistic than most people about their ability to shape their own lives and more pessimistic about government action to solve social problems. This dates back to our founding by Europeans who wanted freedom from social, religious, and government restraints. As individualists today, we tend to be

Author in Abu Dhabi.

8

skeptical of organizations like the United Nations (only four out of ten of us believe it does a good job); but as optimists, we tend to underestimate the dangers and obstacles that lie ahead, as we did in Vietnam. These attitudes, the poll concluded, are likely to create enduring problems for Americans as long as "the most individualistic people on the planet continue to bear the greatest responsibility for solving problems that demand united global action."

> **Hint**: This concept of individualism is a major recurring theme throughout this book. It is important for foreigners to understand how and why it permeates our society if they want to understand why we behave the way we do in so many different situations. Nowhere is this more evident today than Americans taking a strong issue with China's censorship and suppression of human rights. Facebook, our Internet social network that allows one billion people around the world to express their opinions and keep in touch with others, is banned in China. We were shocked when China shut down Google.com because the American-based company refused to censor mail there. Our country was founded on independence, individualism, and freedom from censorship, and the belief that these tenets should extend to all of mankind. Rather than concede to China's demand, Google dropped their service there. We were proud.

Fear Of Immigrants – Along with cultural differences comes a growing fear of immigrants. Tensions over the presence of foreigners with different *cultures* and *values* are a real threat in nations around the world. With the creation of the Common Market, immigration barriers that once separated the various nations in Europe have been lowered and people are now free to seek opportunities anywhere in the Union. As a result, Germany now has a strong Turkish minority; France, a Libyan and Northern African minority. The U.K. has an India/Pakistani minority. A Norwegian anti-immigrant killed 77 countrymen in 2011 and a Swede three in 2012 saying the victims were traitors for embracing multiculturalism. Some of the European population in Australia and New Zealand perceive a rising tide of Asian and Pacific Island people who seek to reclaim their "European-occupied" lands. The native Maori there are regaining land and power just as the natives in our state of Hawaii are recovering their lands.

Author at Papeete archeological religious site in Tahiti.

And even in Hong Kong there is now a backlash against the millions of mainland Chinese tourists flooding the territory. They are accused by locals of littering, spitting, urinating in public, smoking in inappropriate places, and other breaches of etiquette that offend the more fastidious sensibilities of this British-infused culture. Meanwhile in the U.S., the immigration issue is focused on our porous Mexican border. We are passing increasingly strident laws in state after state to stop the illegal flow. In typical fashion, however, many Americans do not support this suppression of individual rights of illegal immigrants who want to start a new life in America. That's the *diversity* thing and *individual rights* that pop up again and again throughout this book.

Tommy Koh, the former Singapore Ambassador to the U.N. and the U.S. [and who endorsed this book], summarizes these misconceptions and basic differences between nations and peoples and the need for us to have a better understanding of each other:

> "Asians and Americans are poorly informed about each other…and inhabit different cultural boxes. Each box is filled with a people's history, memories, conventions, customs, traditions, habits, values, virtues and prejudices. Our cultural box determines the way we think and behave, the way we perceive and interpret reality, and the way we react to others. To increase mutual understanding…we need to understand each other's history and culture."

Tommy Koh

So, welcome to America as you begin your journey to learn more about my country with me at your side. You will also learn about the same history and cultural issues that Ambassador Koh refers to.

Now it's on to the first letter in *A to Z*. In Chapter A, you will learn about the heritage that shaped American culture and made us who and what we are today. To understand complex America, it is important to first understand this historical background. Perhaps your country contributed. As you will learn, many countries did.

SECTION I

AMERICA'S HERITAGE

History is a relentless master. It has no present, only the past rushing into the future. To try to hold fast is to be swept aside.

John F. Kennedy, U.S. president 1961-1963

A

WE THE PEOPLE

America lives in the heart of every man everywhere who
wishes to find a region where he will be free to work out his
destiny as he chooses. – Woodrow Wilson, U.S. president 1913-1921

What is America? What is an American? Ask a hundred people either here or abroad and you will get a hundred different answers. When General Eisenhower, leader of European allied forces in **WWII** (World War Two) and future president of the U.S., became president of Columbia University in the early 1950s, he assembled the faculty and told them *they* were the university, not the buildings, not the laboratories, not the libraries and other trappings.

And in 1863 during the Civil War between our northern and southern states, President Abraham Lincoln made a famous speech at a dedication of a burial ground for fallen soldiers. His **Gettysburg Address** is considered one of the most important speeches in our history (see Appendix 1 for full text). He concluded the 265-word speech with "of the people, by the people, and for the people" that defines what America is all about: the people.

U.S. Constitution.

In the same light, the first three words of our **Constitution** that defines the framework for our government says the same thing: We the people….

But, who are we? This chapter provides a broad overview of America's population—including foreigners—and how we compare to other nations. And you will learn more about us in each succeeding chapter.

SPIRIT OF THE PEOPLE

Americans have a competitive spirit that dates back four hundred years to our founding immigrants dissatisfied with life in their native countries. And for most of the past century this spirit has enforced our belief that the U.S. could be, and was, number one and we **sat on top the world** (were tops in our endeavors). This wasn't about boasting or competition with other nations, it was merely about achievement, an important American underpinning. But things changed. John F. Kennedy, campaigning for the presidency back in 1961, said, "The United States no longer carries the same image of a vital society on the move with its brightest days ahead." Campaigners for offices today still say the same thing. So do voters. But *are* we on a **downward slope** (things are declining)?

Our infrastructure ranks 23rd in the world. We rank 11th in spending for research and development (Germany is first). And according to the World Health Organization, we're 27th in life expectancy, 18th in diabetes, and first in obesity. We used to produce more patents than the rest of the world combined; we now produce half. A generation ago America had the highest percentage of college graduates in the world—today we are ninth. The U.S. is ranked 51st in science and math education. A few decades ago we were in the top echelons of all of these and many other societal markers.

We are still number one in some areas. We have the most guns, the largest debt, the largest military, and the most crime among rich countries. So, contrary to what some foreigners think, America does have its **warts** (unattractive things), something of concern to many of us. But, along with the warts we do have some good stuff.

Polls show the U.S. is the country most foreigners would like to immigrate to. (**Emigrate** means to leave a country; **immigrate** means to enter a country.) We still respond to growing competition around the world, including the glut of cheap labor. So our worker productivity has improved to where one American now produces as much as six Chinese workers, 30 percent more than Japanese and German workers, and 45 percent more than the average European Union worker. And while Japan has the most debt in relation to its gross economic output, the U.S. only ranks seventh.

So, **in a nutshell** (a summary), is the U.S.—make that *we the people*—on the decline as Kennedy said six decades ago and as some foreigners and Americans believe, or is the rest of the world merely catching up with us? It is both, depending on which portal you view America through. This book helps open those portals so you can see what is happening here and can intelligently discuss them with your American counterpart.

As you will learn, underlying our competitive spirit is the belief that individual pursuit of self-interest achieves the best results for a country as a whole, a concept that differs from some countries. Traveling in the former Soviet states that still have not recovered from the legacy of a controlling, centralized government reinforces that belief in me even more.

THE AMERICAN DREAM

You may have heard the popular term **American Dream** that refers to a concept that through hard work, courage, and determination one can achieve prosperity. It reflects who we are as a people and can be credited for our <u>prosperity</u> as a nation. Today, our widely held goals of home ownership, a good job, financial security, and civil and international stability further define the American Dream.

This concept was nonexistent in the homelands of the first Europeans who came to America and brought their dreams with them. Then, our pioneers took three hundred years to settle the country from the Atlantic to the Pacific Ocean in search of their individual dreams, too.

Horatio Alger was a prolific 19th-century American writer whose novels told of impoverished children rising to lives of respectable middle-class security and comfort, sometimes even vast wealth. We still use the Horatio Alger term to describe someone who has overcome great odds to achieve prosperity, including foreigners, some of whom are discussed in various chapters because of their achievements in the U.S.

But our Dream differs from other countries. As Europe emerges as an economic and cultural superpower, its beliefs and traits are often different from ours. Our Dream tends to be somewhat tied to religion, while the European Dream is somewhat secular. Europeans often remark that Americans "live to work," while Europeans "work to live." The average paid vacation time in Europe is now six weeks a year. By contrast, Americans, on average, receive two weeks or less and work longer hours. Our Dream emphasizes autonomy, national pride, and material wealth while Europe's vision of the future for many emphasizes community and quality of life.

IMMIGRANTS

America's history, peoples, and culture today cannot be separated from the history of our immigrants, beginning with Spanish settlers in the sixteenth century and French and English settlers in the seventeenth century. These relatively recent dates are in stark contrast to some countries with civilizations that began more than 4,500 years ago. Almost 60 million of our people today—more than a fifth of our total population—are immigrants or the children of immigrants who have influenced our cultural development.

Since our beginning, the U.S. has received over two-thirds of the world's immigrants: 70 million people. For this reason, America is called a **melting pot**. Since 1990 this influx of immigrants and the children they bore account for nearly 60 percent of our nation's population growth, with Asians one of our fastest growing minority groups.

Legal immigrants here number 850,000 each year; undocumented (illegal) immigrants are estimated to be half that number. They come from various countries seeking opportunities to improve their lives and create a foundation of success for their children to build upon. Along with their dreams, many bring their skills and a willingness to work hard to make their dreams a reality.

Eighteen countries continue to attract more than 70 percent of the potential migrants worldwide. Surveys show the U.S. as the top desired destination for adults who would like to migrate, followed by Canada, the United Kingdom, France, Spain, and Australia. If all of these adults worldwide actually did migrate, the U.S. would see a net population gain of 60 percent with 23 million from China, 17 million from India, and three million from Japan.

In the late nineteenth and early twentieth century, immigrants played an important role in our transition to an urban industrial economy. Also, our language, customs, and traditions today are derived in part from the blending of those who brought their cultures with them. As a result, American culture, like our language and foods, is a rich, complex mix. So, chances are pretty good that you might spot some familiar culture from your homeland somewhere in the U.S. or even in this book.

Nineteenth century American immigrants.

German is our largest heritage ancestry group in America (as it is in the European Union). When I watch documentary WWII films on TV, I'm amazed at how much the German officers look like Americans. Before the start of World War II, Hitler assumed that with our German heritage we would not oppose his expansion efforts in Europe. Had he read this book he would have learned that *freedom*, *independence*, and personal *liberties* are at the top of our list of values. Following German, our other heritage rankings are Irish, English, African, Italian, Mexican, French, and Polish.

POPULATION

Whites comprise 75 percent of our population, followed by **Hispanics** (Spanish speaking native origins of Mexico, Central and South America), African Americans, Asians, and American Indians, who we refer to as **Native Americans**.

Like Europe, we are evolving from a young society to a middle-aged one. Our median age is 37 years, up from 30 in 1980, versus 28 for the world as a whole, because our **baby boomers** are aging. Boomers are members of the large group of people born after the Second World War (WWII) and through the mid-1960s. We have other population terms you will hear. The generation following them until the 1980s is called **Generation X** and are noted as being independent and ambitious. **Generation Y** are those born between the 1980s and 2000 and are achievement-oriented. **Yuppie** (short for young urban professional) refers to a member of the upper middle class in their 20s or 30s. You will hear the term **tweens** who are youngsters between 10 and 12 years of age.

We start school at six years old, vote when we turn 18 years old, and may legally gamble and buy cigarettes and alcohol when we turn 21. The average age at which we marry is 28 for men and 26 for women, versus Germany's 33 for men and 30 for women.

16

Similar to most European countries, normal retirement age in the U.S. is 65 versus 60 in Japan and now 58 in Bolivia. We have some of the world's highest marriage rates, divorce rates, teenage pregnancies, and one-person households.

For the first time, racial and ethnic minorities now make up more than half the children born in the U.S. Minorities comprise one-third of our total population of 310 million, which is projected to grow to over 400 million people by 2050 with minorities accounting for nearly half of the population. In contrast, by 2050 Europe's population will drop 13 percent from today's population of 450 million, a third of all Europeans will be over 60, and the median age of Europe will be 57, up from the 30s today. The big challenge for Europe is keeping its population numbers up and incorporating its immigrants constructively into a future that brings fairness and justice to all, neither of which are big concerns in the U.S. where our immigrant population has always *eventually* been integrated into our society.

In 1950, more than half of us lived in the Northeast and Midwest. Today that number is lower because the population has shifted to southern and western states with favorable climates. Our western state of California has the most people. The population of our farming areas is declining as people migrate to cities for work and a change in living style, similar to what is occurring in other nations.

About three-fourths of us live in **urban areas** *[URR-bun]*, defined as towns with populations over 2500. This is similar to Japan's 78 percent who are urban dwellers, but in contrast to China's 36 percent urban figure. One-fourth of us live in less populated **rural areas** *[RU-ruhl]*.

Suburban neighborhood in Texas.

Many Americans live in what is known as the **suburbs**, collectively called **suburbia**. They are quiet areas outside the busy fringes of our larger cities and are filled with single-family homes separated from retail districts and industrial areas. So, if you are invited to the home of an American, there's a 50 percent chance you'll be going to the suburbs and will see houses with lawns and fences, schools with lawns and playgrounds, and small businesses in quiet shopping streets here and there—the same scenario I found in Australia and New Zealand where home ownership is obviously important, too.

FAMILIES

Our average household size has declined over the last 30 years from 3.2 children per family to 2.6 versus 2.5 for Europe, 3.9 for Colombia, and 3.6 for Chile. There are many reasons for this, not least of which is economics. But we also have shifting lifestyles, like more one-parent households, more independent women who have less time for raising children, medical advances that afford greater control over family size, and on and on. A majority of Americans say that having no more than two children is ideal, while one-third favor having three or more children. Americans with a preference, like the Chinese, would still prefer to give birth to a boy rather than a girl by a 40 to 28 percent margin.

Chances are good that your American counterpart has been divorced because our divorce rate is 48 percent (Sweden's is 55 percent and Italy's 10 percent), a figure that has more than tripled since 1970. Our children live with their parents until they go away to college or until they acquire a job and then move into their own apartments or homes. This is unlike some countries like China, Fiji, and Samoa where parents might live with their grown children, or Peru where grown children build living quarters on top of their parent's home when they can afford to do so.

In the early to mid-20th century, the father typically was the sole wage earner and the mother was the children's principal caregiver. Today, both parents often hold jobs, so adequate daycare for children is necessary for our dual-earner families. Private companies and home-based daycare centers fill some of this need. Increasingly, our corporations offer daycare centers to attract employees who have families, and the government provides assistance to some low-income parents who require daycare. We are even seeing more fathers taking over childcare duties when mother is the **bread winner** (brings home the paycheck).

Our single-parent households have a single adult, usually a woman, with one or more children. They tend to have higher rates of poverty and children of these households are more likely to have educational problems. These families are increasing in number, and the majority of black households are single-parent homes without a father.

According to surveys, the most important financial problem our families face today is a lack of money (17%) compared with 9 percent who say it is unemployment or job loss. The cost of health care takes second place as 12 percent say it is their most important financial problem.

If you are one of the 112 million households in the U.S., various numbers describe your average finances. (How do we **stack up** (compare) with your country?)

- Your family income is $51,000 a year.
- You have $3,800 in the bank and a net worth of $77,000.
- Your debt is $100,000: mortgage $71,000, home equity revolving $9,000, auto loan $6,000, credit card $6,000, student loan $5,000, and other $3,000.
- You spend $14,000 on health care each year.
- One out of two American households doesn't have a retirement account.
- You spend $227,000 on your child from birth until age 17.
- If you own your home, as two out of three families do, its median value exceeds $200,000, down considerably from 2007 at the height of the housing boom and before the recession set in. If you live in Los Angeles County in

18

Southern California or in other large cities, it could easily be double or triple that amount. So, if you are interested in purchasing a home here, you might suffer from **sticker shock** (exorbitant prices).

Further, our families are in better financial shape than our government. If the U.S. government were a family, it would earn $58,000 a year, spend $75,000 while trying to reduce it to $72,000, and have $327,000 in credit card debt with 68 percent due to foreign lenders. Another view: Washington takes in $6 billion per day and spends $10 billion per day, something that some politicians like to **harp on** (continue complaining about).

LANGUAGES

Unlike some countries, the U.S. does not have an "official" language at the national level. Some Americans oppose our conducting classes in Spanish for immigrants and instead propose adopting an official language, which would eliminate them. Eighty-two percent of the population claim English as a mother tongue, while ninety-six percent claim to speak it well. But spoken on a much smaller scale are Spanish, Hawaiian, Korean, Chinese, Vietnamese, French (in parts of northern New England and Louisiana in the South), along with scattered Native American languages and 300 minor languages.

Many of our immigrants speak English as a second language, but some second- and third-generation children do not speak the native language of their ancestors. In China, one spoken Chinese language is not understood in all geographical areas. This separation does not occur in the U.S. although we do have some regional accents that might cause English-speaking foreigners a little trouble, particularly in the South, New England, and the New York area.

STANDARD OF LIVING

Contrary to what many foreigners believe, we are not the richest people in the world. The United Nations places the U.S. in the top ten for our standard of living, which is generally measured by income per person and their access to goods and services. But we consistently rank lower than Scandinavia, Canada, Australia, and Japan.

The United Nations' Human Development Index also combines indicators of a country's life expectancy, educational attainment, and income as a frame of reference for both social and economic development. The U.S. ranks 4th after Norway, Australia, and Netherlands. New Zealand is 5th, followed by Germany 9th, Spain 23rd, U.K. 28th, Turkey 92nd, China 101st, and India 134th.

We view charity, which also contributes to a country's standard of living, as a voluntary, private-sector function compared to Europeans who have compulsory charity in the form of progressive taxation and more government social services. We spend 11 percent of our GDP (gross domestic product) on social services. Europe's 26 percent is derived from higher taxes, something Americans generally disfavor because of our cultural belief in providing for our own destinies. There's that *independence* thing again. However, not all of us are enthralled with the lack of social services in the U.S. It is a continual **tug of war** (pulling on both sides) between the two opposing sides.

Class Division – We have a large middle class in the U.S.—economically between the working class and upper class—unlike some emerging countries that are limited primarily to rich and poor classes, sometimes referred to as the **haves** and **have-nots**. Our our middle class is rapidly decreasing due in part to jobs shifting to cheaper overseas factories. As a result, our richest one percent now own more financial wealth than the bottom ninety-five percent combined. We have a saying that explains what is going on: **The rich get richer and the poor get poorer.**

With this split in standard of living comes class tension in the U.S. According to a Pew Research Center poll, nearly two-thirds of Americans believe the wealth gap is the greatest cause of tension in America today, the highest level since Pew began asking the question in 1987. In 2009, less than half of respondents expressed that opinion. Since then, more traditional sources of friction—race, gender, religion, sexual preference, age, and national origin—have become vastly overshadowed by distrust over wealth.

Poverty – Ironically, with our wealth, we have more people below the **poverty line** than 26 other developed nations. Down from 20 percent in 1960, 16 percent of us live below the poverty line today. This is in contrast to India's 29 percent, Poland's 24 percent, Egypt's 17 percent, Germany's 11 percent, and Belgium's 4 percent. There are now more poor people living in America than in the 16 European nations for which data are available, due in part to their socialized government programs.

The current U.S. poverty line is defined as an annual income of about $22,000 for a family of four. The poverty rate of African Americans is nearly twice the national rate, something you might witness as you travel about here, particularly in our large inner cities such as Detroit and in the South. Poverty in America is a concern to most Americans and is a topic of debate and finger pointing during political campaigns. With 49 million living in poverty, many think this is a national disgrace. The figure helps dispel the popular belief that all Americans are rich, as does the fact that 46 million Americans receive food stamps to help them purchase some of their food for free.

Food stamps.

Health Care – The American health care system, another reflection of our standard of living, is adequate, but is considered one of the worst among developed countries. People, businesses, and politicians have been demanding health care improvements for years. We essentially have an employer-based health insurance system that excludes those with low-paying jobs. This contributes to the 45 million Americans who have no health insurance coverage, something else that some consider a national disgrace. We are still **feeling our way** with the new Obama health plan designed to provide insurance to all, but at a cost. And the U.S. is one of only three industrialized nations that do not require paid maternity or unpaid paternity leave, while most of Europe offers a standard three-month leave with full salary. Americans say they want to choose the doctors they go to. So we worry about changing this when we see those in other countries with government sponsored health care who do not have this option. This is yet another example of our desire to keep government out of our lives, a recurring theme throughout this book.

Life Expectancy – Life expectancy and infant mortality are poor in the U.S. compared to other advanced nations. We are living longer, but not as long as people in 41 other countries including Japan and most of Europe. Europe has more doctors per thousand people (3.22 vs. our 2.79, with Greece the highest), and the U.S. has higher infant mortality. Though the U.S. spends vastly more per person on health care each year than these nations, American women are at greater risk of dying from pregnancy-related causes than in 40 other countries—five times greater than in Greece, four times more than Germany, and three times greater than Spain. Black women in the U.S. are nearly four times as likely as white women to die from pregnancy-related causes.

Material Possessions – It is no secret that we spend a lot of money for material possessions, so some view us as being materialistic. But we don't think of it this way. It is just our way of life. Two-thirds of our giant economy (GDP) is based on consumer spending versus Germany's 55 percent and China's 35 percent. The number of our televisions, vehicles, and other such products per person are considerably higher than in other countries and are confirmation of the American Dream.

The mythical Joneses.

We have a saying in the U.S.: **Keeping up with the Joneses**. This refers to comparing yourself to your neighbor (the fictional Jones family) as a benchmark for social status or the accumulation of material goods as if it were a competition.

It is said that Americans flaunt their wealth while some Europeans hide it. I saw this in Granada, Spain, where some expensive homes surrounded by high walls in upscale neighborhoods had an older car deliberately parked outside to downplay the owner's wealth. In Europe, particularly in Germany, some car owners order expensive cars with no model designation insignia in order to hide the car's identity. Twenty-five percent of Audis are ordered this way, with the practice more common with top models. Perhaps it has to do with security measures, too.

In contrast, some owners in the U.S. upgrade their car's model by putting on the insignia of more expensive cars. On the opposite extreme, the world's second richest man, Warren Buffet, popular head of a large U.S. mutual fund company, still lives in the modest house he bought three decades ago and still drives an older car.

From my experience, this display of wealth—called conspicuous consumption—in the U.S. is probably no different than other countries where it varies among individuals. In fact, a study of Hong Kong immigrants living in Canada concluded that conspicuous consumption is not related to a person's ethnicity.

A U.S. company opened a large mining operation in a remote area of South America. Expecting to attract and retain a sufficient number of local workers as they would in the U.S., they were surprised at the low turnout and retention rates. After a year they realized the natives had little use for money because they could only buy food and other necessities, and any additional money would not be worth working for. So the company introduced stores and catalogs from which the workers could purchase items. From then on they always had full employment and a loyal, dedicated workforce.

The same inducing force is at work in the U.S. and every other advanced nation today, but to varying degrees. China, for example, is witnessing a dramatic increase in the number of people who own automobiles, while Americans, already saturated with cars, are spending their wages on new and improved homes. Once accustomed to having possessions, we all have incentives like the South American natives to maintain or improve our standard of living in our own individual ways.

SOCIAL EQUALITY

Despite what some foreigners believe, like my German friends I spoke of earlier, the U.S. still suffers from some problems of racial and gender inequality. Since the 1970s, traditional gender roles of males and females have been increasingly challenged by the people and our courts. So today fewer roles are restricted by one's sex or skin color. We are making progress.

According to the World Economic Forum, Nordic countries have the greatest equality between men and women, with Iceland ranked first, the U.S. 19th, and France 46th. Our women workers average 78 cents for the same work we pay our men, but they have higher participation rates in the labor force and higher salaries compared to men than in most other countries. (Baton Rouge, Louisiana, in the South pays women 63 percent of what men earn, earning it the title of our worst-paying large city for women.) Women's representation in our senior management positions remains in the 7-16 percent range; before WWII it was less than four percent.

This contrasts with some nations like India where discrimination against women prevails. A world survey reports that 87 percent of women in India, perhaps because of inequality, have the most constant stress, compared to 53 percent in the U.S. and in the

60s in Europe. Although increasing, the percentage of Indian women serving in political or administrative office still remains low and women, unlike the U.S., are rare in senior business positions and in legal and medical professions.

In my travels to Muslim countries, I've observed how American women in our tour groups have harsh views about how women there suffer from inequality of the sexes. This is something that is not only hard for them to accept, but in typical American fashion to not comment on. Women in Saudi Arabia, for example, cannot travel, work, study abroad, marry, get divorced, or be admitted to a public hospital without permission from a male guardian. And the Human Rights Watch (www.hrw.org) has documented Saudi Arabia's systematic discrimination against women in sports. All of this **goes against the grain** (is the opposite of) for our women here. On the other hand, I've noticed my fellow travelers are more accepting of progressive Muslim Turkey where women have more choices about such things as covering their heads and faces with scarves and receiving generous divorce settlements.

However, Americans—especially women—recognize that we still have room for improvement in all these equality areas. We have a saying: **People who live in glass houses shouldn't throw stones.** That suggests we should not criticize others for the very same things that we are guilty of.

> **Hint**: If you are from a country that views the role of women and religious minorities unfavorably, you might exercise caution when discussing these beliefs with an American who is not a close friend.

FOREIGN HERITAGE ROOTS

Americans have foreign heritage roots in one way or another. Some are recent immigrants, some are first generation Americans born here of immigrants (as my father was), and others are from families that have lived here for many generations. Many foreigners were not accepted in the U.S. by the more established groups even up until the mid-twentieth century. Today, however, most are integral parts of our complex society.

Our presidents and government have recently paid respect to these heritage groups by recognizing their contribution to our society.

- *Asian/Pacific Americans* – President Clinton proclaimed May 1996 as Asian/Pacific American Heritage Month. He said our national character has been enhanced by citizens who maintain and honor cultural values and customs brought from other lands.
- *German Americans* – President George W. Bush proclaimed October 6, 2003 as German American Day. He encouraged all Americans to recognize the contributions of our citizens of German descent to the liberty and prosperity of the U.S.

- *Asian Indian Americans* – In 2005, Congress praised our Asian Indian American community and The Indian Institutes of Technology. This was the first time they honored a foreign university for its significant contributions to our society. The congressman who sponsored the resolution said that the U.S. must learn from India and devise a strategy to focus on and improve our studies in math and sciences. Another congressman said, "As the... representative of one of the largest concentrations of Indian Americans in the United States, I have seen firsthand the contributions my friends from India have made."

One characteristic of Americans is we **forgive and forget**, witness our relations today with World War II enemies Japan and Germany. We also like to make amends for past abuses, including the treatment of immigrants, perhaps not doing it as soon as and as often as we should. In 2011, our federal government approved a resolution apologizing for our discriminatory laws that had targeted Chinese immigrants going back to 1882. California, with its large Asian American population, had already put forth a similar resolution two years before. Sometimes slow Washington gets its cues from the states.

In 1988, President Reagan provided $20,000 each and a formal apology to Japanese Americans interned during World War II. And in 2008, an apology was issued to African Americans for their ancestors who suffered under slavery. (These discriminatory times are discussed in Chapter D on history.)

In 2012, the Obama administration announced that it would halt the deportation of some young illegal immigrants who came to the U.S. as children. The policy change would affect about 1.4 million people, many of whom are now educated professionals.

Our four major heritage groups are European, Latin American, African, and Asian, each corresponding to their native continents. If you happen to deal with an American, there is a 90 percent probability he or she will belong to one of these four ethnic groups. They are Americans, but may often retain to one degree or another some of their original cultural traits that are passed on from generation to generation.

Before the turn of the twentieth century, more than half in the U.S. were blue-eyed Caucasians, but that is no longer the case. Several decades ago, more than 40 percent of the population had blue eyes. Most recently, that percentage has dwindled to about 20 percent. Both the huge influx of immigrants and the increased acceptance of interracial relationships and the children born of those unions have caused this shift to a brown-eyed population.

1. European Americans – American culture is essentially European and primarily of British origin. As we discuss in later chapters, our European lineage is institutionalized in the form of our government and civic education. Comprising 61 percent of our population, those of European heritage have the lowest poverty rate and the second highest educational attainment levels, median household income, and median personal income than any other racial demographic in the U.S. except for Asians.

European Americans descended from two big waves of immigration. From 1800 to 1850, Northern and Western Europeans arrived in the U.S., including Germans, Irish, Scots, Welsh, French, Danish, Norwegians, Finns, and Swedes. They arrived with high levels of education and Protestant religions, which we discuss in Chapter F on religion. The second wave arrived from 1880 to 1920s from Southern and Eastern Europe, including Italians, Poles, Russians, Hungarians, Serbs, Ukrainians, Croatians and Bulgarians.

European American actress Penélope Cruz.

2. Latin Americans – The term Latin America refers to all of the Americas south of the U.S., from Mexico to the tip of South America. You will hear two terms, **Latino** and **Hispanic**, which are ethnic terms to categorize a person from Latin America, whether or not the person has Spanish (Hispanic) ancestry. Their presence in the U.S. has existed since the 16th century, earlier than any other group after our Native Americans who migrated from Asia 10,000 years ago.

You are bound to meet Hispanics here because they constitute the largest ethnic minority in the U.S., roughly 15 percent of our population, of which half live in the states of California and Texas. By 2050, one-quarter of the U.S. population will be Hispanic. In 35 of our country's 50 largest cities, non-Hispanic whites soon will be in the minority.

Latin American actress Salma Hayek.

It is estimated that the U.S. has 8 million illegal immigrants from Mexico, something your American contact might discuss with you. This is a hotly contested issue for taxpayers who support these people with health care and education dollars, particularly in our border states. Because the federal government has not stopped the flow of 450,000 of these people into the southwestern state of Arizona, the state has **taken matters into its own hands**. They instituted laws, contrary to federal laws, that ask for identification from suspected illegal immigrants, something that those in other states view as a violation of the constitutional protection from illegal search. To protest this, some organizations have cancelled their annual conferences in Arizona. This is a confirmation, once again, that most of us defend the human rights of all, even those who are here illegally or those in other countries deprived of the same rights that we so enjoy and have fought for.

3. African Americans – The term African American is generally used for Americans with predominantly sub-Saharan African ancestry. We also use the term "blacks," while the terms "colored," "Negro," and "Nigger" were dropped from our vocabulary in the latter half of the twentieth century out of respect to these people, and are terms you must not use. Most are descendants of captive Africans who were enslaved within the boundaries of the present U.S., although some are descended from, or are voluntary immigrants from, Africa, the Caribbean, and South America.

Many believe the U.S. was the number one proponent and user of slavery in the world several centuries ago. However, of the 10.7 million slaves shipped across the Atlantic back then, Brazil took 50 percent of them while the U.S. took six percent. America abolished slavery in 1864 while Brazil in 1888 was the last country in the Americas to outlaw it.

African American TV host Oprah Winfrey .

Blacks comprise 14 percent of our population and are the second largest minority in the U.S. behind Hispanics. Their median income is roughly 65 percent of that of white people; in Brazil it is 57 percent. African Americans are now more involved in the American political process than other minority groups, including immigrants, yet you might observe they still remain at an economic, educational, and social disadvantage in many areas compared to whites. The civil rights movement, which we discuss in Chapter D on history, heavily influenced the civil and social liberties of *all* Americans of varied cultural backgrounds, including immigrants, not just blacks.

4. Asian Americans – The term Asian American originated in the late 1960s when Asian American activists sought to end the use of the word **Orientals**, believing it had a negative image. Today, Asian heritage Americans, like other foreign nationals, are recognized as an important part of the American scene and are viewed as successful, law-abiding, and high-achieving minorities. It wasn't always this way, as you will learn in Chapter D on history.

Asian American newscaster Connie Chung.

More than 18 million Asian Americans (6% of total population) comprise our fastest growing minority group, recently surpassing Hispanic Americans. Three-quarters were born abroad. Those of Chinese heritage (23%) form the largest group followed by Filipino, Indian, Vietnamese, Korean, and Japanese (7%). About half the Asian American population lives in the western U.S., with 4 out of 10 in California. The Asian Indian American population is more evenly spread across the U.S., mainly in urban and large metropolitan areas, with the largest share (31%) living in the Northeast.

Surveys show Asian Americans are the best educated and highest-income racial or ethnic group, they tend to be more satisfied than most Americans with their own lives, and they hold more traditional views than the general public on the value of marriage, parenthood, and hard work. They are also more likely than the general public to prefer a big government that provides more services.

THE ASIAN AMERICAN EXPERIENCE

A broader examination of the Asian American experience in the U.S. provides insight into how members of a large and fairly homogenous group have assimilated American culture. To varying degrees, it is characteristic of how other nationals have faced similar problems and adjusted to life in the U.S.

- *Income* – The median household income for Asian American married couples tops $55,000, while the average for the U.S. is $48,000 per year. Many also operate small businesses. Asian Indian Americans have the highest median income of any ethnic group in the U.S. ($60,093), with nearly 200,000 millionaires. Educated Asian Indians comprise:
    o 38% of our doctors and 12% of our scientists,
    o 36% of NASA (National Aeronautical and Space Administration) employees,
    o 34% of Microsoft and 28% of Intel employees, and
    o 28% of IBM and 13% of Xerox employees.
- *Education* – More than two-thirds of recent adult immigrants are either college students or college graduates. At two of our best universities, Harvard and Yale, Asian Americans now account for 15 to 20 percent of the undergraduate student body. At the elite campuses of the University of California system, Asians outnumber all other groups, including whites. Two-thirds of Asian Indians in the U.S. have attained a bachelor's degree or higher, versus 29 percent of all Americans.
- *Language* – Asian Americans define their lack of English skills as their biggest barrier to job advancement. For those who lack English skills, some start businesses that deal exclusively with Asians. Unfortunately they remain locked in their Asian-only culture in the U.S. (This is why Chapter Y deals with improving English grammar skills and Chapter Z helps improve English speaking skills.)
- *Culture* – Asian American children may find themselves in conflict with their parents' generation and at the same time may not find complete acceptance in American society. Studies show that all immigrant groups experience this upon coming to the U.S., but this conflict eases over time as families become more assimilated. Assimilation, however, has traditionally been less of a problem for Asian Indians because of their English skills and often coming from more prosperous, educated backgrounds in India.
- *Acceptance* – Asians, like other minorities, have faced problems of acceptance in the U.S. But sociologists now refer to Asian Americans as the "model minority," implying an acceptance of Asians, their life styles, and their

cultures. Some Asian Americans, however, who oppose any form of ethnic stereotyping, dislike the use of this term.

- *Help for Asians* – In the U.S., we band together in groups with like interests to make changes and to empower ourselves—this is the "American way." Asian Americans, like other foreign nationals, are slowly beginning to coalesce into representative groups to improve their status. But some don't, so they remain rooted in their own ethnic identities because of language, religion, and even historic rivalries; thus they do not advance culturally. We have a term for this: **stuck in the mud**.

  Help is widely available from both fellow Asians and American organizations that reach out to Asians. The Indian American Center for Political Awareness, for example, has a website at www.collegecostshowmuch.com. And the Organization of Chinese Americans (www.ocanational.org) is dedicated to advancing the social, political, and economic wellbeing of Asian Pacific Americans in the U.S.

  A wide range of publications and media sources also address the needs of Asian Americans. And many Asian-interest websites—some in English and some in their native languages—such as www.goldsea.com represent Asian American interests. One website provides links to a wide variety of Asian American organizations: www.asianamerican.net.

Assist groups like these are also available for other immigrant groups that are operated by likeminded immigrants. You will also find community-based service organizations not formed specifically to help immigrants, traditional groups such as Kiwanis (www.kiwanis.org), Rotary (www.rotary.org), and the Chamber of Commerce (www.uschamber.com). They are there, but you have to search them out.

FOREIGN HERITAGE INFLUENCE IN OUR CITIES

Foreigners influence how our cities develop and grow. During the late nineteenth and early twentieth centuries and continuing today, many sections of our cities were populated by recent immigrants. Chinatowns, Little Tokyos, Germantowns and Little Italys to name a few were established in our larger cities. We have thousands of these communities today that retain their ethnic makeup. New York City, with a population of 8 million, has the largest ethnic mix in the U.S., accounting for 36 percent of the city's population and the 800 languages spoken there. You can probably find one of your ethnic groups somewhere in the U.S. Here is a small sampling.

- South Boston in Massachusetts was long known as a working class Irish American neighborhood. Today it is also home to small but vibrant Polish and Lithuanian communities. The Irish faced severe discrimination a century ago.

28

- Strawberry Hill is a Kansas City Slavic community.
- Green Bay, Wisconsin, is home to large Irish, German, Polish and Scandinavian neighborhoods.
- Historic Filipinotown is a Filipino district of the city of Los Angeles, California.
- Little Bohemia is an historic Czech neighborhood in Omaha, Nebraska.
- Germantown in Louisville, Kentucky, was formed by German immigrants in the 1870s. Today we have hundreds of Germantowns across the U.S.
- Greektown is an historic Greek neighborhood in Detroit, Michigan.
- Little Italy is home to a large and active Italian ethnic community in Baltimore, Maryland.
- Solvang, California, is a Danish Village with old country architecture, windmills, and cobblestone side streets.

Solvang, California

- Brighton Beach, in Brooklyn, New York, is known as Little Odessa—home to 150,000 Russian immigrants who still favor cabbage pies, lard sandwiches, strong vodka, and sentimental music.
- Three of our major metropolitan areas alone have over a million and a half Asians each—Los Angeles, San Francisco, and New York City.

These ethnic communities and neighborhoods provide inhabitants work and social opportunities. But they also limit economic opportunities and development of English speech by keeping immigrants in their own culture. Not all immigrants today live in these ethnic neighborhoods. Our Asian Indian population, for example, which has doubled in the last 10 years, tends to integrate more with non-ethnic neighborhoods, just as immigrant Europeans do. This is another reason these two cultures do so well when they come to the U.S.

The Los Angeles area has a vast array of recent immigrants as reflected in the names of cities on the map. These areas have businesses owned and operated by immigrants. Their business signs are often in their native languages. Many restaurants and schools are geared toward immigrant

(Asianbizguide.com)

29

students, and local governments have strong immigrant representation.

A model for rapid immigrant assimilation and acceptance occurred in Monterey Park, California—a half-hour's drive east of Los Angeles (www.ci.monterey-park.ca.us). Before it became America's first Asian American majority city in the 1980s, it was a predominantly white **bedroom community** (people live there but work elsewhere) and had a small Latino and Japanese American population.

A young real estate agent from Hong Kong knew that tens of thousands of highly educated, upwardly mobile Chinese were moving into the Los Angeles area, so he promoted the city to them. Many Asians moved in, at first causing problems for resident non-Asians. So the city council passed a non-binding resolution declaring English as the official language. Tense battles followed over such things as whether Asian books should be allowed in the library, or if Asian lettering should be allowed on the storefronts of Asian-owned businesses. But the backlash eventually passed as whites and Latinos adapted to the new community and Asian Americans

A model city for immigrant assimilation.

became involved in local government and schools. In the process, both sides adjusted to the culture of the others.

Adjacent Alhambra has seen its Asian heritage population increase from 31 percent in 1990 to 48 percent today. The city of Glendale, California, just outside Los Angeles, has the third largest concentration of Armenians outside of Armenia. Koreatown, a mid-city section of Los Angeles, has seen the Korean population grow to an estimated 160,000, making it the largest concentration of Koreans outside of Korea.

Foreigners can contact a local U.S. Embassy website in their country for more information about America and our relations with their country. For a listing of all U.S. embassies and consulates go to www.usembassy.state.gov.

With this broad overview of America's population and the role of immigrants in our society, let's now examine those factors that helped shaped the development of America and its culture, starting with our government.

B
GOVERNMENT

*Today we can declare: Government is not the problem,
and government is not the solution. We, the American people,
we are the solution.* - Bill Clinton, U.S. president 1993-2001

To better understand Americans, you need to understand our government. To understand our government, you need to understand our history (covered in Chapter D). Our history dictated how our government developed, and our government and history influence how we function as a society today. Incorporating this knowledge in your relations and conversations with Americans will surely boost the image you create for yourself.

The foundation of our government is **democracy**. Its premise is that government exists to serve the people; the people are free; the majority rules while the rights of the minority are protected; there is a rule of law; all people are equal before the law; and there are basic freedoms such as freedom to exchange opinions, freedom to assemble and freedom of religion. These democratic ideas permeate our society and define who we are and how we conduct our everyday lives.

To the American pioneers and immigrants, government was, at best, a necessary evil. Its main duty was to preserve a nation free from tyranny and unnecessary restraints on the individual, something they abhorred in their native homelands. Even today, some Americans see big government as a potential threat to—more than a protector of—our autonomy, property rights, and freedoms. For this reason, our media (and the people) delight in **stirring up the pot** (incite) when reporting on government mismanagement or intrusion into our lives (see Chapter Q - Media).

This contrasts with Europeans who view their governments in a different light and debated over a European Union constitution, something we did three centuries ago. The U.S. was a proponent of the European Union, but, because of our cultural differences, much of the document probably would not be acceptable to most Americans. Although some passages mirrored our own Declaration of Independence and the U.S.

Constitution's Bill of Rights (which we discuss in Chapter D on history), there are other ideas and notions we might consider with suspicion or even as being strange.

For example, there was no reference to God and only a veiled reference to Europe's religious inheritance. While 82 percent of Americans say that God is very important to them, less than 20 percent of Europeans express similar religious convictions. And there was only one reference to private property in the document, and barely a mention of free markets and trade, concepts that are fundamental to the American way of life.

Although our government has vast powers and far-reaching responsibilities, visitors to America are surprised to learn how much is accomplished by the efforts of the public outside the realm of government. For example, in May 1865 one citizen in upstate New York organized an effort to decorate the gravesites of local Civil War (1861-1865) veterans. Today a national holiday honors this effort (see Chapter R - Holidays and Traditions). In the early 1960s, Rachael Carson's startling book drew the nation's attention to the need to clean up and protect our environment; that effort continues in full force today, much of it without the support of government. Any government support it does get is instituted because of the public's will. In fact, because of the public's will, in 2011 Mattel, Inc., the maker of the Barbie Doll line, said it would stop buying paper and packaging that was linked to rain forest destruction in Indonesia.

The unveiling of the World War II Memorial in Washington, D.C. on Memorial Day, 2004 is attributed to the efforts of one man. We had monuments to the veterans of other wars, including the unpopular Vietnam War. One individual citizen who was a WWII veteran thought there should be such a monument to his comrades. After discussing his idea with his state's representative in Congress in 1987, **the ball started rolling** (things went forward) with the help of a former senator, the chairman of a business (FedEx), and spokesman-actor Tom Hanks. The

WWII Memorial - Washington, D.C.

effort raised $193 million and construction began in 2000 with no government money, although it was built on government property.

Jody Williams received the **Nobel Peace Prize** for single-handedly organizing the Ban Land Mines Campaign from her Vermont farmhouse in New England. Her efforts have saved lives and limbs for thousands of people far beyond the boundaries of the U.S. that has no land mines. There are millions of such volunteers in the U.S. helping to enhance life in the U.S. and around the world by simply doing what they feel is the right thing to do. Sometimes the government gets involved, sometimes it doesn't.

"Less government is better government" is heard frequently in the U.S. However, this has led to problems like the collapse of the financial markets in 2008 when banks and financial firms ran amok in highly profitable but unregulated areas, which led to the collapse that echoed around the world. New laws will someday be put into to place. So, we are learning the hard way that the government is indeed needed in some circumstances.

Foreigners might be surprised at how our federal government prefers to have industries, such as the media and film, self-regulate where possible. Unlike India where the states defer much more to the federal government, in the U.S. the federal government (and courts) many times will defer matters to the states to decide individually, and the states might in turn defer to the cities. Our founding fathers who wanted more self-control would be proud of this decentralization of power.

We have four levels of government in America: *federal, state, county,* and *city.* Cities are grouped together to form a county *[KOWN-tee].* Counties are grouped together to form a state, and states are grouped together to form the United States of America. We *are* "united" states. As an example, California is one of 50 states and is located on the West Coast. It consists of 58 counties, one of which is called Los Angeles County. It is the most populated county in the U.S. and covers 10,570 square km (4081 square miles) and contains 88 cities, one of which is the city of Long Beach. They all have governments elected by its residents, unlike some countries where they might be appointed.

> **Hint**: Classic films centered on our government include *State of the Union* (1948), *All the King's Men* (1949), *Mr. Smith Goes to Washington* (1939), *Advise and Consent* (1962), *The Candidate* (1972), and *JFK* (1991). *The American President* (1995) takes you inside the White House.

FEDERAL GOVERNMENT

Our country, like other major countries, has a constitution *[kon-stih-TOO-shun],* which is a body of basic principles and laws by which the people are governed. The **U.S. Constitution** was approved in 1789, 13 years after we obtained our freedom from England. It defines our form of government and the rights and liberties of the people. In doing so, the Constitution gives certain powers to the federal (U.S.) government's three separate branches: *executive* (the president), *legislative* (the Congress), and *judicial* (the courts). Having these three branches prevents any single branch of government from becoming too powerful, yet at the same time allows them to work together. We call this a system of **checks and balances**.

Our federal government resides in the capitol city of Washington, D.C. (D.C. is short for the District of Columbia). It is a "city" but is not part of a state, the only one in America with this singular status. You may hear people refer to it as merely "Washington" or "D.C."

Uncle Sam

33

We have a symbol for our federal government called **Uncle Sam**. You may hear us use the term when referring to the federal government, such as "I owed Uncle Sam 2,000 dollars in taxes this year."

The national symbol of America is the eagle (a symbol of strength) clutching olive branches (a sign of peace) and arrows (a sign of defense). You will see it in logos for various federal departments and on our money. The role of this symbol is similar to the national emblem of France that has a shield with a lion head, eagle head, laurel branch, and an oak branch.

National symbol.

The duties of the federal branches are clearly defined. The **executive branch** consists of the president, vice president, and his **cabinet** consisting of 15 department heads and other staff members. It is responsible for *enforcing* the laws of the U.S. The president is elected every four years and may serve for two terms. Apart from federal matching funds for official presidential candidates, the U.S. government does not use taxpayer money to finance political parties and candidates, as some countries like Germany do.

The president lives and works in the **White House** (yes, it *is* white) with his

administrative staff and appoints the heads of important federal departments, such as the Secretary of State, Secretary of Commerce, and Secretary of Labor, but Congress must confirm these appointments. Unlike India, Germany, and other countries where the role of the president is largely ceremonial and the prime minister or chancellor has more power, in the U.S. we have only a president who is in full charge.

The White House

Hint: The White House is located at 1600 Pennsylvania Avenue, so we sometimes refer to our president or even our government as "1600 Pennsylvania" in the same fashion Brits refer to 10 Downing Street as the headquarters of Her Majesty's Government. In a conversation, you might say, "What do you think 1600 Pennsylvania thinks about that?" The White House has its own website at www.WhiteHouse.org. Tours are limited to local area school children. If you want to send a letter, the official address is 1600 Pennsylvania Ave NW, Washington, DC 20500. You might receive acknowledgement of your letter on White House stationery as I once did.

The **legislative branch**, also called **Congress** is similar to parliament in other countries. It consists of the **Senate** and the **House of Representatives** and is responsible for *making* our laws. Congress is housed in the round-dome building called the **Capitol Building** in Washington, D.C. Each state elects two **senators** who serve six-years each term. Based on its population, each state also elects **representatives** who serve two-year terms. There are 100 U.S. senators and 435 U.S. representatives in Congress. For example, the state of California with the largest population of 37 million people has 53 representatives while the small state of Rhode Island with a population of only one million has two representatives in Congress.

This system gives each state an equal vote on matters before the Senate, but also gives each state a weighted vote on matters before the House of Representatives. Senators and representatives sit on different commissions that oversee the running of the federal government, such as commerce, defense, banking, and other matters. In many cases they establish policy and monitor the performance of the various federal departments—again, a system of checks and balances that our founding fathers established because of injustices they faced in Europe.

The third branch, the **judicial branch**, consists of the federal courts such as the Supreme Court and lower level federal courts. They are responsible for *interpreting* the laws and ensuring that the rights of the people are protected. You will frequently see the **scales of justice** relating to legal matters. It implies that both sides of an issue are given equal review.

Scales of justice.

Our first ten **Amendments** (additions) to the Constitution are called the **Bill of Rights** that guarantee us certain freedoms, such as the right to free speech, to bear arms, to a trial when accused of a crime, to own property, etc. You will read or hear about lawsuits in America where people claim their constitutional rights have been violated. We have lawyers who specialize in this branch of the law. Some nonprofit groups such as The American Civil Liberties Union (**ACLU**) work to insure our rights are not violated, as do our media (www.ACLU.org). As you might expect with our diverse culture, some Americans think the ACLU goes too far in their actions, such as wanting to eliminate prayer in schools, while others support their causes. Some say the strength of America lies in our diversity.

We like to use popular sayings in our everyday conversations that we borrow from numerous sources, including the government. The Fifth Amendment, for example, states that a person does not have to testify against himself in a criminal court proceeding. Sometimes you will hear a person say jokingly, **I am taking the fifth**, meaning they would prefer not to answer your question.

Hint: Feel free to ask Americans their opinion about any official in the federal government, from the president on down. As I learned in Thailand and other countries, you do not speak negatively about the king without serious consequences, but in America you may speak freely. We are very **open** (willing to discuss) about our opinions of our government. To appear knowledgeable, you might use the name of a senator from the state where your counterpart is from. (Use sites on the Internet, such as www.infoplease, or refer to Appendix 9 for how to locate their names.) We tend to know more about our senators than our lower ranking representatives. So, if you are discussing something like your pollution control equipment with a potential buyer, you might ask what his or her senators (using their two names) are doing to control pollution in their state.

STATE GOVERNMENT

Our Constitution states that any powers not given to the federal government are the responsibility of the states. So the states have their own individual constitutions and delight in exercising their rights. In contrast to some countries like China in which the country is divided into administrative areas, regions, and municipalities directly under the central government, our states are quite independent. (There's that *independence* thing again.) Because of this, foreigners are sometimes surprised at the lack of uniformity among the states on various government matters and the powers they have. For example, in 1933 the federal government ended legislation that for 13 years had prohibited the sale of alcohol. The states, however, were given the power to regulate alcohol and a few continued outlawing it for years before finally allowing it.

Each of our states has a **capital city** [note it is spelled "al"] where the state government is located and is housed in the state **capitol building** [note it is spelled "ol"], which often has a round dome like the Capitol Building in Washington, D.C. State governments are organized similar to the federal government with the three independent branches. Each is headed by a **governor** *[GUV-er-nur]* who is elected by the voters in the state. This differs from some countries like India where governors are appointed by the president to a five-year term. Some of our governors have later become presidents of the U.S., including Ronald Reagan.

California, our most populated state, has 40 state senators who serve a four-year term and 80 state representatives who serve two-year terms and all reside in the state's capital city of Sacramento. Surprisingly, tiny Rhode Island has 38 state senators and 75 state representatives with no term limits. As you can see, in America we **do our own thing**, meaning that we like to make our own decisions at the state level about how we govern ourselves. This localized state obsession lead to our Civil War in 1861, which we discuss later in Chapter D on History.

America preaches to the rest of the world the importance of honesty and transparency in government. A study by the Center for Public Integrity released a report detailing the risk of corruption and lack of accountability in all 50 states. The southern state of Georgia was identified as the worst because of the absence of a strong ethics enforcement agency. This was followed by South Dakota, Wyoming, Virginia, and Maine. New Jersey was ranked as the best with some of the toughest ethics and anti-corruption laws in the nation. Next were Connecticut, Washington, California, and Nebraska.

Each state has adopted official names and nicknames that you can use in your conversations if you know the state of your American counterpart. For example, California has the nickname of the Golden State because of gold discovered there. California's motto is **Eureka**, a word meaning, "I have found it!" In 1849 when gold miners found gold in California they exclaimed, "Eureka!" The state flower is the

California poppy, the state bird is the California quail (which came from China, by the way), and the state animal is the California grizzly bear, one of its native animals.

> **Hint**: We still use "eureka" playfully today when we find something important that we have been seeking and are surprised. You might yell out "Eureka!"*[you-REEK-ah]* if you hit a big jackpot on a slot machine, or close a big sales contract. Check out the state motto and nicknames of your counterpart's state and use them in a conversation, such as, "How do you like living in the Golden State (California)?"

Our state mottos, some dating back to the 1700s, give insight into the virtues, values, and beliefs of the American people. Some of the most frequently occurring words in these mottos are "liberty," "independence," "rights," and other related terms. Delaware: "Liberty and Independence," New Hampshire: "Live Free or Die," New Jersey: "Liberty and Prosperity," Pennsylvania: "Virtue, Liberty, Independence," Vermont: "Freedom and Unity," and Wyoming: "Equal Rights." A member of Congress back then, **Patrick Henry** hated British tyranny and is still remembered for saying, **"Give me liberty or give me death."**

In 1999, America began a ten-year celebration of the 50 states using commemorative coins. Each year five quarters (25 cents) were issued for five states in the sequence the states were admitted to the Union. Some Americans collect these coins. You might want to keep one as a souvenir of your visit to a state. When I travel overseas I take these coins and give them as thank you gestures. (Go to www.usmint.gov for more details.)

California quarter.

> **Hint**: If you know the home state of your American counterpart, you will make a nice impression if you refer to it when you talk to them. Ask their opinion of their state or their governor. Be sure to use the governor's name (see Appendix 9 for how to find it). Ask what their governor is doing about education, highways, state taxes, pollution, crime, etc. Ask if their governor will be re-elected, or will run for the U.S. Senate or president as some governors do. Ask if the state has a surplus of money (few do) or if the governor will have to raise taxes. Caution: once started, you may have trouble stopping us from **venting our spleen** (expressing anger) over these controversial subjects.

COUNTY AND CITY GOVERNMENT

Our next level of government below the state is the *county [KOWN-tee],* which administers government as a sub-division of the state. The citizens usually elect a board of supervisors who oversee county services like law enforcement, property assessment, tax collection, public health protection, social services, flood control, parks and recreation, and cultural activities.

The next level of government is the *city,* typically headed by a **mayor** *[MAY-or]* who is elected by the residents in the city and is responsible for running it. Some of the services that counties normally provide might be administered by the larger cities. It might have a voter-elected city council that oversees the mayor. The building that houses city government is sometimes called **city hall**. We have a saying, **you can't fight city hall**, meaning you might not get the results you want from your efforts of appealing to an authority, not necessarily a government agency.

During elections, some residents place small signs in their front yards to promote their candidates or issues to be voted upon. Some citizens become members of a committee to promote a cause or assist a candidate who is running for a public office. Anybody can run for any office or start a campaign to bring about change in their city, state, county, or country. In California, for example, many people stood in front of shopping centers in early 2003 to get enough signatures to place a recall of their governor on the November ballot. For the first time in the state's history, they collected the required signatures to

Front yard sign for candidate.

bring the issue to a vote. He was subsequently voted out of office and actor Arnold Schwarzenegger was voted to replace him, but he didn't do much better either. Wisconsin did the same thing in 2011 over the rights of union representation of certain workers. These are examples of the American people increasingly **taking matters into their own hands** to do what has to be done or be changed. That's the American way. Sometimes this even extends to matters overseas.

Ten Worst Cities To Live In – Sometimes the people do a good job selecting their local officials, sometimes not. Given there are often conditions and influences beyond the control of our government—disasters, world economies, etc.—but you can see by the following lists that it may be true what we say: **You get the government leaders you deserve**. So we only have to look to ourselves for both pride and for placing blame.

Thinking of moving to a city in the U.S.? Using a variety of criteria including unemployment rates, health data, number of home mortgage foreclosures, crime statistics, climate, and other measures of misery, one survey recently came up with an unofficial list of our 10 worst cities to live in, all strongly affected by city government.

1. El Centro, California – Highest unemployment rate in the U.S.
2. Cleveland, Ohio – Unemployment, high taxes, bad weather, political corruption.
3. Detroit, Michigan – Highest violent crime rate in the U.S.
4. Las Vegas, Nevada – Highest home loan foreclosure rate.
5. Oklahoma City, Oklahoma – Unhealthiest city.
6. Los Angeles, California – Air pollution problems, traffic congestion.
7. Phoenix, Arizona – Immigrant problems.
8. Newark, New Jersey – Poverty and toxic waste sites.
9. Miami, Florida – Bad place to raise a family.
10. Memphis, Tennessee – High violent crime rate and government corruption.

Ten Best Cities To Live In – On the other hand, another survey determined the 10 best cities to live in based on such factors as adult education levels, unemployment, high schools, children's hospitals, violent crime rates, and data on parklands playgrounds and other public facilities, all functions of local government. Here is their top ten.

1. Madison, Wisconsin – Growing health and biotech industries, recreational activities.
2. Virginia Beach, Virginia – Prosperous, low crime and unemployment rates, playgrounds.
3. Raleigh, North Carolina – High-tech and biotech industries, low unemployment, top schools.
4. Irvine, California – Perfect city for children to enjoy the outdoors, low crime rates, bike paths.
5. Lincoln, Nebraska – Land dedicated to parks and playgrounds, low unemployment.
6. Scottsdale, Arizona – Highest rate of educated adults, low unemployment.
7. Plano, Texas – Low crime rate earns it title of America's Safest City, top school system.
8. Omaha, Nebraska – Low unemployment, top hospitals, good economy, high graduation rates.
9. Boise, Idaho – One of the safest cities in the country; education has a high priority.
10. Greensboro, North Carolina – Excellent school system, abundant parks, tech businesses.

Most/Least Expensive Cities To Live In – On the subject of our cities, a Kiplinger survey (www.kiplinger.com) identifies our most and least expensive larger cities based on relative pricing of essentials such as consumer goods, housing, transportation, utilities, and health care. However, wage levels typically parallel the cost of living index of our cities.

Most Expensive Cost of Living	Cheapest Cost of Living
1. New York, New York	1. Brownsville, Texas
2. Honolulu, Hawaii	2. Pueblo, Colorado
3. San Francisco, California	3. Fort Hood, Texas
4. San Jose, California	4. Fort Smith, Arkansas
5. Stamford, Connecticut	5. Sherman , Texas
6. Washington, D.C.	6. Springfield, Illinois
7. Fairbanks, Alaska	7. Waco, Texsas
8. Boston, Massachusetts	8. Fayetteville, Arkansas
9. Los Angeles, California	9. Austin, Texas
10. San Diego, California	10. Springfield, Missouri

Hint: You might discuss all these factors about the city in which your American counterpart lives, or pay attention to such lists if you are offered a job opportunity in one of them. You can ask Americans what they feel are the top five problems in their city, and compare them with your city. They will be interested in hearing your comparison. Use the name of their mayor in your discussions by first doing an Internet search on the city's name. Most cities have a website with this information such as this one for Los Angeles: www.ci.la.ca.us/.

POLITICAL PARTIES

Our **political parties** define general political policy, select candidates to represent their party, and help their candidates get elected. Unlike controlling political parties in some nations, we can join a political party by merely signing up. We have always had at least a two-party system with both sides simultaneously holding elected government positions. With recent grumblings about them, more parties are on the horizon. Some voters vote for all the candidates in their party (called a straight ticket). Others vote for the candidate they prefer, without consideration of his or her party affiliation. Anybody in America can vote any way they want, irrespective of his or her party affiliation.

Unlike some countries with dozens of national and regional political parties, the **Democrats** and **Republicans** represent the vast majority of voters in the U.S. We have a few smaller parties such as the Independent Party. Dating back to our founding parties, the general perception was Republicans were for business and states' rights, while Democrats were more concerned about having the government improve conditions for the people. Our stock market dropped the day before the presidential election in 2004 when it appeared Democratic candidate Kerry might win; the next day it soared when republican Bush was announced the winner. The people traditionally vote democratic: professionals (college educated), academicians, youth, labor, women, working class, minorities, and immigrants. Changing from time to time, the Democratic Party currently holds a minority of seats in the House of Representatives, a majority in the Senate, a minority of state governorships, and a minority of state legislatures.

However, these party views are not entirely true because there are so many conflicting issues today and even differences among the people within each party. As an example of this, in the 2004 presidential election, Republican President Bush advocated a constitutional amendment that would outlaw same-sex marriages. His running mate, Vice President Dick Cheney, has a daughter who is lesbian and he has stated publicly that he supports letting individuals do what they want to do on this controversial matter.

Since our founding, Americans have felt free to express their views or protest against things they do not agree with. You might meet an American who is a member of one or more of our numerous protest groups trying to reform government at all levels. The latest is the **Tea Party** movement that is focused on fiscal conservatism. The name is a reference to the historic Boston Tea Party of 1773, a protest by American colonists against taxation of tea by the British government when the colonists had no representation in the British Parliament. The **Occupy Wall Street** movement started in New York City in 2011 and spread across the world, motivating thousands to voice their anger at financial and social inequality, and in some places it merged with existing anti-government protests. The problem, the protesters said, is no one in government has been listening.

So, as a foreigner, don't draw conclusions about the American people on the stance of one person or one protest group or one political party. This includes our president or his political party, neither of which might represent the attitudes of the majority of the American people. Our views about the Iraq and Afghanistan wars are an example of this. Also, don't draw any conclusions about your American counterpart based on his or her political party affiliation because most likely they will probably only support certain party stands. You will learn what is on the collective minds of Americans in Chapter S on what Americans think.

In political cartoons, you might see an elephant represent the republicans and a donkey represent the democrats. The Republican Party is also called the **GOP** (Grand Old Party). You might hear Americans refer to "red" versus "blue" states. A **blue state** may be any state leaning towards the democratic ticket while a **red state** may be any state in which the majority favors the republican ticket. Democrats are more likely than average to be women, nonwhite, less likely to be religious or married, much less likely to be conservative, and much more likely to be liberal than the U.S. population as a whole.

Democrat - Republican

Our parties attempt to define their stand on certain issues so the people will know more about their party. One such issue today is abortion, the right of a woman to terminate an unborn baby. Republicans generally oppose abortion while Democrats feel that a woman has the right to make her own choice on this sensitive issue. Some members have quit their parties because of their personal disagreement with their party's stand on issues like this. We wish more of our politicians would stand up for what they believe and not go along with the **party line**, while others feel the parties (and the government) should not take a stand on issues that are private, such as abortion and gay marriage.

You might hear Americans refer to their elected representatives as being **right wing** (conservative) or **left wing** (liberal). Republicans have traditionally been called **conservatives** and the Democrats **liberals**, although within each party they may have their own liberal and conservative members. Conservatives are considered opposed to change, while liberals are associated with change, but like everything thing else in America, this is in flux. More than half of the residents of Wyoming (53%), Mississippi (53%), and Utah (51%) are identified as conservative, making them the most conservative states in the U.S. The District of Columbia and four New England states have the highest percentage of liberals. You will also hear the term **Left Coast**, a political expression that implies that the West Coast of the U.S. leans politically to the left.

Within these party ranks are **moderates** who sometimes work with the other party. Over the past few years many have been voted out of office because the people were fed up with government and wanted extreme changes made, so they voted for those on the extreme right or left. Consequently, and as a shortfall of this **knee-jerk** (immediate without thought) reaction, it has become harder for bills to be passed in Congress. So government is now viewed by the people as stagnant and at its lowest level in decades. As stated earlier, we get what we deserve when it comes to government.

You will also hear all these various political terms used in conversations outside of politics, such as in business matters or lifestyles.

Hint: If you get into a political discussion with an American, you might ask if they are from a red or blue state, if they are a donkey or elephant, or a left or right-winger; this might bring a smile. Some political issues are personal to Americans, such as abortion, pre-marital or same-sex marriage, and religion, and it is probably best not to venture into a discussion on these topics until you know the person well. However, most Americans welcome your questions about most other political issues. We enjoy expressing our beliefs, including whom we are voting for and why.

WHAT WE THINK ABOUT OUR GOVERNMENT

Our federal government stinks. So say continuing surveys of the American people and their attitudes toward Washington, irrespective of their party affiliation. Many in the U.S. feel that the public's interest loses out to rich and powerful special interests in Washington, D.C. Large majorities believe that big companies, **political action committees** (PACs) that give money to candidates, the news media, and political lobbyists all have too much power and influence in Washington. Over half believe that our TV and radio talk shows have too much political clout. Equally large

U.S. Capitol Building.

majorities believe that small business and public opinion have too little power and influence in the nation's capital. In fact, for the past 10 years three-fourths of Americans say the nation would be better off if leaders followed public opinion more closely, instead of their party.

Here are more findings.

- *Trust* – A Harvard University study reveals the top five reasons why most Americans do not trust the federal government.
    1. Government waste and inefficiency (73%).
    2. Unnecessary partisan bickering (68%).
    3. Special interests having too much influence (65%).
    4. Lack of honesty and integrity among elected officials (64%).
    5. High taxes (57%).
- *Congress* – 88% of Americans disapprove of Congress handling its job.
- *Problem Solving* – 57% have little or no confidence in the federal government to solve domestic problems, while 43% have little or no confidence in the government to solve international problems.
- *Politicians* – 53% have little or no confidence in the men and women who seek or hold elected office.
- *Waste* – Americans believe the federal government wastes 51 cents of every dollar it spends, followed by state (42 cents) and local governments (38 cents).
- *Freedoms* – Half of those surveyed believe the federal government has become so large and powerful that it poses an immediate threat to the rights and freedoms of ordinary citizens, up from less than one-third in 2003 before

the 9/11 attack on the U.S. Americans are willing to accept some restrictions on freedom of speech, but they do not want discrimination against any particular ethnic group. (There's that *equality* thing again.)

- *Less Government* – A Harris poll in the 1970s—a time of great social reform in the U.S.—found that only one-third of respondents agreed with the statement "The best government is the government that governs the least." Today, the views have flipped—57 percent now want less government. This reversal reflects the public's belief that government's role is not to redistribute public wealth or freely spend on social programs as occurred in the 60s and 70s. Instead, we overwhelmingly prefer a government that focuses on spurring economic growth and creating opportunity for all Americans, and then getting out of the way and letting us do our own thing.

- *Business Regulation* – A majority of Americans believe government has gone *too far* in regulating business and interfering with the free enterprise system. Yet, when asked about specific areas that the government now regulates or could regulate—from automobile safety to health care to TV program content—Americans are much more likely to say there is *not enough* regulation than they are to say there is too much. (Does this remind you of the irregularities in the logic of our crazy language, too?)

FOREIGN HERITAGE AMERICANS IN U.S. GOVERNMENT

First- or second-generation Americans are increasingly participating in American government, from local cities to federal government levels. Here are just a few.

- Katherine Ortega's grandparents emigrated from Spain and then Mexico. She only spoke Spanish until she learned English in the U.S. President Reagan appointed her Treasurer of the U.S. in 1983. Ortega credited much of her success to her heritage, saying, "I am the product of a heritage that teaches strong family devotion, a commitment to earning a livelihood by hard work, patience, determination and perseverance."

Katherine Ortega

- In 1990, President Bush appointed Antonia Novello Surgeon General of the U.S. Born in Puerto Rico, she was both the first woman and the first Latin American to be appointed to this post. She won praise for her campaigns to address the health problems of America's young people. After leaving office, Dr. Novello served UNICEF, the United Nations' children's health organization, and was Commissioner of Health for the State of New York.

Dr. Novello

- Piyush "Bobby" Jindal was elected to the U.S. House of Representatives in 2004 from Louisiana and became governor in 2007. He was *India Abroad's* Person of the Year in 2005.

Piyush Jindal

- Elaine Chao became the first Asian American immigrant to be appointed to a cabinet post when President Bush selected her as his Secretary of Labor in 2001. She came to America when she was eight years old and spoke no English.

Elaine Chao

- In the late 1990s, Eric Shinseki, of Japanese ancestry, was one of the youngest Chiefs of Staff in U.S. Army history, one of the top five jobs in the military. He retired in 2003 and President Obama would later appoint him to head the Veterans Affairs.

Eric Shinseki

- Norman Mineta became the first Asian American to be elected mayor of a major U.S. city in 1970. He later became a member of Congress, and President Clinton appointed him Commerce Secretary. President Bush appointed him Transportation Secretary in 2000, the only Democratic cabinet member in his cabinet.

Norman Mineta

- Born into Chinese poverty, Gary Locke's grandfather immigrated to Washington State at the turn of the 20th century where he worked as a houseboy. Locke rose to be elected governor of Washington in 1996, the first Asian American governor in the continental U.S. He was appointed Secretary of Commerce in 2009 and U.S. Ambassador to China in 2011.

Gary Locke

- Born in Czechoslovakia, Madeline Albright's family was given asylum in the U.S. after WWII when the communists took over her country. She got her Ph.D. and worked her way up to become our U.N. Ambassador, her first diplomatic post. Later she became the first female U.S. Secretary of State and the highest ranking women in the history of U.S. government.

Madeline Albright

☺ **Here's an assignment for you.** If you would like to test your general knowledge of American government or learn more about the U.S., Appendix 10 provides a fun quiz about our government and history.

Let's next examine how geography has affected the development of America and its culture.

C

GEOGRAPHY

*This land is your land, this land is my land/From California to the New York
Island/From the redwood forest to the Gulf Stream waters/This land was made
for you and me.* – From a 1940 song by Woody Guthrie, U.S. folksinger and songwriter

To better understand America, it is necessary to understand the underlying influence of our geography. Knowledge of the names and places of our important mountains, rivers, lakes, cities, and states will enhance your conversations with Americans and aid in further understanding our culture. Many of our businesses, schools, and institutions are named after them.

Geography helped mold our national character because of the large and varied landmass that was waiting to be inhabited, cultivated, and developed into states hundreds of years ago. Settlers coped with its vast size with an attraction to certain geographical areas, even influencing where different immigrant groups settled. Americans long regarded the wide-open spaces of the American West as The **Last Frontier**. Many of our values and attitudes can be traced back to the spirit of this **Great Frontier**: self-reliance, resourcefulness, helping others, hard work, independence, and a strong sense of equality.

The story of America is a story about movement and change. Because of the vast expanse and varied geography, it was not until 1869 that trains connected our two shores. And not until 1903 that the first person drove an automobile from coast to coast. It took 63 days on crude dirt roads in an attempt to win a $50 bet. A short thirteen years later as highways were improving drivers crossed it in only five days. America, like its roads, is ever changing and its geography affects many of these changes. During the 1950s and 60s, in a competitive effort to attract engineers, many companies established operations in the more favorable climate areas of the southern one-third of the U.S. It remains our fastest growing area with cultural differences and a faster paced society.

Geography even influences our political process. To appeal to the most voters, many U.S. presidential candidates purposely choose a vice presidential running mate who hails from a different geographical region than their own.

The landmass between the Pacific Ocean and the Atlantic Ocean, known as the **Americas**, is generally divided into North, Central, and South America. People who live in the Americas are sometimes referred to as being American, although the word "American" is used nearly exclusively today to refer to a citizen of the United States of America, and "America" to refer to the U.S. (They are used in this context in this book.)

North American Continent   (Courtesy of MapQuest.com.)

The U.S. is located on the North American continent with 48 adjoining states (called the **continental states**) and two others, Alaska and Hawaii, separate from the others and in the Pacific Ocean. A flight from the West Coast to Tokyo takes 11 hours, and from our West Coast to the East Coast five hours. The longest airplane flight in the world—15,345 km between Singapore and New York City—takes 19 hours.

Our neighbor to the north is Canada where English is widely spoken along with French in some northeastern areas. Our neighbor to the south is Mexico where Spanish is the predominant tongue as it is in Central and most of South America.

Geographically, the size of the U.S. (9.6 million sq. km) ranks third behind Russia and Canada. In terms of population (310 million), we rank third behind China and India. India's landmass is about a third the area of the U.S. and its population density of 941 people per square mile is roughly 12 times greater. To complicate matters, only 10 percent of India's land is fit for growing food, about half that of the productive U.S. We only have five percent of the

U.S. states and their capital city locations.   (Courtesy of www.worldatlas.com)

world's population but consume 25 percent of the world's energy, due in part to our massive industrial base and economy that are enhanced in part by the geography and natural resources of the U.S. (see Chapter U - Business and Finance).

> **Hint**: Want to play a trivia game with an American? Ask them which is farther west, the west coast of South America or New York City on our East Coast. Most will say New York City, in which case they are wrong. Ask them what South American country does not have Spanish as its native tongue. The answer is Brazil where Portuguese is spoken because, unlike the other South American countries, it was founded by Portugal, not Spain, in the 1500s.

Another way to view the **continental** United States is to think of it as a land with four time zones running north to south: Pacific, Mountain, Midwest, and Eastern. Hawaii and Alaska, our other two states, are in still earlier time zones. About 48 percent of Americans live in the Eastern Time Zone, 29 in Central, 6 in Mountain, and 17 in Pacific. We use "a.m." to specify time from midnight to noon, and "p.m." from noon to midnight. When it is 10 p.m. in Rome, Italy, it is 1 p.m. in the Pacific Time Zone. I was surprised to learn that China and India each

U.S. time zones.   (www.worldatlas.com)

only have one time zone. It's amazing what we learn about others when we travel.

Our country's great expanse is made up of mountains and deserts in the West, vast grassy plains in the Midwest, and hills and low mountains in the east. Our climate is varied: tropical in Hawaii and subtropical in Florida, arctic in Alaska, semiarid in the great plains west of the Mississippi River, and the desert areas in the Southwest. Our northern states have lots of snow in the winter while southern states enjoy sunshine and tourists. Similar to China's Turpan Basin that is minus 154 meters, our lowest point is barren **Death Valley** in our western state of Nevada at 86 meters below sea level.

Throughout this vast land the U.S. is blessed with a wealth of agriculture and natural resources including timber, petroleum, natural gas, gold, silver, coal and many minerals, but some say our greatest resource is our diversity of people derived from our immigrants.

Desert landscape in western state of Arizona.

47

MOUNTAINS

Our highest elevation is **Mount McKinley** in Alaska at 6194 m. In the continental U.S., California's **Mount Whitney** (a two-hour drive north of Los Angeles) is the highest point at 4476 m. As a comparison, Germany's highest point is in the Zugspitze Mountains at 2962 m. We have two major mountain ranges in America: the **Rocky Mountains** in the west and the **Appalachian Mountains** *[app-a-LAY-chee-un]* in the East.

Unlike India's east-west lying Himalayan range, The Rocky Mountains, also called the **Rockies**, is that portion of the vast mountain range that flows north to south from Canada through the U.S., border to border, for a distance of 3200 km (and continues down through all of South America where it is named the Andes). As the name suggests, the mountains *are* rocky. (We have a way of being literal when we assign names

Rocky Mountain lake.

to things and places. Unfortunately, as you will learn in the chapter on grammar or already know, the rest of our language is not as logical.)

The Rockies are located in broad portions of several western states: Washington, Idaho, Montana, Utah, Wyoming, Colorado, and New Mexico. So we call most of these states the **Rocky Mountain States**. The **Continental Divide** is the ridgeline of the Rockies, perfectly named because it separates streams that flow westerly into the Pacific Ocean from those that flow eastward; hence, it "divides" our continent.

The Rockies have more than 50 peaks above 4250 meters versus 100 in Switzerland. The overall terrain in this area is elevated compared to the eastern U.S. The highest point in the eastern state of

North America   (Courtesy of www.worldatlas.com)

Pennsylvania is lower than the lowest point in Colorado. Relatively few people live throughout this rugged and sometimes remote region, but because of its spectacular scenery, it attracts tourists. There is also substantial mining activity. To the east of the Rockies, the flat Midwest region begins rather abruptly, but to the west the Pacific Coast region contains many smaller mountain ranges.

The American West, particularly the Rocky Mountain area, had not been explored until the **Lewis & Clark** Expedition first set foot in this remote area in 1804. People had moved from the East across the Midwest region to the Mississippi River by then, but the rugged Rockies were a barrier to further westward movement. It was not until the mid-1800s that **pioneers** (first settlers) started making their way west in covered wagons and on foot through the rugged mountains.

> **Hint**: A book I highly recommend to foreigners who want to learn more about the exciting opening of the West is "Undaunted Courage: Meriwether Lewis, Thomas Jefferson and the Opening of the American West" by Stephen Ambrose.

The **Appalachian** Mountains in the eastern part of North America extend from Canada down through the U.S. into the state of Alabama for 2,400 km. They are much smaller than the Rockies. The area to the west is hilly and descends gently to the Midwest. Our first settlers established colonies in the 1600s in the broad coastal plain area to the east of the Appalachians. The Appalachians were a barrier to westward migration for several hundred years until routes through them were discovered in the early 1800s. Because of the more gentle nature of these mountains, more people live here than in the Rockies. Like the Rockies, they attract tourists and contain natural resources.

The Appalachians harbor areas of poverty similar to other remote places in the world. Our government started the Tennessee Valley Authority (TVA) in the mid-1930s to stimulate the local economy and create jobs. It built 42 dams, improved river navigation, and provided flood control and electric power in the area. It was a massive project, perhaps similar to what is happening in other countries, like the Yangtze River projects in China.

> **Hint**: The movie, *Coal Miner's Daughter,* provides an accurate portrayal of poor life in this area, which we refer to as **Appalachia**.

You might encounter names of other smaller mountain ranges in the U.S., or actually visit them. Some, like the **Cascades** in Washington State and the **Sierras** in California, lie west of the Rockies, but are not considered part of the Rockies. In the East, the mountains are all part of the Appalachian range but have names like the **Great Smoky Mountains** in North Carolina, the **Allegheny** *[ahl-eh-GAIN-e]* **Mountains** in Pennsylvania, and the **Catskills** *[CAT-skills]* in New York. Due to geological forces that created our mountains, most flow in a general north-south direction, but the Uintah Mountains in the state of Utah are one of the few east-west lying mountain ranges.

RIVERS AND LAKES

Our coastlines, lakes, and rivers played a major role in the development of the U.S. Unlike China and India where rivers generally flow eastwardly, in the U.S. they

49

generally flow southward. In the map below are the names of our major lakes and rivers that you might hear us refer to.

Let's start with the **Great Lakes** along the border between Canada and the U.S. Yes, these five lakes—Superior, Huron, Michigan, Ontario, and Erie—*are* great in size

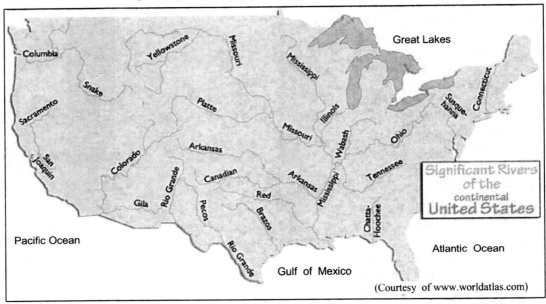

(Courtesy of www.worldatlas.com)

and importance, just like the Rockies *are* rocky. The Great Lakes form the world's largest body of freshwater and are a major source for shipping bulk cargo such as coal, timber, iron ore, and grain between cities located on its shores and even out to the Atlantic Ocean through the **St. Lawrence Seaway** along the Canadian border. Five large industrial cities are located on the shores of these lakes: Chicago, Milwaukee, Detroit, Cleveland, and Buffalo.

North America's longest river, the **Mississippi** *[miss-ih-SIP-ee]* at 3800 km, flows from Minnesota south to the Gulf of Mexico. Like China's Yangtze River that serves as an imaginary dividing line between North and South, the Mississippi divides our East and West and, with a number of smaller rivers running into it, drains the Midwest. In the chapter on American literature, you will learn about Mark Twain, one of our most famous authors, who wrote about 19th century life around the mighty Mississippi. Today, the river is a major artery for moving bulk commodities to and from the Midwest.

You may hear us refer to other major rivers.
- The **Ohio River** *[oh-HIGH-oh]* flows 1600 km southwesterly through a heavily industrialized area from the Appalachian Mountains to the

Mississippi. It forms the northern boundary where people to the south speak with a Southern accent.

- The **Missouri River** *[MIH-zu-ree]* begins in the Rockies in Montana and flows 4100 km southeasterly into the Mississippi. It lacks heavy cargo traffic and major cities along its remote path.

- The **Rio Grande River** *[REE-oh grand]* forms a portion of our border with Mexico and provides water for this dry region.

- The **Colorado River** *[CALL-o-radd-oh]* also originates in the Rocky Mountains but flows 2300 km southwesterly throughout the desert region, separating California and Arizona before flowing into the Gulf of California. It created the spectacular Grand Canyon National Park discussed at the end of this chapter.

- The **Columbia River** *[co-LUHM-bee-uh]* flows 1950 km from the Rockies westward into the Pacific Ocean, forming the boundary between the states of Washington and Oregon. Its dams are a major source of hydroelectricity.

GEOGRAPHICAL REGIONS

In the broadest sense, America has two major regions, West and East. But we also have seven smaller geographical regions, each of which is loosely uniform in terms of landscape, climate, economy, speech, foods, customs, and history. These regions, from west to east, are: Pacific Coast, Rocky Mountain, Southwest, Midwest, Southern, Middle Atlantic, and New England. You may often hear us use these names as well. (You may encounter other definitions of our regions, but the seven presented here are the most clearly defined.)

Geographical regions.

Pacific Coast Region – These states border the Pacific Ocean and have rugged mountains, dense forests, beautiful shorelines, and deserts. The region has fertile farming areas and contains many minerals. It also has more people of Asian ancestry than any other region in the U.S. Major cities include Los Angeles, San Francisco, and Seattle. The states are **California** *[kal-ih-FOR-niuh]*, **Oregon** *[ORE-ee-gun]*, and **Washington** *[WASH-ing-tun]*. The **Pacific Northwest** refers to the states of Washington and Oregon, and the **Pacific Southwest** refers to the Southern California area.

Golden Gate Bridge

Southwest Region – This vast, dry, warm area contains cattle, cotton ranches, oil drilling, and minerals. Because of its warm climate, it has many of the fastest growing cities in the U.S. Spanish people settled this area in the 1500s, so Spanish (the second most common language in the U.S.) is also spoken here by some. English, however, is the common language as it is in all the regions. Phoenix and Dallas are two major cities. The states are **Arizona** *[air-ih-ZO-nah]*, **New Mexico** *[MEX-ih-ko]*, **Oklahoma** *[ohk-lah-HOME-ah]*, and **Texas** *[TEX-us]*.

Grand Canyon - Arizona.

Rocky Mountain Region – This area not only contains the Rockies and other mountain ranges, but it also has deserts and plains. Mining has always been important to the region. It also has farming, cattle, and tourism. Major cities include Denver, Salt Lake City, and Las Vegas. The states are **Colorado** *[call-oh-RAD-oh]*, **Idaho** *[EYE-duh-ho]*, **Montana** *[mon-TAN-ah]*, **Nevada** *[nuh-VAH-duh]*, **Utah** *[YOU-taw]*, and **Wyoming** *[y-OHM-ing]*.

Rocky Mountain National Park - Colorado

Midwest Region – This vast area of land in the middle of the U.S. is relatively flat, has very fertile soil, and produces large amounts of corn, wheat, and livestock. The two major cities, Chicago and St. Louis, are adjacent to waterways. The states are **Illinois** *[ill-ah-NOY]*, **Indiana** *[in-dee-AN-uh]*, **Iowa** *[EYE-oh-wah]*, **Kansas** *[KAN-zus]*, **Michigan** *[MISH-e-gun]*, **Minnesota** *[min-ah-SOTE-ah]*, **Missouri** *[mah-ZUR-ee]*, **Nebraska** *[nah-BRASS-ka]*, **North Dakota** *[duh-COAT-ah]*, **Ohio** *[oh-HI-oh]*, **South Dakota**, and **Wisconsin** *[wiz-KON-sun]*.

Mt. Rushmore - South Dakota.

Southern Region – This area of rolling hills, mountains, and plains borders on the Atlantic Ocean and the Gulf of Mexico. Until the 1950s, it was primarily an agricultural region with warm weather crops such as cotton, sugarcane, tobacco, and rice. Since then, it has experienced strong industrial and tourist growth. People native to this area are called **Southerners**, some of whom speak with a distinctive slower, rounded Southern accent. During the 1600s and 1700s, black Africans were brought as slaves to this region to work on plantations; consequently, a large number of **African Americans** live here today. The **Mason-Dixon Line** is a famous boundary between Pennsylvania and

52

Maryland that signified the geo-political division line between the North and South when slavery was an issue in the 1800s and over which we fought the Civil War from 1861 to 1865 (see Chapter D - History). You might notice that Southerners have an especially strong sense of loyalty to their region and are proud of their history, heritage, and culture.

South Carolina plantation.

Major cities include Washington, D.C., Atlanta, and Miami. The southern states are **Alabama** *[ahl-a-BAM-ah]*, **Arkansas** *[are-CAN-saw]*, **Delaware** *[DELL-uh-ware]*, **Florida** *[FLOOR-ih-duh]*, **Georgia** *[JOR-juh]*, **Kentucky** *[ken-TUCK-ee]*, **Louisiana,** *[lou-eez-ee-ANNA]*, **Maryland** *[MARE-eh-lund]*, **Mississippi** *[miss-sih-SIP-ee]*, **North Carolina** *[care-ah-LINE-ah]*, **South Carolina**, **Tennessee** *[ten-ah-SEE]*, **Virginia** *[vir-JIN-yah]*, and **West Virginia**.

Middle Atlantic Region – This region is the most heavily populated area in the U.S. with large ethnic groups, including African, Latin American, and Asian ancestries. The area has good harbors for international trade, many factories, farms, and forests. Rich coal mining is found in the western part of the region. Major cities include New York City (America's largest), Philadelphia, and Pittsburgh. The states are **New Jersey** *[JUR-zee]*, **New York**, and **Pennsylvania** *[penn-sul-VANE-yuh]*.

New York City

New England Region – This small region in the northeast part of the U.S. is mostly hilly and rocky with beautiful small villages, coastlines, and covered bridges. It is known for its natural scenery and trees that turn bright gold and red in autumn. It has many historical sites relating to America's founding. **New Englanders** (people who live here) are proud of this heritage, which dates back to the 1600s when English immigrants settled the area. They, too, have a unique accent when speaking, in which the letter R is usually replaced with an AH sound, so "park" is pronounced by some as "pahk." (President Kennedy was from this area and spoke with this accent.) The area was our first industrial region and light manufacturing is still important. The major city is Boston. The states are **Connecticut** *[kun-NET-ih-cut]*, **Maine** *[MAY-n]*, **Massachusetts** *[mass-a-CHEW-suts]*, **New Hampshire** *[HAMP-shur]*, **Rhode Island** *[rode-EYE-lund]*, and **Vermont** *[vur-MONT]*.

New England coastline.

OTHER REGIONS

Besides our seven geographical regions, you will also hear us refer to other areas in the U.S.

- The **Bible Belt** refers to a general area throughout the southern states where groups of religious people are strong believers in the Bible (see Chapter F - Religion).

- **Dixie** is region of the southern and eastern U.S. comprising the states that joined the Confederacy during the Civil War (see Chapter D - History).

- The **Borscht Belt** is a region in upstate New York where many Jewish families traditionally spent summer vacations.

- The Midwest states are referred to as **Middle America** or the **Heartland of America**.

- The **Silicon Valley** area in Northern California near San Francisco—just 32 km long—is headquarters for important computer manufacturing, software, and other high-technology industries. This area equates to China's Wuhan and India's Bangalore high-tech areas.

Silicon Valley – California.

- The **Intermountain West** refers to the states amidst the Rocky Mountains to the northeast and the Sierra Nevada and the Cascade Mountains on the west. This includes Wyoming, Montana, Idaho, Utah, Colorado, Nevada, New Mexico, and Arizona.

- The **Desert Southwest**, a dry area to the south and west, includes Arizona, New Mexico, and smaller parts of California, Utah, Colorado, and Texas.

- The **Smoke Stack Belt** refers to the heavily industrialized northeastern area sweeping from Pittsburgh, Pennsylvania (steel making), through Ohio, Indiana (chemicals), Illinois, and then up to Detroit, Michigan, the **car-making capital**[*] of the U.S. This area is also referred to as the **Rust Belt**, because, starting in the 1970s, this formerly dominant industrial region became noted for abandoned factories, unemployment, and overall decline. This was due in part to cheaper foreign imports and migration to other areas in the U.S. Some cities are now recovering with new light industries.

---

[*]Car manufacturing started here because buggy making was concentrated here in the 1800s. This identity is so ingrained that the term "Detroit" can be used to refer to the U.S. auto industry in general, not necessarily the Michigan city.

- The **Sun Belt** is the rapidly growing southern tier of the U.S., primarily Florida, Texas, Arizona, and Southern California, and extends as far north as Virginia on the East Coast. Its growth was fueled by oil booms of the 1970s, aerospace and defense contractors opening plants, and expanding tourist industries, especially in Florida and Southern California.

- The **Great Plains** area lies east of the Rocky Mountains and extends to the lowlands west of the Mississippi River, from the Dakotas in the north to northern Texas to the south. It is sparsely populated, elevated, arid, and has much grassland devoted to farms and ranches.

- To the east of the Great Plains are the wetter **Prairies** that are the original grass-covered, treeless plains of North America, stretching from western Ohio through Indiana, Illinois, and Iowa, up into Canada. Because of favorable climate, fertile soil, and prolific production of wheat and corn, our Midwest is sometimes called the **bread basket of the world.** (The U.S. accounts for half of all world corn exports, 40 percent of soybean exports, and 30 percent of wheat exports.)

OUR LARGEST STATES AND CITIES

If you come to the U.S., you just might end up in one of our largest states or cities. Or, if Americans visit your country, they might be from one of them. You may hear us use these nicknames for some of our cities: Boston-**Bean Town.**, Chicago-**The Windy City**, Detroit-**Motor City** and **Motown**, Las Vegas-**Sin City**, New Orleans-**The Big Easy**, New York City-**The Big Apple**, Minneapolis/St. Paul-**The Twin Cities**, and Los Angeles-**The City of Angels**.

2012 Rank	STATE	2012 Population	1950 Rank	2012 Rank	CITY (State)	2012 Population	1950 Population
01	California (CA)	37.2 m	02	01	New York City, NY	8.2 m	7.8 m
02	Texas (TX)	25.1	06	02	Los Angeles, CA	3.8	1.9
03	New York (NY)	19.4	01	03	Chicago, IL	2.8	3.6
04	Florida (FL)	18.8	20	04	Houston, TX	2.1	0.5
05	Illinois (IL)	12.8	04	05	Philadelphia, PA	1.5	2.1
06	Pennsylvania (PA)	12.7	03	06	Phoenix, AZ	1.5	0.1
07	Ohio (OH)	11.5	05	07	San Antonio, TX	1.3	0.4
08	Michigan (MI)	9.9	07	08	San Diego, CA	1.3	0.3
09	Georgia (GA)	9.7	13	09	Dallas, TX	1.2	0.4
10	North Carolina (NC)	9.5	10	10	San Jose, CA	0.9	1.8

CLIMATE

Still another way to view the U.S. is by its climatic zones. Some of our early immigrants settled in areas with climates similar to their homelands. For instance, Scandinavians settled in Minnesota and other cool northern states, the Irish in rocky

Massachusetts and eastern coastal areas while Germans settled the rich farmland areas of Pennsylvania and the Midwest. The culture of these areas remains a reflection of those early American settlers. Today, our climate still might affect where some immigrants choose to attend school or work in the U.S.

Our country is generally divided into four broad climatic regions—the arid West, the humid East, the cooler North, and the warmer South. The arid West, like the dry northwest area of China, has an increase in precipitation going east.

The western portion of Oregon and Washington on the West Coast is one of the wettest areas in the continental U.S. During the summer, eastern and southern states have much more humidity than the more comfortable western states. Though we don't experience monsoons as some countries do, we have hurricanes that hit from the Gulf Coast up through the East Coast during the summer months, and tornados (cyclones) in the midwestern states. Our Pacific Coast and Rocky Mountain states do not experience these destructive forces of **Mother Nature**, but they are known for their earthquakes. There are approximately 500,000 detectable seismic tremors in California annually, few of which are actually felt.

> **Hint**: Our most famous earthquake was the 1906 San Francisco, California, quake that leveled the city and killed thousands. When you are discussing something devastating, you might say, "The disappointment hit me like the **San Francisco Earthquake** of 1906."

NATIONAL PARKS

In 1872, the U.S. was the first nation to set aside specific areas to protect their beauty, wildlife, history, or natural features. Today, we have 376 national parks, monuments, scenic trails, and cemeteries. Other nations have similar protected areas. Japan has about 80 while China has over 100.

Americans love these sites. If appropriate, refer to them in your conversations or writings. The large number of these protected areas reflects their importance in our culture. Our mint even introduced five new coins a year to honor each one (www.parkquarters.com). Try to visit some. For more information, go to the National Park System's website at www.nps.gov. Tourist agencies can help you plan such trips Some parks require reservations in advance. Here is but a sampling of some of our favorites that you may hear us refer to (state names in parentheses).[*]

---

[*] Photos courtesy of National Park Service.

Bryce *[brise]* **Canyon National Park** (Utah) – This is a sweeping canyon of bright, rust-red eroded rock formations that look like a jungle of pillars and exciting castle towers.

Carlsbad Caverns National Park (New Mexico) – The world's largest known caves were created by 500,000 years of dripping water. The park contains 83 separate caves, including the nation's biggest limestone cave 30-stories tall. Formations are mysterious with lovely pink, beige, and brown colors. These remind me of the world famous caves in Slovenia carved out by rivers.

Crater Lake National Park (Oregon) – This beautiful blue lake, the deepest in the U.S., is a dark clear sapphire jewel formed after the collapse of a volcano 7,700 years ago. Mountains, volcanic peaks, and evergreen forests surround it.

Death Valley National Park (California) – A large, inhospitable, delicately colored desert surrounded by high mountains. It is the lowest point in the Western Hemisphere (-86 m, -282 feet) and holds the record for the highest year-round temperature in the world. You might hear someone say something "was as barren and remote as Death Valley."

Everglades National Park (Florida) – A lush, subtropical area in southern Florida with lakes, birds, and animal life. It is also the only place in the world where alligators and crocodiles exist side by side.

Glacier National Park (Montana) – With Rocky Mountain scenery that includes many glaciers and lakes, this park encompasses 3.6 million sq. km (1.4 million sq. miles) of wilderness and some of the most beautiful mountain scenery in the western United States.

Grand Canyon National Park (Arizona) – This is a gorge 1.6 km deep, 6.5 to 29 km wide, and 350 km long carved out by the Colorado River. Because it is so immense, so colorful, and unlike anything they have ever seen, many first-time visitors don't believe what they are seeing. It is popular for challenging river rafting, hiking,  and an exciting two-day mule ride to and from the bottom of the canyon. You could say, "My love for you is as big as the Grand Canyon."

Mount Rushmore National Memorial (South Dakota) – Carved in a remote mountainside are the busts of U.S. presidents Washington, Jefferson, Teddy Roosevelt, and Lincoln. The rustic lodge below is a beauty that offers wide vistas. (The classic mystery movie, *North by Northwest* (1959), is set in this famous site.) We like to speculate about the next president who should be carved in the mountain. Most choose Ronald Reagan or Franklin D. Roosevelt.

Statue of Liberty National Monument (New York City) – Liberty is our famous symbol of freedom and democracy and a welcome to America for those arriving by ship. It was a gift from the people of France in 1886. A short boat ride takes visitors to the lady who stands in the middle of New York Harbor. They can climb stairs inside her body that lead up to the top of the statue where they are treated to a commanding view of the majestic New York skyline and busy harbor.

Washington Monument (Washington, D.C.) – A tribute to George Washington, the first president of the U.S. A nighttime view shows the Lincoln Memorial in the foreground, the tall Washington Monument, and the U.S. Capitol. Stairs lead to the top of the slender monument, the world's tallest stone structure. The area is a beautiful sight at night when the three are lighted. In the springtime, cherry trees that were a gift from the people of Japan in 1912 are in full bloom throughout the area.

Yellowstone National Park (Wyoming) – This was the world's first national park and has most of the world's 10,000 geysers and hot springs within its borders. The world's largest geyser, **Old Faithful**, shoots 45 meters in the air with regularity. Yellowstone is also a mountain-range wilderness and an open refuge for wildlife, including grizzly bear, elk, American bison, moose, and wolf. It is also a popular camping area with overly-friendly bears seeking food from tourists.

Yosemite *[yoh-SEM-ah-tee]* **National Park** (California) – We love this park's mountains, glacial-carved gorges, and its giant Sequoia *[suh-KWOI-yah]* trees—the world's *largest* living things. A famous tree, General Sherman, is the world's *oldest* living thing at 5,000 years old. It is 84 meters (274 feet) tall and has a giant base diameter of 11 meters (37 feet).

Zion National Park (Utah) – This is a multicolored gorge in the heart of a desert with spectacular cliffs, canyons, and wilderness. It has the world's largest natural arch—Kolob Arch—with a span that measures 94.5 m (310 feet). Nearby, Arches National Park contains the world's largest collection of over 2,000 natural sandstone arches.

National Geographic's 10 Best National Parks – The prestigious *National Geographic* magazine (www.nationalgeographic.com) ranks these as our 10 best parks.
1. Sequoia & Kings Canyon National Parks, California. (www.nps.gov/seki/index.htm)
2. Gettysburg National Military Park, Pennsylvania. (www.nps.gov/gett/index.htm)
3. Alagnak Wild River, Alaska. (www.nps.gov/alag/index.htm)
4. Santa Fe National Historic Trail, Colorado to Oklahoma. (www.nps.gov/safe/index.htm)
5. Statue of Liberty National Monument, New York. (www.nps.gov/stli/index.htm)
6. Blue Ridge Parkway, North Carolina and Virginia. (www.nps.gov/blri/index.htm)
7. New Orleans Jazz Historical Park, Louisiana. (www.nps.gov/jazz/index.htm)
8. Yosemite National Park, California. (www.nps.gov/yose/index.htm)
9. Hawaii Volcanoes National Park, Hawaii. (www.nps.gov/havo/index.htm)
10. Grand Canyon National Park, Arizona. (www.nps.gov/grca/index.htm)

TRIVIA QUIZ

Want to play a U.S. geography trivia game with an American? Here are some interesting questions to ask them about America and its geograpny. A map of the U.S. below helps you understand the areas referred to.
1. Geographically, how many of the smallest states in the U.S. would fit simultaneously within the state of Alaska, our largest state? **Answer:** 21.
2. What two states are bordered with more states than all others? **Answer:** Tennessee and Missouri each have eight.
3. Name the state capitol with the highest elevation. **Answer:** Santa Fe, New Mexico, a Rocky Mountain state at 6998 feet (2133 m).

61

4. What is the southernmost capitol city in the continental U.S.? **Answer:** Austin, Texas.

5. What is the only state that borders only one state? **Answer:** The New England state of Maine

6. What is the deepest lake in the U.S.? **Answer:** Crater Lake in the Pacific Coast state of Oregon at 1932 feet (589 m).

7. What is the highest lake in the U.S.? **Answer:** Yellowstone Lake, located in the western state of Wyoming at 7735 feet (2358 m) above sea level.

8. What was the first state to allow women to vote and had the first female governor (1925)? **Answer:** The western state of Wyoming, which is our least populated.

9. What state was the first state admitted after the original 13? **Answer:** Vermont

10. What is the only state to front two oceans? **Answer:** Alaska (The Arctic Ocean and the Pacific Ocean.)

U.S. states and their capitol city locations. (Courtesy of www.worldatlas.com)

11. What mountain in the U.S. is the tallest mountain in the world? **Answer:** If you account for the entire mountain, Mauna Kea in Hawaii is 33,480 feet tall (10.2 kilometers); however, only 13,796 feet (4.2 kilometers) is above sea level.

12. What is the deepest gorge in the U.S.? **Answer:** Hells Canyon on the Snake River in the western state of Idaho is 7,900 feet deep (2,408 meters).

13. In which state is there not a single billboard advertisement? **Answer:** The New England state of Vermont, another example of states' rights and independence.

With this geographical background of the U.S. in place, let's now examine how the powerful forces of history combined to influence the cultural development of America and its people. Perhaps your country, like many others, contributed to our development, too.

D

HISTORY

The past is a source of knowledge, and the future is a source of hope. Love of the past implies faith in the future. - Stephen Ambrose, historian and author

Compared to other countries with thousands of years of history, America is a **new kid on the block** (newcomer) with a history of only five hundred years. When I travel abroad and see buildings two and three times as old as America, I am reminded of just how young we really are. Because we have had no dynasties or reigning kings to refer to, our eras are usually identified by their century or by important events that occurred, such as our wars. Let's examine each of the last five centuries and discuss how history has shaped America, its people, and its culture. Knowing about these eras will help you better understand our culture and people of today.

THE 1500s – EXPLORATION

Hunters from Asia migrated to North America about 11,000 years ago over a land bridge into Alaska after the retreat of Ice Age glaciers. In the 1400s, Europeans wanted to find a short sea path to Asia, which they called the **Far East**, where they traded for spices, silks, and other valuable commodities via overland caravans. In 1492, **Christopher Columbus** sailed west from Spain looking for a sea route to those lands when he discovered America by mistake. He landed south of what is our state of Florida, thinking he had found the Far East. A new era in Western history began as European nations set sail for the **New World**. We have a national holiday called

Columbus' ship, the Santa Maria.

Columbus Day in October (see Chapter R - Holidays and Traditions). Children learn in school, "In 1492, Columbus sailed the ocean blue."

During the 1500s, Spain (and to a lesser extent Portugal) moved into and settled much of Mexico and Central and South America. For this reason Spanish is the predominant language spoken today by our neighbors to the south. Spain also moved into the southern parts of what would later become the U.S. to seek riches like they had found farther south. They established St. Augustine, Florida in 1565, the first permanent American settlement, which today is a fun tourist spot. While French interests were primarily in Canada, the British explored to the south in what is now the U.S. The individual cultures they brought with them as they settled these areas remain part of our culture today.

THE 1600s – SETTLEMENT

Starting in the early 1600s, England's kings granted charters to merchants that allowed them to establish colonies in America. These merchants recruited people to sail with them across the Atlantic Ocean, and then to govern them even though they were officially under control of the king. During the 1600s and half of the 1700s, small settlements were established along the East Coast from New Hampshire to Georgia. They eventually banded together to form the larger **Thirteen Colonies** that later became our first 13 states (as shown in the map).

13 original colonies. (worldatlas.com)

In 1607, about 100 English people founded **Jamestown** in Virginia that was the first English settlement in America. They were called **colonists** because they established a colony for England.

> **Hint**: **Colonial Williamsburg**, near Jamestown, a 1½ hour drive south of Washington, D.C., is a wonderful tourist site where you can go back to these early times and see how people lived in those days. It is a refurbished village from that era with craftspeople making items the way they were made 400 years ago (www.history.org).

Farther north, New England colonies were founded in 1620 by **Puritans** who had been persecuted by the English because of their opposition to Britain's official church, the Church of England. **Plymouth Rock** is a famous rock on the shore in Massachusetts with the date "1620" carved in it. It is located where the **Pilgrims** (original settlers) were thought to have first set foot in America. Historians disagree, but it still remains a popular tourist site (www.visit-plymouth.com/plymouthrock.htm). It

Plymouth Rock

was this colony that inspired our national holiday in November called **Thanksgiving Day**. It was first celebrated in those early days when the colonists were thankful for surviving with the help of native Indians.

As tobacco farms became prosperous in Jamestown in the early 1600s, new farms and settlements spread up and down the East Coast. Initially, it was a very difficult life for the immigrants because of diseases, lack of food, and some Indian (Native American) attacks. Eventually, they developed farms and businesses, roads, churches, schools, and some learned to keep peace with the Indians.

In 1626, a Dutch colonist bought Manhattan Island from Native Americans for $24 and some beads and New York City got its start. In 1634, English Roman Catholics who were persecuted in England settled in Maryland and prospered with tobacco crops, too. Colonists from Sweden established a small settlement in Pennsylvania in 1643 while the land between Virginia and Florida attracted British settlers. In the South Carolina area, rich landowners established rice and tobacco plantations and brought blacks from Africa to work them. Connecticut and Rhode Island became colonies within 20 years followed by New Hampshire in 1680.

These colonists came to America primarily for religious and economic reasons. It was difficult for many to advance economically or socially in Europe. In America, the opposite was true. With hard work, a person could succeed because land was abundant, people were not locked into a social class, and they had opportunities to start new businesses and trades. They were also free to develop their own political and social beliefs, many different from those in their native countries. This led to a democratic form of government, individual freedoms, and rewards for hard work, all of which remain the foundation of our society today.

The colonists continued to establish settlements during the rest of the 1600s and well into the 1700s. While living under British rule, which they often disliked and ignored (something we are still good at doing), the colonists' increasing desire for independence ultimately lead to an eventual split with Britain in the 1700s.

THE 1700s – INDEPENDENCE

Even though the heritage of most colonists was British, they grew discontented with British rule and wanted more voice in how they were governed. Britain, in opposition to colonists' wishes, taxed Americans for products imported from England such as tea. In 1773, colonists boarded an English ship in Boston Harbor that was loaded with British tea. They tossed it in the water in response to what they called irresponsible "taxation without representation." The incident became known as the **Boston Tea Party**. Taxes on international trade are still a hot political issue with Americans today. By this time most colonists, who now thought of themselves as Americans, not British subjects, hungered for independence. In contrast to our rebellious nature, India's first big uprising against the British would not occur for another 84 years in 1857.

On **July 4, 1776**, Congress—comprised of the 13 original colonies—formally declared independence from Britain and formed the United States of America by adopting the written **Declaration of Independence.** The 13 colonies thus became states. Written by **Thomas Jefferson** of Virginia (who later became our 3rd president), the Declaration opened with the idea that all men are created equal and are entitled to life, liberty, and the pursuit of happiness. It was necessary, therefore, for the colonies to form a new government apart from Britain in order to protect those rights. Americans remember the celebrated opening words of the document. So did Ho Chi Minh when he declared Vietnam's independence from France in 1945 and borrowed some of the same opening words from our Declaration: the "inalienable right of people to life, liberty, and the pursuit of happiness." It would be another 44 years before Mexico would gain independence from Spain, and 91 years before Canada gains freedom from Britain.

The **Liberty Bell** was rung when the Continental Congress signed the Declaration of Independence and is still on display in Philadelphia, Pennsylvania. History tells us that it was rung so long and hard that it cracked. It remains a symbol of freedom for us. Today, **July Fourth**, the anniversary of this signing, is a national holiday celebrated with fireworks, picnics, flag waving, bell ringing, and parades (see Chapter R - Holidays and Traditions).

Liberty Bell

Our first flag was adopted in 1777. Our school children learn that **Betsy Ross** made it with 13 stars and 13 red and white stripes that represented the 13 original states. Today's flag has 50 stars to represent the states, but still has 13 stripes to honor the original 13 colonies.

First flag.

The **Revolutionary War** resulted when Britain invaded America because of our treasonous act of declaring independence. **George Washington** of Virginia was our first commander in chief of the small, poor, unorganized army that fought and defeated Britain, which was then the world's most powerful nation. He later became our first president and is called the **Father of Our Country**.

It ended in 1783 when a temporary peace was achieved. The French Revolution would begin six years later during this period of radical social and political upheaval. Britain was a sore loser. We went to war again in 1812 and again we prevailed.

George Washington

After the Revolutionary War, the 13 states were loosely connected and had their own state constitutions until the **U.S. Constitution** was written in 1787. It became the basic law of the new nation and bonded the states together into one united country. Starting with the words "We the people," it was written by famous leaders in American history, including **Washington, James Madison,** and **Alexander Hamilton**. These men, along with Jefferson, **Benjamin Franklin**, and **John Adams** are referred to as America's **Founding Fathers**. You will see many cities, universities, schools, institutions, and businesses that are named after them.

Among other things, the Constitution defined our government system as having states with representatives in Congress based on population (in order to satisfy the larger states), and equal representation in the Senate (to satisfy the smaller states). Lawyers point out that the Constitution has required few amendments because the people have allowed the courts to interpret the law.

Amendments to Constitution – In 1791, the **Bill of Rights** became the first ten amendments to the U.S. Constitution. It limited the power of the U.S. federal government and enhanced the rights of the individual. It came two years after France's National Constituent Assembly adopted the Declaration of the Rights of Man and of the Citizen. The Bill of Rights' concepts of *equality*, *representation,* and personal *freedoms* are chiseled forever in the cornerstone of our national character.

Hint: The original Declaration of Independence, the Constitution, and the Bill of Rights documents are on display in the National Archives Building in Washington, D.C. (www.archives.gov).The movie, *National Treasure* (2004), is about a fictitious theft of the Declaration document.

Archives Building – Wash. D.C.

The Bill of Rights and the 17 other amendments to the Constitution that followed in succession have a profound effect today in defining our everyday life and culture. Even how we react to other countries that deprive their people of rights similar to those we enjoy. Frequently the media refer to the various Amendments when discussing troubling issues in the U.S. Their topics and the sequence in which they were adopted provide an interesting snapshot of America's changing history. These are of some of the historical amendments and their adoption dates that give insight to the evolution of our culture.

- *1st Amendment (1791)* – Guarantees freedom of speech, freedom of the press, freedom of association and assembly, and the rights of citizens to worship as they please, all of which were suppressed by the British. Today, the freedom of our probing media and press (see Chapter Q - Media) rests squarely on shoulders of this amendment.

  Hint: Neo-Nazi activity appears to be a global phenomenon, with a number of these small groups in the U.S. that attack and harass people with different political or religious opinions. Unlike America, some European and Latin American countries have laws prohibiting the expression of pro-Nazi, racist, anti-Semitic, or anti-gay views, and many Nazi-related symbols are banned in European countries. We also have a hate group called the **Ku Klux Klan** that advocates extremist white supremacy, white nationalism, and anti-immigration. However, given our First Amendment rights, political organizations such as these have great latitude to express their views. While most Americans oppose **what they stand for** (their views), they believe the right of the groups to express their views is more important than silencing their voice. There's that *freedom of expression* thing again.

- *2nd Amendment (1791)* – Protects the individual right of gun ownership, something England did not allow the colonists. Many today want stricter gun controls, while others say that would be unconstitutional.
- *4th Amendment (1791)* – Prohibits police and government from searching peoples' homes or seizing their property without reasonable grounds that a crime has been committed, something the British practiced at free will.
- *13th Amendment (1865)* – Slavery and involuntary servitude are illegal. We fought a civil war from 1861 to 1864 over this issue (more on that later).
- *14th Amendment (1868)* – Anyone born or naturalized in the U.S. is a citizen, including the children of illegal immigrants. This is a hot topic in the U.S. today because a half-million illegal immigrants arrive each year with some giving birth to children who immediately become U.S. citizens.
- *15th Amendment (1870)* – Neither states nor the federal government can stop people from voting because of race or because they were once slaves. This amendment was enforced briefly in the 1870s, but not again until the 1960s when the civil rights movement began (more on that later).

- *17th Amendment (1913)* – Voters in each state will elect two members to the U.S. Senate. Previously this power was given to state legislatures.
- *18th Amendment (1919)* – This ban on the sale of alcohol, known as **Prohibition**, was later repealed in 1933 by the 21st Amendment.

Women prohibitionists.

- *19th Amendment (1920)* – After protesting 50 years, women were finally given the right to vote. (Blacks had this right a few years after the Civil War ended, but it was only a partial vote.)
- *21st Amendment (1933)* – The ban on alcohol was repealed, but states were given the right to regulate alcohol. Some southern states continued the ban for another 20 years. America learned it could not legislate morality, but it is once again become a hot topic for banned substances like marijuana and drugs.
- *24th Amendment (1964)* – Nobody can be barred from voting because they have not paid a poll tax. This ruse was used in the South to prevent African Americans from voting. Note that this was passed one hundred years after blacks had obtained their theoretical freedom and equality that resulted from the Civil War. As I say, we are good at ignoring things when we want to.

Centralized Power – George Washington became our first president in 1789 and was re-elected in 1793. When he took office, America's form of government was a brand new concept, never having existed anywhere in its form, somewhat like today's emerging

European Union. Because people were familiar with kingdoms at the time, they thought Washington should be treated as a king with all the trappings. He knew better. He set the stage for all our presidents who are still viewed as just ordinary citizens entrusted to lead the country. Adams and Jefferson, two more of our founding fathers, followed the example he set as America expanded geographically and culturally.

Throughout the remainder of the 1700s, the nation also slowly adjusted to the young government and the new concept of increased centralized power in the hands of the federal government. True to our independent spirit, there were objections to this radical concept. Pennsylvania farmers refused to pay a federal tax on whiskey they produced and led a famous **Whiskey Rebellion** in 1794. This new tax on a commodity by the federal government established its authority for taxing and enforcing federal laws within the states, the foundation of our government as we know it today.

New York City and Philadelphia initially served briefly as capital cities that housed the federal government. The southern states, suspicious of northern intentions, were concerned about this new centralist power residing in a capital city in the North. In 1790, the rivalry of northern and southern states for the capital's new location ended when the southern states supported a program of federal assumption of state debts in return for an agreement to situate the national capital in Washington, D.C., so named for our first president, and District of Columbia in honor of explorer Christopher Columbus. This new site was 90 km south of the north-south geo-political boundary line that separated Pennsylvania from Maryland. And also separated North from South.

This system of compromise that started two centuries ago remains an integral part of our legislative process. Political parties and the president seldom get all of what they want. They make trade-offs and compromises in order to get at least a part of the legislation they seek. Many Americans wish they would just do what is right for the country and put politics and party lines aside, but we know it will never happen. This **give and take** is part of the American way.

School children learn about another hero from this time, frontiersman **Daniel Boone**. He journeyed westward through the rugged wilderness of the Appalachian Mountains and in 1769 was the first to reach the unexplored area that would later become the state of Kentucky. Thirty years later he again led settlers into what is now the Midwest state of Missouri. Its city of St. Louis became the **jumping off point** (departure area) for mass migration to the vast, unexplored West beyond the Mississippi River well into the 1800s.

Daniel Boone

Hint: In a conversation, you might refer to Boone if you are venturing into an unknown endeavor by saying, "I feel like Daniel Boone venturing into the wilderness of the Appalachians."

THE 1800s – EXPANSION

The 1800s began with visionary **Thomas Jefferson** as president. He believed that America should be a nation of small farmers who direct their own affairs with little federal government interference, a policy still in place in the U.S. At that time, there were few settlements west of the Mississippi. In 1803, he purchased from France a vast area of land for $15 million that ranged from the Mississippi River west to the Rockies, and from the Gulf of Mexico up to Canada. This transaction, known as the **Louisiana Purchase**, doubled the size of the U.S. overnight.

Louisiana Purchase, 1803.   (gatewayno.com)

> **Hint**: Jefferson did not have authority from Congress to make the purchase; he just knew it was the right thing to do. Some say this is still an American custom, "doing what we know is right." Sometimes that includes **going it alone** in unilateral dealings with other countries and issues.

In 1804, Jefferson sent the **Lewis & Clark Expedition** to explore this new land and find a navigable river route through it to the Pacific Ocean that would spur commerce. The two explorers learned there was no such route due to the rugged terrain.

By the 1840s, American **pioneers** slowly made it to the **Far West** on foot, horseback, and in oxen-drawn covered wagons. It could take up to six months to make the coast-to-coast journey in search of dreams. Thus was born the popular slogan, **Go west young man**, originated by an eastern newspaper and symbolic of the government's long-standing desire to settle the West. This is similar to China's Go-West campaign launched in 2000 to help its relatively backward western and central areas catch up with more affluent eastern China.

Covered wagon.

> **Hint**: Popular movies about the Old West include *Broken Arrow* (1950), *High Noon* (1952), *The Big Country* (1958), and *How the West Was Won* (1962). Chapter K on literature discusses author Zane Grey and Chapter M on art discusses Frederic Remington, both of whom share their love of the **Old West**.

This restless, adventuresome spirit of Americans early on continually pushed our frontier farther west. This spirit continues with our yearning to explore the frontiers of space, medicine, oceans, and science.

As the frontier was pushed west, so were the Native Americans (Indians). When Columbus set foot in the New World, it is estimated the

Native American

70

area now known as the U.S. had nine million Indians. By 1900, with wars, disease, and removal from their homelands, they numbered 250,000. To most, this was a sad chapter in American history. Things are changing. Stanford University dropped the "Indians" mascot name in 1972 out of respect to their culture and heritage. Today, 2.5 million Native Americans are reasserting control over their tribal lands, government, economies, and cultures. Many tribes now own casinos on their land like this one in Milwaukee, Wisconsin, our largest: www.paysbig.com.

> **Hint**: An Academy Award-winning movie about Native Americans during this era is *Dances with Wolves* (1990) that depicts history from the natives' points of view. Others include *The Last of the Mohicans* (1992) and *Geronimo: An American Hero* (1993).

In continuing border wars with Mexico, a treaty was finally signed in 1846 that expanded America farther west from Texas and up to Oregon. In 1853, the U.S. purchased a small strip of land from Mexico along the border. At that point we had all the land that we have today in the continental U.S.

The large, profitable cotton plantations (farms) in the South needed slaves to tend to the crops. By the early 1800s, all northern states had outlawed slavery, but the southern states had economies that depended on them. In 1821, there were 12 "free" (anti-slavery) states and 12 states that permitted slavery. Symbolic of the Whiskey Rebellion several generations before, the authority of the federal government was still under attack and not defined clearly. We were the *United* States of America in concept, but not in reality.

Civil War – In 1861, 11 southern states seceded (withdrew) from the U.S., insisting that the federal government had no right to control the states on certain matters, including slavery (there's that *independence* thing again). The North insisted the South had no right to secede and that this union of states must be preserved at all cost. Our president at this time was **Abraham Lincoln** from the Midwest state of Illinois, called **Honest Abe** because of his integrity and sense of fairness.

Abe Lincoln

In 1861, the **Civil War** broke out between North and South. The southern states, called the **Confederacy**, had their own Confederate flag. The North was called the **Union** and continued to fly the American flag. The war took more American lives than any other war in our history (800,000) and left many parts of the South in ruins.

It also created ill feelings between these two peoples, some of which carried over well into the 20th century and still may be found in pockets of the South where Southern pride abounds and the Confederate flag is flown. (The courts have challenged this flag flying.)

Confederate flag.

Ulysses S. Grant led the armies of the North and would later became president. The South was led by **Robert E. Lee**, a U.S. Army officer from Virginia who opposed slavery and his state's withdrawing from the Union. Ultimately, though, he felt his state was protecting the very liberty, freedom, and legal principles for which George Washington had fought.

During the dedication of a Civil War cemetery in the state of Pennsylvania, Lincoln delivered his famous two-minute **Gettysburg Address** in which he said our government is "of the people, by the people, and for the people." (For the full text, see Appendix 1.)

In 1863, Lincoln's famous **Emancipation Proclamation** outlawed slavery in America. It came two years after Czar Alexander II of Russia had eliminated serfdom. It also came four years before Canada was freed from Britain without violence. Many consider Lincoln and George Washington the two most important presidents in our history, similar to how Gandhi and Nehru are viewed in India.

Historians say the Civil War finally brought the states together to form one nation of states *united* with strong federal leadership that we have today. They use the analogy of a blacksmith pounding steel to make it stronger; the war was a hard pounding.

> **Hint**: We have many classic movies about the Civil War, including *Glory* (1989) that gives a stirring account of African American soldiers in the war. Others are *Gone With the Wind* (1939), *The Red Badge of Courage* (1951), *Shenandoah* (1965), *Gettysburg* (1993), and *Cold Mountain* (2003). Some are available as books (see Chapter K - Literature).

America On The Move – For the remainder of the 1800s, industry in America underwent rapid growth. Machines replaced manual labor while ships and trains transported people and goods everywhere. The census of 1890 was the first in which the output of America's factories exceeded the output of its farms, and by 1913 more than one-third of the world's industrial production would come from the U.S.

True to form, in the interest of protecting **the little guy**, the federal government took action to prevent big businesses from ruining smaller ones. In 1890, the **Sherman Antitrust Act** was passed that broke up big businesses that hindered free trade. Today's government is still charged with protecting our smaller businesses, though some believe they could do a better job because of the influence of politics and special interests groups.

Our culture was also becoming more defined and a dramatic transition was occurring in the lifestyles of the average U.S. citizen. People wanted to end corrupt government and to reduce poverty and improve living conditions for the poor. These same issues are still being addressed today.

Work, school, and leisure activities changed rapidly from mostly agrarian activities to the beginnings of an industrial and technological age. Giving women the vote continued to be an issue. A law was established to grant federal government jobs on the basis of merit, not political favors. New jobs were created as cities became bigger and businesses thrived. In 1886, a labor union was first organized to represent its workers, many of which were immigrants.

These quests for *equality*, *harmony,* and *human rights* that started during this period remain firmly in place today and are still being pursued.

Toward the end of the 19th century, however, the government and the people were now faced with something new: an expanding role for the U.S. in an ever-shrinking world, a role that continues to this day.

THE 1900s – CONFLICTS AND REFORMS

Our first president of the 20th century was **Theodore** (Teddy) **Roosevelt**. He is regarded by some as our first to truly use the power of his office to govern, improve, and protect the public interest. Special interest groups had controlled some prior presidents, but not this one. He set the stage for today's presidents. He started the massive construction of the **Panama Canal** between Central and South America in 1904, which allowed ships to pass between the Pacific and Atlantic oceans. (The French had tried but failed.) He broke up large, controlling businesses. He established national parks, protected wildlife and terrain, was the first president to

Theodore Roosevelt

aid workers in a strike against employers, and established acts to regulate the purity of food and drugs. The stuffed toy "teddy bear" was named after him.

Roosevelt became a statesman in international relations, too. He was known for his motto, **speak softly but carry a big stick**. The U.S. was now becoming a mediator in world affairs. Roosevelt was awarded the Nobel Peace Prize for negotiating a peace treaty to end the Russo-Japanese War of 1904-1905. His diplomacy in helping resolve the conflict was a combination of courtesy (speak softly) and show of strength (big stick). Other presidents would subsequently adopt his approach to international relations.

In 1914, problems among European nations led to the outbreak of **World War I**, but America remained neutral until 1917 when unarmed ships were being sunk by Germany. The War ended in 1918. Soon the U.S. economy soared, setting the stage for the Roaring Twenties. The U.S. was opposed to the harsh settlement terms imposed on Germany at the Treaty of Versailles, including harsh territorial concessions and monetary reparations that would have taken until 1988 to fully repay. America knew these terms would eventually lead to Germany going to war again, which it did in 1939.

The Roaring Twenties – The 1920s ushered in the modern society that America enjoys today. With the booming economy came new lifestyles, new attitudes, and a fast paced society called **The Roaring Twenties**. (See Chapter K on literature for F. Scott Fitzgerald's books about this era.) People moved from farms to the city, businesses thrived,

Roaring Twenties styles in America.

73

and people had jobs. They bought newfangled items such as washing machines, telephones, radios, and autos. In 1920, women finally had the right to vote.

Concerned that liquor leads to increased crime, poverty, and violence, coupled with the public outcry of the Protestant view that liquor was evil, an amendment was made to the Constitution in 1920 that prohibited the sale of alcoholic beverages. This era was called **Prohibition**.

> **Hint**: **Gangsters** (criminals) had control of some of our cities during Prohibition. *Al Capone* (1959) is the classic film about a famous Chicago mobster of this time. In some surveys, Chicago still ranks number one today for corrupt city government.

This period provides interesting insight into America's legislative process and the collective psychological makeup of Americans. Although consumption of alcohol fell at the beginning of Prohibition, it subsequently increased. People didn't like being told what to do and what not to do, a trait that continues today. As a result, alcohol became more dangerous to consume because of unregulated, illegal production; organized crime increased; the court and prison systems were stretched to the breaking point; and corruption of public officials was rampant. Further, Prohibition removed a significant source of tax revenue and greatly increased government spending to enforce it. Realizing that they could

Prohibition poster.

not legislate morality nor control the public's desire for alcoholic beverages, Congress legalized the sale of liquor once again in 1933. A Chinese proverb: "The law cannot be enforced when everyone is an offender."

We have something similar going on today regarding the regulation of marijuana. Some states like California (often at the forefront of changes in the states) allow its sale for medical uses, while at the same time federal laws outlaw it. Stay tuned for the eventual outcome of federal law versus state laws on this matter.

Depression Years – After the soaring, roaring 20s, America plunged into an economic hardship in the 1930s that we call the **Great Depression**. It began with the **stock market crash of 1929**. During the 20s, wild speculation took place in the soaring stock market. People borrowed money or spent their savings to buy stocks that kept rising in price to unprecedented levels. Such undisciplined behavior abruptly came to an end with the **October 1929** stock market crash. It forced banks to cut back on loans to businesses, which in turn cut back their production. Millions of people lost jobs and their buying power, and businesses suffered from people not buying their products. It was a

Great Depession bread line.

74

vicious circle. Thousands of banks failed. People lost their life's savings. Millions of Americans lost their homes and went hungry. Former executives were selling apples on the street to earn money.

On top of the Depression, the Midwest experienced a terrible drought during the 1930s. It closed 700,000 farms in that vast area, particularly in the southern plains. This event and era were dubbed the **Dust Bowl.** Its impact worsened and lengthened the depression.

> **Hint**: **John Steinbeck** (see Chapter K - Literature) won the Pulitzer Prize for his 1939 novel, *The Grapes of Wrath,* in which he documented a national tragedy by tracing one family's exodus from Oklahoma because of the great Dust Bowl disaster. The book's blunt style shocked the nation and exposed the exploited masses of the Depression Era. It was instrumental in changing laws to benefit the poorer working classes. The film of the same name is considered a classic, too.

Americans faced hardships they had never faced before. The American Dream was quickly fading. America was on its knees. Ultimately the government learned lessons from this and put into place federal laws and regulations to control wild financial speculation that led to the depression. It ushered in a new concept that continues today: having the federal government regulate and play a more important role in controlling the nation's economy. (However, the government failed to regulate our financial institutions' new speculative ventures seventy years later and a worldwide recession resulted in 2008. We are still learning, and hopefully, re-learning from the past.)

In 1932, President **Franklin Delano Roosevelt** (referred to as **FDR**) was elected president with his promise to end the depression. His **New Deal** promised new reforms and new recovery steps. He pushed public works projects that provided jobs, including building the massive **Hoover Dam** in Nevada that is a spectacular tourist site (www.usbr.gov/lc/hooverdam). He helped farmers and manufacturing firms. He tightened regulations on banks and the stock market. He also started our **Social Security System**

FDR

to provide retirement funding for workers that remains in place today (though studies show it running out of money). Most important of all, he provided the American people with hope for the future. FDR remains one of our most popular presidents for leading the country out of the depression and then through World War II that began in 1941.

The War Years – World War II (pronounced as "world war two" or "the second world war") started in 1939. The U.S. was reluctant to enter until Hawaii was attacked in 1941. When FDR died in office toward the end of the war, Vice President Truman became president. Truman knew that millions of Japanese would be killed with an invasion of Japan if conventional warfare was used to finally end the war. He made the decision to drop two atomic bombs on Japan that ended the war in 1945. (Historians say at least nine million Japanese would have been killed in an invasion.) Instead, and tragically, several hundred thousand were killed and injured with the two bombs.

> **Hint**: A tour guide at the Nagasaki Museum that sits on the site of one of the droppings told our group that the U.S. dropped the bombs to justify spending one billion dollars on their development. As a student of WWII history, I tried to correct her but she refused to listen because she had been instructed what to say. Our **Freedom of Information Act** allows for full or partial disclosure of previously unreleased information and documents controlled by the U.S. government. So wartime files from that era are now public record and there is nothing to support her claim. Also, we spent two billion, not one. As I say, we need to deal with facts so that myths about other countries and peoples are not perpetrated from generation to generation.

When the war ended, America entered its greatest period of economic expansion in its history, setting the stage for today's lifestyle in America. New housing tracts arose in the suburbs to house the millions of returning soldiers and their new families. New industries such as electronics, plastics, pharmaceuticals, and jet engines arose. This prosperity continued into the 1950s as television sets, automobiles, and appliances became common in households.

The U.S. **Marshall Plan** was put in force after the war to rebuild war-devastated Europe, remove trade barriers, modernize industry, and make Europe prosperous again, including those countries that had been our enemies. This is yet another example of America's **forgive and forget** culture. We took similar steps in Japan where the emperor was allowed to remain and with him we paved the way for Japan to become the industrial powerhouse that it became with American assistance and know-how.

> **Hint**: A classic film about the troubled life of a soldier after returning from WWII service is *The Best Years of Our Lives* (1946). *Saving Private Ryan* (1998) with Tom Hanks is an Academy Award winning film about a school teacher who goes to war.

Jobs were plentiful after the war, but not everyone participated in this boom. There were still many poor whites and blacks. And blacks were still discriminated against, one hundred years after the Civil War guaranteed their equality.

Human Rights Era – In 1955, **Martin Luther King**, a Baptist minister, began organizing demonstrations against racial discrimination. Thus began our **civil rights movement** that called for equal rights for all minorities, not just blacks. In one of King's most moving speeches, he said, "I have a dream that my four little children will one day live in a nation where they will not be judged by the color of their skin but by the content of their character." Those lines are still quoted today.

Martin Luther King

As the campaign continued into the 70s, some demonstrations were peaceful as King advocated, while others in our large cities led to violence. Many whites marched alongside blacks to protest the unequal treatment of blacks. There's that *equality* thing again. We now have a Martin Luther King national holiday in January (see Chapter R - Holidays and Traditions) and a monument to him was erected in 2011 in the nation's capital. Civil right efforts that began with King continue today.

Hint: *Malcolm X* (1992) is a film that tells the life story of a slain civil rights leader.

The issue of **women's rights** started anew in the late 1960s and 70s with women like **Gloria Steinem**, an American feminist, journalist, and social and political activist recognized as one of the leaders of the **Women's Liberation Movement**. They fought for equal rights and fair treatment, reproductive rights and control over women's bodies, and basic respect. They also extended that support to the gay (homosexual) community and minorities not only in the U.S. but all over the globe. The belief that women are entitled to the same rights and privileges as men in such areas as business, politics, and sports is still not a full reality. Surveys show that some women today are paid about 25 percent less than men in similar jobs. All these journeys to equality continue today.

Citizens who wanted to advance human rights in the U.S. founded many organizations during the 20th century. The National Association for the Advancement of Colored People (**NAACP**) (www.naacp.org) works to eliminate racial discrimination, while the goal of the National Organization of Women (**NOW**) (www.now.org) is to bring about equality for all women. NOW organized a march on Washington, D.C. in 2004 with millions of supporters who expressed their support of abortion rights that they felt were being eroded in the U.S. This journey also continues today.

It seems as if we are always organizing some sort of effort to protest—or support—issues in the U.S., be it a Boston Tea Party in Massachusetts, a women's march in Washington, D.C., or an Occupy Wall Street sit-in in New York that spread around the world in 2011. It's the American way.

Nixon Era – In 1972, President **Richard Nixon** became the first U.S. president to visit China while in office. When he met with Chairman Mao Zedong, Americans were pleased the leaders of these two nations could put their differences aside and talk. I have spoken to Chinese residents who say they were equally moved by his visit. Following the historic meeting, ping-pong tournaments between our two countries were started. The U.S. media with its ever-present sense of humor called this **Ping Pong Diplomacy**. The U.S. and China would finally establish diplomatic relations in 1979 when President Carter was in office. It would still be another 25 years before our two countries would be closer to more fully normalized relations.

Richard Nixon

In 1974, Nixon became our first president to resign from office because of what the public and Congress viewed as obstruction of justice. This was proof that no one is above the law in America, not even a president. A generation of Americans saw firsthand the unshakable workings of our Constitution and legal system. The situation that led to Nixon's downfall became known as the **Watergate Scandal** because of illegal break-ins in the Watergate office building. He tried to cover up these relatively minor, yet illegal, activities of some of his campaign workers during the election of 1972.

Hint: The movie, *Nixon* (1995), is a powerful story about the downfall of our 37th president. *All the President's Men* (1976) is the true story of how newspaper reporters uncovered Nixon's wrongdoings. (It is also available as a book.) Their story is also testament to the importance of our free press, which is discussed in Chapter Q on media. Another movie, *Frost/Nixon* (2008), dramatizes actual interviews with Nixon in 1977 after he left office. Dozens of books have also been written about his downfall. I still remember the sign that was spray-painted on a wall I saw during the Nixon investigation that said "Impeach the bastard." That's how deeply the American people felt about their president lying to them. It also reflects the credo of the American people that is repeated throughout this book: **honesty is the best policy**.

Cold War Ending – The **Cold War** began soon after the end of WWII when the Soviet Union took control of Eastern European nations. During this era, relations between the U.S. and the USSR were strained and many thought a World War III could be the result. Communism was viewed as an enemy of the U.S. School children in the U.S. regularly practiced hiding under their desks in the event of a Soviet nuclear attack. The closest the world has come to nuclear war occurred with the **Cuban Missile Crisis** of October 1962. The Soviets had installed nuclear warheads in Cuba, 90 miles off our mainland. The U.S. formed a naval blockade of the island. President Kennedy resolved the crisis and the missiles were removed when Kennedy agreed to remove missiles in Turkey aimed at the USSR. The entire world breathed a sigh of relief.

Relations between India and the U.S. were also antagonistic throughout the 1970s, based partially on the U.S. arming of Pakistan. As a means of counteracting Soviet influence in the region, the Reagan administration in the 1980s reexamined its policy toward India and decided to expand economic and scientific areas of cooperation. But in the late 1980s, the U.S. had differences with the India over India not improving its legal protection of intellectual property rights, opening its markets to American service industries, and liberalizing its foreign investment regulations, the same problems that the U.S. is trying to resolve with China today.

In 1987 President Reagan and Soviet leader **Mikhail Gorbachev** signed a monumental treaty to eliminate many of the nuclear missiles of both nations. In 1989, Soviet rule came to an end in Eastern European countries, the people regained their freedom, and the Berlin Wall that separated Germany

Berlin Wall teardown 1989.

was torn down, symbolic of the easing of tensions. President Reagan is remembered by Germans for his speech at the Wall, saying, **"Tear down this wall, Mister Gorbachev."** East Germany was re-united with West Germany in 1990 and, for the first time in 46 years, Germans could move freely about their country and finally be with loved ones. Americans breathed another sigh of relief, knowing that tensions with a former enemy were disappearing *and* the oppressed people were now free to enjoy the same freedoms that we have enjoyed since our founding. (In surveys of Americans' attitudes toward our recent presidents, Reagan remains at number one due in part to his efforts with the Soviets. Clinton remains at number two, with George W. Bush and Nixon at the bottom.)

> **Hint**: Americans are proud of our heritage. Some are aware of the hardships that a nation of **ragtag** (poor, shaggy) immigrants endured to make it what it is today. Feel free to discuss any aspect of our history with us, including our wars. You will get different opinions about our involvement in them, particularly Vietnam and Iraq. Try to use important historic names, dates, and places discussed in this chapter in your conversations. We do not expect friends from other nations to know things like this, but like you, we are impressed when they do know something about our history. Most will not be offended if you choose to offer negative opinions about these issues. They might even agree with you while some will be uninformed.

THE NEW MILLENNIUM

The U.S. lost its innocence in 2001 when two hijacked jetliners rammed the **World Trade Towers** in the worst-ever terrorist attack against the U.S. A third hijacked plane flew into the Pentagon and a fourth crashed in rural Pennsylvania. More than 3,000 people died in the infamous **September 11** attacks. This gave rise to the term **9/11** (nine-eleven). We never dreamed something like this could happen in America. We immediately went after those responsible for the attack.

Trade Towers

Afghanistan War – The **Afghanistan War** began when U.S. and Britain launched air attacks after the **Taliban** government failed to hand over Saudi Arabian terrorist **Osama bin Laden**, the suspected mastermind behind the terrorist attacks. Following air campaigns and ground assaults by coalition and Afghani opposition troops, the Taliban regime that had brutally ruled Afghanistan toppled in December. However, the hunt for bin Laden and other members of the **al-Qaeda** terrorist organization continued. Osama bin Laden was finally found in 2011 and killed by U.S. troops raiding his hideout compound across the border in Pakistan where many Americans believe he was given shelter and protection.

Iraq War – The **Iraq War** began in 2003 with claims that Iraq possessed **weapons of mass destruction**. Some U.S. officials also accused Iraqi President **Saddam Hussein** of harboring and supporting al-Qaeda, but no evidence of a meaningful connection was ever found. After investigations following the U.S. led invasion, it was concluded that Iraq had ended its nuclear, chemical, and biological programs in 1991 and had no active programs at the time of the invasion. Saddam Hussein was captured in 2003 by U.S. troops and executed by the Iraq government in 2006 for the inhumane treatment of his people for the 24 brutal years he ruled. All U.S. troops were withdrawn in 2011. Shortly after, a new wave of sectarian violence erupted across Iraq, raising concerns over a full blown civil war between the main factions of Iraq, most notably the Sunni and the Shia Arabs. This added fuel to those Americans who had argued against the war all along. We have a saying: **What goes around comes around**.

Great Recession – The third big event of the new millennium was the **Great Recession** that started in December 2007 and reverberated around the world for several years. Our politicians and banks had lobbied for deregulation of the banking and investment industries, laws that were put in place in the 1930s as a result of the **Great Depression**. They got their wish in 1999 and abused it with new speculative investments. Banks and mortgage companies started lending money for homes to anyone regardless of their income or credit rating. By the fall of 2008 as housing prices were falling, more and more people owed more than their homes were worth, and defaults and foreclosures were rising.

Banks had severe capital and liquidity problems as home prices fell. People were pulling their money out of banks that were desperately trying to find mergers before they went bankrupt. This was further inflamed by dishonesty on the part of firms that falsely rated securities, and the insurance companies that were involved in new, unregulated, speculative ventures. The damage from the Great Recession of 2008 was the worst recession since the 1930s. At least 8 million jobs were lost. Americans lost $13 trillion dollars of wealth. Hundreds of bank failed. The S&P 500 stock index dropped 57 percent, and one in 45 homes were in default. The recession reverberated around the world, sometimes worse in countries than our setback, reminding many of the saying, **When America sneezes the world catches a cold**. The American people wondered why we didn't learn our lesson from the Great Depression of the 1930s that was fraught with wild greed and speculation, too. There's that saying again: **What goes around comes around**.

IMMIGRATION HISTORY

The history of immigration in the U.S. is the history of the United States itself. Until the 1960s, most immigrants to the U.S. came from Europe. America took a big step forward in 1965 when it passed the Immigration Reform Act that removed many obstacles that heretofore prevented foreigners, particularly Asians, from entering the U.S. As we matured as a nation, we began to realize the importance of immigrants to the development of our country. We have a saying: **We wised up**.

Since the 1970s the leading countries of origin for our legal immigrants have been Mexico (20%), the Philippines (7%), China (4%), India (4%), South Korea (4%), and Vietnam (4%). Economic and educational opportunities in the U.S. have always been the main attraction for them. For others, it is personal freedoms.

Illegal immigration is now a major issue in U.S. politics. Two-thirds of Americans say they are sympathetic toward illegal immigrants and say it is important that we develop a plan to deal with the large numbers who are already living in the U.S. instead of just kicking them out.

The **Statue of Liberty** was a common sight to 12 million immigrants who entered the U.S. through New York Harbor. A gift of friendship from the people of France to the people of the U.S., it is a universal symbol of freedom and democracy. It was dedicated in 1886 with this famous inscription that still reflects the outreached hand the U.S. offers to others: "Give me your tired, your poor, your huddled masses yearning to breathe free, the wretched refuse of your teeming shore. Send these, the homeless, tempest-tost [troubled] to me. I lift my lamp beside the golden door!" (www.nps.gov/stli/index.htm).

Statue of Liberty

Significant Asian immigration first occurred when gold was discovered in California in 1848, and by 1864 20,000 Chinese people were living in California. Because of a lack of workers in the remote West, in 1865 the Central Pacific Railroad imported about 10,000 Chinese laborers to build the railroad across the rugged Sierra Mountains in California. They were paid much less than American workers and faced racial discrimination, as did other minorities in the U.S. at this time. They overcame these obstacles and performed their jobs with honor and pride. Today they are still recognized for their contribution to America's largest civil engineering project before the eras of mechanization and our greater acceptance of non-European foreigners.

When the railroad was finished at **Promontory Point**, Utah, in 1869, America at last had a transcontinental railroad. Many of the Chinese workers then migrated to central California to establish farms and to San Francisco in search of jobs where they continued to experience severe discrimination. They established the Chinatown area in San Francisco to survive the economic restraints put on them by a society that felt "outsiders" were taking away their jobs and should not be allowed to own property. Today, American jobs

Famous photograph: Promontory Point, Utah, 1869.

are being shipped overseas, and with lost jobs some Americans cannot afford homes.

In the early 20th century, Japanese Americans constituted the largest group of Asian immigrants. They engaged primarily in agricultural pursuits in the western states of California, Oregon, and Washington. And then the Immigration Act of 1924 practically barred all Asians from entering the U.S. After the infamous 1941 attack on **Pearl Harbor** that drew the U.S. into WWII, the U.S. government evacuated 110,000 Pacific Coast residents of Japanese descent to internment camps in the interior of the U.S. because they were viewed as security threats. At the urging of the U.S., Peru sent 1,771 Japanese Peruvians to the U.S. who were also interned for the duration of the war. At war's end, Peru refused to allow the detainees to return.

Manzanar Relocation Center, Ansel Adams. 1943.

Famous photographer **Ansel Adams**, aggrieved by this harsh Asian policy, visited the **Manzanar Relocation Center** near California's Sierra Mountains in 1943 and photographed how citizens "had overcome the sense of defeat and despair by building...a vital community." Chapter M on art discusses a Japanese American artist who focuses his art on this internment.

Hint: I had a Japanese American friend who was born in America and lived in Manzanar as a young child during the war. Like all other "Americans" there, she was insulted that she was not considered an American. It is inconceivable to most Americans today, given our protective attitude toward minorities and immigrants, that America could have behaved this way toward groups of people—from excluding the Chinese to relocating the Japanese—merely because of their ethnicity. Some view it as a national disgrace and hope as a nation we have learned from our mistakes. Others may not be aware these things happened back then, while others may not understand that their attitudes against recent immigrants resemble the discrimination and violation of human rights in other countries that we now so detest. As I say, we must learn more about each other to prevent these types of racist, discriminatory actions from ever happening again.

Since World War II, more refugees have found homes in the U.S. than any other nation, with more than two million arriving since 1980. Of the top ten countries accepting resettled refugees in 2006, the U.S. accepted more than twice as many as the next nine countries combined.

No doubt cultural differences account for the disparity. For example, according to the United Nations, in 1999 Japan accepted 16 refugees for resettlement while the U.S. took in 85,010. Throughout history, America has always been viewed as open to foreigners except for a few periods noted above, while others still view Japan today as a closed society, much as it was from 1616 to 1853 when Japan closed its ports to all but a few Dutch and Chinese traders. Back then the U.S. hoped Japan would agree to open certain ports so American and other vessels could begin to trade with the mysterious island kingdom and ships could refuel there.

Commodore Perry, a U.S. naval officer, carried a letter from the U.S. president in 1854 to be delivered to Japan's premier asking him to open its ports. At first he refused, so Perry anchored his four battleships in Tokyo Bay. Japan was so isolated from the world they thought the ships were "giant dragons puffing smoke," and were shocked by the number and size of the guns onboard. After weeks of talks, Perry received a treaty with Japan that broke down barriers separating Japan from the rest of the world. In turn, Japan would use this **gunboat diplomacy** learned from Commodore Perry to force Korea to open its ports to trade.

Nineteenth century gunboat diplomacy.

Some criticize the U.S. today for still using gunboat diplomacy. On the other hand, some activists claim that Japan's immigration laws violate human rights and should be reformed. They say some Japanese don't relate to cultures and peoples different from their own, witness the nightclubs that have signs reading "no foreigners allowed." Further, they say foreigners are oftentimes rejected when applying for apartments without a Japanese guarantor, and some Japanese don't want to sit next to a foreigner on a train, the same things that might happen in the U.S. and in other countries with certain foreigners or minorities. At least these are common *cultural perceptions* of our countries. I find that traveling in Japan is no different than other countries as long as one follows the customs and courtesies of that country. Myths and perceptions are hard to change.

☺ **Here's an assignment for you.** If you would like to test your general knowledge of America's history, Appendix 10 provides a quiz about our history and government. This is the same test our government uses to test applicants for U.S. citizenship.

Underlying this broad historical perspective of America and how it shaped our society and culture, our legal system is discussed next. It has had a similar influence.

E

LAW

Scarcely any political question arises in the United States that is not resolved, sooner or later, into a judicial question. - Alexis De Tocqueville, 19th century French social philosopher[*]

A fundamental principle of life in American is our commitment to the "rule of law," a body of legal rules and regulations intended to maintain order and stability. You have learned that we are a society in which all citizens in theory are equal under the law. These laws are made by officials elected by the people and are enforced by the courts.

American courtroom.

Understanding our underlying legal system provides key insight into American culture and our daily way of life. Even though we may respect our legal system, in true American fashion we sometimes criticize our courts, judges, and their rulings. And sometimes the voice of the public rises up, exerts its influence, and changes the law of the land, such as the legalization of alcohol, women's rights, and abortions.

One of the basic principles of the American legal system is due process of law. It requires fairness in the government's dealing with its people. This concept dates back to England's **Magna Carta** of 1215 that defined basic laws, just as our Constitution does today. This due process incorporates these principles that in some countries are missing.

- The law must be administered fairly and impartially.
- People must be informed of the charges against them and must be given the opportunity for a fair hearing.
- The person bringing the charges must not be allowed to judge the case.
- Criminal laws must be worded clearly so the public understands them.

---

[*]**De Tocqueville's** 1835 classic work on the U.S. political system, titled *Democracy in America*, is one of the earliest studies of American life. The Frenchman explored the influence of social and political institutions on the habits, manners, and culture of Americans and why democracy succeeded in the U.S.

Legal System Differences – Most English speaking countries including the U.S., Australia, India, and Singapore have a common law system that originated in England in the Middle Ages and is based largely on prior court decisions. Civil law systems, however, are based mainly on statutes (legislative acts). In countries like France, Italy, Spain, and most of Latin America, the statutes, rather than the courts, provide the final answers to any law question.

Culture has molded our laws, laws that are sure to differ in some ways from your county's. For example, privacy laws in Europe and the U.S. are so different because Europeans reserve their deepest distrust for corporations, while we are far more concerned about the government invading our privacy. Consequently, our emphasis is on providing a fair trial, which makes the trial itself more adversarial than in some European countries.

In French and German systems—unlike the U.S.—there are no attorneys for the defense or the prosecution. The trial is run by a judge whose job is to find out what happened and has complete power to do so. The European system has faith that the State will do the right thing. In our legal system, juries of fellow citizens participate. While the European system is designed to punish the guilty first and foremost, in the U.S. it is designed to protect the rights of the individual. (There's that *individual rights* thing again.)

With this emphasis on individual rights, our system has developed into a difficult one for others to understand. A survey of 180 corporate lawyers in five European countries identified the U.S. as the jurisdiction in which they were most concerned about facing a major dispute, worse than China or Russia. It said the U.S. system, although less corrupt than most, is "filled with traps in which the inexperienced or uninformed may easily become caught." These traps include targeting corporations as well as individuals in criminal cases and the aggressiveness of American prosecutors and their willingness to apply U.S. laws overseas was another factor.

Independence of Our Courts – As a co-equal branch of government, our judiciary is (theoretically) free of control by the executive and legislative branches so it can decide cases impartially. Frequent Supreme Court decisions magnify this clear separation. In a major defeat for President George W. Bush in 2004, the U.S. Supreme Court ruled that detainees captured in Bush's "war on terrorism" and held at a U.S. base in Cuba or in a U.S. territory have the right to challenge their detention in our federal court system against the wishes of the president's administration.

Hint: Unlike some nations, we are proud that our courts protect the rights of *all* individuals, even if these people are potential enemies of the state or illegal immigrants. This is how firmly implanted this *individual rights* thing is in the American character. Perhaps this helps foreigners understand why we **poke our noses** (become involved) in human rights violations in other nations. That's how deep it goes.

86

However, polls show that the same forces that have caused Americans to lose trust in the presidency and Congress (more on that in Chapter S - What Americans Think) now appear to affect the way Americans view our Supreme Court. In recent polls, two-thirds say they trust the judicial branch more than the executive or the legislative branches. But less than half of us approve of the job the U.S. Supreme Court does, with a third believing it is too liberal versus two out of ten who believe it is too conservative. (There's that *diversity* of opinion thing again.)

Cultural Differences – Because the U.S. is a highly legalistic society in which many of our actions are based primarily on our rule of law, our courts are overflowing with lawsuits. In contrast, the Chinese have historically considered resorting to the law as a sort of moral wasteland when relationships or reasoning fails. A Chinese proverb: "Going to law is losing a cow for the sake of a cat."

Foreigners conducting business here must be aware of cultural differences when dealing with Americans or other Western societies on legal matters. In the U.S. for instance, **a contract is a contract**, meaning that the law will enforce a written agreement that you have signed, unless, of course, fraud is involved. In fact, our courts will often enforce verbal contracts made between two parties. Korean Americans have told me that even though they had a contract in their homeland to rent space for a retail operation, it was not binding and the terms changed frequently, something that has never happened with their contracts in the U.S. So, some American business people are cautious when signing contracts with Asian businesses, knowing they might come back later for more favorable terms. (We discuss these matters in Chapter V - Business Customs.)

A Chinese American friend failed to renew the insurance policy on her car, which is a violation of the law. When she was involved in an accident her license was revoked for six months. Because of her cultural background, she miscalculated the intent of the law in the U.S. and didn't think it was important. This reminds me of Istanbul, Turkey, with cars parked fearlessly in front of "No Parking" signs. In America they would fined and towed away. If you are not sure of our laws, contact a government agency or an American.

Hint: Classic courtroom movies include *12 Angry Men* (1957), *Witness for the Prosecution* (1957), *Inherit the Wind* (1960), and *To Kill a Mockingbird* (1962).

LEGAL VOCABULARY FOR YOU
- **Jurisprudence** *[jurr-is-PRUD-unce]* is the entire subject of law, the study of law and legal questions.
- A **statute** *[STAT-chute]* is a law enacted by a legislative body, such as a state's determination to increase its sales tax rate.

- **Litigation** *[lit-ih-GAY-shun]* is the process of resolving a matter by means of the law. With all of our **lawsuits**, the U.S. is a defined as a **litigious** society. A **litigant** is a person involved in litigation.

- The **plaintiff** is the person or party bringing charges to court. The **defendant** is the one being accused of something.

- The **judge** is the person in charge of a courtroom who hears and sometimes decides cases for the courts if a jury is not used.

- The **jury** consists of up to 12 people selected from the public to decide the outcome of the trial, not the judge.

- A **subpoena** *[sub-PE-nah]* is a command to appear in court to testify as a witness.

- A **judgment** is the court decision, the outcome of the court proceeding.

- A **sentence** is the penalty imposed by a judge upon the defendant, such as the number of years of confinement in prison.

- A **misdemeanor** *[miss-dah-MEAN-or]* is a minor crime that carries a maximum penalty of one year in jail and/or a $2,000 fine.

- A **felony** *[FELL-ah-nee]* is a criminal offense for which a person may be sentenced to a term of imprisonment of more than one year.

- A **capital felony** is a criminal offense in which the death penalty may be imposed. We call this **capital punishment**.

Hint: A common misconception of Americans is that we love the death penalty as much as we love baseball and apple pie. Capital punishment is a hotly contested issue today. While 60 percent in the U.S. approve of the death penalty, its use varies by state, as do so many other things. The 34 states that impose the death penalty have executed about 350 criminals since 1990. Some countries will not **extradite** (return) criminals to the U.S. where they committed a crime because of their opposition to the death penalty. The U.S. ranks fifth in the world for number of executions. China ranks number one followed by Saudi Arabia, Iran, and Iraq.

OUR DIFFERENT COURTS

The U.S. has a three-level court system that you might encounter: U.S. (federal), state, and local.

Federal Courts – These courts handle both criminal and civil cases involving the Constitution or federal laws. They only handle about one percent of the nation's judicial matters. The federal court system has three different levels of courts: district, appeal, and the Supreme Court. Cases begin in district courts and can go to an appeal court to seek a different outcome.

The highest federal level is the **Supreme Court**, which

Supreme Court Building – D.C.

generally chooses to consider only cases of important constitutional significance. If a case is lost in a federal court of appeals or in the highest state court, it may be appealed to the Supreme Court, which in turn may refuse to hear it. It also has jurisdiction over cases involving two states or representatives of other countries. There are nine justices in the Supreme Court, nominated by the president and confirmed by Congress. Unlike India where 25 Supreme Court judges serve until a retirement age of 65, in the U.S. they may serve a lifetime.

Our liberal presidents appoint liberal justices, and conservative presidents appoint conservative justices. Our media and the public like to give their views on the left/right leanings of the justices and the implications for the country. Conservatives (right wing) believe the Court should strictly interpret the Constitution using only the document's specific wording and the original intentions of its authors. Liberals (left wing) believe the Court should be liberal in its interpretation, knowing the authors meant the Constitution to adapt as the needs of the nation changed.

> **Hint**: This matter influenced voting in the 2004 presidential election because the public knew that several justices would retire over the upcoming four years and the president would be able to appoint new ones more in sympathy with his own views. Liberal voters in favor of abortion rights, for example, voted against President Bush's re-election for this reason, hoping to prevent more conservative justices from **taking the bench** who adhered to Bush's views.

State And Local Courts – The states have systems similar to the federal three-tier system. We have a famous American saying: "I'll see you in court." This saying reflects the sheer number of cases considered by these courts each year (25 million). One in nine Americans is directly involved in some sort of law matter during their lifetime. Thus our state and local courts face problems of long delays before trials begin, slowness of the trials, and unequal access to justice between the rich and the poor, which goes against our basic cultural instincts. (More about free legal representation later.)

COURTROOM ALTERNATIVES

Courtroom litigation can be time-consuming and expensive. Because our courts are overloaded with cases, litigation can drag on for years before a final resolution is reached. Foreigners should be aware that we have several alternatives to courtroom litigation, should they become involved in a lawsuit.

One method of resolving a dispute that has become popular is **arbitration** *[are-bih-TRAY-shun]*. If both parties to a dispute agree to take their case to binding (meaning the decision is final) arbitration, then most arbitration proceedings can be completed in less than six months. A relatively informal hearing is conducted at the local office of the arbitrator, sometimes a retired judge—outside the court system—and then a decision is announced. If you visit a doctor, you might be asked to sign a document stating you authorize any claims to be settled by arbitration.

Another source is **mediation** *[meed-ee-A-shun]*. This is a process by which deadlocked parties consider the suggestions of an agreed-upon third party. Unlike arbitration, they are not bound to accept the mediator's recommendations. The decision-making authority rests with the participants themselves. Employee conflicts are often settled using mediation.

LEGAL ASSISTANCE

We have different ways of offering assistance to those in need of legal services.

Gideon Ruling – Americans have always had concern for those who need help, be they an individual or a nation. With the value we place on individual rights, one person *can* make a societal change in the U.S. Since the early 1960s, court decisions and legislation have ensured legal help for criminal defendants too poor to hire a lawyer, thanks to the efforts of one man named Gideon. His case is known as the **Gideon Ruling**. Here is what U.S. Attorney General Robert F. Kennedy (brother of President John F. Kennedy) said about this in 1963.

"If an obscure Florida convict named Clarence Earl Gideon had not sat down in prison with a pencil and paper to write a letter to the Supreme Court, and if the Supreme Court had not taken the trouble to look for merit in that one crude petition among all the bundles of mail it must receive every day, the vast machinery of American law would have gone on functioning undisturbed.

"But Gideon did write that letter. The Court did look into his case and he was retried with the help of a competent defense counsel, found not guilty, and released from prison after two years of punishment for a crime he did not commit, and the whole course of American legal history has been changed."

> **Hint**: The book and film, *Gideon's Trumpet* (1980), tell the true story about Gideon and the Supreme Court's 1963 ruling. (The name Gideon comes from a disadvantaged Biblical character.)

Cheap Legal Alternatives – Public and private legal aid services provide our poor people and charity organizations with free help in private law cases. We call these free legal services *pro bono*, a Latin word meaning for the public good. In typical American fashion, some of our private law firms encourage their lawyers to volunteer a certain percentage of time to the poor and underserved at the firm's expense. One such organization is www.probono.net. Storefront organizations provide forms and general assistance at a low price to assist you in pursuing a legal action without the expense of hiring an attorney. Online firms offer forms and instructions as well, such as legalzoom.com whose services range from incorporation to wills to divorce. Legal action workshops are firms that usually charge low flat fees for a specific legal service and can be found on the Internet, such as www.lawencino.com.

Small Claims Court – Other assistance is available in our **small claims courts** for those individuals who want to pursue legal matters inexpensively but without the use of an attorney. One of my immigrant American friends, who had only lived in the U.S. for a year, signed a contract that was written in English for an acting class she enrolled in. She did not understand what she was signing, but signed it anyway because she was *told* she would get her money back if she didn't like it. She gave the acting school $1500, leaving a balance due of $3,000. After attending one lesson she asked me questions about the school and its program. I was shocked.

I told her to get her money back immediately and cancel the contract because they were charging her way too much. (The slang term we use for this is **rip-off**.) I was furious that they took advantage of a foreigner. She tried, but the school wanted the remaining $3,000 because the *contract* stated that it was due at the end of the first month. She was worried that she would have to hire an attorney or pay the balance. I worked with her to schedule a hearing at a small claims court. For a court fee of $25, a judge heard both sides. I testified because of my acting background and I also acted as an English interpreter for her. Then the judge made his decision and instructed the school to refund her money, including court fees, and to cancel the balance due.

> **Hint**: Unfortunately, there are those in the U.S. who will take advantage of others, particularly the uninformed like newly arrived immigrants who do not understand our language and customs. If you have to sign a contract that you do not understand, take it home and find someone who can interpret it for you. If you are told you have to sign it now and can't take it with you for review, just walk out because it is probably a rip-off. Legitimate firms will not do this.

Small claims courts do not allow the use of attorneys, so anyone—even you—can file a claim and be heard within a few weeks if the claim is for less than generally $10,000. Court personnel will answer your administrative questions, provide forms, and assist you in filing a case. Most states have a website where you can learn about their small claims court, such as this one in the east coast state of Virginia: www.courts.state.va.us/pamphlets/small_claims.html.

LEGAL STATUS OF FOREIGNERS

When you are traveling or living in a foreign country you are subject to its laws and are under its jurisdiction. The rights granted to you in your home country do not necessarily protect you there. As we discussed earlier, your cultural interpretation of laws in your country may adversely affect your interpretation of laws in the U.S. As a non-citizen, you may face the additional punishment of being deported if you meet certain criteria established by the U.S. Citizenship and Immigration Services (www.uscis.gov).

A Japanese couple settled in California in 1984 as immigrants determined to succeed in business. They never became U.S. citizens, but they operated three popular sushi restaurants and did well financially. But after they deliberately underreported their business income in 1991, the IRS **hit them** (assessed them) with $245,000 in taxes and penalties. The couple pleaded guilty and paid in full. However, a decade later, the Immigration and Naturalization Service (**INS**) decided to deport them. The matter made its way to the Supreme Court in 2012 where it was ruled 6 to 3 that the INS acted within its authority. Deportation was once limited to murderers and drug **kingpins** (leaders) but has expanded over the years. The ruling sends an ominous warning to legal immigrants and especially to small business owners whose tax liabilities may attract IRS attention. (There's that *honesty* thing again.)

So, if you are a non-citizen and commit a crime in the U.S., expect to face the consequences. You will be treated like anyone else. If you are charged with a serious offense, insist that your local embassy or consulate be informed. Ask them to notify your family, advise you on local procedures, and put you in touch with a lawyer. Pay attention to the Miranda Rule discussed below. And if you cannot afford a lawyer, the court will provide one for you, courtesy of the Gideon ruling discussed above. Your embassy or consulate will help you, but will probably not pay for a lawyer, give you legal advice, post your bail, or arrange to have you released. So obey our laws to the best of your ability while you are with us, including not parking in front of "No Parking" signs.

LAW PROFESSION

American law students generally must have a four-year college degree in any subject of their choice. They then go on to study public and private law for three years at one of our 220 law schools at a university. This contrasts to civil law countries such as Japan and Western Europe where students study law as university undergraduates and then go to a legal research institute for training in specific areas of law. Today, American women earn nearly 50 percent of law degrees, compared to 7 percent in 1972. One study (www.Top-Law-Schools.com) ranks our top five U.S. law schools in this order: Yale, Harvard, Stanford, Columbia, and University of Chicago. President and Hillary Clinton both studied law at Yale University; Obama attended Harvard.

Yale University law classroom.

Like India and other nations with state regulation of lawyers, each of our states has its own **bar**—a body of lawyers who are licensed to practice in that state. Some are licensed in multiple states. The word *bar* originally referred to the railing that separated spectators from the proceedings in a courtroom. It is said that lawyers represent their clients **before the bar** and are **members of the bar**. States issue a license to law school graduates who pass their state's bar examination. If lawyers conduct themselves in an unprofessional manner, they will be disbarred and lose their license to practice.

Though most of our universities offer degrees in political science, the law profession is often a **stepping stone** for those who wish to seek public office. Two-thirds of our presidents have been lawyers. Congress, state legislatures, and administrative agencies attract more people from law than from any other profession.

RULINGS THAT CHANGED AMERICA

Some relatively recent legal decisions with far-reaching implications provide further insight into how the legal system influences our daily life. They are frequently referred to in the media. Your American counterpart might do the same. If you are familiar with them, you will be **in the know** (knowledgeable about what is going on) about America.

Miranda Rule – The Supreme Court confirmed that **Miranda** warnings are constitutionally required when law enforcers make an arrest. It came about because of a 1966 court case called Miranda v. Arizona (the V stands for versus). When a person is taken into in custody, some version of the Miranda rights, such as the following, must now be read to the individual before questioning.

"You have the right to remain silent. If you give up the right to remain silent, anything you say can and will be used against you in a court of law. You have the right to an attorney. If you desire an attorney and cannot afford one, an attorney will be obtained for you before police questioning."

Occasionally you will see reenactments of this in our **cops and robbers** (crime) movies and TV shows.

Roe v. Wade – In 1973, the Supreme Court decided that a woman could legally have an abortion (terminate the life of an unborn fetus). Roe lived in Texas, a state that prohibited abortions. The Court held that a woman's right to an abortion fell within the *right to privacy* protected by the U.S. Constitution. As a result, the laws of all the states were affected by the Court's ruling. This issue is still of prime importance to many Americans. Some groups who object to abortion are still trying to get the ruling overturned, while others are defending it.

You will hear the terms **right to life** and **pro-life** that imply the unborn child has a right to life. Fifty percent of adult Americans identify with pro-life. On the other hand, a woman's **right to choose** and **pro-choice** define those who support abortion and feel this is a personal decision for the woman and government intervention is an infringement of their right to privacy. Forty-one percent of adult Americans identify with pro-choice. However, that number increases to 58 percent for those with a postgraduate degree, and 68 percent for those with no religion.

Some Americans have switched political

Anti-abortion protesters.

parties because they disagreed with their party's stand on abortion. In theory, the democratic party supports the right to choose, while the republican party supports the right to life. Some who oppose abortion protest in groups outside clinics that offer abortion services to the public. And some anti-abortionists have even bombed and killed at these clinics in order to influence others to abide by their beliefs. **Planned Parenthood** (www.plannedparenthood.org) supports a woman's choice and provides counseling.

The Obama administration wanted to continue funding money to international groups that perform abortions or provide abortion information as part of counseling on family planning and population control. But the House Foreign Affairs Committee that holds the **purse strings** (controls the money) **shot it down** (voted against it).

> **Hint**: As you might learn firsthand, abortion can be a very sensitive subject for some due in part to religious beliefs. You may prefer to avoid the subject even if someone brings it up, unless they are a close friend. Because certain foreigners can be more practical and detached on the subject due to their culture, they may not understand how emotional some Americans are about this issue. For instance, I met a woman in China who was **matter of fact** (forthright) about the need to have an abortion should she accidentally become pregnant. She already had her one state-allowed child and knew she would lose her government job if she had another child.

Affirmative Action – This refers to court decisions, laws, and policies intended to increase the opportunities afforded people to **level the playing field** (create equal opportunities) for those discriminated against in the past. This includes people from certain social groups in employment, education, business, government, and other areas. Women are included along with minorities such as African Americans, Asian Americans, disabled people, and veterans to name a few. Some organizations use numerical quotas to ensure they are included in predetermined proportions. On the other hand, some programs seek to remove barriers so all people may compete equally. There is wide disagreement

Affirmative action affects students.

in the U.S. about the fairness of either one of these approaches to eliminating **discrimination** *[dis-crim-in-AY-shun]*.

In a 1995 ruling, the Supreme Court ruled that a federal program requiring preference based on a person's race is unconstitutional unless it is to make up for past In 1996, California voters approved a proposition that banned the use of race or gender considerations in public hiring, contracting, and education. But, where affirmative action has been abolished, some universities circumvent it by having other admission policies to ensure diversity. Minority foreign students in America, even with their usually high class-rankings and good grades, might be affected positively or negatively by affirmative action, depending on the college at which they seek enrollment.

Segregation – Segregation *[seg-reh-GAY-shun]* is the separation of groups of people, by custom or law. It can be based on differences such as race, religion, culture, sex, or wealth. It can occur in places such as housing, education, employment, and public facilities. It almost always involves some kind of discrimination when members of a dominant group limit the opportunities of a less powerful group. Foreigners and most Americans find it difficult to understand how segregation and discrimination still exists in American where the basic premise of our society **since day one** (from our beginning) has been equality of the people. We are slowly making changes.

It was not until the 1950s and 60s that our courts became active in outlawing segregation, and not until the 1960s that Presidents Kennedy and Johnson ushered in laws against segregation and discrimination.

In 1954's **Brown v. Board of Education**, and again in 1969, the Supreme Court ruled against segregation in public schools. An infamous event occurred in 1957 when federal troops escorted black students into a white school in **Little Rock, Arkansas**. This incident ignited the modern day civil rights movement.

Armed intervention at Little Rock High School, 1957.

Hint: While on the decline, racial discrimination is still a hot topic in America. Some people are against affirmative action programs and busing of students in poor neighborhoods to more affluent schools. Others feel they are necessary to give disadvantaged minorities an equal opportunity. Americans will discuss these matters with you if you bring up the subject. How you approach the subject might affect how they view you. My recommendation is you let them present their views while you reserve your opinions unless they ask for them. If they use the term Little Rock High when addressing a ground-breaking event, you will know it is a serious matter.

Title IX – Landmark legislation, called Title IX (pronounced nine) that bans sex discrimination in schools in both academics and athletics was passed in 1972. Schools that did not comply did not receive federal funds, a common method used by Washington to force states to comply with federal laws.

Patsy Mink, of Japanese heritage and the first non-white woman to serve in Congress, led the push for passage of the bill. The new law worked. Women today participate in sports far more than those who grew up before Title IX.

Hint: When my daughter was in high school in the late 1970s, there was not a girls' water polo team, so she tried out and became a member of the boys' team, the first girl ever on any boys' team at that school, perhaps in our city or state. Prior to Title IX, girls' teams would not have been allowed in rough sports. Today, in accordance with Title IX, if there is enough interest on the part of the girls, chances are pretty good they will have their own teams.

95

Over half of the post-Title IX generations now participate in high school sports, compared to a third for the pre-Title IX generation. More women are also receiving athletic scholarships and thus the opportunity for higher education than would have been possible otherwise. And the number of women in high school sports has increased by a factor of nine, while the number of women in college sports has increased by more than 450 percent.

High school soccer players.

Although athletics has created the most controversy regarding Title IX, its gains in education and academics are also noteworthy. Before Title IX, many schools refused to admit women or had strict limits on their admission. Today, women account for half of medical and law school applications—up from the low teens before Title IX—and 45 percent of our doctoral degrees are awarded to women—up from 25 percent.

FAMOUS COURT CASES

It seems like our media is always reporting on court trials that capture the public's attention. Some of these might come up in your conversations with Americans. If you are familiar with them you might want to join the conversation when the subject comes up.

Scopes Trial – The famous 1925 **Scopes Trial** in Tennessee reveals the delicate boundary between education and religion in the U.S. and how, given our diversity, some states are slow to change. John T. Scopes, a high school biology teacher, was accused of having violated a Tennessee law that forbade the teaching of the **theory of evolution** (humans evolved) in public schools because it contradicted the Bible's account that God created man in God's image. The trial received worldwide publicity and was called the **Monkey Trial**. He was convicted and fined, but the state supreme court later reversed the verdict on technical grounds. The law **remained on the books** until 1967. Some of our states–some *people*–can be slow to change. Only recently Texas outlawed text books that mention our great third president Thomas Jefferson because he endorsed religion in a nontraditional way, and because of his love affair with one of his black slaves.

Hint: *Inherit the Wind* (1960) is an award-winning movie about the Scopes Trial.

O.J. Simpson Trial – Perhaps the most famous recent trial was the **O.J. Simpson** trial, called the "Trial of the Century" because the case received more media coverage than any other criminal trial. Simpson, a former outstanding football player and celebrity, was accused of slashing to death his beautiful ex-wife and her friend in June 1994. The trial, which allowed TV cameras in the courtroom, lasted nine months. Although the jury acquitted Simpson in October 1995, polls showed that

O.J. Simpson

the majority of the public thought he was guilty. When he was tried again on civil (non-criminal) charges, he *was* found guilty.

> **Hint**: Americans like to use popular sayings in a humorous way to make a point. If something is obviously true and we want to emphasize that, we might sarcastically say "Was O.J. guilty?" to make our point. For instance, you know how important it is that you complete your work before going on vacation. If your supervisor asks, "Are you going to be able to finish all your work before going?" your response might be, "Was O.J. guilty?" or "Is the pope Catholic?" to show that of course you will finish it.

Martha Stewart Trial – It is against the law for an individual who has personal insight into a company's operations to make financial gains in the stock market because of that unique knowledge. (There's that *level playing field* thing again.) When they do, we call it **insider trading**. Stewart was a wealthy TV celebrity and head of a billion dollar merchandising company. She was also a friend of the head of a corporation that was awaiting government approval to begin marketing a new drug. Her friend advised Stewart to sell her stock in that company just days before the government was about to announce the drug would not receive approval and the stock would drop significantly in price.

She was found guilty for lying in court about the advance information she received. Many wonder why she didn't admit her guilt and face a small fine. Instead, she went to court and lost, had to resign Martha Stewart from her chief executive and TV roles, and went to prison. She was also given a five-year ban on serving as an executive of a public company. Americans often **forgive and forget** when people have **paid their debt to society**. She completed her jail time and is now a TV star again.

Micael Jackson Trial – Michael Jackson was 50 when he died in 2009 as he was preparing for a comeback tour to restore him as a superstar. A highly publicized six week trial was held two years later in which fans waited outside the courtroom each day with signs proclaiming their love for Jackson. Jackson's doctor who administered him injections of a risky and  controlled drug was found guilty of involuntary manslaughter (unintended death) that led to the death of the singer who the media called the **King of Pop**. Michael Jackson

Roger Clemens Trial – This trial was more about the use of illicit drugs in sports in America than it was against Roger Clemens. The government began its inquiry after Clemens was named in a 2007 government report that exposed widespread steroid and human growth hormone use in Major League Baseball (see Chapter N - Sports). Mr. Clemens, 44-years old at the time and formerly one of the game's best pitchers, was charged with one count of obstructing Congress, three counts of making false statements, and two counts of perjury in connection with his testimony to a 2008 House committee denying he used drugs. He was found innocent in 2012 when he was tried for the second time. In the final analysis it amounted to the jury believing Clemens over a witness who testified against him. Despite the verdict, it is widely believed that Clemens did use steroids of some kind over the later years of his career and his legacy will be tarnished as a result.

Clemens in court.

Clemens' acquittal followed the **slap on the hand** (very minor punishment) received by another baseball player in 2011, all-star **Barry Bonds**, with two trials that took seven years to prosecute, cost tax payers millions and yielded little in return. He was convicted of obstructing justice when he misled a grand jury investigating use of performance-enhancing drugs among elite athletes. He was sentenced to 30 days of house arrest but appealed his conviction.

Bonds

A two-year, multi-continent investigation of famous cyclist **Lance Armstrong** was closed with no charges brought, though the U.S. Anti-Doping Agency filed formal accusations in 2012 that could strip the seven-time Tour de France winner of his victories in that storied race. Armstrong denies any doping.

Armstrong

The Clemens verdict was a blow to the government's legal pursuit of athletes accused of illicit drug use. Some say this case was about appeasing the egos of glory-seeking Washington politicians who went on a **witch hunt** (pointless harrassment) and less about any real evidence. They say this will probably mark the end of the government's reach into sports and steroids.

Others say these trials of elite athletes must continue because they are about the core values of fair play and a **level playing field** that define America.

Next we examine religion's powerful influence on our culture and beliefs, something that dates back to our founding four hundred years ago.

F

RELIGION

*My religion consists of a humble admiration of the illimitable
Superior spirit who reveals Himself in the slight details we are able
to perceive with our frail and feeble mind.* - Albert Einstein, physicist

Just as East Asian cultures are generally derived from ancient Chinese thought and philosophy of the schools of Confucism, Buddhism, and Taoism, our Western philosophy is infused in a similar fashion by Christianity and Judaism. Perhaps more than any other aspect of America culture, an understanding of the role of religion in our lives provides key insight into the character, principles, values, and souls of the American people.

Sunday religious service.

Religions are highly complicated, interwoven and controversial. With the aim of acquainting you with our religious diversity, this chapter provides overviews of religion and its effect on our culture, politics, and the spiritual lives of Americans. It is meant to give you just an **inkling** (hint) of this vast subject that would take volumes to explain.

Our churches and religious organizations continue to play important societal roles. They:

- Provide moral guidance and places for worship and social gatherings.
- Operate many elementary and secondary schools, colleges, universities, hospitals, and nursing homes.
- Provide aid for the poor, the elderly, refugees, orphans, and other people in need, both in the U.S. and around the world.
- Take active roles in discussing such issues as birth control and rights for minorities, immigrants, and women.

We have three fundamental religious types in America.

- *Christian* – The vast majority (79%) of Americans are Christians, a religion based on the teachings of Jesus Christ. The three basic Christian groups are:
  o Protestant – 51%.
  o Roman Catholic – 24%
  o Eastern Orthodox – 0.6 %.
- *Judaism* – The next largest type comprises about 1.7 percent.
- *Others* – This includes Buddhism, Hinduism, Islam, and miscellaneous others that comprise 2 percent.

Importance of Religion – America is regarded among the most religious and religiously diverse countries in the world where 95 percent say they believe in God, 60 percent are members of an organized religious group, and nearly two-thirds call religion important in their lives. In Poland, 35 percent say religion is important; in Britain it is 33, Canada 30, Italy 27, Germany 21, Russia 14, Japan 12, and France 11 percent. Latin American attitudes about religion compare closely with the U.S.

Fifty-eight percent of Americans say it is necessary to believe in God to be a moral, good person. Thirteen percent of the French, 25 percent of the British, and 27 percent of Italians agree. Mississippi is the most religious U.S. state, with almost six in 10 residents classified in one study as "very religious." Vermont and New Hampshire are the least religious states where less than one in four qualifies as "very religious."

While many in the U.S. still cling to the traditions of their religion, 44 percent of us do not go to church. And many believe that a person can still be a good person even if they do not practice their religion or do not have a religious faith, a change that came about in the 1960s.

Religious Influence – In contrast to countries that have one dominant religion, we have hundreds of organized religions. In some nations, religion can be a unifying influence. In America it is another source of our diversity. In our early days, religion had a major, controlling influence in the everyday lives of Americans. Today it has relatively less influence. Marriage between members of different religions, once frowned upon, is now commonplace, as is not attending weekly church services. And the role of women in religious ceremonies is increasing.

For most Americans, religion is a personal matter usually not discussed in everyday conversation as it once was. This is in contrast to India and Muslim countries where the vast majority of people engage in daily rituals, making religion one of the most important facets of life. We are free to criticize religions here, unlike some Muslim countries where it might land people in jail.

New Religions – Despite the traditional popularity of Christianity in America, many people have turned to new religions or movements, another indicator of our

100

diversity and the restless spirit of Americans. More than one-quarter of American adults have left the faith in which they were raised in favor of another religion or no religion at all. While nearly one-in-three Americans (31%) were raised in the Catholic faith, today fewer than one-in-four (24%) describe themselves as Catholic. Some Americans have sought the teachings of Asian religions such as Buddhism, Hinduism, and Islam. Some have turned to astrology and spiritualism, and some **mix and match** these paths to spirituality.

Preachers of religion on TV attract about a fifth of Americans and their financial donations. Even though sexual and financial scandals have affected many of the biggest names in television **evangelism** (preaching beliefs to those who do not hold those beliefs), religious broadcasting is stronger and more diverse now than ever.

Some religious leaders today still travel from town to town the old fashion way and conduct spirited **gospel** (teachings of Christ) meetings in tents, quote the Bible, and instil the fear of God in worshipers.

> **Hint**: One of my favorite movies and books, *Elmer Gantry* (1960), is about such a preacher who travels from town to town to save sinners who violate the teachings of the Bible. A memorable line from the movie as he addresses the assembly: "I have here in my pocket—and thank heaven you can't see them—lewd, dirty, obscene, and I'm ashamed to say this: French postcards. They were sold to me in front of your own innocent high school by a man with a black beard...a foreigner." Yes, even back in 1927 when the story takes place, foreigners were viewed with caution. The movie is a good reminder of how **narrow thinking** can infect attitudes in our lives. (The book or movie can be ordered online through Amazon.com at http://amzn.to/GantryMovie.)

Church and State – Unlike some countries, we have always had a separation of church and state. Europeans who did not want to conform to a religious belief dictated by their government left their homelands in the 1600s and sailed to America. Consequently, today our government does not control religion, and religion does not control our government, at least in theory. In reality, Christian fundamentalist groups have become a powerful factor in U.S. politics and society. Their influence ranges from domestic affairs (law, health care, education, science) to international politics. It is even a key factor in elections. This contrasts with China where Catholics, evangelical Christians, Muslims, and Buddhists still report varying forms of government repression. In spite of our separation of government and church, two-thirds say the president should be guided by his faith when making policy decisions.

Unlike Europe, God is often mentioned by American politicians. Here, religious freedom was at the foundation of the U.S. where many Pilgrims came to freely practice their religion. In France, the separation of church and state was to shield the state from the socially dominant Catholic Church. That gave roots to secularism, which basically sees religion as a threat to democracy and to a republican state. So strangely in the U.S. it is politically correct to be religious, while in Europe—France in particular—it is politically correct to be secular.

Even though our Constitution requires a separation of religion and state, this whole issue is **somewhat muddy** (not defined clearly). On the one hand, Judges have overturned plans calling for the government to give the same financial aid to religious schools that is being given to public schools, and have ruled unconstitutional a number of programs to teach the Bible or recite prayers in public schools. Yet our currency has "In God We Trust" printed on it, and some local government officials might begin a meeting with a prayer. Crazy, huh?

What Surveys Say – Over a third of Americans say they go to religious services at least once a week. The top 10 states in church attendance other than Utah are in the South. At the other end of the spectrum, the states with lowest attendance are either in New England or the West. Other findings:

- *Heaven* – More than three out of four adults expect to go to heaven where they will have eternal life, while just two percent think they will be condemned to hell.

- *Catholics* – The story of America is a story of change and shifting views. In an ABC News/Washington Post poll, about six in ten Catholics felt the church was out of touch with their views, including premarital sex, birth control, the death penalty, ordaining women, and allowing priests to marry, all of which are opposed by this church. Two-thirds say the pope should focus less on traditional policies and more on changing policies to reflect the attitudes and lifestyles of Catholics today.

U.S. Nat'l Cathedral – Wash. D.C.

- *Prayer* – Nine out of 10 Americans say they pray to God. They pray for these things most often: their own families (98%), world's children (81%), world peace (77%), and co-workers (69%). Fewer than half believe that God is a man, while 43 percent say God doesn't have a gender. One percent thinks God is a woman.

Let's look at our three fundamental religious types: Christianity, Judaism, and other minor religions. You will learn about their history, their differences, their basic beliefs, and key terms that you can use in your conversations with Americans. This understanding might also provide insight into the general moral code of your American contact. Keep in mind that the religious community in the U.S., like everything else, is very diverse. This discussion is only meant to give you a broad overview.

CHRISTIANITY

Christianity *[kriss-tee-AN-ih-tee]* is based on the life and teachings of Jesus Christ. It is believed that God sent Jesus to the world as the Son of God, and that man can achieve eternal life by believing in Jesus. Born about 4 BC to Mary and Joseph in a manger—a housing for farm animals—His birth is celebrated on December 25th as Christmas, one of our national holidays (see Chapter R - Holidays and Traditions). Jesus taught that man could enter the kingdom of God (eternal life) with a change of heart and repentance for sins, love of God and neighbor, and a concern for justice.

Symbol of Christianity.

Jesus was crucified (nailed to a cross where he died) in 30 AD by the Romans because of his religious teachings. For this reason, the cross became the symbol of Christianity. Besides appearing in our churches, on gravestones, and sometimes hanging on walls in our homes, you will see the cross worn as jewelry.

The Rocky Mountain state of Utah is the most Christian state with around 78 percent identifying as Christian adherents; Maine is the least with about 27 percent.

The Bible – This name is given to several collections of writings held sacred by the Jewish and Christian religions. The Bible is the most widely distributed book in world history and has been translated more times, and into more languages (2200), than any other book. Scholars value the Bible not only as an important religious document, but also as a great literary work. Some Americans, both young and old, attend Bible study classes.

When an American president takes the Oath of Office, he places one hand on a Bible. But he does not swear an oath to his God; he swears to "support and defend the Constitution of the United States." Witnesses in court are sworn in by placing their hand on the Bible and swearing to tell the truth, "…so help you

Christians' holy book.

God." If you visit a hotel in America, you will probably find a Bible in your room that was put there by a Bible society. You will hear public speakers quote lines from the Bible. Some high school students attend private Bible study classes before the start of school each day in Utah. In religious based school they might be part of the curriculum.

> **Hint**: We have many award-winning movies based on biblical times, including *Samson and Delilah* (1949), *Quo Vadis* (1951), *The Robe* (1953), *The Ten Commandments* (1956), *Ben Hur* (1959), and *The Passion of Christ* (2004).

The Ten Commandments – Christian ethics derive to a large extent from the Jewish traditions in the Old Testament book in the Bible, including the Ten Commandments. This is a list of rules for living and worship that, according to the Bible, God wrote and, in theory, is supposed to guide our conduct.

1. You shall have no other gods before me.

103

2. You shall not make any graven image of me.

3. You shall not take the name of the Lord thy God in vain.

4. Remember the Sabbath day (Sunday or day of worship), to keep it holy.

5. Honor your father and mother.

6. You shall not murder.

7. You shall not commit adultery.

8. You shall not steal.

9. You shall not bear false witness against your neighbor.

10. You shall not covet [desire] your neighbor's house, wife, or other possessions.

The Lord's Prayer – This is a simple Christian prayer that many learn by heart. It is sometimes used in public and private prayers and invites man to draw near to God. For some, calling God "Father" does not mean that God is masculine because He is beyond the categories of gender. Some religions, however, *do* view God as a man.

"Our Father, who art in heaven, hallowed be thy name.

Thy Kingdom come, thy will be done, on earth as it is in heaven.

Give us this day our daily bread.

Forgive our trespasses, as we forgive those who trespass against us.

And lead us not into temptation, but deliver us from evil.

For thine is the kingdom, and the power, and the glory, for ever and ever. Amen."

Forgiveness and loving and helping our neighbor are at the heart of Christian ethics and, in turn, our culture. The Prayer suggests we should forgive others who do wrong deeds to us before we can ask forgiveness for our own misdeeds. When Jesus was dying on the cross, he said to God of his slayers, "Forgive them Father, they know not what they do."

In more recent times, a mentally deranged young man shot President Reagan in 1981. Reagan, who was a member of the Presbyterian Church, believed he could not pray to God to spare his own life as long as he had hatred in his soul for the man who tried to kill him. So, the president forgave and prayed for the young man, then began to pray for himself. He eventually healed. Let's now look at our various religions.

PROTESTANT CHURCHES

The largest group of Christian religions in the U.S. are called **Protestants**, derived from the word "protest." Besides disliking the corruption and power of the Catholic Church in the 1600s, Protestants wanted the Bible translated from Latin into the common language of the people. They also thought that each person should think and grow in the Christian life and not rely on a formal church structure to make decisions for them.

We call this period of time the **Reformation** *[ref-or-MAY-shun]* (to reform is to change). America has not become as secularized (non-religious) as Europe due in part to our Protestant churches. You might hear the demographic term **WASP**, which refers to a person who is a **w**hite, **A**nglo-**S**axon, **P**rotestant whose ancestry is typically Northern European.

The following are our five most popular Protestant churches. Chances are pretty good that an American you meet might belong to one of these. Feel free to ask questions and discuss their church with them.

Lutheran Church – Born in Germany in 1483, **Martin Luther** is known as the Father of Protestantism. He hoped the Catholic Church would reform its practices. It didn't, so there was a separation from it. Based on its number of church members, it is the fourth largest religion in the U.S. (www.elca.org)

Baptist Church – Each local Baptist church appoints its own leaders (**ministers**) for preaching and teaching. These local churches are self-governing and self-supporting, ranging in size from twenty or so members to many hundreds. It is the second largest organized religion in the U.S. (www.abc-usa.org)

Methodist Church – The Church encourages members to think for themselves. So they don't necessarily share the same opinions about every faith issue or social concern. It has 36,000 churches in the U.S. and is our third largest religion. (www.umc.org)

Presbyterian Church – The Church is governed at all levels by a combination of clergy and church members, men and women alike. Like many other Christian churches, they engage in missionary activities to alleviate hunger, foster self-development, respond to disasters, preach the gospel, heal the sick, and educate new generations for the future. It is our fifth largest religion. (www.pcusa.org)

Episcopal Church – The Episcopal *[ih-PISS-kuh-puhl]* Church traces its roots to the Church of England, which, in turn, developed from the Catholic Church. During the 1600s, English Protestants, called **Puritans**, sought more reforms and sailed to America when change did not come. In 1789, after our Revolutionary War, settlers in the colonies separated from the Church of England and formed the Protestant Episcopal Church. It is our seventh largest religion. *A Man for All Seasons* (1966) is a classic film about King Henry VIII's decision to break from the Roman Catholic Church to form his own Church of England. (www.ecusa.anglican.org)

ROMAN CATHOLIC CHURCH

The Roman Catholic Church in the U.S. has the second most members after the Protestants (www.usccb.org). Roman Catholics believe that God has given a person called the **pope** the authority to speak on God's behalf. Roman Catholics are far more unified than Protestants, due in part to their hierarchical structure and insistence on certain core beliefs. Many schools, orphanages, and hospitals have been started by Catholic priests in response to needs throughout the world. Catholic schools and universities are numerous in the U.S., with Notre Dame University the most famous. The National Catholic College Admission Association, a non-profit organization of our  Catholic colleges and universities, promotes the value of Catholic higher education and assists students in the transition to college (www.catholiccollegesonline.org).

EASTERN ORTHODOX CHURCH

Eastern Orthodox, the third largest Christian group in the U.S., is divided by national origin. The Greek Orthodox and Russian Orthodox Churches are the two largest branches in the U.S. In 1054 the Eastern Church separated from the Roman Catholic Church over several issues. Consequently the Orthodox Church became a federation of self-governing churches with a head of church in each area, generally a nation. (www.oca.org)

JUDIASM

After Christianity in general, Judaism *[JOO-dah-is-um]* is the second largest fundamental religion in the U.S. with about four percent of our religious population. The Jewish identity is a mixture of historical, ethnic, and religious factors. Both Christianity and Islam are rooted in Judaism. (www.ou.org)

Jews worship in **synagogues** *[SIN-ah-gogs]* and **temples** while Christians worship in churches and cathedrals. German dictator Adolf Hitler and his Nazi Party killed about 6 million of the 8 million Jews in Europe. Because of Israel's ongoing conflict with Muslims who live there, some criticize America for its support of Israel.

Hint: This conflict is a hot topic of discussion with Americans and even influences how we are viewed by other countries. Some Muslims believe that Israel should not be allowed to exist as a nation, even though the United Nations granted it title and statehood in the area they now occupy. Consequently there is bloodshed between the Palestinians there and the Jews. America is deeply concerned for the people on both sides of this issue, even though it supports Israel as a legitimate nation. It has tried unsuccessfully for years to mediate peace between these warring parties. President Clinton came close in the 1990s. With the help of the U.S., Egypt, and a few other Muslim countries that once were at war with Israel and are now friendly, they too are trying to help solve this conflict. Ask Americans what they think about this. Some may have no opinion or conflicting opinions. An award-winning movie (and book) that deals with the establishment of Israel is *Exodus* (1960). *The Ten Commandments* (1956) is a classic movie about a Hebrew leader.

OTHER FUNDAMENTAL RELIGIONS

The third and smallest group of other fundamental religions practiced in the U.S. include Asian-based religions and Islam. These religions appeal to some Americans because of their alternative views to Christianity and Judaism.

- **Hinduism** *[HIN-du-is-um]* with 1.5 million members in the U.S. is in direct opposition to America's idea of equality. It has a strict system of social classes, ranging from the priests and scholars at the top, down to servants at the bottom. At the same time it offers spiritualism, culture, and history that appeal to many.

- **Buddhism** *[BOOD-is-um]* has 800,000 followers in the U.S. More recently, Tibetan Buddhism has entered the mainstream American consciousness fuelled by the influence of the free-Tibet movement, the charisma of the Dalai Lama, and the interest of Hollywood personalities like Richard Gere, Martin Scorsese, and Steven Seagal.

- **Confucianism** *[kon-FU-she-is-um]* is viewed by some more as a philosophy than a religion. It stresses a well-ordered society in which parents rule their children and emphasize deep respect for one's ancestors and the past. Don't be surprised if you hear Americans utter one of his beliefs, such as "Confucius says, never impose on others what you would not choose for yourself."

- **Islam** *[IZ-lhom]* believers worship God directly without the intercession of priests, clergy, or saints. People who practice the religion of Islam are called **Muslims** *[MUHZ-lums]*. It is estimated that North America has about 5 million Muslims. (www.masnet.org)

NON-MAINSTREAM RELIGIONS

As you are learning, America is a land of variety and constant change. During the 1800s America changed geographically, socially, and religiously as new religions arose. And today, if a particular religion does not fit the beliefs of some in the U.S., they might form a new religion, just as our ancestors did in Europe during the Reformation. You might come into contact with members of these non-mainstream Christian religions.

Amish – Amish *[AIM-ish]* people live in settlements in 22 states. The oldest group—about 16-18,000 people in the eastern state of Pennsylvania—stress humility, family and community, and separation from the world. They come from a mainly German background, ride horses and buggies rather than cars, do not have electricity in their homes, and send their children to private, one-room schoolhouses only through the eighth grade. After that, they work on their family farms or businesses until they marry. Many who belong to

Amish family.

more progressive Amish groups in other localities do attend high school and even college. *Witness*, the popular 1985 movie with Harrison Ford, centers on an Amish farm family. (www.amish.net)

Christian Scientists – This church, founded in the 1860s, interprets the Bible in a distinct way, focusing on the life of Jesus as a model of healing by prayer. They believe physical illness and injury result from error or wrong belief and can be healed through one's own prayer or with the help of a Christian Science practitioner. (www.christianscience.com)

Mormons – The Church of Jesus Christ of Latter-day Saints (called Mormons) was established by Joseph Smith (1805-1844) in 1830. Because of their beliefs, they were persecuted as they moved about the country. They finally settled in the remote western state of Utah in 1847. The church is home to the world's largest collection of genealogical (family tree) data. They emphasize the family unit, strong personal principles, and living free of alcohol, caffeine, tobacco, and other body and mind altering substances. They have 50,000 missionaries around the world. They have a membership of 15 million followers. (www.LDS.org)

Mormon Temple, Salt Lake City, Utah.

Seventh-day Adventists – This religion is traced to a preacher who proclaimed that Christ would reappear sometime in 1843-1844. Unlike most of our Christian religions, they choose Saturday for worship and rest. They practice vegetarianism and avoid alcohol and caffeine. They accept the Bible as the word of God and still await the coming of Christ. (www.adventist.org)

Jehovah's Witnesses – They believe an end of the world will come with a great war as described in the Bible. They do not salute flags or join the military. (www.watchtower.org)

G

MEASUREMENTS

*A foot can be too long and an inch
can be long enough.* - Chinese proverb

Foreigners can be baffled by our crazy measurements just as they are by our crazy language and a host of other things. On your first visit here, you are bound to compare how we measure things to how it's done in your country.

As you probably know, Americans can be stubborn about some things. The way we measure things is a good example. Nations began to adopt the metric system in the 1840s, and by 1900 most commercially advanced countries of the world had adopted it. The U.S., India, and U.K. and were the main holdouts, but in the 1950s and 60s India and the U.K. began a changeover to the metric system.

"Have I lost inches?"

The U.S. has never fully converted to it, even with nudging by government and business. Today we tend to use a **mixed bag** (a combination) of both. No, we don't do this to confuse foreigners who see our gasoline priced by the gallon and our vegetables priced by the pound.

The nudging got pharmacists to use metric units to fill prescriptions in the 1950s. In 1975, Congress passed a law establishing a policy of *voluntary* conversion to the metric system. Congress amended this law in 1988, naming the metric system the *preferred* system of weights and measures for U.S. trade and commerce. By the early 2000s, an increasing amount of scientific and engineering work in the U.S. was done using metric units. Also, major industrial firms converted their U.S. facilities to metric, but packaged consumer goods were labeled in both metric and inch-pound units. (There's that *individualism* thing again that pervades our society in which we like to make our own choices.)

In spite of all this nudging, the public still deals mostly with our inch-pound system. So, what are you to conclude from this? On certain things perhaps it is better to continually nudge Americans rather than force them. Are we different from other

109

peoples? Hitler, with all his power, reportedly learned the same lesson with his people when he was powerless to install speed limits on his newly built autobahns.

This chapter will help you understand our units of measurements and how to make quick conversions to and from the measurements you are probably accustomed to using. Websites like www.calculateme.com are also available for exact conversions.

> **Hint**: Instead of worrying about exact conversions, at first just try to get a general sense of our key measurements, such as how long our mile is, how heavy a pound is, and how much gasoline is in a gallon. Then, relate these in general comparative terms to your kilometer, kilogram, and liter. If you need to make an exact conversion, I provide tables and formulas below.

WEIGHT

We weigh things in **ounces** and **pounds**. There are 16 ounces in one pound. There are 2,000 pounds in a **ton** (short ton). (To confuse you, the "long ton" is the British ton of 2240 pounds.) The post office computes mailing charges based on ounces and pounds. Vegetable scales in our markets are in ounces and pounds. Autos and elephants are weighed in tons.

> **Hint**: We also use the word **ton** to denote a lot of something: "He won a ton of money gambling in Las Vegas."

Pounds to Kilograms Scale

lb	1	2	3	10	100	150	200	250
kg	0.5	0.9	1.14	4.50	45.4	68.0	90.70	113.4

Ounces to Grams Scale

oz	1	2	3	4	5	6	7	8	9
g	28.3	56.7	85.0	113.4	141.7	170.1	198.4	226.8	255.1

Weight and Mass Conversion

When you know:	Multiply by:	To find:
ounces (oz)	28.350	grams
pounds (lb)	0.4536	kilograms
tons (t)	0.9072	metric tons
grams (g)	0.03527	ounces
kilograms (kg)	2.205	pounds
metric tons (t)	1.102	short tons

VOLUME

Most measuring cups used in our kitchens have two scales on them: cups and ounces. Dry foods are measured using **cups**, while liquids are measured in **ounces**. In the kitchen, three **teaspoons** is equivalent to one **tablespoon**, and 16 tablespoons are equal to one cup or 8 fluid ounces. We also have **pints**, **quarts**, **and gallons**. We use the saying

Mind your Ps and Qs that originated in old England's pubs when they cautioned heavy drinkers to keep track of the **p**ints and **q**uarts of ale they drank. These are our volume equivalents:

1 cup (c)	= 8 fluid ounces (fl. oz.)
1 pint (pt)	= 2 cups (c)
1 quart (qt)	= 4 cups (c)
1 gallon (gal)	= 4 quarts (qt)

Packaged ice cream is sold in pints, quarts, and gallons. Some cans of soda are labeled on the front as "12 Oz. (355 ml)." Bottles of water might read "1.5 liter (50.7 fl oz)" or "1.5 liter (1.58 qt)." Our gasoline is sold by the gallon. We measure a car's gas consumption rate in **miles per gallon** (over 25 mpg is considered good).

Hint: A rule of thumb I use to convert the foreign price per liter of gasoline into our familiar U.S. price per gallon is to multiply the liter price by four and subtract 10%. Either way, gasoline is expensive.

Fluid Ounces to Liters Scale

fl oz	1	2	5	10	20	25	30	35
liter	.03	.06	0.15	0.30	0.59	0.74	0.89	1.04

Pints to Liters Scale

pt	1	2	3	4	5
liter	0.57	1.14	1.70	2.27	2.84

U.S. Gallons to Liters Scale

gal	1	2	3	4	5
liter	3.79	7.57	11.36	15.14	18.93

Volume and Capacity (liquid) Conversions

When you know:	Multiply by:	To find
fluid ounces	29.57	milliliters
cups (c)	0.2366	liters
pints (pt)	0.4732	liters
quarts (qt)	0.9464	liters
gallons (gl)	3.785	liters
milliliters (ml)	0.03381	fluid ounces
liters (l)	4.227	cups, U.S.
liters	2.113	pints, U.S.
liters	1.057	quarts, U.S.
liters	0.2642	gallons, U.S.

LENGTH

There are 12 inches in a **foot**, 3 feet or 36 inches in a **yard**, and 1,760 yards or 5,280 feet in a **mile**. Within an inch, we use fractions like 1/2, 1/4, 1/8, and 1/16. Written inches are indicated with two quote marks (") and feet are indicated with one ('). Two-feet-six inches is written as 2'6". Decimals are used, too, such as 6.5" for six and one-half inches or 6.25' for six and a quarter feet.

In our sporting track events, we have measurements in both metric and yards, such as the 400-meter race and the 100-yard dash. Our football fields have 10-yard lines. Clothing waist, leg, and neck sizes are made in inches. School children carry a ruler in their backpacks that is 12 inches in length. Carpenters use a tape measure in their work. You will hear people say, **if I give him an inch and he will take a foot**, meaning that the other person will always want more than what you give him or her.

Tape measure.

Just for fun, here are some equivalent measurements. The famous Empire State Building in New York City, the world's tallest from 1931 to 1972, is 1,472 feet tall (448 meters). The driving distance from San Francisco, California, to New York City is 2930 miles (4726 kilometers). The average U.S. woman is 5'3.7" tall (162 centimeters) and weighs 152 pounds (69 kilograms). The average U.S. male stands 5'9.1" tall (180.1 centimeters) and weighs 180 pounds (81.6 kilograms). The Great Wall of China spans five provinces for 4,162 miles (6,700 kilometers).

Inches to Centimeters Scale

in	1	2	3	4	5	10	16	20	24
cm	2.5	5.1	7.6	10.2	12.7	25.4	40.6	50.8	61.0

Feet to Meters Scale

ft	1	2	3	4	5	6	8	10
m	0.30	0.61	0.91	1.22	1.52	1.83	2.44	3.05

Length and Distance Conversions

When you know:	Multiply by:	To find
inches (in)	2.54	centimeters
feet (ft)	30.48	centimeters
yards (yd)	0.9144	meters
rods (rd)	5.029	meters
statute miles (mi)	1.609	kilometers
fathoms (sea depth)	1.829	meters
nautical miles	1.852	kilometers
millimeters (mm)	0.03937	inches
centimeters (cm)	0.3937	inches
meters (m)	1.094	yards
kilometers (km)	0.6213	miles

1,472 feet tall.

SURFACE OR AREA

The U.S. Census measures the number of people per **square mile** to define a city's population density. Contractors first compute the total **square footage** of a job to lay floor tiles before quoting a price to a customer. The size of a farm, housing tract, or public park is measured in number of **acres** *[AKE-ers]*. The acre, by the way, was originally an English unit of measurement that described the area that oxen could plow in a day. It was ultimately fixed at 4,840 square yards. It can be any shape as long as its area is 43,560 square feet, so a square-shaped acre is about 209 by 209 feet.

Alaska is our largest state with 656,425 square miles, and Rhode Island our smallest with 1545 square miles. Washington, D.C. has 68 square miles (176 sq. km) compared to Beijing, China, that has 6,487 square miles (16,800 sq. km). The population density of the U.S. is 76 people per square mile versus South America's 73, Europe's 134, and Asia at 203.

Surface or Area Conversion

When you know:	Multiply by:	To find
square inches (sq in)	6.452	square centimeters
square feet (sq ft)	929.0	square centimeters
square yards (sq yd)	0.8361	square meters
square miles (sq mi)	2.590	square kilometers
acres	0.4047	hectares
square cent. (sq cm)	0.1550	square inches
square meters (sq m)	10.76	square feet
square kilo. (sq km)	0.3861	square miles
hectares (ha)	2.471	acres

TEMPERATURE

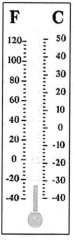

The zero point on the **Celsius** temperature scale that most foreigners are accustomed to using is the freezing point of water. At sea level, water boils at a temperature of 100°C. Normal body temperature for human beings is about 35°C.

We still use the **Fahrenheit** *[FAIR-un-hite]* system in which water freezes at 32°, water boils at 212°, and normal body temperature is 98.6°. The highest temperature ever recorded in the U.S.—134°—occurred in 1913 at Death Valley in California. The lowest temperature in the 48 states—minus 69.7°—occurred in Montana in 1954 on the Continental Divide. Temperatures in our office buildings are generally set at a comfortable 72 degrees.

Hint: If someone says **my blood is boiling**, that means they are extremely angry about something. You might want to back away from them or change the subject.

Degrees Fahrenheit to Degrees Celsius Scale

°F	25	30	35	40	50	65	75	85	100
°C	-4	-1	2	4	10	16	24	20	38

Temperature Conversion

When you know:	Multiply by:	To find:
°Fahrenheit (°F)	5/9 (after subtracting 32)	°Celsius
°Celsius (°C)	9/5 (then add 32)	°Fahrenheit

Hint: A quick conversion method I use to approximate Fahrenheit temperature is to double the Celsius temperature and add 27. Example: 25° Celsius equals 25+25+27 = 77° Fahrenheit. To convert from Fahrenheit to Celsius, subtract 27 and then divide the result by 2. Example: 77° Fahrenheit equals 77-27 = 50/2 = 25.

MONEY

Compared to our inches and pounds, you will probably need to get a bit more exact with our money. But it won't be hard because our money is metric, so to speak. The U.S. monetary system is a decimal system (which, by the way was developed in India 100 BC) with one **dollar** equal to one hundred **cents**, just like India's rupee is divided into 100 paise.

One dollar, sometimes referred to as a **buck**, is written as $1.00. One cent, called a **penny**, is written as 1¢ or .01. Some Americans can be **tight fisted** with their money (tightly control their spending) and tell you that **a penny saved is a penny earned**, which American statesman Benjamin Franklin preached back in the 1700s.

Two dollars and eighty-five cents is written as $2.85. Sometimes we eliminate the two zeros after the decimal point and just show the dollar amount, such as $2 instead of $2.00. Dollar amounts are written with a comma every three digits, so one thousand dollars is written as $1,000.00.

Paper currency is mostly used for amounts of $1 or more, even though we have a dollar coin that nobody likes, so coins are used for amounts under $1. Because America is ever changing, you might end up with a two-dollar paper bill or coin, both of which were dropped a few years back because we didn't like them either. Yes, they're still good but you might get a double look from a merchant you give one of these to.

Coins – Starting with our penny shown below on the left, these are the coins we use, all with U.S. presidents on one side.

Coin	Figure on Front	Value ¢	Value $	Color
Penny	Lincoln	1 cent	0.01 dollars	Copper
Nickel	Jefferson	5 cents	0.05 dollars	Silver
Dime	Roosevelt	10 cents	0.10 dollars	Silver
Quarter	Washington or State	25 cents	0.25 dollars	Silver
Half Dollar	Kennedy	50 cents	0.50 dollars	Silver

Hint: Ask your American counterpart why the penny is the only one with the president facing right. The answer is the sculpture's original plaque from which the coin was designed faced right. Ask how many ways a dollar can be comprised of coins. The answer is 293.

We have fun using coins to help us make decisions. The front of the coin with the figure's face is referred to as **heads** and the reverse side **tails**. If you need to make a choice, such as deciding who will buy drinks, you might toss a coin and call heads or tails while it is still in the air. If the side you call is face up after the coin lands, you win the coin toss and the other person gets to pay for the drinks. You might hear the saying, **the opposite side of the coin**, when someone is discussing both sides of an argument, such as "I want to buy a new car, but on the opposite side of the coin, my house needs repairs."

Hint: As another example of our crazy language that we discuss in Section IV on America's language, coins are *minted* (made) at the *U.S. Mint*. Something is in *mint* condition if it appears to be brand new. We have a green aromatic plant called *mint* that is used in teas and to flavor foods. And we have candy *after-dinner mints* made with chocolate and the flavoring from mint plants.

Currency – Our paper currency is most often circulated in denominations of $1, $5, $10, $20, $50, and $100. You might occasionally see a $2 bill. The denomination of all currency is marked clearly on the bottom of both sides of the bill, and on all four corners. Some of our bills were recently redesigned to make it more difficult to counterfeit. They are a little more colorful. So you may see both new and old bills and both are still good.

Because our currency is printed using lots of green, the U.S. dollar is sometimes referred to as the **greenback**.

The majority of American paper currency is actually held outside of the U.S. because the dollar is used as the standard unit of currency in international markets for commodities such as gold and oil. The average lifespan of our well-traveled dollar bills is 20 months.

Each of our currency denominations listed below has a picture of a famous American statesman on the front. For that reason, you might hear someone refer to $100 bills as Benjamins, named after penny-saved-penny-earned Benjamin Franklin. (Note the famous portrait of George Washington on the $1 bill above. We discuss its painter in Chapter M on art.) The patriotic motto **E Pluribus Unum** that appears on our currency is Latin for "out of many, one," and refers to the original 13 colonies banding together to form one nation. Here is a list of our **paper bills**.

Denomination	Portrait on Front	Illustration on Back
$1.00	George Washington	Great Seal of the U.S.
$2.00	Thomas Jefferson	Declaration of Independence
$5.00	Abraham Lincoln	Lincoln Memorial
$10.00	Alexander Hamilton	U.S. Treasury Building
$20.00	Andrew Jackson	White House
$50.00	Ulysses S. Grant	U.S. Capitol Building
$100.00	Benjamin Franklin	Independence Hall

Hint: When I was in Europe, I met a couple from Germany who had spent time in the U.S. on business. I asked them, as I do all foreigners I meet, if there was something about America they didn't understand or would like to know more about. Number two on their list of eight items was the pyramid and the eye on the back of our one-dollar bill. "What does it stand for?" they asked. Here's the answer. The eye is positioned above an unfinished pyramid with thirteen steps, representing the original thirteen states and the future growth of the undeveloped country. The lowest level of the pyramid shows the year 1776 in Roman numerals. The combined implication is that the eye, or God, favors the prosperity of America. Americans are naturally suspicious, so some might tell you the symbols are connected to mysterious political or religious meanings, something my Germans friends had heard. Others **won't have a clue** (unknowing).

Numerous websites will accurately convert the value of your native currency into American dollars and vice versa, like www.xe.com/ucc/. However, unlike many countries where merchants take American dollars, we don't take foreign currency in the U.S. So convert your money at the airport or a bank before or after you arrive in the U.S.

In my travels I always use a handy **rule of thumb** (broad approximation) to make quick conversions. You can do the same here. Recently, for the Chinese yuan I divided the yuan amount by six to arrive at dollars, or multiplied the dollars by six to roughly approximate the yuan.

Now that you understand how our heritage helped shaped America and our behavior, we can next examine America's culture today. We explore everything from our everyday life, to customs and etiquette, to what's on the minds of Americans, to education, literature, movies, and a whole lot more. Even what we think of foreigners and what they think of us.

SECTION II
AMERICA'S CULTURE

Culture is the name for what people are interested in, their thoughts, their models, the books they read and the speeches they hear, their table-talk, gossip, controversies, historical sense and scientific training, the values they appreciate, the quality of life they admire. All communities have a culture. It is the climate of their civilization.

Walter Lippmann, American journalist 1889-1974

H

CUSTOMS AND ETIQUETTE

Culture is the widening of the mind and of the spirit. - Jawaharlal Nehru, India nationalist, statesman

The term **culture** refers to the general patterns of behavior and thinking that people in different countries learn, create, and share. Each country's culture is defined by such things as customs, etiquette, beliefs, rules of behavior, food, religion, language, art, dress, lifestyles, and political and economic systems to name just a few. This book in its entirety is all about America's culture.

So far you have learned how our history, political structure, and other influences helped define America's culture. Later chapters discuss other factors such as our literature, dress, and film. Understanding our culture will help you better understand Americans and enhance your personal relationships with us.

An international consulting firm recently did a survey of unsuccessful cross-border business mergers and alliances. They found that cultural difference was a significant contributor to failure. So, for these and many other reasons, it is in our best interest to learn more about the culture of other nations with which we deal, be it for personal or business matters. (Our business related customs are discussed in Chapter V.)

Francis Bacon (British philosopher and author 1561-1626) said, "People usually think according to their inclinations, speak according to their learning and ingrained opinions, but generally act according to custom."

In this chapter you will be introduced to some of America's beliefs and rules of behavior that we call our **customs**, which are part of our culture. Customs are those behaviors we have had in the past and will most likely continue to have in the future. Such things as traditions, values, how we do things, habits, ideals, general practices, and etiquette influence these. To help you understand them, comparisons are made to other nations. You will note that our country is learning to adapt to an increasingly diverse population so we must learn to change our ways to accommodate them, too, particularly in the business world.

Our culture and customs are rooted in traditional Western thought based on the cultures of ancient Greece, Rome, and Christianity. **Homer's** two epic poems written in 800 BC, the **Iliad** and the **Odyssey**, and other Greek writings and myths are central in the definition of Western culture.

Culture and customs travel from one country to another. Our founding immigrants brought them from Europe to our shores. So English-speaking countries generally have similar customs, but there can be major differences among us. Although India, for example, is a political democracy like the U.S., in daily life there is little advocacy of equality as is the custom in the U.S.

Our differing customs affect our everyday beliefs. An informal poll asked Asians and Americans this question: "You are on a boat with your mother, your spouse and your child and the boat begins to sink. If you can only save one of them, whom do you save?" Sixty percent of Americans said they would save their spouse, while the other 40 percent would save their children. The typical Western reasoning was "My spouse is my partner for life and I can have more children." However, among Asian cultures or Americans of recent Asian descent, nearly 100 percent would save the mother. The rationale was "My mother gave me life, I owe her my life. I can marry again, I can have more children, but I cannot replace her or otherwise repay the debt I owe her."

Customs also vary within a country. Mark Twain (1835-1910), the famous American humorist and writer we discuss in Chapter K on literature said, "In Boston they ask, 'How much does he know?' In New York 'How much is he worth?' In Philadelphia, 'Who were his parents?'" The customs you are about to learn are fairly standard throughout the U.S., although as you can see from Twain's observation, we do have regional and local differences. For example:

- **Southerners** tend to place less emphasis on the clock and lead a slower life.
- **Northerners** might be more traditional and conservative than those in rapidly growing southern areas like Florida, Texas, Arizona, and California.
- **Midwesterners** (also called **Heartlanders**) are more **down to earth** (grounded) and less impressed with status, are honest, help their neighbors, and are known for their common sense. In fact, when I sit in airports overseas and people-watch I can generally spot these Americans because of their simple dress, friendliness, and relaxed demeanor. They stand out in contrast to intense Europeans and serious looking Japanese. After you spend time here, you will come to recognize them, too.

Hawaii

120

- **Hawaiians** – Life on these tropical islands is a more relaxed, outdoor style.
- **New Englanders** are more impressed with one's family history and status. Being on time, as with Midwesterners, is generally important for them, too.

At least these are some commonly perceived regional differences. Your country probably has them, too. One can generalize between Northern and Southern Europeans, and in China where Northerners can be perceived as louder and warmer in character than the more reserved Southerners.

FOREIGN vs. AMERICAN CUSTOMS

Customs vary by country where they are learned. So Americans and foreigners have different customs—lots of them—that can affect our relationships and how we interpret the actions of each other.

Individuality – In one study, 70 percent of Asians emphasized the importance of an orderly society compared to just 11 percent of Americans. At the opposite extreme, 80 percent of Americans emphasized the importance of personal *freedom* and individual *rights* compared to just 30 percent of Asians.

This emphasis on individuality in the U.S. is further explained in an Oregon university study in which students were asked to list situations in which they felt *they* were winning or losing. The American students focused more on ways in which they won *individually*, while Asian students won when the *group* with which they were associated enjoyed a success.

Gestures – We smile at people on the street, at the airport, in restaurants, shopping malls, and so on. We consider it a friendly gesture. However, in other cultures a smile can be considered insulting or signal embarrassment. (Do you remember our discussion of Walmart in Germany where this practice was stopped?) Americans fail to realize that common gestures such as shrugging one's shoulders or scratching one's forehead can be misinterpreted by someone from another country. And with a display of frankness, so common to Americans, the Japanese think the American people exhibit a lack of discipline.

The Poor – Americans live in a society that is open, where the poor have every opportunity and where, if you don't take advantage of those opportunities, you are in some sense unworthy of government assistance, though that is changing given the current economic climate. Europeans, by contrast, believe they live in a class-bound society where position is determined by birth and other factors. So, in the U.S., 60 percent believe that the poor are lazy versus just 26 percent of Europeans. Twenty-nine percent of

Americans believe the poor are trapped in poverty versus 60 percent of Europeans; in fact the probability of moving out of poverty is about the same on both continents.

Social Behavior – Americans are generally more relaxed than other cultures when it comes to proper social behavior. We use the term **faux pas** *[foe paw]*, a French word, to define a social blunder. Some foreigners can be embarrassed by the slightest infraction of cultural protocol. When U.S. President Bill Clinton was in South Korea, for instance, he embarrassed Korean officials, confused his translator, baffled some dinner guests, and delayed dinner briefly by committing a faux pas. What did he do? He placed a human translator between himself and the Korean president. In Korea, it can be an insult for

Bill Clinton

anyone to stand between two heads of state. In America, where we are more practical and less formal, we see such a move as a way to improve the communication between the two men. As you will learn, *practicality* sometimes takes a **front row seat** (is most important) for Americans.

Another reason some nations place much more emphasis on proper social behavior might be related to the language they speak. In Japan, for example, there are six different ways to say "wife," based on the social setting or audience, and it is socially unacceptable to use the wrong one. Our language is less nuanced in many respects.

My advice: Don't worry too much about making a bad social error with us to the extent you might in your own country. We put less emphasis on such things and can have a sense of humor about them when they do occur, probably as Clinton did.

European Differences – Despite our European roots, there are even big difference between European and North American customs.

- *American Dream* – While the American Dream emphasizes economic growth at any cost, the European Dream stresses sustainable and environmentally safe development.
- *Benefits* – Europeans prefer social benefits that guarantee everyone the same outcome. Americans prefer a system in which the benefits of all rise constantly even though some receive more, and some less.
- *Formality* – In North America, informality is more prominent compared to Europe, so people dress and act more casually here.
- *Greeting* – In Europe, there is an order and structure for greetings in which younger greets older, man greets woman, and children greet adults. In North America, rules like this have diminished to the point where they don't exist.
- *Happiness* – Americans achieve happiness by self-reliant accomplishment of goals on their own; in Europe, a full and meaningful life requires lots of communities and relationships.

- *History* – Europe is long on history and tradition while the U.S. is a relatively new country by comparison and overall doesn't have this focus.
- *Individuality* – The American Dream is personal; the European Dream is communal.
- *Religion* – The American Dream is somewhat tied to religion while the European Dream for some can be secular.
- *Security* – Risk-taking has long been beneficial to Americans. Europeans have experienced disruption and insecurity for millenniums and might instead favor stability, security, and predictability.
- *State* – Europeans value security-state benefits whereas we prefer liberty and independence with government at arm's length.
- *Work* – Americans embrace the work ethic while Europeans strive for more fun and leisure.

HOW OTHER NATIONS VIEW AMERICANS

Because of our differing customs, cultural anthropologists note that people from other nations sometimes describe Americans in these terms.

- *Americans are always in such a hurry to get things done.* – We tend to use achievements and accomplishments as a measure of a person's worth. The more Americans accomplish, the more we feel respected. We don't want to waste opportunities. Many cultures believe that slower is better and that building and maintaining relationships takes priority over getting things done at the expense of those relationships. We often say, "**make hay while the sun shines**," "**no time like the present**," and "**the early bird gets the worm**."
- *Americans insist on treating everyone the same.* – This attitude comes from our beginning as a free nation with a deep instinct toward social equality and a class-free system. Our proverb "**do unto others as you would have them do unto you**" reflects this belief in equality.
- *Americans always have to say what they're thinking.* – We value assertiveness and being open and direct about our thoughts and feelings. Honesty is important and we believe that being direct is the most efficient way to communicate and get things done. You will often hear us say, "**tell it like it is**," "**speak your mind**," and "**mean what you say**." Being direct is generally valued over "**beating around the bush**" in which people are not forthcoming. In some Asian countries—where negative replies are sometimes considered impolite—instead of saying "no" they might answer "maybe," "I'll think about it," or "we'll see," and then deal with the specifics later. The Japanese saying, "The nail that sticks out gets pounded down," suggests that it is more important to be alike than different. In contrast, we say, "**the squeaky wheel**

123

gets the grease." I'm reminded of the Ethiopian cab driver in Los Angeles who I asked, "What's the best thing about America?" He responded, "The honesty and forthrightness of the people."

- *Americans always want to change things.* – We believe things can always be better and that progress is inevitable. Because our nation is relatively young, our culture tends to be a positive one. Many Americans believe it is "good" to initiate change and "bad" to resist it. We say, "**Never put off until tomorrow what can be done today**."

- *Americans don't show much respect for their elders.* – Americans believe that by their actions people will earn any regard or respect they are given, regardless of their age. Merely attaining a certain age or holding a certain position does not in itself signify achievement nor place someone in a higher class here, as it does in many other cultures.

- *Americans always think things are going to get better; so optimistic.* – Because of our vast resources and past successes, we have always had a culture of optimism. Americans believe they are in control of their own destiny rather than being influenced by fate, government, or an emperor. Many Americans believe that The American Dream can be achieved by anyone who is willing to work hard enough and the only obstacle to making things better is not trying hard enough. This even extends to such things as sports and business. We say, "**Every cloud has a silver lining**," meaning even though things look bad, the bad is only hiding the good things to come.

- *Americans want to control the world.* – We are fiercely independent and, contrary to some cultures, we generally view ourselves first as individuals and then as members of a group or nation. Consequently our behavior reflects this underlying belief that came ashore with the first Europeans settlers who sought the elevation of the individual and the establishment of a **level playing field** (all play by the same rules). For this reason, we are attuned to how individuals are treated, and when we see anything that interferes with the rights of the individual, either here or in other nations, we speak up as we have done for centuries.

Hint: Unfortunately, foreigners and their media view this control thing as a desire for U.S. dominance instead of what it really is—simply a concern for fellow human beings. Trust me on this one: The last thing the average American wants is to dominate other nations; we have enough problems just **taking care of business** (attending to matters) at home. In a poll, Americans were asked how they felt when a McDonald's restaurant was about to open in another country. Over half had a negative feeling about exporting American culture there. And in response to the recent uprisings in Egypt, Bahrain, Jordan, Saudi Arabia, Syria, and Yemen, the overwhelming majority of Americans in a poll said the U.S. should not take a position. On the other hand, they expressed concern for the *people* in these countries and thought we should do something to help them individually.

INFLUENCING FACTORS

Why are our customs and beliefs so different from those in many parts of the world? A number of factors influenced how they developed, including the time when early immigrants came to America and found space—lots of it. Unlike the more crowded living conditions they were accustomed to in Europe, they had a great expanse of land to settle, which helped mold our customs. For example:

- *Self-Dependence* – Their farms and settlements were widely scattered, forcing the inhabitants to be *self-dependent*, a strong characteristic of Americans today.

- *Helping Neighbors* – These distances instilled in them a need to **help thy neighbor**. This custom continues today, whether it is helping our next-door neighbors or giving a **helping hand** (assistance) to other nations. Americans are *generous*, a trait they learned from helping each other.

- *Individualism* – Because of the problems living in these vast remote spaces, we learned *individualism*. In contrast, some countries such as those in Asia, people identify with groups that protect them in exchange for loyalty and compliance to the group. However, Americans *can* work for a common cause when necessary but still retain their individualism.

- *Density* – Given this vast space orientation, a large number of Americans today still live in private dwellings at a distance from their neighbors. **The American Dream** includes home ownership that gives us space. About 66 percent of Americans and Britons own their own homes versus 39 percent in Germany. American visitors to some nations are surprised by the general absence of houses, fences, and grass, and by the abundance of apartment buildings. We do have dense living in our large cities, but our suburbs are filled with individual houses that provide privacy and **elbow room** (room to move freely). As a comparison, Japan—with its

American Dream

126 million people—is geographically the size of our western state of Montana that has a population of less than one million. And England's density rate of 395 (Europe's highest) is 12 times our rate.

Hint: Search the Internet for "song: Don't fence me in" and listen to it. It captures the spirit of the American West's open spaces with lines like: Oh give me land, lots of land, under starry skies above, don't fence me in....

- *Our Imaginary Circle* – This concept of open space also affects the way we drive, work, stand, walk, talk, and relax. It is important for foreigners to understand that Americans have a personal, imaginary circle around them of about an arm's length. People accustomed to crowded conditions generally have a smaller circle. You must be careful not to intrude into this imaginary circle in different ways with your actions, noises, or smells. Please keep this in mind as we discuss some of our customs and you try to understand why we behave the way do.

    Hint: If you notice an American backing away from you a step or two, it might signal that you are too close to him or her, not that they don't like you. I was standing at the rear of a cafeteria line at an Asian university campus where I was teaching when a student stepped in line in front of me. I thought it was rude until I realized that he assumed I was not standing in line because of the one-meter space I left in front of me.

- *Speech Circle* – Our small imaginary circle can be invaded by speech as well, so you must be careful not to be too loud in public places like offices and restaurants. Out of cultural habit, some immigrant Americans speak loudly (and rapidly) to their friends in their native language, perhaps louder than they would speak to an American in English. I was in an Asian consulate in the U.S. and heard two Asian men over on the far side of a giant room loudly discussing a visa form. It was distracting and annoying. I was in an American restaurant and an immigrant party of 12 people occupied three tables in front of me. The tables were separated by walkways, yet one man used a loud voice to carry on a conversation the whole time with the others two tables away from his, a common practice in their country. This, too, is considered rude.

    Hint: I have to be honest. Certain Asian cultures speak with a rapid, high-pitched, piercing, nasal voice that is most unpleasant to the American ear. It is even worse when they speak loudly to their fellow countrymen in a group. Don't be surprised if you receive looks from an American to suggest you **cool it** (tone it down) because you are invading their circle. We do the same thing to those near us who are using cell phones in a loud manner.

- *Class Rankings* – Titles meant nothing on the American frontier; survival did. Americans for the most part are informal when it comes to titles and class ranking, something our ancestors left behind in Europe 400 years ago. Unlike some cultures, U.S. parents try to treat all children in the family equally. Some cultures give special status to wealthy people. We do it but to a lesser extent. Even our employer/employee relationships are more informal. On an American flight to Tokyo, a Japanese businessman was offered a free upgrade to business class but refused it because his boss was in business class. We do not have this degree of deference in our culture. But we do have trouble understanding or accepting formal caste systems where people are ranked according to power and wealth. It's not the American way, just like it wasn't on the frontier.

With this broad background of cultural differences, let's now examine three general customs that apply to everyday situations you might encounter with an American either here or in your country.

✓ How you meet and greet people.
✓ How you conduct yourself at a social gathering, called etiquette.
✓ How to carry on conversations in person or on the telephone.

GREETINGS CUSTOMS

You will be more comfortable when greeting Americans if you understand how we shake hands, use names and titles, and what we say upon greeting each other.

I remember a sign in the office of the college admissions officer when I took my son to be interviewed. It said, "You never get a second chance to make a good first impression." Unlike some cultures, Americans make a special effort to make a very good first impression when meeting someone.

> **Hint**: With the exception women from the Middle East or Muslim countries, I find that immigrant women tend to convey a warmer feeling than immigrant men when introduced to Americans. The men seem to be either more reserved or masculine acting, which might have something to do with the respect they are showing or the male behavior in their native countries. Unfortunately, most Americans do not know about these customs and might misinterpret their greeting as unfriendly.

Introducing Others – If you are talking to someone and another person walks up to greet you, it is important you introduce the other person to the newly arrived person, even if you don't remember their name. Let's assume you are talking to John when Mary walks up. You should first greet Mary, then introduce her to John by saying, "Mary, I would like to introduce you to my friend John." If you have just met John and can't remember his name, you might say to John, "This is my friend Mary," at which time he would probably say, "My name is John. Very nice to meet you." Or, you might ask John's name again, "I'm sorry, I forgot your name," and then introduce him to Mary.

Shaking Hands – Because your handshake speaks volumes about who you are as a person, I teach my classes on our culture how to shake hands and to project an interested, positive image—and that includes women. When a woman here shakes hands it shows she is up-to-date and assertive. The important thing to remember is that you want to appear interested in meeting the other person. Some foreigners do not do this; instead, they appear to shake hands just to get the formality out of the way. These hand-shaking tips will help you create a good impression.

- *Who Initiates?* – Unlike some countries where you might wait for your counterpart to initiate the handshake based on social position, anyone can initiate it in the U.S. And unlike Sweden where the man waits for the women to do it (as we used to do in the U.S.), a man can reach out for a woman's hand first.

- *Lean In* – We often lean forward to grasp a hand, a clear sign we are interested in meeting the other person. If you have a cigarette or toothpick in your mouth, discard it first.

- *Touching* – Other than shaking hands, we usually don't touch people on a first meeting, but you might on subsequent meetings after you know a person—man or woman. Some American men hug once they develop a close relationship, though it is rarer than in some cultures. And men rarely cheek-kiss as they do in Europe, the Mediterranean, the Middle East, and Latin America, but women do so more often.

- *Firm Squeeze* – When shaking, right hands are clasped at waist level and at arm's length while the base of the thumbs meet. If they don't meet, you end up shaking fingers and this is considered a weak shake. Give a firm squeeze while you raise and lower the hands slightly. Don't squeeze too tightly, and don't hold on too long. This process should not take more than two to three seconds. In some countries like China it is customary to use a weak handshake; in America it says you are not interested in meeting the other person and you lack self-confidence.

    Hint: I auditioned for a movie role with an Asian director who gave me a weak handshake when we first met. I immediately felt rejected and thought he wasn't interested in meeting me, until I remembered that his handshake was customary in his country. If you do this in a business situation with an American, it could kill an opportunity you are seeking.

- *Eye Contact* – As you shake hands, be sure to make eye contact and give a very clear and strong greeting (do not mumble) and smile. (The movie directed noted above also failed to do this, which only added to my angst.) Do not talk to someone else as you are shaking hands with a person. Your full attention goes to the hand shaker.

- *Seated* – A seated man should rise to shake hands with another person who is standing. Should a seated woman stand up? The answer used to be no, but today things have changed. In a non-business environment, she can make her own choice. But in today's business environment in which women want to be treated the same as men, she should rise.

Names And Titles In Greetings – Our names, titles, and how we use them may differ from your country.

- *Name Components* – Westerners usually have three names stated in this sequence: a given *first name* (John), a *middle name* (David) and a *family name* that we also call the *last name* or the *surname* (Jones). Sometimes you will fill out a form asking for your last name first, then your first name. So, if you see an American name that is listed first with a comma after it, that means the last name is first, as in "Jones, John D." Asians (and Hungarians as I learned the hard way in my travels there) who are accustomed to using their family name first should be sure to reverse it in America, otherwise someone will address you by your last name, thinking it is your first, and vice versa. That applies to your business cards that you have made, too.

- *Common Names* – The most common first names in the U.S. are James for men and Mary for women. Smith is our most common last name. Some of our first names are shortened for informal purposes, so your counterpart might be called by different names. James becomes Jim; Robert becomes Bob, Rob, or Robby; William becomes Bill; and Richard becomes Rick or Dick. Some of our family names might give a hint as to one's ancestry, such as Mc or O' prefixes for Irish names and Mac for Scottish names. Names that end in "son" might be Swedish such as Johnson, "sen" might be Danish as in Jensen, and Armenian endings can be "ian" or "yan."

- *Named After Parent* – You might see Roman numerals after a name when a son has the identical name as the father, such as John D. Jones II [pronounced "the second"] to identify the son, or John D. Jones III [the third] to identify the grandson of the original John D. Jones. Sometimes you will see "Jr." [pronounced "junior"] to indicate the son, and "Sr." [senior] to indicate the senior father. (Generally not used for daughter/mother.) When addressing these people in speech, they are seldom used, so they would be addressed as just Mr. Jones. Do use them, however, when sending a letter.

- *Nicknames* – We also use nicknames, so you might meet someone who goes by Shorty (short in stature), Lefty (left handed), Doc (a doctor), or Junior (the younger) on an informal basis, but their proper name is used in formal correspondence.

- *Choosing an American Name* – Many Asian Americans and other foreigners choose to adopt an American first name to make it is easier for Americans to remember and pronounce. If you should choose to do so, you can probably find a similar sounding American first name among the 5,200 we have. My Chinese friend Lee Bing did when she chose "Leigh" as her American name. ("Lee" in the U.S. is considered male.) Some Asian Americans also use hyphens to tie together two first names or two last names to clarify how they should be used, such as Song-Lee Dang. You may hear the term **Tom, Dick, and Harry**, which means everyone, as in "They allow every Tom, Dick, and Harry into the night club."

Addressing Someone By Title – These four name titles can precede a *last* name.

Miss (single woman)

Mrs. [pronounced *MISS-es*] (married woman)

Mr. [pronounced *MISS-ter*] (adult male)

Female   Male

Ms.* [pronounced *mizz*] (woman whose marital status is unknown, or sometimes for addressing a woman in business.)

- *Introduction* – If someone is introduced to you with a title, such as "Peter, this is *Mr. Jones*," which is formal, address him the same way, as in "Hello *Mr. Jones*, I am Peter Smith." When children are introduced to an adult, they too should use formal titles such as Mrs. or Mr. unless told to use first names.

- *Officials* – Address a college professor as Mr. or Professor, a doctor as Dr., and only a high-ranking government official, such as a mayor or governor, using their official title, such as Mayor Jones.

- *Adults* – An adult might address a much older person with the Mr. or Mrs. title, thus showing respect. But in contrast to some countries, we do not use formal titles with older family members.

- *Business* – In a business situation, you might address an older person higher in your organization as Mr., but not by their title such as Manager Jones or Director Jones as is done in some countries.

- *First Name* – In Korean and other societies, it is generally considered rude to address anyone by their first name, particularly with adults or one's elders. But Americans usually introduce themselves or others more informally by using first names ("Hi, I'm John Jones. Call me John."), in which case you can address them by their first name ("Hi, *John*, I'm Peter Smith. ") unless you know that more respect is required, as noted above for a senior. However, if you prefer to use someone's last name as is customary in your country, that is okay, too, but if they request you call them by their first name, it's probably best to comply.

- *Unknown* – When writing a letter to an unknown person, you might address it as "Dear Sir" or "Dear Ms," but a better solution is to learn the

---

*Ms. originated in the 1960s when women said they should have a title similar to Mr. that did not indicate their marital status.

name of the person you are writing, or use a gender-neutral salutation such as "Dear Customer" or "Dear Colleague" or "Dear Friends." Remember, half our workforce is female.

Greeting Someone New – As you are greeting someone, what do you say? This depends on whether you are being introduced to someone new, or, if you are meeting someone you already know. In either case, just like shaking hands, you must make the other person feel that you are genuinely pleased to meet him or her. It is not disrespectful to show warmth as seems to be the custom in some countries; it is expected and respected here.

These are some greetings to use when you are being introduced to *someone new*, or what Americans might say when being introduced to you.

- *How are you? or How do you do?* – These are probably our most common greetings. Even though they appear to be questions, they are not intended as such. A typical response might be "Fine, thank you, how are you?" Do not say, "I have stomach pains," or tell them about other problems. You could, on a more casual basis, give them an answer that would enhance your meeting, such as, "I'm just fine! I won $5 million dollars in the lottery this morning." In this case, it provides a warm welcome and gives you both something to talk about at that moment. We call conversation openers like this **ice breakers**. ("How are you?" in the U.S. might be equivalent to the Chinese asking, "Have you eaten?" or "Where have you been?")

- *Nice to meet you.* – If you use this response, it is a nice touch if you attach their name, either first or last depending on the formality required, such as "Nice to meet you, John." Repeating the person's name in your greeting also helps you remember it. Grammatically, this should start with *It is* as we discuss in Chapter Y on using better English grammar, but it is less formal and okay with greetings. Your English grammar will not be judged on a greeting, but your warmth and sincerity will.

- *It's a pleasure to meet you.* – Use this response when you *are* pleased to meet someone; otherwise, you will appear insincere. You will also occasionally hear a shorter version of this, "My pleasure."

- *Hi or Hello.* – These can be used any time, but are more appropriate in casual situations. Make sure you smile and make eye contact, and possibly use their name, too. If you don't, you will appear curt (rudely brief) and uninterested with this curt greeting.

Greeting Someone You Know – These are greetings you can use when you meet someone you know or you just want to acknowledge them, such as when walking on the street or in your office building. How well you know them will determine what you say and whether you stop to talk. After making your greeting, as a courtesy wait for a response before immediately talking about something else or moving on. Because of our friendliness, don't be surprised if someone you don't know greets you with one of these.

- *Hi or Hello* – Use this when you don't plan to stop and talk to them. It is just a greeting to acknowledge them in passing. Again, make sure you make eye contact and give a little smile or a nod.
- *How are you?* – This can be used both when stopping or not stopping to chat. You don't need to pause for an answer because it is not really a question.
- *How is ...?* – You fill in the blank. If you know something about their job, family or other personal matters, it is okay to ask them about it, such as "How's the family?" or "How's the job?" or "How was your vacation?" or "How's that new car?" You do not have to first say, "How are you?" and then ask this type of question because your question *is* a greeting. Unlike some countries, it is not considered impolite to ask personal questions as long as you are asking about things you know they will be happy to talk about. This might then entail a short pause for an answer.
- *Good to see you.* – This is a warm, short greeting when said with sincerity.
- *How's it going?* – This is a very informal greeting usually used among young men. It is similar to "How are you?" in that it is a question, but an answer is not expected. Because of its slangy tone, it is probably one you should avoid. Also, do not use "Hey, Dude" except with close friends because it is considered lower class. (A **dude** is someone who surfs or skateboards, but has come to mean a young man of a similar status as you.)
- *Hey there.* – This is used more and more by close friends and in the movies.
- *Long time no see.* – Although grammatically incorrect (as you will also learn in Chapter Y), this is used informally to recognize a person you haven't seen in a long time, or, as a joke when you just saw them a short time ago. Also in this ungrammatical category, three of my personal favorites are "Morning" instead of good morning, "Evening" instead of good evening, and "Howdy" instead of how do you do. I give a nod or smile along with them.

A cute, rhyming saying some of us use when departing from close friends is "**See you later alligator**," to which they respond "After while crocodile."

SOCIAL GATHERING ETIQUETTE

20th century English novelist W. Somerset Maugham had a guideline for proper social behavior: "At a dinner party one should eat wisely but not too well, and talk well but not too wisely." In other words, use good manners and etiquette. Etiquette is defined as the rules of behavior, while good manners are all in how you treat people.

Now that you know about our greetings, let's assume you have been invited to a social gathering (perhaps at someone's home) hosted by an American, either here or in your country. The relationship between the host and guests might be less formal than what you would expect in your country. To begin with, here are some general pointers.

- *Shoes* – In many countries, including Asia, Scandinavia, and the Middle East, visitors might take off their shoes before entering the host's home. We do not do this. However, if you want a visitor to your home to do this, it is okay to ask them to do so. Americans will respect your culture and find it interesting.
- *Coat* – Your host should take your coat and hang it up or place it on a bed, just as you will do when you are a host.
- *Admiration* – As part of the custom in some countries like Russia and in Asia, if you overly admire something in your host's house, he may feel obligated to give it to you as a gift. We don't have this custom, so just casually admire it.
- *Smoking* – Never light tobacco in someone's house. Ask your host where you might smoke and you will most likely be directed outside.
- *Car* – Park your car in a space on the street, not in your host's driveway.
- *Telephone* – Do not use your host's telephone without first asking. Go to another room or outside to use your cell phone.

Here are social customs you should know about: receiving an invitation, arriving on time, and giving a gift to your host.

Invitation – If you receive a written invitation to a party, you might see the letters **RSVP**, a French term meaning "please respond." That means you must let your host know if you will or will not be coming. It is considered rude not to respond at all. Not responding to the invitation and still attending is rude. Saying you will attend and then not showing up is rude. Sometimes an invitation says "**Regrets Only**," which means you should notify the host only if you cannot attend.

A party invitation.

Unlike some cultures, it is not rude to be honest and tell a host that you will be unable to attend. Try to be polite in your refusals and give some kind of a *brief* explanation. I know foreigners who decline an invitation by saying bluntly "I can't go." This gives the impression they don't want to go. If you simply do not want to go, say "I'm sorry; I will be unable to make it." If you have a schedule conflict, you might tell them very briefly what it is or just say, "I'm sorry, I have a conflict that day."

On occasion someone might invite you verbally with "Let's get together this weekend," or "Drop over to the house next week." If you plan to take them up on their invitation, be sure to establish a time beforehand, or at least call them before going to their house because they might have forgotten about their informal invitation.

Time – If you receive an invitation, try not to arrive more than ten minutes early. Arriving more than ten minutes late might also be considered rude. In the Philippines, sometimes the more important the guest the later he or she arrives. In America, we generally do not do this, although we have some who like to make grand entrances. If you are invited to an **open house**, you will be given the time frame, such as 7 p.m. to 10 p.m. You can come and leave anytime between these hours. Although some hosts do not request a response from their open house invitations, they might be please you let them know. Do not arrive or leave beyond the stated hours.

Gift For Host – In some cultures, you always take a gift when visiting someone. In Russia, for example, a host might prepare for company by cooking their best dishes and buying delicacies that they normally wouldn't for themselves. If after all this effort guests show up without even a flower, Russians can be offended.

Our gift-giving protocol is not this rigid. We, too, prepare party foods in advance, but whether or not we give our host a gift depends on the nature of the social event. If, for example, a friend invites you and a few other people for dinner at their house, you might take a bottle of wine, a gift basket of fruit, a box of candy, a small potted plant, or a small bouquet of flowers.

"Thank you for inviting me."

If instead they take you out to dinner to a restaurant, a gift is not necessary and a "thank you" will suffice. If the event is for a large office staff at the home of a superior, a small gift is a nice gesture. If your friend holds a party for you in your honor (you had a baby, you were promoted, etc.), take a gift. In every case, a follow-up note or a phone call to thank your host is considerate and a sure way to make the best impression.

If you are unsure about giving a gift, feel free to give one. Gifts should be modest. An expensive gift might make your host feel uncomfortable and perhaps obligated to give you an expensive gift in the future. Avoid personal items such as perfume or toiletries. To most, the thought of your giving a gift is more important than the gift itself. Some Asians like to hand a gift to the host with both hands. In America we don't have this two-handed custom, so don't be offended if someone gives you a gift with one hand and a hug with the other.

The host often doesn't open a gift until after the guests have left because it might create a situation where gifts are compared with each other. That might embarrass those who brought inexpensive gifts or none at all. If, however, you think it would be appropriate to open it because it is candy or food that everyone could enjoy, then suggest

134

the host open it. If you bring wine or flowers and you see the host is busy, ask if you can put the flowers in a vase or open the wine bottle for them.

As part of their culture, some people in China might politely refuse three times before accepting a gift from someone. We don't have this custom. So, if an American gives you a gift, accept it immediately; otherwise, they will think you *really* don't want it or are being ungracious. Also, in some countries like Japan, the rules for wrapping gifts seem complicated, at least to an American. White and blue in China are reserved for times of mourning while red has special meanings of good luck. Black in some countries connotes death.

In America, however, we are less formal with giftwrap colors, although we do use colors for specific holidays (see Chapter R - Holidays and Traditions) such as green and red for Christmas, pastels for Easter, red for Valentine's, and black, though worn at funerals, can be elegant anytime. Stores where you purchase your gift can help you with gift wrap colors. Tell them what occasion it is for, if it is for a man or a woman, a couple, or a child; this will influence the color and style of wrap. Some charge for wrapping, some don't.

> **Hint**: It is also fine to bring unwrapped gifts with only a small gift card attached, especially for items like flowers, candy, and wine.

Dining Differences – Our general rules of table etiquette are discussed in Chapter O on food and dining. There are broad cultural differences you need to know in order to feel more comfortable eating in an American's home or at their hosted dinner in a restaurant. The secret, however, is to be relaxed and not worry about committing a social error when dining.

After finishing dinner it is customary for everyone to move to another room to socialize, or to sit awhile at the dinner table. Feel free to offer to help clear the table of dishes or assist in the kitchen. It is best not to plan to leave immediately after eating, but if you must (baby sitter, work, etc.), briefly explain this and apologize as you get ready to leave. A thoughtful host will escort you to the door.

CONVERSATION CUSTOMS

Don't worry about violating an unknown social custom at a social gathering such as a dinner or cocktail party when you talk with your American host and other guests. You are not judged by how well you perform culturally as you might in your country. Breaking a custom in America is not viewed as seriously as it is in some cultures. In Japan where dining and entertaining in the home is viewed more formally, some Americans are accustomed to saying to a host upon leaving their house, "Shitsurei shimasu," which means please excuse me for any social blunders I may have made. If you are worried about making a **boo-boo** (slang for dumb mistake) in the U.S., this will restrict what you do and say. Practical Americans would rather you have a good time.

Stereotypes *[STAIR-ee-oh-types]* are widely accepted views we have of others but not necessarily based on fact. For example, a common stereotype we use to describe some Asians (particularly the Japanese) is **inscrutable**, meaning mysterious and impenetrable. Americans like to see reactions from others while talking to them. So, if you are overly formal rather than open, it might send a signal that you are not interested in us, don't like us, or find us boring. So be careful not to reinforce negative stereotypical messages that might be part of your culture. We should do the same.

Small Talk – "Small talk" is a discussion that deals with a simple subject like weather or sports as compared to large topics like the elimination of world poverty. Americans love small talk at social gatherings and may avoid talking about controversial, deeper issues that might not appeal to the group. They may also avoid strictly personal topics unless you are a good friend. Americans, unlike some foreigners, are uncomfortable with **lulls** (long pauses) in conversations. For this reason, they will bring up small talk topics to keep the conversation going.

Topics – Your host may indicate the direction of conversation in his house. Some people love to discuss politics, and others don't, so he may steer the conversation in or out of politics. It is not considered impolite, as it is in some countries, to ask others what they do at work, which makes a good topic. Conversely, in other cultures where it might be done, do not ask about another person's salary, marital/dating status, or age. Americans love to talk about geographical locations in the U.S., probably because they have lived or vacationed in several states. We like to share stories about our family, too. But in some cultures like Russia where making jokes about one's parents is considered in bad taste, we sometimes do it with affection.

> **Hint**: To be on the safe side, avoid telling jokes about minorities, ethnicities, races, and religions. It's also best to avoid telling **off-color jokes** (jokes with sexual overtones) unless you are with close friends.

Questions – Americans are curious and like to ask questions, plus we believe it is polite to show interest in others by asking questions of them. Because of your foreign background, do not be surprised if you become the center of attention in your host's house. You will find some Americans fascinated with your customs, life style, and certain aspects of your life back home (I know I would). If you feel a question is of a very personal nature, just tell them that. It might be considered rude in your country to ask so

136

many questions about a person, but here it is not. Conversely, it is okay for you to ask the same questions about them.

> **Hint**: I had a friend in New York City whose parents were immigrants and she was trained as a child to not ask any questions of others. Consequently, as an adult her conversational skills were limited. She is the exception, but you still might encounter someone like her who appears not to show interest in you because of this behavior. This is important for Koreans raised in this culture.

Truth – We like to think and talk in linear terms where we move from one topic to the next when we are sure we understand the previous one. So we deal with truth, facts, and evidence and might probe you to seek more information. This is not a personal thing against you, and it is not considered rude to question you as it might be in your country. One of our Midwestern states, Missouri, has the nickname of the "Show Me" state, which means give me the truth, make it clear to me, show the results, or show me how.

Relaxing – Socially, it is okay to relax and stretch out when away from the dinner table. Americans may talk to you in the living room or on the patio while sitting in a more relaxed position than what you are accustomed to. They are not showing disrespect. If, however, your host puts his feet on his own coffee table while relaxing, you should not do it.

Complaints – Complaints can be overdone in social situations and create the wrong impression. Be honest in your conversations, but don't be overly negative about things in your life as some foreigners (and Americans) do. If, however, you think your host or another guest can give you advice on a non-serious matter, ask for their opinion. Americans love to express their opinions and offer help to others, something you might also find differs from your country. Reserve your serious problems, however, for your close friends.

Children – Your host's children might attend a party in their house. This may be contrary to what you do in your country. You may also find that some American children are more assertive and talkative. This is not a sign of disrespect. Parents in the U.S. like to expose their children to different social situations as a learning experience. However, do not take your children with you unless they have been invited or you have permission. If they do go with you, do not be surprised if someone rubs your child on his or her head or pinches their cheeks. To us, this is a show of affection and we will be unaware this might be a violation in your country.

TELEPHONE ETIQUETTE

We have general rules of etiquette for speaking over the phone that are just as important as talking to people face to face. Also, because we sometimes have trouble understanding foreigners on the phone, useful tips are provided to improve your communication skills. The pages at the front of most telephone directory books give useful information such as help lines, maps of local areas, and government agency telephone numbers.

> **Hint**: Keep in mind we don't call someone at home before 9 a.m. or after 9 p.m. unless we were asked to do so or it is an emergency.

Telephone Numbers – Like many countries, the basic telephone number in America has seven digits, such as 123-4567. The left-three digits usually signify an area within a city. In addition we have other numbers.

- *Area Codes* – In addition to the seven digits, we use three more numbers to specify a larger area called the **area code**, such as (639) 123-4567. If you call a number in the U.S. that is in a different area code from where you are calling, you must first dial a "1" and then the area code, and then the seven-digit number. If you are calling within the same area code—termed a **local call**—with a few exceptions you merely dial the seven-digit number. Some small states may have only one or two area codes while our large cities have multiple area codes like New York City with six. You can refer to this website to lookup an area code: www.whitepages.com/area-codes.

- *Customer Service* – Some companies use customer service area code numbers like (800), (866), (877), or (888) that are toll free (in Europe they might charge for their equivalents). But you must be very careful dialing other profit-making codes for which you will be charged upwards of five and ten dollars a minute, such as those that begin with 7 and 9. Some (809) calls can also be scams with excessive charges.

- *International Calls* – To call an international telephone number, dial 011, the country code, the city code, and the telephone number. Omit any leading zeros from the country code. Find a list of country and city codes in the front of our telephone directories or on Internet sites like www.countrycallingcodes.com.

- *Directory Assistance* – If you need someone's telephone number but do not have a telephone book to look it up, you can use the Internet or call for directory assistance. For local directory assistance (within your area code), dial 555-1212 or simply 411. To reach **long distance** (outside your area code) directory assistance, dial 1, the area code, and 555-1212. To find the toll free number for a company with a toll-free 800 number, call 1-800-555-1212.

- *Emergencies* – We have an emergency call system called **911** that receives 240 million calls a year. This corresponds to the 112 number in Sweden, 997 in Poland, and 112 in Germany. Dial 911 to report an emergency and request help from medical personnel, the police, or fire departments.

Phone Greetings – When the phone rings, we pick it up and merely say "Hello," as is done in other countries. Only uninformed people would say "Yes?" On a holiday such as Christmas, I might say "Merry Christmas." When saying hello, it is important to use a rising tone of voice and elongate the "oh" sound in "Hello" (something we discuss in Chapter Z - Let's Speak Better English). Say it as a question, because it will sound friendly and invite a response. A decreasing tone sounds dull and uninviting. Say these two sounds out loud and notice the difference:

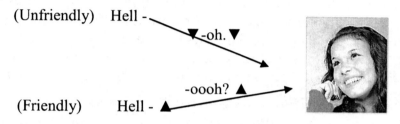

(Unfriendly)   Hell - -oh. ▼

(Friendly)   Hell - -oooh? ▲

Here are different ways to handle calls politely.
- A business might answer, "ABC Widgets, this is Shirley, how may I help you?"
- If the caller asks for you and you know them, say, "Hi John, how are you?"
- If the caller asks for you and you don't know them, say, "This is he or she." (Notice the good grammar of *he/she* that we discuss in Chapter Y?)
- If the caller asks for someone who is not there, say, "He is not here. *May* I take a message?" (Notice the *may*, not *can*, which we also discuss in Chapter Y?)
- If the caller asks, "Can [it should be *may*!] I talk to Susan?" you might respond, "Yes you *may*," or "Certainly, I'll get her."
- If the caller asks, "Is Susan there?" you might respond, "Yes she is. One moment *please*," or "Who is calling *please*?" It is rude to just say "yes" and then go search for the other person. To American ears, this abrupt handling of a call is considered rude.
- When you call someone and another person answers the phone, it is polite to first identify yourself. Say "This is Peter Bennett. Is John there?" If you know the person who answered, use their name, such as "Hi Mary, this is Peter, is John there?"

- When you answer the phone and the call is for another person who is there, after the proper greeting place the phone down *quietly* and go search for the person. Do not yell for them and do not drop the phone down on a hard surface, which the caller will hear. There's that imaginary circle thing again.
- If you call a friend at work you might first ask if they "have a minute to talk." Likewise, if a friend calls you at work and you are busy, it is okay to tell them you will call back when you have the time.

Sales Calls – Businesses make telephone calls to homes to sell something, primarily in the evening. Most of us consider this **telemarketing** a nuisance. You might receive three or more calls in one evening. Up to now you have been instructed to be polite on the phone. You may be more abrupt with telemarketers. Do not feel obligated to listen to their whole sales pitch—that might take five minutes. If you don't know fairly quickly what they are selling, interrupt and ask for clarification. If you are not interested, say, "I'm not interested" and hang up. They will make every attempt to keep you listening by making you think you are being rude to them. Never give out your credit card number, your address, or other personal information on these sales calls, either.

Hint: In 2008, the federal government developed the National Do Not Call Registry where you can list your number to indicate you do not want to receive telemarketing calls. Many telemarketers ignore the list, but you can register a complaint at this website: www.donotcall.gov/.

Cell Phone Manners – Because it is a relatively new invention and manners have not yet been well defined, we all need to be more polite using our cell phones. When you are using one around others, keep your voice down. Remember the arm's length personal circle Americans have that we spoke about earlier. Don't intrude with your voice beyond the imaginary circle.

Hint: While standing in a line, I often hear someone behind or near me speaking loudly on their cell phone. I don't like it and I will turn and give them a look that says so. Sometimes this happens in restaurants, too. If someone gives you a disapproving look while you are using your cell phone, it is an indication you are not obeying the imaginary circle rule. If it is essential for you to talk in a public place, take your phone into a quiet corner or step outside.

I have an immigrant American friend who, in the middle of our conversation, will spend 5 to 10 minutes socializing with a friend who has called her on her cell phone. Most Americans consider this rude. If your cell phone rings and you must answer, say "Excuse me" to the person you are with, answer your phone, then tell your caller you will call them back. If you do need to talk to your caller, excuse yourself, move to another area, and keep the call as short as possible. It is best to leave your cell phone turned off when you are in business meetings, theatres, and other public places around others.

140

Speak Up/Slow Down – Foreigners who are worried about their English vocabulary, diction, and grammar have a habit of speaking to an American in soft tones, even on the phone. If you have an accent, this low tone makes it all the more difficult to understand you. Don't be afraid to speak up. It amuses me that I will be with a foreigner who is speaking loudly, almost shouting, on the phone to a friend in their native tongue. But when they speak to an American a few minutes later on the phone, they speak considerably softer. If you make a business call, this low volume might suggest you are not sure of yourself and could create a wrong image of you or your business. Also, slowing down will improve your communication as we discuss in Chapter Z on speaking better English.

> **Hint**: If the American you are speaking to on the phone keeps asking you to repeat yourself, that is your cue to speak louder, slow down, enunciate, or all three of these that we discuss in Chapter Z.

DRINKING AND SMOKING CUSTOMS

You might quickly learn that many Americans are health conscious, particularly about drinking and smoking. Foreigners must be careful not to impose their smoking and drinking customs on Americans at social gatherings. Americans should do the same.

Smoking – Smoking has become less socially acceptable in the U.S. due in large part to health risks. So foreigners must be careful where they **light up** in the U.S. Unlike some countries, it is prohibited in most enclosed areas such as on airlines, buses, and trains, and in government and public buildings, sports stadiums, theatres, airports, and even in restaurants. The sign to the right means that smoking is not permitted in that area. Some of these facilities provide areas where it is allowed.

Do not light a cigarette in someone's home, office, or car unless they begin to smoke first. It is impolite to blow smoke in someone's direction or allow your smoke to drift near them. Do not allow a cigarette to hang from your lip or wave it in your hand while talking.

> **Hint**: If you are smoking and someone near you coughs lightly, it may be a signal that they don't like your cigarette smoke. They may even do this without looking at you. Take the hint and move away or put your cigarette out. A simple apology, such as "I'm sorry" is nice, or a quick glance at them with a nod or smile before you move or put it out.

Drinking – In some countries like China, Korea, and Japan, drinking can be a vital part of making and nurturing personal, business, and political relationships. In China it is sometimes proper to decline a drink (and a meal, gift, or favor) while it is up to the host to politely persist until the guest accepts. Don't expect that here. Some Koreans tend

141

to be aggressive in their drinking and expectations of others to **follow suit** (do the same thing). Don't expect that here, either.

Americans view drinking differently. Some may or may not serve it in their homes or at parties. We decline a drink because we don't want it. Some view it as religiously wrong. Others view it as unhealthy. Others simply do not like its taste.

Some belong to Alcoholics Anonymous (AA), an organization where problem drinkers can go for help (www.alcoholics-anonymous.org). They find it difficult in social situations when someone tries to pressure them to drink. Do not try to impose your drinking-related customs onto them.

There is nothing wrong with you ordering an alcoholic beverage while an American orders a soft drink, or vice versa. Most Americans do not judge you by whether or not you drink, or by the number of glasses you consume. Remember, in America we **do our own thing**. (There's that *independence* thing again.)

We have very serious penalties for people who drive automobiles while intoxicated. On some holidays, such as New Year's Eve, some police departments set up roadblocks to test the sobriety of drivers on busy streets. If the police ever stop you for any reason, they may test your sobriety if they suspect you are under the influence of drink or drugs. If you are impaired, you will go to jail. **DUI** (driving under the influence) is a serious crime and you could lose your driver's license. Instead, have a sober friend drive you home or call a taxi.

The organization called MADD—Mothers Against Drunk Driving—attempts to reduce drunk driving and to increase the penalties for DUI (www.madd.org). As one more example of how an individual in the U.S. can effect change, a Texas mother founded the organization in 1980 when her 13-year old daughter was killed by a drunk driver. With this program, alcohol-related traffic fatalities have decreased nearly 50 percent and over 383,000 lives have been saved. With mothers around the world protective of their children, MADD is now located in five other countries.

AUTOMOBILE CUSTOMS

While we're on the subject of driving, you need to know about our customs and laws. Because autos play a major role in our everyday lives, the average household owns two vehicles. Europeans on the other hand own 30 percent fewer cars per person and drive about 35 percent fewer miles per car. As I can attest to, they simply have better alternate transportation systems than we do and are not in love with their cars as we are.

Possible Cultural Differences – Here are auto customs and laws you need to know if you drive in the U.S., some of which might differ from your country.

142

- *Accidents* – It is a *very serious* violation of the law if you are in an accident with damage generally over $750 or someone is hurt and you leave before the police arrive or before you give your name to the other party involved. If you bump into an empty car, leave your name and telephone number on the windshield so they can contact you. Get the car's license number in case your insurance company gets involved. (The southern state of Mississippi has the most number of auto accident deaths per 100,000 population.)

- *Alcohol and Guns* – In some states it is against the law to carry an open alcoholic beverage or gun in an automobile.

- *Cell Phone Use* – Talking on a cell phone or texting while driving makes a person four times more likely to be in a crash. In many countries, from Austria to Zimbabwe, driving while using a cell phone is illegal. The U.S. has been slow to impose these restrictions; as a result the law varies among jurisdictions and states.

- *Driver's License* – If you have a foreign driver's license that is written in a language other than English, it is best to have an international driver's license in case you are stopped by the police. If you are a U.S. resident you must apply for a driver's license if you want to drive. This government website defines a resident: www.irs.gov/publications/p519/ch01.html. Driving without a license is punishable by law. Each state has a Department of Motor Vehicles that gives you a written and an actual driving test to determine if you are a safe driver. If you are, you are issued a driver's license that has your picture. It also serves as a personal identification when you cash a check or when your age needs verification before entering a nightclub or casino or when buying cigarettes or liquor.

Los Angeles freeway.

- *Flashing Headlights* – During the day if an approaching automobile flashes its headlights on and off several times, it is a courtesy signal that you are approaching an area that has a **cop** (police) car looking for speeders. (There's that *help thy neighbor* thing again.) If this happens at night, it could mean you failed to turn on your headlights, or your headlights are on high-beam and should be turned down. If a car behind you flashes, you are probably going too slowly and they want to pass you, so move to the right.

- *Insurance* – The law states that you must have insurance on an automobile you own. If you plan to rent a car in the U.S., check to see if your own auto insurance will cover an accident here before you leave home. It probably won't, but you can purchase it at the time you rent your car here.

143

- *Parking Laws* – Unlike some countries, we enforce driving and parking laws. I was amazed at the lack of enforcement in Istanbul and Odessa where cars were parked in front of "no parking" signs, and double-parked along busy streets and even in the middle of busy intersections. If you try that here your car will be towed away and you will pay a hefty fine to get it back.

- *Pedestrians* – In some countries like China, cars rule on crowded streets because of their size, followed by bicycles, and last by pedestrians. I call it the rule of the Jungle. The opposite is true in the U.S. Pedestrians come first and drivers *must* stop for them, not vice versa. Hitting a pedestrian with an automobile is a serious crime. And failing to yield to a pedestrian crossing the street in or out of a painted walkway might get you a **ticket** (citation) as well.

- *Sig Alert* – If you listen to the radio while driving, you might hear the term "Sig Alert," which is a **heads up** (alert) signal of an accident or unplanned event that is causing the closure of one or more lanes of traffic that you might want to avoid.

- *Smog Inspection* – Because of environmental concerns, some states, with California at the forefront, require an annual smog inspection of your car to insure it does not pollute the air. License plates expire yearly. You will not get new ones if you do not have the car inspected and it passes. Driving with expired plates (or car insurance if you are stopped) can result in a fine.

Bumper Stickers – As you are learning, we like to express our personal interests as well as poke fun at ourselves. We have lots of different outlets for doing this. Some states allow car owners to customize their license plates with a unique saying, such as "ILOVEU." We also use printed T-shirts or bumper stickers to proclaim, pronounce, profess, protest, or just to have fun.

Humorous bumper sticker.

Bumper stickers are small signs (about 10 cm x 20 cm) placed on a car's bumper to convey a message. Frequently they are seen during presidential elections to promote the driver's favorite candidate, or to indicate the driver visited a national park, attends a certain university, or has a favorite sports team.

Examples of other bumper stickers you might spot, starting with my favorite: "Be nice to America or we'll bring democracy to your country." – "World peace begins with me." – "Make love, not war." – "I hate bumper stickers." – "My child was elected student of the month at [school name]." – "Never forget 9/11." – "The #1 cause of divorce is marriage." – "Save gasoline. Drive a camel." – "Why do I have to take an English class? I'm never going to England." – "A clean desk is a sign of a cluttered drawer." – "I love cats." – "I ♥ New York City."

ENVIRONMENTAL CUSTOMS

Although America's interest in the environment may not be apparent when our government represents us at some worldwide environmental conferences like the Kyoto Accord, the majority of Americans are concerned about it. One-fifth say they are active participants in the environmental movement, while two-fifths are sympathetic but not active. Six out of ten say the movement has done more good than harm, while a third believes the opposite. Again, more diversity of opinion as you would expect in the U.S., but we still lean toward caring.

In 1963, American author Rachael Carson wrote an important book titled *Silent Spring* that brought attention to how we were mistreating our environment, which, in turn, was affecting human health, air, oceans, lakes, soil, streams, and wildlife in America. Over the intervening years, Americans have become very conscious about the world we live in, from the use of pesticides, to artificial ingredients in our food, to the hazards of smoking, to recycling, to environmental pollution.

You might hear the names of our volunteer groups that help protect and improve our environment such as the **Sierra Club** (www.sierraclub.org). Their efforts have spurred the government to address environmental concerns for such things as clean water, global population, human rights, national forests, responsible trade, urban sprawl, global warming, and wild lands. Another organization is international **Greenpeace** (www.greenpeace.org) that exposes environmental criminals and challenges government and corporations when they fail to safeguard the environment. Again, more examples of how the people bring about change in the U.S.

As an example of our environmental concerns, you will sometimes see signs along freeways with the names of volunteer organizations that pick up litter in that area. Or see people walking around their neighborhoods each morning picking up litter even though the city probably does it weekly or monthly. Many are opposed to billboards in our cities. Giant banner advertising signs like those draping the fronts of buildings in China are not used in the U.S. because we find them intrusive. Smoking is no longer allowed along a 38-mile stretch of beach near Los Angeles because of the abundance of cigarette butts that were contaminating the beaches.

Non-smoking California beach.

So, don't be surprised if you talk to an American who seems overly concerned with these matters, or if you encounter environmental issues that are handled differently than your country. Foreign businessmen must be aware of our environmental customs, too, when selling products to America.

Graffiti And Litter – Like Ecuador and numerous other countries where I've seen it, America has problems with **litter** (garbage) in the streets and **graffiti** *[grah-FIT-ey]* (spray painting on walls). When I visit countries like Costa Rica and the Emirates, I am amazed at the absence of both and wonder why. When you are in the U.S., here's is a good rule to follow: Don't litter or **tag** (spray paint) anywhere. You might be fined for doing it, sometimes $500 and up.

Graffiti spraying in Hawaii.

Recycling – Some of our cities have recycling programs where garbage is separated into different categories—glass, metal, and paper items—so they can be reused. This decreases the land required to dispose of garbage, and also saves our valuable natural resources. You may be at a public function that has garbage cans for this purpose with the symbol shown to the right printed on the container. Embrace this program by discarding your castoffs— Americans will make note of it.

PLEASE RECYCLE

Recycle symbol.

You may also see products with "Made from recycled material" proudly displayed on our wrappers. An "Organic" label indicates the food is free from exposure to synthetic pesticides, food additives, and fertilizers. "Green" is often also printed on labels to indicate efforts were made to reduce the impact of modern human life on the natural world. Foreign businesses should take note of these labels if their products are to be sold in the U.S.

PET CUSTOMS

It is said in China and Hong Kong that cats bring good luck. The Japanese keep birds and crickets as pets. In Arab countries, dogs are considered unclean. Italians have little use for dogs but find cats charming and companionable. The Inuit Eskimos of Northern Canada adopt bear cubs, foxes, birds, and baby seals. Animals are rarely kept as pets in Africa. Half of the households in England have a pet, usually a cat or bird. And so it goes around the world.

In America, we love our pets and treat them like family members, particularly cats and dogs. You will see framed pictures of pets in our homes next to pictures of children and spouses. You might be surprised at our closeness between pets and owners. In case you are wondering, for two decades now the beloved Labrador retriever has been our favorite **pooch** (dog).

One happy family.

It may be best not to discuss how animals that we consider pets are treated differently in your country. As an example, seventy-five percent of Koreans favor eating

146

dog meat and 500 restaurants in Seoul serve it. This might be disturbing to some Americans.

If you are invited to an American's home and are comfortable with animals, make a big fuss over their pets (and their children). It is also acceptable to tell your host you are uncomfortable with them so they can be moved to another area. If you are in an office and you see a picture of a pet, you can be sure it will be a welcome topic of conversation.

States have laws to protect animals. Organizations also help, such as the American Society of Prevention of Cruelty to Animals (ASPCA). Don't be surprised if someone gives you a frown if you are wearing a fur coat because many feel animals should not be killed for fashion. The public in the U.S. is also demanding better treatment of laboratory animals, so you might see "no animal testing" or "cruelty free" printed on a product's wrapper, or "free range" printed on meat and poultry packages to denote the animal was not confined to a cage and it had access to natural feed. Foreign businesses should take note of this as well.

WALKING CUSTOMS

When you are in the U.S., "Keep to the right" is a good motto to remember. Unlike some countries, we drive on the right side of the road. We form lines and walk on the right side of the sidewalk. We walk up and down stairs and go in and out of doors on the right side. If a man walks with a woman it is customary for the man to walk on the woman's right side or nearest to the road.

> **Hint**: We frequently encounter foreigners walking on the wrong side. It is difficult for visitors and immigrants to change, but they should try. If you find yourself in this situation and you come face to face with another person, say **"I'm sorry"** or **"excuse me"** and move to your right. I do the same when I'm on the wrong side in their countries.

Good manners are associated with walking and moving about. Some foreigners are surprised at how often people in the U.S. say "excuse me," even when we barely touch someone, interfere with them, or are about to cut in front of someone who has the right of way. For Americans, saying "excuse me" exhibits culture and class. On occasion we encounter foreigners who have not learned to use these words and we feel offended when bumped, interrupted, or interfered with and they just continue on their way with no apology. There's that imaginary circle thing again.

Here are more behaviors by foreigners (and Americans) that happen and are considered rude.

- Foreign heritage teenage girls walking arm-in-arm along sidewalks in America, not allowing anyone to pass by. Or groups of people standing and talking and blocking the walkway.

- When exiting from a crowded room I politely let people to the side of me exit first. Sometimes foreigners will push from behind and cut in front of me or the people I am letting out the door.
- Cutting across the line directly in front of me, even stepping on my toes, and not saying "excuse me." If you ever have to cut across a line, say with a gesture, "Excuse me; may I get through?" or just "May I?"
- Stepping rudely into an elevator before the people inside have fully exited.

I understand these actions result from cultural difference for those foreigners who come from crowded cities, but most Americans will not. Unfortunately, actions like these reflect poorly on those foreigners as a whole in the minds of Americans who witness it.

SUPERSTITIONS

A superstition is a belief or practice generally regarded as irrational and implies a belief in unseen and unknown forces that can be influenced by objects and rituals. All people are susceptible to superstitions, and it is fun to compare them. Centuries ago the number 9 was special in China because it was the highest single number. I visited a park in Beijing where the emperor had groups of nine steps and nine circles used in the construction of his temples. Because the number 8 symbolizes wealth in China, the beautiful Jin Mao building in Shanghai is 88 stories high with an observation deck view I found thrilling. And certain numbers and colors have special meanings in most if not all cultures.

Some U.S. businesses are learning the hard way about foreign superstitions and customs. The entryway of the then-newly opened giant MGM Hotel & Casino in Las Vegas featured a gold lion with an open mouth through which patrons entered the casino. After several years they realized Asians considered this bad luck because it suggested that the lion was devouring the visitors; hence, an expensive new entrance was installed.

Bad luck casino entrance.

> **Hint**: Two of our large drugstore chains merged a few years ago and the new OSCO name was found to be offensive to some cultures. It, too, was later changed and the signs on their stores had to be remade. More and more of our businesses are now carefully reviewing their product names to insure minorities will not be offended by what at first appears to be an innocent name in the U.S. We are slowly learning about the customs of other cultures. If you find a cultural boo-boo in the U.S., you know it is done out if ignorance.

You probably don't need to be concerned with superstitions in America because few take them very seriously, but some might change a behavior to accommodate them.

We do have fun with them though. You might impress an American if you encounter a situation where you can jokingly refer to one of these.

- *7/11* – Gamblers find numbers 7 and 11 lucky because they can be winners in the dice game of craps.

- *Birthday Candles* – Blow out all the candles on your birthday cake in one breath and your wish will come true.
- *Black Cat* – If a black cat walks across your path it brings bad luck.
- *Breaking a Mirror* – Will cause seven years' bad luck.
- *Coin in Fountain* – Make a wish while throwing a coin into a fountain and it will come true. (A popular movie based on this superstition and set in Italy is *Three Coins in the Fountain*.)
- *Crossing Fingers* – Brings good luck when index and middle fingers are crossed in hope of something happening or not happening.
- *Four Leaf Clovers* – Finding one brings good luck.
- *Horseshoe* – Brings good luck when hung on a wall above a door.
- *Number 13* – Because the number 13 is considered unlucky, some of our buildings do not have a 13th floor. Friday the 13th is said to be unlucky.
- *Open Ladder* – Don't walk under an open ladder or it will bring bad luck.
- *Rabbit's Foot* – Brings good luck when carried on a person.
- *Sidewalk Crack* – We say, "Step on a crack, break your mother's back."
- *Stars* – Wishes made upon seeing a shooting star are supposed to come true (unlike Japan where it forebodes). Children love this poem (so do a lot of adults): "Star light, star bright, First star I see tonight, I wish I may, I wish I might, Have the wish I wish tonight."
- *Umbrellas* – If you open one indoors, it brings you bad luck.
- *Weather* – Another poem: "Red sky at night, Sailor's delight. Red sky at morning, Sailors take warning."

THANK YOU CUSTOMS

"Thank you" creates a nice impression for Americans, whether spoken, written, or even suggested as a nod. If someone hands you something like a store receipt or money change, say thank you. We consider it rude if you take it and just walk away. If you and another person are about to enter a door simultaneously and the other person directs you to proceed first—and perhaps says "after you"—say thank you. If someone in front of you exits and then holds the door open for you as you exit, say thank you softly. If someone says thank you for something you did, say "you're welcome" in return or perhaps "my pleasure." If you don't acknowledge such small favors, or respond in some way even with a nod or smile when others thank you, it feels like a violation of etiquette to us. From my experience, some foreigners need to be careful with their etiquette.

Upper class Americans like to send—and expect to receive—thank you notes. They are an expression of appreciation for a thoughtful act, expression, or gift. Their use creates a very nice impression of you. Generally notes should be sent within a week of receipt of the gift or gesture. Your handwritten message on it should be brief, personalized, and sincere.

Always send notes in the following situations.

- To the host after a party was given in your honor.
- For gifts that you received by mail or in person.
- After being entertained by your boss.
- Gifts received during a hospital stay.
- If you were a houseguest for one or more nights.
- To accompany notes or gifts of congratulations you send to someone. When a floral shop sends flowers to someone, they will ask what message you want on the card that accompanies them. You might thank them for a favor they did. You can order flowers or gifts online from numerous websites such as www.1800flowers.com.

Fold-over thank you note.

Thank you notes are not required in the following situations, but would still be considered a nice gesture.

- After being a guest at a dinner party.
- For birthday gifts that were received and opened in person, and you already thanked the giver personally.
- When a friend has helped you out with a special favor such as babysitting or preparing a meal when you were sick.
- To a sales representative who has entertained you personally as part of a business relationship.
- After a job interview (not required, but definitely a smart idea), preferably within 24 hours. (More about job searching customs in Chapter X - Getting a Job.)

If you write a thank you note in a business situation, it should be typed on your company's letterhead unless someone did a favor to you personally. If you write a thank you note for a social occasion, write it by hand using black or dark blue ink.

If you send a thank you note for a gift you received, you should specifically mention the gift in your note along with a brief personal comment about it. For example: "Thank you for the floral bouquet. Yellow roses are my favorite."

You can purchase thank you notes individually or in boxes of 8 to 12. Our stationery and drug stores carry many different styles.

> **Hint**: The ultimate thank you note is custom made with your initials engraved—not printed—on the front. Although expensive, sending these creates a very nice, high-class impression of you. Here is one firm that provides them: www.crane.com/home.

Another way of saying thank you is to use an Internet e-mail message, an e-card, or through a social network such as Facebook. Various websites have e-mail greeting cards that you can send such as www.americangreetings.com (for a fee) and www.123greetings.com (free).

These are less formal (and less professional) than a thank you note and should only be used for small favors, things for which you might not otherwise use note cards and postage stamps.

Mailing Your Thank You – When writing an address on your envelope, put your full address in the upper left hand side of the envelope front or on the back flap. This is called the return address in case the post office must return it to you. The address of the person you are writing to goes in the middle and to the right side on the front of the envelope.

States have a two-digit state postal code, such as NC for North Carolina. (Appendix 9 provides a listing of these.)

Each address in America has a five-digit **ZIP code** after the state code. Like the telephone area code, the ZIP code signifies a specific geographical location. The lower number codes

Sally Student
302 Red, White and Blue Ave.
Wilmington, NC 28409

Sam Student
405 Liberty Lane
Wilmington, NC 28409

Envelope addresses. (www.nhcs.net/parsley/)

start in the New England states while the high numbers end up in the Pacific Northwest. Sometimes you will see a dash and four more digits after the Zip code, such as 28409-1234, to specify a more detailed address location. Failure to use a ZIP code or an apartment/suite/office number might cancel or delay the delivery of your mail. Use this post office website to look up ZIP codes and state codes: www.usps.com.

> **Hint**: If you want to quiz an American about its meaning, ZIP stands for **Z**oning **I**mprovement **P**System; few will know the answer to your question.

I

EDUCATION

He who learns but does not think, is lost! He who thinks but does not learn is in great danger. – Confucius, 6th century BC Chinese philosopher

This chapter provides information for those who will become involved with our schools or those who just want to know more about the American education system.

Our school systems vary from state to state and even within cities. Families relocating to the U.S. might ask prospective employers and colleagues for information about local school districts to help locate the best ones, which will then aid them in locating housing in that area. They also may inquire at a school district's office about the emphasis of the curriculum, the school's resources, its counseling and college placement services, and its extra-curricular activities. Most public schools do not offer English as a second language course unless they are located in areas with large non-English speaking populations.

High school building.

International students who accompany parents who are working, studying, or performing diplomatic service in the U.S. usually attend public elementary and high schools tuition-free just as our own students do. The student's visa status is based on that of the parents, as explained at: www.travel.state.gov/visa/temp/types/types_1268.html.

However, international students who attend school on their own require an individual student visa and need to be knowledgeable about our schools' application processes discussed in this chapter.

Literacy – As a reflection of our educational system, approximately 97 percent of the people in the U.S. are **literate** *[LIT-er-uht],* meaning they can read and write. This compares to Norway and Finland's 100 percent, China's 82 percent, and India's 65 percent.

Our literacy rate, like so many other things, varies by geographical area and the quality of the schools within the area. Our five top-ranked cities for literacy have largely Euro-American cultures; lower-ranked cities often have large numbers of immigrants. Asian Indian Americans have the highest educational qualifications of all national origin groups in the U.S. Even though our school systems are important for assimilating immigrants into a literate American culture, like everything else in the U.S., some do a good job, some don't.

Government Involvement – Below the college level, we offer free education that is paid for with our taxes. Our state governments control school systems but with some assistance from the federal government whose aim is to monitor and improve our schools. Germany and other countries use a similar approach. Many of our states devise standardized tests to measure student abilities in reading, math, writing, and science. Students who do not pass are not allowed to progress into the next grade or to graduate. Some feel these tests are not fair for immigrants and culturally deprived students. Each state has its own public university system, too. We also have many privately run lower-level schools, colleges, universities, and trade schools, some of which are affiliated with religious organizations.

Right To An Education – Our general attitude is that **higher education** (after high school) is a privilege, not a right. So it is proper for our students to assume some of the cost of their education through work and loans, although most of our universities offer academic scholarships and need-based aid. This popular saying is typical of that belief: **You reap what you sow**. In other words, you must do what you have to do to get an education if you want to reap the rewards of an education. This attitude is unlike many countries in Europe, but it seems to work reasonably well here because six percent of our population is enrolled in college versus three percent in Great Britain and France.

Failure Of Public Education – We recognize that the educational achievements of our schools are behind other nations. We hear about it in the media every day, but not much seems to be done about it. The Organisation for Economic Co-operation and Development reveals that our 15-year-olds rank 17th in the world in science and 25th in math. Among developed nations, only New Zealand, Spain, Turkey, and Mexico have lower high school completion rates than the U.S. One study of students at 55 of our universities found that over a third were unable to identify the U.S. Constitution as the document establishing the division of powers in our government and 40 percent could not place the Civil War in the correct half-century. (I hope you remember these two points from Chapter D on our history!)

Despite this, much of our population is educated beyond high school—we are second only to Canada and well ahead of most European nations. And our college and university systems are respected and are among the world's most accessible. It is our public elementary and high schools that we view as the problem. You might, too.

It is hard for us to understand why our system excels in some ways and fails in others. That makes it difficult to fix the problems we are experiencing. But educators say the blame for America's sagging academic achievement does not lie solely with our public schools, but also with dysfunctional families and a culture that increasingly undervalues education. In contrast, South Korea is an economic dynamo due in part to its educational attainment, which has a 96 percent high school graduation rate—the world's highest. The U.S. rate is 75 percent, up from 69 percent in 2007.

Views Of Americans – How do Americans view our educational system? Here are results from numerous surveys and what we have to say.

- *Priority* – Our highest legislative priorities should be improving our schools.
- *Ranking* – Public schools are the most important public institutions in their communities, ranking higher than churches or hospitals.
- *Teacher Quality* – We rate teacher quality as the most important factor for improving student learning. The second most important is equalizing funding between our rich and poor schools.
- *Academic Achievement* – Parents in the U.S. want their children to succeed socially and academically, but, in contrast to some Asian cultures, many are skeptical of the value of high academic achievement.
- *Sexuality* – Nine out of ten support teaching sex education, including information about AIDS, to high school age students.
- *Religious Teaching* – Seven out of ten say the Bible should be used in classes.
- *Career Success* – Only one in ten teachers say academics are the most important factor in career success. Instead, they think developing inner drive and knowing how to deal well socially with people are more important. This conflicts with educational attitudes in those countries where academics come first.
- *Sports* – About two-thirds say our colleges place too much emphasis on sports, that professors should not be granted jobs for life, and that minority students who have lower grade-point averages and test scores than their peers should not be admitted. (The latter attitude explains why many see a need for **affirmative action** legislation in the U.S. that fosters admission exceptions for minorities and immigrants.)

Too much emphasis?

- *Degree* – Only half of us say a college or university degree is essential, while eight out of ten Asian Americans say it is.

LOWER LEVEL SCHOOL FUNDAMENTALS

Referred to as our **lower level schools**, about 75 percent of our nation's **elementary** (grades 1-6) and **secondary schools** (grades 7-12), are **public schools** offering free education. (In the U.K., "public" refers to certain private schools.) The rest of our schools are **private schools** run by religious or private organizations and typically charge a fee.

Our cities have geographical **school districts** that define which public school elementary and secondary level students will attend based on where they live. This is unlike some nations like Germany where the parent can decide.

Typical elementary school classroom.

Some private schools and a few public schools require students to wear uniforms. Unlike Japan and some countries in the Southern hemisphere where the school year starts in April, our school year generally runs from September through June with a summer vacation. Some cities now have staggered year-round education in which student vacation months rotate. Typical school hours are from 9 a.m. to 3 p.m. Monday through Friday.

In contrast to some countries where elementary classes might approach 60 students, we try to limit students to fewer than 30 per class if possible. Some parents choose to educate their children at home. This is called **home study**. To do this, parents must have permission, be certified, and use guidance that is provided to them.

Here are more terms and facts about our lower level schools.

- *Private Schools* – Private schools are not affiliated with the government and cost money to attend. Private **boarding schools**, perceived by some as the most prestigious, allow students to live at the school. **Parochial** *[pah-ROW-kee-uhl]* schools are private schools operated by a religious group. These are the only schools in the U.S. allowed by law to teach religious beliefs because of our separation of church and state. Six in ten parents with children in public school say they would send their children to private schools if they could afford to do so because they think they do a better job in areas they are most concerned with—school safety, higher standards, order, and smaller classes.

- *Preparatory Schools* – Secondary schools that prepare students for college are called **preparatory** or **prep schools**. They are private and academically more difficult and usually more prestigious than public schools. Top colleges may admit students who graduate from these more readily because of their higher educational achievement. A good one might charge over $12,000 for tuition each year. The top prep school in the U.S. is the Trinity School (www.trinityschoolnyc.org) in New York City that has one teacher for every six students and an annual tuition of $35,000, though the school does offer financial aid to some qualified lower- income students.

- *Authorities* – The head of elementary and secondary schools is called the **principal**. At some private schools, the head might be called the **headmaster**. School districts usually have a **superintendent** who is in charge of all of its schools and a **board of education** that consists of elected people who monitor education in the city. As part of America's widespread system of checks and balances, we have both elected and appointed officials overseeing our school systems, from city governments to the federal government.

- *Teachers* – In some nations, teachers are viewed with the same respect paid to doctors and other professionals. We used to be like that, but things have changed. A third of new lower-level teachers in the U.S. leave the profession within three years; half leave after five years. Our schools have trouble attracting teachers who instead can take their skills to private businesses and earn considerably more. A shortage of up to 700,000 teaching instructors in the U.S. draws our school administrators to India where they recruit teachers who might make $2400 a year, but when they come to the U.S. they may earn over $40,000.

- *Special Schools* – You might hear the term, **charter schools**, which are publicly funded elementary or secondary schools freed from some of the rules, regulations, and statutes that apply to other public schools. They are leading the reform of our public schools and are similar in concept to the independent schools in New Zealand, U.K., Chile, and Canada. Our **magnet schools** attract students from outside an assigned neighborhood attendance zone for the purpose of achieving diversity by offering a distinctive curriculum or instructional approach. The Performing Arts High School in New York City is a famous one that gives students special skills in drama, music, and dance.

- *Disadvantaged Kids* – Some school districts offer a school busing program in which students (including immigrants) who live in poorer areas in the school district are bused to schools that are more economically, culturally, and educationally advanced. A school district office can inform you of these.

Hint: The movie *Stand and Deliver* (1988) is a true story about an immigrant teacher from Bolivia who transformed a tough Los Angeles high school by motivating struggling students to excel at advanced math and science. At first he was discouraged by the school's culture of low expectations, gang activity, and administrative apathy, which is typical of our **inner city** (poor areas in large cities) schools. Gradually, he overhauled the school's math curriculum and enabled students who were previously considered un-teachable to master the **advanced-placement** (qualified to enroll in college-level classes) calculus test. The school had more advanced-placement calculus students than all but four other public high schools in the U.S. He shattered one of the most dangerous cultural myths of our time: Inner city students (including immigrants) can't be expected to perform at the highest levels.

SCHOOL DIVISIONS

We have eight different kinds of schools in America based on the level of education they teach. They range from nursery schools to colleges.

1. Nursery Schools *[NURR-sir-ee]* – These are generally for 3 to 4-year old children and attendance is optional. We also call these **preschools**. The children learn to work and play together and are prepared for the next level of school, which is kindergarten. About a third of our children attend nursery school. Most are privately owned, small, and charge a fee. Mothers who work may use them as daycare centers for their children. Corporate daycare centers are provided onsite by some corporations for their personnel who are parents of young children. Immigrants should explore this with prospective employers and factor it in as part of their salary.

2. Kindergarten *[kin-der-GAR-ten]* – This is a one-year grade for children 5 to 6 years old, usually taught for a half day before they start the first grade in elementary school. For many children it is their first experience with formal education. Most are located in and administered by public elementary schools. ("Kindergarten" is a term borrowed from German. *Kinder* means children and *garten* means garden; hence, a pleasant garden-like atmosphere for young children.) If you see the term **K-12**, it refers to grades kindergarten through grade 12.

3. Elementary Schools *[ell-ih-MEN-tah-ree]* – Elementary means basic. These schools have six to seven grades, starting with the first grade. They teach children from ages 6 to 12 or 14 basic subjects such as reading, writing, and arithmetic. These are also called **primary schools**, **grammar schools**, and **grade schools**, so take your pick.

4. Junior High Schools *[JUNE-yurr]* – These schools offer two or three years of education, usually grades 7 thru 9, after six years of elementary school. They introduce students to the kind of class schedule and assignments they will have in high school. Students choose some of their subjects, rotate to different classrooms, and learn from different teachers in each subject.

5. Middle Schools *[MID-dull]* – In the 1960s, some communities replaced their junior high school systems with middle schools. (You will hear our middle schools and junior high schools referred to as **intermediate schools**. These schools usually consist of grades 6 or 7 thru 8, when children start maturing. They then move on to high school in the 9th grade. Some educators believe this system allows each child to better advance at his or her own speed and to receive more individual help from teachers.

6. High Schools – Our high schools are also called **secondary schools**. (Out of confusion I learned in New Zealand that secondary school is often called college, from year 9 to 13.) These schools provide the last grades before students move on to college, vocational schools, or to work when they graduate with a **diploma** *[dih-PLOM-ah]* (document) upon completing the 12th grade. High schools consist of grades 10 thru 12 in communities with three-year junior high schools, or grades 9 thru 12 for those with middle schools. Vocational programs

High school building in Virginia.

provide training in job skills such as carpentry and auto repair for those who do not plan to enter college.

All high schools have required courses, but students might elect other courses such as music, foreign languages, and drama. Only 60 percent go on to college, another concern for some Americans.

Many high schools have reunions for their graduating classes long after they have left school, such as 5, 10, 25, and 50-year reunions. These often help keep communities together and offer their graduates networking opportunities (something we are good at doing) in the business world to nurture success.

These high school procedures and activities may differ from your country's.

- *A Second Chance* – Just like our culture, our educational system gives individuals second and third chances to succeed. There is hope for those who drop out of high school before graduating but wish to later resume their education. They can study and then be tested to receive a High School Equivalency Diploma (HSED). Our colleges and employers view them the same as they would a normal high school diploma. This can be done online: www.ehow.com/how_6401381_ged-test-online.html.

- *SAT Test* – Before graduating, high school students take an **SAT** (Scholastic Achievement Test) that ranks the students academically based on their score. Colleges rely on these scores as a predictor of how well students will perform in college. A perfect score is 2400, with an average of 1500. However, the average score of entering freshmen at our top colleges is over 2100. A good SAT score carries weight, but our colleges consider other factors. For example, the prestigious University of California at Berkeley with its high average SAT scores admitted 400 students with lower scores because they showed motivation in other areas. High scores can lead to scholarships, too.

- *Tutoring* – We have private businesses in the U.S. that provide tutoring for high school students, such as the national chain of Sylvan Learning Centers (www.tutoring.sylvanlearning.com). Also, some high school students take classes from private firms after school to learn how to achieve a high grade on SAT exams, such as www.KlassTutoring.com and www.CollegeBoard.com.

- *Outside Activities* – Unlike nations like Germany where some schools are strictly for learning and lack social events, most of our high schools offer activities outside the classroom in the belief they produce well rounded individuals. These activities include athletics, dance, music, theatre, club activities, honor societies, and producing the school newspaper. High schools usually have about five dances each year and students may bring dates.

- *Yearbook* – Students also may work on their school's yearbook, something many foreigners are not familiar with. They are part of almost every American's life and memories. Published at the end of the school year, they contain individual photos of students and teachers and summarize the year's activities. Students eagerly await these books that are issued a week or two before the end of the school year when classmates sign each other's yearbooks and write comments in them. Most people keep them a lifetime. Sometimes our media will show the yearbook picture of a celebrity when he or she was in high school.

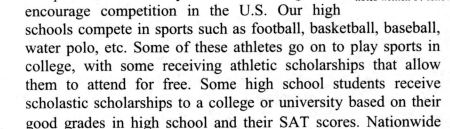

Page from a high school yearbook with notes written by fellow classmates.

- *Competition* – As you are learning, we encourage competition in the U.S. Our high schools compete in sports such as football, basketball, baseball, water polo, etc. Some of these athletes go on to play sports in college, with some receiving athletic scholarships that allow them to attend for free. Some high school students receive scholastic scholarships to a college or university based on their good grades in high school and their SAT scores. Nationwide **Spelling bees** are held each year in which students under 16-years old compete to become the best speller in the U.S. **Scholastic bowls** are competitions in which a school's team of five or six students competes against other high schools by answering academic questions.

President Obama yearbook photo.

- *Comparisons To Europe* – Here are a few general comparisons between U.S. and European high schools.
    - ○ *Gymnasiums* – American school facilities are much larger than their European counterparts because European schools don't have **gymnasiums** and adjacent athletic fields. (European countries use the term "gymnasium" to refer to a middle or secondary school. In the U.S. it refers to a facility where physical education and sports are conducted. We shorten the word and call it a "gym.")

High school gym.

    - ○ *Sports* – As you will learn in Chapter N on sports, we love sports and they are an essential part of high school life. In comparison, sports teams are generally lacking in European high schools.
    - ○ *Lockers* – European schools don't have the lockers that line our school hallways. Unlike U.S. high schoolers, European students can be in the same classroom all day, with three- or four-minute breaks when teachers rotate instead.
    - ○ *Parking* – European schools lack parking lots that our high schools have. So, in public-transport-friendly Europe, students take buses, trains, trams, and bikes to school. And in most European countries the driving age is 18 versus 16 in the U.S., so few students have a license or a car as they do in the U.S.
    - ○ *School Day* – In France, some school days can be considerably longer than in the U.S.: 8 a.m. to noon in the morning, and then 2 p.m. to 6 p.m. in the afternoons. Wednesdays are half days as are Saturdays. Our schools have shorter days and are closed on Saturdays.
    - ○ *Teachers* – Foreign students in the U.S. say their American teachers seem to relate to them better because our teachers also oversee student extracurricular activities and get to know the students both in and out of the classroom.

Hint: Classic films about high school life include *Blackboard Jungle* (1955), *The Breakfast Club* (1985) and *Coach Carter* (2005).

7. Community Colleges *[come-UHN-ah-tee]* – These are also called **junior colleges (JCs)** and **city colleges**. Most provide a two-year program of study after high school. Some offer broad programs with courses similar to those taught the first two years at our four-year colleges or universities. Some offer specialized job training for those students who will not continue their education at a four-year university or college.

161

The U.S. has about 1,500 community colleges, of which two-thirds are public. The average annual price for tuition and fees is $3,000, which is usually much less than a four-year college or university. Visit this website for information about a typical community college located in the southwestern state of Arizona, and study the different tuition categories: www.gc.maricopa.edu. Note that their tuition varies for local residents and out-of-state students. (To compute sample costs based on credit hours taken, the average fulltime student takes about 12 to 15 credit hours per semester.)

Another website that you will find interesting is for a typical community college in the midwestern state of Iowa: www.highline.edu/home/home.htm. Note their helpful guidelines for admission requirements for foreign students.

The degree granted by community colleges is called an associate degree in art or science (AA or AS). Students with low grades in high school might attend a community college for one or two years to boost their grades (or improve their English), then apply to a four-year university or college of their choice and enter at an advanced grade level. Some junior colleges offer guaranteed admission to top state universities to those students who achieve stellar grades at the community college level.

Florida community college building.

The overall enrollment of community colleges is generally smaller than universities and colleges, and their class sizes are sometimes smaller. Most do not offer student housing. Many offer excellent English language classes for foreign students who want to improve their English language skills. These classes are called **ESL**, which stands for English as a Second Language.

> **Hint**: Community colleges can be an excellent choice for foreigners who want to study in America. I have foreign heritage friends who just take English language classes at these colleges at night or on weekends. They are not working toward a degree but are trying to improve their language skills. They are available to anyone who wants to study either during the day or at night, part time or full time. I strongly recommend these for immigrants.

8. Colleges And Universities – At the highest level, we have about 4,800 colleges and universities that offer more than 900 fields of study that foreigners can choose from. We use the term "college" to refer to both of them collectively. Forty-five percent of these institutions of **higher learning** are public. Some have international student advisers to assist foreigners make the most of their education.

Unlike the low ranking of our public elementary and high schools, many U.S. colleges are highly regarded worldwide. According to a widely used global ranking, the U.S. has 17 of the world's top 20 universities. Because of an increasing global demand for American-style higher education, some of our universities, including New York University and Yale University are building campuses overseas.

America's universities currently employ 70 percent of the world's Nobel Prize winners, publish 30 percent of the world's output of articles on science and engineering, and 44 percent of the most frequently cited articles. Ten years ago, 50 percent of European graduates of American universities returned to Europe; today the figure is 25 percent, which, among other things, is an indication they can find jobs here.

UCLA - Los Angeles, California.

What is the difference between a college and a university? To begin with, a college is smaller than a university. A university can consist of different "colleges" that specialize in specific areas of study like the "College of Nursing," etc. (We sometimes call these **schools** within the university, such as the business school, dental school, etc.) Thus a college might be a school within a university, or it can be an independent, smaller institution specializing in a narrow branch of knowledge.

A **liberal arts college** is an independent college that only teaches liberal art subjects such as art, history, music, literature, etc. We also have teacher's colleges and agricultural colleges. Most independent colleges do not offer masters and doctorate programs as our universities do.

> **Hint**: Because we use the term "college" to refer to both colleges and universities, if someone says, "Are you going to college?" or "Where did you go to college?" they mean any higher education, including either a university or a college. You might also hear the term "**old college try**" used to indicate maximum effort will be given to achieve success. For example, "We might not make the deadline, but we'll give it the old college try."

These higher institutions offer advanced study in a variety of fields after high school or junior college. Unlike some countries with three-year degrees, ours have four-year programs that offer a bachelor's degree in the arts or sciences. The **BS** degree is the **Bachelor of Science**, and the **BA** degree is the **Bachelor of Arts**. Some offer programs leading to a **master's degree** (MS, MA, MBA, etc.) that require two more years of study, or a **doctorate degree (Ph.D.** for four more years of study (for a total of 10 beyond high school). A graduate of a medical school is awarded an **MD** (medical doctor) and a dentist a **DDS**, which you see after their names on their diplomas hanging on their office walls.

Let's now discuss various aspects of our colleges, ranging from their operations, to applying for admission, to getting financial aid, to classroom culture that probably varies from your country.

COLLEGE FUNDAMENTALS

Being accepted to study at our colleges and universities is based on merit, unlike some countries like India where caste affiliation may be recognized criteria for admission. Most of our universities and colleges allow both men and women (60 percent of our students) to attend, although a **handful** (very few) of liberal arts colleges allow only women or men. These schools will point this out in their **school catalog**. Harvard's acceptance rate is six percent, while Yale receives 27,000 applications and accepts 1,350 for the freshmen class each year.

The **campus** is the land that the school stands on. On it are the classrooms, administration buildings, libraries, laboratories, gymnasiums, athletic fields, athletic stadiums, and **dormitories** where some students live. Students can also live in apartments or rented homes off campus if they don't live at home with their families.

Classes consist of lectures in classrooms of maybe 15 to 30 students, but a teacher can have hundreds of students in a classroom for one of the school's required introductory or core courses. A student will generally spend about 15-20 hours each week in class (about 3-4 hours a day), plus extra time for laboratory work. The rest of the time is free for study, recreation, or a job.

Hint: Classic films that take place in university settings are *Animal House* (1978), *Good Will Hunting* (1998), and *A Beautiful Mind* (2001).

Major – Most schools require students to take a broad number of defined courses their first two years, giving them a solid educational background. Their last two years is then spent in their field of specialization called their **major**. The number one major today is business (22%).

U.S. census figures show that over an adult's life high school graduates who do not attend college will earn $1.2 million, while those with a bachelor's degree will earn $2.1 million. Figures also show that the average starting salary for college graduates is almost double the figure for high school graduates who do not go to college. Here is a ranking of the average annual starting salaries for a bachelor's degree for recent graduates with these majors:

1. Chemical Engineering $64,902
2. Computer Engineering $61,738
3. Computer Science $61,407
4. Electrical Engineering $60,125
5. Engineering $59,254
6. Information Sciences $52,089
7. Civil Engineering $52,048
8. Finance $49,940
9. Economics $49,829
10. Accounting $48,993

164

School Officials *[oh-FISH-uhls]* – The head of the university is called the president or chancellor. A **dean** or director heads each school or college within the university. The teachers collectively are called the **faculty** *[FAK-uhl-tee]*. They are assigned to a specific department, such as English, math, or history. Each department is headed by a chairman who is usually a senior **professor** *[pro-FESS-or]*. Other faculty members with sufficient years of experience also have that title.

Students – The **student body** consists of **graduates** working on a master or doctor's degree and **undergraduates** studying for their bachelor's degree. Based on the number of classes they have completed, undergraduates are in one of four groups, each of which has a name. These same designations are also used in our high schools for the 9th through 12th grades. (Juniors and seniors are referred to as **upperclassmen.**)

- First Year - **Freshman** *[FRESH-man]*
- Second Year - **Sophomore** *[SOFF-oh-more]*
- Third Year - **Junior** *[JUNE-yerr]*
- Fourth Year - **Senior** *[SEEN-yerr]*

Many students work to put themselves through college and do not carry a full load (about 15 hours) of classes. Some might take a year off to work or to travel during enrollment. So the average time it takes a full-time student to complete a four-year degree is now 4.7 years; part-time students need an additional five months on average.

At the start of the school year in the fall, a student election is held that is similar to those in our cities and states. Students elect fellow students for school president, class presidents, and other student body offices. These class officers plan student activities and represent the students on school matters. (There's that *representation* thing again.)

Hint: As you are learning, representation and civic responsibility are so important in our culture. We even encourage this in our schools in order to have our groups represented by one of our own. I was a class officer in the 6th grade. I was only 12 years old and we were electing representatives!

School Year – Our schools use one of two time periods for the school year.

- Semester – *[seh-MESS-ter]* This is the most common and divides the school year into two halves, about 16 weeks each. The first semester generally begins around September and the second one in January. Many schools also have a six- to eight-week summer session that students can choose to attend.
- Quarter – *[KWOR-ter]* The year is divided into four quarters of 10-12 weeks each. We call these fall quarter, winter quarter, spring quarter, and summer quarter. Many do not attend summer quarter but choose to work as **interns** (trainees) to advance their skills or at summer jobs to finance their schooling.

Curriculum – The courses offered by a college or a university are called the school's **curriculum** *[kurr-ICK-you-luhm]*. Each school publishes a catalog before the beginning of the school year that outlines the complete curriculum for the coming year. It defines the requirements for taking each course, as well as the **credits** given. Each course completion gives a student a specified number of credits. These usually equal the number of classroom hours devoted each week to the course. A course that meets two hours a week usually awards two credits for its successful completion, and so on. The catalog also defines how many total credits are required for graduation. (You can request a university you are interested in to mail their catalog to you. Most have course descriptions online as well.)

Each course is given a number to identify it and to indicate the required grade level the student must have achieved to take it. For example, some schools assign numbers in the 100 and 200 series for freshmen and sophomores. Those in the 300 and 400 series are primarily for juniors and seniors and can require completion of certain 100 and 200 courses as prerequisites before enrolling.

> **Hint**: "**101**" is a common number assigned to a basic, required course, such as "English 101." It is pronounced as "one-oh-one," not "one-hundred and one." Frequently you will hear someone refer to "101" when talking about something fundamental but not related to school. For example, if a manager is discussing how customers are to be treated, he might say, "Customer Relations 101 says telephone customers should never be put on hold for more than two minutes."

Cheating – This is an area where students from other cultures get into trouble. Unless the professor has indicated otherwise, students should do all work on their own. Studying with others is okay, but hand-in assignments should be completed individually. Quoting a text word-for-word (or even part of it) without properly attributing the source is considered cheating.

Some students download papers from the Internet and submit them as their work. Because of their popularity, some professors recognize them immediately, and now there are online sites where teachers can check for these borrowed (stolen) papers. **Cliffs Notes** (www.cliffsnotes.com) are used notoriously by students for copying rather than as study aids and teachers know it.

All cheating is grounds for failing a class or even expulsion from school. We had a scandal at our prestigious Air Force Academy a few years ago where a few cadets **got their hands on** (acquired) a copy of an upcoming test and were expelled. There's that *honesty* thing again.

Grades – Your final course grade is based on your scores on tests, quizzes, and assignments. If the class allows for recitation, discussion, or asking questions, active participation can improve your grade. The better the professor and teaching assistants know you and your work, the better they will be able to assess your progress.

Hint: You might hear the terms **brown nose**, **teacher's pet**, or **apple polisher**. They define those students who make an extra special effort, such as frequent participation in class discussions, to be on good terms with a teacher in order to get a good grade. These are intended as negative terms, but you should do what you must to achieve good grades ethically and ignore teasing by others who might not be goal-oriented like you.

In America you will hear the term **GPA** *[g-p-a]* (**grade point average**). Unlike some countries that use a numerical system, letters are used to report your final course grade. An "A" grade is the highest grade, and then B, C, D, and F for failure. Sometimes a "+" (plus) or "-" (minus) is used for further assessment. To compute your GPA, assign a 4 to an A grade, 3 to a B, 2 to a C, and 1 to a D. Next, multiply the number of hours the course was rated as, such as 5, 4, 3, or 2. Compute an average as shown in this example:

Course: English Grammar –   5 hours   Grade: A = 5x4 =   20 points.
Course: English Speech –   3 hours   Grade: B = 3x3 =   9 points.
Course: American History –   4 hours   Grade: C = 4x2 =   8 points.
                                              12 hrs.   37 points
$37 \div 12 = 3.08$ grade point average = B

Our colleges use an applicant's high school GPA when evaluating him or her for admission. The prestigious University of California, like other schools systems, raised its GPA requirement in 2004 from 2.8 to 3.1 in order to further narrow the growing list of high school candidates from which it would choose.

Costs – Tuition *[too-ISH-uhn]* is the fee you pay for enrolling in one or more classes. **Room and board** refers to cost of a room in which you live and the expense of meals. College costs vary widely and are increasing an average of five percent each year. Most college catalogs list their average living costs for one year along with tuition and other fees. (Midwest schools and those in smaller cities can be cheaper.) These are the average charges just for tuition for full time students per year.

- Public four-year colleges for residents of the same state - $8,000.
- Public four-year colleges for out-of-state students - $12,500.
- Private nonprofit four-year colleges - $28,500.

Social Groups – Some universities and colleges have social groups called **fraternities** *[frah-TURN-ih-tees]* for men and **sororities** *[suh-RORE-ih-tees]* for women that date back to the early nineteenth century. Their names are derived from Latin, meaning brothers and sisters respectively. In Europe, student organizations are termed "corporations," and "nations" in Sweden, Finland, and Scotland.

The groups select their own members and abide by the school's regulations (most of the time). The membership in each organization will probably number less than 100 each school year, and friendships might be made for a lifetime. Many are national organizations with chapters on numerous campuses nationwide. They are given Greek letters to signify their names, such as alpha, beta, etc. Members meet in **chapter houses** that are usually located adjacent to the school campus, and some students live in the houses. Studies show that Greek affiliation leads students to significantly higher levels of general education gains, volunteerism, civic responsibility, and participation in student organizations.

In typical American fashion, many Greek letter organizations also make philanthropy an integral part of their objectives by reaching beyond their own group to support others. There is also competition between the "houses" on campus, including best grade averages, fund raising, and sporting events.

Sporting Events – Sporting events between schools is an important activity for the students, the community, and for the school's graduates. Most athletes who participate in professional sports come from colleges and universities. The most popular sporting events include football in the fall, basketball in the winter, and less popular baseball and track in the spring. They have other events such as swimming, tennis, golf, and volleyball. Tiger Woods played golf for Stanford University in California before turning professional. Soccer (which is called football in other countries) is less important in America than in most of the rest of the world. Women have competing events, too.

Cheerleaders.

Alumni *[ah-LHUM-ni]* are people who have graduated from the school. They might continue to attend games or watch their teams on TV. College teams have student **cheerleaders** at games to encourage vocal support for their team from the spectators. Some of our celebrities who were once cheerleaders include Madonna, Arnold Schwarzenegger, Meryl Streep, Michael Douglas, Dwight D. Eisenhower, and Ronald Reagan. Texas is the cheerleading capital of the world and sponsors lots of competitions. There's that *competitive* thing again.

COLLEGE RANKINGS

Contrary to what some foreigners might think, Harvard is not the only good university in the U.S. Many other colleges and universities have fine reputations. Appendices 2, 3, and 4 summarize an annual study by a national magazine that ranks the top schools in America. You can also use their website to research these and many other institutions not included in the lists. The Princeton Review, which administers college entrance exams, also provides annual rankings of our colleges and universities for over 60 different categories (www.princetonreview.com). For example:

- *Best Party School* - University of Texas at Austin.
- *Best Campus Life* - Brown University in Rhode Island.

- *Most Beautiful Campus* - Pepperdine University overlooking the Pacific Ocean just outside Los Angeles.
- *Best Overall Teachers* - Middlebury College in Vermont.
- *Hardest to get Into* - Massachusetts Institute of Technology (MIT), followed by Princeton, Harvard, Brown, and Yale.
- *Most Diverse Students* - DePaul University in Chicago. Illinois.

Pepperdine University – Los Angeles.

Each year *Forbes* magazine ranks over 600 colleges not on their reputations but on things that matter the most to students: quality of teaching, career prospects, graduation rates, and low levels of debt because of financial grants discussed below (www.forbes.com). This is their recent top 10 rankings and their states where located.

1. Williams College, Massachusetts
2. Princeton University, New Jersey
3. United States Military Academy, New York
4. Amherst College, Massachusetts
5. Stanford University, California
6. Harvard University, Massachusetts
7. Haverford College, Pennsylvania
8. University of Chicago, Illinois
9. Massachusetts Institute of Technology, Massachusetts
10. United States Air Force Academy, Colorado

Williams College

APPLYING TO AN AMERICAN COLLEGE

Each year over a half-million international students come the U.S. to study in our educational institutions at all levels. The number has increased by 22 percent since 2007. President George W. Bush said, "We encourage international students to take part in our educational system. The relationships that are formed between individuals from different countries—as part of international education programs and exchanges—foster goodwill that develops into vibrant, mutually beneficial partnerships among nations."

You can use various websites to learn more about studying here. For example:

- This government website is an excellent source of information for studying in the U.S.: www.ed.gov/NLE/USNEI/us/study-us.html.
- This State Department website explains getting a visa, student aid, and a host of other subjects: www.educationusa.state.gov. Their education bureaus are located in major cities around the world, including inside U.S. embassies and consulates. They can also let you know if representatives from U.S. colleges are planning a visit to your country.
- A fun, informational website with lots of information about the U.S. and getting an education here is www.USA.gov. Also, for information on the application process and funding try www.collegeboard.com.

The leading country of origin for international students in the U.S. is India, with China, South Korea, Japan, and Canada **close on their heels** (not far behind). On the other hand, top destinations for U.S. students studying abroad are the United Kingdom, Italy, and Spain.

Visas – The best possibilities for young people who want to work in the U.S. while touring the country are student visas or cultural exchange programs. Student visas (J-visas) are available to students who are accepted into an approved educational program in the U.S. They do not automatically allow employment, but many work-study provisions are available. A U.S. embassy or consulate in your home country is the best place to get complete and accurate information about visas. Another good source is the U.S. State Department's website: www.state.gov.

Application – Many websites offer advice on choosing a university or college to attend in the America. Most colleges offer virtual tours on their websites—a good resource for students who cannot visit in person. Each university or college has its own application process and you need to contact each one of your choice for its requirements. Ask for their catalog and application papers, some of which you might find online.

In general, they require completion of a high school curriculum, although there can be exceptions to this. Most require that certain basic courses have been taken in high school. Others will not consider students whose grades are below a certain level.

Some schools might administer entrance exams before they make their selections. You will be

Harvard University.

asked for a copy of your **transcript**, which is a certified listing of all courses completed in high school or other colleges and the grade you attained in each course.

The admission procedures for international students may not be the same as those required of American students. There will be differences in the tests administered and financial disclosures required. For an example of this, Harvard University's website summarizes their requirements at www.admissions.college.harvard.edu/index.html.

American colleges and universities welcome your inquiry and will help you with your application for entrance. Some are flexible when applying the rules of acceptance to foreign students. Once students are accepted, schools continue to assist them to insure they make the most of their educations.

Here are more tips to consider when applying.

- *Location* – If you don't know where to start your search for a school to attend, start by looking for schools in a geographic area that interests you. If you know the name of a city, you can go to that city's (or state's) website and

170

search for a list of colleges and universities and then connect to their websites. Also, consider climate—what you are accustomed to and what you prefer. Our northern states are cold and snowy in the winter and our southern states can get hot and humid in the summer. Consider diversity, too. You'll find more Asians in the West due to its closer proximity to Asia, and perhaps more Europeans on the East Coast and Latinos in our southern states for similar reasons. Our small Midwestern schools might be cheaper to attend than those in the big cities. Choosing a course of study might also dictate a geographical location, such as marine biology dictating a coastal state, mining engineering a Rocky Mountain state, agriculture in a Midwestern state, etc. Sometimes a little-known university has a strong reputation in a specific discipline.

- *English Test* – Typically, you must be fluent in English to attend a U.S. college, so some students must take English-language programs before applying. If English is not your native language, you will have to take a test called **TOEFL** (Test of English as a Foreign Language). It may be taken at an educational testing service in your native country or in America. Websites such as this one provide testing locations and tips on taking the test: www.toefl.org.

- *Graduate Tests* – Graduate study requires separate tests, such as LSAT (Law School Admission Test), or MCAT (Medical College Admission Test). Factor in the timing of taking these when considering the application deadline. U.S. schools will not consider your application until they receive your test scores. Usually it takes 6-8 weeks for your scores to be reported.

- *Deadline* – Start your search early because schools have deadlines for applications, ranging from six to twelve months before the school year begins. That means that if the school starts in September, as is typical, you should start taking tests in September or October of the prior year.

COLLEGE FINANCIAL ASSISTANCE

With the average college student graduating with some $28,000 in debt, many seek financial help. Inquire if a school can offer you financial aid. About two-thirds of our undergraduates and 30 percent of international students in the U.S. receive some form of financial aid from universities that averages $9,100. This website offers assistance to international students seeking financial aid: www.iefa.org. Of those students who receive aid, nearly half receive **grants** averaging $3600—money that doesn't need to be repaid and effectively reduces the price paid for college.

Scholarships – Numerous scholarships are also available, including those awarded specifically to foreign students. They may be awarded for a variety criteria including advanced achievements, interests, skills, or even your major. Foreign graduates of a college sometimes establish a scholarship for fellow countrymen. The school you choose will have an office that advises and assists you with obtaining scholarships.

Loans – Some universities make loans that must eventually be repaid by the student. Low-interest loans are also sponsored by the federal government. Private loans tend to have higher fees and interest rates than federal government loans and do not offer the opportunities for cancellation or loan forgiveness that are available on many federal loan programs. So it makes good financial sense to exhaust your federal loan options (as well as grants and scholarships) before considering loans from private companies. To learn more about federal government loans and whether or not foreigners can apply, visit www.FederalStudentAid.ed.gov. To be considered for government money, students should submit the FAFSA application form (Free Application for Federal Student Aid). Do it as soon as possible because aid is given to qualified students on a first-come, first-serve basis (www.fafsa.ed.gov).

> **Hint**: I had a combination scholarship and university loan when I was in graduate school. Without these I could not have attended one of the best and most expensive schools in the country. Each year, as many other alumni do, I contribute to the school's scholarship fund to aid current students in need of financial support so they can benefit as I once did. Hopefully, they will do the same after they graduate. We call this **paying it forward**: doing a good deed for the next person who in turn will do it for the next person when they are able to do so.

Predatory Private Loans – We have a term, **tread lightly**, that means proceed with caution. Private, predatory loans are largely unregulated and have variable interest rates that are **sky-high** (excessive). The interest they charge can be up to 20 percent per year (four times federal rates). You might be paying off a loan like that the rest of your life. The majority of borrowers taking out those riskier private loans are students at for-profit colleges (institutions run by private companies trying to make money) where 42 percent of students have private loans. Some of these include DeVry University and Phoenix University.

If you are considering a private student loan, it's *important* to know with whom you're doing business and the terms of the loan. Do an Internet search on the name of the lender to see if others have had trouble with them. Check blogs and review sites like www.Yelp.com. The U.S. Education Department (www.ed.gov) offers these tips to help you recognize questionable private student loans.

- Some private lenders use names and seals to create the impression they are affiliated with the federal government. If you receive a student loan solicitation, it is not from Education Department.
- Don't let incentives like gift cards, credit cards, and sweepstakes prizes divert you from assessing whether the key terms of the loan are reasonable.

- Don't give out personal information unless you know with whom you are dealing. Private student lenders typically ask for your student account number or social security number saying they need it to help determine your eligibility. Because they can misuse this information, it is critical to provide personal information only if you have confidence in the lender with whom you are dealing.
- Check out the **track record** (record of performance) of particular private student lenders with your state Attorney General (www.naag.org), your local consumer protection agency (www.consumeraction.gov), and the Better Business Bureau (www.bbb.org).

Generous Colleges – The Princeton Review compiles a financial aid ranking of 613 colleges.(www.princetonreview.com.) They consider how many students receive aid compared to the number who need it, how much of their financial needs are met, and how satisfied students are with their awards. They advise getting current information about a school's financial aid offerings before crossing a school off your list because of its high **sticker price** (cost) stated in its catalog. Sometimes, the most expensive colleges are the most generous with their grants and aid. They rank these alphabetically as our top 10 most generous schools:

- Carleton College (Northfield, MN)
- Claremont McKenna College (Claremont, CA)
- Columbia University (New York, NY)
- Franklin W. Olin College of Engineering (Needham, MA)
- Pomona College (Claremont, CA)
- Princeton University (Princeton, NJ)
- Swarthmore College (Swarthmore, PA)
- Thomas Aquinas College (Santa Paula, CA)
- Vassar College (Poughkeepsie, NY)
- Yale University (New Haven, CT)

Princeton University

FREE COLLEGES

Some countries like Sweden, Germany, and Venezuela offer free college for their students. This is rare in America, but like everything else, we do have exceptions.

- *Alice Lloyd College* – Four-year liberal arts institution providing leadership education. (www.alc.edu)
- *Barclay College* – Degrees in various ministries and Christian education. (www.barclaycollege.edu)
- *Berea College* – Free laptops and on-campus jobs for liberal arts students with high academic achievement. (www.berea.edu)

- *City University of New York Teacher Academy* – For students talented in mathemetics and science who want to become teachers in those fields. (www.york.cuny.edu/centers-institutes/teacher-academy)
- *College of the Ozarks* – Presbyterian liberal arts college. (www.cofo.edu)
- *Cooper Union for the Advancement of Science and* Art – The only private, full-scholarship college in the U.S. dedicated exclusively to preparing students for professions in architecture, art, and engineering. (www.cooper.edu)
- *Curtis Institute of Music* – One of the finest music conservatories in the world for the musically gifted. (www.curtis.edu)
- *United States Military Academies* – These schools include the U.S. Military Academy at West Point (www.usma.edu), U.S. Air Force Academy (www.usafa.af.mil), U.S. Naval Academy (www.usna.edu), U.S. Coast Guard Academy (www.cga.edu), and the U.S. Merchant Marine Academy (www.usmma.edu). The tradeoff for free college is 5 to 9 years of service in the military and/or reserves after graduation.

U.S. Military Academy - New York State.

- *University of the People* – New online university dedicated to the global advancement and democratization of higher education and backed by the United Nations. (www.uopeople.org)
- *William E. Macaulay Honors College at City University of New York* – Liberal arts students receive a computer, funds for research, and internships. (www.macaulay.cuny.edu)
- *Webb Institute* – Students complete a double major in naval architecture and marine engineering. (www.webb-institute.edu)

FOREIGN STUDENTS IN AMERICAN COLLEGES

To make a fellow foreigner's stay in America more rewarding, organizations comprised of foreign students offer information and social interaction. Contact the university to provide you with lists of these, or search an organization's website and let them help you with your questions. For example, UCLA's (University of California at Los Angeles) International Students Association (ISA) is an organization that provides guidance and help. They also organize social activities that help diffuse the belief of many students that cultural groups tend to separate students from other cultural and ethnic backgrounds.

In addition to student organizations, college administrators offer assistance to foreign students attending their schools. They might have orientation classes that last from one day to one week. They might also have their own websites or publications that discuss American culture and customs, and provide information about the surrounding area and other topics that will make your stay with us easier. Some even have classes that teach American slang to ESL students. Check the school's career center for help.

Cultural Differences – Once enrolled, many international students are surprised by the cultural differences between schools in their homelands and America. Lawyers from foreign countries recently discovered these cultural classroom differences while studying American law at a university in Southern California. What surprised a Tokyo lawyer about American education was the informality of the classroom and the interaction between teachers and students. In Japan, he said, professors lecture and students listen, but here they exchange ideas and professors like to ask students questions. He was nervous the first time he was called on and became flustered when the professor continued with follow-up questions. He said that culturally it is an uncomfortable thing for an East Asian.

In the class was a lawyer from Britain who said professors in the U.S. are extremely accessible and go out of their way to help their students. One teacher said the law students learn to understand that their teacher's view of legal education is not the only view there is, that there are many other systems that approach the world in different ways. Another Japanese lawyer said he wasn't used to the freedom American students exercise to ask questions in the classroom. He rarely asked questions because of his cultural inhibition. If he did ask a question, he felt it must be a good question and would not impose on other students' time without a good reason.

Memorization – With orientation toward class discussion and analysis, we place less emphasis on rote memorization than many foreign classrooms, particularly those in Asia. Some educational systems in Asia do not teach students how to *apply* knowledge, but rather they learn to memorize, pass examinations, get into a good university, and ultimately get a good job. They will learn about this different orientation firsthand when they are enrolled in the U.S. and are quizzed in a manner different than they are accustomed to in their native country. They will learn that test answers and essays might get better grades if the student expresses his or her own opinion, supported of course by viable reasons for having that opinion.

> Hint: I had a teacher in graduate school who exemplified this different orientation when, on the first day of school, he told us he would be a "lamplighter, not a bucket filler." In other words, his emphasis would be getting us to think, analyze, draw our own conclusions and express them clearly—not to give us endless pages of notes to memorize. I loved his class.

Blackboard – Some foreign students expect an instructor to write down all important points for the lesson on the blackboard and feel they must copy everything that is written. They find it difficult to make notes from just listening to the instructor. It can take practice for these students in U.S. classrooms to quickly summarize the important points of a lecture, very often without information from a blackboard.

> **Hint**: To alleviate this note-taking stress, become friends with an American student in your class and ask to review and compare his or her class notes. You might learn some good techniques. Also, some schools offer study skill classes to help you develop these techniques. Some tutoring businesses like Kaplan offer classes in study skills as well (www.kaplan.com).

Class Participation – In the U.S. you will not be viewed as a troublemaker—as some foreign students believe—if you question the instructor. Some cultures, such as those in Asia, train children to listen more than to speak, to speak in a soft voice, and to be modest in dress and behavior. For this reason they are reluctant to raise their hands to ask questions or to offer their ideas or opinions in American classrooms. Foreigners might also be afraid of using English in front of American students. They fear they will take too long to express their opinions and the classmates and the instructor might think they are wasting time. This is probably not true.

> **Hint**: I was always told by my teachers that, "there is no such thing as a dumb question." My advice is to take small steps to overcome this fear. Start by asking a simple question in class, then graduate to making an observation. It also helps to establish a more personal relationship by talking to a professor after class, either in the classroom or in his or her office during posted office hours. Confidence builds upon confidence. We call this process **taking baby steps**.

Answering Questions – If someone in the U.S., perhaps a teacher, asks, "Do you understand?" some foreigners interpret this incorrectly as meaning "Did you hear me?" and will answer "yes" even if they don't understand. Or, some who don't understand will answer "yes" out of respect to their cultural rules of politeness because that is what they think the questioner wants to hear. Along the same line, the question "Do you have any questions?" will elicit a "no" from some even if they do have a question because they are trying to be polite, or in their culture they lose face if they are less than perfect. In our culture it is more important to be direct. Over time, foreigners will develop the confidence to answer a question honestly when they understand that there are no cultural overtones when we ask them questions. Remember our saying: **Tell it like it is**.

CULTURAL COURSES FOR INTERNATIONAL STUDENTS

Many of our colleges and universities have one- or two day orientation classes to help foreign students adapt to life in the U.S. Some have websites that do this. The University of Southern California (USC) in Los Angeles started a class titled "The United States: An American Culture Series" to help its international students learn about our "crazy" food, difficult idioms, and bewildering customs that surround them (www.usc.edu).

176

Because the university has the largest contingent of foreign students of any U.S. university (7500 students, with Asian Indians number one and Chinese second), it offered this free, non-credit course in American culture. The class met for two hours once a week for 12 weeks on an experimental basis in 2009. It was such a success it was expanded the next year to five classes on an on-going basis.

To succeed academically, the university said foreign students must adjust both *culturally* and *socially* to their new surroundings. So part of their goal was to ease international students' isolation. Some students said they felt trapped by their heavy academic loads, strong accents, shyness, and cultural confusion.

USC administration bldg.

Many topics discussed in this book were topics in the class. For example, the teacher taught the class about baseball (see Chapter N - Sports) and the sayings that spring from it that we use frequently: **Step up to the plate** (move into position to do a task). **Knock it out of the park** (do an outstanding job). **Cover all the bases** (make preparations thoroughly). **Don't drop the ball** (follow through to completion of your task). They also attended a football game, another popular sport here.

Numerous other topics were discussed.

- What are tailgate parties? (See Chapter O - Food and Dining)
- Who do you give Christmas gifts to? (See Chapter R - Holidays and Traditions)
- Is it an insult to call someone a **couch potato**—a person who spends too much time sitting or lying down, usually watching television? I say, why not if they are a close friend and you want to **shape them up** (improve them) or if you are teasing them in a good natured way.

"Couch potato."

- For what emergencies should you call the police? (If you feel in danger.)

The class explored mass transit and downtown Los Angeles landmarks, such as the Walt Disney Concert Hall. (See Chapter M - Art) They also went on fieldtrips.

- The California African American Museum (www.caamuseum.org) where they learned about the historical treatment of blacks and slaves in the U.S. (see Chapter D - History).
- The world-famous Getty art museum; see Chapter M - Art (www.getty.edu).
- An In-n-Out Burger drive-in, a favorite of many Southern California students (www.in-n-out.com).

They also participated in Halloween, Thanksgiving, and Christmas rituals (see Chapter R - Holidays and Traditions) and tasted related foods.

They studied idioms (see Chapter Z - Let's Speak Better English), including:

"Bent out of shape."

- **"Bent out of shape"** (aggravated or overly annoyed).
- **"Beat around the bush"** (delay or be indirect).
- **"Grab a bite"** (eat a quick snack).

Using practical exercises to better understand our sayings, the teacher asked the class who the **head honcho** (Spanish term for person in charge) was in the U.S. They replied "Barack Obama."

Broadening a student's social experiences and helping them meet new people outside their own culture was another goal of the program, another principle discussed in this book (see Chapter J - Relationships). It

"Head Honcho"

was difficult for many students to break out of their own national circles at school because their groups were large and concentrated in engineering programs, particularly for those from India and China. So they were encouraged to join campus clubs and volunteer efforts outside their immediate circles.

A Chinese graduate student said she felt she could interact more easily with Americans because of what she learned in the class. She said it also gave her topics for conversations with American classmates and, more importantly, taught her to express her own opinion, one of the objectives of our schools of higher learning and this book.

KAHN ACADEMY ASSISTANCE

The Khan Academy (www.kahnacademy.com) is a unique U.S. Internet-based, non-profit organization changing education for the better by providing an education to anyone anywhere. It can be a powerful learning tool for foreigners with its broad selection of topics. It doesn't matter if you are a student, teacher, home-schooler, principal, or an adult returning to the classroom after 20 years. Their materials and resources are completely free. Many schools in the U.S. and around the world now use this program so their students can learn at their own pace and leave teachers more time for individual instruction. (Bill Gates of Microsoft helped fund the academy.)

Students can access Kahn's extensive video library, practice exercises, and receive assessments on their progress from any computer with access to the Web. Their library of 3000 videos covers K-12 math, the sciences including biology, chemistry, and physics, and even delves into finance and history. Each video is an easily-comprehended segment approximately 10 minutes long. The step-by-step sessions are guided with the voice of a teacher who uses a magic pen, just as if the video were a classroom teacher with a blackboard.

J

RELATIONSHIPS

One word frees us of all the weight and pain in life.
That word is love. – Sophocles, ancient Greek playwright

Foreigners sometimes have difficulty figuring out how Americans form and maintain friendships because we have a different cultural definition of friendship and what friendship entails. A Japanese student studying in the U.S., for instance, took her visiting sister to a department store. A smiling clerk greeted them and said "Hi! How are you today?" Surprised by this warm greeting, the visiting sister asked "Do you know her?" Another foreign student was confused about why everyone was so nice and polite to her on her first day in the U.S. Social differences even extend to such things as marriage. In India, marriage is deemed essential for virtually everyone, marking the transition to adulthood. In America, our social attitude is some people want it, some don't.

Good friends.

It is difficult to provide an accurate guide to our social relations and customs because situations differ so greatly. Because we **do our own thing**, it can be difficult for foreigners to **pinpoint** (precisely define) our social customs and find a comfortable way to adjust to our ways. So, do not assume that you are not liked or respected by an American because he or she does not meet the expectations you have for friends in your native country. If you do, you might cut off a friendship unnecessarily and miss what it has to offer. Instead, just **chalk it up** (attribute it to) to cultural and social differences and keep working at it.

It is worth your effort to **get a handle** (understand) on how we view relationships so you can expand your relations with us. Here are some social factors about Americans you should keep in mind that might help you better understand our friendship process.

- *Friendliness* – In some cultures it can be difficult to make friends with someone unless you are properly introduced, and it might take a long time to be accepted. Many foreigners are surprised and pleased at their immediate acceptance by Americans who might be more **open** (willing to discuss) about a broader variety of subjects than some cultures that are initially more reserved.

- *Casualness* – Unlike some cultures, Americans might move seven to ten times in their lives, might change schools and jobs frequently, might join various volunteer organizations, and might change love interests. Because of this, we learn to make friends quickly. However, these casual friendships might not become the deep friendships that some foreigners expect. They are easily made and easily dissolved, so you might feel that our friendships are superficial and manipulative.

- *Directness* – Americans prefer to be direct in dealing with problems and conflicts or in discussing topics that other societies would share only with the immediate family. The concept of saving face is not as important in the U.S. as it is in many other cultures such as in Asia. We **tell it like it is**. In spite of this, there are certain areas of discussion that are considered private to some Americans and should be approached gently, such as personal finances, age, religious beliefs, sexual behavior, and political views.

- *Hygiene* – Most Americans place emphasis on personal hygiene and habits, and that can affect relationships. Because we are conscious of body odors, we use a variety of toiletries such as shampoos, perfumes, deodorants, and mouthwashes, and we generally bathe and change our clothes daily. We are **turned off** (offended) when others appear unhygienic by our standards. We also react negatively toward foreigners with annoying habits,  like those who noisily suck mucus down their throat and then spit it out or those who pick their noses in public.

- *Informality* – As long as one does not infringe on the rights of others, we accept a great deal of flexibility in personal expression. This informality is reflected in our casual relationships between persons of different ages and status. With this informality (and contrary to some cultures) we routinely address one another by their first (given) name even if we have just been introduced.

- *Rushed* – Life in the U.S. might at first seem rather rushed. We are usually time conscious, so punctuality is important to many, even among friends. This preoccupation with time can also cause us to appear impatient and abrupt when we encounter delays.

- *Independence* – Americans strive to be autonomous and self-reliant. We view ourselves more as individuals than members of a nation, community, or family, and dislike being dependent on other people or having others dependent on us, including friends. Because of these attitudes and beliefs, foreigners must be careful not to view us as being self-centered or unfriendly.

- *Privacy* – An old American proverb says "Friends are like fiddle strings; they must not be screwed too tight." Because we value our privacy and independence, we might prefer doing some things ourselves rather than asking for help. And we might feel we are imposing on others' privacy when we ask for too much help. As a result we tend to expect others not to impose on us.

- *Friends and Relatives* – In some countries like India, friends and relatives **pop in** (make unannounced visits) and their friends tend to **drop everything** (stop what they are doing) and enjoy their company. In America, neighbors who seem friendly might never pop in or visit. If they do, it might be set up formally because of their busy schedules. So foreigners may find the American single-minded focus on accomplishment disconcerting. However, once involved in the American workplace, newcomers often eventually adopt the same behavior with friends and relatives.

- *Gay-Lesbian Relationships* – A recent survey estimates that 3.5 percent of adults in the U.S. identify as lesbian, gay, transgender, or bisexual, with bisexuals making up a slight majority of that figure. Fifty percent of Americans believe same-sex marriages should be recognized by law as valid, with the same rights as traditional marriages. Forty-eight percent say such marriages should not be legal. In one survey, only a third favor amending the U.S. Constitution to make it illegal for homosexual couples to marry, whereas six out of ten say each state should make its own laws on gay marriage. (There's that *states' rights* thing again.) Over two-thirds at the time favored allowing military service by openly gay men and lesbians, which is now allowed thanks to the Obama Administration tossing out the old rule of "Don't ask, don't tell" that hid these secrets. The Administration also announced it would confront other nations that criminalize homosexual conduct, abuse gay men, lesbians, bisexuals or transgendered people, or ignore any abuse against them. (There's that *individual rights* thing again.)

Because of these and many other cultural differences, foreigners must not judge our social behavior in the same light they judge people in their native countries. If they do, they might deprive themselves of friendships. You also should not take our behaviors personally. Just accept it. It is often Americans who are missing out on having closer relationships.

With this background on our friendship process, let's now discuss how our friendships can evolve romantically from dating to engagement and then to marriage, perhaps a process you or your American counterpart will encounter.

DATING AND COURTSHIP

As you might expect, there is a wide array of romantic possibilities in American relationships. There is no set pattern and it is changing so quickly that the meaning might differ between generations, regions, and partners in a relationship.

Dating in the U.S. differs from some countries where free association with the opposite sex is limited and dating in the Western sense, such as in India, is essentially done by members of the educated urban elite. We might date many persons at the same time before going steady with one, whereas in France there is more commitment early on. American women complain that, unlike American men, their French boyfriends 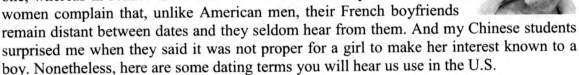 remain distant between dates and they seldom hear from them. And my Chinese students surprised me when they said it was not proper for a girl to make her interest known to a boy. Nonetheless, here are some dating terms you will hear us use in the U.S.

- *Boyfriend/Girlfriend* – Romantically, when you claim someone as one of these, you are probably inferring that you are not dating someone else. In other cultures, however, the term might not imply as serious a relationship as it does here. If there is no romance involved we refer to that person as a "male friend" or "female friend".

- *Dating* – This is the process that occurs when a couple spends time together, typically in a public place like a restaurant in order to learn more about each other. Some also call this **going out**.

- *Hanging Out* – You are spending time together in a casual or relaxed way with no romance.

- *Hooking Up* – This term has largely replaced the term dating with one important distinction: there is a sexual connotation.

- *Lover* – This implies that you are having sexual relations with this person, either with or without a serious relationship or emotional attachment. An emerging trend in our colleges, due to time and financial pressures of going to school and graduating, is the use of convenient "lover" relationships where there are none of the emotional and financial demands associated with a committed relationship.

- *Seeing Someone* – You've dated someone for a little while and it is getting serious.

- *Significant Other* – A person, such as a spouse or lover, with whom one shares a long-term sexual relationship. A colloquial term for this is **main squeeze**.

- *Steady* – This says that you are only dating one person steadily and no one else. You might refer to this other person as your "steady" or say you are "going steady."

Starting To Date – It is against the law to date in Iran where teens are separated until marrying age. In Japan and Korea, most high school students don't date or go to parties so they don't generally begin dating until college. In Central and South America, dating is not allowed until the age of 15. But in America, our teens start dating around age 15 or 16 by first attending mixed group activities, and then later attending with a partner. Parents frown upon a child dating only one person and becoming serious at this young age. A 19 year old Hawaiian tour guide said her mother forbid her from dating.

Asking Someone Out – Asking someone **out** means asking for a date. Men still tend to initiate invitations to dances, films, and other events more than women do. But it is also acceptable (contrary to our social customs thirty years ago) for a woman to ask a man to go out. Most men do not view a woman who does this as too assertive, as might be the case in some cultures. If the man invites, he will usually pay for the expenses incurred on the date. If a woman invites, the man might pay too, unless the woman offers to pay. Or, each will pay their portion, which we call **Dutch treat**. This arrangement is often used by college students with limited funds or suggested by women who want to assert their independence.

Equality In Dating – Many dating Americans like equality in their relationships, unlike Japan and Korea where the boy makes the date and pays for it, or in Russia where a woman would never think of paying. In the U.S., both share in the decisions about where they will go, who will drive, who will pay, etc. (There's that *equality* thing that you've heard so often in this book! Welcome to America, the land of equality.) Try to remember the equality word if you are dating an America. Feel free to question or offer your advice or opinion to your date, whether you are a man or a woman. You will be respected for this.

Public Affection – In most of the Western world such as Europe, Australia, New Zealand, Canada, and the U.S., we see people holding hands, hugging and kissing in public. In South Africa, it is against the law for anyone under the age of 16 to take part in any public display of affection; in India it is a criminal offense; in Pakistan couples can be arrested; and in South Korea it is improper and unacceptable. Also in America, a *casual* hug or kiss on the cheek is not an invitation to more intimacy. It can merely be a show of friendship. After a couple in America has become serious with each other, they might hold hands while walking or kiss on the lips in public. It is **no big deal** (nothing to be concerned about) as it might be in your country unless it is overdone.

Hint: I was in a stage play rehearsal with about 20 other actors in which a young actor and actress were frequently quite physically affectionate with each other in front of the rest of us. It made us feel uncomfortable and distracted us. Sexually suggestive behavior is not appropriate in public situations, especially not in business, though what we consider suggestive may differ from what others cultures find suggestive. So try to **tune in to** (observe) how we behave in groups with the opposite sex.

Just Be You – Foreigners need to be themselves on dates and not worry about how they think they should act with an American. This is one of the first things they teach us in acting school when we are learning to perform at auditions. If we actors are trying to figure out what we think *they* (the directors) want from us, we won't deliver what *we* are the best at delivering, which is *us*. Be honest in your opinions and feelings. Don't say what you think your date wants to hear. And if you don't understand something they say because of language differences, don't be embarrassed to say so (as is common in some cultures) and ask for clarification. In short, just be you.

Dating Safety – Because it is often difficult for newcomers to read the subtle physical and verbal cues in an unfamiliar culture, counselors suggest that foreigners interested in dating stick to group and **double-dating** (two couples) situations. That way they get to know new people and can get recommendations from trusted friends. There is relative safety in school, church, and neighborhood dating functions with group activities and/or adult supervision. Also, a good first date might be a coffee date or a public function and at a time no later than mid-afternoon. This allows the woman to learn more about her date in a safe environment and become comfortable with him. Here are additional suggestions that counselors say make dating safer.

- *Bad Feeling* – If you ever feel uncomfortable on a date, put politeness aside and go home immediately. If you didn't drive, call a taxicab or a friend.
- *Drinking* – For us, drinking is not ritualized as it is in some countries. But we do have problems with some college students who, for the first time in their lives, are overexposed to drinking and might behave differently than they would otherwise. (See Chapter H - Customs and Etiquette.)
- *Driving* – Drive yourself to the location on the first date so you can leave when you want.
- *Drugs* – Unfortunately, in America and other countries date rapes occur when drugs are put in a date's drink causing her to lose consciousness. Never let a drink out of your sight. If you go to the restroom, take your drink with you or order another one when you return. Some women order soft drinks or water in their original cans or bottles and they open them themselves.

- *Internet Dating* – Be careful with Internet-arranged dating. We frequently hear stories about these dates that have ended up in trouble. Some dating websites offer you the world in their advertisements, but just take your money. Ask your friends if they have had success with a particular one, or search Internet blogs for comments on them.
- *Background Check* - Internet firms such as www.ussearch.com can do a background check on an individual, including current address, phone number, address history, bankruptcies, civil judgments, liens, criminal background records and more.
- *Money* – If a date asks you to loan money to him or her or to use your credit card, do not cooperate and arrange to leave quickly.
- *Personal Info* – Do not tell a first date where you live or work or give out your telephone number until you get to know him or her better on subsequent dates. Never give out your social security number or allow a first date to see your driver's license or a bill that has your address.
- *Tell Someone* – Before leaving on a date, tell your roommate or friend who you are going with, where you are going, and when you will return.

Workplace Dating – One survey suggests that some 60 percent of our workers have **taken a shot at** (attempted) some kind of workplace romance, which is a worry to some employers. Of 617 companies that responded to a survey of their policies on workplace dating, 72 percent did not have a written policy; 14 percent said they had an unwritten but well understood norm in their workplace; thirteen percent did not have a policy. A personnel consultant says that if an employee's actions are polarizing a workgroup or causing it to lose its effectiveness, or if the employee is doing something that could embarrass the company, he or she is at risk. He adds, "If you're having a relationship and you think anybody in the place might be jealous or resentful of that, or might see it as distracting or potentially risky to the organization, you're better off not having that relationship. Or handle that relationship with absolute discretion." The heads of our Boeing aircraft and HP computer companies didn't and they were **canned** (fired).

On the **opposite side of the coin**, there are numerous examples of successful couples whose romances began and flourished on company time. Bill and Melinda Gates met when Melinda began working at Microsoft in 1987. They married in 1994. President Barack Obama worked as an intern for his future wife Michelle when she was an associate at a Chicago law firm. They married in 1992.

My advice: be professional in *all* aspects of your job.

Dinner Dates – Americans like to go to restaurants on dates. Chapter O on food and dining deals with dining etiquette, but there are a few general dating guidelines you should know. Be honest and tell your date what you like to eat. A pizza date might be all

185

you want instead of getting **dolled up** (dressed up) for a formal dinner somewhere else. In nice American restaurants, a host escorts the man and woman to a table and pulls out a chair for the woman to sit on. Because this is not a custom in some cultures, some women will sit down in another chair instead of the one intended for her. If the host doesn't pull out her chair, then her date should.

Feel free to ask your date what he or she would recommend eating. The man should order his date's drink first by saying "Would you like a drink?" Unlike some foreign customs where everyone is expected to drink, it is okay for your date to consume alcohol drinks while you don't, or vice versa.

Male Behavior – How should men behave on a date? Here is what counselors say about gentlemanly behavior that appeals to women in the U.S.

- *Confidence* – American women like men who are confident, but there is a fine line between confidence and cockiness, arrogance, or dominance that males in certain cultures display. Confidence is an attitude of "I'll do my best to deal with it."
- *Doors* – When entering or exiting a car, some men like to walk around to the passenger side and open the door for the woman. This is not as important as it once was, but it is still a nice gesture. Unlike some cultures, you politely let the woman walk through a door before you do. This is the mark of a gentleman.
- *Equality* – Women like to be treated with respect and equality. Treat her like a partner when making dating decisions.
- *Feelings* – Women like men who are willing to talk about their feelings and who are sincerely interested in theirs.
- *Flowers* – If you, sir, pick a woman up for a date, you might give her a small bouquet of flowers. It's the thought that counts for her.
- *Parents* – If you meet her parents or roommate, be gracious. They *will* discuss you and they will pass judgment even though it was a brief meeting. (Review conversation skills in Chapter H - Customs and Etiquette.)
- *Time* – Be on time. Yes, you might have to wait for her to get ready, but you still win points for being on time.

An article in America's *Playboy* magazine discussed things men can do to enhance their image with women (www.playboy.com). On your date, you should:

- *Assist Her* – Be a gentleman. A willingness to open doors, help on with coats, and pull out chairs for her shows you are a man **in the know** (knowledgeable) she can count on and look up to.

186

- *Reliable* – Keep your word and be reliable. Show up when and where you say you will. Do what you say you will do. Don't make promises you can't fulfill and don't be boastful.
- *Share* – Be willing to reveal some personal information about yourself. It isn't necessary to reveal everything, but your date shouldn't get the idea that you are keeping secrets.
- *Waiters* – Be patient with service people (waiters, clerks, etc.) because she will be looking to see how well you treat people. In my observations, some foreigners are lacking in this department; again, a cultural thing. Be sure to make eye contact when greeting your server. How well you treat them might in turn affect the service they afford you.

Female Behavior – How should women behave on a date? A recent magazine survey listed those things about women that attract men the most. Personality *[purr-son-AHL-ah-tee]* (socially attractive qualities) comes first followed by beauty, sense of humor, smile, intelligence, and finally legs (yes legs, mind you).

Men appreciate women who are honest in sharing their opinions and feelings, but not too aggressively. Some foreigners have a cultural habit of saying with ease what they *don't* want, but have difficulty explaining what they *do* want. This can drive guys nuts and they might mutter to themselves "**Give me a break!**" (help me out here). Learn to say what you want. Other suggestions from experts, some of which might differ from your customs back home:

- *Boyfriends* – Don't discuss your past or present boyfriends with him.
- *Calling Him* – If you, madam, call a man once and invite him out and he declines, tell him to call you if he wants to get together in the future, and then do not call him again.
- *Doors* – If you want him to open the door, pause in front of it to give him a chance to open it. If the door opening doesn't matter to you, then go ahead and open it yourself—he will appreciate your honesty.
- *Dress* – Don't under- or overdress on dates. Some foreign women have a problem selecting the right dress for a date. If you aren't sure what is appropriate dress for the occasion, ask him. If he plans to wear a tie, you should **dress up** as well. (Chapter P on dress and appearance deals with dressing for different occasions.)
- *Flowers* – When a man picks you up for a date, he might bring you flowers. Be gracious as the two of you put them in a vase. If you pick him up, however, flowers or a gift are not expected. Yes, we *do* have double standards, but not many in our culture of equality.

- *His Past* – Don't pry into his personal affairs, such as his past girlfriends, how much his job pays, etc. On the other hand, do show some interest in him by asking non-personal questions. Don't make the conversation all about you.
- *Makeup* – Don't look repeatedly in a mirror at your makeup and hairdo when you are with him. This sends the message these things are more important than he is and that you lack self-confidence.
- *Smells* – Use only a small amount of perfume or none at all; Americans are sensitive to smells.
- *Sports* – Some guys love to talk about sports. Pay special attention to Chapter N - Sports. Ask what his favorite team or player is and why. You might tell him a little about sports in your own country. But if you hate sports it is okay to be honest and just say so.
- *Tab* – If you invite him out, offer to pay when the time comes to pay. He might decline your offer and pay himself, but give him the option, or you might just split the bill.
- *Time* – Be on time.
- *Walking* – Allow your date to walk on the street side of the sidewalk.

At the end of the date, give your date some indication as to whether or not you would like to see him again. You could say "I had a wonderful time, let's be sure to do it again." Or, you might suggest another meeting, like "I had a great time. Would you like to join me tomorrow night for a four-hour English grammar lecture on past tense perfect progressive verbs?" (which we discuss in Chapter Y on using better English grammar). In other words, your date *wants* to know if the dating door has been closed or left open for him. If you don't want to date him again, be polite and just thank him for taking you out, but no more. Most guys will get your message.

> **Hint**: Just as women like men who are confident, most American men like women who are confident. If a woman is shy and unable to express her opinions and wishes, as some foreigners can appear to be, she will not impress most American men. On the other hand, if she is controlling and domineering, she won't either. Try to strike a good balance.

Interracial Dating – Helen Keller, a famous blind and deaf American educator, said, "The highest result of education is tolerance." Americans are approaching unanimity in our acceptance of marriages between races. Over the past century, intermarriage has evolved from being illegal, to being **taboo** (a moral restriction), to being unusual. And with each passing year, it becomes less unusual. As an example, 86 percent now approve of such unions between blacks and whites versus four percent in 1958.

A Pew study found that 15 percent of U.S. marriages in 2010 were interracial: white/Hispanic (43%), white/Asian (14%) and white/black (10%). This is up from 3.2 percent in 1980. Race relations improved when the Supreme Court in 1967 barred race-based restrictions on marriage. Minorities, young adults, the higher educated and those living in western or northeastern states are more likely to say mixed marriages are a change for the better for society. Hispanics and Asians remain the most likely, as in previous decades, to marry someone of a different race.

(www.socialtikmag.com)

Hint: Classic films about interracial love stories include the musical *South Pacific* (1958) and *Guess Who's Coming to Dinner* (1967). *Bad Day at Black Rock* (1955) is about a small town's Japanese American prejudice.

When I am asked about the question of foreigners dating Americans, my answer is always "Don't worry about it. Be yourself and be proud of who you are. Be proud of your heritage. Do what *you* want to do, not what you think others think you should do." As a nation we are becoming more tolerant of others, but you still might find some people who are not. I view this as their problem, not yours.

Hint: I have a wonderful black American friend who was married to a white Swedish woman and had two beautiful daughters. I was shocked when he told me they had received negative comments or looks from white strangers on the street who did not approve of blacks being with whites. He also told me, to my astonishment, that when he was recently in New Orleans, Louisiana, a white store clerk ignored his asking for help and waited on white customers instead. If you are a student coming to college in America or live in a larger city, you will probably be in a liberal environment where you will not experience such bigotry that usually develops in the family and is passed on.

Ethnicity and religion are personal beliefs that are developed in the family unit and can take generations to change. I have a first-generation Korean American friend whose 19-year-old son was not allowed to date non-Korean girls. But I have other Asian American friends who date interracially and have married interracially. As you are learning, here in America we **do our own thing** and sometimes go outside the bounds of family traditions. If you do not feel comfortable with those of a different religion or race, it is best not to put them (or you) in an uncomfortable position by accepting a date with them. On the other hand, you might just **broaden your horizons** (expand your knowledge) from going on such a date.

Hint: I was surprised when a friend told me that he loved to date Asian women in the U.S., but only those who were immigrants, not those who were born and raised here. He said immigrants are more appealing because they have not adopted the sharper edge that American women have, are more feminine acting, and do not have attitude issues that affect their personality negatively. This is yet another example of how our cultures affect who we become.

An Asian American reporter in San Francisco examined the dating relationships of Asians and Americans, and why some Asian American women prefer to date whites, or not date at all. The social dynamics might be relevant to other cultures as well.

- Asian American men are too old-fashioned, too sexist, or too short.
- Asian American men are thought of as inarticulate, unromantic, unfeeling, and only interested in money and material goods.
- Japanese American men tend to keep their emotions hidden, which distances them from wife and children.
- Traditional male gender roles of authority cause some Asian American women to seek relationships with those of other ethnic backgrounds.
- Because Asian American women tend to become acculturated faster than Asian American men, there is greater incentive for them to adapt because they gain more power and freedom. There is less incentive for men because they already are held in high esteem in their own cultures.

Dating And Sex – If you are **going steady**, that is, dating one person exclusively, there might be certain things expected of you. Counselors say you need to have a clear understanding with your partner what the expectations and boundaries are of going steady, and be ready to express yours. This also applies to the role of sex in your relationship. Sex, of course, can occur whether or not you are going steady, but is probably more likely with a "steady" partner.

Studies indicate that more than 75 percent of young people in the U.S. have had sexual intercourse by the age of 19. In recent years, however, student and teen organizations have promoted the virtues of abstaining from sex until after marriage. Aside from our religions and individual family values, there are no set rules today regarding sex as there was prior to the 1960s when sex before marriage was culturally frowned upon. If you are both at that stage in your relationship where you feel ready to engage in any sexual activity, counselors say that talking about it first will help you be informed about the potential physical, emotional, and health risk-reducing options available to you.

Hint: Counselors say you need to be honest with yourself and your beliefs and those of your partner. Do not be pressured into having sex because you think it is "the right thing to do," or it is the custom in America. AIDS and other sexually transmitted diseases are a big concern to Americans. In addition, unwanted pregnancies are on the rise. If you choose sex, counselors say to practice safe sex by using condoms and common sense. Condoms can be purchased at most drug stores and supermarkets. If your partner refuses to respect your concern, you should leave the relationship. **Caution for males:** Some women will lie and tell their partner they are on **the pill** (pregnancy prevention) so it is okay not to use a condom. They will do this to get pregnant and force the man to marry her and take care of her financially.

If someone forces sex on you against your will in the U.S., they have committed a serious crime and should be reported to the police. In many parts of the world, marriage is interpreted as granting men the right to unconditional sexual access to their wives and the power to enforce this access through force if necessary. Because of this, many women agree to have sex even if they do not want it. For example, in the Western Visayas region of the Philippines, four out of ten married women surveyed said they were afraid to refuse their husbands' sexual advances, often because refusal might cause their husbands to beat them. **In the U.S., any woman, married or not, can say no to sex for whatever reason and her wishes MUST be respected. If she is beaten, she should report it to the police. This is a serious crime. Foreigners could be deported if found guilty.**

> **Hint**: The University of Michigan website at www.uofmhealth.org/health-library discusses many health issues. Click on Safe Sex to learn about sexually transmitted diseases and tips for participating in safe sex.

Living Together – When two unmarried people of the opposite sex live together without marriage, we call it **cohabitation** *[ko-hab-ih-TAY-shun]*, **living together,** or the slang phrase **shacking-up**. In the U.S. today, about two-thirds choose to live with their partners before marriage (or before breaking up) compared to 10 percent in the 1950s. The number in England is 70 percent. In Denmark and Sweden, 90 percent cohabitate. Despite its popularity in the diverse U.S., be aware there are those who still might view you in a negative light if they learn you are shacking-up, including employers.

Couples choosing this lifestyle give reasons like economics and getting to know their partner better. Yet a Yale University study concludes that after marriage, cohabiting women were 80 percent more likely to separate or divorce than were women who had not lived with their spouses before marriage. Another study found that one of the major reasons men say they are reluctant to get married at all is because they can live with a woman and enjoy the benefits without the responsibilities. You may hear the saying, **why buy a cow when you can get the milk free,** that reflects this belief.

ENGAGEMENT

After a couple has been dating and concluded they want to eventually get married, they can first become **engaged** for a period of time, generally six months to a year but there is no fixed time. Long-term engagements have become quite common, especially if the couple is young and trying to finish school or build up savings for the wedding. When couples become engaged, each partner vows to limit their dating to each other. If you or your American friend might become engaged, there are a few things you should know.

The Proposal – Typically the man asks the woman if she will marry him; we call this the **proposal.** In more informal situations, a couple might discuss getting married and simply agree to become engaged. The traditional idea is that he will get on one knee, as

191

men did in the old days, and open a box with an engagement ring in it, then propose marriage. In the old days, a man first asked the father of the woman if he approved of their marriage. If he objected, the engagement did not proceed. Today, most couples first become engaged and then tell their parents about it. Depending on the family structure, some children still marry even if the parents object. This is quite a contrast to more formal procedures like those in the Philippines where the groom and his family might visit the bride's family to ask for permission and discuss wedding plans.

A proposal.
(WeddingsAvenue.com)

Occasionally the media will report a man making a proposal in front of thousands of people at a sporting event before the game begins. Other "romantic" proposals might occur at a woman's job with all her workers there to observe. Billboards (large outdoor advertisements) and airplanes pulling banners for all to see have been used. There is no end to American ingenuity when it comes to marriage proposals. So don't be surprised if you experience one of these that would be considered weird in your country.

Once engaged, the man is called the **fiancé**, and the woman is called the **fiancée**. Both are pronounced as *fee-ON-say* even though they have different spellings. (Yes, these are two more borrowed French words in our crazy language that we discuss in Chapter Y on using better English grammar.)

Selecting The Ring – Typically the couple chooses two rings for the potential bride—the **engagement ring** and the **wedding ring**—and a wedding band for the man. Like everything else in America, we like options about rings, too. The woman or man may also choose not to wear a ring. Depending on finances, a couple might decide to forgo an engagement ring and just acquire a wedding ring when the time comes to get married. The engagement ring might be selected by the couple before the engagement

His and her rings.

is announced or by the man if he wants to surprise his love. Typically the wedding rings might be simple bands and her engagement ring might have diamonds, the average price of which is $3,500 today.

Parties Before Wedding – Some cultures have an engagement ceremony, like the Japanese *yunio* ceremony, in which the engagement is sealed and symbolic exchanges of gifts are made. In America, we are less formal, but some engaged couples might celebrate with an **engagement party** that introduces the two families and their friends to each other. There are no set rules for who hosts it. It can be informal, like a backyard barbeque, or it can be a formal affair in a banquet hall. Gifts are not expected at engagement parties, but they are a nice gesture.

Girlfriends of the bride will usually give her a **bridal shower** where she is "showered" with gifts. Usually a shower is for women only, but sometimes the groom and his friends are included, too. They often have a theme where gifts are chosen for a specific need. The party might be a kitchen shower, bathroom shower, gourmet shower or a personal shower.

The male friends of the groom might provide him with a **bachelor party** to which women are not invited.

> **Hint**: The humorous young Tom Hanks film, *Bachelor Party* (1984), is about a party thrown by his friends on the eve of his wedding. It explores the temptations of being unfaithful to his fiancée. A similar film is *The Hangover* (2009) in which the groom-to-be and his friends celebrate his bachelor party in Las Vegas. Classic romantic films include *It happened One Night* (1934), *An Affair to Remember* (1957), *When Harry Met Sally* (1989), and *Sleepless in Seattle* (1993).

WEDDING

An American friend may invite you to attend or participate in his or her wedding ceremony. The following will give you a **heads up** (a necessary understanding) about the ceremony and perhaps what your role might be.

Marriage begins with a formal ceremony known as the **wedding** that unites the couple. In some cultures, marriage involves the formal transfer of property from parents to their marrying children or from one set of parents to the other. This formal exchange of property, known as a **dowry** *[DOW-ree]*, is not done in America where marriage is supposedly based on love, not wealth or possessions. In India where dowry was outlawed in 1961, a bride still might be expected to bring gold into the marriage, a form of dowry nonetheless. Also, marriage in some countries where they are arranged by parents is viewed as a coming together of families. In the U.S. it is more a coming together of a couple.

Weddings can be attended by just the couple or by hundreds of guests. Often the high cost of weddings might limit who attends. Once the wedding date is decided, the bride or her family sends out **wedding invitations** with names chosen by both families.

Chinese and Vietnamese couples might consult a lunar calendar to determine the best day for marriage. In Odessa, Ukraine, I witnessed numerous weddings on Fridays, which I learned gives the couple a longer window for a honeymoon. In America, good old practicality rules and the date chosen is a matter of convenience. June is our most popular month for weddings because students have just graduated or have a break in their college studies or work, plus the weather is nice throughout the U.S.

Unlike women in Asian, Muslim, and other countries, most women in the U.S. adopt the last name of their husband. Today, less than eight percent do not. This is down from 23 percent in the 1990s when our Women's Rights Movement that started in the

1970s was in **full swing** (highest level of activity). Some women also choose to hyphenate their "old" (called the maiden name) and "new" last names.

Types Of Weddings – Our wedding ceremonies range from informal to formal, and religious to civil. Religious ceremonies are conducted by a clergy member in a traditional religious setting. Each of our religions has its distinctive wedding customs and ceremonies. On the other hand, some couples prefer to have a civil wedding ceremony in a commercial wedding chapel or reception hall, home, courthouse, or government office. These ceremonies are conducted by a judge or clerk and can be simple and less expensive that a more formal wedding.

Formal weddings have become expensive, averaging $26,000. This includes costs for the minister, chapel or hall, the food, invitations, wedding dresses, etc. Unlike countries like China and the Middle East where the groom usually pays for the expensive wedding reception, the bride's family is often responsible for the major cost of the wedding in the U.S. unless the couple is older and on their own. But our groom pays for the minister or the person officiating at the ceremony and for the **rehearsal dinner** for the parents and attendants who will be in the wedding ceremony. Some couples and parents might choose to split the costs or make other arrangements. (Are you getting the impression that, like our founding immigrants, we are open to discussing how something will be done rather than just relying on tradition?)

If a couple decides not to have a formal wedding ceremony, they might **elope**, *[ee-LOPE]* a cheaper alternative where they choose to go out of town and marry, usually in a civil ceremony. Many go to the western gambling resort town of **Las Vegas, Nevada**, called the **Wedding Capital of The World**. It has 100 wedding chapels that perform over 120,000 weddings ceremonies each year, some starting at $100. Even celebrities like Elvis Presley and Frank Sinatra were married there.

Wedding Capitol of the World.

Traditional Wedding Ceremony – At a traditional wedding ceremony, music is played as the father escorts the bride from the back of the room or church, past the seated guests, down to the awaiting minister or official where the bridegroom is standing. The **bride** is usually dressed in white. Because of the expense of buying a dress, some brides rent wedding gowns. The **groom** and his attendants are dressed in tuxedos (formal attire) that are probably rented, too. Standing with the groom is the **best man** who holds the bride's wedding ring and the **matron of honor** who holds the groom's wedding ring. Other attendants include **bridesmaids** who usually carry flowers and **ushers** or **groomsmen** who are friends of the groom and show guests to their seats before the ceremony begins. In Christian ceremonies, friends and relatives of the bride traditionally

194

sit on the left side, and those of the bridegroom on the right. In Jewish ceremonies the opposite is true.

The **ceremony** *[SERR-ah-mon-ee]* (spoken words) begins when the bride stands facing her husband-to-be to exchange vows (spoken promises). In some cases, the couple writes their own words for the ceremony beforehand. But traditionally the minister asks the bride and groom if they "promise to love, honor and cherish,* for better and for worse, for richer and for poorer, in sickness and in healthy, until death do you part," to which they respond "I do."

Wedding ceremony in a church setting.

Wedding Reception – Following the wedding ceremony, a **reception** is customarily held where friends and family gather to eat, drink, dance, and make toasts to the bride and groom. Sometimes the bride and groom and their parents form a reception line where they greet and thank each guest for attending their wedding as guests enter the reception room.

Sometimes buffet lines are used to serve food. Other times sit-down meals are served. Toward the end of the reception the couple cuts a wedding cake that is then shared with the guests. The cake topping is often a bride and groom figure that becomes a souvenir for the couple. Those who attend can sign a **guest book** that the couple keeps for a lifetime.

Wedding cake.

People may bring gifts and leave them in a specific area during the reception, but it is better etiquette to send gifts to the couple before the wedding. Many couples use a **bridal registry** service offered by retailers that specifies the types of items they would most like to receive, a convenience now offered in Japan, too.

During the reception, an American bride may toss her floral bouquet over her shoulder to a group of single women. It is believed that the woman who catches it will be the next to marry. The bridegroom removes a garter (stocking supporter) from the bride's upper leg and tosses it to a waiting group of single men. The man who catches it is believed to be the next man to marry. Sometimes the best man and the other attendants secretly decorate the groom's car with sayings like "just married" and with objects like tin cans and old shoes tied to the rear bumper to announce their marriage. Another tradition is the tossing of rice at the couple as they exit after the ceremony.

---

*Up until the 1970s, the word "obey" was used instead of "cherish" when this question was asked of the bride. This reflects the female-related cultural advances we've made in the U.S. over the last thirty years.

The Honeymoon – After the wedding, the couple usually leaves for a vacation away from friends and family. This might last for a few days to several weeks, depending on the couple's financial and time constraints. Some parents might give the bride and groom a honeymoon as a gift. Favorite honeymoon spots are Hawaii, the Caribbean, and Mexico. **Niagara Falls** *[nye-AG-rah]* in New York State is a traditional honeymoon destination where 3,160 tons of water flows over the falls every second. (A popular movie about this spot is *Niagara*, starring Marilyn Monroe.) Some hotels in the U.S. have romantic **honeymoon suites** designed for newlyweds, but not limited to use only by them.

Niagara Falls, New York.

> **Hint**: We have a saying, "**The honeymoon is over**," that we apply to non-wedding situations to indicate that things are back to normal. For example, when our new president takes office there is always a friendly relationship between the White House and Congress where each pledges to work with the other and put politics aside to do what is best for the country. After several months, however, "the honeymoon is over" and things return to normal when friction develops and political posturing resumes.

DIVORCE

The U.S. has the 5th highest divorce rate in the world with 3.4 divorces per every 1000 people. That equates to about one out of every two marriages. Due to male infidelity and abusive treatment of wives, Russia now has the world's highest rate: 5 divorces per 1000 people. This is why some Russian women prefer to have relationships with foreign men and use Internet dating sites.

Surveys show that forty percent of Americans believe that lack of effective communication very frequently causes a marriage or relationship to end. Money problems are the second most divisive factor followed by interference of relatives or in-laws (14%), sexual problems (12%), previous relationships (9%), and children (7%).

An interesting study by Cornell University defined the prescription for a healthy marriage in America. They interviewed 1200 Americans, most of who were age 70 or older and had experienced all the **ups and downs** (good and bad times) marriage brings. Here are their conclusions.

- Marry someone a lot like you. Similarity in core values in particular is the key to a happy marriage. (Foreign heritage values might cause problems for those who marry outside their culture.)
- Marry someone for whom you feel deep friendship as well as love.
- Don't keep score. Don't take the attitude that marriage must always be a 50-50 proposition because you can't get out exactly what you put in.

196

- Talk to each other. Long-term married partners are talkers to one another and about things that count.
- Don't commit to your partner; commit to marriage itself.

However, divorces do occur and their proceedings differ from one country to another. Divorce is not permitted in some countries such as Malta and the Philippines where marriages are dissolved by annulment (voided). In India where arranged marriage is still prominent, divorce is not deemed acceptable so a concerted effort is made to work through relationship problems or to remain in unhappy marriages. But in the U.S. where half our marriages end in divorce, we do not have a stigma against divorce as we did 50 years ago except in some religions like the Catholic Church.

Divorces can take a year or more if the matter proceeds to a court trial. The legal process can be complicated with issues of spousal support, child custody and support, distribution of property, and division of debt. Like other issues in the U.S., our courts prefer the parties negotiate their own settlement rather than impose its decisions. So 95 percent of divorces in the U.S. are uncontested because the two parties are able to come to an agreement and they don't have to **fight it out** in court.

In the U.S. there are nine community property states: Arizona, California, Idaho, Louisiana, Nevada, New Mexico, Texas, Washington, and Wisconsin. In these states the property acquired by the husband or the wife during the course of the marriage is divided equally upon divorce. Our state with the lowest divorce rate is Massachusetts, and couples in New York City have the lowest divorce rate of our metropolitan areas.

"Your divorce is granted. Case closed."

Our "wedding capitol of the world"—Las Vegas, Nevada—has the highest divorce rate in the U.S. because couples from all over the nation use it for a **quickie divorce**. There, a Nevada resident can get a divorce in as little as one to two weeks while non-residents can use Nevada's short residency statute that allows them to establish residency in only six weeks and one day (compared to six-months to a year in other states). Based on average hourly billing rates of lawyers across the country, the most expensive city in America for getting divorced is Los Angeles, California. Second to that is New York, followed by San Francisco and Miami.

The subject of celebrity divorces may come up in conversations with your American counterpart. Given our one-out-of-two divorce rate, it seems that when celebrity couples get married it isn't too long before we learn they, too, are divorcing. This website tracks these breakups: www.whosdatedwho.com/sections/celebrity-divorces/.

K

LITERATURE

A bookstore is one of the only pieces of evidence we have that people are still thinking. - Jerry Seinfeld, comedian

Noted 20th century author **C.S. Lewis** said, "Literature adds to reality, it does not simply describe it. It enriches the necessary competencies that daily life requires and provides; and in this respect, it irrigates the deserts that our lives have already become." An understanding of our literature can do the same for your perspective of America and its people.

This chapter discusses key American authors and their works that have remained popular for generations. Some are required reading in our high schools and colleges. The selection provides a good cross section of our fiction, drama, and poetry. You might choose to read some of the works mentioned, see movies based on them, or just familiarize yourself with their names and titles. Whatever you choose, referring to them in a conversation might impress your American counterpart. You will find, however, that not all Americans will be familiar with them.

As we discuss these authors and their works, several prestigious awards are mentioned. Starting in 1901, the **Nobel Prize** *[no-BELL]* was the first annual international award for achievements in literature as well as physics, chemistry, medicine, and peace. It was not until 1930 that Sinclair Lewis was the first American to win the prize for literature.

Nobel Prize for literature medal.

In 1917, Joseph Pulitzer, publisher of a New York newspaper, established the **Pulitzer Prize** *[PULL-its-zerr]* through an endowment to Columbia University in New York City. Annual Pulitzer awards are given for books by American authors and other categories (www.pulitzer.org). The only U.S. president awarded a Pulitzer Prize for literature was John F. Kennedy for his *Profiles in Courage* book. Appendix 6 contains a selected list of Pulitzer Prize-winning fiction authors and their books that some Americans will recognize if you use their names.

When you read the works of these American authors, you might recall the names of your country's writers and begin to see more similarities in our lives. For instance, the novels of China's great writer Luhsun (1881-1936) encompass the sorrow, struggles, and pain of his people. American writers **Faulkner**, **Hemingway**, **Hawthorne**, **Melville**, and **Steinbeck** explore these same topics. Literature reveals how our basic human struggles are the same around the world.

HISTORICAL PERSPECTIVE

America's literature reflects our changing culture down through the centuries. Much of our early literature evoked a European style placed in a **New World** (Western Hemisphere) setting. Then in the 1800s our literature changed as our culture changed.

The 1800s – In 1836, ex-minister **Ralph Waldo Emerson** (1803-1882) published a startling nonfiction work called *Nature* in which he claimed it was possible to dispense with organized religion and reach a lofty spiritual state by studying and responding to the natural world. **Henry David Thoreau** (1817-1862) was a nonconformist whose radical writings expressed a deep-rooted tendency toward individualism in the American character, something you have already learned about in this book. As our literature progressed during this era, America was also finding its cultural identity.

The 1900s – At the beginning of the 20th century as America was growing socially, economically, and internationally, American novelists expanded to encompass both high and low life. In addition to fiction, the 1920s were a rich period for drama. There had not been an important American dramatist until **Eugene O'Neill** (1888-1953) wrote his plays. Another strikingly original American playwright was **Tennessee Williams** (1911-1983) who expressed his Southern heritage in poetic yet sensational plays, usually about a sensitive woman trapped in a rough environment. His plays are still performed today and some have become popular movies, including *A Streetcar Named Desire*, *Cat on a Hot Tin Roof*, *Sweet Bird of Youth*, *The Night of the Iguana*, and *Baby Doll*.

Today – After World War II, mainstream America became receptive to the diverse voices of black writers and eventually fiction by members of other minority groups emerged. Many people in the spotlight today write books. Bill and Hillary Clinton told their stories. Our former head of counterintelligence told how the Bush administration ignored his warnings about a terrorist attack before 9/11. The list is endless for these popular **tell all** books, many by celebrities.

Authors widely read today in the U.S. include John Grisham, John Irving, Scott Turow, Nora Roberts, Danielle Steele, Stephen King, Dan Brown, Sue Grafton, and Toni

Morrison. Our classic authors, however, from Hawthorne to Steinbeck that we discuss below are still widely read.

SELECTED AMERICAN AUTHORS

Old Chinese proverb: "A book holds a house of gold." In keeping with this sage observation, here is a chronological selection of classic American authors and their works of gold that span a broad spectrum of U.S. history, culture, and writing styles. Many are required reading in our college English literature classes. (Some of their works can be downloaded as e-books or ordered in print from www.Amazon.com and other sources.)

NATHANIEL HAWTHORNE *[HAW-thorn]* (1804-1864)

Hawthorne

Hawthorne gained international fame for his novel ***The Scarlet Letter*** (1850), considered a masterpiece of American literature. Probing the darker side of human nature, he set many stories against the somber background of **Puritan** (adheres to strict religious principles) **New England**, the world of his ancestors. Hawthorne believed that sin (like adultery in *Letter*) results in the isolation of the sinners and more suffering until the sinners either destroy themselves or seek forgiveness and rejoin the community.

"Happiness is like a butterfly which, when pursued, is always beyond our grasp, but, if you will sit down quietly, may alight upon you." - Nathaniel Hawthorne

HENRY WADSWORTH LONGFELLOW (1807-1882)

Longfellow

Longfellow was the most widely published American poet of the 1800s. Many of his poems remain among the most familiar in American literature, including "Evangeline" and "The Courtship of Miles Standish." Among his popular shorter poems are "The Village Blacksmith," and "The Wreck of the Hesperus." "The Song of Hiawatha," published in 1855, captures the humanity and nobility he saw in American Indians. (The poem can be read at www.theotherpages.org/poems/hiawatha.html.)

"**Paul Revere's Ride**" recounts Revere's historic ride through his New England village to alert his neighbors to the oncoming British army during the American Revolution in the 1770s. (The full poem can be found at poetry.eserver.org/paul-revere.html.) Some adults might still remember these introductory lines they learned in their early school years.

> "Listen my children and you shall hear
> Of the midnight ride of Paul Revere,
> On the eighteenth of April, in Seventy-five;
> Hardly a man is now alive...."

EDGAR ALLAN POE (1809-1849)

Poe

Perhaps our first writer to produce bold new fiction and poetry, Poe explored levels of human psychology that were never previously discussed. He pushed the boundaries of fiction toward mystery and fantasy. His tales include decaying castles, forbidden passions, and guilt-ridden and insane criminals. His short story, "The Murders in the Rue Morgue" (1841), is considered the first modern detective story. "The Raven" (1845) is Poe's best-known poem.

"Poetry is the rhythmical creation of beauty in words." - Edgar Allen Poe

HERMAN MELVILLE *[MEL-vil]* (1819-1891)

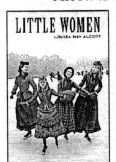

Melville

Melville wrote *Moby-Dick* (1851), a great novel upon which his reputation largely rests. But many of his other works are literary creations of fact, fiction, adventure, and symbolism. *Moby-Dick* is a fierce white whale supposedly known to sailors of Melville's time. The captain of a whaling ship lost a leg in an earlier battle with the whale and is determined to catch it. *Moby-Dick* is a symbolic story in which the whale represents the mysterious and complex force of the universe, and the captain symbolizes the heroic struggle against the limits that confront man. (The film was made in 1956.)

"Life's a voyage that's homeward bound." - Herman Melville

LOUISA MAY ALCOTT *[AL-kot]* (1832-1888)

Alcott

Alcott is best known for her novel *Little Women* (1868). It tells the story of four sisters growing up in a New England town and the courage, humor, and ingenuity they display to survive poverty and the absence of their father during the Civil War. Two of the sisters fall in love while the heroine develops a career as a writer. The book is popular among young American girls and is required reading in some high schools. (The film of the same name was made in 1994.)

"Life is my college. May I graduate well, and earn some honors!" - Louisa May Alcott

MARK TWAIN (1835-1910)

Mark Twain changed what Americans expected from their literature by having his characters speak like real people and sound distinctly American. He used regional slang accents. Considered the greatest humorist in American literature, he says, "Humor is the great thing, the saving thing. The minute it crops up, all our irritations and resentments slip away and a sunny spirit takes their place." Coupled with his humor about life, he wrote about racism, class conflicts, and poverty. His stories about the Mississippi River are especially popular among modern readers who learn about life in the mid-1800s.

Twain

The Adventures of Tom Sawyer is a classic novel read by children and adults alike. Published in 1870, it tells of life in small-town America before the outbreak of the American Civil War in 1861. The book's hero is a mischievous but good-hearted boy living in a Missouri town along the Mississippi River. Tom and his friend Huck Finn accidentally witness a murder and Tom later reveals the real killer. (You can read it free at this website: www.online-literature.com/twain/tomsawyer/.)

Adventures of Huckleberry Finn, considered Twain's greatest work, was published as a sequel to *Tom Sawyer*. A teenaged **misfit** (unacceptable) finds himself floating on a raft down the Mississippi River with a young escaping slave. Tom Sawyer reappears and his antics provide the familiar Twain humor. It was a controversial book when first published. Some people still dislike the novel because of Huck's unrefined manners and language. (Read it free at etext.virginia.edu/twain/huckfinn.html.) The Mark Twain Boyhood Home Museum has this website: www.marktwainmuesum.org.

"The human race has one really effective weapon, and that is laughter." - Mark Twain

SINCLAIR LEWIS (1885-1951)

Lewis gained international fame for his novels by attacking the weaknesses he saw in American society. In 1930, he became the first American author to win the Nobel

Lewis

Prize for literature. *Main Street* (1920) caused a sensation and brought him immediate fame. The book is a penetrating satire on the dullness and lack of culture that exist in a typical American small town, and the narrow-mindedness and self-satisfaction of its inhabitants. Written in minute detail, it shows the fruitless efforts of the heroine to awaken and improve her town.

Babbitt (1922) focuses on Lewis' idea of a typical small city businessman. The novel describes the futile attempt of its central character to break loose from the confining life of a "solid

American citizen"—a middle-class, middle-aged realtor. Possibly no two works of literature did more to make Americans aware of the limitations of their national life and culture than did *Main Street* and *Babbitt*.

"Intellectually I know that America is no better than any other country; emotionally I know she is better than every other country." - Sinclair Lewis

F. SCOTT FITZGERALD *[fits-JERR-uld]* (1896-1940)

After World War I, the stories and novels of **F. Scott Fitzgerald** captured the restless, pleasure-hungry, defiant mood of the 1920s that eventually propelled our society into the Great Depression of the 1930s. Fitzgerald was the leading writer of America's **Jazz Age**—the prosperous and flamboyant 1920s also called the **Roaring Twenties**. He

Fitzgerald

was both a leading participant and observer of the high life he described. His own life, reflected in his books, is a tragic example of the joys and tragedies of young love, wealth and success, and excess and failure. While he lived, most readers considered his stories a chronicle and even a celebration of moral decline. Later readers realized that Fitzgerald's works had a deeper moral theme.

The Great Gatsby (1925) was his masterpiece and the first of three successive novels that gave him literary importance. The deeply moral novel centers on a wealthy **bootlegger** (an alcohol smuggler) during Prohibition, a time when alcohol was outlawed in the U.S. It presents a criticism of the moral emptiness Fitzgerald saw in wealthy American society of the 1920s. His next novel, *Tender Is the Night* (1934), is an account of the general decline of a few glamorous Americans in Europe. (Both of these were made into films.)

"Show me a hero and I'll write you a tragedy." - F. Scott Fitzgerald.

Hint: In a discussion with an American, you might describe a situation of wealth and/or excesses as "straight out of F. Scott Fitzgerald."

WILLIAM FAULKNER *[FALK-nur]* (1897-1962)

Faulkner expressed a range of humanity and showed how the past—especially the

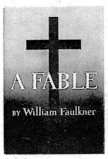

Faulkner

slave-holding era of the American South—endures in the present. The traditions, history, and social and moral life of the South were favorite Faulkner themes. He saw slavery and racism as the great sins haunting Southern history. Most of Faulkner's novels have a serious, even tragic, tone. But in nearly all of them tragedy is mixed with comedy. He was influenced by the humor of Mark Twain. Besides receiving the 1949 Nobel Prize for literature, he won

204

the Pulitzer Prize in 1955 for *A Fable* and in 1963 for *The Reivers*. *Fable* is set in the trenches of World War I in France and deals with mutiny in a French regiment. *Reivers* (1962) is a humorous story of a young boy's adventures during a trip from Mississippi to Memphis. (Faulkner's works are not easy reading—only those fluent in English should attempt it.)

"Always dream and shoot higher than you know you can do. Don't bother just to be better than your contemporaries or predecessors. Try to be better than yourself." – William Faulkner.

ERNEST HEMINGWAY *[HEM-ing-way]* (1899-1961)

Hemingway saw violence and death first-hand as an ambulance driver in World War I. The senseless carnage persuaded him that vague, abstract language was empty and misleading. He eliminated unnecessary words from his writing, simplified sentence structure, and concentrated on concrete objects and actions. You have learned Americans

can be direct and honest. Hemingway's writing style reflects that tendency in our character. He also developed a type of male character who faced violence and destruction with courage and grace under pressure, much like the founders of our country. One of the most famous and influential American writers of the 1900s, he received the Nobel Prize for literature in 1954.

Hemingway

Hemingway's most famous novels are two of his early works, *The Sun Also Rises* (1926) and *A Farewell to Arms* (1929). *Sun* portrays a group of Americans disillusioned by World War I. *Farewell*, set in Italy in World War I, is a tragic love story. In *The Old Man and the Sea* (1952), he revived his theme of a strong man courageously accepting fate. The hero, an old fisherman, catches a giant marlin fish after a long and brutal struggle, only to have the fish eaten by sharks. He was awarded a Pulitzer Prize for this novel. All three of these were made into films, as were most of his other writings.

"There is no friend as loyal as a book." – Ernest Hemingway.

Hint: Hemingway's short stories with blunt prose provide an easy introduction to American literature.

JOHN STEINBECK *[STINE-beck]* (1902-1968)

Steinbeck's best-known books explore sympathetically the struggles of poor people. His most famous novel, *The Grapes of Wrath* (1939), won the 1940 Pulitzer Prize. The novel tells the story of a poor Oklahoma farming family that migrates to California in search of a better life during the Great Depression of the 1930s. Steinbeck shows how the struggles of one family mirrored the hardship of the entire nation during that time. They learn that the poor must work together in order to survive. Steinbeck set much of his fiction in and around his birthplace in northern California.

Of Mice and Men (1937) is a short novel that Steinbeck adapted into a popular play. It is a tragic story about a physically powerful but mentally retarded farm worker and his best friend and protector. Steinbeck's most ambitious novel is *East of Eden* (1952) that follows three generations of a California family from the 1860s to World War I (1914-1918). *Cannery Row* (1945) explores people who live on a street where fish were canned during the Depression. In his nonfiction work *Travels with Charley* (1962), Steinbeck describes a car trip across America with his pet poodle named Charley. It paints a picture of the diverse U.S. in the early 60s. Steinbeck won the 1962 Nobel Prize for literature "for his realistic and imaginative writings, combining as they do sympathetic humor and keen social perception."

Steinbeck

Movies and plays have been made from 14 of his works in which change is thematic. The National Steinbeck Museum is located in the northern California city of Salinas (www.steinbeck.org).

"Men do change, and change comes like a little wind that ruffles the curtains at dawn, and it comes like the stealthy perfume of wildflowers hidden in the grass." - John Steinbeck.

OTHER NOTABLE AUTHORS

In addition to those discussed above, these authors are famous for their works, too, some of which are public favorites.

- *Arthur Miller* (1915-2005) – Leading American playwright famous for his blunt dialogue in *Death of a Salesman*. Forthrightness pervades his personal observations, too. "I have made more friends for American culture than the State Department. Certainly I have made fewer enemies, but that isn't very difficult."

- *Carl Sandburg* (1878-1967) – Two major themes: the meaning of American history and his enthusiasm for the common American man. His writings on President Abraham Lincoln, a common man who deeply influenced American history, are classics.

- *Dr. Seuss [suus]* (1904-1991) – Writer and illustrator of humorous books for children that combine delightful nonsense, humorous drawings, and social commentary. Famous works include *How the Grinch Stole Christmas* (1957) and *The Cat in the Hat* (1957), both of which were made into movies enjoyed by both children and adults.

- *Harriet Beecher Stowe* (1811-1896) – *Uncle Tom's Cabin* (1851) tells of the abuses and ills of slavery, one of the first to address this issue.

- *J.D. Salinger [SALL-in-jerr]* (1919-2010) – His only novel, *The Catcher in the Rye* (1951), explores the intellectual and emotional struggles of a generation of 1950s high school and college students who are alienated from the shallow, materialistic world of their parents. It is usually assigned in basic English classes in high school or college.

- *Margaret Mitchell* (1900-1949) – *Gone with the Wind* (1936), a romantic story of the South during the Civil War, won the 1937 Pulitzer Prize for fiction.

- *Robert Frost* (1874-1963) – A pastoral poet associated with rural New England, Frost's poems transcend regions as he discusses the doubt and uncertainty in each of us. His works won the Pulitzer Prize for poetry four times.

- *Stephen Crane* (1871-1900) – *The Red Badge of Courage* tells of a young Civil War soldier struggling amid shock and confusion.

- *Zane Grey* (1872-1939) – His 50 novels about the Wild West, including *The Last of the Plainsmen* (1908) and *Riders of the Purple Sage* (1912), tell of cowboys and heroes overcoming the challenges of the Old West.

BEST SELLING FICTION

Based on the number of books sold, these are all-time best selling fiction books, each of which has sold over 10 million copies worldwide. Many have been made into movies.

- *1984* and *Animal Farm* by George Orwell – In *1984*, London is a grim city where the government is always watching you and the police can practically read your mind. *Farm* is a satire of the Russian Revolution as farm animals struggle to transform a farm into a democratic society, only to slip back into totalitarian rule.

- *Catch-22* by Joseph Heller – Hilarious yet penetrating examination of the absurdity and futility of war set in the closing days of WWII, a metaphor extending to life itself.

- *God's Little Acre* by Erskine Caldwell – Sociological and economic impact of the Great Depression on the lives of Southern poor people who lust for more.

- *Jaws* by Peter Benchley – Thriller about the struggle to kill a giant shark that threatens a seaside community.
- *Jonathan Livingstone Seagull* by Richard Bach – Flight is a metaphor for a story told by a seagull seeking a higher purpose in life.
- *Peyton Place* by Grace Metalious – Dark underside of a small, respectable 1950s New England town, its secrets and scandals.

- *The Carpetbaggers* by Harold Robbins – Early 20th century as seen through the lives of an ex-gunfighter, a Hollywood actress, a movie company executive, and the proverbial prostitute with a heart of gold.
- *The Exorcist* by William Blatty – Child is exorcised of an ancient, evil demon.
- *The Godfather* by Mario Puzo – Organized crime in the 1940s and a Mafia family drawn together and ripped apart by their criminal life.

- *The Thorn Birds* by Colleen McCullough – Romeo and Juliet love story set in the Australian Outback in the years surrounding WWII.
- *To Kill a Mockingbird* by Harper Lee – Depression era Southern story of race, class, justice, the pain of growing up, and of a man of tolerance defending what he believes in.

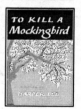

FOREIGN HERITAGE AMERICAN WRITERS

Irish novelist **James Joyce** contributed to the change in U.S. book censorship laws. His *Ulysses* book was published abroad in 1922 but was banned in America. In 1933 a major U.S. publisher's attempt to import the book was at the center of a major court case. *Ulysses* won, forever changing U.S. censorship laws.

Just as they contribute to our culture as a whole, Americans of foreign heritage also contribute to our literature. This globalization of American literature plays a part in shaping the way we view our lives, and in turn, the way Americans and our literature are viewed abroad.

The history of the Nobel Prize for literature reflects cultural changes that have affected our literature. From 1930 to 1962, the list of Americans who won the Prize included **Sinclair Lewis, Eugene O'Neill, Pearl Buck, T. S. Eliot, William Faulkner, Ernest Hemingway**, and **John Steinbeck** (all native born). Except for Toni Morrison, however, the list from 1962 through 2000 contains *no* native-born Americans. Instead, there are only those who by naturalization, long residence, or significant achievement within the U.S. can in a sense be designated "American." Another indicator of this

208

literary shift comes from the Library of Congress where two of the six **poets laureate*** of the U.S. appointed in the 1990s were born abroad.

Here is a small sampling of foreigners who have contributed to our literature.

- *Czesław Miłosz* – Widely considered one of the greatest poets of the 20th century. The Polish poet and prose writer immigrated to the U.S. in 1960. His works had been banned by the communist government. In 1980 he was awarded the Nobel Prize for literature. His *The Captive Mind* has been described as one of the finest studies of the behavior of intellectuals under a repressive regime.

Milosz

- *Isaac Bashevis Singer* – Polish-born novelist, short-story writer, and essayist came to America in 1935 and won the Nobel Prize for Literature in 1978. Singer's chief subject was the traditional Polish life in various periods of history, largely before the Holocaust. His best known works include *The Family Moskat* and *The Estate*.

Singer

- *Saul Bellow* – Canadian-born American writer of Russian-Jewish origin, Bellow was awarded the Pulitzer Prize, the Nobel Prize for literature, and the National Medal of Arts. He is the only writer to have won the National Book Award three times. Widely regarded as one of the twentieth century's greatest authors, Bellow has had a huge literary influence. His best known works include *The Adventures of Augie March, Herzog, Mr. Sammler's Planet*, and *Seize the Day*.

Bellow

- *Alexander Solzhenitsyn* – Russian born, he made the world aware of the Soviet Union's forced labor camp system with *The Gulag Archipelago* and *One Day in the Life of Ivan Denisovich*, his two best-known works. For these efforts Solzhenitsyn was awarded the Nobel Prize for literature in 1970. He was imprisoned for years and then exiled from the Soviet Union in 1974, lived in the U.S., and then returned to Russia in 1994.

Solzhenitsyn

- *Amy Tan* – Awarded the National Book Award in 1989 for her first book, *The Joy Luck Club* (www.nationalbook.org.) The book addresses the generational attitudes of Asians in America, starting with four Chinese families in 1949's San Francisco.

Tan

---

*Officially appointed by the government and often expected to compose poems for State occasions and other government events, poets laureate are appointed by many states and countries. In the United Kingdom, this has been the title of the official poet of the monarch since the time of Charles II (1600s).

This first generation Chinese American uses wit and sensitivity to examine the sometimes painful, deep connection between mothers and daughters. Her work has been translated into 35 languages and a movie.

- *Iris Chang* – The daughter of two university professors who immigrated from China, she became a best-selling author, a human rights activist, and a role model for young American students of all foreign descents. Her bestseller book, *The Rape of Nanking, The Forgotten Holocaust of World War II,* chronicles the 1937 Japanese army invasion of the ancient Chinese city of Nanking. Within weeks, more than 300,000 Chinese civilians and soldiers were systematically raped, tortured, and murdered—a death toll exceeding that of the atomic blasts of Hiroshima and Nagasaki combined. Using

Chang

extensive interviews with survivors and newly discovered documents, Chang wrote the definitive history of this horrifying episode. It also tells about the small group of Americans and Europeans who bravely stayed behind in Nanking to protect the remaining Chinese population who did not flee the Japanese army's advance.

She was compelled to write the book after her parents told her the story of her grandparents who had fled as the violence began. Her book was on the prestigious *New York Times* **Best Seller List**[*] for weeks. She said, "I bring up these crimes to remind us of the potential for evil that lives in us all. The Pacific War was not some tragic flaw, but an indication of a universal condition of human nature." Tragically, she died in 2004 at the age of 36 from a self-inflicted gunshot.

(The book is available online from various sites including Amazon.com in print, audio, and Kindle format at http://amzn.to/NankingHolocaust.)

---

[*]Widely considered to be the preeminent list of best-selling books in the U.S. since 1942, it is published Sundays in the Book Review insert in the *The New York Times* and online. Its sales figures represent books that have actually sold at retail, rather than possibly inflated wholesale figures provided by publishers (www.nytimes.com/pages/books/bestseller/).

L

FILM

"You know what your problem is, it's that you haven't seen enough movies – all of life's riddles are answered in the movies." - Steve Martin's movie lines, actor

Films are an integral part of American life. They entertain, educate, inform, enlighten, and challenge our way of life. So viewing them will provide you with additional insight into our culture and lifestyles.

Also known as movies, motion pictures, flicks, movie pictures, cinema, and the screen, they are the most influential art form of the 20th century. Some historians say America's major contribution to the art world has been our films. We have had a love affair with them since the first crude video boxes in the early 1900s. Annual movie attendance approaches one billion paid-admissions with box office receipts exceeding $10 billion. Home videos and DVD sales now outperform theater ticket sales.

In the U.S., films are shown at one-screen theaters and at multi-complexes with as many as 30 screens. We combined our love for autos and movies when our first drive-in theater opened in 1933. By 1958 we had 4,000 outdoor theaters, but they have since declined to 370.

Modern 14-screen movie theater complex.

Movies reflect how we really speak, which makes them handy and entertaining tools for improving communications with Americans. Many of our sayings originate in our movies and become part of our everyday **patter** (trivial talk), such as "Are you talkin' to me?" "Go ahead, make my day." "Houston, we have a problem." "I'll be b-a-c-k." "That's all folks," and "Life is like a box of chocolates—you never know what you're gonna get."

Foreigners love American movies, too. On average, 60 to 80 percent of all films shown in cinemas across Europe are products of the Hollywood factory system, while most European-made films only reach a limited audience in our largest cities. However, more Asian films are now being shown in the U.S., particularly those from Hong Kong and India, some of which have won prestigious awards here. (Did you know India makes 1000 films each year vs. our 500? Did you know one won an Academy Award in 2008?)

Global distribution of American movies (and TV shows) helps shape the world's perception of the U.S., both accurately and inaccurately. Because of this, many perceive America as the land of fast paced life, fast cars, fast food, fast music, fast women, fast dissolving relationships, fast guns, and fast spent money. They incorrectly assume that these narrow segments define our entire culture, just as Americans assume from watching French movies that all married Frenchmen have a mistress or two on the side.

Because **Hollywood**—an area of Los Angeles City in Southern California—is synonymous with the film industry, we refer to movie making in the U.S. as "Hollywood," just as **Detroit** is shorthand for our automotive industry and **Madison Avenue** (a New York City street with our largest advertising firms) for our advertising business. Visitors to Hollywood can tour film studios and view the

Hollywood sign.

world-famous 15-meter tall **Hollywood Sign** set atop the Hollywood hills. The sign is a metaphor for American ingenuity. Erected in 1923 as an advertisement sign for a local real estate development, it read "HOLLYWOODLAND." The last four letters were removed in 1945 after Hollywood had become the world's movie capital, and the rest is history.

Hollywood is famous for its **Hollywood Walk of Fame** where 2,400 bronze star plaques imbedded in the sidewalk pay tribute to past and present entertainment stars. A public ceremony is held each time a celebrity is given his or her star. World famous

Hollywood Walk of Fame

Grauman's *[GROW-manz]* **Chinese Theatre** in Hollywood is renowned for its courtyard with foot and handprints of stars dating back to 1927. Universal Studios conducts tours of its facilities.

After World War I, filmmakers gravitated to Southern California with its mild climate and varied scenery. During the so-called **Golden Age of Hollywood**—the 1930s and 1940s—Hollywood studios were prolific. Hollywood changed in the late 1940s when a federal antitrust action prohibited the studios from both

Grauman's Theatre

producing films and owning the theatres where they were exhibited, thus removing monopolistic control of this industry. (There's that *fairness* thing again.)

America likes to reward achievers. **Academy Awards** are voted each year by thousands of members of the film industry. Five or fewer potential recipients are first nominated for 24 different categories, including best picture, actor, director, and writer. The event is televised in March to millions of viewers in 150 nations around the world. A statue called **Oscar**

Oscar

212

is awarded to the winner. (Appendix 7 provides a listing of past Oscar winners for Best Picture.)

We are concerned about what our children watch in movie theatres. To help parents judge which movies they will allow their children to see, most movies receive a rating. The movie rating system is a voluntary system sponsored by filmmakers and theatre owners. Americans prefer industries—not the government—to regulate themselves when possible. These ratings vary from "G" that means anyone can see it, to NC-17, which means no one 17-years old or younger will be admitted. Parents demand similar ratings on our videos, computer games, and TV programs.

TOP 20 AMERICAN FILMS

The chapter on literature introduced you to what many consider our classic books. We also have classic films. Many in the U.S. recognize and use their titles and stars' names in conversations. Viewing them might provide further insight into American life and culture. These movies appear frequently on TV and can also be purchased or rented on DVD or watched online, such as at www.netflix.com.

In 1998, The American Film Institute (AFI) commemorated the first 100 years of American movies by selecting the 100 greatest American movies of all time (www.afi.com). More than 1,500 leaders from the American film community made their selections. The following are AFI's top 20 films, many of which have won Academy Awards and withstood the test of time.

1. Citizen Kane (1941) – Starring and directed by **Orson Welles**

Ranked number one, this film is noted for its innovative narrative, photography, and sound track. It tells the story of a publisher's ultimately empty rise to power and is based loosely on the story of America's newspaper tycoon William Randolph Hearst. It received nine Oscar nominations and won Best Original Screenplay.

Welles

2. Casablanca (1942) – Starring **Humphrey Bogart**, **Ingrid Bergman**

Bogart plays an American nightclub owner in French Morocco who sacrifices a great love to join the world's fight against the Nazis in World War II. Two men vie for the same woman's love. A song in the film, "As Time Goes By," was voted AFI's number two all-time best song. The film won three awards: Best Picture, Best Director, and Best Screenplay.

Bogart

Bogart's famous line as he toasts Bergman, "Here's looking at you, kid," is sometimes used by an American man as he toasts a woman.

213

3. The Godfather (1972) – Starring **Marlon Brando, Al Pacino**

Brando is the sympathetic head of a New York crime family. Based on the book of the same name, this epic story traces the history of their close-knit Mafia family over a ten-year period. It is an insightful study of power, violence, honor, obligation, corruption, justice, and crime in America. The film won three Oscars: Best Picture, Best Actor (Marlon Brando), and Best Screenplay

Pacino

Pacino's famous line: "I'll make him an offer he can't refuse."

4. Gone With the Wind (1939) – Starring **Clark Gable, Vivien Leigh**

Novelist Margaret Mitchell's immortal tale of the Old South is retold on the screen with Leigh as **Scarlett O'Hara**. She struggles to find love during the Civil War years and afterwards seeks refuge for herself and her family at her beloved plantation. The burning of Atlanta provides screen excitement. It received 13 nominations and eight Oscars, including Best Picture, Best Director, Best Actress (Leigh), and Best Screenplay.

Gable

Gable's famous line as he leaves Scarlett: "Frankly my dear I don't give a damn."

5. Lawrence of Arabia (1962) – Starring **Peter O'Toole**

The film retells the exploits of a rebellious, desert-loving British officer who aided the Arabians against the Turks (an ally of Germany) during World War I. It received ten Academy Award nominations and seven Oscars, including Best Director, Best Picture, and Best Music Score.

O'Toole

6. The Wizard of Oz (1939) – Starring **Judy Garland**

Dorothy is transported from her black-and-white Kansas home to the colorful **Land of Oz** by a tornado. She then journeys down the **Yellow Brick Road** and is helped by a Scarecrow, a Tin Man, and a Cowardly Lion on their way to see the Wizard. You may hear Americans use the term "Land of Oz" to describe a unreal, magical place, and "yellow brick road" to describe a road leading to a promised land of one's hopes and dreams. Nominated for six Academy Awards, it won Best Song and Best Original Score.

Garland

The film's "Over the Rainbow" tune was voted AFI's number one all-time movie song. The song reflects our American Dream today that is just over the rainbow, and the dreams of those who set sail for America in the 1600s as suggested in these lines:

Somewhere over the rainbow
way up high,
there's a land that I heard of
once in a lullaby.

Somewhere over the rainbow
skies are blue,
and dreams that you dare to dream
really do come true.

214

Garland's famous line to her dog **Toto**, "**I don't think we're in Kansas anymore**," is used by Americans to jokingly denote a shift in location or thought, or that they are no longer in quiet and comfortable surroundings.

7. The Graduate (1967) – Starring **Dustin Hoffman**

Hoffman

The film captures the spirit of our late 1960s culture. Hoffman, a recent college graduate, is alienated in the shifting social and sexual values of that era. As an innocent and confused youth, he is exploited, misdirected, seduced (literally and figuratively), and betrayed by a corrupt older generation. The movie's "Mrs. Robinson" song was voted seventh in AFI's all-time list of movie tunes. The film was nominated for seven Academy Awards and won the Best Director award.

Hoffman's famous line: "Mrs. Robinson, you're trying to seduce me...aren't you?" (Just so you know, the answer is yes.)

8. On the Waterfront (1954) – Starring **Marlon Brando**

Brando

Brando is a longshoreman who rebels against his brother and corruption on New York City docks in the 1950s. He joins forces with a courageous priest and a loving woman to seek reform and challenge the mob. He portrays a struggling hero who is a small-time ex-boxer. The film won eight Academy Awards including Best Picture and Best Actor (Brando).

Brando's famous line, "I coulda [could have] been a contender," meant he could have been a champion fighter if things had gone differently in his life. We use it, too, to mean we could have reached for success but something happened.

9. Schindler's List (1993) – Director **Steven Spielberg**. Starring **Liam Neeson**

Neeson

Neeson plays the fictionalized version of a real-life German industrialist who saves hundreds of Jews from death camps during World War II by giving them jobs in his factory. It recreates authentically a frightening period when Jews in Nazi-occupied Poland had their businesses and homes taken from them. They were placed in **ghettos** (poor isolated areas) and labor camps, and finally resettled in concentration camps where they were executed. It won seven Academy Awards, including Best Picture and Best Director (the first for Spielberg).

10. Singin' in the Rain (1952) – *Starring* **Gene Kelly**

This musical is set in 1927 Hollywood when movie studios were converting from silent to sound films. Kelly sings, dances, and splashes in puddles. It has delightful song and dance numbers, and "Singin' in the Rain" was voted AFI's all-time number three movie tune. The film received two Academy Award nominations but no Oscars.

Kelly

11. It's a Wonderful Life (1946) – Starring James Stewart

Stewart

This Christmas classic features Stewart as a suicidal man redeemed by friendship and the recognition that each person's life touches many others. It was not a commercial success at the time of its release, but became a movie classic in the 1960s with repeated television showings at Christmas time. It received five nominations but won no Oscars.

Stewart's character learned that "One man's life touches so many others; when he's not there it leaves an awfully big hole."

12. Sunset Boulevard (1950) – Starring Gloria Swanson, William Holden

Swanson plays a reclusive, former silent screen star who kills her screenwriting playboy boyfriend. The black and white film exposes the corruptive influences of the New Hollywood and the studio system. It portrays the decline of old Hollywood legends many years after the coming of sound films. It received 11 Academy Award nominations and received three Oscars.

Holden

Having starred in 80 movies, the role in which Holden took the most pride was that of a conservationist dedicated to preserving Africa's wildlife. His effort later expanded throughout the world as he instilled a reverence for nature's creatures through his foundation (www.whwf.org/history.htm).

Swanson's famous line: "I am ready for my close-up, Mr. De Mille." (De Mille was a famous movie director.)

13. The Bridge on the River Kwai (1957) – Starring William Holden, Alec Guinness

Based loosely on a true World War II incident, allied POW's (prisoners of war, pronounced P-O-Ws) from 1942 through 1943 were ordered to build two Kwai River bridges in a Thailand jungle to help move Japanese supplies and troops from Bangkok to Rangoon. Guinness is a rigid British officer who refuses to bow to torture in a Japanese prison camp. Holden is an American who escapes from the camp, then returns to blow up a bridge constructed by POWs under Guinness' command.

Guiness

The story's theme is the futility and insanity of war, and the struggle of wills between a British and a Japanese colonel. The two leaders are symbols of different cultures who actually have much in common: pride, dedication, and obedience to their military codes and rules. It won seven Oscars, including Best Picture and Best Actor (Guinness).

Guinness' famous line: "One day the war will be over. And I hope that the people that use this bridge in years to come will remember how it was built and who built it. Not a gang of slaves, but British soldiers…even in captivity."

Hint: I had the experience of walking across the bridge that is now open to tourist traffic. It is a three-hour drive from Bangkok for those who might want to cross it, too. During its construction, approximately 13,000 prisoners of war died and were buried along the railway. An estimated 100,000 civilians throughout the area also died in the course of the project, chiefly forced labor who suffered from starvation and brutal treatment by the Japanese soldiers, as did the POWs.

14. Some Like it Hot (1959) – Starring **Jack Lemmon, Marilyn Monroe**

This comedy is a clever spoof of 1930s gangster films. Sex symbol Marilyn Monroe is teamed with two male rivals dressed in female attire to elude gangsters pursuing them. It received six nominations and won one Oscar. Monroe remains a screen legend icon though she died in 1962. She is buried at Westwood Memorial Park in Los Angeles where tourists can visit the gravesites of world famous stars.

Monroe

15. Star Wars (1977) – Director **George Lucas**. Starring **Harrison Ford**

This is landmark science fiction film is about Luke Skywalker who embarks on an adventure to rescue a princess and save the galaxy from the evil empire. One of the most popular and successful science fiction, adventure-fantasy films of all time, it helped resurrect this film category. Director Lucas borrowed from Kurosawa and Japanese sword master tales. Nominated for ten Academy Awards, it won six, most of which were technical.

Ford

It popularized the phrase, "May the force be with you."

16. All About Eve (1950) – Starring **Bette Davis**

About the world of New York City's Broadway Theater of the 1950s, it tells the story of female actresses who seek success without regard to scruples or feelings. It was nominated for 14 awards—more than any other picture in Oscar history until *Titanic* (1997) matched the same feat 47 years later. The film won six Oscars, including Best Picture.

Davis

Davis' famous line: "Fasten your seat belts; it's going to be a bumpy night."

17. The African Queen (1951) – Starring **Humphrey Bogart, Katharine Hepburn**

Spinster Hepburn and drunkard boat captain Bogart battle each other and an uncharted river in this love story set in Africa at the outbreak of World War I. During the course of hardships and quarrels along a river filled with many dangers including enemy Germans, they develop love and respect for each other. Aside from the destruction of an enemy warship, they must overcome the various psychological obstacles that stand between them during their journey. This movie is often used by educators to help children understand human relations set against a backdrop of history and the hardships of nature. Nominated for four Academy Awards, it received the Best Actor award (Bogart).

Hepburn

Hepburn's character says to the captain, "Nature, Mr. Allnutt, is what we are put into this world to rise above."

18. Psycho (1960) – Director **Alfred Hitchcock**. Starring **Anthony Perkins**

Alfred Hitchcock's complex psychological thriller is perhaps the best known of all our modern horror suspense films. Leigh runs away with stolen money and makes the mistake of checking into the **Bates Motel** run by Perkins and his mother. The film is best remembered for the murder scene in the shower. It ushered in an era of inferior thrillers with graphic, shocking killings, all avoided by Hitchcock who left much to the imagination. It received four Oscar nominations but won none. The term "Bates Motel" and its famous

Perkins

shower scene still instill fear in the minds of some. Universal Studios' theme park in Hollywood (www.universalstudioshollywood.com) has a Bates Motel.

19. Chinatown (1974) – Starring **Jack Nicholson, Faye Dunaway**

Nicholson plays a private detective in 1930s Los Angeles lured into the world of water rights and land deals while investigating the death of Dunaway's husband. The film blends mystery, romance, suspense, and detective elements. The screenplay was partially based on a true Los Angeles land scandal. It was nominated for 11 Academy Awards, but only won one.

Dunaway

20. One Flew Over the Cuckoo's Nest (1975) – Starring **Jack Nicholson**

Set in a mental hospital, a wise guy antihero rebels against authority. By doing so, troublemaker Nicholson sparks new life in the downtrodden inmates, giving them purpose and self-worth. The mid-70s counterculture was ready for a film dramatizing rebellion against oppressive bureaucracy on the one hand, and an insistence upon rights on the other. It was nominated for 11 Academy Awards and was the first film to take all the major awards (Best Picture, Best Director, Best Screenplay, Best Actor, and Best Actress) since *It Happened*

Nicholson

One Night (1934). Movie star Michael Douglas produced the film.

> **Hint:** Although it is ranked 91st, I include *My Fair Lady* because I frequently give a video of this film to foreign friends seeking to improve their English diction. It is a delightful movie about a poor British girl who attempts to learn to speak English like the Queen. I recommend you view it, too.

91. My Fair Lady (1964) – Starring **Rex Harrison, Audrey Hepburn**

This romantic musical comedy was one of the top five films of 1964. It has clever lyrics, wonderful tunes, and lavish sets and costumes. Harrison's Henry Higgins takes a bet that he can transform the young, lower class **Eliza Doolittle** (Hepburn) into a proper lady in this musical adaptation of George Bernard Shaw's play, *Pygmalion*. It was honored with 12 Academy Award nominations and eight wins, including Best Picture,

218

Best Actor (Harrison), and Best Director. (It can be purchased online from various sources including Amazon.com at http://amzn.to/FairLadyStudy.)

Like other stars in Hollywood who reach out to the less fortunate, Hepburn devoted the last years of her life to helping children around the world as a goodwill ambassador for UNICEF, the United Nations International Children's Emergency Fund.

Harrison's famous line: "Why can't a woman be more like a man?"

Hepburn

OTHER PUBLIC FAVORITES

Our Favorite Actors – Each year a Harris Poll surveys American adults to determine our favorite movie stars, some of whom you may hear us talk about. Our top actors can command $20 million per picture. The rankings change each year based on the success of their latest films, but some remain favorites year in and year out. Some have their own websites. This was the ranking of our top ten favorites in 2012.

1. Johnny Depp
2. Denzel Washington
2. Clint Eastwood
4. Tom Hanks
5. John Wayne *
6. George Clooney
7. Sandra Bullock
8. Harrison Ford
9. Will Smith
10. Adam Sandler

Our Most Inspiring And Romantic Films – According to the American Film Institute, a jury of 1,500 film artists, critics, and historians ranked these classics as the 10 most inspiring films and the greatest love stories of all time.

Most Inspiring Films:
1. *It's a Wonderful Life* (1946)
2. *To Kill a Mockingbird* (1962)
3. *Schindler's List* (1993)
4. *Rocky* (1976)
5. *Mr. Smith Goes to Washington* (1939)
6. *E.T. the Extra-Terrestrial* (1982)
7. *The Grapes of Wrath* (1940)

Greatest Love Stories:
1. *Casablanca* (1942)
2. *Gone With the Wind* (1939)
3. *West Side Story* (1961)
4. *Roman Holiday* (1953)
5. *An Affair to Remember* (1957)
6. *The Way We Were* (1973)
7. *Doctor Zhivago* (1965)

---

* Wayne, who starred primarily in cowboy westerns and died in 1979, remains among the most popular actors of his generation, evidenced by the continual re-releases of his films on home video (www.johnwayne.com).

8. *Breaking Away* (1979)
9. *Miracle on 34th Street* (1947)
10. *Saving Private Ryan* (1998)

8. *It's a Wonderful Life* (1946)
9. *Love Story* (1970)
10. *City Lights* (1931)

Our Box Office Favorites – These films achieved the world's top box office receipts ($ millions) by 2012. This shows that our best films are not necessarily the ones that attract the most viewers.

1. *Avatar* (2009) $2,782
2. *Titanic* (1997) $1,843
3. *Harry Potter and the Deathly Hallows-Part 2* (2011) $1,328
4. *Transformers: Dark of the Moon* (2011) $1,123
5. *The Lord of the Rings: The Return of the King* (2003) $1,119
6. *Pirates of the Caribbean: Dead Man's Chest* (2006) $1,066
7. *Toy Story 3* (2010) $1,063
8. *Pirates of the Caribbean: On Stranger Tides* (2011) $1.039
9. *Alice in Wonderland* (2010) $1,024
10. *The Dark Knight* (2008) $1,001

FOREIGN CONTRIBUTORS TO FILM INDUSTRY

As with other aspects of American culture, foreigners have influenced our theatre arts. The U.S. film industry was practically invented and long sustained by non-Americans, mostly Europeans. Some of the biggest names among early studio bosses, directors, and actors were European-born and produced some of our most popular American films. And during the Golden Era of Hollywood in the 1930s and 40s, many foreign-born actors had leading roles.

The internationalization of Hollywood continues today In fact, nine of the 20 acting or supporting Oscar nominations in 2008 went to foreign-born movie stars. And for the first time since 1965, all four best-acting 2008 Oscars went to non-Americans: Britain's Tilda Swinton, Britain/Ireland's Daniel Day-Lewis, France's Marion Cotillard, and Spain's Javier Bardem.

You might hear Americans discussing our foreign-born actors and their movies. Here is a *small* sampling of expatriate achievers.

- *Arab* – British actor and Arab American F. Murray Abraham won Best Actor for the 1984 movie *Amadeus*.
- *Asia* – James Shigeta dignified the Asian American male image. Nancy Kwan's performance in *The World of Suzie Wong* made this Eurasian beauty the epitome of Asian beauty in the 1960s. Bruce Lee was well known for his Kung Fu movies in which an Asian hero offered physical virtue and emotional power.

Kwan

- *Australia* – Cate Blanchett, Russell Crowe, Nicole Kidman, and the late Heath Ledger.

- *Austria* – Arnold Schwarzenegger put aside his acting career to become the governor of the state of California from 2003 to 2010.
- *Canada* – Mary Pickford won Best Actress and co-founded United Artists studio. Jack Warner founded Warner Brothers. Other Canadian actors include Walter Pigeon, Mack Sennett, Norma Shearer (Best Actress), Fay Wray, Rachel McAdams, and Marie Dressler (Best Actress). There have been hundreds nominated in all Academy categories, including Ryan Gosling's nomination for Best Actor in 2007.
- *France* – Maurice Chevalier received a special Oscar in 1958 for his contributions to the world of entertainment for more than half a century.
- *Germany* – Maximilian Schell made his Hollywood debut in 1958, then in 1962 won the Academy Award for Best Actor in *Judgment at Nuremberg*. Marlene Dietrich was a German American actress and singer who became a U.S. citizen in 1939. In 1999, the American Film Institute named Dietrich the ninth greatest female star of all time.

Dietrich

- *Italy* – Marcello Mastroianni received three Oscar nominations. Anna Magnani, Sophia Loren, and Gina Lollobrigida were fan favorites, too.
- *Mexico* – Anthony Quinn was born in Mexico in 1915. His family came to the U.S. via a coal wagon and eventually moved to Los Angeles where he shined shoes and sold newspapers. He took up acting and eventually won two Academy Awards.

Quinn

- *Spain* – Antonio Banderas and Penelope Cruz (Spain's first Oscar winning actress, 2009).
- *U.K.* – Kate Winslet won the Academy Award for Best Actress in *The Reader* (2008). Oscar winner Anthony Hopkins eventually obtained U.S. citizenship after coming to the U.S. following stardom in Britain, as did two-time Oscar winners Michael Caine and Peter Ustinov.

This foreign influence extends to other areas, too, including directing. Akira Kurosawa *[ah-KEY-rah koo-ROW-saw-wah]* (1910–1998) was one of the world's great directors. Many of today's best filmmakers claim him as a primary influence on their work. In *Rashomon* (1950), he introduced Western audiences to Japanese film. His 29 films often adapted Western literature classics to Japanese settings and attitudes. In 1989, he received an Academy Award for his lifelong body of work.

Kurosawa

M

ART

*No great artist ever sees things as they really are, if he did he would
cease to be an artist.* - Oscar Wilde, Irish poet and dramatist 1854-1900

Like our literature and film, American art reflects the culture of our independent thinking, realism, and truth. This chapter acquaints you with a few of our best-known American artists and their works. Use of their popular names or a simple observation such as, "That is right out of Norman Rockwell," or "This reminds me of Winslow Homer's *Breezing Up*," will bring instant respect from an American who is familiar with these artists. They will also be pleased that you understand that our culture is more than our famed movies and celebrities, as some foreigners do.

Freeway art in California.

Our art is everywhere—in our advertisements, offices, homes, and the media. Some freeways and office buildings have pictures painted on their walls by artists—sometimes authorized, sometimes not. Adults and children build creative sand sculptures on our beaches. Artistic tattoos appeal to some. Computer graphics design is a rapidly expanding field of art. And we have thousands of museums, including the world famous Metropolitan Museum of Art in New York City (www.metmuseum.org) and the National Gallery of Art (www.nga.gov) in Washington, D.C.

Given our centuries-old freewheeling culture in which individuality is pursued, American artists today tend not to restrict themselves to schools, styles, or a single medium. They **do their own thing**, though we have gone through different artistic periods over the centuries.

Native Americans were the first American residents to create art thousands of years ago. These works were painted, carved, woven, sewn, or built for use in daily life as well as in ceremonies. Americans today wear silver and turquoise Indian jewelry produced by various tribes in the U.S., and you will see some homes decorated in this Southwestern style.

In the late 1500s, watercolor art by European immigrants portrayed animals, plants, and Indians in English settlements in Virginia. Portraits became popular in the last half of the 1600s, followed by three-dimensional sculptures of ship figureheads and wooden trade figures in the 1700s such as cigar store Indians that stood outside shop entrances. We refer to the antiques of this period as being part of **Americana** *[ah-mer-ih-KAHN-ah]*. People collect these items while others decorate their homes in this style today.

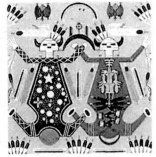
Indian sand painting.

In the 1800s, our artists, influenced by European art, portrayed American heroes at important events and gave visual expression to landscapes that the public was unfamiliar with, somewhat like television does today and books did before that.

Until World War II (1939-1945), American art was considered provincial compared to the best that Europe offered. In the 1950s, however, the U.S. (particularly New York City) took the lead with its own movement called Abstract Expressionism that shared an outlook characterized by a belief in freedom of expression. Typically American, these artists felt ill at ease with the constraints of conventional subjects and styles.

Cigar store Indian, circa 1900.

SELECTED AMERICAN ARTISTS

The following is an alphabetic listing by last name of selected classic American artists and their famous works. A frequent theme among them, like the culture in which they thrived, is their desire to break away from prescribed styles and do their own thing. (Does this repeated American theme sound familiar?)

AUDUBON *[AW-deh-bonn]*, John James (1785-1851)

Audubon was a naturalist and artist noted for his realistic portrayals of American wildlife. One of America's first wildlife artists, he began drawing and studying American birds at the age of 18. His reputation rests primarily on his first major work, *Birds of America* (1838), a collection of 435 life-sized, hand-colored pictures depicting native birds. Working with other naturalists, he produced several more volumes of fine illustrations combined with descriptions of behavior and

Audubon

(Courtesy Audubon Society)

224

characteristics of American birds.

He went into the field to collect specimens to work from in his studio. His work has the clarity and attention to detail that characterizes high-quality scientific illustrations and line quality that characterizes fine art.

Our **National Audubon Society** was founded in his honor. Its mission is to conserve and restore natural ecosystems, focusing on birds and other wildlife and their habitats for the benefit of humanity (www.audubon.org).

HOMER, Winslow (1836-1910)

Homer is considered one of the greatest American 19th century artists and a foremost exponent of Realism, the truthful and accurate depiction of nature and contemporary life. He was famous for stirring paintings of the sea. His fishermen and sea captains were symbols of the rugged quality of all people who follow the sea, and typically American because of our vast shorelines where we work, play, and fish.

Breezing Up (A Fair Wind), 1873-1876.

Homer

Homer's vision took American art out of the Romanticism of the mid-1800s that favored emotion over reason and senses over intellect. He carried it to the heights of Realism with light, shadow, and composition playing expressive roles in his images. He was almost entirely self-taught as a painter. Based on personal observations, his work revealed American life that went unrecorded by other artists and then until his death it dealt with mortality and the forces of nature.

LICHTENSTEIN [LIKT-uhn-steen], Roy (1923-1997)

Roy Lichtenstein was a painter, sculptor, and graphic artist best known for his large-scale paintings and prints inspired by comic strips, newsprint, and advertising. Along with fellow American artist Andy Warhol, Lichtenstein was a central figure of the American Pop Art movement in the 1960s that celebrated popular, commercial images. (www.lichtensteinfoundation.org)

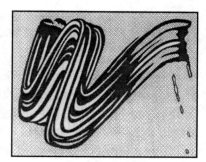

Brush Stroke, 1965.

Lichenstein

225

"[Pop Art] is an involvement with what I think to be the most brazen and threatening characteristics of our culture, things we hate, but which are also powerful in their impingement on us." – Roy Lichtenstein.

O'KEEFFE *[oh-KEEF]*, **Georgia** (1887-1986)

One of America's most celebrated woman painters, Georgia O'Keeffe was an influential member of the New York art scene during the 1920s and 30s. She created a

O'Keeffe

Shell No. 1, 1928.

highly original body of work that played a vital role in the development of modern styles in U.S. art. It ranged from nature studies and depictions of magnified blossoms, to striking portrayals of the southwest desert of New Mexico. She painted desert stones and flowers, cow skulls bleached white by the sun, crosses left by Spanish Catholic missionaries in the 1600s and 1700s, and old adobe churches. The Georgia O'Keeffe Museum in Santa Fe, New Mexico, has a website at www.okeeffemuseum.org.

"To create one's own world in any of the arts takes courage." – Georgia O'Keefe.

POLLOCK *[PULL-ock]*, **Jackson** (1912-1956)

Abstract is a synonym for art completely without recognizable subject matter. Jackson Pollock, the master, developed a technique for applying garish colored paint by pouring or dripping it in a circular pattern onto huge canvases laid on the floor to exude physical energy. With this method, he produced intricate interlaced webs of paint. His

(Courtesy Fine Arts Mag.)

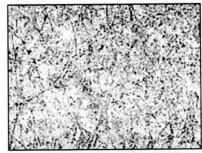

Number 1, 1950 (Lavender Mist), 1950.

rapid and seemingly impulsive execution became a hallmark of Abstract Expressionism that emphasized the spontaneous gestures of the artist.

Pollock was dubbed "Jack the Dripper" by *Time* magazine in 1956 for his revolutionary technique of painting that freed generations of American artists from academic restrictions. His style reflected his own manic-depressive personality. His "Number 5, 1948" sold for $140 million in 2006, then the highest price ever paid for a painting. An American movie titled *Pollock* (2000) explores his turbulent life.

"Every good painter paints what he is." – Jackson Pollock.

Hint: If something is confusing to you, you might say "It's as confusing as a Jackson Pollock painting."

REMINGTON *[RHEM-ing-ton]*, **Frederic** (1861-1909)

Remington was a 19th century painter famous for his lively scenes of the **Old West** (second half of the 19th century) that portray the frontier as a masculine, rugged existence. As a young man on the East Coast, he headed west and worked as a cowboy, sheep

rancher, and gold prospector. He studied and sketched the land around him, insisting on realism in every detail. Like the tales of the Old West books by American writer **Zane Grey**, Remington's heroes were the everyday people

Remington

of the frontier. The Frederic Remington Art Museum is located in Ogdensburg, New York (fredericremington.org).

Burgess Finding a Ford, 1895.

ROCKWELL, **Norman** (1894-1978)

Between 1916 and 1963, Rockwell's 321 artwork covers on *Saturday Evening Post* gave him an audience larger

than that of any other artist in history. His favorite subjects were everyday events that celebrated small-town life, and patriotic themes that reflected simple 20th century life. Frequently seen were Boy Scouts, mothers, children, and grandparents. They were often humorous and executed with such minute attention to detail that they frequently

Rockwell

resembled photos. He often said, "I paint life as I would like it to be."

Magazine, *Ride 'em Cowboy*, 1933.

The Norman Rockwell Museum is located in Stockbridge, Massachusetts, where he spent the last 25 years of his life (www.nrm.org).

Hint: You can say to an American, "It was right out of a Rockwell painting" if you want to comment on a pretty small-town scene with **down-to-earth** (ordinary, sensible) people. His art is the subject of many **coffee-table books** (oversize books of elaborate design that you might see displayed on coffee tables in Americans' living rooms, even mine).

STUART *[STEW-ehrt]*, Gilbert (1755-1828)

Stuart was an American portrait painter in colonial America influenced by the work of English portrait painters. He is probably America's best-known portrait painter, renowned for his portraits of nearly everyone of

Washington, 1795

prominence in government then. His famous 1795 portrait of President Washington hangs in our schools, government offices, and is on our one-dollar bill. Stuart was always low on money and was known for his erratic behavior, which some attributed to his genius. He is buried in Boston in an unmarked pauper's grave.

WARHOL *[WAR-haul]*, Andy (1928-1987)

Warhol was an American painter, publisher, motion-picture director and producer. He was a leader of the Pop Art movement, basing his artwork on images taken from mass or popular culture. His work and ideas both reflected and helped shape American mass media and popular culture. One of his most important innovations was

Warhol

Green Marilyn, 1962.

his use of enlarged photographic images silk-screened onto canvas and/or paper.

He produced quickly and cheaply a series of images that he marketed to the public with a flair that matched his creative genius. Popular objects such as soup cans, U.S. dollar bills, Coca-Cola bottles, and the various faces of celebrities and politicians became highly sought after by art lovers in the 1970s. His "Eight Elvises," painted in 1963, is the fifth most expensive painting ever sold ($100 million in 2008).

We might quote one of his sayings when someone **pops into the headlines** (suddenly becomes known to the public for whatever reason): "In the future everyone will be famous for fifteen minutes."

WHISTLER *[WHISS-lerr]*, James (1834-1903)

Whistler was one of the most influential late 19th

Whistler

century American painters. He assimilated Japanese art styles, made technical innovations, and championed modern art. He was a catalyst for those who wanted to break away from prescribed academic styles, a frequent theme in American art, literature, and culture.

Portrait of the Painter's Mother (1871)

He is credited with being the first American

228

Modernist to influence European art. His art is the opposite of his aggressive personality: discreet and subtle.

His *Portrait of the Painter's Mother* is perhaps the most famous painting in America. We affectionately call it *Whistler's Mother*. Its flattened forms, single color tone, and unsymmetrical composition are characteristic of his style.

"Paint should not be applied thick; it should be like a breath on the surface of a pane of glass." – James McNeill Whistler.

WOOD, Grant (1891-1942)

Wood was born on a small Iowa farm to a deeply religious family. His images of small-town folks and fertile Midwestern landscapes reflect his upbringing. Wood trained in Paris and on a trip to Germany in 1928 was inspired by Flemish and German artists. He soon produced paintings that were easy to understand and had an unassuming Midwestern charm.

Grant

Wood's *American Gothic* is another one of our most famous paintings. It transcends the seriousness of most art with humor that comes from Wood's placement of a typical American farmer and his daughter with European Gothic-style windows in the background.

"In making these paintings...I had in mind something which I hope to convey to a fairly wide audience in America—the picture of a country rich in the arts of peace; a homely lovable nation, infinitely worth any sacrifice necessary to its preservation." – Grant Wood.

American Gothic, 1930

WYETH *[WHY-eth]*, Andrew (1917-2009)

Wyeth ranks as one of the most popular American painters of his time. He is known for his realistic and thoughtful pictures

Wyeth

of people and places in rural Pennsylvania and Maine where he had a summer home. His paintings— reminders of earlier American life—show old buildings with bare windows and cracked ceilings, and abandoned boats on deserted beaches.

Wyeth worked in the tradition of

Brandywine Valley, 1940

229

Thomas Eakins and Winslow Homer, two American Realist painters of the late 1800s. He painted in egg tempera, a medium made of egg yolk that allowed him to represent details and gave his pictures a smooth, delicate surface.

"I prefer winter and fall, when you feel the bone structure of the landscape—the loneliness of it, the dead feeling of winter. Something waits beneath it, the whole story doesn't show." – Andrew Wyeth.

OTHER ARTISTIC ACHIEVERS

Ansel Adams *(1902-1984)* – Photography has played an important role in American art history. Many Americans recognize the name of Ansel Adams for his dramatic photographs of the West. His interest in preserving wilderness areas made him an active participant in the conservation movements. (www.anseladams.com)

Adams' "Farmworkers and Mt. Williamson."

Frank Lloyd Wright *(1867-1959)* – He is considered one of the greatest figures of 20th century architecture. While most American architects in the early 1900s looked to Europe for ideas, Wright found Japanese design and art more inspiring. The originality of his designs, his buildings' surroundings, and his creative use of materials are his hallmark. His homes and buildings are artistic national landmarks; the most famous is "Falling Water" house. (www.franklloydwright.org)

Famous "FallingWater" house.

Frank Gehry *(1929-)* – Believing that "architecture is art," Canadian-born Frank Gehry has lived in Los Angeles since 1947. He is celebrated today for his bold creations, including the Disney Concert Hall in downtown Los Angeles and the Guggenheim Museum in Bilboa, Spain. With his radical designs, some have called him "the apostle of chain-link fencing and corrugated metal siding" (www.foga.com)

Disney Concert Hall

FAVORITE MUSEUMS

The U.S. has about 18,000 museums and 14,000 art galleries. Some of our museums are not world-famous, but that does not lessen their appeal. Many are filled with art treasures and help dispel the notion some foreigners have that America is barren of culture. I am frequently asked by foreigners to name my favorites, so here they are.

- *Getty Villa* – By far my favorite, this stunning Villa overlooks the Pacific Ocean near Los Angeles. Filled with antiquities, it is patterned after an ancient villa in Herculaneum near famed Mt. Vesuvius. Entry is free, reservations are necessary. It makes for a lovely luncheon spot. (www.getty.edu/visit/)

- *Autry Museum of Western Heritage* – This intercultural history center in Los Angeles is dedicated to exploring and sharing the stories, experiences, and perceptions of the diverse peoples of the American West, including cowboys and Indians. (www.theautry.org)
- *National Gallery of Art* – This national art museum in Washington, D.C. was established in 1937 by a joint resolution of Congress with funds for construction and a substantial art collection donated by banker Andrew W. Mellon. (www.nga.gov)
- *Phoenix Art Museum* – This largest art museum in the southwest features 17,000 works in its collection, including Frederic Remington, Georgia O'Keeffe, Albert Bierstadt, and more. (www.phxart.org)
- *Metropolitan Museum of Art* – This New York City favorite dates back to 1866 Paris, France, when a group of Americans agreed to create a national institution and gallery of art to "bring art and art education to the American people." (www.metmuseum.org)
- *Huntington Gardens, Library and Museum* – This world-renowned center of art and culture is located just outside Los Angeles. It has four art galleries and a library with magnificent collections of rare books and historic manuscripts such as the Gutenberg Bible and Chaucer's *The Canterbury Tales*. Its priceless works of art include Gainsborough's *Blue Boy* and works by Reynolds, Sargent, Cassatt, and Hopper. (www.huntington.org)

FOREIGN CONTRIBUTORS TO AMERICAN ART

Unfortunately, traditional American art history tends to ignore or minimize the contributions of minorities and immigrants. And many American artists of the late 19th century were strongly influenced by foreign styles and aesthetics. Throughout the centuries, foreign heritage Americans have produced a wide variety of art in the form of paintings, photographs, sculptures, architecture, gardening, furniture, crafts, and other media. All of these contribute to our culture. Their works are displayed in many of America's (and the world's) prestigious museums. Here are but a few.

India – Natvar Bhavsar (1934–) came to the U.S. to study when he was 28 years old. His work is part of the permanent collections of museums such as the Boston Fine Arts Museum, the Metropolitan Museum of Art, and the Whitney Museum of American Art in New York.

Natvar Bhavsar

231

China – Maya Lin (1959-) is a contemporary Chinese American architectural talent. When she was 21 and a college student at Yale University School of Architecture, she was selected in a national contest to design the originally controversial, but now much admired, **Vietnam Veterans Memorial** in the Washington, D.C. Area.

This is one of the most acclaimed U.S. public monuments built in the last decades of the 20th century. It has two highly polished black granite walls 150 m (493 ft) long.

Lin

Vietnam Veterans Memorial

The names of more than 58,000 American men and women killed or missing as a result of the Vietnam War (1964-1973) are inscribed in them.

The monument focuses attention not only upon itself, but also changes one's perception of the surrounding area. Tearing across the ground as a metaphor for an emotional scar, the wall of names depicts the enormity of the suffering, by both soldiers and the civilians, through that turbulent period. It evokes raw emotions from visitors who can see their own faces reflected as they search for names of loved ones. It is not uncommon to see friends, relatives, and war companions rubbing names off the wall onto paper, or leaving flowers and pictures. Lin also designed a Civil Rights Memorial in Montgomery, Alabama.

China – Ieoh Ming Pei (1917-) left for the U.S. in 1934 to study architecture at MIT (Massachusetts Institute of Technology) and the Harvard Graduate School of Design. Designing over 50 projects, he has won numerous awards and media attention for

Rock and Roll Hall of Fame.

incorporating bold geometric and high-tech designs into buildings such as the Javits Convention Center in New York City, La Pyramide du Louvre in Paris, and the Rock and Roll Hall of Fame in Cleveland. In 1982, the deans of the architectural schools of the U.S. chose Pei as the best designer of significant non-residential structures. Ever the perfectionist, he said, "Doctors can bury their mistakes, but architects have to live with theirs."

232

Japan – Roger Shimomura (1939-) is a third-generation Japanese American who creates paintings and theatrical performance pieces by blending an ironic mixture of Japanese imagery and American popular culture. He and his family were removed to an American internment camp for Japanese Americans during World War II (1941-1945).

Shimomura

Diary: December 12, 1941, 1980
(Courtesy of Mr. Shimomura.)

Much of his work explores the emotional and psychological hardships of that internment experience based on the diaries of his grandmother. More recently he has taken a more light-hearted approach to the serious themes of racism and cross-cultural relations.

"Too many people blur the distinctions between Japanese, Chinese, Korean, Vietnamese, and other Asians," he says. Shimomura's works play with these misconceptions. In his paintings, brick walls and screens represent the arbitrary barriers that often separate races and cultures in this country. He also draws attention to the sometimes hilarious ways in which different cultures overlap.

The prestigious **Smithsonian Institution** (www.si.edu) in Washington, D.C., the world's largest museum and research complex with 19 museums and 9 research centers, is collecting his personal papers.

Romania – Saul Steinberg (1941-1999) was a cartoonist whose work began to appear in *The New Yorker* magazine (www.newyorker.com) in 1941, a year before he arrived in the U.S. He was featured in this prestigious magazine's pages throughout his life. Since the 1940s his work has been exhibited in museums and galleries.

He elevated the cartoon to a fine art by employing humor often tinged with irony and portraying the richness of the American scene.

One his most famous *New Yorker* covers represents New Yorkers' shortsighted view of the world with a large Manhattan Island and a tiny world west of the Hudson River. (This is the same near-sighted view some foreigners say America as a whole has in relation to the rest of the world.)

N

SPORTS

Sports is the toy department of human life. - Howard Cosell, sportscaster

Even though America is often described as the most diverse country in the world, sports is a bond that brings us together irrespective of race, gender, age, ethnicity, country of origin, or religion.

Sports is a **big deal** (important) for Americans. This chapter familiarizes you with a few of our popular ones. As we enjoy more leisure time and become more aware of their health benefits, we participate in more sports and recreational activities. We also enjoy watching games in person and on TV and have our favorite high school, college, and professional teams and players. You might be asked to go to a game with us or participate in a sport. Given our competitive nature, some corporations even have teams of employees that compete against each other in various sports.

With this popularity of sports comes various sports-related words and terms we use. Knowing them and the names of our athletes and teams will enhance your understanding of our pastimes.

Collectively, sports is big business in the U.S. Manufacturers pay millions of dollars to get our top professional athletes to endorse their products. Tiger Woods earned ten times more from sponsor endorsements in 2009 than from his $10 million in prize winnings. Some of us even wear sports clothing with the names of our favorite teams and players.

Thirty million of our children are involved in organized youth sports, some beginning as early as age six. Little League Baseball, for example, which started in the U.S. in 1939, today has 3 million kids on 7,000 teams participating around the world, including Canada, Mexico, Asia Pacific, Japan, Europe, Middle East, Africa, Latin America, and the Caribbean.

Many (but unfortunately not all) of our professional and college athletes serve as positive role models for our kids. We don't much like it when they don't. We believe competitive sports build character and self-confidence, teach team effort, and encourage sportsmanship and fair play that carry over into adult lives. (There's that *competition* and *fairness* thing again.)

> **Hint**: Some parents feel that instead of learning fair play and teamwork, some children are learning that winning is the only thing that matters. So, some parents and coaches try to downplay this aspect of these games and make participation more fun and less competitive. Occasionally the media reports on a spectator parent who was removed from a game because of their aggressive behavior and disrespect shown to the officials. Or a coach who was dropped from a team because of his win-at-all-cost philosophy.

Our daily newspapers have comprehensive sports sections. We have sports-only cable TV channels such as ESPN, which bills itself as The Worldwide Leader in Sports (www.espn.go.com). *Sports Illustrated* (www.si.com) is one of many popular sports magazine in the U.S.

Regulation – As you might expect, our different sports govern themselves in America, so the government is not involved. The National Collegiate Athletic Association (**NCAA**) regulates amateur athletics (colleges) while our professional sports have their own governing bodies. Indirectly, however, the government can get involved in such things as defining illegal sports-enhancing drugs and eligibility requirements for a college player to go to a professional team. There are times Americans wish for more regulation. As an example, professional boxing in the U.S. is viewed by many as corrupt and unregulated. Sometimes boxers are taken advantage of by fight promoters and they **come out on the short end** (are cheated) of their financial earnings.

> **Hint**: Classic films dealing with boxing are *Rocky* (1976), *Raging Bull* (1980), *Ali* (2001) the story of Muhammad Ali, and Academy Award winner *Million Dollar Baby* (2004).

Most Popular Sports – Our 15 most popular *recreational sporting activities* that we participate in are swimming, walking, bowling, bicycling, weight lifting, fishing, camping, treadmill exercise, billiards, basketball, stretching, hiking, jogging, and golf. In addition to these, we have dozens of others such as skydiving, hang gliding, bungee jumping, snow and water skiing, and tennis. Our sporting goods stores are **packed to the rafters** (full to overflowing) with equipment to support a vast array of these activities.

A skiing family.

Ranked by popularity, our top 10 *spectator sports* that we follow by attending games, watching on TV, listening to on radio, or reading about are: professional football in the number one position followed by professional baseball, college football, professional basketball, auto racing, professional hockey, high school football, and professional soccer at number 10.

National Anthem – If you should attend our games, you will notice the crowd stands before the game starts and they sing the **Star Spangled Banner**, our National Anthem (a solemn hymn). They are sometimes led by a member of the public or by a celebrity singer. Written in 1814, our national song's ending line reflects our heritage: "…and the home of the free." The song is also played when medals are awarded to Americans at the Olympics. (You can hear and read the words at kids.niehs.nih.gov/lyrics/spangle.htm.) It is not unlike the anthem of other nations, including India's *Jan gana mana,* Japan's *Kimigayo,* and England's *God Save the Queen*.

Equality – As you might expect, our culture influences how our teams compete. Equality, once again, plays a role, as it has in so many other aspects of our lives since our founding. We adopt measures to create a **level playing field** for the teams to compete. For example, baseball teams in our larger cities take in more money and can thus afford to pay to get the best players. To offset this, baseball assesses money from teams whose payrolls are above a certain limit and then redistributes the money to the smaller teams. Professional football and basketball teams also have similar **salary caps**. Further, professional football teams must interview at least one minority for a coaching position.

Since many Americans follow organized sports (57% of men, 35% women), your American contact probably has an interest in at least one or more of our three most popular spectator sports discussed below: baseball, football, and basketball. A basic understanding of each may enhance your conversations and relationships; even your understanding in case you are taken to a game or get caught up in the fervor. (Golf is also discussed because it is both popular and widely used today for business entertaining).

BASEBALL

"Whoever wants to know the heart and mind of America had better learn baseball, the rules and realities of the game."

Those words, written by a cultural historian in 1954, remain an insightful commentary on both Americans and baseball. Baseball is called **America's favorite pastime**. Fans love to sit in the ballpark and eat hotdogs, drink beer, and hope they will catch a souvenir ball hit in their direction. We love to yell encouragement to our team. Youngsters hope someday to be playing on the same field just as their heroes are doing. Watch a game is a good way to escape the pressures of everyday life. Famous actor Humphrey Bogart once said, "A hot dog at the ball park is better than steak at the Ritz [a fancy hotel]."

Baseball

Fifty percent of Americans are baseball fans. Although it began in America, its popularity has spread to other nations, particularly the Caribbean and Japan. It was introduced to the Olympics in the 1992 but was dropped 20 years later. Just as soccer is played around the world, we play baseball on local playgrounds, parks, empty lots, and farm fields. We have various leagues for young children, high school, college, and professional teams.

Besides the **minor leagues** where young players start their careers, we have 30 Major League Baseball (**MLB**) teams (www.mlb.com) from coast to coast and in Canada that play 162 games from April to September. The teams are divided into the National and American Leagues and the victorious team from each league meet in early October in our famed **World Series**. The **New York Yankees** have won the most World Series titles (27) (www.yankees.com). In fact we have a popular musical stage play and movie titled *Damn Yankees!*. More than 100 million people in 224 countries around the world viewed a recent World Series on TV, with Korean and Japanese viewers

Baseball stadium.

making up about 47 million of that total. The average major league salary is about $3.3 million per year. Top players earn as high as $25 million a year.

The Baseball Hall of Fame Museum in central New York State contains over 30,000 objects representing all facets of the game from its inception to the present. It is an honor for the few players elected to the Hall (www.baseballhalloffame.org).

> **Hint: Pete Rose** achieved the most number of hits in a career but was forbidden election to the Hall of Fame because he bet illegally on his team's baseball games when he was a manager. About two-thirds of fans think he should be eligible, which fits with our idea of forgive and forget. But it doesn't fit so well with our belief that honesty is the best policy. Feel free to ask your American counterpart what he or she thinks about this controversial issue.

The first African American to play in the major leagues was **Jackie Robinson** (1919-1972), an outstanding player with the Brooklyn Dodgers (now the Los Angeles Dodgers). He **opened the door** (set the precedent) for other minorities to play in the **majors** (MLB), including foreigners. **Babe Ruth** played in the 1920s and remains our most famous player of all time.

> **Hint**: Popular baseball movies include *The Natural* (1984) with Robert Redford, *Bull Durham* (1988) with Kevin Costner, and *Field of Dreams* (1989) with Kevin Costner. (Costner played baseball in college.) *A League of Their Own* (1992) with Tom Hanks deals with women's baseball during World War II when male players were away at war.

Baseball is a reflection of our culture, and vice versa, and that includes personal freedoms. From the 19th century through 1976, baseball players were bound to one team for life. Teams could renew contracts for one year for as long as they wanted to keep the player. Then in 1969 a player was traded to another team and he refused to report because he didn't want to play for that team. He appealed to the U.S. Supreme Court but lost.

Then in 1975, two players played without a contract, arguing that their contract could not be renewed by the team if they never signed it. An arbitrator agreed and they were declared free agents (free to negotiate with other teams) and now had control over their own futures. The players' union and the owners then agreed to the new rules governing free agency that the teams and players would follow. Yet another example how "we the people" bring about change in the U.S.

The Teams – This table provides the location and names of our major league teams. Refer to these names and locations if you are meeting with Americans and know what city they live in. Most likely they will be fans of the nearest baseball team. Each team has its own own website.

AMERICAN LEAGUE TEAMS		
Eastern Division	**Central Division**	**Western Division**
Baltimore Orioles (Maryland)	Chicago White Sox (Illinois)	Anaheim Angels (S. California)
Boston Red Sox (Massachusetts)	Cleveland Indians (Ohio)	Oakland Athletics (N. California)
New York Yankees (New York)	Detroit Tigers (Michigan)	Seattle Mariners (Washington)
Tampa Bay Devil Rays (Florida)	Kansas City Royals (Kansas)	Texas Rangers (Near Dallas)
Toronto Blue Jays (Canada)	Minnesota Twins (In Minneapolis)	

NATIONAL LEAGUE TEAMS		
Eastern Division	**Central Division**	**Western Division**
Atlanta Braves (Georgia)	Chicago Cubs (Illinois)	Arizona Diamondbacks (In Phoenix)
Florida Marlins (In Miami)	Cincinnati Reds (Ohio)	Colorado Rockies (In Denver)
Washington, D.C. Nationals	Houston Astros (Texas)	Los Angeles Dodgers (S.California)
New York Mets (New York)	Milwaukee Brewers (Wisconsin)	San Diego Padres (S. California)
Philadelphia Phillies (Pennsylvania)	Pittsburgh Pirates (Pennsylvania)	San Francisco Giants (N. California)
	St. Louis Cardinals (Missouri)	

The Game – Famous scientist Albert Einstein said, "You teach me baseball and I'll teach you relativity...no.... You will learn about relativity faster than I learn baseball." Actually, baseball is not that complicated once you **get the hang of it** (grasp the fundamentals) even though the teams do execute lots of strategies, which keeps the game interesting.

A batter and a catcher.

The goal of the game is to score more **runs** (points) than the opposing team. That's easy, right? A run is scored when a runner circles all three **bases** and touches **home plate**. In each of 9 **innings**, a team will send a **batter** to the **plate** (home plate) to hit the ball with a wooden **bat** that is thrown by the opposing **pitcher** to his **catcher** squatting behind home plate.

The batter tries to get on base by either safely hitting the ball that is not caught by the opposing team, or by a **walk** in which the pitcher throws four balls outside the strike zone. Once on base, the player must be advanced to home plate by teammates at bat in order to score a run. A minimum of three batters will come to the plate for a team in each inning. When three **outs** have been made, the team has completed its half of the inning and the opposing team comes to bat. The only major team sport played in North America without a time clock, the game usually lasts two to three hours with multiple trips to the food stands by the fans. (Are you still with me?)

The most exciting play in baseball, the **home run**, occurs when the ball is hit out of the baseball park over the fences. We have a saying, **swing for the fences**, which comes from this effort. If there are three runners on the bases (the bases are "loaded") when the home run is hit, it is called a **grand slam** and four runs are scored. (The New York Yankees in 2011 became the first team in major league history to hit three grand slams in a game.) **Hank Aaron** retired in 1974 with 755 career home runs, a record that still stands. **Barry Bonds** hit 73 home runs in 2001, setting a new single-season record; however, many believe he took steroids to achieve it so his record is tarnished.

So, was that so hard? Start with these basics and your knowledge will grow.

Everyday Terms – Like many other sports terms, baseball terms are used in our everyday talk in other contexts besides baseball. It will benefit you to understand them or even use them when you talk to an American, or if you visit a real baseball game.

- **Home run** and **grand slam** denote a very special success. For example, "I hit a home run when I wrote up a million dollar sales order."
- The ball used in baseball is called a hardball as opposed to a softball that is used in the similar game of softball. The term **hardball** can mean to get tough or firm in negotions.
- A **curveball**, which is thrown by the pitcher that curves and is therefore hard to hit, denotes an unexpected turn of events. In everyday life, this might occur when you are about to sign a contract and unexpectedly your counterpart makes a demand for something that was never discussed. You might say, "He threw me a curveball," or "it came unexpectedly  out of **left field**, which is one of the three outfield locations in the park that are far removed from home plate.

Umpire signaling "You're out!

- **Three strikes and you're out** could mean that you will be allowed three attempts to accomplish something before you will be relieved by someone else. **I struck out** means you did not achieve what you were trying to accomplish, just like the batter who swings at the ball three times and misses, thus not getting on base.
- The baseball umpire yells **let's play ball** to begin play. You could say it to initiate the action of others, such as at the beginning of a business meeting to get it started.
- Players have a **batting average** that indicates as a percentage how frequently they successfully hit the ball; a .300 average or above is excellent. **Batting 1,000** indicates 100 percent success in multiple situtations. A salesman who "closes a deal" (writes an order) in ten out of ten sales calls is "batting 1,000."
- A **fastball** is the pitcher's hardest thrown pitch to the batter, sometimes exceeding 185 kph. If you **throw a fastball** to someone, you give your best effort to win or achieve something over them. A lawyer could deliver a powerful fastball (or hardball) interrogation in a courtroom trial.
- An **All Star** game is played once a year with the best players voted into the game by the fans. If you have done something particularly well, you might be complimeted for your **all-star performance**.

Foreign Heritage Baseball Players – Of the 846 major league baseball players beginning the 2011 season, 28 percent were born outside the U.S. They came from 14 countries with the vast majority from Latin America. In a few years the mix is expected to approach 50 percent, the same percentage of foreign-born minor leaguers playing today. The Dominican Republic lead with 86 players, Venezuela was second with 62 and Puerto Rico third with 20. You might hear the names of these foreign heritage players.

- Fernando Valenzuela was born in a small town in Mexico. He was a dominating pitcher most notably for the Los Angeles Dodgers from 1980 to 1990. He touched off an early 80s craze dubbed "Fernandomania." He became the only player to win both the **Rookie of The Year** (first year player) award and the **Cy Young Award** (for best pitcher) in the same season.

Valenzuela

- Roberto Clemente was the first Latin American to be elected to the Hall of Fame posthumously (after death) in 1973. He played in the majors from 1955 to 1972, winning the National League **Most Valuable Player Award** (MVP) in 1966. He died in a plane crash in 1972 en route to delivering aid to earthquake victims in Nicaragua.
- Hideo Nomo was the first Asian-born player to join a major league U.S. team. After playing professionally in Japan, his 1995 signing with the Los Angeles

Dodgers led to other Asian athletes following in his footsteps. Many Japanese traveled to the U.S. to watch him play, and the games in which he pitched were shown on Japan TV.

Nomo

- Kauhiro Sasaki, a pitcher, set a Seattle Mariners' record in 2001 and was voted the league's Rookie of the Year in 2000 and voted by the fans to the All Star Game in 2001.
- Chan Ho Park was the first Korean to play in the **big leagues**. In 2001 he pitched with the Los Angeles Dodgers and was also selected to the All Star Game.
- Ichiro Suzuki of the Seattle Mariners was the first non-pitcher from Japan to sign with a major league team. In 2004, 30-year old Suzuki broke an 84-year-old record with 262 hits and became the first player in major league history to collect 200 hits in his first four seasons.
- Hideki Matsui, a hero in Japanese baseball, joined the New York Yankees in 2003 and helped them go to the World Series with his strong batting skills. He also helped them win the 2009 World Series and was selected the series' Most Valuable Player.

Matsui

FOOTBALL

In most countries, "football" is known as the game Americans call "soccer." In America, football is football, not soccer. Soccer uses a round ball and football uses an oblong ball. Our game of football is somewhat similar to soccer, however, as points are scored by advancing the ball into the opponent's goal. But rugby is the sport most similar to American football. American football got a boost from the launch of the NFL Europe league in 1991, but it was terminated in 2007 after incurring financial losses, a reflection of the popularity of soccer there.

Football

Roughly 60 percent of adult Americans claim to follow professional football regularly, and about 45 percent follow college football. Youngsters play football anywhere, from vacant fields to parks to backyards, and on grass, asphalt, and dirt.

As with baseball, there are organized football leagues for youngsters of all ages. High schools and colleges have football teams that compete with each other. At halftime, their schools' marching bands provide colorful entertainment. Although baseball is America's

Carolina Panthers football stadium.

Favorite Pastime, football is the number one competition sport between our schools. In

242

smaller towns, particularly in our state of Texas, the high school football team's success might be the focus of the entire community. Schools and professional teams usually play once a week for about three months in the fall.

Professional football is played in the **National Football League (NFL)** that, like baseball, has National and American Conference teams (www.nfl.com). The ever-popular **Super Bowl** is played in early February between the two conference winners to determine the one best team. It is one of the world's most watched sporting events, with one-third of the people in the U.S. gathered in front of their TVs. **Super Bowl Sunday** is now considered an unofficial holiday with records for the second largest day for U.S. food consumption (particularly home-delivered pizzas); Thanksgiving Day is first.

> **Hint**: Popular football movies include *Brian's Song* (1970), *The Longest Yard* (1974), *North Dallas Forty* (1979), and *Jerry Maguire* (1996) with Tom Cruise. Sandra Bullock won the Best Actress Academy Award staring in *The Blind Side* (2009) that tells the true story of a **well-to-do** (rich) family **taking under their wing** (guiding and protecting) a homeless black teen who grows to become a star NFL athlete. You don't have to be a football fan to enjoy them, and they will give you an understanding of how central the sport is to American life.

The Teams – This table provides the names and divisions of the 31 NFL teams. If you plan to meet with an American and you know where they live, check this table and remember the name of the closest team—it might be their favorite. Fans take their teams seriously, so if you ask them how their team is doing, some might use profanity if their team is not doing well. Others might **light up** (look pleased).

AMERICAN FOOTBALL CONFERENCE		
Eastern Division	**Central Division**	**Western Division**
Buffalo Bills	Baltimore Ravens	Denver Broncos
Indianapolis Colts	Cincinnati Bengals	Kansas City Chiefs
Miami Dolphins	Cleveland Browns	Oakland Raiders
New England Patriots	Jacksonville Jaguars	San Diego Chargers
New York Jets	Pittsburgh Steelers	Seattle Seahawks
	Tennessee Titans	

NATIONAL FOOTBALL CONFERENCE		
Eastern Division	**Central Division**	**Western Division**
Arizona Cardinals	Chicago Bears	Atlanta Falcons
Dallas Cowboys	Detroit Lions	Carolina Panthers
New York Giants	Green Bay Packers	New Orleans Saints
Philadelphia Eagles	Minnesota Vikings	St. Louis Rams
Washington Redskins	Tampa Bay Buccaneers	San Francisco 49ers

Team names can reflect the culture of their area. The San Francisco 49ers name derives from gold seekers in that area in 1849. The Minnesota Vikings from the Scandinavian influence in that area. Dallas Cowboys is a tribute to horseback riding cowboys that herd cattle in the area. And Pittsburgh Steelers reflects the history of steel making there.

Use the teams' websites to learn more about them. The league has worked for years to re-establish a team in Los Angeles after the owner moved it to the Midwest city of St. Louis in 1994.

The Game – **Vince Lombardi**, a famous winning football coach, drew a similarity between football and our culture: "Football is like life—it requires perseverance, self-denial, hard work, sacrifice, dedication, and respect for authority."

Simplified, this is how the game is played. A rectangular-shaped field of natural grass or artificial turf is marked with ten white **10-yard lines**. It is played in four periods, or quarters, of 15 minutes playing time for each. Two opposing teams try to score points against each other, most commonly by advancing the ball across the opposing team's **goal line** (6 points)—called a **touchdown**—or by kicking the ball between the opponent's H-shaped goalposts (3 points). Defensive players try to tackle the offensive ball carrier to prevent a touchdown. Because of the often violent bodily contact and aggressive play, players wear protective equipment. The team scoring the most points by the end of the game wins.

Everyday Terms – We use football **jargon** (specialized language) in everyday talk.

- When you score a **touchdown**, you complete something successfully that you've been working on, like making a large sale for your company.
- If **the ball is on the 1 yard line**, the team is very close to making a touchdown. You could say, "We've developed this new technology for five years and we are now **on the one yard line** before we start marketing it."
- A **goal-line stance** indicates the defensive team is closely guarding its goal line to prevent a touchdown by the opposing team. You might be in a goal-line stance if you are strongly defending your position that is verbally under attack from others.
- A **fumble** occurs when the ball is dropped and the other team recovers it. "I **fumbled** the ball when I neglected to research my competitor's prices and they were awarded the contract."
- If a player **runs interference**, he is running in front of his teammate (who is carrying the ball) in order to deflect the opposition from tackling the runner. Similarly, a manager might tell a subordinate to "**Run with the ball** and I will **run your interference**," meaning the manager will attempt to remove obstacles so the project can advance without interruption from others.

Foreign Heritage Football Players – Though their numbers are small, foreign-born Americans are slowly adapting to professional football. They number about 100, nearly double the number ten years ago. Samoa averages about 30 players each year.

244

- *Ukraine* – Igor Olshansky immigrated with his family to the U.S. at the age of seven and is the first player from the former Soviet Union to be drafted by an NFL team.

- *Scandinavia* – Morten Andersen (Denmark) is the all-time leading kicker. Ove Johansson (Sweden) is the holder of the longest field goal in NFL history at 69 yards.

- *Germany* – Players include, Ivan Jurkovic, Horst Muhlmann, and Sebastian Vollmer.

- *Netherlands* – Harald Hasselbach played in the NFL for six years and was a starter in a Super Bowl game.

- *Vietnam* – Dat Nguyen, born in Vietnam, set an all-time Texas A&M college record for tackles and then played for the Dallas Cowboys.

- *Philippines* – Roman Gabriel, son of a Filipino immigrant, was the first Asian American to **start** (begin a game) as an NFL **quarterback** (offensive leader) in 1962, and was named the NFL's Most Valuable Player in 1969.

Roman Gabriel

BASKETBALL

This game seems to be the easiest for foreigners to learn because it merely involves throwing a round inflated ball through a suspended basket to make points. Foreigners also enjoy the game because of its continuous action and frequent scoring. You might see our homes with basketball hoops attached to garages where parents join their children in a game. Our playgrounds, parks, and school grounds have basketball courts, too.

Basketball

About 40 percent of Americans are basketbll fans. Our high schools and colleges have men's and women's basketball teams that compete separately. In March, a national college tournament is held to determine the best men's college team out of 64 entrants. In case you meet someone from these winning states, North Carolina's Duke University won the men's 2010 trophy, the University of Connecticut in 2011, and the University of Kentucky in 2012. UCLA (University of California at Los Angeles) has won the most: 11.

The men's professional league is called the **National Basketball Association (NBA)** (www.nba.com). Most NBA players played in college. The NBA playoffs are held in May and June. The **Los Angeles Lakers** won the championship in 2009 and their sixteenth again in 2010. The Dallas [Texas] Mavericks won the title in 2011. The **Boston Celtics** *[SELL-ticks]* from Massachusetts have won the most NBA titles with 17. The individual record for the most points scored in a

Playing basketball on a school playground.

game is 100 by **Wilt Chamberlain** in 1962. The average NBA salary is $5.3 million. The Women's National Basketball Association (WNBA), a relative newcomer, is composed of twelve teams that play from June to September when the NBA is on vacation.

Though basketball started in the U.S. in 1891, it is now recognized as a national sport in 213 countries. A number of Americans play on professional European teams, and vice versa. It was the first U.S. professional organized sport to stage regular season games outside America when two games were played at Tokyo in 1990. Since then, NBA teams have opened the season in Japan six other times. The Chinese took to basketball like **ducks to water** (natural attraction), making it their most popular sport when countryman **Yao Ming** became a star in the NBA and his games were broadcast on Chinese television.

The NBA follows a tradition in our other professional sports. An NBA Most Valuable Player (**MVP**) is selected as the best player at the end of each season. They also elect their best players—both men and women—to The Basketball Hall of Fame in Springfield, Massachusetts, in recognition of their achievements during their careers that have since ended (www.hoophall.com).

Hint: Popular movies about basketball include *Hoosiers* (1986), *He Got Game* (1998), *Coach Carter* (2005), and *Glory Road* (2006).

The Teams – Chances are good that an American you meet will have an interest in one of our NBA teams. There is one in most of our major cities and one in Canada. For a great conversation starter, learn the name of your new friend's hometown team. Here are the 29 teams, their states, and the divisional alignment. All have websites that provide more information you can use in your discussions with American basketball fans.

NBA TEAMS - EASTERN CONFERENCE

Atlantic Division

Boston Celtics (MA)	Miami Heat (Fl)
New Jersey Nets (NJ)	New York Knickerbockers (NY)
Orlando Magic (FL)	Philadelphia 76ers (PA)
Washington Wizards (DC)	

Central Division

Atlanta Hawks (GA)	New Orleans Hornets (LA)
Chicago Bulls (IL)	Cleveland Cavaliers (OH)
Detroit Pistons (MI)	Indiana Pacers (IN)
Milwaukee Bucks (WI)	Toronto Raptors (Canada)

NBA TEAMS - WESTERN CONFERENCE

Midwest Division

Dallas Mavericks (TX)	Denver Nuggets (CO)
Houston Rockets (TX)	Minnesota Timberwolves (MN)
San Antonio Spurs (TX)	Utah Jazz (UT)
Memphis Grizzlies (TN)	

Pacific Division

Golden State Warriors(CA)	Los Angeles Clippers (CA)
Los Angeles Lakers (CA)	Phoenix Suns (AZ)
Portland Trail Blazers(OR)	Sacramento Kings (CA)
Seattle SuperSonics (WA)	

Hint: Like our other professional teams, names of some NBA teams reflect the culture of their locations. Boston Celtics: Irish heritage. Philadelphia 76ers: 1776 American history. Detroit Pistons: automotive capitol of America. San Antonio Spurs: cowboy heritage. Denver Nuggets: gold mining history in the Rocky Mountains. Phoenix Suns: warm climate. Seattle SuperSonics: aircraft manufacturing center. Portland Trail Blazers: Early settlers who pushed west through Oregon's vast forests. New Orleans is known for its jazz music, so the Utah Jazz name came from the New Orleans Jazz team that moved to Utah. The Los Angeles Lakers name came from the Minneapolis Lakers team that moved west from the Midwest state known as The Land of 10,000 Lakes.

The Game – The basketball **court** is a rectangular area and at each end is a vertical backboard anchored to a wall or suspended from the ceiling with **baskets** attached firmly to the backboards. When a player makes the ball fall down through the net basket, points are scored.

A basketball team has five players on the floor at any given time. The team that gets the ball tries to advance it toward the basket defended by the opposing side trying for a **field goal** (a basket) that scores two points. A player may advance the ball by passing it to a teammate or by dribbling (bouncing) it while running toward the basket. After a basket is scored, the team scored upon puts the ball into play from behind its end line and in turn tries to move the ball up court to score at the opposite end of the court.

Everyday Terms – You might hear us use basketball terms in our everyday talk.
- A **slam dunk** occurs when a player jumps up and slams the ball down through the 18-inch hoop, so that it is almost impossible to miss. When something is extremely likely to occur for you, like completing a big sale for your company, you can say confidently, "It will be a slam dunk, boss."
- A **prayer** is a shot from a long distance that has no hope of going through the rim. If you have little or no hope of doing something that will succeed, you might say, "I will **give it a shot** (will try) but I don't think we have a prayer."

- A **hot dog** is a player who shoots the ball with such unconventional form that some consider the player showing off or trying to embarrass his opponent with fancy play. (Our hot dogs are an American sandwich with lots of fancy, appealing condiments heaped upon them, too.) A fun hot-dogging team that plays for show instead

The other kind of hot dog.

of competition is the **Harlem Globetrotters**. You may even have a flashy co-worker or friend you would describe as a hot-dogger.

- A **fast break** occurs when the offensive team quickly moves the ball up court before the opposing team can set up in their defensive position. You could say, "Let's make a fast break and score before our competition knows **what hit them** (they were caught off balance)."

Hint: One of our most moving speeches from someone in athletics came from North Carolina State basketball coach Jim Valvano *[Val-VON-o]* whose underrated 1983 team won the NCAA Men's Basketball Championship. Valvano was diagnosed with bone cancer in 1992. He spoke at a banquet the following year where he was given a courage and humanitarian award. In accepting the award, he is remembered for saying, **"Don't give up. Don't ever give up,"** something he instilled in his **underdog** (weaker rated) teams, and a motto he used in fighting his cancer. He died two months after his famous speech. You might hear an American who admires Valvano use these words of encouragement, even outside the realm of sports.

Foreign Heritage Basketball Players – European players were first **drafted** (selected) by NBA teams in 1989 and the first Asian made it to our shores in 2000. Today, Brazil, Japan, Germany, France, and Spain are among the nations that support leagues that develop the skills of international players and feed the NBA. About a fourth of NBA players are foreign-born. In 2010, the NBA had 83 players from 35 countries, including France 10, Serbia 6, Spain 5, Slovenia 5, Argentina 5, Africa 5, Australia 4, England 4, Italy 3, and China 2, plus others. The numbers change each year as players come and go and teams strive to put the best players on the floor.

Here is a sampling of foreign-born players who have excelled in the NBA.

- *Argentina* – Manu Ginobili earned three NBA championship rings and was named an All Star twice from the San Antonio Spurs (Texas).

Manu Ginobili

- *Belgium* – Tony Parker was born in Belgium, raised in France, and his mother was a Dutch model. He helped the San Antonio Spurs win three NBA Championships from 2003 to 2007 and was selected as an All Star three times.

- *China* – Zhi Zhi Wang became the first Asian to play in the NBA when drafted by the Dallas Mavericks (Texas) in 2000. Yao Ming, a star in China, joined the Houston Rockets (Texas) in 2002 and was selected to the NBA All

Star Game in each of his first seven seasons. Because of his outgoing personality, he was featured in commercials and became an instant celebrity known for his sense of humor. **Nagging** (continuing) injuries force him to retire in 2011.

- *Germany* – Dirk Nowitzki is an all-purpose basketball player for the Dallas Mavericks and regarded as one of the best players in the NBA. In 2007, he became the first European-born player to receive the league's Most Valuable Player (MVP) award. He led his team to the championship in 2011 and was named the series MVP.

Dick Nowitzki

- *Spain* – Pau Gasol was the NBA Rookie of the Year in 2002 and led the Los Angeles Lakers to championships in 2009 and 10.

GOLF

Golf is called a "gentlemen's game." because players are surrounded by beautiful scenery and they pay attention to etiquette and polite behavior. In the past, mostly people of higher economic status played it. Today, it is popular with everyone, including women and children.

The game was invented in Scotland where it was titled **G**entlemen **O**nly **L**adies **F**orbidden—thus

Golf course in desert area of Southern California.

the word GOLF entered into the English language. America has 30 million golfers, so chances are pretty good you will meet an American who plays the game. Strike up a conversation about his or her game to quickly make friends. Business people frequent the golf course to discuss business in an informal, relaxed setting. States in our warmer climates are noted for their year-round courses, particularly Florida, California, Arizona, and Hawaii.

Most cities have public courses where anyone can play. The charge for this averages about $35-40 per day. Private clubs limit play to their members only. The Resort at Pelican Hill (www.pelicanhill.com) near Los Angeles is the number one rated golf resort in the U.S. *Golf Digest* (www.golfdigest.com) and *Golf Magazine* (www.golfmagazine.com) are two of our popular golf magazines.

High schools and colleges have golf teams that compete, and we have amateur tournaments each year to determine the best young golfers. Korean American Grace Park won the 1998 Women's Amateur Championship and went on to a professional career winning $5.5 million. Tiger Woods was a collegiate champ, too.

The Professional Golfers' Association of America (**PGA**) directs professional play of its several hundred male members who tour the country playing in major PGA tournaments (www.pga.com). The Ladies Professional Golf Association (**LPGA**) has about 300 tournament players doing the same (www.lpga.com). Players from other nations have won both of these important tournaments many times.

The Game – Golf is an outdoor game for one or more players (usually in groups of four), each of who uses specially designed clubs to hit a small hard ball over a field of play known as a **course** or links. The standard course is about 5900 to 6400 m (about 6500 to 7000 yd) in length. The object of the game is to sink the ball in each of 18 holes while using the fewest strokes possible.

Golf ball.

The individual holes may vary in length from each other anywhere from 90 to 550 m (from 100 to 600 yd). Each hole has at one end a starting point known as a **tee**, and imbedded in the ground at the other end marked by a flag on a pole is a **cup** (also called a hole) into which the ball must be hit in order to complete play at each hole. The short-cropped grass surrounding the cup is called the **green**.

Golf tee.

The courses are long enough for players to get walking exercise if they don't want to use an electric golf cart to get around. As in other American activities, etiquette is an important part of golf and because of the **honor system** (no one is checking on you), cheating is strictly forbidden.

Par is the term applied to the number of properly played strokes an expert golfer would be expected to use in completing a particular hole. Par-5 is considered a long hole, while a par-3 hole is a short one requiring fewer strokes. The aggregate for all of the holes is **par for the course**, which is usually about 72. If your score is less than the posted par for the course, you did well. Average weekend golfers might shoot 90 to 100.

The cup or hole.

On a rare occasion, a player drives the ball from the tee into the cup in one stroke, thereby making a **hole in one**. A score of one less than par on a given hole is referred to as a **birdie**. A score of two less than par (like a score of 3 on a par-5 hole) is called an **eagle**. One stroke over par is called a **bogey**, a term familiar to weekend golfers, as is double bogey.

Golf clubs.

Everyday Terms – You might hear these golfing terms away from the golf course.

- **Par** is used in situations other than golf to indicate normality. For example, someone who is not feeling well might say, "I'm not feeling up to par."
- A **hole-in-one**, also called an ace, is used to indicate something was a **long shot** (low probability) but it succeeded. "I made a hole in one when I gave my sales pitch and they immediately gave me a large sales order."

- A **chip shot** is a short, easy-to-make shot to the green. If something is going to be easy, you could say, "Making this sale is going to be a chip shot."
- Because there are 18 holes on a golf course, the **19th hole** refers to the clubhouse where drinks and food are served. If you make a business call to a person you know is a golfer, you might ask if they have time to visit the 19th hole after work. They will know you are referring to getting a drink somewhere, but not necessarily at a course.
- A **tee** is a small peg stuck in the ground on which a golf ball is placed before the hitter swings at the ball to begin play to the next hole. You can use this term to indicate to others that they need to get ready to do something, like starting a business meeting, by saying, "Let's tee up and get started."
- **Water hazards** are ponds, lakes, rivers, or ditches on the course, and **sand traps** are scooped-out areas filled with sand, both of which make playing difficult if your ball lands in them. A manager who plays golf might say to his project team, "Let's try to identify all water hazards and sand traps before committing more money to this project."

In major U.S. tournaments, the winner can earn up to $1 million, while second and third place winners can win half that amount. Spectators are allowed to watch, and most PGA events are televised. There are many tournament winners in America whose names are recognized. Perhaps the two best known are **Jack Nicklaus** and **Arnold Palmer**. Palmer was the best player in the 1950s and 60s, and Nicklaus in the 70s and 80s. **Tiger Woods** was the successor to the crown that Nicklaus wore for so many years.

> **Hint**: Our famous movies dealing with golf include *Caddyshack* (1980), *Tin Cup* (1996), *Happy Gilmore* (1996), and *The Legend of Bagger Vance* (2000).

Foreign Heritage Golfers – Golf in America is very popular with immigrant Americans. Some of our best professional players are of foreign heritage. Recently the last four U.S. Open champions were born outside the U.S. and together they reflect golf's new global order.

Ten years ago, there was one South Korean woman on the LPGA Tour. Now there are three among the top six money winners and 11 overall. Only Australia and England boast more international players. The last time a non-immigrant player topped the money list was in 1993.

Tiger Woods is the only man ever to hold all four major PGA titles in the same year (2001). By publicly embracing his mother's Thai heritage, he became an inspiration to Asian Americans and other minorities in the U.S.

Tiger Woods

Hint: As you are learning, America is diverse and we embrace forgiveness. Because of the scandal surrounding Woods' marital infidelity and the apology he made to the public, 55 percent of us said he was sincere in his apology and would forgive him, more than those who said he was insincere or were not ready to forgive. A fourth said forgiveness is not theirs to offer. About 30 percent said his wife should have forgiven him, the same percentage that said she should not have. They were divorced in 2010.

- *Japan* – Shigeki Maruyama joined the PGA Tour in 2000. His 2001 victory made him the first Japanese player to win a PGA Tour event on the U.S. mainland.

- *Korea* – Kyoung-Ju Choi was the first Korean to win on the PGA Tour. In 2002 he earned over $2 million for the first time in his career. Later in his career he donated 10 percent of a $810,000 winning check to underprivileged South Koreans back home and to the Christian church his family attends near Houston, Texas. When Se Ri Pak joined the LPGA in 1998, she was the only Korean player. Ten years later she was one of 45 Koreans on tour. She was the youngest player to win the U.S. Women's Open.

Se Ri Pak

- *Mexico* – Nancy Lopez won five tournaments in her first year in 1977, breaking the record for both men and women **rookies** (first-year player). She was admitted into the Hall of Fame in 1987.

- *Sweden* – Annika Sörenstam is ranked as one of the most successful golfers in LPGA history. In 2003 she was the first woman since 1945 to play in a men's PGA Tour event.

- *Taiwan* – In 2011, Yani Tseng was the youngest player ever, male or female, to win five major championships, and was ranked number 1 in women's golf.

Annika Sörenstam

FAN FAVORITES

Though Americans **pull for** (support) **underdogs** (losing record), we also love perennial winners. Use of these winners' names might elicit a favorable response from your American counterpart. In a 2011 Harris Poll, we said these were our favorites.

- *Athletes* – Top five male favorites:
    1. Derek Jeter (baseball).
    2. Peyton Manning (football).
    3. Kobe Bryant (basketball).
    4. Michael Jordan (basketball).
    5. Tiger Woods (golf). [*]

---

[*]Before Wood's fall from grace due to marital infidelity that shattered his image and led to his divorce.

- *NFL Football Team* – A tie between the Dallas Cowboys in Texas and the Green Bay Packers in Wisconsin. The Cowboys are referred to as **America's Team**.

Dallas Cowboys.

- *College Football Team* – The "Fighting Irish" of Notre Dame University, a Catholic school in the Midwest state of Indiana.
- *College Basketball Team* – University of North Carolina.
- *Baseball Team* – New York Yankees

OTHER FOREIGN HERITAGE SPORTS FIGURES

More and more immigrant athletes are participating and succeeding in other American sports as well. In our cities that have professional sport teams with foreign-born players, American children with the same heritage now have role models.

- *Figure Skating* – Michelle Kwan is an Olympic Bronze Medalist figure skater admired by all Americans for her grace and beauty on and off the ice. In 1992, Kristi Yamaguchi won the Olympic gold medal and now skates professionally. and encourages underprivileged children to pursue their dreams.
- *Gymnasts* – American gymnast Mohini Bhardwaj was the first Indian American Olympic medalist winner (Rome 2004). Amy Chow was a member of the first-ever U.S. Gold Medal Olympic Gymnastics Team in 1996.

Gretzky

- *Hockey* –In 1991, Jim Paek was the first Korean to play in the National Hockey League and the first Korean whose team won the championship. Canadian-born pro hockey player **Wayne Gretzky** had an outstanding career playing for Los Angeles.
- *Olympics* – Foreign-born athletes competing for the U.S. at the Beijing Olympics in 2008 numbered 33, compared to 27 at the 2004 Summer Games. They included four Chinese-born table tennis players, a kayaker from Britain, Russian-born world champion gymnast Nastia Li, and seven members of the track-and-field team.

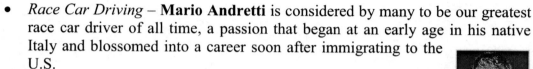
Andretti

- *Race Car Driving* – **Mario Andretti** is considered by many to be our greatest race car driver of all time, a passion that began at an early age in his native Italy and blossomed into a career soon after immigrating to the U.S.
- *Soccer* – In 2007, the Los Angeles Galaxy signed English superstar **David Beckham** in a deal worth $250 million, the highest-profile signing in the history of Major League Soccer.

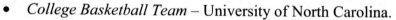
Beckham

- *Tennis* – Originally from Czechoslovakia, **Martina Navratilova** was stripped of her citizenship in 1975 at the age of 18 when she asked the U.S. for political asylum and was granted temporary residency. At the time, Navratilova was told by the government that she was becoming too Americanized and that she should go back to school and make tennis secondary. She became a U.S. citizen in 1981 and in 2008 had her Czech citizenship restored. She's been called the best female tennis player of the 20th century. When not playing tennis, Navratilova is involved with various charities that benefit animal rights, underprivileged children, and gay rights.

Naratilova

She also speaks out on a number of volatile political issues, including her opposition to communism and the former Eastern Bloc power structure that compelled her to flee her native Czechoslovakia. She told a German newspaper, "The most absurd part of my escape from the unjust system is that I have exchanged one system that suppresses free opinion for another. The Republicans in the U.S. manipulate public opinion and sweep controversial issues under the table. It's depressing. Decisions in America are based solely on the question of how much money will come out of it and not on the questions of how much health, morals or environment suffer as a result." Many Americans will agree with her.

O
FOOD AND DINING

*You can tell a lot about a fellow's character by his way of
eating jelly beans.* - Ronald Reagan, U.S. president 1981-1989

One question I always get about America from foreigners has to do with our "crazy" food and table manners. Understanding our differences, including the food terms discussed in this chapter, will add to your pleasure and may affect how you are viewed if you have the opportunity to dine with an American.

Our **cuisine** *[kwi-ZEEN]* (food style or method of cooking) like everything else in America is varied because of the borrowed cuisines from our immigrants' cultures, coupled with native foods unique to our continent and the U.S.

Now that both adults in our families are working full time more than ever before, Americans eat outside the home more often and rely on fully prepared meals to help busy families juggle their schedules. It is estimated that half of the money we spend on meals is spent in restaurants or for **takeout food** (ready-to-eat) prepared in restaurants and taken home and eaten. **Delicatessens** *[dell-ih-kah-TESS-uhns]* offer prepared foods that customers can take home or eat in the store. Many of our large food stores now cater to this growing need with delicatessens and dine-in areas.

> **Hint**: You should have no difficulty finding a restaurant in our larger cities that serves your native dishes. The same with ethnic food stores. Look in the "yellow pages" (business listings) of the telephone directory or on the Internet. However, your favorite dish here may be geared more toward the American palate. You may have difficulty finding exotic delicacies here that you might eat in your native country that we consider endangered species or are basically unappealing to us.

Cultural Differences – There are many cultural differences between American and foreign dining, food, and even our food stores, also called **grocery stores** and **super markets**. Here is a sampling.

- *Bread* – A couple from Germany asked me, "Why do you find muffins so appealing? We like bread so much more." My answer: "Darned if I know. Just what we're used to, I guess." (Though we do like bread, too.)

- *Cooking* – We generally view food preparation as a craft. This is unlike some cultures where cooking is an art, food preparation is more meticulous, and consumption is ceremonious.

- *Food Choices* – Americans are surprised at what some foreigners eat on their platter (dish) while foreigners are surprised at what Americans don't eat. For example, in South China it is said that everything with four legs is eaten except the dinner table, and everything that has two wings except an airplane.

- *Health* – Some cultures have long understood the medicinal value of food. Americans are starting to adopt these healthy views as we pay more attention to waistlines and diets. Healthy salad bars are now common and many of our restaurants offer low calorie or low fat items on their menus, even in our fast food restaurants. McDonald's now provides a calorie count for each item. But only a few restaurants offer organic foods and foods free of artificial colorings, flavors, and chemicals.

- *Hours* – Some restaurants in Europe don't start serving dinner until 7:30 at night; in the U.S. some start serving at 5:00 p.m. We have a saying, "**Early to bed, early to rise, makes a man healthy, wealthy, and wise.**" As I quickly discovered, parts of Europe and South America even shut down for several hours over the lunch hour, something that never happens in **on-the-go** U.S.

- *Lunch* – Americans might skip lunch or will snack at their desks at work. My European friends think that is odd because they seldom skip lunch.

- *Markets* – Large, central outdoor markets in populated areas, such as those in Casablanca and Barcelona that so impressed me, offer an immense array of food for the shopper, from hundreds of vendors and from **soup to nuts** (every possible item). Foreigners in the U.S., however, will generally shop for these same items in our individual food stores that we call **supermarkets**.

- *Ratings* – Some of our cities have rating codes that restaurants must display in their windows that show the result of a recent government inspection; an "A" rating is the best. If restaurants do not pass minimum standards, they must close, correct the problem, and then be reexamined.

- *Speed* – In contrast to some countries like Chile and in most of

Restaurant rating.

Europe where I found service pleasantly unhurried, some Americans like faster service from waiters. They tend to place greater emphasis on relaxation than we do, which extends to savoring each course and enjoying lengthy conversation.

- *Spices* – For some nationalities, our food is too bland, while for others it is too spicy. This is probably one of the hardest adjustments Asian Indian Americans encounter because of the lack of flavor and spices in our cuisine. But my Danish friends dislike our spicy Mexican food.

- *Tailgating* – You might be invited to a **tailgate party**, a social event held on and around the open tailgate of a vehicle in parking lots at sporting events, rock concerts, and the like. It involves consuming beverages and grilling food. People participate even if their vehicles do not have tailgates that fold down as a serving table.

Tailgate party.

- *Take Out* – Americans tend toward fast food and dining on the go. Some of our fast food restaurants have signs reading "take out," so I chuckle at signs in other parts of the world that say "quick take" and "take with."

- *Tips* – In the U.S., the tip is usually added after the waiter initially runs the credit card through the machine but before we sign the receipt. I discovered the opposite in South America where the waiter needs to know the tip first.

- *Utensils* – A Norwegian couple asked me, "Why do you cut your food with a knife and then put it down and switch the fork to the other hand before biting the food, something Europeans don't do?" I told them this is yet another difference between European and U.S. culture. (This is explained later.)

- *Vegetarian* – Our population of vegetarians is growing. We choose this for environmental, health, or spiritual reasons. Though we have very few such restaurants, many offer items on the menu to accommodate "vegi" eaters.

- *Vendors* – Americans are surprised at the large numbers of individuals cooking and selling food on the sidewalks of foreign cities. I was impressed by all the unique smells coming from stalls in Bangkok. Dispensing food this way is not allowed in America because our cities have food safety rules that define where and how prepared food may be served. We do have licensed trucks that dispense food and are monitored by health officials.

Traditional Cuisine – Traditional American cuisine has been defined as **meat and potatoes**, suggestive of a fairly simple basic menu that our immigrants brought with them from England and Germany centuries ago. The following three **meals** are typical of

257

what Americans have generally eaten for generations and which you might be offered if you dine with us.

- *Breakfast* – A hearty breakfast of eggs along with pancakes, waffles, or french toast served with bacon or sausage and hash brown potatoes. Others prefer a lighter breakfast of toast or a pastry, or cereal with milk and fruit. Orange juice and coffee are favored drinks.
- *Lunch* – Hamburgers, hot dogs, or sandwiches filled with meat, sliced sausage, cheese, and peanut butter. We mix mayonnaise with tuna or chopped chicken to make chicken or tuna salad sandwiches, which didn't seem much like a "salad" to my Danish friends.
- *Dinner* – Meat and potatoes served with a lettuce salad, vegetable, and rolls or bread. Favorite dinner meats include ground beef or steaks, chicken, ham, and turkey. Fish, shellfish, and such dishes as pizza and spaghetti also serve as main courses. We also eat lamb, pork and other meats, but not as often.

Most Popular Dishes – A recent study identified the 10 most popular dishes that Americans eat. Chances are good that during a stay in the U.S. you will have an opportunity to enjoy one or more of them.

1. *Apple Pie* – This is one dish so closely identified with the U.S. that it is mentioned in our famous saying "**mom, apple pie, and baseball**," all symbols of simple, basic American lifestyles. It is a European favorite, too.

Slice of apple pie.

2. *Barbecue* – Barbecued spareribs or other meats was a regional food that become popular across the country.
3. *Chili* – Contests to determine the best-made chili, called chili cook-offs, are as popular as this spicy bowl of beans.

Fried chicken.

4. *Chocolate Chip Cookie* – A world survey says "9 out of 10 people like chocolate. The tenth lies."
5. *Fried Chicken* – Countless variations appear in cookbooks and on restaurant menus.
6. *Hamburger/Cheeseburger* – It is estimated that Americans consume three per week.

Jell-O

7. *Jell-O* – The Jell-O brand dessert has been around over 100 years, but gelatin-type dishes date back to the Renaissance.
8. *Macaroni and Cheese* – Little pasta noodles shaped like pipes with melted cheese. A favorite with kids, too.
9. *Pancake* – Round plate-size patties made from flour with maple syrup and butter on top, a breakfast favorite.

Pancakes with syrup.

258

10. *Pizza* – The average American eats 10 pizzas a year, accounting for 13 percent of all restaurant orders. Americans are often surprised at how ours differ from Italy's that have thinner crusts and less generous toppings.

EVERYDAY FOOD TERMS

A **dish** is a plate on which you eat your food, but it also refers to the particular meal you are having—"I will have the chicken *dish*." A **bowl** is used to serve food that is not appropriate on a dish —"I would like a bowl of chicken noodle soup." An **entree** *[ON-tray]* is the main serving at a meal, such as chicken, that can be preceded by soup and/or a salad. A **side order** refers to a small serving of food that normally does not come with a meal—"I would like a side order of fruit."

You might hear food and cooking terms used in our everyday language, some with meanings that are different from the obvious.

- **Food for thought** does not refer to food, but to an idea that causes someone to think about something, such as, "When my boss offered me a 20 percent pay raise, it was food for thought because I had been planning to leave the company."

- **Sunny side up** refers to fried eggs that are not cooked on top, thus allowing the yolk to remain soft and yellow. You might describe a person's happy, colorful disposition as sunny side up.

"Sunny side up."

- If you say, **the glass is half-full**, you are an optimist; if you view it as half-empty you are a pessimist who expects it to be empty soon.

- A **baker's dozen** refers to 13 items, not 12. Some pastry shops give an extra pastry free with the purchase of a dozen.

"In a stew."

- Mothers tell their children, **an apple a day keeps the doctor away**.

- A person is **in a stew** when they are in trouble. They are not floating around in a bowl of vegetables and meat with a soup-like sauce.

- To **chew the fat** means to casually sit around and discuss something that's unimportant.

A fun restaurant.

- **Upper crust** refers not to the top layer of a piecrust, but to someone or something that is upscale or expensive such as a beautiful jewelry store.

- **Buffalo wings** are chicken wings baked and coated with a spicy sauce. Our Buffalo is a large cow-like native American

"Twisted like a pretzel."

259

animal that does not have wings, so don't fall for this joke.

- A **square meal** consists of a well-rounded, healthy assortment of food, not the angular arrangement of food on a square dish.
- If something is **twisted like a pretzel**, such as the plot of a movie or book, it has lots of twists and turns.
- If many people are close together in a small space, you might say they are **packed in like sardines**, referring to the little fish crammed into a small can.
- If something appears to be dishonest, like a business proposal, you might say it **smells fishy**.
- If someone says, **I'm so hungry I could eat a bear**, that means they are *really* hungry. (Sorry, you will not find bear meat on our menus.)
- If you placed more food on your plate than you can eat, you might say **my eyes were bigger than my stomach**. It can also apply to any situation in which you made a hasty error in judgment because the situation was most appealing at the moment.

Our South American tour guide learned that what we call a **hole-in-the-wall** restaurant is one that is small, out of the way, **off the beaten path**, and unpretentious, like the one he took us to for lunch. And that **brown-bagging it** is packing a lunch in a paper sack to eat later. He laughed at our **tongue-in-cheek** (amusing, facetious) proverb that warns about getting married: "The most dangerous food to eat is the wedding cake."

REGIONAL U.S. CUISINES

Perhaps like your home country, different regions of our country offer specialty foods. Each is influenced by the nationality of the colonists who settled in the area and by local ingredients. Although some of the special foods in these areas can be found in other regions, many claim they don't taste the same. Here are five unique regional U.S. cuisines you might have the opportunity to enjoy or hear referred to by your counterpart.

New England Style Cooking – New England is known for its hearty dishes introduced by British colonists and for its cold-water seafood harvested by the local Atlantic fishing fleet. Yankee pot roast, Boston baked beans, New England clam chowder, and Maine lobster are specialties, all claimed by New Englanders to be the best in the world.

Maine lobster.

Southern Cooking – The cuisine of the southeastern states is called **southern cooking** or **down home cooking**. It is characterized by generous farm-style portions with deep fried foods, heavy sauces and sweet desserts. Southerners love **barbequed** meats (**BBQ** is the

Barbequed ribs.

260

acronym for *bar*be*q*ue) that are well spiced or marinated and slowly cooked over glowing coals.

New Orleans Cajun Cooking – This city is situated at the mouth of the Mississippi River and was greatly influenced by Spanish and French colonists and African immigrants. The cuisines, including a bowl of gumbo soup, sea foods, and rice were influenced by these cultures and are spiced with African and West Indian flavors, just as the music there is **spiced up** (added liveliness), too.

Bowl of gumbo.

Southwestern And Tex-Mex Cooking – Native Americans, early Spanish settlers, and our Mexican neighbors influenced the cuisine in our southwestern states. This food includes a variety of dishes prepared with local ingredients, Mexican spices, meats, and chili. It is famous for salsa, nachos, tacos, and burritos, which we have in restaurants across the country. Because of the many cattle ranches in the area, Texas is known for its beefsteaks.

Steak on a grill.

California Cuisine – Because of its warm climate, California has a year-round supply of fresh fruits, vegetables, and abundant seafood. A diverse ethnic population has influenced its foods, but Californians have developed a healthy cuisine that utilizes fresh ingredients flavored with unusual combinations of spices and garnishes on its own. It is usually served in smaller portions than other parts of the country. Almost any combination of ethnic food styles can be found in California restaurants. California wines are taking their place among the world's finest, accounting for 90 percent of U.S. production and ranked as the world's fourth largest wine producer.

California wine.

DINING OUT

When Americans say "**let's eat out**," they mean eating outside the home in a restaurant. These sites vary from very formal to casual, from family-oriented to fast food. The terms **cafe** and **coffee shop** suggest a less formal establishment than a "restaurant." Here are tips for selecting and eating out in a fairly nice sit-down restaurant, as opposed to a fast food restaurant.

Four Seasons Resort, Lanai, Hawaii.

Dress – Casual dress (see Chapter P - Dress and Appearance) is usually appropriate in all but the most expensive restaurants. Restaurants in downtown locations, business areas, or in private clubs tend to have a more formal dress code. Their dress code may require men to wear a suit or sport coat and tie. If you don't have these wardrobe items, they can sometimes loan you one. If you have doubts, phone first. If someone invites you out, ask them about proper dress.

Choosing a Restaurant – Locals (people who work or live in the area) are a great source of information for restaurants. I was in Bangkok for three days and could not find a restaurant that served American food that fit my special diet. I finally asked a local who directed me to an excellent one. Of course, if you are walking about you can also look for menus posted in the windows or near the entrances of our restaurants to guide your choice. If a restaurant offers a foreign cuisine, they might incorporate that in their name, such as Andes Peruvian Restaurant.

Reservations – Make reservations as soon as possible for a table at fine restaurants. Many restaurants in tourist areas do not accept reservations and you might have to wait 10 to 45 minutes for a table. Sometimes I avoid waiting by eating early (before 5 or 6 p.m.).

Smoking and Drinking – Smoking is generally not allowed in most restaurants and is now banned in all elevators, public buildings, hospitals, busses, trains, and airplanes. Laws prohibit anyone under 21 years old from buying, owning, or drinking any alcoholic beverage. Bars and nightclubs will not permit anyone younger to enter even if parents accompany them. However, restaurants that serve alcohol will allow children to enter and eat but will not serve them alcoholic beverages.

Ordering – As you a walk to your table, discreetly look around at what others are eating. This will give you an idea of what you might want to order and will also show you the size of the portions served. Some restaurants have "specials" for that day, sometimes at reduced prices, and posted on a board just inside the entrance. Your server will verbally offer this information, too. It is also appropriate to ask your waiter what their most popular dishes are or the specialties of the house. Or you can ask your host what he or she recommends. The **menu** lists the various dishes available and their prices. If menu prices are not posted, you are in a very expensive restaurant where their patrons are not concerned with price.

Better Service – The better you treat your waiter, the better you will be treated. If you had a long wait before being seated, it was not your waiter's fault. Some foreigners are known for their cold treatment of waiters perhaps because in their culture they are looked down upon. This attitude may reflect unfavorably upon you if it is noticed by an American. Be warm to them and make eye contact—you will get better service. If you appreciate their excellent service, tell them so and tip accordingly when you pay the bill.

262

Yes, there are times when I only leave a small tip or none at all because of the service received. You probably do the same thing back home.

Paying Bill – In some countries, one person **picks up the tab** and pays the restaurant bill because it is considered impolite to pay your own. If we meet friends at a restaurant in the U.S. and there is no particular host, we often pay for our own portion of the bill, which we call "Dutch treat." Sometimes couples give their credit cards to the waiter with instructions to simply split the check equally between the parties. Most restaurants take credit cards, even McDonald's. We also use the term "check" for the bill.

Tipping – While tipping is not done in some cultures like China, it is expected in the U.S. at sit-down restaurants. If you receive good service, it is customary to tip 15 to 20 percent of your bill. Unlike many countries and Europe, most U.S. restaurants do not automatically include a tip on the bill. But a few will add a tip of 15 to 20 percent if you have a large party and will be so noted on the menu or your bill.

TABLE ETIQUETTE

Our rules of table etiquette *[ET-eh-ket]* (manners) have changed over the years. An etiquette writer of the 1840s advised, "Ladies may wipe their lips on the tablecloth, but not blow their noses on it." Today, both are considered bad manners.

In a formal dining situation, such as a dinner in one of our first class restaurants, try to use table manners that we discuss in this section. We are less formal at a fast food restaurant or with families at home. However, some of the good manners you learn about formal dining will apply to informal eating with friends, too.

As you are dining, try to be yourself and have a nice dining experience. Your dinner guests will not be watching to see if you are using the correct fork or knife. They know your customs differ from ours. If you can master a few of our rules of etiquette, however, you may feel more comfortable.

A properly set table.

For purposes of our discussion, let's assume you are eating in a nice restaurant (or at your host's home) with other guests. These are good manners you should be aware of.

Hint: You will learn in Chapter Y on using better English grammar that we have three levels of grammar: formal, general, and informal. I suppose you could say we have the same levels for table etiquette based on who you are eating with. I must admit I do not practice all of the good manners, especially when I am with close friends or in a fast food restaurant. Just be aware that the more of our rules you practice the more favorable you will appear. Over time you will note the manners used by your counterpart and will see which ones are most important to him or her.

Table Setting – At a formal dinner, a server will bring you different **courses** of food throughout the dining experience. These courses are, in this sequence, **appetizer** (small foods to nibble on that may be shared), **soup**, **salad**, **main course**, and finally **dessert**. After you have finished one course, the server removes your plate and sometimes the utensils you used, and brings the next course. If you are from China where multiple main courses are served, expect only one here.

Utensils used in formal settings, also called **silverware** (because they were originally made of silver) or **cutlery**, are the small tools you use to handle your food, some of which are used for specific courses. These consist of **knives**, **forks**, and **spoons** all of varying shapes and sizes. In formal dining, your utensils will be placed on the table in a prescribed format before you arrive at the table. If you are accustomed to using chopsticks, using these utensils might be confusing to you at first.

> **Hint**: When I am in an Asian country, I use chopsticks if my hosts use them. It creates the impression that I am respectful of their culture and want to learn about it. You might want to do the same thing in the U.S. with our utensils except when you are in an Asian cuisine restaurant that offer chopsticks.

The maximum 15-piece layout for a formal dinner setting is shown below. In some circumstances, the teaspoon (9), dessert fork (4) and dessert spoon (8) might be placed to the top instead of to the side of the plate as shown below, or other pieces will be missing. At an informal meal, the coffee cup and saucer (15) are placed on the table setting in advance or at the end of meal when dessert is served. Keep in mind this is at a formal setting. At informal restaurants and coffee shops, you might only have a knife and a fork in front of you. This is how your table might look:

1. Napkin 2. Salad fork 3. Dinner fork 4. Dessert fork 5. Bread and butter plate with spreader
6. Dinner plate 7. Dinner knife 8. Dessert spoon 9. Teaspoon 10. Soup spoon 11. Cocktail fork
12. Water 13. Red-wine 14. White-wine 15. Coffee cup and saucer.   (www.recipehut.com)

The silverware placed on the table indicates how many courses you are going to be served. Silverware is placed in the order of its use. So, for each new course, you pick up the silverware piece *farthest* away from the plate. In other words, you work from the outside in, towards the plate, as the meal progresses and different courses are served.

Alcohol – Before dining, your host will probably ask if you would like something to drink. Some cultures enjoy testing the ability of a foreigner to handle his or her alcohol. This is not acceptable in the U.S. If you do not drink alcoholic beverages, do not feel embarrassed, as you might in your country. You might choose to order a non-alcoholic drink instead, or just politely refuse any drink. It is not rude if the host tells you to pour your own drink in his house while he is busy doing something else and wants you to **feel at home**. (See alcohol discussion in Chapter H - Customs and Etiquette.)

Seating – The host usually sits at one end of the table and his spouse at the other end, unlike some cultures where the oldest person might sit at the end. When guests approach the table to sit down, the host may point out a specific chair for each guest, usually in a man-woman-man sequence. With larger groups or more formal affairs, name cards might be used. Either way, remain standing behind your chair until the host says to be seated or begins to seat himself. Unlike some cultures, we do not have a set order of who may be seated first among men, women, old, and young. A man should pull out the chair of a woman next to him and assist her as she sits down by pushing her chair toward the table. She should softly say thank you.

Ceremony – Before we begin eating, a prayer (a blessing) might be offered at a family dinner or some official dinners. This is also called **saying grace**, which almost half of American families do before their meal. When this is done, we close our eyes, bow our heads, and sometimes hold hands. If wine is served, sometimes a host will first make a ceremonial **toast** in which good wishes are offered to the guests who then clink their glasses together. Feel free to speak up and make your toast, too. A toast might also be made at the conclusion of the meal. So, if your host says "let's make

Saying grace.

a toast," he is not suggesting that you heat bread up to make it crispy, which is our other "toast."

Napkin – As soon as you are seated, remove the napkin from your place setting, unfold it, and place it in your lap. Some hosts use napkin rings, in which case you remove the napkin from the ring and place the ring to the side. Some creative restaurants will place the napkin in an empty water glass, or fold it into a fancy shape and place on your dinner plate. Do not be surprised if the waiter unfolds and places your napkin in your lap. Some Asians leave their napkin hanging down from the table edge; we don't do this. If you need to leave the table during the meal, place the napkin on the *chair* and slide the chair under the table. When you leave the table at the end of the meal, place your napkin loosely next to your plate to signal that you are through.

Napkin ring.

265

Left/Right – Your beverages should be on the upper right side of your plate and food like bread and salad on separate plates on your upper left. You need to know this rule in order to help you avoid eating or drinking from someone else's place setting. Occasionally, even we make a mistake and use a plate intended for the one next to us. When it does, most Americans just make a joke of it as they switch plates.

> **Hint**: To keep this arrangement straight in your mind, think of the beginning and ending letters in the word "**Food**" in which the **F** (for **f**ood) is on the left, and the **D** (for **d**rink) is on the right side.

Ordering – If there are items on the menu that you are uncertain about, ask your server or your host any questions you may have. Some of my foreign friends ask me to order for them. It is an easy task because most of them like fish and vegetables, but I often encourage them to sample different foods. I chuckle at my Asian friends who discover that they like our brown rice better than the white rice they have eaten all their lives. So, experiment. You might be pleasantly surprised with your discoveries. If you don't like spicy foods, be sure to ask your server if a dish you are interested in is "spicy." Sometimes we use the term "hot" to describe a very spicy food. But if you use this term, your server might think you are referring to food temperature, not spicy taste.

Wine – If you want to order wine, you might ask the host or waiter to recommend something. White wine is recommended for fish, chicken, and vegetables; red for red meat and heavy dishes. You can order by the glass or by the bottle as some hosts do. If someone orders wine by the bottle for the table, he or she will first have the waiter pour a small amount into his or her glass to taste it. They will smell it delicately, sip it, roll it around on the tongue, and then swallow. Unless it tastes like vinegar, we nod our head and say something like, "Excellent" or "Very good." Also, in some cultures it is a polite gesture to pour another person's drink *without* first asking them for permission. However, in America, *always* ask someone if they want something before giving it to them, food or wine.

Posture – Sit up straight and keep your arms and elbows off the table. Your idle hand should be in your lap. If you are accustomed to using chopsticks, you may be in the habit of leaning down to your food. Instead, bring your utensils to your mouth. Leaning forward slightly is okay when spooning soup.

Selecting Food – We do not use a turntable containing large platters of food from which we select our food as is customary in some cultures. We eat family style like we do at home where dishes of food are placed on the table. We select what we want and put it on our plate then pass the dish to the next person. If you are asked if you would like something from a dish at the table, you can say "no thank you" if you don't want it, though it is more polite to put a small portion on your plate and sample it.

Utensil Selection – If you are unsure about using your utensils, watch your host or others around you. Use them delicately so you avoid making a noise as they touch the plate. Once you have used a piece of silverware, never place it back on the table; place it on the edge of a plate. Do not leave a used spoon in a cup; place it on the saucer that the cup is sitting on. Any unused silverware is left sitting on the table in its original position. Do not play with your utensils (something I do when I am bored with the conversation at an informal dinner with friends).

Eating Your Food – You do not have to eat something you do not want to try. This is in contrast to dining in some cultures like Singapore where it is polite to try everything offered by your host as a show of respect for his choice of food. I felt uncomfortable once at a dinner in China when I was frowned upon for not eating different animal parts we don't eat in the U.S. like fish eyes We consider such criticism ruder than the original infraction of not trying an unfamiliar food. Also, if you don't like something you have eaten, you don't have to eat it and don't have to explain why.

Passing Food – Do not reach for something on the table that is not in front of you. Instead, ask the person nearest to it to pass it. If someone asks for the salt, pass both the salt and pepper. In some Asian cultures, the host might use his own chopsticks to serve you food. As food plates are passed to us, each should have a  serving spoon or fork on it that we use to remove food if we want some. Do not use your own utensils to place food on your plate; it is considered unsanitary. Then, pass the food to the next person to the *right* of you, leaving the serving utensil in the serving bowl. We don't use two hands as a sign of respect to pass food as they do in China, so passing with one hand is okay. Softly say "thank you" if

Family style meal. (SimonSaysPlease.com)

someone hands you a platter of food or drink. Also, do not tap your fingers on the table as a gesture of thanks as some Asians do—we might think you are nervous or uncomfortable and want to leave.

Soup – It is polite to scoop up your soup by moving the soupspoon in a direction away from you. Do not make a sucking noise as some cultures are accustomed to doing. Put the spoon on the plate the bowl is sitting on when finished. Do not blow on soup or food that is hot. Wait until  it cools or skim some from the top of the bowl. Do not pick up or tilt the bowl to make scooping easier, though I admit to doing this at home when I'm not being observed.

Soup bowl and spoon.

Knife – When you must cut food, hold your knife gently and use pressure from your index finger and thumb to cut as you hold your fork with the other hand to stabilize what you are cutting. Only cut off a small piece that you plan to put in your mouth. After

267

you have cut a piece of food, put your knife down on your plate with the blade (cutting edge) to the inside and switch your fork to your other hand to eat. Europeans don't switch hands as we do and some Americans find this eating style too aggressive. I don't switch either when I'm at home, but I would if invited to a White House dinner.

> **Hint**: I mentioned at the beginning of this chapter the Norwegian couple who asked me about this knife business. Remember the imaginary circle that we discussed earlier? Good etiquette at the dinner table dictates it must not be violated by two things: noise and aggressive eating, both of which relate to the knife. Striking the plate with the knife is rude. Also, keeping the knife in one hand and the fork in the other the whole time gives the appearance of aggressive eating. As my father used to tell us kids, "Don't shovel your food!" meaning, take it easy and put the knife down now and then. And don't rush the fork to your mouth. As he would say, "You are not animals."

Bread and Butter – When butter is passed around on a butter server, cut off a piece (about a spoonful) and place it on the edge of your bread-and-butter plate. Do not scoop from the butter plate directly to your bread or roll. Once it's on your plate, tear off a small piece of your roll or bread and apply the butter only to what you will eat in the next bite. Lay your butter knife down (for the same reasons discussed above) on your bread-and-butter plate with the blade to the inside while you eat that piece. Remember, the butter knife is the small one with the rounded tip, the large one is your cutting knife.

Taking Bites – If you are accustomed to picking up large pieces of food with a fork or chopsticks and taking multiple bites from it, you *must* change your habit. Only pick up a piece of food of a size that can be put in your mouth. Do not put your face close to your plate as you might if you use chopsticks. We don't leave food on our fork and continually bite at it. Keep your mouth closed and finish chewing before getting another piece of food ready to eat *and* continuing your conversation.

Eating noodles.

Do not suck up long noodles into your mouth. Cut them with your fork or twirl them into a neat little package around your fork so they will fit easily into your mouth.

Fish Deboning – Unlike Asia where it might be considered unlucky, you may debone a fish yourself. However, your host or waiter might ask if you want them to separate the fish skeleton and flesh. They will also help you with lobster. The choice is yours. I usually let the waiter **do the honors** (perform the task) to avoid looking clumsy.

Fingers – A question I am asked frequently about American culture is "when is it okay to use my fingers while eating?" Use your knife or a piece of bread, not your fingers, to help push small pieces of food on your plate onto your fork. It is okay to pick up the following foods with your fingers: artichokes, corn on the cob, spareribs, crabs, clams and oysters on the half shell, chicken wings and bones, sandwiches,

Corn on the cob.

certain fruits, celery, and cookies. If in doubt, observe the other diners and see how they are doing it. **Hors d'oeuvres** *[or-DURVS]* are small finger foods served at cocktail parties. Although they are often picked up with a toothpick, we often use our fingers with small items like baby carrots.

Socializing – It is polite to try to talk a little to people seated at both sides of you and across from you. When you are at a large sit-down dinner, talk to those around you, but don't yell at someone down the table. Of course, don't talk when your mouth is full of food either.

Eating Speed – In some cultures, eating fast and making noises is a show of approval for the host's food. In the U.S. it is bad manners. When dining with others, everyone should start and generally finish at about the same time. If you are a fast eater, try to pace yourself. You could make the others feel uncomfortable if you finish long before they do or if you appear to eat aggressively. If you finish one course, politely wait for the others to finish before beginning to eat the next course, even if the waiter places it in front of you.

Things to Avoid – By our standards, some cultures are more aggressive in their eating habits. Burping is not used to express our satisfaction with a meal as it is in some cultures. Communal cups are not passed around the table for everyone to drink from; it is considered unsanitary. Some of my foreign friends will comment on the small amount of food I have eaten and insist I eat some of their food. Don't do this. Food quantity consumed does not necessarily equate to food quality or appreciation, especially for those on a diet. Do not smoke at the table because of health considerations. Today, guests go outside to smoke.

Coffee/Tea/Water – If coffee or tea is served, it usually comes with a teaspoon resting on its saucer, which you can use to stir your sugar and cream. After using it, place it back on saucer. For sanitary reasons, use the spoon in the sugar bowl to add sugar to your cup, not the spoon on your saucer. Then use your own spoon to stir it. If a teapot is left on the table, do not be offended if the spout is pointing at you because Americans are not aware this is considered bad luck in some cultures. Do not slurp (make a noise) as you drink a liquid or chew on the ice in your drink. Unlike some countries, our public drinking water is safe, so you can drink it instead of ordering bottled water if you so choose.

Dessert – The dessert fork or spoon will either be above your plate when you first sit down, or will be brought to you when the dessert or fruit is served. It is polite to wait for everyone to finish their main course so all can begin to eat dessert at approximately the same time.

Private Moments – We do not offer toothpicks between courses or at the conclusion of a meal as some cultures do, so do not use your own at the table. Some restaurants offer toothpicks in a little dispenser at the cashier stand near the door. Use the restroom to pick food out of your teeth or repair your makeup. If you are in a high-class restaurant, you might find an attendant in the restroom whom you may tip if service is provided to you.

Finished – In some Asian cultures like China, leaving a clean plate means you were not given enough food and might be considered an insult; conversely, leaving food untouched on your plate will also offend. It is not uncommon for a Chinese host to order enough food for ten people at a table of five. He or she loses face if there are not leftovers at the end of the meal. We do not have these customs, so eat what you want and do not worry about offending anyone by what you eat. Do not push your plate away from you when you have finished eating; leave it in the place setting. Do not stack plates. The common way to show that you have finished your meal is to lay your fork and knife diagonally across your plate with the handles resting on the rim of the plate, fork ends turned down and the knife blade turned in toward the center of the plate. Unlike some countries like Italy where it is considered rude and not done, our restaurants offer containers in which leftover food can be taken home. If we choose to do this, we ask for a **doggie bag**.

NATIONAL FAST FOOD RESTAURANTS

In typical American entrepreneurial spirit, when a restaurant **catches on** (becomes popular) with the public, it sometimes expands nationwide and even globally. Many of them are owned and operated by individual owners but overseen by the parent company that sold the rights to the owner. We call franchising. (Refer to Chapter W on owning a business for information on franchising opportunities.)

Those that do not lend themselves to chains, like French, German, Middle Eastern, Thai, Korean, etc. are most likely individually owned and operated, perhaps by an immigrant or a first generation American.

Here are a few of our favorite chains that **started from scratch** (initially just one site).

Top Rated Chains – Zagat (www.zagat.com) surveys name these as our best national **fast food restaurants** where inexpensive food is prepared and served quickly. You can access their individual websites to obtain locations and menus.

- *Best Breakfast* – IHOP (www.ihop.com)
- *Most Popular Chain* – Wendy's (www.wendys.com)
- *Most Popular Fast Food* – Panera Bread Co is also rated number one for healthiest menu. (www.panerabreadco.com)

- *Most Popular Full-Service* – Outback Steakhouse (www.outback.com)
- *Best Physical Facilities* – Cracker Barrel (www.crackerbarrell.com)
- *Best Chicken* – Chick-fil-A (www.chick-fil-a.com)
- *Best French Fries* – McDonald's (www.mcdonalds.com)
- *Best Hamburger/Cheeseburger* – Wendy's (www.wendys.com)
- *Most Child-Friendly* – McDonald's (www.mcdonalds.com)

Pizza Chains –For nine years running, Papa John's pizza has received the highest customer satisfaction rating. We have others as well, including Domino's, Little Caesar's, Pizza Hut, Round Table, and Shakey's.

Mexican Chains – Three of our national Mexican fast food chains are *Taco Bell* (www.tacobell.com), *Chipotle* (www.chipotle.com), and *Del Taco* (www.deltaco.com).

Asian Chains – Yes, we even have national Asian food chains.
- *Benihana* – Upscale Asian restaurant set in a Japanese garden where a chef chops and juggles food at your table with its own grill. (www.benihana.com)
- *P.F. Chang's* – Operates 200 upscale, full service restaurants in the U.S., Puerto Rico, Mexico, Kuwait City, and Dubai. (www.pfchangs.com)
- *Panda Express* – Expanding quick-service Chinese style chain. (www.pandaexpress.com)*
- *Yoshinoya* – Popular Japanese fast food chain with 100 outlets in America and 1,000 in the world. (www.yoshinoyaamerica.com)

An immigrant American successstory.

Full Service Dining – Our full-service restaurant chains offer menu dining with a wide selection of foods and table service. They include *Applebee's, Chili's, Denny's, Red Lobster, Ruby Tuesday,* and *TGI Friday's* that has over 1000 locations worldwide.

An 18-month study reports that ninety-six percent of main entrees sold at top U.S. chain eateries exceed daily limits for calories, sodium, fat and saturated fat recommended by the U.S. Department of Agriculture. Surprisingly, the entrees at these family-style restaurants exceed those at fast-food restaurants.

American Foods Disliked By Foreigners – Foreigners frequently say they are surprised by the large portions served in Americants restaurants, the free refills of

---

*This is yet another example of how foreigners have succeeded in the U.S. A Chinese immigrant family established their first fast food restaurant in California in 1973. Today, Panda Express is the largest chain of Chinese fast food restaurants in the U.S. with 1,300 outlets in 38 states.

beverages, and eating three warm meals a day. These are examples of American food that some also find find bizarre.

- American processed cheese
- Bacon and eggs
- Biscuits and gravy
- Corn on the cob
- Grits
- Hot dogs

Pumpkin pie.

Bacon and eggs.

- Marshmallows
- Mayonnaise
- Pasta and broccoli
- Peanut butter (and jelly sandwich)
- Pumpkin pie
- Root beer
- Salad dressings
- Soft squishy bread
- Sweet potatoes

Biscuits and gravy.

Grits and butter.

Food Foreigners Take Home – This is a sampling of American foods that foreigners might take home from their visit to the U.S. or will be asked by friends in their native countries to bring back. Interestingly, many of these are considered junk foods that foreigners criticize Americans for consuming.

- A1 steak sauce
- Bottled spice mixes
- Boxed cake mixes
- California pistachio nuts
- Cheez-Its and Goldfish snack crackers
- Corn tortillas
- Cracker Jack popcorn
- Cracklin Oat Bran cereal
- Hershey chocolate syrup and chips
- Maple syrup peanut butter
- Reese's peanut butter cups
- Sour kids candies
- Sugar Frosted Flakes cereal

P

DRESS AND APPEARANCE

It is an interesting question how far men would retain their relative rank if they were divested of their clothes. - Henry David Thoreau, 19th century author

This chapter will acquaint you with some basics of our dress. As you might expect, fashion in America is as varied as everything else you have learned about us. You will not be expected to dress like us, but you might choose to adopt some of these tips especially if you conduct business with Americans or come to live or study here. It might also help you assess others in your personal endeavors and even help you decide which of our styles you prefer to adapt or avoid.

President Obama at work dressed in business suit.

In major cities, residents may dress with more polish and style than those in smaller communities. Many Americans prefer jeans, a T-shirt and athletic shoes with optional baseball cap after work or on weekends. Our casual dress has been influenced by our interest in fitness and health, which translates into easy and comfortable fabrics and fit. According to a travel magazine's annual survey, Anchorage, Alaska, is the "worst-dressed city in America" where the dress code leans toward practicality rather than fashion, and where fashion trends take longer to reach this hinterland. It is followed by Salt Lake City, Utah; Baltimore, Maryland; Orlando, Florida; and San Antonio and Dallas/Fort Worth, Texas.

You might notice that those on the East Coast generally tend to dress less casually than Westerners. Residents of cooler northern states wear heavier clothing. In our beach areas, especially California, Hawaii, and Florida, skimpy clothing might be acceptable in all but the most formal settings. You will spot Western wear (**cowboy**) hats, boots, and large silver belt buckles in the Southwest and rural West, particularly in Texas and Arizona. President Bush, from Texas, was sometimes depicted in foreign newspaper cartoons dressed in a

Cowboy boot.

cowboy outfit. With all this variety of styles throughout America though, we do have some general dress standards.

Cultural Differences – Some foreigners dress differently than Americans; some dress similarly. To me, the people in Madrid, Spain, are among the best dressers in the world, along with Paris, Milan, and New York City. I spent time in a modern mall in Shanghai and noticed world-famous designer clothing names on storefronts—the same ones we have in America. As I sat and watched the shoppers, I noticed their Western style dress was often more stylish than what I would expect to see in a typical mall in the U.S. In India, I noticed that Western style clothing has virtually replaced traditional dress for men, especially in the north. However, in the U.S. we occasionally see Asian Indian Americans—particularly women—dressed in their native dress.

Russians sometimes dress up on more occasions than Americans do. A woman may wear high heels and a nice dress even to go for a casual walk. They explain it this way, "We only live once; I want to look and feel my best." In America, you might witness some of this in congested cities like New York City, but most likely they will wear sweats, jeans, or exercise clothes on a casual walk.

Indonesia's Religious Affairs Minister recently ignited a firestorm when he proposed making miniskirts a porn crime, something that would never happen here given our personal freedoms. There are no rules how we or foreigners should dress. As you would expect, it is up to the individuals to decide if they should wear their ethnic clothes on a daily basis at work, home, or play. We see just about everything. However, if you associate with Americans you might consider some changes to feel more comfortable or to create a more favorable image of yourself in business or other situations. Some of my foreign-born American friends have retained portions of their native country dress while also assimilating new Western styles in the U.S. It makes a nice mix.

> **Hint**: An old Chinese proverb says, "A wise man makes his own decisions, an ignorant man follows the public opinion." You may see girls in America wear **hip hugger** or **low rise** pants that expose their hips or midriff. Some wear short blouses that expose their stomach area or reveal some of their bust. Just because these things appear to be in style doesn't mean *you* have to wear them. If you don't feel comfortable with a fashion, don't dress that way. You will not be considered out of style because many American women also avoid them.

Everyday Terms – You will hear fashion-related terms in our everyday language.

- **Cinch up your belt** means you have to prepare yourself for more difficult times ahead, such as when a company has to cut expenses.
- A **white collar** worker is an administrator; a **blue collar** worker works with his or her hands.
- You **roll up your sleeves** when you are about to begin a difficult physical task, like painting your house or coming up with a new business plan.

274

- **Deep pockets** refers to someone with a lot of money.
- You **click your heels** when you snap to attention in the presence of another person.
- A **clothes horse** is someone who dresses well and has lots of clothes to select from.
- If you wear fancy or formal clothing and make a nice impression, we might say you are **all dolled up, dressed to the nines** ("9s"), **spruced up, spiffed up,** or **dressed to kill.**

Shopping – Some immigrants are intimidated by Americans and our culture. Because of this, they tend to shop in places run by people who speak their language. Native tastes and dress mistakes are then passed from one member of their community to another. They are only mistakes when someone works at assimilating our trends but they don't quite **get it** (understand) or are getting bad advice from others who also don't get it. I often see an immigrant-owned store in the U.S. that has a grammatically incorrect storefront sign and I know an immigrant-owned American business made the sign.

Clothing store in a mall.

Those who want to adapt to our culture for business, school, or even social situations might consider going to our mainstream clothing stores to purchase garments and receive good advice on up-to-date fashions. Here are more shopping tips.

- *Consignments* – Because fads date clothing quickly and many in the U.S. are thrifty, people have started taking their unwanted clothes to **consignment stores** *[kon-SIGN-ment]* to be sold. These stores take a percentage of the sales price if the item is sold. Women are pleasantly surprised at the low prices they pay for expensive designer clothes at these stores, such as $100 for a famous designer dress that sold new for $1,000. (These stores are listed in the telephone book's **yellow pages** (businesses) or on the Internet under "Consignment Stores.") A drawback is you might not find this year's most popular colors or cuts.
- *Fads* – A fashion that quickly comes and goes is called a **fad**. America is subject to these frequent changes. I have ties that have been in and out of style at least four times over the last 20 years. Later you will learn how to keep up-to-date with these changes.
- *Hours* – General shopping hours in our malls are from 10 a.m. to 9 p.m. on weekdays and from 10 a.m. to 6 p.m. on weekends. Ethnic stores in major commercial districts might have longer hours. Refund and exchange policies

can vary among our stores, so be sure to keep your sales receipt and return items within their terms, usually within 30 days.

- *Images* – Use the images in our magazines or outfits on mannequins in stores as models for outfit selections. If the outfit on the mannequin does not have a teddy bear backpack or a flashy gold belt, do not add one. Pay attention to the type of shoes selected for the outfits. Ask your sales person for advice on shoes if you are not sure of the best style, or take your newly purchased clothing over to the store's shoe department for a good match.

- *Layered Look* – The popular layered look allows you to combine garments and expand your wardrobe. Chain stores like the Gap (www.gap.com) and The Limited (www.thelimited.com) have layered clothing appropriate for most age ranges. Although the garments might cost a little more there than in small immigrant-owned stores, they will allow you to buy clothing with more confidence in style and colors.

- *Prices* – The price of clothing and other goods at our large department stores and malls are generally non-negotiable. At indoor and outdoor markets you can sometimes bargain with independent merchants, but you can't shop there with the fashion confidence or expertise found in malls and chain stores.

- *Salesperson* – Sales associates in our better stores can be a wealth of information and can help you put together culturally appropriate garments. Some can even help you assemble a **wardrobe**—an assortment of garments that can be mixed-and-matched for an assortment of different outfits. Some of our fine department stores even have shopping consultants to help you.

Designers – We have famous American clothing designers whose **labels** (clothing lines) are found in our stores. Here are a few that many of our immigrants and shoppers around the world have come to favor.

- **Calvin Klein** is famous for stylish casual designs. (www.calvinkleininc.com)
- **Donna Karan** *[KARE-an]* creates clothes primarily for businesswomen. She also designs a popular, less expensive line called **DKNY** [New York]. You might see those big letters on jeans and shirts we wear. (www.dkny.com)
- **Ralph Lauren** *[LORE-ehn]* has the Polo/Ralph Lauren label that focuses on a traditional look of quality, simplicity, and durability in his designs. For fun, check out his America-influenced clothing with flags, red/white/blue, and other American motifs. (www.RalphLauren.com)
- **Liz Claiborne** *[KLAY-born]* provides clothes for work or leisure. Cleanly sculptured silhouettes and splashes of color mark her designs. (www.lizclaiborneinc.com)

Ethnic groups might be attracted to certain designers. When Asian Americans were surveyed and asked to identify the fashion brands that are most flattering on Asian women, Calvin Klein was ranked number one, followed by DKNY, Emporio Armani, Chanel, Versace, Prada, and Bebe. These all are popular upscale labels in the U.S.

DRESSING TIPS FOR FOREIGNERS

Because of our cultural diversity, Americans are generally accepting of foreigners who dress differently. However, foreign-born Americans who have assimilated our dressing styles can be the harshest critics of the clothing of newly arrived or uninformed members of their culture. Don't be surprised if one of them offers you dressing advice without your asking for it.

Foreign Women Survey – When foreign-born women were asked in a survey to name the four most common dressing errors they see committed by their fellow women in the U.S., this was their response, starting with the most serious mistake. (They are common to American women in general.) If you are not sure about your outfit, a sales clerk will offer his or her opinion if you ask for it.

1. Wearing colors that are wrong for their coloring or features.
2. Wearing cuts that are wrong for their proportions and/or size.
3. Dressing inappropriately for the occasion.
4. Wearing clearly outdated styles. You can refer to fashion magazines (listed at end of this chapter) and go to various websites with current and forecasted trends, such as www.trendstop.com.

Common Dressing Errors – To add to these dressing problems, fashion consultants say the following are some of the most common "errors"—by American standards at least—that are made by uninformed foreigners in the U.S.

- *Casual Footwear* – Flip-flops (cheap thong-type sandals) and flimsy house-type shoes should be reserved only for the most casual situations. House slippers should never be worn outside of the home.
- *Cheap Garments* – Cheap, flimsy, and poorly cut clothing can cause a person to be perceived as lower class or unprofessional. Newly arrived immigrants tend to shop in immigrant-owned stores that might carry inexpensive clothing.
- *Childlike Choices* – Adults should not wear childish hair ornaments, ponytail holders, and barrettes with eye-catching ribbon, sequins, and beads. As for clothing, images of cartoon characters, teddy bears, puppies, kittens, and some floral prints may be fun but are best reserved for children under 15 years old.
- *Copying Others* – Not all Americans use proper English grammar, as you will learn in Chapter Y. The same is true with the way we dress. Ask questions,

use your judgment, and do some research before you commit to something you are not comfortable with. When in doubt, choose conservative styles and colors.

- *Furs* – Some Americans are opposed to people wearing fur coats made from animal skins. They might give you a nasty look if you are wearing one.

- *Hair Styles* – Choosing a beauty parlor in an ethnic American community might lead to inappropriate styling advice. Find an established salon outside that area where stylists are up-to-date in American styles.

- *Knock-offs* – Watch for cheap imitations of famous designs. Their cheap construction signals you are trying to appear affluent with a fake item. Also, be aware it is illegal to copy or buy these copyrighted fake designs.

- *Makeup* – Makeup artists at cosmetic counters at major department stores will provide a "makeover" for you at no charge. It is important you communicate to them your own likes and dislikes in makeup. The artist then selects the best colors and products for you and teaches you how to apply them. It is a courtesy to buy at least some of the products they show you. They might cost less in drug stores, but the professional advice regarding your image is worth the investment. At a later date when your products have been used up, you can probably find a

Cosmetic counter.

close match with similar but cheaper brands somewhere else if you so choose.

- *Mixing Patterns* – Be careful about mixing patterns and colors. Don't mix a skirt with a floral print with a shirt with polka dots. Be careful with colors, too, such as navy colored stockings with a pastel outfit that looks out of place to us.

- *Sparkly Daytime Garments* – Some immigrants wear sparkly or shiny garments with sequins and gold embellishments during the day. This is an outdated daytime look but is acceptable at dressy evening events. A Korean American friend, who once attended a nighttime party I hosted, came dressed in her sparkly native Korean wear and she was beautiful and the **hit of the party**.

- *Stockings* – Do not wear **socks** (stockings) or nylons with sandals or open-toed shoes. Wear nylons or tights well above your knee so the tops do not show. Men wear sports socks with sports shoes and dress socks with dress shoes. Women seem to favor bare legs in most occasions these days.

- *What to Wear* – Dress according to where you are going to be seen. If in doubt, ask someone who is known for their fashion sense. I have taken immigrant friends to places where they have chosen unwisely. I took an actor

278

friend to a stage play where Americans tend to dress up a bit and he was in jeans and sneakers, though admittedly there were some Americans dressed like that, too. Still, such casual wear is not quite appropriate. Now I always explain the dress code when inviting immigrant friends.

DRESSING STYLES

American dress styles can be divided into four general appearance groups: grungy, casual, business, and formal. Circumstances will dictate which style is proper for you to wear. Here are tips for you to consider.

1. Grungy Dress – Grungy *[GRUNN-gee]* is a term for sloppy, very casual dress. Typical dress includes T-shirt, shorts, tank tops (sleeveless T-shirts), athletic wear, oversized baggy pants, skateboard attire, and sandals. This kind of clothing should be limited to around the house or to the beach or mountains, although you might see people attend movies and go to the local market in this garb, especially during warm weather. Do not  wear grungy clothing where more upscale casual clothes would be more appropriate, such as a nice restaurant. Many schools provide dress standards that prohibit grungy dress (see below). Never wear grungy to work on a casual workday unless you know for sure it is acceptable.

2. Casual Dress – This is appropriate for those informal situations where a tie is not required for a man, and this category has different levels, from street casual to business casual. Jeans and a T-shirt, for example, would be very informal casual dress, while jeans accompanied with a collared shirt and a sport coat could be upscale casual. From my observations, immigrant Americans have no problem with casual dressing. If anything, some may tend to overdress. There is nothing wrong with this, but you might be more comfortable in certain situations by dressing more comfortably. Our schools have special dress codes to define casual dress.

Obama family casual dress.

- *High School Dress* – Many junior and senior high schools define minimum standards of dress for their students, hoping to avert grungy clothing and gang behavior. Such codes can work as guidelines for casual dress in general. This is a typical dress and grooming code used by a school system in Texas.

  "All students are expected to wear clothing that fits appropriately and covers the shoulders and the midriff; oversized or excessively tight clothing (such as spandex) is not permitted. Students may not wear short shorts, biking shorts, or miniskirts. Students are expected to be neatly groomed. Excessive jewelry, decorative contact lenses, and tooth caps and any other items deemed to be distracting are strictly prohibited. Clothing with

279

inappropriate messages related to alcohol, drugs, sex, violence, or vulgarity are prohibited. Also, thongs, backless shoes, and house slippers are not allowed."

- *College Dress* – Casual dress dominates in college, too. Because of cultural differences though, some foreign students may not dress as casually as American students. A Korean college student attending a U.S. college commented on these differences.
  - o Koreans wear more formal clothing at school. U.S. students dress casually for school but dress up during the weekend similar to Korean students.
  - o Most Korean women wear makeup in a public place or even to a meeting with a professor. Americans are more relaxed.
  - o In Korea, students wear sweatpants at home is viewed as impolite if worn to class as Americans do. Unlike casual America, Korean professors do not like students to wear sandals in the summer.
  - o American students tend to pay little attention to others' opinions about themselves compared to Korean students who are somewhat conservative due to their culture.

- *Casual Dress Stores* – Many stores in the U.S. sell casual wear, from small independents to large chains. Many are found in our large malls, including **factory outlet malls** where manufacturers sell their products directly to the public through their own stores at a reduced price. Lands End (www.landsend.com) is a popular casual wear retailer, as are Gap (www.gap.com), Abercrombie & Fitch (www.abercrombie.com), LL Bean (www.llbean.com), Eddie Bauer (www.eddiebauer.com), Banana Republic (www.bananarepublic.com), and Old Navy (www.olddnavy.com). Their websites show the latest in current styles. Some also mail seasonal catalogs to their customers. Sign up to receive them and they will serve as quick-study guides for casual dress. Some of our expensive high-design houses also offer casual clothing, but it is not necessary to pay their high prices to look stylishly casual.

Casual outfit.

3. Business Dress – Your clothes convey much about your intelligence, competence, and creativity. Clothes can be a distraction; you want attention paid to you, not your clothes. Proper employee dress varies from business to business. Some industries like startup Internet companies allow their employees to be comfortable with informal dress. Some may even allow grungy. Others like banking, finance, and corporations located in our larger cities require professional business attire. Successful corporate executives sometime council younger employees to dress and groom now for the job they aspire to; it will aid them in their climb up the **corporate ladder** (to move up in the hierarchy of a corporation).

280

Business dress for women means a suit or tailored dress in conservative colors (black, navy, gray, beige) with low-heeled shoes and simple jewelry. For men, business dress means a conservative **suit** (pants match the jacket, not a **sports coat** where pants do not match) with similar conservative colors, plus a long-sleeved shirt, tie, and leather shoes. A white dress shirt with tie conveys professionalism; a colored shirt suggests more informality.

Business dress.

If you are calling on an American company to discuss business matters, dressing properly will create a professional image for you and your company. If you normally wear a suit in your business calls and are calling on a company that dresses casually all the time, go ahead and wear your suit. Do not feel that you have to dress according to their standards; dress to yours. If you are in an informal conference meeting and would feel more comfortable taking off your jacket and/or tie, go ahead and do it if that is how the others are dressed. The decision is yours to make. A thoughtful counterpart might even suggest you do it, something you will do if your counterpart visits your office.

Business suit.

- *Business Dressing Tips* – Regardless of where you work, consultants say these tips will enhance your business image.
  - o *Accessories* – Keep your accessories up-to-date, including eyeglasses, watchband, briefcase, and jewelry. If you miss the little details in your office dress, people might think you miss the details in your office work, too.
  - o *Consistent* – Don't change your hair color every few months. Don't show up in a suit most days and jeans on the others.
  - o *First Impressions* – These are based mostly on appearance. People hire and promote people who appear to be like themselves, and dress is one of these factors.
  - o *Grooming* – Grooming shortcomings create a bad impression, including dirty and long fingernails, hair or eyebrows too long, body odor, wrinkled clothes, food stains on clothes and teeth, unshined shoes, ill-fitting clothes, unshaven, poorly matched clothing colors, and mismatched or casual stockings worn with dress shoes.
  - o *Look About* – Use the wardrobe of successful fellow employees and your boss as a guide. Look in business magazines for photos of leaders—wear what they wear. Notice things like shoe color, hair length and cut, and how they put outfits together.
- *Business Casual* – Starting in the 1990s, some businesses selected one day a week, usually Fridays, in which employees were allowed to dress casually. It

is estimated that as many as 50 percent of our companies now have a **business casual** dress policy on a daily basis, up from about 33 percent a few years ago. Such policies are intended to create a relaxed workplace where individuality is accepted and where skill and talent are given a higher priority than wardrobe. Business casual means a tie isn't necessary. Some men may choose a sports coat or sweater. This day for women usually means a dress, skirt and blouse, or slacks and blouse with comfortable low–heeled or flat shoes.

Men can't go wrong with lightweight cotton pants called **chinos** *[CHEEN-ohs]*, suntans, or khakis with a long-sleeved shirt on casual dress days. Popular chinos colors are beige, khaki (gray/green), and beige. They all look nice with practically everything. Since chinos are a more relaxed look, it is okay to wear them with **loafers** (shoes with no laces) rather than more formal dress shoes or sneakers.

Chinos.

- *Business Dress Stores* – Most department stores offer business attire, including shoes. Some have a department called Career Dressing where consultants can assist you in selecting the correct style for your office. They will need to know the dress policy of your employer in order to help you. If you are new to the company, ask your colleagues. One of our best-known, upscale men and women's chain stores for business dress is Brooks Brothers (www.brooksbrothers.com) that has worldwide stores I have spotted from Chile to **Park Avenue** (upscale street in New York City) to the United Arab Emirates.

4. Formal Dress – If formal dress is required for an event, your invitation will specify it using one of special terms listed below. (A little sparkle for women works for any of these more formal situations, sometimes merely a beaded evening purse.)

- *Black Tie* – Men wear tuxedos. Women wear **cocktail** (short) dresses, long dresses, or dressy evening separates.
- *Business Formal* – The same as semi-formal for him, but more tailored dressy suits and dresses for her; nothing too sexy, but still dressed up.

Tuxedo

- *Cocktail Attire* – Short, elegant dresses for her and dark suits for him. The little black dress is the ultimate cocktail dress and appropriate for most special occasions. (Dress shown is from Banana Republic.)
- *Daytime Semi-formal* – A suit for him (not necessarily dark) and an appropriate short dress or dressy suit for her.

Cocktail dress.

282

- *Evening Semi-formal* – Also called **after five**, tuxes are not required, nor are long dresses. A dark suit for him and a shorter cocktail dress is fine for her.

Those who do not own tuxedoes can rent them. Look in the telephone directory or Internet under "tuxedos and formal wear." Participants in a formal wedding ceremony often wear such attire. This website of a nationwide tuxedo rental firm offers suggestions for making the right selection: www.jimsformalwear.com.

FASHION MAGAZINES

We have many publications that provide readers with advice, trends, and latest styles in U.S. fashion and grooming. Most have websites, too. Here are some popular ones.

- *Cosmopolitan* – The largest-selling young women's magazine in the world aimed at the sexy youth market. (www.cosmomag.com)
- *ELLE* – International fashion magazine devoted to the sophisticated and well-traveled woman, covering style and beauty. (www.elle.com)

- *Esquire* – Appeals to men who are interested in new fashions and current events. (www.esquire.com)
- *Glamour* – For young women interested in fashion, beauty, career opportunities, image building, and personal issues. (www.glamour.com)
- *GQ* (Gentlemen's Quarterly) – The ultimate authority for men's style news. (www.gq.com)

  Hint: If you are dressed well, someone might say, "You look like you just stepped out of GQ."

- *Harper's Bazaar* – Addresses varied interests of upscale women who seek the best for their careers. (www.harpersbazar.com)
- *Marie Claire* – Monthly guide for the sophisticated woman. (www.marieclaire.com)
- *Men's Health* – Men's magazine covering fitness, fashion, grooming, and health issues. (www.menshealth.com)
- *Seventeen* – World's most popular magazine for the modern teenage girl, including those who may be searching for her first job. (www.seventeen.com)

- *Vogue* – The latest high style trends in women's fashion, style, and beauty (www.vogue.com). The movie, *The September Issue* (2008), is a documentary that provides a rare glimpse into the life of *Vogue's* world-renowned fashion editor.

CLOTHING SIZES

Clothing sizes are not measured in the same units around the world. An American size 8 shoe, for example, equates to a 7.5 in Britain and a size 40 in Europe. Most of our stores cater to American sizes, which might cause problems for some foreigners. For example, nearly half of all Asian American women wear size 6 or smaller, while sixty percent of American women wear a size 14 or larger. For this reason, some stores may not have a good selection of smaller sizes to choose from. Some stores now have sections called "Petite" for small women.

American clothing sizes are expressed three different ways.

- Some garments, like men's jackets, have a numerical number, such as "44" to indicate its size relative to the other numbers.
- Other articles, like men's shirts, have neck and sleeve length sizes expressed in inches, such as "16 (neck size) X 35" (sleeve length).
- Other clothing sizes are merely expressed in general terms like extra small (XS), small (S), medium (M), large (L), and extra-large (XL).

Our stores allow us to try on clothing and most allow their return—if they are still in good condition—for credit or exchange within 30 days of purchase with the sales receipt. Some stores do not allow items bought at a discount or on sale to be returned.

These general conversions will aid you in understanding U.S. sizes. They vary between manufacturers and even between different designs by the same manufacturer. Use these charts for approximation only. But to insure a good fit, always try on clothing in the private fitting room in the store before purchasing.

Men's Jackets

U.S. Sizes	36	38	40	42	44	46	48
Asian Sizes	46	48	50	52	54	56	58
European Sizes	46	48	50	52	54	56	58
U.K. Sizes	36	38	40	42	44	46	48

Men's Shirts

U.S. Sizes	14	14½	15	15½	16	16½	17 (in inches)
Asian Sizes	36	37	38	39	40	41	42
European Sizes	36	37	38	39	41	42	43
U.K. Sizes	14	14½	15	15½	16	16½	17

Men's Pants

U.S. Sizes	30	32	34	36	38	40 (in inches)
Asian Sizes	46	48	50	52	54	56
Int'l (cms)	76	81	86	91½	96½	101½

Shoe Sizes

U.S. Sizes	6	6½	7	7½	8	8½	9	9½
Asian (cm)	23	23	23½	24	24	24½	25	25½
European Sizes	37½	38	38½	39	39½	40	41	42
U.K. Sizes	5 ½	6	6 ½	7	7 ½	8	8½	9

Women's Dress, Suit, and Jacket Sizes

U.S. Sizes	2	4	6	8	10	12	14	16	18
Asian Sizes	32	34	36	38	40	42	44	46	48
European Sizes	32	34	36	38	40	42	44	46	48
U.K. Sizes	4	6	8	10	12	14	16	18	20

Women's Blouse, Sweater, Shirt Sizes

U.S. Sizes	24	26	28	30	32	34	36	38	40	42	44
Asian Sizes	32	34	36	38	40	42	44	46	48	50	52
European Sizes	40	42	44	46	48	50	52	54	56	58	60
U.K. Sizes	34	36	38	40	42	44	46	48	50	52	54

U.S. Dress Measurements Per Size

U.S. Number Size	2	4-6	8-10	12-14	16
Other Size	XS(34)	S(36)	M(38)	L(40)	XXL(42)
Body Bust	32"	34"	36"	38"	40"
Body Waist	24"	26"	28"	30"	32"
Body Hips	34"	36"	38"	40'	42"

FOREIGN HERITAGE DESIGNERS

Like so many other things in America, international talents have inspired and succeeded in our clothing industry. Many of our largest clothing companies were founded by immigrants, including New Balance Shoes (England), New Era Caps (Germany), Levi Strauss & Co. (Bavaria), Guess (Morocco), and Columbia Sportswear (Germany).

First Lady (our president's wife) Michelle Obama, known for wearing simple and relatively inexpensive clothing from our popular chain stores, was once criticized for not wearing these same domestic brands when she traveled overseas with her husband. Instead, she wore clothes of foreign-born American designers such as Jason Wu (Taiwan) and Isobel Toledo (Cuba), and new foreign names such as Azzedine Alaia (Tunisian-French) and Junya Watanabe (Japanese). For her meeting with her French counterpart Carla Bruni, Mrs. Obama opted for a coat and dress by Thakoon Panchigul, a Thai-born designer who moved to the U.S. when he was 11. As we say, **"You can't please all of the people all of the time**," even when it comes to the clothes we wear.

First Lady

285

Here is a sampling of foreign-born American designers/clothiers who have achieved success in the U.S.

- *Belgium* – Diane Von Furstenberg was born in Brussels, Belgium and moved to New York City in 1969. She started her own business selling knit dresses and expanded to perfumes, home furnishings, and cosmetics. She was ranked among the "Top 10 U.S. Businesses Run by Women" in a *Savvy* magazine annual survey. (www.dvf.com)

Von Furstenberg

- *China* - Fashion designer Vera Wang was the youngest-ever fashion editor and stylist for one of our popular fashion magazines. She now has her own luxury clothing business. Her bridal gowns and evening dresses are world famous. Celebrities often wear her designs to our star-studded Academy Awards ceremony. (www.verawang.com)

Wang

- *Germany* - Levi Strauss was born in Germany and at the age of 18 sailed to America. In 1873, he received a patent for using copper rivets to strengthen the pockets of denim work pants. Levi Strauss & Co. began manufacturing the famous Levi's brand of blue jeans. Today the company employs a staff of 10,500 people and has worldwide sales of $4 billion. (www.levi.com)

Strauss

- *India* – Naneem Khan learned from both his father and grandfather who designed for royal families. He later apprenticed in America as a teenager and presented his debut collection in 2003. His celebrity clientele includes singers, actresses, and princesses. Khan's collection is carried by Saks Fifth Avenue, Bergdorf Goodman, Neiman Marcus, and other upscale stores in the U.S. (www.naeemkhan.com)

Khan

- *Italy* – Donatella Versace was born in Italy and took over her late brother Gianni Versace's design house when he died in Miami, Florida. Following in his footsteps with the same passion, Donatella has become known for her sexy yet elegant designs. (www.versace.com)

Versace

- *Taiwan* – David Chu came to America in the late 1960s and eventually took up clothing design on the advice of an instructor at a college he attended. He established his Nautica clothing company in 1983 that now has global sales exceeding $1 billion. Many of his designs reflect the national colors and symbols of his adopted country. (www.nautica.com)

Chu

Q
MEDIA

Television is an invention that permits you to be entertained in your living room by people you wouldn't have in your home. - David Frost, British TV personality

Americans want to be informed about their country and the world. Our media help provide this service. You will gain insight about America by experiencing our media firsthand. But let's face it. Media sources around the world affect us all in terms of how we view and understand each other. Some do a good job, some not so good—both here and abroad.

We use the term **"the press"** to generally refer to print media like newspapers and magazines. **"Media"** is a broader term that includes newspapers, magazines, TV, radio and the Internet. However, we use them interchangeably as our media conglomerates own newspapers and other non-press media as well, and most newspapers now have online editions. So we now use "media" to refer to organizations and "press" for the all-important reporting aspect of the media.

In a world study, Americans gave relatively low marks to our news media—only 65 percent said it was a good influence—while Vietnam, the Philippines, and China give their media higher marks. Two-thirds of us believe our news media are biased when reporting politics and social issues, and over half believe our news stories are filled with wrong information. Further, three-fourths believe our TV and movies are largely responsible for juvenile crime. Seven out of ten Americans believe

that radio stations do a good job of providing a variety of programming. No matter what people think though, it is free speech and free press that contribute to a free nation and keeping its people informed.

Free Speech - The cornerstone of our media is the right to free speech, a vital part of our democratic heritage. Under the First Amendment of the U.S. Constitution, we have the right to speak our minds and publish our thoughts. So, when President Nixon went to court to stop *The New York Times* and *The Washington Post* newspapers from publishing the **Pentagon Papers**[*] in 1971, the Supreme Court ruled that neither the president nor the courts could constitutionally limit that right. This is in contrast to China where in 2012 President Hu Jintao called for increased government control of culture in television, film, and the performing arts. He warned of "hostile foreign powers" that are attempting to infiltrate China's "ideological and cultural sphere."

At the same time and during the presidential race in Russia, the Kremlin shuffled management of the Echo of Moscow radio station, considered one of the country's few stalwarts of free speech that had been critical of Prime Minister Putin who was seeking his third presidential term. In America, our media are neither owned nor controlled by the government, so free speech abounds and we expect to be told the truth or at least discover the truth from our many media sources.

The Press – The framers of our Constitution believed that a well-informed people is the strongest guardian of our liberties. Today, **the press** (our media reporters) functions as watchdogs over government and business by calling attention to official misdeeds and violations of individual rights. Our media perform this oversight function superbly, perhaps better than what you experience in your homeland.

President Kennedy (1961-1963) said, "There is a terrific disadvantage in not having the abrasive quality of the press applied to you daily. Even though we never like it, and even though we wish they didn't write it, and even though we disapprove, there isn't any doubt that we could not do the job at all in a free society without a very, very active press."

Most Americans agree that a healthy debate keeps our democracy flourishing. In contrast, many say the European press contains less diversity of opinion than the U.S. press. For example, at the beginning of the Iraq War when it was a hotly debated topic in the U.S. with strong divergent views, most European papers held a common view with little dissent. (See Chapter T on what foreigners think about America for more on this.)

Does our press do a good, unbiased job? In the 1970s, veteran TV broadcaster **Walter Cronkite** was voted in a poll as "the most trusted man in America." During that era, 70 percent of us trusted the press. Today we are largely distrusting, with only 45 percent saying they have some trust in the media to report the news fully, accurately, and fairly. One out of two believes the media is too liberal and 15 percent too conservative.

Truman, Election Day, 1948.

---

[*]A secret government report detailing negative implications about the unpopular Vietnam War.

288

You might hear us talk about the most famous example of inept reporting. It occurred during the presidential election in 1948 when some newspapers incorrectly reported prematurely that Dewey had defeated President Truman.

> **Hint**: We still use the term "**Dewey Defeats Truman**" jokingly in sarcastic speech when someone makes a statement that is obviously in error. For example, if someone says they are going to win the upcoming lottery, you might say "Sure, and Dewey defeated Truman."

Press Reporting – Our news gathering system is unlike some countries like China where the media receive news from an official government agency. Our agencies that provide reporting and article services are privately owned. More importantly our individual media outlets do their own investigative reporting and try to get a **scoop** (inside, revealing story) before the rest do. As a result, our officials and government are highly scrutinized. There's that *competitive* thing again that is part of our culture.

Due to our changing, more liberal culture, we have witnessed a fundamental change in what our press reports and how we view this information. Through the 1960s, reporters virtually conspired with politicians, celebrities, and other public figures to keep the public from knowing about their personal weaknesses, and this included our presidents. In the 1930s and 40s, President Franklin Roosevelt's crippled body was not talked about nor was he ever photographed with his crutches. The press equally ignored President Kennedy's numerous escapades with women in the 60s, believing this was a private matter, which was quite different from how President Clinton's private life was exposed in the 90s.

So today, this invasion of privacy is a hotly debated issue by Americans— whether any area of a person's life should remain off-limits once he or she becomes a public figure. Some believe this prying of the press deters capable people from going into politics and public service. Some believe the public has a right to know, especially those who believe private matters indicate character, which, in turn, can influence public policy. If carried too far, freedom without responsibility can do harm as well as good.

Slanted Reporting – When people in America and foreign countries misunderstand each other, the press is often at fault. Americans will tell you our media is biased in one direction or the other. Even a husband and wife might disagree with each other about the bias of their daily newspaper. I have found this obvious bias when reading foreign newspapers that report about the U.S.

As a case in point, when U.S. President George Bush did not sign the important Kyoto Agreement—which would lead to reduced greenhouse gases affecting our atmosphere—some foreign newspapers did not report Bush's legitimate concerns such as his not wanting exemptions allowed. Instead, they simply reported the U.S. was not interested in environmental issues. Unfortunately, they did not report that the U.S. has some of the strictest environmental standards in the world. Many foreign-built cars, for example, are not allowed in the U.S. because of our strict air pollution standards. We have some of the strictest water, power plant, factory, and mining pollution standards in the world, and our scientists take global warming seriously.

On the other hand, the general impression in the U.S. media is that China and other rapidly expanding economies are lax when it comes to pollution and the environment. I know China is doing much more than is being reported in the press here, witness the shuttering in 2007 of their old production facilities producing millions of tons of iron, cement, steel, and calcium carbide. And Ambassador Zhou Wenzhong (who endorsed this book) says, "Climate change is very high on the agenda of strategic economic dialogue between China and the United States. There is a lot we can do together." I don't think our press is deliberately misrepresenting China's efforts; it is simply ignorant of the real facts, perhaps because China's political process is not as open as ours. Our press may also commit errors of omission when reporting, thus affecting how we view China, its people, and government.

Before moving to the U.S., my foreign-born American friend had read in newspapers about all the different colors of people in the U.S. After living here for years and never seeing any blue-colored people, she finally asked a stranger where they were located. She had been a victim of misleading media reporting in her home country.

For these reasons, I caution my students to exercise care before drawing conclusions about the U.S., just as we should do with their country. We have an appropriate saying: **Don't believe everything you read**. I would add that we should all put things in proper perspective, consider the source, get the real facts from multiple sources, and keep learning before we pass judgment on other countries and peoples. (Do you remember our discussion of the the tragic consequences of our not understanding the intentions of the people of Vietnam that led to that war?)

Corporate Influence – The extent to which the interests of its advertisers affect the reporting (editorial policy) of a media outlet is a subject of frequent controversy in the U.S. Would a newspaper or TV network run a negative story about the crash worthiness of a car if the automaker is one of its advertisers? Also of concern to Americans is the power a corporation wields over public opinion by having controlling interests in our media outlets. At the end of World War II, four out of five newspapers were locally owned. By 1990 four out of five were controlled by outside corporations and the number is still growing. We had more than 1,600 daily papers in 1990 with only 15 chief executive officers responsible for the majority of the circulation. Today, six corporations account for the bulk of our magazine business, and some of the biggest are foreign-owned corporations that have been caught using **shady** (not honest) reporting tactics. So, we wonder if we are getting objective reporting in the media today. We have to **stay on our toes** (be alert) to get the truth.

Hint: Loosely based on the true story about a powerful newspaper publisher's rise to power in the U.S., the film *Citizen Kane* (1941) is regarded by many as one of the most popular films of all time. (The film is discussed in Chapter L - Film.) Other popular films dealing with the media include *Network* (1976), *All the President's Men* (1976), *Absence of Malice* (1981), and *Broadcast News* (1987).

Immigrant Media – Studies show that a significant percentage of immigrant Americans prefers their own media over our English language counterparts. The Asian American media, for example, reach 75 percent of the Asian population of California. This means they are probably getting news reported to them by immigrants and they may not be balancing that news with other more reliable information closer to the source.

Second-generation Asian Americans report that their parents' English language has never substantially improved, due in part to this isolation from English language media, friends, and businesses. Asians in the San Francisco Bay area where there are twelve Chinese dialects are further isolated because there is not one tongue as there is for Spanish-speaking Latinos in the U.S. This separation also applies to my isolated Armenian American friends who get most of their information from Armenian TV, press, friends, and schools.

Hint: I tell my students and foreigners to try to get different perspectives on what occurs in the U.S. by reading one of our newspapers daily, even if they only read one article or scan the front page. This will help them learn about topical issues in America as well as improve their English and conversational skills. Unfortunately, many only read an ethnic paper because they have difficulty reading English. It's a vicious circle.

NEWSPAPERS

You will sometimes hear us use the term **Fourth Estate** when we refer to our newspapers. This is because in early England the lowly press ranked fourth after the king, lords, and commoners. The government in the U.S. does not own or control our newspapers as they do in some countries. Most are issued on a daily basis, primarily in the morning or weekly. Many colleges, staffed by student reporters and editors getting a start in this profession, print a daily newspaper to inform their student body of what is happening locally or on campus. Most

Daily U.S. newspapers.

countries have national newspapers, such as the U.K. with its 12. We have five papers with limited national distribution including *The New York Times* and *USA Today*.

Role Of Newspapers – Nearly six out of ten adults in the U.S. read a newspaper daily, but readership is declining. Only 28 percent express a great deal of trust in our papers. By the time we see a newspaper, we have already learned about news stories on television, radio, or the Internet. But we rely on our newspapers to provide more detailed background information and interpretation. Thus, our newspapers help shape American attitudes and opinions with this in-depth analysis. As an example, *The Washington Post's* 1970s investigation into the **Watergate Scandal** lead to the resignation of President Nixon* for which the paper received a Pulitzer Prize for its investigative reporting.

Besides reporting news, our papers, probably like yours back home, also provide readers with a host of other topics ranging from comics to sports. Earl Warren, a 20th century governor and Supreme Court Justice, said, "I always turn to the sports page first, which records people's accomplishments. The front page has nothing but man's failures." He does have a point, doesn't he?

Editorial Slant – You will note that the **editorial page** of our large daily papers carries the *opinions* of the papers' editors on various subjects, including the government. This page defines the **editorial policy** of the paper. Readers know this one page is opinion, not fact. If they are informed and careful readers, they might also notice the same editorial slant in the paper's reporting of news stories. Some of our newspapers have reputations for leaning toward Democrat or Republican issues, or have a subtle liberal or conservative bias in their reporting and editorials. Responding to media bias, Ben Bradlee, the former late-20th century *Washington Post* executive editor said, "To hell with the news. I'm no longer interested in news. I'm interested in causes. We don't print the truth. We don't pretend to print the truth...." Wasn't this the same attitude our founding fathers had when their cause was to liberate us from England and give us freedom? The **op-ed page** (opposite the editorial page) prints the opinions sent to the paper by its readers, including scholars, homemakers, and celebrities. *The New York Times'* op-ed page is an example of this (www.newyorktimes.com).

Tabloids – A Japanese proverb: "If you believe everything you read, better not read." In addition to our regular size newspapers, we have physically smaller papers called **tabloids**. The term **tabloid journalism** refers to newspapers that carry stories about celebrity scandals, crime, gossip, and the outrageously bizarre under sensational headlines. Our supermarkets sell these national tabloids with grabbing headlines, such as the **National Enquirer** (www.nationalenquirer.com) that prints stories that would not appear in a normal newspaper. Do not judge American culture by these

A tabloid.

---

*During Nixon's re-election campaign in 1970, some of his election staff broke into the **Watergate Office Building** in search of information on his opponent. *The Washington Post* unveiled Nixon's deliberate cover up of this, which led to impeachment hearings that forced him to resign from office, the first president to do so. A wonderful movie that deals with this is *All the President's Men* (1976) with Dustin Hoffman and Robert Redford as the investigative newspaper reporters who uncovered the cover up.

tabloids! And do not believe everything you read! Even my immigrant American friends love these publications because they **uncover the dirt** (reveal the hidden) on celebrities.

Hint: Because it is printed in a tabloid format does not mean it is a **gossip rag**. Some tabloid-size newspapers are legitimate papers such as the *New York Daily News*, the *Chicago Sun-Times*, and the *Boston Herald*. Many good little local papers are formatted this way, too.

International Papers – There is international demand for some U.S. newspapers, perhaps by those who want to get our **slant** (view) on the news. *USA Today* (www.usatoday.com) is composed in Virginia and then transmitted via satellite to printing plants serving Europe and Asia. The *Wall Street Journal* (www.wallstreetjournal.com) transmits European and Asian editions. The *International Herald Tribune* (www.global.nytimes.com/?iht), owned by The New York Times Company, is a global newspaper printed via satellite at 38 sites throughout the world and sold in more than 160 countries.

Hint: American travelers overseas enjoy reading the *Tribune*. I read it when traveling to keep up with sports scores. If you want to pleasantly surprise American visitors to your country, you might present them with a copy of it so they can learn what is happening back home. Some large hotels overseas carry the paper in their lobby shops.

Newspaper Rankings – Columbia University's esteemed School of Journalism in New York City conducted a survey to determine our best newspapers. Judging was based on such factors as writing and reporting quality, integrity, accuracy, fairness, vision, innovation, and influence in their community, the same factors that you are learning are theoretically the underpinnings of American culture. This is their ranking of our top newspapers.

Rank	Paper Name	City/State	Circulation
1.	*The New York Times*	New York, NY	1.6 million
2.	*The Washington Post*	Washington, D.C.	1.1
3.	*Wall Street Journal*	New York, NY	1.7
4.	*Los Angeles Times*	Los Angeles, CA	1.4
5.	*The Dallas Morning News*	Dallas, TX	0.8
6.	*Chicago Tribune*	Chicago, IL	1.0
7.	*The Boston Globe*	Boston, MA	0.8
12.	*USA Today*	Arlington, VA	2.1

Hint: Using the names of these papers or referring to an article in them in a conversation with an American might put you in a favorable light. And if you want an objective view of America, you might temper what you see on TV or read in another newspaper with what you read in these papers. However, you will see that even *The Washington Post* and *The Washington Times* that are both located in the same city can have different views on the same subjects.

Ethnic Newspapers – Dozens of English language newspapers in the U.S. have closed in recent years thanks to the **new media** (Internet). At the same time, however, ethnic newspapers have been building circulation in cities with large ethnic populations. The Vietnamese American market, for example, now offers readers more than 60 newspapers to choose from, and Latino, Chinese, and Russian papers are gaining readers. In the last ten years, Asian American print media have increased 300 percent to over 600 publications, of which 100 are in English but written for Asian Americans. New York City alone has 200 magazines and newspapers published in 36 languages. At the opposite extreme, many older publications aimed at Western European immigrants are losing readers to our mainstream English language media, an indication that they more quickly assimilate U.S. culture and language.

Ethnic newspaper.

The ethnic American media do not always cover the same news as our mainstream media because of their focus on news from their homeland. This further handicaps their readers or viewers from assimilating or understanding America if this is their only news source. On the other hand, our mainstream media may not provide relevant information about what is going on in the homelands of these readers, so I advise immigrants to strike a happy balance between the two.

While corporations own 86 percent of English-language newspapers in the U.S., many of our ethnic publications are family-owned. There are exceptions, such as media companies in Taiwan and Hong Kong that own the major Chinese papers in New York, and *The Korea Central Daily News* that is the U.S. edition of a daily in Korea.

This website provides links to 20,000 newspapers and other news sources in the U.S. and most countries in the world: www.kidon.com/media-link/us_ethnic.php.

MAGAZINES

We have 11,000 magazines on virtually any subject, with names and topics ranging from *Tennis, Antiques,* and *Trailer Life,* to *Model Railroading.* Our more academic magazines, called journals, are supported by research and include *National Geographic* (www.nationalgeographic.com), *The Smithsonian* (www.smithsonianmag.com), *Nature* (http://magazine.nature.org/), and *Scientific American* (www.scientificamerican.com). Ethnic magazines in the U.S. are less common than our ethnic newspapers. But studies show that Asian Americans are 70 percent more likely to read a fashion magazine than the average American, perhaps due to their desire to assimilate American culture.

News Magazines – These are excellent places to get indepth coverage of all kinds of stories from business to politics to the arts. Our three leading weekly newsmagazines will provide you with good in depth coverage of what is going on in the U.S.: *Time* (www.time.com), *Newsweek* (www.newsweek.com) and *U.S. News and World Report* (www.usnews.com). *Time* and *Newsweek* are center-left (somewhat liberal) while *U.S. News and World Report* tends to be center-right (somewhat conservative).

First *Time.*

Introduced in 1923, *Time* magazine was the first to offer weekly in-depth analyses of national and international developments. It is the world's largest circulation weekly news magazine with a readership of 25 million, of which 20 million are in the U.S. *Time Asia* is our number one news or business magazine in circulation across East and Southeast Asia.

Magazines Bring Cultural Changes – *Playboy* magazine's (www.playboy.com) first edition in 1953 was a reflection of onrushing sexual cultural changes in the U.S. With sexy movie star **Marilyn Monroe** shown in a bathing suit on its cover, it caused a sensation. It also set new publishing standards and by 1969 it contained photos of nude women along with intellectual articles by some of our best authors. Similar magazines arose. It is still our largest selling men's magazine, about 1.5 million copies a month in the U.S. Some states like Utah ban selling it to boys under 16 years old.

First *Playboy.*

As another example of how American culture differs from other countries, *Playboy* today is banned in many parts of Asia (except Hong Kong), including Singapore, India, mainland China, Myanmar, Malaysia, Thailand, and Brunei. In Japan, genitals of models cannot be shown, so a separate edition is published for that country. It is also banned in most Muslim countries (except Lebanon and Turkey), including Iran, Saudi Arabia, and Pakistan.

International Audiences – Like their newspaper counterparts, our magazines meet the demands of international audiences. *Newsweek* and several others print special international editions geared to geographical regions. *Time* transmits its entire magazine from New York to Hong Kong and Singapore each week. Two of our women's magazines, *Cosmopolitan* and *Vogue,* have had international followings for years. These magazines can provide foreigners with excellent insight into America from afar.

Circulation – Like publications in other countries, a magazine's influence in the U.S. is based on its circulation. Ranked by readership, these ten most-read general magazines in the U.S. can add insight to your understanding of our culture.

1. *Better Homes & Gardens* – Features on food, home, gardening. (www.bhg.com)
2. *Reader's Digest* – Condensed articles from other publications. (www.rd.com)
3. *National Geographic* – Information and maps about other

nations, world issues, and the environment. (www.nationalgeographic.com)

4. *Good Housekeeping* – Information on home, food, beauty, health. (www.goodhousekeeping.com)

5. *Woman's Day* – Health, fitness, crafts, cooking, relationships, beauty tips. (www.womansday.com)

6. *Family Circle* – Fashion, beauty, family life, home improvement. (www.familycircle.com)

7. *People* – Inside news about famous people as well as interesting ordinary people. (www.people.com)

8. *Time* – Weekly in-depth reporting and analysis of U.S. and world events. (www.time.com)

9. *Ladies Home Journal* – Social issues, food and nutrition, health, exercise. (www.lhj.com)

10. *Sports Illustrated* – Photography and in-depth coverage of various sports and athletes. (www.si.com)

Hint: Beware of telephone sales pitches for free, pre-paid, or special magazine subscription deals. An impulse purchase could leave you with years of monthly payments for magazines you may not want or could buy for less elsewhere. In some states, you're legally obligated to pay for a subscription once you verbally agree to it. Ask questions. If you don't get answers that they're willing to back up in writing, consider doing business elsewhere. Beware of emotional appeals by someone selling door-to-door such as a "student" selling magazine subscriptions using the appeal that your sale will help him/her get a college scholarship or other such rewards. Many are not students and the subscriptions may be more expensive. Don't be intimidated or fooled by them.

RADIO

Commercial stations are owned by private companies and make profits from advertisements. Public stations like PBS (www.pbs.org) receive contributions and generally do not have commercials. They provide intellectual programming like world affairs, poetry, the arts, and literature that might appeal to a relatively narrow segment of the population. Some colleges have radio stations that appeal to, and are staffed by, its students and heard by the public as well in surrounding communities.

Our 14,000 radio stations are almost evenly divided between AM and FM broadcast spectrums. AM broadcasting consists mostly of talk programming, including telephone call-in shows, all-news formats, religion, and sports coverage. Most major league sports teams broadcast their games on a local AM station as our ethnic stations do.

Disk jockey.   (voices.com)

Most FM stations provide music formats, such as rock, country, rap, classical, or other types that appeal to particular audiences. Hosts of our music programs are called **disk jockeys** or **DJs**, a term dating back to the early days of radio when they played records (round disks).

Call Letters – Like other countries, our radio and TV stations use **call letters** comprised three or four letters, such as WJR or KVST. These equate to the use of AX in Australia and R in Russia. Our stations with call letters beginning with W are located east of the Mississippi River, while those beginning with K are west of it. As a small boy, I would listen at night when radio signals travel farther. I became excited when a distant radio station announced its call letters and the location of its city.

Satellite Radio – For a small fee each month, a listener is offered dozens of static-free, commercial-free radio formats beamed by a satellite in space to a special radio anywhere in the U.S. This is particularly helpful in the vast, remote areas of our western states that have weak or no AM or FM radio signals. One operator is SiriusXM (www.sirius.com) that offers 140 different channels ranging from music to sports to news of all kinds.

Ethnic Stations – We have ethnic stations in areas with matching populations. The Los Angeles area, for example, has 21 of the 1330 Spanish speaking radio stations in the U.S. and seven Asian language stations. These ethnic radio stations have huge audiences and can help their listeners adapt to everyday life. A website where you can search for ethnic radio stations in the U.S. is www.radio-locator.com.

Talk Radio – As you have been learning, Americans like to express their opinions. Our popular **talk radio** shows started in the late 1970s with 75 stations. Because of their popularity, we now have over 1400. Each features a host, a celebrity, or an expert on some subject, even government officials, and allows listeners to call in and ask questions or express their opinions on the air, something we are good at doing.

Some talk radio programs are heard nationwide, but most are produced for local areas. And you may notice that most of the hosts lean to the political and social right (conservative) that has the country's largest audience. This is in spite of what you may hear about our media favoring the left (liberal). Your American counterpart might refer to one or more of these national hosts.

- *Howard Stern* – Described as a **shock jock** because of his offensive language and topics, he has been fined over the years for abusing the public airwaves. The movie, *Private Parts* (1997), is an auto-biographical story of this radio rebel, TV personality, and author. (www.howardstern.com)

Howard Stern

- *Rush Limbaugh* – Openly supportive of Republican administrations and critical of Democrats. (www.rushlimbaugh.com)

- *Bill O'Reilly* – Outspoken about government mismanagement and ineptness. (www.foxnews.com/oreilly)
- *Dr. Laura* – Provides callers advice on relationships and moral dilemmas. (www.drlaura.com).

Hint: You can refer to these national media celebrities if you want to make a point in a conversation with an American. For example, if someone is criticizing our democratic president, you might say, "You must be a big Rush Limbaugh fan." Or, if someone is criticizing inept management in Washington, D.C., you might say, "Sounds like you'd like to see Bill O'Reilly clean up the mess." If someone confesses their emotional problems to you, you could say, "I wonder what Doctor Laura would say about that." Or if someone shocks you with their weird behavior, you might say, "Have you been listening to Howard Stern too much?" You'll probably get a smile from your American counterpart and a nod that says yes.

Internet Radio – Many of our radio stations now send their signals over the Internet in addition to the airwaves. You can locate these from your computer at www.live-radio.net/info.shtml. (Click on USA and then on a state on the U.S. map to get a listing of stations that stream onto your computer.) You can test your understanding of English by clicking on one of these two popular talk radio stations: **WABC** in New York, or **KABC** in Los Angeles. You can also listen to ethnic stations in the U.S., hear our popular music, or learn about the news. We also have Internet-only radio stations like www.Pandora.com that do not broadcast over the airwaves.

TELEVISION

We have 1,200 commercial and 370 public TV stations that reach more than 99 percent of homes in the U.S. The broader more diversified European Union has 6500 channels. Similar to our newspapers, only 27 percent express a great deal of trust in TV.

Our radio and TV stations are not owned or operated by a government agency as they are in some countries. But the airways they use *are* limited by a government license. Our government has banned cigarette advertising on TV, but does not regulate the advertising minutes per hour. This limited role of the government in regulating our airwaves contrasts with those countries where program content is closely defined. European Union legislation, for example, limits the time taken by commercial breaks to 12 minutes per hour. China

TV studio control room.

regulates this, too. In the U.S. it is voluntary, but amounts to about 18 minutes. This is a good example of our stance that industries, not the government, should self-regulate where possible, an affirmation that **less government is better government**.

Hint: A current hot topic in the U.S. deals with the question of how far the government should go in regulating what is said and shown over our airways in free-speech America. Because of increasing violence, offensive language, and sexual overtones, some want the government to impose stricter standards; others say the government would be violating our freedom of speech if they did. This issue gives good insight into how Americans and their government attempt to approach and resolve its differences. In the U.S., there are always two sides to issues to be explored. Many times public outcry initiates media investigation, which, in turn, can result in government investigation and action.

One of my immigrant friends came to America and learned English primarily from watching TV. She loved our cartoons because of their simple language. In short, you can learn a lot about America from TV, just as we do, but keep in mind that it may sometimes not depict the real America, especially our drama series that many foreigners love.

There is no question that TV impacts our lives. During the Vietnam War in the 1970s, protests against the war were reported daily on TV newscasts. The war was widely debated on other non-news programs. Nightly TV images of body bags containing dead soldiers being brought back home as they were lifted off of airplanes had a powerful influence on shaping the people's opposition to the unpopular war.

About three-fourths of all commercial television stations in the U.S. are affiliates of one of the four major national networks: **ABC**, **CBS**, **NBC**, and **FOX**. These networks create some of their programs and buy others from independent producers. Even our movie studios produce shows for TV. In addition, we have hundreds of national cable channels, some of which are seen overseas.

Television awards are presented each year by a number of organizations. The best known awards, the **Emmys** (www.emmys.tv), are given to recognize achievements of the preceding year. Like the Academy Awards for film and the **Tony Awards** for stage plays, a statuette is awarded for various TV categories.

Emmy Award

Hint: Attending the filming of our TV programs is a popular free activity for tourists in New York City and Los Angeles. They might see a favorite celebrity in person. This website provides information for getting tickets: www.studioaudiences.com. Tickets should be obtained well in advance.

Overseas Interest – Foreign interest in American entertainment is pronounced, even in our television shows. In many countries, particularly in Europe, our shows, once relegated to late night, are now shown in prime time. In the Middle East with negative views of the U.S., there is an understanding of the difference between our government and the American people because of our TV shows shown there.

I learned this first hand when a refined woman I met on a New Zealand train thought all Americans were loud because people on our talk shows that she watched were loud and sometimes overbearing. I assured her they do not represent the vast majority American people. Like our tabloids that want to attract attention and increase readership by dealing with the unusual, our talk shows increase viewership with this loud behavior.

Since 1992, almost 30 U.S. cable channels have been launched in Latin America, including NBC, Cinemax, Discovery, ESPN, Fox, HBO, MTV, and Cartoon Network, all of which are successful in the U.S. I was surprised at the significant number of these I saw in Chile while **channel surfing** (switching channels) one night. They expose viewers to a good cross section of American culture and language, even our talk shows.

TV In Politics – Politicians can purchase commercial time during elections. This is quite unlike some countries like France where political advertising on television is heavily restricted and Norway where it is banned. During the election season our politicians participate in debates with other candidates on TV, which in turn can affect our political opinions. On Sunday mornings you may see a government official on TV being questioned at length by an interviewer.

You might hear about the first live telecast in 1960 of a debate between our two presidential candidates, Kennedy and Nixon. Some say TV brought out Kennedy's youthful appeal and got him elected. Interestingly, it would be another 50 years before gentlemanly England had its first televised debate of candidates for prime minister. (It was also England at the outset of WWII that stated, given the opportunity, it would not attempt to assassinate Hitler because it was not sportsmanlike; that soon changed after Hitler's relentless bombings and the deaths of Londoners.)

Kennedy-Nixon TV debate, 1960

Types Of Programs – You might hear Americans discussing a TV program, sometimes **at the water cooler** the next day at work. (In the old days, workers would fill their cups at the water cooler where they would gossip or casually talk. Today it might be the coffee machine but you'll still hear the term used.) You might be invited to the home of an American to watch their favorite program, including American Idol, a reality television singing competition based on the Idol franchise in the U.K. It is our most watched TV series and the only program to have been number one for eight consecutive seasons.

- Action-packed Dramas – About detectives, doctors, lawyers, and police officers.
- Documentaries – Nonfiction programs, mostly educational, such as National Geographic's.
- Game Shows – Wheel of Fortune and Jeopardy have been popular for years.
- Light Dramas – Also called situation comedies.
- Movies – Reruns of older theater movies, but also some made expressly for TV.
- News – Local, national, and international news daily. Objective BBC is a favorite for some.
- Reality Shows – Real people, not actors, participate and compete, such as American Idol.
- Soap Operas – Daily serial dramas that were originally sponsored by advertisers of soap.
- Talk Shows – A host who interviews people. *Leno* and *Letterman* are two late-night favorites.
- Sporting Events – Many teams broadcast their games to their local audience. Some games such as our Super Bowl and World Series are broadcast around the world.

Hint: Professional football, as pointed out in Chapter N on sports, is very popular with Americans, so it is to your advantage to learn about the game and discuss it with your American counterpart. The high TV ratings of these games reflect this popularity, especially when the two best teams eventually play in the Super Bowl in February.

Ethnic TV – We have numerous ethnic TV stations. And because of growing advertising revenue, these same cable and satellite companies are retransmitting shows from the United Arab Emirates, Russia, Poland, Greece, Israel, Italy, Vietnam, China, South Korea, and elsewhere to America. Ethnic American TV stations are now pooling their resources to create national networks of their own for their followers here. Univision, for example, is our largest Spanish-language broadcaster with 62 TV stations. And popular American TV programs are broadcast in English on these ethnic stations and abroad. Their viewers follow native language sub-titles across the bottom of the TV screen, providing them another good way to brush up on their spoken English.

INTERNET

Digital technology is enabling more people to get involved in social change faster than ever before and is creating a shift in how it comes about. The Internet has become an important media source in the U.S. where two-thirds of Americans use it—averaging 32 hours a month at home and three-times that amount at work. We account for 14 percent of the world's total Internet usage versus Asia's 43 percent and Europe's 24 percent. We are the only

Internet Explorer

major country without a national policy to promote high-speed Internet access, but like a lot of other things, **it's in the hopper** (the government's working on it). As with other media in the U.S., the **Net** (slang for Internet) has had a profound effect on our lives. For the first time, in 2010 Americans said they would prefer to surf the Net instead of watch TV if they had to make a choice. And a majority of Americans who use the Internet now consider it their most important source of information, more than television and newspapers. However, you should view the reliability of Internet data to be less reliable than our other media, particularly our mainstream newspapers and magazines.

Do we get too much of a good thing? By their own admission, many young Americans, aged 18 to 29, say they spend too much time using the Internet (59%), their cell phones or smartphones (58%), and social media sites such as Facebook (48%).

Cultural Differences – E-mail styles differ between America and other countries. For some Europeans, e-mail has replaced the business letter. For Americans, it has begun to replace the telephone. Europeans comment than an American's e-mail can be informal and chatty and is likely to begin with a friendly "Hi" and end with a "Bye." And it might contain a smiley face ☺ or "xoxo" meaning hugs and kisses. Some say our e-mails are rambling and yet direct, deferential yet arrogant. In other words, Amerimail is America.

On the other hand, Americans might say Euromail can be stiff and cold, often beginning with a formal "Dear Mr. X" and ending with a brusque "Sincerely" and is all businesslike. Unlike **on-the-go** U.S. where responses are immediate, it might take days, even weeks, to receive an answer from Europe. Euromail is also less confrontational and rarely filled with the directness that characterizes American e-mail disagreements. In other words, some say Euromail is exactly like the Europeans themselves.

> **Hint**: We should be aware of these differences if we want to make the right impression with our counterparts. We should also try not to generalize because Americans also use e-mails for serious business letters, and some Europeans have come to appreciate America's more relaxed style.

Most Visited Web Sites – Although they change regularly, these are the current rankings of our most visited websites. To gain further insight into what Americans are **up to** (what they are doing), you might want to explore them.

1. Google.com – Search the Web, Usenet, and images.
2. Facebook.com – Online directory connecting people through social networks.
3. Yahoo.com – Multi-faceted resource from advanced search engine to free e-mail.
4. YouTube.com – Upload, tag, and share videos worldwide.
5. Amazon.com – Largest online retailer in the U.S., offering everything from **soup to nuts** (vast array), including a huge catalog of books—both paperbooks and e-books—like this one you are reading.
6. Wikipedia – Online collaborative encyclopedia.
7. Twitter – Source of instantly updated information on a wide variety of topics.
8. Blogspot – Web blog publishing tool for sharing text, photos, videos, thoughts.
9. Craigslist.org – Centralized network featuring free online classified advertisements.
10. MSN.com – Microsoft network and content provider.

Internet Greeting Cards – Americans send 7 billion printed greeting cards each year, half of which are for holidays. We have websites with e-mail greeting cards you can send on the Internet such as www.123greetings.com (free) and www.americangreetings.com (for a fee). There is an e-card for any occasion you can think of. Some are humorous and some are serious depending on the occasion. On-line cards are less formal than cards sent via the post office, so use them in

Happy B'day!
(123greetings.com)

situations when a more formal card would not be required (see Chapter H - Customs and Etiquette).

302

FOREIGN HERITAGE AMERICANS IN THE MEDIA

Foreign heritage Americans have always had a strong presence in our media. Here's a few.

- *Canada* – Peter Jennings was a beloved Canadian American journalist and reporter who became a U.S. citizen in 2003. He was the popular anchor of ABC's World News Tonight from 1983 until his early death in 2005 of lung cancer from smoking cigarettes.

Jennings

- *Germany* – A refugee from Nazi Germany, Max Frankel couldn't speak English when he arrived in the U.S. as a boy. He worked for *The New York Times* for 50 years, rising from college correspondent to reporter to executive editor from 1986-1994. He won the Pulitzer Prize for his coverage of President Nixon's trip to China in 1972.

Frankel

- *Asia* – Lisa Ling was on a popular nationally televised morning program for several years and does other national TV broadcasts. Many Asians, particularly women, are popular local newscasters on TV, particularly in the San Francisco and Los Angeles areas. Connie Chung is one of a very small group of women who achieved prominence in American network news. Ann Curry has also done nationally televised programs. Stephen Chao, a movie producer and TV executive, was president of Fox TV and Fox News.

Ling

- *India* – Writer and journalist Fareed Zakaria, born and raised in India, specializes in international relations. He writes regular columns for *The Washington Post, Newsweek,* and *Time* magazines. He was an analyst for ABC News and his book, *The Future of Freedom*, was a *New York Times* bestseller.

Zakaria

Dr. Sanjay Gupta is a CNN TV senior medical correspondent. He is also a frequent guest on other TV news shows. From 1997–1998 he served as advisor to First Lady Hillary Clinton.

Gupta

R
HOLIDAYS AND TRADITIONS

Christmas is not a time nor a season, but a state of mind. To cherish peace and goodwill, to be plenteous in mercy, is to have the real spirit of Christmas. - Calvin Coolidge, U.S. president 1923-1929

Our holidays, annual events, and their related customs reflect America's diversity and culture. Although the word "holiday" literally means "holy day," most American holidays are not religious. An understanding of our special days not only provides insight into our national character and heritage, but also allows you to participate more fully on these special days if you have the opportunity. Some of our holidays such as Independence Day may be similar to those in your native country.

Some countries use the term "holiday" to describe what we call a "vacation." For us, a holiday is a day of observance with religious, national, or cultural significance and often accompanied by festivities. "Vacation" describes recreational travel or a journey away from work or home.

> **Hint**: If you are communicating with Americans a week or two before one of our holidays, you might wish them a happy holiday. After a holiday, you might ask them how their holiday was. This will reflect favorably on your understanding of and interest in our culture.

In 1971, the dates of many of our federal holidays were officially moved to the nearest Monday, because three-day weekends give us more time to celebrate and relax, similar to what other countries do. But unlike some of those countries, there is no one rule that determines when our businesses, schools, retailers, and offices must close or stay open.

You will discover that our government offices, banks, and schools are generally closed on the *federal* holidays discussed below. But to confuse matters, our schools and some businesses close on other major holidays while many retail establishments remain open.

Our holidays and celebrations fall into five general categories: federal holidays, national celebrations, religious celebrations, fun days, and ethnic celebrations.

FEDERAL HOLIDAYS

The federal government proclaims ten holidays per year. On these days, schools, banks, and government offices are closed, but not all businesses and retailers. (There's that *individuality* thing again where we like to make our own choices.)

New Year's Day (January 1) – New Year's holiday is January 1, but Americans begin celebrating on **New Year's Eve** the evening of December 31. New Yorkers, for example, gather in **Times Square** for a celebration that first started in 1907. There, at one minute before midnight, a lighted ball drops slowly from top to bottom of a pole that sits atop a tall building. As the ball drops, the 750,000 people crammed into the Square count down in unison. When it reaches the bottom, the new year's number is lighted to applause, shouting, horn tooting, and kissing as confetti (small paper bits) rains down on them.

On New Year's Day, some Americans make promises to improve their lives in the new year. They might even write down **New Year's resolutions**. (It's a joke that whatever the resolution, most of them are broken or forgotten by February.) Some visit friends, relatives, and neighbors. Many watch the Tournament of Roses parade* and the Rose Bowl football game in Pasadena, California, either in person or on TV. There

Confetti-filled Times Square, New Year's Eve.

are also popular college playoff football games in other warm regions. Their names are characteristic of their state: the Orange Bowl game in Florida, the Cotton Bowl in Texas, and the Sugar Bowl in Louisiana. (Chapter N on sports discusses this popular game.)

Martin Luther King Day (3rd Monday in January) – In 1957, Dr. (Ph.D.) King began the civil rights movement in America. In the years that followed, he organized protests against unequal treatment of African American people urging his followers to demonstrate *peacefully*.

In August 1963, a crowd of 250,000 people gathered in Washington, D.C., black and white, to march to the Capitol Building in support of passing laws that guaranteed every American equal rights. Dr. King was at the front of this "March on Washington." On the steps of the

King, 1963

Lincoln Memorial that day, Dr. King delivered a famous speech titled "**I Have a Dream**." These words from his speech will long be remembered: "I have a dream that my

---

*The surfaces of all floats in this unique parade must be covered with live flowers or plant materials. Many people volunteer to help cover them a week or so before the parade.

four little children will one day live in a nation where they will not be judged by the color of their skin but by the content of their character."

One year later, Congress passed the Civil Rights Act of 1964 that guaranteed equal rights in housing, public facilities, voting, and public schools. In the same year Dr. King won the Nobel Peace Prize for his leadership role in that movement. In 1968, he was assassinated while leading a workers' strike in Memphis, Tennessee. The world grieved the loss of this man of peace. The holiday was not observed until 1986. Schools, banks, and government offices are closed, but most businesses remain open.

Presidents' Day (3rd Monday in February) – We once observed the birthday of Abraham Lincoln on February 12 and George Washington on February 22. Washington was our first president and Lincoln preserved the Union during the Civil War and freed the slaves. In 1971, Presidents' Day was proclaimed as a single federal public holiday to honor all past presidents of the U.S. But most relate to Washington and Lincoln on this day. Most businesses remain open. Department stores advertise big President Day sales.

Memorial Day (last Monday in May) – On this day cities hold parades and ceremonies to pay respect to the men and women who have died in wars or in the service of our country. Families and individuals also honor the memories of their loved ones who have died. Church services, visits to the cemetery, flowers on graves, or simply silent tributes mark the day with dignity and solemnity.

Memorial Day parade.

On this day our president lays flowers at the **Tomb of the Unknown Soldier** at Arlington National Cemetery[*] near Washington, D.C. (www.arlingtoncemetery.org). On the tomb are three Greek figures representing Peace, Victory, and Valor. Inscribed on the back of the tomb are the words "Here Rests in Honored Glory an American Soldier Known But to God." We are no different than many other countries that pay this tribute, including Argentina's Metropolitan Cathedral in Buenos Aires, Australia's War Memorial in Canberra, and Austria's Heldenplatz in Vienna.

This day also signals the upcoming closing of the school year and the beginning of summer. It also gives Americans a three-day weekend to spend at the beach, in the mountains, or at home relaxing. Some families might do the "annual spring cleaning" of their home or garage. Since 1911, the **Indianapolis 500** motor race (www.indy500.com) is run in Indiana and televised live to 255 million homes in 184 countries. Most businesses are closed on this day, but retailers have big Memorial Day sales and many people shop for **big ticket items** (expensive) like cars and TVs.

---

[*]John F. Kennedy, his wife Jackie, and 260,000 service personnel and their families are buried here.

Independence Day (July 4th) – Akin to National Day in China, Russia's June 12, August 15 in India, September 16 in Mexico, July 9 in Argentina, and similar celebrations in numerous other countries, we celebrate July 4th to mark the birth of our country, more specifically the completion of the draft of the Declaration of Independence in 1776 that announced the separation of our 13 original colonies from Britain. Our War of Independence dragged on until 1783 when Independence Day was made an official holiday.

The portion of the document that most Americans recognize are the words "We hold these truths to be self-evident, that all men are created equal, that they are endowed by their Creator with certain unalienable rights, that among these are life, liberty and the pursuit of happiness."

4th of July parade.

This is one of our most festive holidays of the year and is celebrated with vigor. Colorful fireworks displays are popular on this day, a day we simply call **The Fourth**. Some cities outlaw the use of dangerous fireworks by the public, so they offer public displays instead. We wave flags at parades, go to movies and baseball games, and eat potato salad, watermelon, and apple pie at picnics. Government offices, schools, and most businesses are closed.

Labor Day (1st Monday in September) – In the 1880s, 12-hour workdays, low pay, and deplorable working conditions were commonplace in America (and the rest of the world). Laborers in cities planned a holiday on the first day of September to spotlight the hardship of workers, a day halfway between Independence Day and Thanksgiving Day. In 1894, Congress voted it a federal holiday.

Some cities today have parades and community picnics. Many politicians running for office begin their political campaigns by holding rallies on the holiday, hoping they will be elected in November. Most Americans consider Labor Day the end of summer, so our beaches, campgrounds, and other popular resort areas are filled with people enjoying one last three-day summer weekend. In colder climates, resorts close for the year after this holiday and reopen the following spring. Many schools that have been closed for summer vacation reopen soon after or just before Labor Day.

> **Hint**: Depending on location, some airlines and many hotels in tourist areas reduce their prices after this holiday because of the decline in their tourist business.

Columbus Day (2nd Monday in October) – The 15th century saw many explorers set sail to find riches in distant lands. European spice merchants who had been sailing south around the tip of Africa or making long overland trips were looking for an easier route to Asia. **Christopher Columbus** convinced Queen Isabella of Spain that it would be easier to sail directly west to find the rich treasures of India and Asia. In August 1492, he and 90 men set sail westward in three ships. On October 12th, they landed at what is

308

now the Caribbean area south of our state of Florida, and so discovered the **New World**. (Historians claim that Zheng He of China discovered the Americas 72 years before Columbus, but most Americans have not heard of him.)

The Italian people of New York City first celebrated the discovery in 1866, and in 1937 October 12th was proclaimed Columbus Day. A popular parade in New York City marks the day and in some schools children reenact the event. Most businesses remain open and department stores have Columbus Day sales. Have you noticed free enterprise in the U.S. allows profits to be made on holidays and the general population does not object to this commercialization? We have a saying: **A penny saved is a penny earned**.

Hint: As you are learning, Americans always have always had concern for the welfare of others, both here and abroad. The 500th anniversary of Columbus' discovery was celebrated in 1992. Shortly thereafter some began demonstrating against this holiday. They opposed the treatment of the native peoples of the New World that came after his discovery. Besides stealing their riches, Spaniards enslaved and killed natives and introduced new diseases, all of which wiped out three-fourths of the native tribes. Because of this concern by the public, the importance of this holiday has been diminished substantially.

In case you want to quiz your American counterpart (who won't have an answer), *America* was named after *Amerigo* Vespucci who made two voyages to the Americas. His first was seven years after Columbus' journey. He was not the first European of his era to set foot on the mainland, but was probably the first to realize that the land he helped explore was a separate continent and not merely part of Asia as Columbus and others initially believed.

Veterans Day (November 11th) – World War I ended on the 11th hour of the 11th day in the 11th month in 1918 when a cease-fire agreement (an armistice) was signed by Germany and the allies. Congress voted Armistice Day a federal holiday in 1938. In 1954 the name was changed to Veterans Day to honor veterans of all U.S. wars.

Veteran's Day parade.

Besides paying tribute to fallen Americans and **vets** (those who have served in our armed services) on this holiday as we do on Memorial Day in May, we also reflect on those now serving and on world peace and the hope that wars will not be necessary to resolve world disputes. Starting at 11:00 in the morning, some cities have parades with marching bands from local high schools that play our well-known marches written by American composer John Philip Sousa. (Visit this website to listen to Sousa's spirited, uplifting marches: www.dws.org/sousa/works.htm.) Bystanders wave small flags. Small children sit on their parents' shoulders to see the colorful display. And some Americans observe a moment of silence, remembering those who served.

Some veterans of military service raise funds for disabled veterans, their widows and orphans by selling paper poppies handmade by veterans. This bright red wildflower became a symbol of World War I after a bloody battle in a field of poppies called Flanders Field in Belgium. I experienced this in New Zealand, too, during ANZAC day when they paid tribute to their fallen WWI soldiers.

Our unpopular Vietnam War in the 1970s changed the face of this holiday that resulted in fewer military parades and ceremonies. But the Iraq and Afghanistan wars brought back its popularity as a tribute to those serving and those who have fallen. Some gather at the **Vietnam Veterans Memorial** in Washington, D.C. that has polished black granite walls chiseled with the names of 58,000 Americans who were killed in that war. Families and friends see the inscribed names of loved ones and cry, and then turn their thoughts toward peace and the avoidance of future conflicts. (Chapter M on art has a picture of the impressive wall and discusses the young Asian American woman who designed it.)

Vietnam Veterans Memorial

∞

This seems like an appropriate place to discuss America's place in the world war complex. One of the strongest impressions foreigners have of Americans is that we love war. Americans hate war. Because Veterans Day is not a celebration of war but a tribute to those who serve, we avoid the large display of military equipment in our parades that might be seen in other countries like Russia that show off their tanks and giant missiles.

For the first 160 years, America had a distrust of a large armed force. In fact, there was a prohibition against a standing armed force. Americans viewed war not as a profession but as an emergency disruption of life. And once a war was over most of the forces were disbanded and weapons scrapped. Two years prior to the beginning of World War II, U.S. armed forces ranked 17th in size in the world and only had one operational division versus 200 for Germany and 100 for Japan.

During the 20th century, slowly America learned the hard way that war could be prevented not only with a strong defense but also by becoming involved in issues before a war starts. At the start of World War I, America was allied with the European nations involved but had a firm policy of isolationism, wishing not to get involved in others' wars. Three years after WWI started, America had no choice but to send troops in when our unarmed ships and those of other friendly countries were being sunk. The war ended within a year. The same thing happened in World War II when America was allied with the warring nations and felt it should not get involved until three events occurred: we were attacked in

World War II poster.

310

Hawaii, Hitler had conquered most of Europe, and China and other Asian countries were under siege. We finally learned that isolationism was no longer acceptable, but also that all efforts must be exercised to avoid war. These tenants remain in place today and are a reminder of President Teddy Roosevelt's "speak softly but carry a big stick" policy that had been abandoned prior to these two wars.

Because of these lessons, we often speak up when people are deprived of life, liberty, and the pursuit of happiness, the cornerstones of our society. This, unfortunately, creates the impression that America wants to be the policeman of the world when in reality Americans simply want to avoid war and prevent human suffering. We also wonder why other nations don't **pick up the ball** (become involved) and assist in this effort, too. (With our aversion to war, our War Department's name was changed to the Department of Defense in 1947 and is housed in the **Pentagon** in Washington, D.C.)

Today our military-industrial complex contributes significantly to our economy and jobs as well as to those of other nations. Upon retiring in 1961, President Dwight Eisenhower, who was also the leader of allied troops in WWII Europe, gave the nation a dire warning about the military-industrial complex, a formidable union of defense contractors and the armed forces. He saw the possibility that as the military and the arms industry gained power, they would be a threat to democracy with civilians losing control of the military-industrial complex. So far he has been wrong.

The ten biggest defense budgets in the world total $1.1 trillion, with America's accounting for $700 billion. But when defense spending is compared to each country's economy, Saudi Arabia tops the list at 10 percent of gross domestic production (GDP) spent on defense, more than double the 4.6 percent spent by America. China ranks second with $100 billion, about 1.5 percent of its GDP, and is expected to be $240 by 2015.

Thanksgiving Day (last Thursday in November) – In 1620, a boat filled with 100 Pilgrims sailed across the Atlantic Ocean. They became the first to settle in what is now the state of Massachusetts. They arrived too late in the year to grow many crops, and without fresh food half the colony died from disease. The following spring the Iroquois Indians *[IRR-ah-coy]* taught them how to hunt, fish, and grow corn and other crops in the unfamiliar soil and climate. In the autumn of 1621, bountiful crops of corn, barley, beans, and pumpkins were harvested, mostly crops unfamiliar to these Europeans. In following years, many of the original colonists celebrated the autumn harvest with a feast of

Thanksgiving turkey dinner.

thanks. At the end of a long and bloody Civil War, Abraham Lincoln asked all Americans to set aside the last Thursday in November as a day of general thanksgiving.

Some of us decorate our homes, schools and businesses for this holiday. Turkey, corn, pumpkins, and cranberry sauce are symbolic of the first Thanksgiving. Now all of these symbols are seen on holiday decorations and greeting cards. I was in Bangkok,

Thailand, on a Thanksgiving Day and enjoyed a Thanksgiving dinner at a hotel. I thought it was nice that they had prepared a buffet with many of these traditional Thanksgiving foods. Many of our restaurants offer a similar **plate** (meal) all year long.

Another Thanksgiving tradition is the **Macy's Thanksgiving Parade** in New York City. Giant helium-inflated balloon-like objects float in the air along the parade

route instead of rolling on the ground like motorized "floats" in most parades. The parade started in the 1920s when many of Macy's Department Store employees, who were first-generation immigrants and proud of their new American heritage, wanted to celebrate the American holiday. Some across the nation watch this parade on TV. *Planes, Trains, and Automobiles* (1987) is a humorous movie about a man struggling with a series of unfortunate events as he tries to get home for Thanksgiving.

Macy's Parade float.

Hint: As you have learned, Americans like to deal with the truth and to pay respect to those who deserve it. In the 1980s, Americans began to reexamine our early history, just as they would do later in the 1990s with Columbus Day and its implications. Over 40,000 people gathered in New York on Thanksgiving night 1988 to acknowledge the importance of Indians in the first Thanksgiving 350 years before. Among them were Native Americans representing tribes from all over the country and descendants of pilgrims who had immigrated to the New World. Until then, many believed that the pilgrims cooked the entire Thanksgiving feast and offered it to the Indians. In fact, the feast was planned to thank the Indians for teaching them how to cook those foods. Without the Indians, these first settlers would not have survived. (A book you and your children might want to read is *Pilgrim Girl* by Jule Selbo and Laura Peters. Find it at amzn.to/PilgrimGirl. It is also available as an e-book at www.ebookad.com.)

Christmas (December 25) – Christmas is a religious holiday to celebrate the birth of **Jesus Christ**. We discussed Christianity based on his life in Chapter F on religion. Christmas in the U.S. remains a festive season of giving and receiving gifts and reflecting on our blessings.

Starting shortly after Thanksgiving Day, many of us—including many who are not Christian—purchase a Christmas tree (an evergreen tree) for our home from a neighborhood vendor and decorate it with electric lights and colorful ornaments. A familiar sight this time of year is a Christmas tree strapped on the top of a car for its trip to someone's living room. The annual lighting of a giant Christmas tree at the White

House that is usually trucked in from a New England state is widely reported in the media. A huge tree installed at Rockefeller Plaza in New York City is equally famous.

We place wrapped gifts under our tree where they stay until opened on Christmas morning. Some people string electric lights outside their house or in their windows. Many businesses and schools decorate for Christmas, too. Some cities have lighting

Santa with Christmas gifts.

312

and decorations along their busy streets, a delightful sight I experienced in Singapore, but to my surprise religious Mexico and South America don't. Some of our radio stations play Christmas music for a month or so before Christmas.

Christmas stockings.

Young children believe that **Santa Claus** *[claws]* lives at the North Pole where he has little helpers called elves who make toys and wrap presents. On **Christmas Eve**, December 24, Santa Claus hitches his eight reindeer to a sleigh and loads it with presents. The reindeer pull him and his sleigh through the sky to deliver presents to good children all around the world. Before going to bed, children leave cookies and milk for Santa, and Santa leaves gifts for kiddies under their Christmas trees and in stockings hanging from fireplace mantels.

On Christmas Eve, some children also listen to their parents read the "**The Night Before Christmas**," a poem written in 1828 that heightens the excitement of Christmas Eve. It starts with "'Twas [it was] the night before Christmas, and all through the house, not a creature was stirring, not even a mouse." This free website has the poem in full: www.christmas-tree.com/stories/nightbeforechristmas.html. (Or, you can buy the beautifully illustrated book to read or give to your children at http://amzn.to/NiteB4Xm.)

In 1897 an eight-year-old girl named Virginia sent a letter to a New York City newspaper asking if there was a real Santa. The newspaper printed a response to her question, which included "**Yes, Virginia, there is a Santa Claus**," and it has become part of our Christmas lore. The famous article is an appeal to everyone in the hope that the joy of Christmas remains in mankind's soul forever, regardless of our age. (A copy of the printed article is shown in Appendix 8.)

Christmas card. (HP.com)

Gifts are given to close friends and relatives, but some also give token gifts to those who serve us all year like newspaper carriers, pool cleaners, hair dressers, etc. We send **Christmas cards** or more general holiday cards to friends, family, and business acquaintances to express the sentiment of the season. Some are religious in nature; others are secular, even humorous. Because of our mobile society, this is one way we stay in touch with distant friends. In addition to sending cards, some people send a newsletter telling their friends about their past year.

> **Hint**: Many who are not Christians still participate in the celebration of Christmas. This includes some of my immigrant American friends who instead send "happy holiday" cards and give gifts. This is a nice way for them to participate in the fun and spirit of this festive holiday season.

This is also a time when people might struggle with feelings about things in their lives that are not ideal, needs that are not met, families that are not intact, or losses that are still painful. Happy images portrayed in the media may only heighten those feelings for some who are reminded that everyone should be happy during this holiday. Counselors say that one of the best remedies for "holiday blues" is being around people who care about us. So, many look forward to being at home during this festive holiday.

Hint: Thanksgiving and Christmas holidays are the busiest times of the year at our airports, train stations, bus depots, and stores. If you plan to travel in the U.S. at this time, be sure to obtain your tickets well in advance and expect long lines. Expect to pay more for your ticket, too.

The Christmas Day table looks much like a Thanksgiving feast. At Christmas gatherings adults drink **eggnog**, a drink made of cream, milk, sugar, beaten eggs, and brandy or rum. Plenty of eggnog, hot apple cider, or hot cocoa is on hand in colder climates for **carolers** [CARE-ol-ers], people who go from house to house to sing Christmas carols to their neighbors. White and red striped candy canes are a symbol of Christmas. Besides being eaten, they are sometimes seen on dinner tables, hanging on Christmas trees, and tied to decorative bows on a gift.

Carolers in costumes.

Giving gifts is a Christmas tradition. However, in recent years, some complain that Christmas is too commercial. They believe that the origin of Christmas has been lost and that commemorating the birth of Jesus Christ should be central to the celebration. You will sometimes see Christmas written as "Xmas." This shorthand version might offend those who consider this a holy day rather than a secular holiday. More diversity of opinion in the U.S.

Although we donate to those less fortunate throughout the year, Americans caught up in the Christmas spirit make a special effort at Christmastime to support organizations that provide shelters and food for homeless people. Movie stars and other celebrities join the public and visit shelters on Christmas Day to serve food to hundreds of homeless people.

Perhaps like your country, members of charity organizations such as the **Salvation Army** (which is found in 124 countries) dress up as Santa Claus and ring bells outside stores to collect money to operate **soup kitchens** (meals) for the poor. Our Marine Corps and some city police departments supervise a **Toys For Tots** campaign in which people contribute new or used toys for poor children and those in hospitals and orphanages.

Salvation Army "bell ringer."

Such giving emphasizes the true message of Christmas—to share what we have with others less fortunate. Some wonder why we can't be this charitable all year long, including nineteenth century British writer **Charles Dickens**: "I will honor Christmas in my heart, and try to keep it all the year."

Hint: You can get a feel for this holiday by watching some of our well-known Christmas movies. As explained in Chapter L on Film, *It's a Wonderful Life* (1946) is shown on TV each Christmas season. This classic deals with a suicidal man who, at Christmas time, is shown by an angel what life for others would be like if he never existed. *The Grinch Who Stole Christmas* (1966) is a perennial favorite of children and adults. Other favorites include *Holiday Inn* (1942) and *White Christmas* (1954) that portray our traditional views of Christmas. *Home Alone* (1990) is a comedy about a youngster who is accidentally left home by his parents when they go on a Christmas vacation. *Miracle on 34th Street* (1947) is a classic tale about a nice old man who claims to be Santa Claus and is defended in court by a lawyer claiming his client is indeed the real Santa Claus.

NATIONAL CELEBRATIONS

In addition to our federal holidays, we have other special days. On these days though, schools, businesses, and government offices are not normally closed.

Earth Day (April) – When pioneers settled in the midwestern state of Nebraska in the 1840s, they found few trees to build houses or to burn for fuel. In 1872, citizens set aside April 10 as a day to plant one million trees; that became our first **Arbor Day**. A visitor to Nebraska today would never guess that it was once a dusty prairie.

In 1970, Arbor Day activities were modified to emphasize the critical importance of the earth's environment and to make the American public aware of the ongoing destruction of the earth's natural resources. The sponsors of this day, now **dubbed** (called) **Earth Day**, hoped to start an environmental movement that would alter industrial practices and human consumption. Within three years, President Nixon signed into law most of the resulting major environmental legislation that resulted from this effort.

2009 Earth Day stamp.

Earth Day is a good example of how we bring about change in America. We call this a **grass roots** movement when the public identifies problems or offers solutions and the government becomes involved—sometimes due to public pressure—and passes legislation or lends a hand to facilitate change. This contrasts with some nations where environmental protection changes traditionally start not with the public but at the top.

Mother's Day (2nd Sunday in May) – On this day we try to show in a tangible way how much we appreciate our mothers. Some children serve their mothers breakfast in bed and some give them gifts they made themselves in school or purchased. Adults also give gifts or flowers to their mothers. If our mothers are deceased, we may put flowers on their gravesites on this day. On mother's special day, family members do not want **Mom** (mother) to cook dinner. So, this is the busiest day of the year for our restaurants. A popular mother's song was written in 1915 that many Americans still recognize:

Mother's Day card.

315

M... is for the **Million** things she gave me,
O... means only that she's growing **Old**,
T... is for the **Tears** she shed to save me,
H... is for her **Heart** of purest gold;
E... is for her **Eyes**, with love-light shining,
R... means **Right**, and Right she'll always be.
Put them all together, they spell MOTHER,
a word that means the world to me.

President Abraham Lincoln said, "All that I am or ever hope to be, I owe to my angel Mother." All mothers (bless 'em) like to give advice to their children. Here are some typical American motherly sayings.

- Wear clean underwear; you never know if you'll be in an accident and have go to a hospital.
- Don't make that ugly face; it might freeze in that position.
- Eat all your food. There are children starving in the world.
- Don't talk with your mouth full. Don't sing at the dinner table.
- What if everyone jumped off a cliff? Would you do it, too?
- You have enough dirt behind those ears to grow potatoes!
- Close that door! Were you born in a barn?
- If you can't say something nice about somebody, don't say anything at all.
- Don't put that in your mouth; you don't know where it's been!
- Take the garbage out and then do your homework.
- Don't chew food with your mouth open.
- I'm going to tell your father.

Are mothers the same around the world?

Flag Day (sometime in June) – On this day, which is selected by the president, Americans are encouraged to display the **Stars and Stripes** (our flag) outside their homes and businesses. The flag is flown from public buildings and some cities have special ceremonies. School children learn that **Betsy Ross** designed the first flag shortly after we became a free nation. The present flag has 13 stripes (symbolic of the original 13 colonies) and 50 stars for each state. Schools, businesses, and government offices remain open on this day of observance.

Stars and Stripes

On this day some will say the **Pledge of Allegiance**, a solemn promise of loyalty. It reads: "I pledge allegiance to the flag of the United States of America, and to the Republic for which it stands, one Nation under God, indivisible, with liberty and justice for all." Some schools have their students recite the Pledge before the start of school each day, too.

Hint: Because of the constitutional separation of church and state in America, there are those who say the use of the word God in the Pledge violates the Constitution and should be removed.

Father's Day (3rd Sunday in June) – The U.S. is one of the few countries that has an official day on which fathers are honored by their children. Fathers might be given presents, treated to dinner or otherwise made to feel special, just like mothers are in May. When children can't visit their fathers or take them out to dinner, they send a greeting card or gift. Some cards are whimsical and make fathers laugh when they open them. Some also give heartfelt thanks for being there whenever the child needed **Dad** (father).

A typical fatherly saying: "Talk to your mother about that," or "I'll think about it." We generally think of these things they do when we think about our fathers.

- Drink beer on the weekend while relaxing and watching sports on TV.
- Mow lawns on weekends.
- Take out the garbage.
- Avoid going shopping with his wife.
- Avoid frequent restroom stops on long family road trips.
- Reluctantly clean out the garage.
- Avoid changing diapers.
- Bounce kids on his knees.
- Repair broken toys and bicycles.
- Drop kids off at school on his way to work.
- Teach his teenagers how to drive.
- Assure his teenage daughter she is beautiful in her first dance dress.
- Teach sports to his kids.
- Work hard to provide for his family.
- Tuck children in at night with hugs and kisses.

Are fathers the same around the world?

RELIGIOUS CELEBRATIONS

Easter (a Sunday in March or April) – Christians commemorate **Good Friday** as the day that Jesus Christ died on the cross and **Easter Sunday** as the day that He was resurrected and brought eternal life to mankind. Some who are not Christians celebrate the day as the beginning of spring.

On Easter Sunday, some children wake up to find the **Easter Bunny** left them colorful baskets filled with cellophane grass, candy, and pastel-colored eggs. (Crusaders returning from the Middle East during the Middle Ages spread the custom of coloring eggs. Europeans then began to use them to celebrate Easter and other warm weather holidays.) Decorated eggs are hidden by parents, and children compete to find the most. Even neighborhoods and

Easter basket.

organizations hold Easter egg hunts. There is an annual Easter egg party for local children on the lawn of the White House, a tradition since 1878.

Dating back to the Civil War, New Yorkers used this day to bring out their spring wardrobes, which they wore to church that day. Women displayed their new Easter bonnets (hats) as they strolled around town. This led to the American custom of Easter parades, which are not real parades but rather people strolling about in their spring finery. Today, some children might be given new spring clothing on this day to wear to church.

Many schools give their students a week off in the spring, called **spring break**, generally just before or after Easter.

Jewish Holidays – There are many Jewish holidays, of course, but two of particular note that most Americans, Jewish or not, are aware of. **Rosh Hashanah** is the celebration of the Jewish New Year and is observed in the fall. It marks the beginning of a ten-day period of prayer, self-examination, and repentance, which culminates on the fast day of Yom Kippur. **Chanukah**, meaning "dedication" in Hebrew, refers to the joyous eight-day celebration with gifts and food to commemorate the victory over

Happy New Year
(123greetings.com)

the armies of Syria in 165 BC and the subsequent liberation and rededication of the Temple in Jerusalem. Some Jewish businesses and schools are closed on these holidays.

Islamic Holidays – Muslim Americans have four major holidays. But **Ramadan** *[RHOM-ah-don]* is the one the public is most familiar with. It is a month of blessing marked by prayer, fasting, and charity. Muslims believe that during the month of Ramadan in 610 AD the first versus of the **Q'uran**, the holy book of Islam, were revealed. As the month draws to a close, Muslims are reminded to share their blessings by feeding the poor and making contributions to mosques where they worship, just as Christians do on their special holidays.

U.S. Islamic stamp.

FUN DAYS

Valentine's Day (February 14) – This is a day when you show friends or loved ones that you care. It is celebrated around the world, including Italy, U.K., Australia, New Zealand, Denmark, Mexico, France, Germany, Austria, Spain, and Japan. You can give candy, flowers, or greeting cards called valentines to someone special. Valentines can be sentimental, romantic, funny, or friendly.

Cupid *[Q-pid]*, a symbol of love with his arrows of passion, appears on some valentines that can be heart-shaped or have pictures of hearts. In elementary schools, children make valentines for their

Cupid

318

classmates and put them in a large decorated box, similar to a mailbox. On February 14, teachers open the box and distribute the valentines to each student. After the students read their valentines they have a small party with refreshments. All schools, businesses, and government offices remain open on this red and pink fun day.

> **Hint**: In the Middle Ages, young men and women drew names from a bowl to see who their valentine would be. They then wore these names on their sleeves for one week. Today, if someone says to you "You wear your heart on your sleeve," it means that you are visibly showing your feelings toward another person.

April Fool's Day (April 1) – Some Americans may play small tricks on friends and strangers alike on the first of April. One common trick that children play on April Fool's Day is to say you have dirt on the back of your shirt and you will try to twist and look at your back. Whatever the trick, if the innocent victim falls for the joke, the prankster then yells **April Fools**! Most of the time everyone laughs, especially the person on whom the joke is played. Schools, businesses, and government offices remain open.

Mark Twain (see Chapter K - Literature), with his infinite gift for humor, said, "Let us be thankful for the fools. But for them the rest of us could not succeed." He also reminds us, "The first of April is the day we remember what we are the other 364 days of the year."

Halloween (October 31) – This day is celebrated in one form or another in such places as North America, Austria, Belgium, China, Czech Republic, England, France, and Germany. In the U.S., on the evening of October 31st children dress as little pirates, monsters, princesses, ghosts, and popular heroes of the day. They knock on neighbors' doors and yell **"Trick or treat"** when the doors open. The kids then hold bags open to catch candy or other goodies that the neighbor drops in. In larger cities, costumed children and their parents might do this at shopping malls early in the evening.

Trick-or-treaters.

Teenagers enjoy costume dances and parties. You might be invited to a party where you bob for apples. It is a Halloween party game in which one person at a time has to get apples from a tub of water—without using hands—by sinking his or her face into the water and biting an apple. Sometimes we place dry ice in a punch bowl of apple cider to make it look like a gurgling witch's brew alongside donuts (round dough pastry with hole in center) that we often serve at Halloween parties.

Halloween originated as a celebration connected with evil spirits. Because of this, we decorate our houses, stores, businesses, and schools with silhouettes and sculptures of witches, ghosts, skeletons, and black cats. These symbols are also popular for trick-or-treat costumes, table decorations, and greeting cards. Black and orange are the traditional Halloween colors.

Pumpkins, an orange colored squash, are also a symbol of Halloween. Carving pumpkins into **jack-o-lanterns** is a Halloween tradition. We carve out the inside of a pumpkin, carve a scary or happy face into it, and then place a candle inside. A jack-o-lantern in the window of a house on Halloween signals costumed children that there are goodies waiting for them. A jack-o-lantern seen in a business signals they are participating in the fun, too.

Jack-o-lantern.

Hint: Several years ago I showed some immigrant American friends how to carve a pumpkin. They now do it every year and participate in the festivities. But you can do it without instructions. Just slice off the top, dig out the inside, carve a face in one side and you have a jack-o-lantern.

ETHNIC CELEBRATIONS

Mardi Gras *[MARR-dee graw]* (springtime) – Mardi Gras combines religious tradition with a carnival to welcome spring. It is similar to India's Goa Carnival and Rio's annual celebration. In 1829, some young men returned to New Orleans, Louisiana, from a visit to Paris. Carrying on a lively French custom, they dressed in costumes and masks and paraded through the narrow streets of the French Quarter area. From that time on, masked walking parades highlighting colors of purple and gold became fashionable in New Orleans in the springtime. Though it is only a holiday in Alabama, Florida, and some counties of Louisiana, many in the U.S. travel to New Orleans to join in the festive celebration.

Mardi Gras parade.

Chinese New Year (sometime between January 21 to February 19) – From ancient times to the present, Chinese people have welcomed in the New Year and scared away evil spirits with noisy firecrackers. Today, large crowds gather in the narrow streets in the Chinatowns of New York, San Francisco, and many other cities. A huge cloth dragon might sway back and forth chasing a red sun ball or a white pearl ball, followed by people playing drums and gongs, and dancers with paper lion heads on sticks. Store and business owners come outside to cheer and toss money. Hotel-casinos in Las Vegas provide a festive atmosphere and events for celebrants with red the dominant color.

Chinese New Year parade.

Saint Patrick's Day (March 17) – Every year on March 17, our cities with a large Irish heritage population have parades. New York City has the largest parade that dates back to 1766. Green, one of the signs of spring, is the color of the day. People wear green shirts, ties, hair ribbons, and hats. School children pinch other children if they do not wear green on this day. Many American bars even serve green beer. The leprechaun

[LEPP-reh-con] is a smiling, merry little elf and a symbol of this day for the Irish. This is a popular Irish blessing known by most Americans.

Leprechaun

> May the road rise up to meet you,
> may the wind be always at your back,
> may the sun shine warm upon your face,
> and the rain fall soft upon your fields,
> and until we meet again,
> may God hold you in the palm of His hand.

Kwanzaa *[KWAN-zah]* – This is the African American holiday celebrated from December 26 to January 1. It is not a religious holiday, nor is it meant to replace Christmas. A professor of black history created it in 1966, a time of great social change for African Americans in the U.S. It is a celebration that honors the values of ancient African cultures and inspires African Americans who are working for progress for their race.

OTHER DATES AND TRADITIONS

In addition to our holidays and celebrations, we have other days that have special meaning.

Groundhog Day (February 2) – Pennsylvania German immigrants in the 1840s believed they could predict the weather for the next six weeks by observing a groundhog. A groundhog is a cute, furry animal that sleeps all winter underground. If it sees its shadow on a bright and clear day on February 2nd, it is believed that six more weeks of winter lie ahead. Although few take this folklore seriously, which has its origins in ancient European weather lore, the media make an event of this day each year. We have a humorous, popular movie titled *Ground Hog Day* (1993).

Groundhog.

Daylight Saving Time – This starts when we turn our clocks forward one hour from standard time on the second Sunday in March and set them back on the first Sunday in November. Britain and Germany began using the concept in World War I to conserve energy. We used it for a brief time during the war, but it didn't become widely accepted in the states until after World War II.

Today, approximately 70 countries utilize Daylight Saving Time. Japan, India, and China are the only major industrialized countries that do not, along with 161 other countries. Given the desire of our states to determine what is best for them, a few of them do not observe daylight saving time either, including Hawaii and Arizona. Our scientists say there are almost no energy savings

"Forward?"

associated with it, yet we continue doing what we have done for years, even though 50 percent of the public says it is not worth the hassle.

> **Hint**: To avoid confusion with these yearly spring and fall clock changes, we remember the slogan, "Spring forward-fall back:" move the clock forward in the spring, move it back in the fall.

Election Day – Every four years, on the first Tuesday after the first Monday in November, we set aside a day for electing our president. Most states and cities also have their elections on this day. Citizens go to a local house or building in their neighborhood to vote. If you are a resident citizen 18 or over and registered, you can vote. I was surprised in Slovenia to learn that 16 year-olds can vote if they have a job. Some of our voting places give buttons or stickers to those who voted, hoping they will remind others to vote. Some homes fly the flag on this day. Schools, businesses, and government offices are open normal

Voting ballot box.

hours. The media enjoys projecting the winning candidates weeks before Election Day. However, out of fairness and not wanting to sway voters, on Election Day our television networks have voluntarily adopted the policy of not projecting any victor within a state until all polls have closed.

You may hear **sore-loser** used to describe those who can't accept defeat. Voters use the term **stuffing the ballot box** when their candidate loses an election. It means supporters supposedly filled a ballot box with illegal votes (more votes than the number of actual voters), something that rarely happens because of our tight controls. However, we are always reading about this happening in other countries, like Russia in 2012 when Putin, to the surprise of many, was re-elected president.

Unlike other countries that have compulsory voting, such as Argentina, Ecuador, Brazil, Peru, Chile and Turkey, in the U.S. it is voluntary, which contributes to our low voter turnout. In our 2008 presidential election, for example, the turnout was 63 percent while in Australia and in Malta, which also have compulsory voting, participation reaches 95 percent.

> **Hint**: You may have heard about the voting controversy in our state of Florida during the 2000 presidential election. Most of our states use computer punch cards in which the voter pushes a metal rod that punches a small hole into the card to record their vote. Due to Florida's defective equipment, many of the holes were not cleanly punched out. We still make jokes about this when we meet people from Florida. You might want to do the same by saying to Floridians something like, "Oh, you're from the punch-card state." Typical of most Americans, they will have a good sense of humor about this and joke along with you.

Federal Income Tax – Mention **April 15th** to most Americans and they might start shaking, sweating, and feeling weak. Federal and state income tax forms must be filed by April 15th to avoid financial penalties. Many fill out their forms at the last minute. Some post offices remain open until midnight to accommodate these last-minute procrastinators (people who wait until the last minute to do things). See Appendix 5 for a sample form.

Spring Break – This is a weeklong recess from studying in the early spring at our universities and schools. Students in other countries like Canada, China, Korea, Japan, Taiwan, and Mexico celebrate in similar ways.

Party time during spring break.

During this **spring vacation**, college students go to warm resort areas to party, drink, and meet members of the opposite sex.

Resort areas in Florida have traditionally been their prime destination. Panama City, Florida, is ranked number one with its 500,000 students each spring. Other spots now include Texas, California, Mexico, and the Bahamas. Cancun, Mexico, is considered the number one international spring break site with visitors numbering 250,000. Some students, in lieu of frolicking in resort areas, form groups to perform services for the unfortunate such as painting houses, cleaning yards, harvesting crops, and attending to the needs of the poor.

Hint: *Where the Boys Are* (1960) is an American coming-of-age comedy film about four Midwestern college co-eds who spend spring break in Fort Lauderdale, Florida. Aimed at the teen market, the film featured sun, sand, and romance. Released in the wintertime, it inspired thousands of additional American college students to head to Fort Lauderdale for their annual spring break. It was one of the first teen films to explore adolescent sexuality and the changing sexual morals and attitudes among American college youth of the 1960s just as Playboy magazine did in the 1950s that we discussed earlier. This is another example of the role movies have in shaping our culture and habits.

State Celebrations – Most states have their own important dates and traditions, some of which are holidays. Utah, for example, celebrates July 24th as a holiday to commemorate the arrival of the first pioneers in July 1847 with parades and fireworks. Some states celebrate Admission Day, the day they were admitted to the Union. Others celebrate the birthday of a president who was born in their state.

Hint: If you plan to travel to an American city on business, you might want to first check a state's website to ensure that an important day on your schedule is not a state holiday when businesses are closed. (See Appendix 9 for a convenient way to do this.)

S

WHAT AMERICANS THINK

Americans are not a people like the French, Germans, or Japanese,
whose genes have been mixing with kindred genes for thousands of
years. Americans are held together only by ideas. – Theodore White, writer

This chapter provides insight to the ideas, attitudes, beliefs, character, and personal values of the American people. Surveys, polls and studies are always being conducted in the U.S. to measure the mood of the country and to shed light on what we think about a lot of issues.[*] These results will help you better understand our culture and who we are as individuals.

The story of America is a story of change, and given our diversity, Americans will always have differences of opinions, and as you will see, are subject to change.

MOST ADMIRED PEOPLE

The people we most admire reflects our core values and beliefs. A poll asked Americans to name 20th century people they most admired. Most esteemed were those who contributed to the betterment of mankind. Ranked by popularity, Americans will recognize these ten names if you use them in a conversation with us.

1. Mother Teresa *[terr-REE-suh]* (1910-1997) was a Roman Catholic nun who received the 1979 Nobel Peace Prize for her work with the poor. She founded a religious order in India that provides food for the needy and operates hospitals, schools, and orphanages. She said, "Spread love everywhere you go. Let no one ever come to you without leaving happier."

Teresa

---

[*]Some of the polls cited in this chapter are respected scientific studies and their names are identified. Others are more informal and, for purposes of brevity, are not identified.

2. Martin Luther King, Jr. (1929-1968) was a minister who lead the civil rights movement in the U.S. during the 1950s and 60s. He won the 1964 Nobel Peace Prize for leading nonviolent civil rights demonstrations. He cautioned that, "We must learn to live together as brothers or perish together as fools."

King, Jr.

3. John F. Kennedy (1917-1963) was our youngest elected president. His tenure in office was named after legendary Camelot (a blissful place of English legend) because of his and his wife's appeal. **JFK** urged Congress to pass legislation outlawing discrimination on the basis of race. He was assassinated after two years in office. He is most remembered for the lines he spoke at his 1961 inaugural ceremony: "And so, my fellow Americans: ask not what your country can do for you—ask what you can do for your country." The movie, *PT 109* (1963), is about JFK's courageous rescue of fellow sailors during WWII.

JFK

4. Albert Einstein (1879-1955) was the most important physicist of the 1900s and one of the most famous scientists of all time. Americans appreciated his humor. "The hardest thing in the world to understand is the income tax."

Einstein

5. Helen Keller (1880-1968) was an example to all of us that physical disabilities can be conquered. She could not hear or see but gained international fame by helping disabled people live fuller lives. She gives us vision by saying, "The best and most beautiful things in the world cannot be seen, nor touched...but are felt in the heart."

Keller

6. Franklin D. Roosevelt *[ROH-zuh-velt]* (1882-1945) was our president for more than 12 years, longer than any other president. **FDR** led the U.S. through its worst depression and World War II despite a crippling physical disability. He said, "The only thing we have to fear is fear itself," as he led the nation during these two very difficult times. *Sunrise at Campobello* (1960) is a film about FDR's life.

FDR

7. Billy Graham (1918-) is a world-famous **evangelist** (preacher of fundamentalist Christianity). He preached peace and the word of God around the world. His popularity reflects the beliefs of those who value his Christian principles. He said, "God has given us two hands, one to receive with and the other to give with."

Graham

8. Pope John Paul II (1920-2005) was the first non-Italian pope (Polish) of the Roman Catholic Church since 1522. The most traveled pope, he visited over 60 countries—the majority of them developing nations—to promote peace and caring for others. He warned, "As the family goes, so goes the nation and so goes the whole world in which we live."

Paul II

9. Eleanor Roosevelt *[ROH-zuh-velt]* (1884-1962), the wife of President Franklin D. Roosevelt, was one of our most active **first ladies** (a president's wife). She won fame for her humanitarian work and became a role model for women in politics and public affairs. She cautioned, "We have to face the fact that either all of us are going to die together or we are going to learn to live together, and if we are to live together we have to talk."

Roosevelt

10. Winston Churchill (1874-1965) was the heroic prime minister of the United Kingdom during World War II. He offered his people hope as they struggled to keep their freedom. Churchill also was a noted author and speaker: "If the human race wishes to have a prolonged and indefinite period of material prosperity, they have only got to behave in a peaceful and helpful way toward one another."

Churchill

In a yearly 2011 study, the Gallup Poll asked Americans to name the Most Admired Woman living anywhere in the world. Hillary Clinton, Secretary of State and wife of former President Clinton, was named for the 16th time. No other woman has been named as many times as Clinton. Eleanor Roosevelt is second with 13 number-one finishes, followed by Margaret Thatcher (U.K.), Jacqueline Kennedy, and Mother Teresa. President Barack Obama topped the list for the fourth time in a row as the Most Admired Man; former President and five-star general Dwight Eisenhower holds the record at 12.

Clinton

TOP GOVERNMENT ACCOMPLISHMENTS 1950 - 2000

As you have learned, we view our government as "of the people, by the people, and for the people." Thus, its accomplishments might be viewed as achievements by the people. At the start of the 21st century, a survey was made to define what we think were the 50 greatest accomplishments of the U.S. federal government in the second half of the 20th century. Although some believe our government creates more problems than it solves, the survey suggests that it probably deserves more credit than it gets. In

U.S. Capitol building.

order of importance, we ranked these as our top eight accomplishments during that time period. (The websites of related government agencies are included.)

1. We rebuilt Europe after World War II. Massive outlays of economic and other aid went to countries that were both enemies and allies during and long after the war ended. (As a small child I remember my parents mailing clothing to relief agencies in these war-ravaged countries, as did many other American families after the war.) The U.S. also formed two international financial institutions that still help nations in trouble: The World Bank (www.worldbank.org) and The International Monetary Fund (www.imf.org).

World War II devastation.

2. We expanded the right to vote. New laws insured Americans were not deprived of their voting rights due to their race, religion, or ethnicity. The voting age was lowered to 18 in 1971 when young men were dying for their country in Vietnam but not allowed to vote.

3. We promoted equal access to public accommodations. Discrimination based on race, religion, or ethnicity across a broad spectrum of public accommodations was now prohibited. (www.justice.gov)

Circa 1940s legacy.

4. We reduced disease. We discovered how to prevent and cure diseases both in the U.S. and around the world. Polio, a major concern in the 1950s, has practically disappeared. (www.nih.gov)

5. We reduced workplace discrimination. Fewer people, including women, immigrants, and minorities, suffer discrimination in hiring based on factors unrelated to potential job performance. (www.justice.gov)

6. We ensured safe food and drinking water. Laws ensured the safety of our food and drinking water to a greater extent than ever before. (www.epa.gov)

Interstate Highway System

7. We strengthened our nation's highway system. Congress funded a massive construction plan in 1956 for the development of a modern highway system that took 35 years to complete. Today we have over 75,000 km (46,000 miles) of interstate highways from coast to coast. (www.dot.gov)

8. We increased older Americans' access to health care. In 1965, Congress passed Medicare, a package of health benefits that covers a large portion of hospital and nursing home expenses for Americans that begins when we reach age 65. (www.medicare.gov)

Medicare card.

GOVERNMENT'S TOP PRIORITIES IN 21st CENTURY

What do we want from our government? After the conclusion of the 20th century, some of America's top historians, political scientists, and sociologists were asked what they felt were the federal government's top 10 priorities for the 21st century. In addition to continuing work on some of the accomplishments noted above, this is what they listed in order of importance.

All remain priorities today by the American public, too. We are still struggling with numbers 2, 5, 8, and 10, and lately new issues have brought numbers 3 and 4 to the forefront. Sometimes it seems like we take two steps forward and one back on major issues like these. Is it the same in your country?

1. Increase arms control and disarmament.
2. Increase health care for low-income earners.
3. Expand and protect the right to vote.
4. Promote financial security in retirement.
5. Provide assistance for the working poor.
6. Improve air quality (tie).
6. Improve health care for older Americans (tie).
8. Improve elementary and secondary education.
9. Reduce workplace discrimination.
10. Streamline the national defense.

TOP EVENTS OF THE 20th CENTURY

How do Americans define significant events in their lives? *Time* magazine conducted a survey of the American public at the beginning of the 21st century to determine what they regarded as the most important world events in their lives in the 20th century. These are their top 10 events you might hear us refer to. Number 1 is a total surprise to me and others. Maybe those being polled felt he helped release people from the narrow societal confines of the 1950s with his music? What about your country?

1. Elvis teaches American teens to rock 'n' roll (1954). Americans love their music. It is said that America's number one export is its music. **Elvis Presley** (1935-1977), one of the first American stars of rock music, changed the musical culture of America. Elvis' website is www.elvis.com.

Elvis

2. First landing on the moon (1969). As U.S. astronaut **Neil Armstrong** was about to become the first person to set foot on the moon, he said to everyone on Earth 385,000 km (239,000 mi) away, "One small step for man, one giant leap for mankind." He and Buzz Aldrin spent 21 hours on the lunar surface and returned 46 pounds of rocks that were sent around the world so many countries could benefit from their scientific study and public display.

Moon landing, 1969. (NASA)

3. Gandhi opposes Britain. He freed India from British control with his peaceful demonstrations.

4. World War II. This war (1939-1945) had more far-reaching consequences than any other world war in history. The battlegrounds included Europe, Asia, deserts of Northern Africa, and islands in the Pacific Ocean. It is estimated that over 70 million people were killed, including 55 million civilians who died as a result of starvation, bombing raids, massacres, epidemics, torture, and other war-related causes brought on by Germany and Japan.

Los Angeles demonstrators.

5. U.S. civil rights movement. Events and new public attitudes brought dramatic social changes to the U.S. starting in the 1960s. Blacks and whites together staged demonstrations for rights and equality. American Indians, Mexican Americans, women, and other minorities also began demanding fuller rights.

6. The Holocaust (1933-1945) *[HOL-uh-kawst]*. This was the systematic, state-sponsored murder of Jews and others by Adolf Hitler and the Nazis during World War II. By the end of the War, they had killed 15 million who were considered undesirable, including 6 million Jewish men, women, and children—more than two-thirds of the Jews in Europe.

The Holocaust

7. Invention of the microchip (1958). Two U.S. inventors developed the microchip (integrated circuit) that contained all the components of an electronic circuit that today are widely used in computers and other electronic equipment.

8. Internet created (1969). The U.S. Government began investigating means of linking computer installations via communication lines. This led to the development of today's Internet.

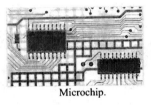
Microchip.

9. Model T Ford introduced (1908). Henry Ford introduced the famous Model T in 1908, affectionately called the Tin Lizzy. He established the first production line that reduced the cost of his cars that made them affordable for the average family for the first time.

10. Theory of relativity (1916). German-born American physicist **Albert Einstein's** theory explained the behavior of

Ford's 1920 Model T.

matter, energy, and time and space. It is the foundation upon which modern physics is built.

OTHER AMERICAN BELIEFS

How does one go about defining an American? Hopefully this book comes close to painting that puzzling, complex picture. But in the meantime, what's on our minds? What are our personal beliefs? How do we feel about various issues? Do our beliefs mirror those of our government and vice versa? What changes would we like to see in the U.S.? What do we think about other nations? How do our beliefs and values compare with other nations? Are we really what the rest of the world **paints us** (views us) to be?

This section gives you the results of hundreds of surveys that have tried to answer these and many more questions that help define an American. In turn, the findings reflect how we conduct our lives every day. The surveys are snapshots of the public's attitude in the 2010-12 era. Undoubtedly we will continue to change over the coming years.

Some of these surveys give the impression Americans are not happy. However, a respected world survey finds that Americans are ranked as one of the highest among nations for satisfaction with their *personal* lives. On the other hand, a Gallup poll (www.gallup.com) finds that an average of only 17 percent of Americans say they are satisfied with the way things are "going in our country as a whole." That is the second-lowest annual average, after the 15 percent in 2008 when the economic collapse occurred. This satisfaction rating averaged as high as 60 percent in 1986, 1998, and 2000.

These findings that illuminate the beliefs and behavior of the U.S. public are listed in alphabetical order. They range from things that annoy us the most to what we think about our work. Are we any different than you or your country?

Annoyances – *Consumer Reports* magazine (www.consumerreports.org) asked Americans to rank these 20 annoyances in decreasing importance. Record your personal rankings to the right of our rankings. Do any **ring a bell** (sound familiar) with you?

1. ___ Hidden fees when signing up for something.
2. ___ Not getting a human on the telephone.
3. ___ Tailgating (a car following your car too closely).
4. ___ Cell phone use by drivers.
5. ___ Inability to understand bills.
6. ___ Dog droppings.
7. ___ Unreliable Internet service.
8. ___ Waiting for repair people to arrive.
9. ___ Spam (flooding the Internet with same message).
10. ___ Shrunken products (getting less than we pay for).
11. ___ Very slow drivers.
12. ___ Unreliable cell phone service.
13. ___ Traffic jams.
14. ___ Noisy neighbors.
15. ___ Poor airline service.
16. ___ Shouting on TV and radio shows.
17. ___ Long checkout lines.
18. ___ Speeding drivers.
19. ___ Passwords and PINs (for Internet use and banking).
20. ___ Inaccurate weather forecasts.

#13 - Dreaded traffic jam.

#17 - Dreaded checkout line.

Business – Americans are concerned about the influence of big business interests, the need for more regulation, excessive executive pay, and corporate scandals.

A Gallup survey shows that Americans are almost uniformly positive in their reactions to three business terms: "small business," "free enterprise," and "entrepreneurs" (which we discuss in Chapter U - Business and Finance). But we are divided 50-50 on "big business" and the "federal government." We are more positive on capitalism (61%) and, as you might suspect, more negative on socialism (36%). Here are more findings.

- *Business and Government* – According to a *New York Times* survey, Americans say business interests have too much influence in the Republican Party and the following businesses should be more regulated by the government: managed health care, health insurance, pharmaceuticals, and the oil industry. The majority thinks their expensive prices are contrived by their industries to improve profits.

- *Executive Salaries* – Almost nine out of ten believe most top company executives are paid more than they deserve, and that they become rich at the expense of ordinary workers. **CEO**s (chief executive officers) in 350 of our top corporations make an average of $11 million in total annual compensation. That is over 600 times that of a full-time minimum wage earner; back in 1980 it was 42 times. (The average starting salary for a Walmart or similar retail worker today is about $9.00 per hour and $7.50 at McDonald's.)

- *Serving Customers* – When asked to define how well our industries serve their customers, this is how we rank them.
  - o Hospitals, computers, and food industries are at the top.
  - o Car manufactures, with emphasis now on improved auto safety, gas mileage, and reliability are now viewed favorably.
  - o Health maintenance organizations (HMOs) that provide care to enrolled members and their families are toward the bottom. They are viewed as more interested in making money than in taking good care of their patients.
  - o Real estate and the related legal field are ranked poorly because of publicized corporate scandals in recent years that contributed to the collapse of the housing market and then the economy.
  - o Oil companies' high gasoline prices and environmental concerns place them at the bottom. Tobacco companies fare no better because of massive health lawsuits, and banks because of the bad publicity from their role in the recession.

- *Customer Complaints* – Americans are not pleased with the customer service they receive from nine businesses in particular. Auto dealers are ranked as the worst of the worst.
  1. Auto Dealers – Sales practices (misrepresentation of automobile and purchase/lease terms).

Auto dealership.

2. Television Connections – Misleading cancellation options.
3. Cellular Phone – Contract issues (not getting the price promised).
4. Banks – Billing issues (unnecessary fees, inaccurate information).
5. Collection Agencies – Harassing tactics.
6. Auto Repair – Failure to fix problem.
7. Furniture Stores – Failure to issue refunds.
8. Internet Shopping – Failure to issue refunds.
9. Mortgage Brokers – Not honoring promised rates or terms.

Charity – Americans have always believed **a friend in need is a friend indeed**. As a result, seven out of ten households contribute to charities each year, averaging about $1,100 per family. Total charitable contributions from American individuals, corporations, and foundations were estimated at $291 billion in 2010, of which the public donated $212 billion and corporations $15 billion.

- *Foreign Aid* – Congress allotted $18 billion for aid to foreign countries in 2004 and $58 billion in 2011. Budget cuts in 2012 dropped it to $42 billion. Six out of ten Americans say they favor the U.S. providing this economic assistance, the highest level of support since 1974. Others question this policy when surveys show that 15 percent in the U.S. cannot afford food regularly (versus 4% in Japan) and one in five of our children go hungry part of every month.

- *Food Donations* – Seventy percent of total food aid distributed around the world to poor countries comes from Americans who donate time and money to these causes. We have numerous organizations doing this, including World Vision (www.worldvision.org) that is in 100 countries helping families and communities fight poverty, hunger, and injustice.

- *Volunteer Work* – As individuals, we know our government cannot do everything to help those in need, so some feel a responsibility to help out. The Labor Department estimates that 60 million Americans perform volunteer work that averages 52 hours per year. We tutor, mentor, build affordable housing, teach computer skills, clean parks and streams, and help communities respond to disasters not only in the U.S. but overseas as well. Actor Brad Pitt started the

Actor Brad Pitt building houses.

Make It Right foundation (www.makeitright.org) with a $5 million donation to build 150 affordable, green, storm resistant homes for the poor to help replace the 4,000 houses lost in the Katrina flood of New Orleans in 2005.

Others volunteer to help nonprofit health organizations and charities that operate homes for three million homeless people in the U.S., a condition most view as a national disgrace. Some organizations operate volunteer-staffed emergency shelters that provide care to women and their children in crisis. Our religious-based rescue missions are staffed by ordinary citizen volunteers. Some schools encourage or require teens to volunteer in some way. Our Boy and Girl Scout organizations do the same.

Hint: The 2009 film, *The Soloist*, is a true story about a *Los Angeles Times* columnist befriending a homeless and mentally impaired but talented musician and the struggle he had getting him into a shelter.

- *Health Events* – Americans participate in thousands of health events, like an annual 5-kilometer walk/run outside Los Angeles that draws 50,000 participants to raise awareness about breast and ovarian cancer as well as raise money for their research, treatment, and prevention. An annual AIDS walk in Los Angeles attracts 25,000 participants to raise money for research.

AIDS walk raises $3 million.

Children – Surveys show that many Americans believe that helping kids get a good start in life is one of the most important issues facing them and the future of our nation. A majority believes too many youngsters lack basic values, saying that failing to learn such character traits as honesty, respect, and responsibility is the most serious problem affecting kids. (Haven't parents been saying this for the last two hundred years?)

The public tends to hold parents responsible for how well our kids are doing and for the needed guidance they receive. They are most likely to look to our schools, employers, and community-based organizations—and not the government—for solutions to problems facing youngsters.

Here is what other surveys say about our teenagers.

- *Marijuana* – One out of every 15 high school students smokes marijuana on a near-daily basis, reaching a 30-year peak even as use of alcohol, cigarettes, and cocaine among teenagers continues a slow decline. Their perception is that marijuana use carries little risk of harm.
- *Marriage* – Eight out of ten teenagers say they will most likely get married someday. But only six out of ten expect to stay married to one person for life, probably due to divorces experienced in their own families or their friends.
- *Religion* – Almost nine out of ten youths aged 11 to 18 believe religion is an important part of life.

Families here have a tough job to do under difficult circumstances. Outside forces—such as drugs, crowded schools, both parents working, violence, and crime—

sometime undermine parents' efforts to raise good kids. Studies reveal that some things are improving while others are worsening for our teenagers.

- 9% have tried cocaine in their lifetime, up from 6% in 1991.
- 42% have had sex, down from 54% in 1991.
- 50% try marijuana before they graduate from high school.
- 63% say their schools are drug-free; nearly double the number in 1998.

Hint: *Rebel Without a Cause* (1955) is a classic film dealing with disaffected youth. *Bye Bye Birdie* (1963) provides a humorous look at American teenagers in the Rock 'n' Roll years of the 1960s. Hilarious *Ferris Buehler's Day Off* (1986) will give you a more up-to-date glimpse. It is important to remember that when watching our films, the economic and social circumstances portrayed are not an indication of how all of us live, perhaps only some of us. Also, our culture varies somewhat from decade to decade.

Crime And Safety – The U.S. does not lead the world in crimes committed, but we want to see changes in our criminal justice system, want gun regulation, and have a favorable image of our local police.

- *Criminal Justice* – A study finds that most Americans believe our criminal justice system comprises an ineffective, purely punitive approach to crime. Instead, Americans want a system that is used by other countries:
  - Attack the underlying causes of crime rather than the symptoms.
  - Prevention should be the nation's top criminal justice goal.
  - Harsh prison sentences reconsidered as a primary crime-fighting tool.
  - Drug abuse considered a medical problem and handled through counseling and treatment rather than as a crime.

Famous Alcatraz Prison, San Francisco Bay.

- *Crime Rates* – Americans can be misinformed. The majority of Americans continue to believe the nation's crime problem is getting worse, as they have believed for most of the past decade. Foreigners I talk to believe this, too. However, violent crime rates have declined since 1994 and are now at the lowest level ever recorded. Of the 100 largest countries in the world, on a per capita basis America ranks 24th for murders, 11th for robberies, and 8th for overall crimes.
- *Guns* – Most Americans think the average citizen should have the right to own a handgun. They believe it is guaranteed in our Constitution, but what "the right to bear arms" means is hotly debated. Nearly 60 percent of our gun owners get their first gun by their 20th birthday. Half report they have a gun in

335

their home or elsewhere on their property, which is the highest recorded since 1993. But half also want the government to regulate gun ownership while a record-low 26 percent favor a ban on handguns.

When citizens were asked, "Do you feel that the federal government should pass a law holding parents responsible when their child commits a crime with a gun?" two-thirds responded yes. Women think having a gun in the home makes it less safe to live there, while a large majority of men think just the opposite. Guns are virtually the last consumer product that has remained federally unregulated for health or safety due to the strong gun **lobby** (firms that influence government decisions)—another hot topic in the U.S. The U.S. ranks eighth in the world on a per capita basis for murders committed with firearms.

- *Police* – Most Americans have generally favorable attitudes toward their local police and give them high marks in most areas.
    1. Helpfulness and friendliness – 73% approval rating.
    2. Quick responses to calls for help – 68%.
    3. Not using excessive force – 67%.
    4. Preventing crime – 65%.
    5. Solving crimes – 61%.

During the social unrest of minorities in the 1960s and 70s when rioters burned parts of our major cities, our police would have received much lower ratings. Today, blacks, Hispanics, and other minorities still rate their local police lower than whites. We still read and hear about police brutality occurring when undue force is used to subdue a person.

As you have learned, Americans are not reluctant to express their opinions. A famous incident occurred in 1991 when Los Angeles police brutally beat **Rodney King**. The incident was captured on a video camera by a bystander and shown on TV. When the four officers were not found guilty by the court of using excessive force, blacks started the Los Angeles riots of 1992 with over 7,000 fires, 52 deaths and 4,000 injured. When interviewed about the riots by the press, King's famous words were, "**Can we all just get along**?"

King

Environment – Americans are less worried about a series of environmental problems than at any time in the past 20 years. Thirty-six percent say they worry a "great deal" about air pollution and 48 percent about pollution of drinking water. Both figures are down more than 20 percentage points from the year 2000. In an effort to appeal to customers

Energy polluter.

336

who are concerned about the environment, many of our companies advertise that their products or packages are made from recycled materials in support of a greener environment. Here are more facts.

- *Energy Developnment.* – For the first time in 10 years, Americans favor the U.S. prioritizing development of energy supplies over prioritizing protecting the environment. However, Americans continue to advocate greater energy conservation by consumers (52%) over greater production of oil, gas, and coal supplies (36%) as a means of solving the nation's energy problems.

- *Environment vs. Economics* – Asked whether the environment should be given priority, even if it means curbing economic growth, almost half of us favor environmental protection, while four out of ten choose economic growth. This is similar to India where environmental protection is also given precedence over economic growth.

- *Immediacy* – Only 25 percent of Americans agree that damage to the environment is a serious and immediate problem versus seventy percent in Europe who show concern.

- *Individual Efforts* – Large majorities report recycling, reducing household energy use, using fluorescent and energy saving-light bulbs, buying environmentally friendly products, and using reusable shopping bags.

- *Kyoto* – Most Americans say they have seen, heard, or read about the theory of global warming. Three-fourths believe that increased carbon dioxide and other gases will lead to global warming. Of those who have heard of the Kyoto and Bonn agreements that would limit emissions of greenhouse gases, three-fourths approve of them and over half think that the Bush administration was wrong not to accept these agreements.

Hint: The movie *Erin Brockovich* (2000) won Julia Roberts an Academy Award. It tells the true story of a woman who discovers a systematic cover-up of the industrial poisoning of a city's water supply that threatened the health of an entire California community.

Feeling Good – A world survey a few years ago measured how satisfied people were with the lives they lived. The nation with the highest rating was Canada at 67 percent. The U.S. was 64 percent. Other numbers were South Korea (53%), Japan (39%), Philippines (31%) and China (23%). Asians, however, were more optimistic about prospects for the next generation than were Americans or Europeans. Countries with low scores all gave money a strong concern except for Japan.

What do Americans feel good about?

1. Relations with family (98%)
2. Home (95%)
3. Quality of life overall (92%)
4. Social life (91%)
9. Marriage (66%)
10. Children's future (63%)
11. Job (60%)
12. Financial security for future (62%)

5. Health (88%)
6. Standard of living (85%)
7. City where they live (84%)
8. Morals and values of people in community (77%)

13. State of the nation (55%)
14. Morals and values of Americans (55%)
15. Nation's economy (43%)

As for **looking down the road** (the future), 53 percent of Americans rate their expectations for their lives in five years high enough to be classified as "thriving," compared to 52 percent of Britons and 41 percent of Germans. Other survey results:

- *Feel Good States* – A survey of Americans in 2010 resulted in a well-being index for each state based on such factors as how residents rate their personal life situation, physical and emotional health, and access to basics of life. Nine of the top 10 states are in the West or Midwest, with Hawaii ranked number one, followed by Utah, Montana, Minnesota, Iowa, Vermont, Colorado, Alaska, North Dakota and Kansas. Among the nation's 52 largest metropolitan areas, San Jose, California, residents had the highest well-being score followed closely by Washington, D.C. Las Vegas, Nevada, had the lowest ranking.

Hawaiians feel good.

Each year a national survey asks respondents to answer the question, "If you could live in or near any state in the country except the state you live in now, what state would you choose to move to?" This was their recent response: 1-California, 2-Florida, 3-Hawaii, 4-Colorado, 5-North Carolina, and 6-Arizona. It is no coincidence these are some of our fastest growing states.

San Francisco, California

- *Getting Rich* – A poll finds that a third of us expect to get rich at some time in our lives, and another two percent volunteer that they already are rich. The public's definition of rich means an annual income of about $150,000, or $1 million or more in savings and investments. Over half of Americans under 30 expect to be rich someday, but by the time they reach age 65, only eight percent still have that dream. Oh well, it's fun to dream while we're young. The world has about 10 million millionaires (net assets excluding home exceed $1 million), with 3.3 million in the U.S., 2.9 million in Europe, 2.8 in the Middle East, and 2.6 million in Asia-Pacific.

Health And Safety – We think the most important health issues facing the nation are cancer (36%), AIDS/HIV (21%), cost of health care (19%), obesity (9%), and our health insurance program for seniors called Medicare (8%). We have other concerns, too.

- *Believing the Government* – Women essentially rejected a 2010 government-sponsored scientific guideline on mammograms, another indicator that we increasingly question what the government tells us. The guidelines called for no mammograms before the age of 50. Yet 84 percent of women aged 35-49 said they would continue to have mammograms regardless. The majority dismissed the guidelines as attempts by the government to save money at the expense of their health.

- *Overweight* – A frequent question I get asked about America is, "Why are Americans fat?" Eight out of ten of us *are* overweight, up from six out of ten in 1983. The proportion of these adults who are seriously overweight (**obese**) has increased from 15 percent in 1983 to 27 percent today, contrasted with slim France where it is three percent. However, our obesity rate recently stabilized for the first time. The majority thinks it is not right for companies to refuse to hire people because they are significantly overweight or smoke; fourteen percent say the practice should be allowed. Again, America, the land of diversity of opinion.

"Back to my diet."

The vast majority of American adults say diet and nutrition are important, yet only 40 percent feel they are doing all they can to achieve a healthy diet. They say an unwillingness to forego their favorite foods is the main reason they are not achieving a healthy diet.

Hint: Instead of saying someone is "fat," educated people will use the term "obese." The western state of Colorado has the lowest obesity rate nationwide at 18 percent. West Virginia has the highest at 35 percent in case you happen to travel there and notice it.

- *Exercise* – A recent survey found that eight out of ten Americans rank exercise and physical activity just as important to their overall health as a nutritious die. Forty percent of us are inactive versus 60 percent worldwide. Americans most likely to report exercising frequently are residents in the West, men, seniors, and young adults. Those most likely not to exercise are probably too busy to do it, typical of the busy American lifestyle.

Working up a sweat.

- *Health Care* – A universal health insurance program is preferred by most Americans instead of an employer-based system. If, however, we have a limited choice of doctors or waiting lists for non-emergency treatments, support falls to fewer than four in ten. As you are learning, we like to make our own choices. There's that *independence* thing again.

Annual exam.

- *Alternative Medicine* – Over a third of U.S. adults say they use acupuncture, chiropractic, herbs, special diets, and megavitamins, many of which are important in other cultures.

- *Prescription Drugs* – Americans believe drug prices are excessive and they are making their demands known to the government. Medications can be more than twice as expensive in the U.S. as in bordering cities in Canada and Mexico. So millions of Americans purchase their drugs illegally outside the U.S. via the Internet or by traveling across the border. This is another example of how the government can respond too slowly to the demands of the public.

  "Expensive."

- *Stem Cell Research* – This exciting new field of health science is another hot topic in the U.S. Anti-abortionists oppose the killing of an embryo, which they consider a human being at instant of conception. Public support is increasing however, from 58 percent in 2001 during the Bush administration to 70 percent today. Bush opposed federal funding of stem cell research. So some states like California funded stem cell research on their own, another example of how the people circumvent Washington on what they consider important issues. President Obama reversed the government's position upon taking office.

- *Stress Levels* – In a 2010 survey, Americans were asked to define their stress levels. Residents of the western state of Utah ranked first with the most stress, followed by Kentucky, West Virginia, Idaho, and Massachusetts. (Utah is reported to have the highest per capita use of pornography; are the two related?) Hawaiians say they have the least stress, followed by Wyoming, North and South Dakota, and Washington, D.C.

- *Seat Belts* – Perhaps the biggest single public health success story over the last twenty years came with the passage of *state* laws that mandated seat belt use. Eight out of ten adults say they wear seatbelts when in the front seat of a car, a huge increase over two out of ten in 1983. Since then, states have also mandated motorcycle and bicycle helmets, which some view as government intrusion. We say we want less government, yet we want the government to promote child

  Lousiana warning to motorists.

  safety seats and bicycle and motorcycle helmets and to reduce drunk driving. And seven out of ten consider it "very important" for the federal government to provide comparative crash ratings on the safety of new vehicles to aid in their car selection. Volvo and Germans cars have fine safety reputations in the U.S.

Institutions – Each year a poll asks Americans to express the degree of confidence they have in our institutions. Here is a recent ranking. As you can see, we're a pretty distrustful bunch, perhaps born of our idea that things can always be made better.

Military	75%	Criminal justice system	29%
Small business	63	Newspapers	25
Police	56	Television news	21
Church/religion	44	Banks	21
Medical system	41	Organized labor	21
Supreme Court	37	Big business	21
The presidency	37	Health maintenance organizations	19
Public schools	29	Congress	13

Big business has not been helped by widely reported corporate scandals, exorbitant salaries, and irresponsible use of power. A large proportion of Americans blame our big financial institutions for the global financial crisis of 2007-2010. And four-in-five believe President Obama was right to describe Wall Street bankers as **fat cats** (wealthy and privileged) because of their excessive bonuses, something the bankers did not like hearing about when millions of Americans were losing their jobs.

Low rating of Congress.

Helping to explain the low ranking for Congress, sixty-four percent of Americans rate the honesty and ethics of members as low, tying the record low for any profession, including lobbyists and car salespeople. When given a choice, almost two-thirds say big government is the biggest threat to the country versus a fourth who say big business is. Relatively few name big labor as the greatest threat any more.

International Relations – Americans are aware the U.S. is not liked or trusted by many foreign nations. We have been concerned with this decrease in popularity over the last decade, especially during President Bush's first term in office when a CNN news poll revealed two-thirds of Americans felt he should "pay more attention to the views of other countries."

Frequently my foreign students ask me how much Americans know about their country. My response is, "You know more about America than we know about you." This is because foreign schools teach about the U.S.; because their media report on events in the U.S.; because vast oceans separate us from you; and because of the busy lives we lead in the U.S. Unfortunately my students misinterpret this ignorance as meaning that as a nation we do not like foreigners or don't care, which is simply not true. Our focus and interests are just different. I tell them not to be insulted, because in some U.S. polls only half can name the vice president of the U.S. That makes them feel better.

Here are some thoughts Americans have about our relations with other countries.

- *Arab Spring* – In terms of the American response to the 2011 uprisings in Bahrain, Jordan, Saudi Arabia, Syria, and Yemen, the overwhelming majority of respondents in each case said the U.S. should not take a position. In Egypt and Tunisia, however, they felt we should be part of a coalition force, just as it turned out, because of our support for democracy that the people were trying to achieve there.

Americans supports Egypt uprising.

- *China* – As you have learned, Americans believe in fairness. A Gallup Poll a few years ago asked Americans which comes closer to their view about what China represents to the U.S. Their response: unfair competition 55 percent versus a large potential market 34 percent. When asked to select how Chinese businesses were capturing more and more business in the U.S., their response was unfair trade tactics 51 percent versus better product or price 32 percent. Like so many other issues, our media bring these matters to the public's attention and stir up sentiment.

- *Foreign Languages* – A majority of Americans feel that foreign languages should be required in our high schools, colleges and universities. Yet less than one in ten studies a foreign language, and half of those study Spanish because of our close proximity to Mexico.

- *International Trade* – Our views on international trade are both a hot topic and complex. A study shows that although Americans view trade as beneficial to business and the wealthy, they think it has not benefited American workers and has widened the gap between the rich and poor. Americans are concerned that trade has been harmful to the environment and to international labor standards. They also believe that, while U.S. trade practices are fair, most other countries' are not. They want the U.S. to re-examine its trade relations in order to **level the playing field** (everyone plays by the same rules) and keep jobs in the U.S.

A poll revealed that if we had to choose between an American made product or a foreign-made product at a lower price, 54 percent would select the higher priced U.S. product vs. 40 percent for the cheaper foreign product. If the foreign made product was the same price as the U.S. made product, 93 percent would purchase the U.S. made product.

Because of the public's high quality standards, attempts by Chinese companies to bring Konka TVs and Xiali cars to the U.S. in the late 1990s failed, mostly because their products did not meet the quality standards U.S. consumers demand.

- *International Understanding* – Our media reports on jobs going to less expensive sites overseas, so two-thirds of working adults strongly agree that international issues will affect their future careers. About half believe it is very important to know about the cultures and customs of others in order to successfully compete in a global economy, yet from my experience Americans are quite lacking in this area. Some of our businesses, too.

- *Peace Corps* – Americans are proud of our **Peace Corps** (www.peacecorps.gov). There are now 8,700 Americans serving in the cause of peace by volunteering to live and work in 76 developing countries that want help. Their projects include bringing clean water to communities, child education, AIDS education, information technology, and environmental preservation. The Ukraine currently has the most volunteers; Kenya has received the most volunteers over time. Over 200,000 volunteers have helped promote a better understanding between Americans and the people of 139 countries in which they have served since 1961 when President Kennedy started the program.

- *Student Exchange Programs* – Because of their belief in learning about others, many American students participate in student exchange programs with other nations. American Field Service (www.afs.org) is one of the most active. Students who participate love the experience and return home to share what they learned about other nations. Some programs also arrange for American families to host students from other lands in their homes. I had my children participate in these programs and recommend them to families in the U.S. and abroad.

- *Our Views of Other Countries* – In a 2012 Gallup survey, Americans were asked about their views of 25 countries and their relationship with the U.S. The top eight countries with a favorable rating by a majority of Americans were Canada (96%), Australia (93%), Great Britain (90%), Germany (86%), Japan (83%), India (75%), France (75%), and Israel (71%). Those countries with less favorable approval include Mexico (51%, because of Mexican illegal immigrants in the U.S. and drug wars), Russia (50%, down from 61% in 1991), Saudi Arabia (42%), China (41%), Cuba (37%), and so on down to North Korea (13%) and finally Iran in last place at 10 percent.

Morals And Values – Americans like to tell the truth but aren't too pleased with our collective moral values that differ from other cultures. Two-thirds say our moral values are poor to fair, not getting better, or are good but getting worse.

- *Immoral Rankings* –A recent Gallup survey shows the percentage of Americans who regard these acts as immoral.

Marital infidelity	91%	Wearing animal fur clothing	39%
Polygamy	86	Gay/lesbian relations	39
Cloning humans	84	Medical testing on animals	38
Suicide	80	Sex between unweds	36
Pornography	66	Gambling	31
Cloning animals	62	Human embryos for stem cell research	30
Abortion	51	Death penalty	28
Doctor assisted suicide	48	Divorce	23
Babies born outside marriage	41		

- *Marital Infidelity* - In a worldwide study of marital infidelity, 80 percent of U.S. respondents condemned extramarital relations as wrong, exceeded only by the Philippines (88%) and Ireland and Northern Ireland (81%). Other countries that were not as **uptight** (concerned) were Spain (76%), New Zealand (75%), Poland (74%), Israel (73%), Norway (70%), Sweden (68%), Italy (67%), Great Britain (67%), Netherlands (63%), Hungary (62%), Japan (58%), Slovenia (57%), Germany (55%), Bulgaria (51%), and Russia (36%).

- *Truth And Honesty* – Our popular saying, "Honesty is the best policy" reflects the fact that 90 percent of American adults say it is hard for them to tell a lie. For this reason, we like to be told the truth, too. We use the term **little white lies** when we **bend the truth** a little.

  Many say it is fiction, but our young children learn in school that when President George Washington was a young boy he chopped down a cherry tree. When his father asked him if he was the one who did it, he responded, "I cannot tell a lie. I did it."

  Young George Washington

  Another president, Abraham Lincoln, said, "I am a firm believer in the people. If given the truth, they can be depended upon to meet any national crisis. The great point is to bring them the real facts." Unfortunately we have some individuals in our society whose dishonesty reflects negatively on the rest of us. Many of them are in jail.

- *Basic Values* – Americans and East Asians (Japan, Thailand, China, Korea, Malaysia, Singapore, Indonesia, and Philippines) were asked to choose the societal and personal values that they regard as core and critical to them personally. The survey confirms that Americans place higher values on *individual freedom*, *self-reliance* and *personal achievement* than do Asians who are more group oriented and have a greater concern for an orderly society and a respect for learning.

344

Presidents – We are demanding of our presidents. Gallup Polls are conducted each month in which the public is asked, "Do you approve of the job the president is doing?" A president is lucky if he (perhaps someday a "she") receives a majority approval rating. We have high hopes when a new president takes office, but things change during their term. Since Roosevelt in the 1940s, President Clinton is the only one who had a higher approval rating when he left office. President Obama dropped from 64 to 50 percent his first year in office, typical of the initial drop our presidents experience.

- *Informal Poll* – The National Park Service conducts an informal poll asking visitors to Mount Rushmore (see Chapter C - Geography) to name their favorite president. Since the beginning of this poll in 1997, Abraham Lincoln remains number one. The others in order of preference are Ronald Reagan, George Washington, John F. Kennedy, Bill Clinton, George H. W. Bush (senior), Franklin D. Roosevelt, Theodore Roosevelt, Harry Truman, and Thomas Jefferson. (Lincoln and Jefferson are my favorites.)

- *Grading Recent Presidents* – A 2010 Siena College poll of 238 presidential scholars ranked former president George W. Bush 39th out of 43 with poor ratings in handling of the economy, communication, ability to compromise, foreign policy accomplishments, and intelligence. Meanwhile, Barack Obama with several years in office **under his belt** (completed) was ranked 15th out of 43, with high ratings for imagination, communication ability, and intelligence; and a low rating for background (family, education, and experience).

The Oval Office in the White House with President Obama and staff.

Tobacco and Marijuana – The proportion of American adults who smoke cigarettes has fallen from 30 percent in the 1970s to 19 percent today versus Germany and Japan (34%) and France and England (27%). The state of Kentucky has the highest rate (28%). While Finland might become the first country to totally outlaw smoking, fewer than twenty percent of Americans favor making it totally illegal. Now being enforced and expanded in many of our cities, a majority of Americans (59%) support bans on smoking in all public places for the first time since Gallup initially asked the question in 2001.

- *Trying To Stop* – Eight out of ten smokers know the dangers of smoking but keep smoking anyway. Some 44 percent have tried to kick the habit at least once the past year. A recent survey shows that those who are socially and economically disadvantaged tend to have worse health behaviors than people with more education and higher incomes. The lowest proportion of those smoking cigarettes is found among our college graduates (16%).

- *Cigarette Industry* – Americans have a very unfavorable image of the cigarette industry. The government requires cigarette packages to be labeled: "Caution: Cigarette Smoking May Be Hazardous to Your Health." Smoking kills 430,000 people in the U.S. each year, a number approaching China's half-million. To the delight of many, in the 1990s the Clinton administration filed lawsuits against the tobacco companies because of deaths and health costs the U.S. incurs as a result of cigarettes. Our courts required the cigarette companies to pay billions of dollars to states and individuals who had been harmed by smoking.

A judge tossed out a federal mandate in 2012 requiring tobacco companies to place graphic images of diseased lungs on their products to warn of the dangers of smoking. In his ruling, he said government can compel speech in some cases, like making companies put warning labels on their products (as noted above). But when the compelled speech goes from information to advocacy, it becomes unconstitutional. There's that *fairness* of the law thing again. This hands-off approach contrasts with New Zealand where the government advocates snuffing out smoking, so they have the world's highest tobacco tax that will approach $15.00 per pack by 2016. (The average state tax in the U.S. is $1.50)

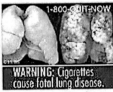

Not allowed to be shown.

- *Marijuana* – Marijuana use in the U.S. is an even more controversial subject. A record-high 50 percent of Americans say marijuana use should be made legal and the government should treat it the same way it treats alcohol: regulate it, control it, tax it, and only make it illegal for children. Sixteen states, eight of which are in the West, have legalized its use for medical purposes even though federal law makes this use illegal. Eighty percent of California voters support doctor-recommended use for illness, but only half support legalization of general or recreational use. Here's another example of our crazy states' rights versus federal regulation, a **tug of war** (pulling on two different sides) that is always being reevaluated by our courts.

Marijuana plant.

Space Programs – When Russia launched Sputnik in 1957, the first satellite in orbit, Americans were embarrassed that they **beat us to the draw** (were first) and the Space Race began. We accelerated our space program and have since led the international community for the exploration and peaceful uses of outer space. Our astronauts are viewed as heroes. **John Glenn** was our first to orbit the Earth in 1962 and later became a

U.S. senator from Ohio. Like China's first astronaut Yang Liwei, Glenn provided inspiration for others (including women eventually) to pursue their dreams and to work in this exciting new field. Today, one out of three in the U.S. would like to travel to outer space. **NASA** (www.nasa.gov) is our government agency responsible for space programs.

- *Government Spending* – We are divided over government spending for the space program, which we call The **Last Frontier**. Almost half think we spend too much, due in part to the long lead-time required to reap the rewards of space probes and the billions of dollars expended that could be spent on more **down-to-earth** (fundamental) things. Some change their negative views of spending once there is finally scientific payback, but our agencies do a poor job of getting the word out about the huge number of scientific and other benefits reaped from these programs.

- *Space Programs* – Examples of these expensive programs include the U.S. led development of the **International Space Station**, which drew upon the scientific resources of 15 other countries. The **Hubble Space Telescope** was built in 1990 by NASA with contributions from the European Space Agency. It remains in operation, helping resolve long-standing problems in astronomy. Our **Cassini** space probe took seven years before it arrived to circle Saturn and transmit data from the depths of dark space for the international

  Image of Saturn sent back to Earth by Cassini.

  scientific community to analyze. It took our **Mars Rover** seven months to land before it began to explore the surface of that next door planet. In classic American fashion, more than five percent believe the 1969 **Apollo Moon Landing** was an elaborate deception conducted in a TV studio.

Hint: A classic film dealing with the early astronaut program is *The Right Stuff* (1983).

UFOs – Half of all Americans are convinced that UFOs (unidentified flying objects) have visited Earth in some form, and would be interested in personally encountering extraterrestrial life here on Earth. Even more believe there is intelligent life on other planets and think they are friendly rather than hostile. Three out of four Americans believe the government is not telling the public everything it knows about UFO activity. Tales abound in the media about recovered spaceships the government is hiding from the public, especially in the Southwest city of Roswell, New Mexico. There, in

Imaginary UFO?

1947, an object crashed and Roswell UFO proponents today still maintain that the alien craft and bodies were recovered and the military has engaged in a cover-up. (There's that *not trusting* what our government tells us thing again.)

Taxes – We have a saying: "**Two things are certain: death and taxes.**" Two-thirds say their *overall* taxes are too high and believe that the maximum tax burden a family should pay is 25 percent for all taxes from all levels of government. The total percentage collected in 1955 was 28 percent; today the typical American family pays 38 percent—more than it spends on food, clothing, and shelter combined. Yet on a per capita basis, the U.S. only ranks 27th in the world for taxes paid. Sometimes we do not know how well off we are.

Forty-six percent of Americans believe the amount they pay in *federal* income tax is too high while 47 percent consider it about right and 3% consider their taxes too low. This is a turnaround from shortly after President Bush took office in 2001 when two-in-three said it was too high. Perhaps we are now realizing the cost of wars and health care. The typical middle-income taxpayer has to work from January 1 to April 19 to just cover federal and state income taxes. In 1930 it only took 30 seconds. Similar to what is occurring in France, Spain, and Germany today, there is a talk in the U.S. to increase taxes on the wealthy, something the Republicans are fighting against.

Here are results of a tax study by Harvard's Kennedy School of Government.

- *Cutting Taxes* – Most Americans believe that other things are more important than cutting taxes. An overwhelming 80 percent of those polled believe it is more important to maintain spending on popular domestic programs like education, health care, and social security than it is to cut taxes. And by a 5-to-4 margin, frugal Americans think it's more important to keep down the federal deficit than it is to lower their taxes.

- *Revamp System* – The Harvard study also found that a majority of Americans believe there is so much wrong with our convoluted federal tax system that Congress should completely overhaul it. The Tax Code has 600 forms and a whopping 72,000 pages. It takes an average of 44 hours to fill out the basic tax forms if you do it yourself. Many **throw their hands in the air** (give up) and hire professionals to prepare their returns that are due by April 15 each year. (See Appendix 5 for sample form.)

Threats – One year after the 9/11 terrorist attack on U.S. soil in September 2001 that demolished the World Trade Towers in New York City, nearly all Americans (91%) believed terrorism was a "critical" threat to the U.S. Ten years later and after the killing of Osama bin Laden, a CBS/*New York Times* poll revealed 44 percent thought the U.S. and its allies were winning, while 45 percent thought neither side was.

Trade Towers

Three-fourths of Americans have confidence in the U.S. to protect its citizens, down from 81 percent in 2004. Large majorities of Americans support the use of military force to combat terrorism.

Other threats:

- *Enemies* – Sixty-one percent of Americans said the military power of Iran was a critical threat to U.S. vital interests. Of seven international issues, Americans rank Iran second only behind international terrorism (81%) as a threat to the U.S. When asked to name our top five "enemies" in 2012, Americans most frequently mentioned Iran (32%), followed by China (23%), North Korea (10%), Afghanistan (7%), Iraq (5%), and Russia (2%). However, when Chinese Vice President Xi embarked on a five-day tour of the U.S. in 2012, a poll was taken of young American adults ages 18-29 that reveals 76 percent view China as an economic and/or military threat. In addition, 62 percent believe the top national security issue is the U.S. debt, followed by our energy dependency and indebtedness to foreign powers, the same things our press keeps **harping on** (repeatedly discusses), too.

- *Immigration Levels* – Six out of ten Americans believe present immigration levels are a "critical threat to the vital interests of the United States." In fact, on no other foreign policy issue do average Americans disagree more with government and business leaders than on immigration. Nearly two out of three want to see immigration levels decreased. It is estimated that 10 percent of the U.S. population consists of illegals who cost taxpayers billions of dollars each year to support medical, schooling, and other needs. Unfortunately, their contributions to our culture and economy are often not deducted

Immigrant farm workers.

from these statistics, because many perform menial jobs that Americans do not want and they contribute to the tax base with their expenditures.

- *Muslims* – After 9/11, Arab Americans experienced verbal and physical abuse but also acts of support and solidarity from the general population. Like other Americans, Arab Americans feel less safe and secure as a result of 9/11. In 2010, more than 4 in 10 Americans admitted to feeling a little prejudice toward Muslims—more than twice the number who said the same about Christians (18%), Jews (15%) and Buddhists (14%). Seventy percent of surveyed Americans said they believe Muslims worldwide want peace, but two-thirds view Muslims as not accepting of other religions.

Muslim Americans

- *National Defense* – When asked about the government's spending on the military and national defense, which accounts for 19 percent of our annual budget, Americans are split, 36 percent saying the government is spending about the right amount, 34 percent too much, and 27 percent too little; one more example of the diversity of opinion in the U.S.

- *Nuclear Disasters* – Despite concerns about a possible nuclear reactor disaster in the U.S. like Japan experienced, six out of ten Americans still think U.S. nuclear power plants are safe, while a third say they are not. We are divided on the issue of increasing the number of our nuclear power plants, but these attitudes remain unchanged from 10 years ago.

Voting – Given our unyielding stance on democracy and the right to vote, foreigners (even Americans) are surprised to learn that the U.S. only ranks 35th in voter turnout among the world's prominent democracies. A little over half of our eligible voters cast ballots during the last four decades in presidential elections. That is far less than Britain (75%) and Japan's (71%) rates. Better educated, higher earning Americans, however, vote at 70-80 percent levels, while less than forty percent of our working class bothers to vote.

This voter apathy is due in part to voters' dislike of the campaign process and a disconnection with Washington and our leaders. In recent voting surveys:

- *Ethics* – 70 percent feel that unethical campaign practices happen fairly often.
- *Money Spent* – 94 percent believe too much money is spent on campaigning (advertisements, mailers, travel, appearances, staff, etc.).
- *National vs. Local Issues* – By 55 percent to 39, more registered voters now say a candidate's stand on *national* issues— rather than his or her district level— is what matters more to them in voting for members of Congress. This reversal has occurred over the past 20 years as Americans become concerned about the direction the U.S. is moving in.

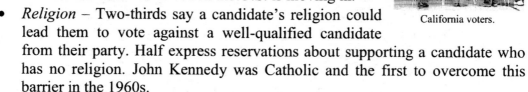

California voters.

- *Religion* – Two-thirds say a candidate's religion could lead them to vote against a well-qualified candidate from their party. Half express reservations about supporting a candidate who has no religion. John Kennedy was Catholic and the first to overcome this barrier in the 1960s.
- *Representation* – Only 25 percent believe their representative in Congress is the best person for the job. Moreover, voters are nearly twice as likely to say they would rather vote for a congressional candidate with no prior experience in Congress than one who served previously in Congress.
- *Special Interests* – 87 percent think candidates go against the public's interests and instead support special interests that donate money to finance their campaigns.

Wars – Some foreigners might believe that the American public's views are in concert with their president's views. Often they are not, especially on the subject of war.

- *Iraq* – In January 2003, two months before the Iraq invasion:
  - Eight out of 10 Americans supported going to war *if* the United Nations backed the action *and* it was carried out by a multinational coalition.
  - Without U.N. approval and allies, only a third of the public would support the war.
  - Two-thirds said the U.S. should continue working toward achieving its goals in Iraq without war.
  - Only a fourth favored quick military action, which is the way it turned out. Thus many foreigners assume that Americans favored rushing into war.
  - The Obama administration's plan to remove all troops from Iraq by the end of 2011 was favored by 70 percent, but only 40 percent were somewhat confident that all U.S. troops would be withdrawn. They were withdrawn by December 2011 against the advice of some in Congress who feared uprisings would occur again.
- *Afghanistan* – When Afghanistan was overrun by the Soviet army 20 years ago, Americans provided arms and supplies to enable the people to win back their country. And by September 11, 2001 when terrorists struck America and we went to war in this country that most of us knew little about, Americans had given more than any other nation to the poor there. The percentage of Americans who favored the war wavered as it dragged on. In 2001, 88 percent were in favor, then 56 percent in 2007, and 33 percent by 2011. Then in 2012, fifty percent said the U.S. should speed up withdrawal of its troops, while 24 percent preferred sticking to the timetable to leave by the end of 2014, and 21 percent said the U.S. should stay as long as it takes to accomplish its goals.

  A Washington Post-ABC News poll also revealed that "Americans are broadly skeptical of President Obama's contention that the war in Afghanistan is necessary for the war against terrorism to be a success, and few see an increase in troops as the right thing to do." Many, however, are concerned about a return of the brutal treatment of women when we decide to leave.
- *What Our Soldiers Believe* – One in three U.S. veterans of the post-9/11 military actions that were surveyed believe the wars in Iraq and Afghanistan were not worth fighting. A majority thinks that after 10 years of combat America should focus less on foreign affairs and more on its own problems. This mirrors a Pew survey (www.pewresearch.org) of the public that found 6 in 10 saying we should pay less attention to problems overseas and instead concentrate on problems at home. This comes more into focus when the media reports on suicide rates of our soldiers.

There were 154 U.S. military suicides in the first 155 days of 2012, up from 130 over the same period the prior year. Historically, the suicide rate has been significantly lower in the military than among the U.S. civilian population. But that began to change as the wars in Afghanistan and Iraq—initially thought of as short-term affairs—dragged on for years. More critical than their duration was the fact that a relatively small number of U.S. troops kept being sent back for multiple combat tours.

Women's Rights – Women are demanding and finally attaining their rights in the U.S. A survey by the Center for the Advancement of Women identifies the top three priorities for the women's movement in the U.S.

1. Reducing domestic violence and sexual assault – 92%.
2. Equal pay for equal work – 90%.
3. Keeping abortion legal – 41%.

To the surprise of many, a recent government survey affirmed that sexual violence against women remains endemic in the U.S. Nearly 1 in 5 surveyed said they had been raped or had experienced an attempted rape at some point, and one in four reported having been beaten by an intimate partner.

THERE CAN BE NO HUMAN RIGHTS WITHOUT WOMEN'S RIGHTS
(Pittsburgh Human Rights.org)

Some golf clubs in America are still for men only, including a famous one, Augusta National, in Georgia. This exclusionary policy remains a hot topic. While a majority of women surveyed do not like its male-only policy, seven out of ten believe Augusta should be allowed to set its own rules. This is typical of a number of controversial issues in the U.S. where, although we don't like what's happening, we respect the rights of the offender; in this case the golf club.

Work – The Conference Board (www.conference-board.org) published results of a survey showing that 55 percent of American workers are dissatisfied with their jobs, the highest rate in 22 years. Workers are getting grumpier because they don't find their jobs interesting, their pay is not keeping up with inflation, and the high cost of health care is taking a toll on their incomes. Here is more of what we think about our jobs. How do we compare to your country?

Machine shop workers.

- *Quitting* – Fifty percent of our workers have recently thought about quitting and one-in-five have applied for another job in the past six months. The top reason is unhappiness with salaries (47%), followed by workload (24%), lack of opportunities for advancement (21%), and employee's manager or supervisor (21%).

- *Too Job Focused* – Surveys also show that more than eight out of ten of us believe we are too focused on working and making money and not enough on family and community. They believe that American society is too materialistic and that we shop and spend too much. (Both of these are common views foreigners have of us, too.)

- *Goodbye American Dream* – Nearly two-thirds report that the American Dream is harder to achieve than it was even ten years ago, and less than half believe they will achieve it themselves. When asked why, three in four cited financial debt while six out of ten said it is hard to live on the money they make. With more debt, more pressure is put on the worker.

- *Long Hours* – Americans work more hours than any other industrialized nation, with Japan a close second. We tend to do that because of our **Puritan work ethic** that dates back to our early settlers whose religion-based philosophy said hard work brings a good life. We are split as to whether the hard work and long hours today have a positive (33%) or negative (31%) effect on our culture. A third of those polled say they postpone fun because they feel guilty when they are not doing something they believe is productive. (Sounds like me.)

- *Job Stress* – One-third say their jobs have little or no stress, are modestly stressful (43%) or very stressful (24%).

- *Job Loss* – Six in ten Americans are concerned that they, a friend, or a relative might lose a job because the employer is moving that job to a foreign country. As companies announce the transfer of jobs to cheaper overseas sites and the media reports on this, it affects public's negative attitudes toward the companies as well as the nations.

- *Vacation Time* – Japanese workers get 25 annual paid vacation days; the European Union a minimum of 20 days. Unlike many other nations, the U.S. has no federal laws mandating vacation time. The typical practice among our large companies is two weeks paid vacation. However, only 14 percent of Americans plan to take this allotted vacation time. At the **bottom of the totem pole** (lowest hierarchy), almost one in four U.S. workers receive no paid days off.

Alaska totem pole.

- *Retirement* – Retirement in the U.S. comes at age 65, which is also customary in most of Europe. However, the average non-retired American now expects to retire at age 67, up from age 63 a decade ago and age 60 in the mid-1990s. The overwhelming majority (95%) also plans to do some work after retirement and two-thirds want to continue to learn, to try new things, to travel, and to have a new hobby or interest.

353

Some can't afford to retire. Many who have retired find they didn't plan properly for their retirement and now work to supplement their retirement funds, even those on Social Security. Two-thirds of pre-retired workers are worried they will not have enough money for retirement while fifty-eight percent, a new high, are worried about not being able to maintain their living standard in retirement.

Retired lifestyle.

HOW WE VIEW OUR FUTURE

Over the past half-century, the Gallup Poll has asked Americans what step of a ladder the U.S. was on, with 10 the best possible situation for the nation and zero the worst. The average response has ranged from a high of 6.7 in 1959 (at the end of President Eisenhower's era) to a low of 4.8 in 1974 during the Watergate crisis and Vietnam War. We were half way up the ladder in early 2010. Those polled recently predicted the U.S. would step up to a sunnier 5.7 by 2015. In 11 specific areas, a majority said things would stay the same or get better in all aspects of life. However, there was one exception: the state of moral values would get worse.

What is the source of this generally positive American attitude? The root is probably our own revolutionary tradition, the idea of beginning anew, says a historian. "We came from England where there was a corrupt church and state, and we wanted to create a better society. It's the idea of American exceptionalism." He theorizes this conviction fueled our country's founding, the westward expansion, and our determination to persevere through the Great Depression and World War II.

More predictions from various polls describe how we view the next 20 years.

- *Economic Power* – Three in four say the U.S. will only be one of several economic powers then, including Brazil, Russia, India, and China, referred to collectively as BRIC. Most believe China will be the leading economic power.
- *Military* – Although two-thirds in a national newspaper (*USA Today*) poll say the U.S. is number one militarily now, a majority predicted it will only be one of several military powers in 20 years.
- *Youth* – More than six in 10 Americans say it is likely that today's youth will have a better life than their parents, a precept of the American Dream.
- *Strengths* – Americans were asked by *USA Today* to define one or two strengths of the U.S. that made them most optimistic about the future of the country over the next 20 years. By frequency of occurrence, this was their response: Strength and will of the American people (35%), military and homeland security (14%), technology and innovation (6%), government leadership (6%), and individual freedoms (5%).

T

WHAT FOREIGNERS THINK ABOUT AMERICA

*America is a large, friendly dog in a very small room. Every time it wags
its tail, it knocks over a chair.* - Arnold Toynbee, British historian 1852-1883

Now you know what Americans think about a lot of things. But what do foreigners think about America? A good way to gain insight about America and its people is to look through the eyes of foreigners who have actually experienced the U.S.

Asian American playwright David Henry Hwang puts his experience and our cultural differences in perspective:

"I don't see it so clear cut that there's a sort of Chinese way of doing things and an American way of doing things and you're either in one or the other. I think that there are a lot of different gradations between. You can only accommodate so many things in your life, so you do gain things and you give up things. And the question is simply, what is the balance that's best for you?"

A Pew survey polled residents of 24 countries on a range of attitudes about America and its people. In 14 countries, over 50 percent had a favorable view of Americans. Foreigners, however, distinguished between the American *people* and the U.S. as a whole, so the U.S. itself was well regarded in only nine of those foreign countries.

Foreign visitors at U.S. immigration station.

Where are Americans most likely to be welcomed? As it turns out, the countries that Americans travel to the most are the countries that best like Americans. Among Americans' top 10 travel destinations, the nations in which we are most liked include Great Britain where 70 percent of residents say they have a good opinion of us, as do Australians. Opinions of Americans are also high in Canada (76%), Japan (65%), France (64%), Italy (62%) and Germany (55%). Mexico is actually our number one country visited but only 44 percent there have a favorable opinion of us, probably because of our mishandling of their illegal immigrants. China ranks ninth in travels (38%) and Spain tenth (41%).

Not in the top 10, about a third of respondents in Jordan and Egypt give an approval rating to Americans, a quarter in Argentina, and a fifth in Pakistan. The least favorable rating comes from Turkey where only 13 percent voice a positive opinion of us.

And what does the world think about our *leadership* in the U.S.? A Gallup poll revealed that perceptions of U.S. leadership worldwide improved significantly from 34 percent in 2008 to 51 percent in 2009 with the change from the Bush administration to the Obama administration. Today, worldwide approval of Germany's leadership ties that of the U.S. at 46 percent. Among the other major powers, the United Kingdom earns the next highest rating (40%). China is 32 percent and Russia 28 percent.

Among the **Group of Twenty** (G-20) members*surveyed, approval ratings also increased substantially with the incoming Obama administration. Russia, however, had the lowest approval rating of America at 20 percent, which comes as no surprise. Russians have long been suspicious of the West, even before Peter the Great struggled to infuse aspects of European culture into his homeland in the 1700s.

THE UGLY AMERICAN

The term **ugly American** has sometimes been used to describe Americans traveling or working abroad who are loud, arrogant, and ignorant of the language and customs of the country they are visiting. *The Ugly American*, a book first published in 1958, became a national bestseller for its exposé of American arrogance, incompetence, and corruption in a fictional Southeast Asia country. (It was made into a movie in 1963 starring Marlon Brando.) It was an **eye opener** (big surprise) for the average American who knew very little about Asia and less about how we were viewed abroad, something some of us are still guilty of.

Ugly American?

In the book, a fictional Burmese journalist describes Americans: "For some reason, the people I meet in my country are not the same as the ones I knew in the United States. A mysterious change seems to come over Americans when they go to a foreign land. They isolate themselves socially. They live pretentiously. They're loud and ostentatious. Perhaps they're frightened and defensive, or maybe they're not properly trained and make mistakes out of ignorance." The novel applies this description to the Foreign Service and other American government workers—the people who frequent embassy parties and choice restaurants. They drive fancy cars and work on the problems they like to solve—the high profile expensive projects—ignoring the problems of the local people.

---

*Members include Argentina, Australia, Brazil, Canada, China, France, Germany, India, Indonesia, Vietnam, Italy, Japan, Mexico, Russia, Saudi Arabia, South Africa, South Korea, Turkey, U.K., U.S., and also the European Union represented by the rotating Council presidency and the European Central Bank.

Ironically, the book's "ugly American" is a hero, a physically unattractive engineer who was brought to advise the American Aid people on the placement of dams and roads. In contrast to today's meaning of "ugly American," he lives among the native people and learns *their* culture. He identifies the greatest need of the people—not dams or roads, but simply a way to get water up on the hillsides to irrigate rice. The American Aid people ignore him because of his unusual views, so he quits the project and designs a bicycle-based water pump that can be built from plentiful, local materials. When he has his design, he enlists the help of a local mechanic to refine the design and help set up a factory to build and sell the pump. He treats his assistant like the equal that he is. He turns out to be quite the opposite of an "ugly American"

The book's message on how to deal with the problems of the local people and communism got lost in Washington as we waged the Vietnam War, a conflict that took the exact course predicted by the book. The book may have influenced President Kennedy's establishment of the Peace Corps (see Chapter S) a few years later in which volunteer Americans live and work with deprived people around the world. They learn about their culture and needs in order to help the people there better their lives.

> **Hint**: As a student of foreign culture, I pay particular attention to other Americans when I travel in foreign countries. I observe their actions and the response they elicit from the native people. Yes, our behavior can make us appear to be the "ugly American," loud and at times demanding. From my experience though, most American tourists I have been with *are* respectful of foreign cultures, but simply don't know how to make adjustments to *appear* more respectful—much like foreign visitors behave in the U.S.

How do foreigners in their native countries—as well as those living in the U.S.—view America? Are we "ugly" or more like the hero of this famous book? Or both? Let's look at what others think: A Frenchman, a group of India/Pakistan/Bangladesh university students who studied in the U.S., an Englishman, an Asian educator, Muslim Americans, and a Vietnamese immigrant. We'll then look at the results of a study of immigrant students and their experiences in the diverse, complex, and sometimes crazy U.S.

A FRENCHMAN

No matter where we go around the world, there is one sporting obsession that unifies the entire human race: America-bashing. So says **Jean-Francois Revel**, the distinguished French writer who chose to take a path of cultural nonconformity. Specifically, Revel chose to confront the entrenched anti-Americanism of generations of European and other intellectuals, particularly the French.

In Revel's 2004 book, *Anti-Americanism,* the author reveals that he lived and traveled frequently in the U.S. between 1970 and 1990. During this time, he had conversations with "a wide range of Americans—politicians, journalists, business people, students and university professors, Democrats and Republicans, conservatives, liberals and radicals, and people I met in passing from every walk of life."

This simple concept—talking to Americans and asking them what they think, as opposed to just mirroring European conventional wisdom about what Americans think—is what separates Revel from the multitudes in his culture. He says that for generations the majority of his peers "cherished their prejudice against Americans too greatly to face the possibility that real, live Americans might not conform to it."

Eiffel Tower.

In Revel's 1970 *Without Marx or Jesus*, he was "astonished by evidence that everything Europeans were saying about the U.S. was false." His *Anti-Americanism* book 34 years later revealed that the situation had not changed. Indeed, if anything, he says, the conventional wisdom about the U.S. was even more wrong now than it was when he wrote his first book.

Revel identifies the main reason for this entrenched belief: Envious resentment due to Europe's loss of leadership status in the Western world during the post-WWII era. He believes that America will be despised no matter what policy option it selects. Further, the only rational reaction Americans could have to this situation, he says, is to keep their own counsel when it comes to foreign policy, and leave their **fair-weather friends** (only good friends when they choose to be) at arm's length. Revel sites how other countries also ascribe their own worst faults to the U.S. We have an appropriate saying in the U.S. that reflects this all-too-human tendency: **People who live in glass houses shouldn't throw rocks.**

Revel also points out the petty criticism of the U.S. in international press coverage. He says it never misses an opportunity to America-bash, even when reporting on subjects that are in essence non-political, such as economic statistics and scientific discovery. He cites a prestigious French economics journal that gleefully announced "The End of Full Employment in the USA" when the U.S. unemployment rate climbed to 5.5 percent in early 2001. Yet, at the same time, the French government was congratulating itself for reducing French unemployment to 11 percent.

More recently, and even in the country of our closest ally, the British Broadcasting Corp. gave extensive coverage to a technical problem with the U.S. Mars Rover, but barely mentioned the successful effort that solved the problem and the wealth of information Rover was beaming through space for the world's scientific community. He says this editorial bias and countless others like it are typical of an environment in which balanced, accurate news coverage has become secondary to the task of denouncing the U.S. We have another saying in the U.S.: **Don't believe everything you read.** So, question what you read or hear about the U.S., just as we should do with your country.

FOREIGN EXCHANGE STUDENTS

The U.S. sponsors exchange programs for students from around the world to develop cultural understanding between our countries. Numerous programs of varying lengths are available. For some, high school students have the opportunity to live in the U.S. with host families and attend high school for an academic year.

Youth Exchange and Study Program – Nada, a Kuwait student on the YES program (www.yesprograms.org) sponsored by the U.S. State Department for high school students from significantly Muslim countries said:

Students from around the world for the 2012 Youth Exchange and Study Program.

"...coming here made me realize that the United States is more than a movie on TV or a politics article in a newspaper. It shocked me how people who don't know you and never met you in their lives would open their houses unconditionally for you and treat you like a part of their family. They worry when you are sick, they listen to you when you have something to say... it all began to feel right...."

Muhammad, an exchange student from Pakistan, said:

"I think that the main purpose of YES program starts now, to pay it forward. Now I'm a more responsible citizen, a loving son, and a better student. I now understand the importance of U.S. ties with Muslim world. Due to a better understanding of American political culture, I understood the fact that people run the government, governments do not run people."

South Asia Muslim Student Program – Another student program was sponsored by the U.S. State Department. A group of 21 young Muslim students from universities in India, Pakistan, and Bangladesh were taught American history in the U.S. during the summer of 2004. The students were able to point out our downfalls. But they were also frank in their admiration of what Americans have achieved and were hopeful for their own fragile efforts to build democracy in their homelands as we have done.

The program was divided into six different themed weeks in the U.S.

- Week 1–Birthrights. They explored early American history and made a visit to a simple seventeenth-century religious meetinghouse that provoked a conversation about similarities between Islam and some of the sects during our colonial period. The Muslim students considered Christians and Jews to be fellow "people of the Book" and far closer to their tradition than Hindus and Buddhists. Conversations about the American Revolution prompted comparisons to various features of the South Asian experience. They could see that their South Asian nations were still faced with the same tensions over representation that the American founders faced three centuries ago.

- Week 2–Civil Rights. They studied the American experience and how our different groups have been denied political participation, including African-Americans, women, and immigrants. A day devoted to slavery and the Civil War prompted comments about the caste system in South Asia and the civil wars that gave birth to all three South Asian nations. The author of a recent book on gay marriage led a group discussion about human sexuality and ways of incorporating minority rights into majority cultures. Since several of the students were already expecting to enter into arranged marriages back home, there was sympathy (and some

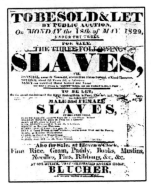

1829 slave poster.

opposition) to the argument that marriage is a right, and that love should have something to do with it as it does here.

- Week 3–Exploration. Exploring the small Maryland town in which the college was located, they saw how Americans actually live their lives, far from the history books. A session was spent with the town's mayor who impressed the female students with her standing up to her mostly male opponents and her successful campaign to keep Walmart (a giant retailer) out of her small, historic town with **mom-and-pop** (small family) businesses. On another day, a local congressman spent two hours with the students, answering every question they could throw at

A "mom and pop" business.

him. After hearing from a lot of democratic academics, they were glad to get a republican who spoke openly about his reservations over U.S. foreign policy. We have a saying: **"Tell it like it is."**

- Weeks 4 & 5–Foreign Policy. Students were given a chance to vent their irritation with our foreign policy, including Iraq and the Middle East, and the dismissive way in which the U.S. is *perceived* to treat Muslims, given our Guantanamo prisoner camp in Cuba that President Obama would say he wanted to eliminate. They used our history and traditions to argue against some of our policies. To their credit, the students wouldn't let the teacher and guest speakers just quote slogans about democracy—they wanted to see the real thing, and they wanted a single standard for all people. It was difficult to argue with their

Guanatanamo prisioner camp – Cuba.

criticism that most Americans have little understanding of how our foreign policy actually affects their lives living on the other side of the world.

- Week 6–Traveling. They spent time in New York City and then Washington, D.C. They visited the shrines of American democracy (see Chapter D - History), worshiped at a mosque, took in an exhibit on Islamic art at the National Gallery of Art (www.nga.gov), and attended a final briefing at the State Department. At a banquet in a Lebanese restaurant, many cried because their enlightening time together in the U.S. would come to a close.

Reflecting back on the summer, the teacher said, "I take heart from the fact that there are so many young people out there trying to build a future that works. …Fifty-four percent of India's billion people are under age twenty-five, and surely it makes sense, from every conceivable viewpoint, to engage them."

AN ENGLISHMAN

Alistair Cooke was a small boy in England during World War I and had exposure to **Yanks**[*] stationed near his home. This is what he says about his experience with Americans.

"Everything about them [American soldiers] was peculiar and fascinating. All their ranks had identical table manners, and…identical accents. They treated my mother with a New World courtesy that kept them strangers. But they addressed children as equals, and I was treated as a sort of regimental pet. They were taller than our soldiers and uniformly paler. My father [incorrectly] explained to me that their complexions were due to the famous skyscrapers, which kept the sun off their faces the year round. But I believe that the preconceptions about another country that we hold on to most tenaciously are those we take in, so to speak, with our mother's milk. The infection of these old prejudices is still widespread."

When he grew up, Cooke came to the U.S. in 1932 to study drama for one year at Yale University. Typical of foreigners, he was curious about America and its people so he decided to journey across the country by car to learn firsthand about the real U.S. "That trip was an absolute eye-opener for me," he later recalled. "Even then, even in the Depression, there was a tremendous energy and vitality to America. The landscape and the people were far more gripping and dramatic than anything I had ever seen. It truly changed me. You see, I began to take up what I felt was the real drama going on—namely, America itself."

Alistair Cooke

---

[*]The word Yank is derived from Yankee, an American Indian word referring to those from New England, now used to refer to Americans in general as Cooke did.

Cooke remained in the U.S. as a foreign correspondent for a British newspaper and in 1951 started his Letters from America radio broadcasts to Britain in which he discussed the passions, manners, and the flavor of the way of life in the U.S. to the curious British. This continued for fifty years. The genteel Cooke hosted cultural TV programs in the U.S. including a 13-week series in which he educated Americans about their own country, much as he had been describing America to Britons. This led to his 1973 classic book, *Alistair Cooke's America,* in which he describes the essential forces that make America work and provides insight to our national character. It still sits on the coffee tables of some Americans.

These are some of his firsthand observations about the U.S. Although written decades ago, they are still relevant today.

- *Character* – "While the Europeans attribute America's bounty to the luck of her [natural] resources, Americans on the other hand like to ascribe it to nothing but character. It usually required a combination of both."
- *Complicated* – "It is a bitterly, and sometimes rousingly, complicated place, this land thrashing over such incessant contradictions as control and permissiveness, the radical young and the conservative middle, the limitlessness of civil rights and the limitations of presidential power."
- *Diversity* – "In a continent of [then] forty-eight governments [states], a half-dozen radically different climates, a score of separate economies, and a **goulash** [a stew] of ethnic ingredients, nothing that you say about the whole country is going to be true." [This is what I emphasize throughout this book.]
- *First Impression* – "Most people, I believe, when they first come to America, whether as travelers or settlers, become aware of a new and agreeable feeling, that the whole country **is their oyster** (is perfect for them). They may, in fact, settle down in one place and stay there."
- *Materialism* – "Every other country scorns American materialism while striving in every big and little way to match it. Envy obviously has something to do with it, but there is a true basis for this debate, and it is whether America is in its ascent or its decline."
- *Self-Reliance* – "One of the oldest of American **chestnuts** (bits of wisdom) is that line of the Italian immigrant asked to say what forty years of American life had taught him: **There is no free lunch** [meaning you have to work for what you get]."
- *Size* – "The first thing a foreigner has to try to take in about America...is the simple size of the place and the often warring variety of life that goes on inside it."
- *Tradition* – "While the American tradition is a conservative one, what it has struggled to conserve are often very radical principles indeed."

AN ASIAN TEACHER

Ting Ni came to America with an understanding of an old Chinese proverb, "Better to light a candle than to curse the darkness." She grew up in China during the Cultural Revolution and had no access to schools that were closed from 1966 to 1976. Sent to a peasant village to work, in the evening hours Ni taught herself English by listening to a radio and reading books her mother sent to her. "The five-year intellectual void...gave me a profound respect for the role knowledge plays in shaping my personal growth," she said. In 1978, when colleges and universities were reopened, she took an exam to enter a school. With only three months to study, Ni passed and was accepted. She studied world history and in 1984 earned her master's degree in American History.

Ting Ni

Ni studied American history because she wanted to know why America could achieve so much in such a short period of time while China could not. In 1987, she was awarded a Fulbright Scholarship (this is *very* prestigious in the U.S.) and traveled to the U.S. where she earned her doctoral degree in 1996, became a teacher at a university in the U.S., and has taught here since 1997.

After a 2002 visit to China, the animosity young Chinese students felt for Americans troubled her. "This young generation in China harbors such strong anger of America. This can be dangerous. It is important to bridge. I would like to do something, to use my personal experiences to illustrate the differences between the two societies. It's going to be a very challenging job."

Ni returned to China in 2004 to teach American history because she realized building a relationship between our two countries was crucial. She hopes to avoid future instability and hostility between the two countries by educating the next generation and exposing them to a more comprehensive view of how American society and government operate (which is one of the goals of this book, too). Perhaps this is what Winston Churchill had in mind when he said, "If you have knowledge, let others light their candles with it."

MUSLIM AMERICAN SURVEY

Surveys were made of Muslim Americans on the 10-year anniversary of the 9/11 Muslim bombing in the U.S. Two-thirds of those surveyed were immigrants who represented 77 countries. Surprisingly, it revealed that our Muslim community is largely content with its place in our society and are optimistic about our country's direction. This is in spite of concerns about anti-Muslim discrimination in the years since the September 11 attacks.

The study found that most Muslims who come to the U.S. want to adopt American customs and ways of life. Two-thirds said life in the U.S. is better than in most Muslim countries. However, nearly half admitted that being a Muslim in the U.S. had become more difficult since 2001. About a quarter reported being treated suspiciously, called offensive names, or felt singled out by airport security. Conversely, over a third reported having someone express support for them and their faith, and half said they believed that Americans are generally friendly. Interestingly, Muslim Americans are more likely to express traditional American ideals than the public at large. Three-fourths, for example, believe that most people can get ahead if they work hard, compared with 62 percent of Americans overall. They also believe that most American Muslims are able to blend into U.S. society without having to abandon their faith and their roots.

Muslim Americans

A VIETNAMESE IMMIGRANT

Thao Le moved from a Vietnamese refugee camp in the Philippines to our East Coast city of Philadelphia, Pennsylvania, in 1980. Nicknamed the City of Brotherly Love, she still found the city loud and crowded with rude people, and it was hard to find work. "I was totally astonished and disappointed," she said. "The life was different than the life I saw in the movies. It had very old houses and narrow roads. The people were very mean and blowing [car] horns."

Fourteen years later, she moved down the coast to smaller Raleigh, North Carolina, to manage a Vietnamese restaurant that she now owns. There she found the U.S. that she had dreamed about. "I feel that in Raleigh, you welcome people with all kinds of ethnic backgrounds. I love this place. I love the pine trees," she said.

Vietnamese Americans celebrating Lunar New Year in California.

Le is one of the thousands of Asians who moved to this southern state in the 1990s, making them the state's third-largest racial group behind whites and blacks. "I think we are very welcome in this area," she said. "We feel comfortable. This area is getting more and more like California. It's kind of a mixture of people."

Le thinks of her two teenage daughters as mostly "American," although she works to instill Vietnamese culture in them. As a child in Vietnam, she said she "had to work weekends to **come up with** [obtain] money for food," something her girls do not have to do. She is pleased that her community has a Chinese American Friendship Group that operates a school on Saturday for kindergartners through eighth-graders to learn the Chinese language, culture, painting, and martial arts.

Le thinks she has succeeded as other Asians have in the U.S. because "In Asian country, we usually have a rough time and being street smart is essential to survival," she said. "We have to be quick to adapt." For example, few Asian cities have the kind of organized law enforcement that the U.S. does. "Here you call 911 for fire, car wreck, or if you think there's a stranger in your backyard," she said. "You call 911 and they're there in five minutes. It's not like that in Oriental cities. You have to be self-sufficient and self-defensive."

FOREIGN STUDENTS IN THE U.S.

An Internet website asked Chinese Americans their thoughts about their experience in America. Most were graduate students who had to adjust to a new country and who experienced language and cultural problems. Their answers give general insight to the overall foreign-student experience in America.

Two-thirds ranked these as the three biggest impediments to their career advancement in the U.S., major topics that are all addressed in this book.

1. Deficient English as a second language.
2. Lack of know-how to break into American social circles.
3. Lack of business understanding and training.

Interestingly, despite problems encountered here, almost six out of ten wished they had come earlier, and a third wanted to become U.S. citizens and remain here. Asked to define the biggest reward they received by coming to the U.S., the top reward, as one might expect, was mastering English and seeing the world. However, the next reward was "getting to be myself regardless of other people's opinions." This response points out one of the major differences between our two cultures. Others are more group oriented while we are more independent and adhere less to group thinking. They also indicated they most liked our open and culturally diverse society; again, more cultural contrasts.

Obama with students in Shanghai after speech.

When asked what they disliked about the U.S., the most frequent response was "self-righteousness and a superiority complex in world affairs." When I ask foreigners I meet about their perceived dislikes of the U.S., I generally get the same response. I understand why they might have this negative perception, given our leadership position in the world and how our overreach is reported in the media.

But in all honesty I simply do not believe that the average American believes his or her country is "superior" to others around the world. I think Americans know they have something very special going for them and are thankful, but most don't gloat over what they have. We have more important things to think about. As history shows, we want to share this with others. Further, in my discussions with immigrants who have assimilated our culture and come to know the true America, most eventually alter this popular negative view of Americans.

A respected foreign educator gave me his perspective on this *perceived* superiority complex of Americans that foreigners have. He said that truth is hard to find in a world that is filled with myths, misinterpretations, and slanted media. Since the collapse of the USSR, the U.S. is now the only superpower. And he said humans like to take **potshots** (be critical of) at what they perceive as the biggest or the best, be it a neighbor, a celebrity, a company, or a country. He pointed out that if smaller countries did the same things it would go unnoticed. Yes, the U.S. makes foreign policy mistakes like most nations do. But he reminded me that American citizenship is eagerly sought even in nations where it is not politically correct to "like" Americans. He thinks the U.S., in part, is simply a victim of its own success and has become a popular target for a world that always needs a target to shoot at, especially when envy is involved.

Reflecting on his view, I saw a parallel between our famed New York Yankees baseball team and U.S. sports fans. The Yankees are the most successful team in the U.S. They have won more World Series than any other club. Yet there will always be those who dislike the Yankees—we even have a play called *Damn Yankees!*—because of their success and because of their owner who was viewed by some as loud and demanding of his players. He also spent more money than any other team to get the best players in order to become a winner. Yet, those fans who hate the Yankees admit their players are respectful to other teams, do not flaunt their

Yankee Stadium, New York City

achievements, and that the owner was the epitome of a winning owner, a quality they would like to see in the owners of their own favorite teams. In some respects, the Yankees team, like the U.S., is a victim of its own success. As the educator points out, humans are quick to both criticize and admire achievers depending on **which way the wind is blowing** (depending on the situation at the time) and the portal through which they are viewing the U.S.

Next, we'll examine business in America that pervades our society. You will learn about our complex business environment, operations, customs, and why American businesses are successful around the world. Information is also provided for dealing with American business personnel, starting and operating a business of your own as many foreigners do, as well as how to increase your chances of being hired by an American employer here or abroad.

SECTION III
AMERICA'S BUSINESS

The chief business of the American people is business. We make no concealment of the fact that we want wealth, but there are many other things that we want very much more. We want peace and honor, and that charity, which is so strong an element of all civilization.

Calvin Coolidge, U.S. president 1923-1929

U

BUSINESS AND FINANCE

*It is not the employer who pays the wages; he only handles the
money. It is the product that pays the wages.* - Henry Ford, industrialist

I sat next to a high-level executive on an overseas flight who was in charge of dozens of U.S. operations around the world. I explained a little about this *A to Z* book that I was thinking about writing back then. He showed an interest and asked what I would have in the business chapter. I told him it would have a few pages of introductions and terms. He started explaining the problems he had training local managers for his overseas operations that were caused by cultural differences. My **ears perked up** (I paid attention).

Ford Motor Company assembly line.

He said he wished he could find a book for them that not only explained our culture and how it impacts business decisions, but also how we do business. He said that after training his people they would lapse into their old ways because they didn't fully understand the culture and why we conduct business as we do.

He convinced me to expand the chapter to include the "big picture as well as the details" so that if he gave the book to his managers they would "**get it** [understand] once and for all." So, that is what this chapter is all about. It broadly examines the culture and the general organization and operations of our business and financial systems that permeate our society—the "stuff" the executive said he wanted his managers to learn about, understand, and then institute.

Mirroring this same problem, a recent study of Africa reveals that poor management is hurting the effectiveness of corporations there, too. One executive told me, "One of the biggest constraints of going into new markets in Africa is the limited availability of people to manage new business." So, many times middle managers are hired from elsewhere because local managers sit around waiting to be told what to do. As part of the culture in many African (and Asian) countries, younger people or subordinates are expected to do things only when told to do them. The opposite is expected in the U.S.

You will learn terms, concepts, how we conduct business, and our differences. Hopefully, if you manage an operation for a U.S. company here or abroad, you, too, will "get it." Banking and finance, the lubricant for the wheels of industry, is also discussed. Given the financial success foreigners achieve, the chapter may also be valuable for those who wish to invest in our stocks, bonds, real estate and other opportunities.

> **Hint**: Some portions of this chapter are general while others are detailed. If you have a **passing interest** (not serious), you might choose to skip over those areas not relevant to your needs. However, this chapter is important for any foreigner who wants to **advance through the ranks** (promotions) working with an American company either here or overseas. Portions of this chapter are geared for higher management and much of what is summarized is what we teach in our college businesses courses. But some of the concepts may also be important for those who want to operate their own businesses or make investments here as well.

American culture sets the operational framework for our businesses. Customs and traditions relating to the *people* aspects of business in America are discussed in Chapter V - Business Customs. Chapter W discusses owning a business in the U.S. and Chapter X gives pointers on how to get a job with an American employer.

CAPITALISM

Capitalism *[cap-ih-TULL-izh-um]* is the term used to describe the U.S. free enterprise system. **Capital** refers to money and material, such as equipment and buildings, used by businesses. In a **free enterprise** system, the managers of businesses decide what goods and services will be produced, what their prices will be, and what labor force is needed.

If a government makes those decisions, it is called **central planning**. Some nations such as China have a combination of the two. However, China's leaders are recognizing that state enterprises can be inefficient and must be reoriented to the outside in order to compete in the world marketplace. It now relies far more on taxes from private commerce and less on revenues from the declining state sector.

The American free enterprise system emphasizes this private ownership in which businesses produce most of our goods and services. Its three basic types of businesses are manufacturing (producing), merchandising (distributing), and services. Two-thirds of our nation's economic output goes to individuals for personal use (the remaining one-third to government and business) in contrast to about one-half in China and 58 percent in France and Germany where free enterprise is also embraced. The consumer role is so great in the U.S. that we are characterized as having a **consumer economy**.

This emphasis on private ownership arises, in part, from our belief that an economy characterized by private ownership is likely to operate more efficiently than one with substantial government ownership or control. For this reason, our government relies on industries to self-regulate where possible to achieve efficiency.

Our capitalistic system stresses profits, efficiency, innovation, shareholder value, and a motivated workforce. Most jobs are based on a 40-hour workweek, five days a week (Monday through Friday), eight hours per day. The U.S. has minimum wage laws ($7.25 in 2012), though a number of employment sectors are excluded and some states have even higher minimum wages. (There that *states' rights* thing again.) Paid vacations are usually two weeks, and some businesses offer health insurance for their employees. Americans usually retire at the age of 65, but may retire earlier if their pension plans permit or later for economic reasons. **Blue collar** refers to workers doing manual or industrial labor as opposed to **white collar** workers in administrative jobs. **Rank and file** refers to the main body of workers, excluding management.

In our capitalist economy, we have three fundamental components that keep the wheels of business turning efficiently and dictate how we operate our businesses.

- **Supply and demand** mainly determines the prices of labor, capital, goods, and services. Supply is the availability of a good or service that is offered for sale. Demand is the amount of a good or service that users would like to buy at various prices. Generally, prices fall when availability is high, and rise when supply is low. In theory, this tends to produce the right combination of goods and services. It is a fundamental component of capitalism.

- **Profit** *[PRAW-fit]* is the primary motivator of businesses. It is the difference between money taken in (usually in the form of sales) and money going out (expenses). Most business policies are based on this profit motive. Many managers are judged on how well their operation contributes to the overall profit of a business, something the executive on the airplane had difficulty instilling in his managers who tended to be isolated in their thinking.

- **Competition** *[komp-ah-TISH-un]* exists when many suppliers try to sell the same kinds of things to the same buyers. A supplier that charges lower prices or improves the quality of its products can take buyers away from competitors. This promotes efficiencies among suppliers that, in turn, reduce their operating costs, allowing them to charge lower prices. Everyone then benefits from competition, the third cornerstone of American business.

GOVERNMENT INVOLVEMENT

Following the old adage, **what's good for General Motors is good for America**, our government provides an environment for capitalism to thrive. Its role may differ from your country's. We use the term **laissez-faire** to describe in a broad sense our government-business relationship. The term is French and means "let do," so it implies minimal government involvement where possible in conducting business.

However, on a narrower scope, foreigners conducting business in the U.S. might be surprised at the number of organizations both in and out of government that can indirectly affect their business decisions. A single federal government agency may issue regulations for an industry where public safety is a concern. But there is a good chance more than one agency will have input. In addition, nonprofit public agencies and lobbyists may exert influence.

As an example, the U.S. auto industry is given safety guidelines by a federal agency. Some states might have additional requirements like California's limits on smog emissions for cars sold there. Our insurance companies have a testing agency that rates the crash worthiness of cars and their findings affect car design. The American Automobile Association (AAA) provides assistance services for car owners and also makes their voice heard in Washington. Thus, when doing business in the U.S., you may not be able to go to one source to explore business options and get answers. We have many consultants and lobbyists in Washington to help businesses through this government/private sector maze.

Congressional meeting in U.S. Capitol.

Unlike some countries, we only have a few government-owned projects in the U.S. They tend to provide vital public services. State governments may construct bridges, toll roads, historic sites, and recreational facilities. Local governments (city/county) might own public utilities such as water and electricity systems. In some countries, the government owns the transportation and communication systems. In America, they are privately owned but regulated by our government.

From an economic point of view, our federal government provides three important services that you might encounter: it ensures competition, looks out for the public's interest, and maintains the economy. (This website provides information on U.S. government departments and agencies that provide these services: www.firstgov.gov.)

Our Government Ensures Competition – Our government ensures there is fair competition among those who provide goods and services. We use the term **level playing field** when that fairness is achieved. If a few firms have too much power because of their large share of sales, they can limit competition that restricts the entry of competitors into their industry. When this occurs, the virtues of capitalism are at risk and artificial pricing and control replace the benefits of a free marketplace.

In the late 1800s, huge **monopolies** [mo-NOP-oh-lees] (sole control) that had no competition dominated many industries in the U.S. The government passed the famous **Sherman Antitrust Act** of 1890 that outlawed them. It broke up huge petroleum and railroad companies into smaller independent companies that reestablished free enterprise within these industries. To foster more competition, our government explored the

372

possibility of breaking up our huge IBM Corporation in the 1970s followed by Microsoft in the 1990s.

Mergers are economically justified on the basis that like-operations can be combined, redundancy eliminated, personnel dismissed, and the end result is lowered operating costs and increased profit. (**M&A** is our short term for these **mergers and acquisitions**.) The government continues to examine proposed large mergers and industry dominance to insure competition is not stifled. One such recent ruling was the government's blocking of AT&T's proposed $39 billion acquisition of T-Mobile, which would "substantially lessen competition" in the wireless market.

The U.S. government also wants to stimulate our world trade, but also wants to protect its own businesses and jobs by insuring that all participants **play by the same rules** to ensure competition. For example, to protect their own local car makers, Chinese tariffs on U.S. vehicles sometimes result in a retail price in China of three times what the vehicle costs in the U.S. The U.S. and other Western countries also worry that some foreign governments, especially in Asia, will not protect our patent and intellectual property rights and strive to eliminate counterfeit operations. For example, it was reported that 90 percent of the popular Viagra pills sold in Shanghai in 2000 were counterfeit because China did not recognize the U.S. patent on this medicine.

> **Hint**: It was inevitable. A U.S. senator proposed legislation that will stop federal money going to companies that send jobs out of the country. He say he is responding to the proliferation of companies that are sending jobs to cheaper overseas sites to increase profits while placing more Americans out of work. He says that 40 percent of **Fortune 500** companies (our 500 largest) are outsourcing jobs to foreign countries and the list is expected to grow. The bill would require that all contractors performing services for the federal government do that work in the U.S. As with most of our issues in the U.S., there are always two sides to them. In this case, those businesses deprived of cheaper labor would be less profitable and their goods would cost the government and the public more to buy when made here.

Our Government Protects Public Interest – In capitalist economies, the government tries to ensure that society and the environment are considered in business decisions. To protect the public, our federal government has guidelines for industries such as banking, airlines, railroads, and radio and television broadcasting. It also regulates those industries that have monopoly power but are sanctioned by the government, such as utilities and telephone companies. These are some of our federal government agencies that regulate or support our businesses that you might encounter with your business dealings here.

- **Environmental Protection Agency** (EPA) – Helps ensure that clean water and clean air will not be impacted by business. (www.epa.gov)
- **Federal Trade Commission** (FTC) – Maintains free and fair competition and protects consumers from unfair practices. (ww.ftc.gov)

- **Small Business Administration** (SBA) – Promotes and protects small businesses by offering aid in the form of loans, counseling, and information on business management. This is a big aid to those immigrants who want to start their own business here, something we discuss in Chapter W on owning a business. (www.sba.gov)
- **Food and Drug Administration** (FDA) – Monitors the purity and safety of medicines and food, including those imported from foreign countries. (www.fda.gov)
- **Department of Labor** (DOL) – Ensures labor regulations are met by businesses to protect our workers, including foreign owned firms. (www.dol.gov)

Hint: You will probably discover that our federal government more closely regulates some American companies than is typical in your native country. Try to learn what these regulations are before your first business meeting with your American counterpart; they could affect you and your business dealings.

Our Government Maintains The Economy – Our federal government also plays a role in regulating the economy. Swings between good and bad times are called **business cycles**. A **recession** occurs when the overall output of goods and services falls for six consecutive months. A **depression** is worse; it involves a 10 percent or more decline in the GDP. **The Great Depression** occurred in the 1930s when many American banks and businesses closed and millions of jobs were lost. We had a 25 percent unemployment rate versus five percent in normal times and the GDP declined 33 percent.

From this we learned that our government must monitor the health of the economy, abandon its centuries-old **hands-off policy** that permeates most of America, and put rules and regulations in place to prevent a similar event from occurring. We are relearning many of these lessons and hoping Congress will install new rules and regulations to prevent a reoccurrence of the 2007-2010 financial collapse.

Inflation occurs during periods of economic growth when prices rise because of excess demand and decreased supply. The government's Consumer Price Index (**CPI**) is a key inflation gauge. Our **Federal Reserve Bank** (www.federalreserve.gov) is the central bank of our government, akin to the European Central Bank. It adjusts interest rates and other factors to stimulate or restrain economic activity. The **Treasury Department** (www.ustreas.gov) also helps stabilize the economy with its monetary actions that affect availability of money for businesses and personal loans.

INTERNATIONAL DIFFERENCES

As an overview, here are some general differences between business operations and environment in the U.S. versus other countries.

374

- *Collaboration* – A survey was taken of 120 European CEOs from Germany, France, U.K., Italy, Poland, and Spain plus 50 U.S. managers from companies of various sizes and industries. Nearly 95 percent of the European managers consider international collaboration important. By contrast, 40 percent of Americans describe closer relations as unimportant, but only 12 percent say transatlantic collaboration up to now has led to positive results. On the other hand, recognizing the economic importance of the European Union, our giant General Electric Co. moved its European headquarters from London to Brussels where the EU is headquartered.

- *Competition* – The U.S. believes in unhindered competition among businesses, while the European Union unifies standards of operation and government guidance to enable competing companies to coordinate for efficiency and greater overall productivity. This suits high-tech industries well, perhaps giving collaborative Europeans an advantage over the **go-it-alone** competitive American approach. As a component of competition, U.S. businesses collectively spend 2.5 percent of GDP on research and development (**R&D**), while Europe spends 1.9 percent and innovative Japan 3 percent.

- *Decision Making* - The way people interpret facts influences how businesses are managed. A study revealed that when senior executives in the U.S. were asked why their firms existed, most answered "to create shareholder value." It found that private firms in China exist to provide shareholder value like their U.S. counterparts but only for people at the very top of the firms. The purpose of Japanese firms was defined to not only solely maximize shareholder value, but to take care of employees. South Korea resembles Europe more closely than Japan or China, but also has an eye towards employees and society.

- *Gross Domestic Product* – In 2011, American companies sold over $15 trillion worth of goods and services. We define this sum total produced by a nation as its **Gross Domestic Product (GDP)**. Together, the U.S. and Europe account for almost 50 percent of the world's economic activity. Sixty of the world's largest 140 companies are European and 50 are American. Although a GDP reflects the market value of the goods and services an economy produces, it is not a measurement of a nation's quality of life or such things as personal happiness, security, clean environment, and good health.

The following table provides a ranking of the world's top ten GDPs. It also shows how the economies of the **BRIC nations** continue to expand. BRIC is a relatively recent acronym that refers to the countries of Brazil, Russia, India, and China that are all deemed to be at a similar stage of newly advanced economic development. They account for more than a quarter of the world's land area and more than 40 percent of the world's population. Studies show that their combined economies could eclipse the combined economies of the current richest countries of the world by 2050.

2011 Top Ten GDPs [*] (BRIC nations in bold)

2011 Rank	Country	GDP ($billion)	2010 Rank
	World	78,852	
	European Union	15,788	
1	United States	15,064	1
2	**China**, People's Republic	8,200	2
3	**India**	4,469	4
4	Japan	4,395	3
5	Germany	3,089	5
6	**Russia**	2,376	6
7	**Brazil**	2,309	9
8	United Kingdom	2,253	7
9	France	2,216	8
10	Italy	1,828	10

Factors accounting for America's giant GDP include its large geographical size and population, its vast natural resources, but perhaps more importantly a society that supports and rewards businesses that contribute to the economy. The U.S. *service economy,* with industries that range from banking to retail to travel, account for 80 percent of U.S. economic activity. It is said that if the state of California, our most populous state, were an independent nation, it would have the world's tenth largest GDP, about the size of Italy's.

Per capita GDP (total GDP divided by population size), a reflection of a nation's efficiency and worker output, is lower in most European countries than in most individual states in the U.S. The same applies to the economic growth rates of European nations, which have lagged the U.S. in recent decades. Economists say our latest U.S. recessions with GDP growth rates of 1-2 percent would represent boom conditions in some EU nations like Germany. This is not to brag, but simply illustrates the importance of other nations and companies understanding the driving forces behind America's business model.

- *Tax Burden* – International economists ascribe U.S. economic success to its overall low tax burden (about 28 percent) as a percentage of the GDP. Sweden has a 52 percent rate, the EU average is 40 percent, and Ireland is the lowest of the 14 nations at 32 percent. The common view is that the higher the tax burden the larger the public sector and the greater the power of political

---

[*]From International Monetary Fund.

decision makers and the public bureaucracy. Higher taxes also generate incentives not to work and limit entrepreneurship incentive. As you have learned, Americans believe that less government is better government and these are some of the reasons why. (More about entrepreneurship in the U.S. later in this chapter.)

- *Labor Force* – In contrast to America, Europeans prefer to work less, earn less, live more simply, and play more. Their per capita income is a third less and they work fewer hours. Seventy percent of Americans believe the rich are rich because they are smarter and work harder, and the poor are poor because they are slackers; only 40 percent of Europeans agree with this viewpoint.

  Given our large businesses, less than 50 percent of employment in the U.S. comes from small and medium businesses as opposed to 70 percent in Europe.

  In most European countries, once you are hired you can only be fired for cause, a strong tradition for the last hundred years. In the U.S., unless you have a contract you can be fired for any reason except for racial or gender discrimination, a reason we work hard with personal responsibility.

  About half our population forms our labor force, but less than one percent are employed in our highly mechanized agriculture industry, unlike India's 60 percent. It is our open workforce coupled with our abundance of natural resources and determination that allows the U.S. to be a leading industrial nation. Other labor facts:

  o *Wages* – Our executives are well paid; some say too well paid. While the typical high-income earner in the U.S. earns over five times that of the low-wage earner, the same ratio in Europe is 3 to 1. America's minimum wage is 40 percent of the average wage; in Europe it is 55 percent.

  o *Unemployment* – The U.S. consistently has one of the lowest unemployment rates in the world, averaging about 5 to 6 percent. A lower average rate is usually found only in Japan and higher rates in places like India (9%), Brazil (9.5%), and Poland (15%).

  o *Women* – About 60 percent of our workforce is women, compared to France's 48 percent and Japan's 40 percent. Unlike the U.S., negative stigma is still attached to women's employment in some countries, including India. (We did have this stigma up to the 1950s when one of three women participated in the labor force because many thought a woman's role was in the home raising her family.)

Hint: Many of our movies are about business and finance, including classics like *The Man in the Gray Flannel Suit* (1956), *The Apartment* (1960), *How to Succeed in Business Without Really Trying* (1967), *Wall Street* (1987), *Working Girl* (1888), and *Other People's Money* (1991).

INTERNATIONAL TRADE

America relies heavily on trade with other nations, which in turn influences our relations with those countries. Canada purchases most of our exports (22%), followed by Mexico, China, Japan, and the U.K. Most of our imports come from Canada (19%), followed by China, Mexico, Japan, and Germany. In terms of total trade dollars exchanged, Canada is first ($600 billion). China advanced from fifth place seven years ago to second today ($500 billion).

Since World War II, the U.S. has sought to reduce trade barriers and enhance the world economic system. We not only see open trade as a means of advancing our own economic interests, but also as a key to building peaceful relations among nations. Prince Albert of Victorian England sought the same thing when he established the first world trade exposition of manufactured products in 1851. (Later they would be called world fairs.) An open trading system requires that countries allow fair and nondiscriminatory access to each other's markets. To that end, the U.S. grants countries favorable access to its markets if they reciprocate by reducing their own trade barriers. (There's that *level playing field* thing again.) However, all is not **hunky-dory** (quite satisfactory) on this front as some countries do not reciprocate. Some Americans want to block their imports.

Trade Deficits – Back in 2006, we exported only $1.4 trillion worth of goods and services, and imported $2.2 trillion. This all-time high $800 billion shortfall was upsetting to many Americans. Although reduced somewhat in the following years and then climbing to $560 billion in 2011, **trade deficits** are still a concern to many. The public wants our government to take a hard look at our trade policies with those nations with whom we have trade deficits. President Bush faced political pressure from the public over soaring trade deficits with China. Americans were pleased when Chinese Premier

Foreign containers unloading in U.S. port.

Wen Jiabao visited the U.S. in 2003 and said China was committed to increasing imports of U.S. products to level the trade balance between the two nations. However, nothing changed. Deficits with China increased steadily from $162 billion in 2004 to $295 billion in 2011. For this reason some politicians and the public wants the U.S. to **crack down** (take firm action) on China.

Job Loss – Americans are also concerned about job losses when items that were once made here are now manufactured overseas more cheaply and then imported to the U.S. Due to trade deficits with China between 2001 and 2011, the U.S. lost 2.8 million jobs, of which 1.9 million were in manufacturing. Jobs were also lost when customer call centers were transferred overseas to handle calls from Americans to U.S. companies. The list of exported jobs also includes back-office information technology (IT) operations,

378

research, bookkeeping, medical transcription, and the work of attorneys, accountants, medical specialists, and scientists, things that are hard to do that people overseas do well and for substantially less money.

Anywhere from one-half to two-thirds of our **Fortune 500 companies** (500 largest) outsource jobs to India alone, achieving potential labor cost savings of 70 percent. This is hard for our executives to ignore with their eye on the **bottom line** (net profit). Some Americans boycott those companies when the media reports they have outsourced jobs overseas.

> **Hint**: This can be a sensitive topic for Americans when discussing nations with whom we have a trade deficit or have lost jobs to, especially if those nations have restrictions on what they can import from the U.S. As you have learned, Americans like equality in all aspects of their lives. Numerous U.S. manufacturers conspicuously display "Made in America" on their products' packaging to bolster their image. A number of Asian and European automakers now build their cars in the U.S. using local labor and materials, which allows them to sidestep this problem.

Other Concerns – Americans also argue that other countries should not receive the benefits of free trade if their employers exploit workers or damage the environment in an effort to compete more effectively in international markets. Reacting to such demands, many U.S. companies now monitor these overseas manufacturing facilities to insure their workers are not exploited. Apple Inc., for example, issues an annual report that details their efforts to monitor its suppliers to ensure they are operating within legal codes and are following the company's policies on environmental standards, human rights, and occupational health and safety. Some of our technical associations do the same for its members. The net result is better working conditions around the world.

You may see public demonstrations against our retailers who import clothing items made in poor countries where young children are forced to work long hours at low wages. Others boycott products that were made by testing them on animals, so you might see labels stating they have not been subjected to this. You may see similar statements at the end of our movies stating that animals were not harmed in the making of the movie. Foreign manufacturers who want to sell products to America should be aware of these important trends.

Feel free to discuss all these trade differences with your U.S. counterpart if you have an interest in conducting business here and want to **head off at the pass** (deal with it early on) before you encounter trade problems.

INTERNATIONAL BUSINESS MODELS

Some foreign businesses have adopted American business models and operational techniques to achieve success both in the U.S. and in their homelands. Japan and China provide interesting case studies of contrasting styles used to achieve business success in the U.S.

Japanese vs. Chinese Approach – For about 20 years after World War II, Japan was a maker of cheap products that had little or no brand recognition in the U.S. In the 1970s and 80s, once Japanese businesses had mastered the complicated task of developing international brand recognition, their economy soared as business prospered. They brought their companies, products, and culture to the U.S. But they often operated their businesses in the U.S. in the same way they did in Japan, and that sometimes created resentment among their American workers and the buyers of their products.

> **Hint**: The 1986 movie, *Gung Ho*, was an accurate portrayal of the backlash Japanese companies actually faced here at the time because of our different cultures and business operations. It is about a Japanese car company that buys an American automobile manufacturer and the clash of work attitudes between foreign management and local workers.

In terms of business, China, which is slowly moving beyond a producer of cheap goods from low-wage factories as Japan once did, is taking a different approach than Japan did. In 2004, China's Lenovo Group, China's largest **PC** (personal computer) maker, announced it was purchasing the personal computer business of America's IBM Corporation, the founder of the PC business. There were questions about whether the Chinese had developed the sophisticated management know-how needed to compete globally. Virtually unknown outside China, the purchase would make Lenovo the world's third-largest seller of PCs. The purchase would give it an internationally recognized brand and access to IBM's technical *and* management capabilities. Many viewed this purchase as symbolic of the new China business model: Buying their way to economic status, as opposed to Japan's lock-step installation of homeland businesses on foreign shores.

As China continues on this international acquisition of companies today, the resentment that the Japanese encountered three decades before no doubt will be stirred up abroad with job losses a big concern. For example, China's Minimetals' proposal to buy Canada's largest mining company created tense debate because Canadians feared their miners would lose jobs. Workers in a shoemaking town in Spain set fire to Chinese-owned warehouses and demanded the Spanish government restrict imports of shoes. Even with incidents like these, China will probably not create the animosity in the U.S. that Japan did because of these differing approaches to global expansion.

- *Open Markets* – China is slowly opening its own markets wider to foreign nations. Japan was more restrictive with imports, which **added fuel to the fire** (made worse) on the issue of a level playing field.
- *Open Minds* – Chinese companies appear more interested in learning our business techniques rather than imposing their way of doing business as Japan did here at first.

- *Open Pockets* – Flush with American dollars, Japanese firms purchased many American landmarks, such as Rockefeller Center in New York City, Columbia Pictures in Hollywood, and many of our office towers and large hotels. Because these were high-profile purchases, they made great news stories that created cultural backlash. (This is probably the same reaction foreigners have had when Americans bought into their countries.)

Compared to Japan's auto industry, China has been unsuccessful in the U.S. and international automobile markets. Its inexpensive Geely automobiles could not pass U.S. road standards. Auto analysts said there were two ways Geely could advance on the world market. One was to take years to methodically improve its quality like Toyota and Honda did in the 1960s and 70s, or shortcut the process by buying a global brand. In 2010, it purchased Sweden's popular Volvo Cars from U.S. based Ford Motor Company in an effort to quickly expand its presence. They also said that because of cultural differences, Geely should allow Volvo to operate largely independently or risk weakening the Swedish company's fine image. It pursued the latter course. China, with annual sales of 19 million autos, has now replaced the U.S. from its former number-one auto market position of 13 million sold.

What A Chinese Executive Learned – Liu Chuanzhi, the founder of China's Lenovo Group, provides interesting insight to what he learned from American businesses and how he applied it to make his own company successful. Lenovo started in Hong Kong as a trading company because China would not grant him a license. He next set up a factory and transferred the operation to China in 1984. As a distributor for foreign companies, such as our leading computer maker Hewlett-Packard Co., he discovered that *management* was something they must learn if they were to succeed. From this international relationship, his company learned how to organize sales channels and how to effectively market its products. He says he constantly read foreign management journals and attended management seminars in the U.S.

Liu Chuanzhi

When asked to define how his firm became China's largest producer of PCs with its Legend brand, he said he focused on three areas that were based on the U.S. business model.

- *Publicly Held* – Even though his company was partially owned by the government (57%), he restructured it as a **publicly held company** and sold shares of stock to the public, believing that would place the company in the same light as publicly held foreign firms. It also enabled him to offer stock options to the company's employees, which turned out to be an excellent motivator. It also increased the firm's ability to obtain capital and it brought pressure from stockholders to perform. It also forced the company to be more transparent in its dealings, something we take for granted in the U.S. but which is less common in other countries, notably Asia.

- *Management Structure* – His second area of focus was building a solid **management structure**. Based on his Western exposure, he developed our traditional marketing, sales promotion, and logistics management techniques that are based on decades of testing and refinement. This is one reason our business schools like to use case studies that show the consequences of management actions.

- *Cultural Differences* – It was more difficult to change ingrained cultural habits, especially motivating workers and instilling new ethical standards. He feels American businesses have a strong sense of their markets and *business ethics*, coupled with a loyal and *motivated workforce*. He says state-owned businesses in China have compensation limits that can stifle responsibility by key managers. He strived to develop a culture, similar to that found in the U.S., in which employees are more self-motivated and allowed to express opinions and are not expected to **parrot** (repeat) what they think their supervisors want to hear.

The components, structure, and principles of the American business model that Liu refers to are now discussed in this chapter, while the cultural/personnel aspects follow in the next chapter.

BUSINESS ETHICS

You have learned throughout this book that Americans believe in equality and fairness. This applies to business, too. We have rules of competition to ensure that all businesses operate within the same guidelines. In general, you should find many (but not all) American business people honest by our Western standards because of the laws and culture under which we operate.

Because business practices vary by country, business ethics and governance also vary. As an example, in China *Yanjiu, Yanjiu* is a word play on cigarettes and wine often used to **grease the wheels** (facilitate getting things done). And *ban shi yao kan qian hou* is word play on thick money, meaning a reward is expected to facilitate progress. What they may consider to be a normal business practice, we might consider unethical or even illegal. The terms we use for this are **bribes** and payments **under the table** (hidden and usually unlawful).

It is against the law in America to offer money or substantial gifts in order to conclude a business deal and can be punishable by fines or jail or both. For this reason,

Americans place much more emphasis on constructing the right business deal at the right price. Do not even hint that you would consider giving or accepting a bribe or **kickback** (secret return of money paid out). It might offend your counterpart, weaken your professional image, and kill your business deal. If, however, you can tie in another business deal with this deal, and at a more favorable price, that would be welcomed because it is business, not personal gain.

Based on a survey of business executives, Transparency International (bpi.transparency.org) annually ranks 28 of the world's largest economies according to the perceived likelihood of companies from those countries to pay bribes abroad. The least likely countries are the Netherlands and Switzerland tied for first place followed by Belgium, Germany, and Japan. Companies from the BRIC economies are led by Brazil at 14, India at 19, China at 27, and Russia last at 28. The Emerates, Indonesia, and Mexico complete the overall bottom five spots. The U.S. ranks 10th, followed by France, Spain, and South Korea. So, the U.S. is not as **squeaky clean** (free from moral fault or taint) as we think we are. (In my travels to former Soviet states, they are still struggling mightily to rid this corruption legacy they inherited.)

The perception we have of some foreign business people is that they may come to an agreement on something, and later they will insist on better terms than were originally agreed to in writing. Do not do this! We consider it unethical! If you do, you will lose respect and will lose a business partner. In the U.S., as explained in Chapter E on law, we say **a deal is a deal**.

American business people are very troubled with **counterfeit** *[KOWN-ter-fit]* (fake) products that compete with their products. So, some global businesses fear going to China, for example, because of the risks to their **intellectual property** (IP). Because of cultural differences, there is little understanding of, or respect for, IP because it is difficult to conceptualize in those societies where copying is often a sign of flattery and efficiency. To them, copying is merely a low risk, smart way to do business. Because IP piracy is culturally acceptable in Spain, Apple's iTunes does not sell movies or television shows there, while other studios are on the brink of not distributing their movies there as well.

> **Hint**: Keep in mind that innovation and inventors are major factors in making America a leader in business. These are often ideas developed by individuals, so naturally we are protective of them.

The U.S. International Trade Commission (www.usitc.gov) said piracy and counterfeiting of U.S. software and a wide range of other intellectual property in China alone cost U.S. businesses an estimated $48 billion and 2.1 million jobs in 2009. And the U.S. Trade Representative's office (www.ustr.gov) listed China for the seventh year as a country with one of the worst records for preventing copyright theft.

Further, often American products manufactured overseas are illegally sold as originals by the very manufacturers employed by the U.S. companies to make them. Our media reported an Asian shoe manufacturer that had a contract to make all the athletic shoes for a big American company, but they were also making and selling the same items for their own profit in Asia, unknown to the U.S. company.

Unfortunately, reports like these on the illegal dealings of a few reflect unfavorably on a country's people and businesses in general. A Japanese proverb: "The reputation of a thousand years may be determined by the conduct of one hour." So, when dealing with a U.S. firm, be prepared to put at ease any concerns they might have about intellectual property security. These findings might kill a deal for companies in nations that sanction piracy and want to do business in the U.S., or for U.S. companies considering business relations there.

Hint: You should make a special effort in your business meetings to convince your American counterpart that you and your firm are *honest* and have *integrity* and *credibility* by American standards. To do this you may need to offer the names of other companies that have used your services and can vouch for your fine principles. As foreign economies mature, the need for honesty and integrity by Western standards will become more important in their international dealings. Long-term financial growth will become more important than illegal short-term gains.

DEFINITIONS AND TERMS

You might encounter frequently-used business words and terms in a business meeting. If you do not understand something, feel free to ask for clarification. A misunderstanding of a word or term could negatively affect your business deal.

- **Accounts receivable** refers to the money that is due from customers. **Accounts payable** is money that a company is expected to pay to another company.
- **Assets** are anything owned that has monetary value, such as cash, stocks, inventory, buildings, patents, and equipment. The opposite, **liabilities**, is debt owed, such as a loan.
  - **Current assets** are assets that can be converted into cash within 12 months, like bonds.
  - **Fixed assets** are held by the business rather than for sale or conversion into cash. These include fixtures, equipment, buildings, patents, trademarks, etc.
- **Budgets** are used by businesses to control their operations. They plan their anticipated sales for a year, then prepare operating budgets for various departments. During the course of business, management personnel monitor financial reports to insure budgets are met. Some items in a budget are *variable* (subject to change, such as sales dollars) and others are *fixed* (fairly constant and predictable, such as rent and utilities).
- **Cash flow** refers to the movement of cash in and out of a business from day-to-day operations. If the money paid out for operating expenses, such as rent, salaries, materials, etc. exceeds the cash coming into a business, it has a *negative cash flow*. Often businesses that have seasonal swings in their cash flow will obtain a **working capital line of credit** with a bank to temporarily add to their cash.
- **Consumers** are people who use goods and services. **Durable goods**, such as cars and refrigerators, are defined as products that are intended to last three or more years.

- **Cost of goods sold** refers to the costs directly associated with the production of goods or services sold. This usually includes materials, labor, and production costs. General corporate costs such as advertising and accounting are excluded.

- **Depreciation** refers to a portion of the purchase price of an asset that the government allows a business to claim as an expense on their taxes. For example, if a building is purchased for $30 million, the business might be allowed to claim $1 million each year for 30 years as depreciation. This is viewed as a "wearing out" expense. The government allows accelerated depreciation in order to recapture more costs early in the life of the asset, thus decreasing taxes. This in turn encourages them to make investments in new buildings, equipment, etc.

- **Economics** *[ek-o-NOM-iks]* is the study of how goods and services get produced and distributed.

- **Equity** is the difference between a company's total assets and its liabilities (money it owes). It represents the value of ownership in the company. If a company has $10 million in assets and $8 million in liabilities, its equity is said to be $2 million. **Net worth** is another term used to define this value of a company (or an individual).

- **Enterprise** is another term for a business. **Firm** is sometimes used, too.

- **Financial year** refers to the period of time for which a financial report is made. If a company reports its operating results for the January 1 to December 31 period, this is referred to as a **calendar year** period. Most corporations, however, have a **fiscal** *[FIS-cull]* **year** of 12 months other than the calendar year, such as April 1 to March 31 or any other period that best suits their operation. **Accounting period** refers to the date stated on a financial report, such as month, quarter, or fiscal year end.

  > **Hint**: The fiscal year of an American company might influence your business dealings with it. For example, if you are attempting to sell something to a company in January that has a fiscal year end of March 31, you might be told to come back in a few months when the manager knows what his budget will be for the upcoming fiscal year.

- **Income** *[IN-come]* and **revenue** refer to the money coming into a business, such as sales, as opposed to money going out which is called an **expense**.

- **Income tax** refers to a tax that is paid by businesses to the government. Within several months after the end of their fiscal year, forms are filled out and filed with federal and state governments showing the computation of the business taxes owed. Congress wants to eliminate some, but not all, of the taxes on overseas profits of U.S.-based companies. This is a hot issue today because they don't transfer the funds back to the U.S. where they will be taxed a second time after first being taxed in the host country.

- **Investment** *[in-VEST-ment]* is the use of savings to produce future income, either by an individual or a business. A business will invest funds in **capital goods**, such as buildings and equipment that will later provide future income. The purchase of a corporation's stock by an individual or another business is also an investment.

- **Letter of credit** is a document issued by an importer's bank to an exporter. It guarantees that the exporter's goods will be paid upon their arrival. American companies that import international goods commonly use this form of payment.

- **Liabilities** *[lie-ah-BILL-ih-tees]* are the opposite of assets. They are what the business owes, such as loans and debts.
  - **Current liabilities** are short-term obligations that must be paid in less than 12 months.

- o **Long term liabilities,** such as large loans used to finance the expansion of a business, have longer due dates.

  The ratio of current assets to current liabilities is one indicator of the **liquidity** *[lih-QUID-ah-tee]* (speed with which cash is available) of a business. The higher the ratio of these assets to liabilities the more liquid the company. This ratio is called the **current ratio**. Potential creditors use this ratio to measure a company's ability to pay off short-term debts. Though acceptable ratios may vary from industry to industry, a current ratio of 2 (assets) to1 (liabilities) is considered the norm.

- **Multinational** *[muhl-tie-NASH-uhn-ul]* describes a business organization that is based in one country and has branches, subsidiaries, and plants in many countries. Many large U.S. companies are multinational, a trend that started in the late 1940s when opportunities arose overseas. Many multinational companies overseas have branches in the U.S., too.

- **Overhead** is an expense, for accounting purposes, that is not attributed to any one single part of the company's activities. Security, computer operations, rent, and accounting are examples.

- **Price** is the amount of money for which something can be bought or sold.
  - o The **retail price** is the price that the public pays for something.
  - o The **wholesale price** is the price that another business might pay for something that it intends to resell at retail to the public.

- **Profit margin** is the difference between the sales price and the cost of producing a product (or service).

- **Pro forma** *[pro-FORM-ah]* is a projected report of revenue and expenses that uses hypothetical dollar and numerical values. This aids management in its decision making process by analyzing financial results by varying different financial factors. If, for example, you are selling a major piece of equipment to an American firm that will help to lower its costs and increase its sales, the business might ask you to help them prepare a pro forma statement to examine the economic impact it will have on their business. The report might show such things as the cost of the machine, projected personnel costs, production costs, lowered selling prices, and increased sales numbers—all of which affect profits.

- **Retained earnings** refers to the portion of net income which is retained by the corporation rather than distributed to its owners as dividends. They are the cumulative additions each year to capital earned since a company's founding.

- **Trade** is the exchange of goods and services. Within a country, it is called **domestic trade**. Between nations, it is called **international trade**. **Globalization** *[globe-uhl-ah-ZAY-shun]* is a term for the trend toward increased cultural and economic connection between people, businesses, and organizations throughout the world.

- **Working capital** is the monetary excess of current assets over current liabilities that keeps the business financially working day to day.

BUSINESS STRUCTURES

We have three main types of business ownership structures in the U.S.: single proprietorship, partnership, and corporation.

Single Proprietorship *[pro-PRY-ah-torr-ship]* – These businesses are owned and operated by one person or a married couple. We have about 17 million of them in the U.S. and immigrant Americans own many. The owner makes all the decisions, receives all the profits, and is personally responsible for debts incurred. Setting up a proprietorship requires a relatively small amount of capital and few legal formalities. In many cases, the owner merely applies for a license from the city to begin. Many are small service and retail businesses, such as gift and clothing stores, beauty parlors, and repair shops.

Typical single proprietorships.

Hint: Immigrant American small business owners might be surprised at the requirements placed on U.S. businesses to maintain accurate financial records. In some countries, sales receipts are not given, or if they are they are not itemized or dated. In the U.S., a government agency may audit a business to insure it is paying all of its taxes, so sales receipts and bank accounts may be examined to insure that all sales dollars have been reported.

Partnership *[PART-nerr-ship]* – A partnership is formed when two or more partners sign a legal agreement that specifies the amount of work and capital each contributes and the percentage of profits each receives. These are commonly used for law, medicine, real estate, and small retailing organizations. The partners are generally responsible for its debts incurred. A lawyer's services are usually required to formalize a partnership. Occasionally you will see the letters **LLC** after the name of a business organization to specify a limited liability company. The LLC is a relatively new type of business structure that provides

Typical partnership business.

the limited liability features of a corporation and the tax efficiencies and operational flexibility of a partnership. (Some German firms use "GmbH" after their names for this same purpose.)

Corporation *[core-por-AY-shun]* – A corporation, our third type of business structure, is a form of business ownership that has an existence of its own, separate from its owners. For this reason, corporations are more permanent entities because they do not stop operating when the people running it quit, retire, or die. You will see our corporations identified by the inclusion of the words Limited (Ltd), Incorporated (Inc.), or Corporation (Corp.) after the company's name. German companies that are publicly

A public corporation.

traded have the letters AG after the company name, the full name of which translates to corporation in English. Throughout the world, S.A. is also used.

Corporations are more difficult to establish and operate because of government regulations. The stockholders (owners) have no liability if the corporation goes into debt. For this reason, there is a trend today for our doctors and other professionals to incorporate in order to eliminate personal liability in case they are sued.

A **stock certificate** states how many shares of stock the stockholder has in the named company. (There is an industry-wide effort to eliminate paper stock certificates and move toward electronic ownership.) In a small corporation, the business owner may be the only **stockholder**. In large corporations, the shares may be owned by millions of stockholders.

Stock certificate.

A corporation's **market value** is computed by multiplying the stock market price of the stock by the total number of shares outstanding. In 2012, Apple Inc. had the world's highest market value at $500 billion. Profits from the corporation in the form of **dividends** *[DIV-ah-dends]* may be paid out to the stockholders, usually on a quarterly basis.

A popular form of employee compensation, called **stock options**, is usually given to executives as an incentive to boost the company's stock price. The options allow them to buy stock in their corporation for a given number of years in the future at or below the price the share was when the option was granted.

The value of their assets defines a corporation's size. Large corporations are defined as having have assets over $250 million. They represent less than one percent of all U.S. corporations but control over 80 percent of total corporate assets. (Apple Inc. had total assets of $140 billion at the beginning of 2012.) **Conglomerates** *[kon-GLOM-er-ats]* are typically large corporations that own a number of other companies, some of which may be in unrelated industries.

The stockholders of a corporation elect the **board of directors** who appoint and oversee **top management**. Top management usually consists of the president or the chief executive officer (**CEO**) as he is sometimes called, the executive vice president, and senior vice presidents. The president is responsible to the board of directors. A typical board might have ten members who are usually from outside the company, along with a few members of top management. The head of the board of directors is called the **chairman of the board**. Interlocking board directorates are where a board member simultaneously serves on the board of a competitor. Unlike some countries, those corporations would violate our **antitrust laws** if combined into a single corporation they hurt businesses or consumers or both, or violated standards of ethical behavior. (There's that *level playing field* again.)

> **Hint**: Officers and directors of our public companies face the increasing possibility that their decisions will be challenged by investors, regulators, and even criminal prosecutors. So it is important that if you serve on a board you understand your obligations and potential liabilities. Lawsuits have arisen in the U.S. because of corporate scandals where top management was not monitored properly by their boards. Many times board members were close friends of top executives and lacked objectivity. The Walt Disney Company underwent a board transformation in 2003 because stockholders felt the chairman had handpicked board members who supported him at the expense of shareholders. To reverse this trend, stockholders are demanding that board

members be totally independent of management so the stockholders' interests are protected. A recent Delaware decision establishes that in certain instances, directors can be liable for excessive compensation decisions under a theory that by making the payments, they are wasting assets.

The corporation generally has departments (or divisions) that report to the president or CEO and perform the three basic operations in a business.

- Production *[pro-DUCK-shun]* involves the planning, designing, and creation of products and services.
- Marketing *[MARR-cut-ing]* identifies those goods and services that customers need and want, and provides them at the right price, place, and time.
- Finance *[FY-nance]* involves the management of money within the business.

One yardstick by which a corporation's performance is measured is **earnings per share**. It is calculated by dividing its net profit by the number of shares outstanding. Typically this is reported to shareholders and the public each quarter and at the end of the fiscal year with comparisons to prior periods. Good earnings can give rise to the price of a company's stock and vice versa with poor earnings.

Corporations must provide their shareholders and the government with an **annual report** that includes financial reports and a discussion of the year's operation. Before preparing the annual report, corporations have an independent **annual audit** performed by an accounting firm to verify the integrity of financial numbers presented in the report. Individuals who are certified by a state to perform this are called **CPAs** (certified public accountants).

Accounting standards in the U.S. are rigid compared to more relaxed international standards because they are established by our Securities and Exchange Commission (SEC), the American Institute of Certified Public Accountants, and the Financial Accounting Standards Board. You might see the term "US GAAP" that is used by some foreign companies when reporting their quarterly operating results in the U.S.; it means **G**enerally **A**ccepted **A**ccounting **P**rinciples in the U.S.

One of the Big Four.

Our four largest public accounting firms—known as the **Big Four**—also offer tax and management consulting services, as do some smaller firms and individual professionals. International in scope with offices around the world, the Big Four are PricewaterhouseCoopers (the world's largest) (www.pwc.com), Ernst & Young (www.ey.com), Deloitte & Touche (www.deloitte.com), and KPMG (www.kpmg.com).

Hint: Companies that hide bad information from the investing public or falsify their numbers can be prosecuted in court. A recent example of this is the widely discussed giant Enron Corporation that deliberately falsified their financial reports, primarily by inflating sales figures. Their large accounting firm, Arthur Andersen, was ordered dissolved and Enron's corporate leaders were sent to jail. When this happened, our Big Five became the Big Four. This is proof that even the "big guys" are not immune from following the law and must pay the consequences. Names of other recent fraudulent companies recognized by Americans include QwestCommumications, Tyco, WorldCom, Adelphia, and HealthSouth Corp. Europeans familiar with Italy's Parmalat case call it Europe's Enron, suggesting that multi-billion dollar frauds are not limited to the U.S.

SMALL BUSINESSES

Most foreigners view America as a land of giant corporations. But small businesses—defined as having fewer than 500 employees—are much more prevalent and have a major influence on our economy. Of the 26 million businesses in America, we have 22 million small businesses of which 16 million have no employees (are owner operated). Women are the full or part owners of nine million businesses and the primary owners in five million of them. Small businesses in the U.S.:

- Represent more than 99% of all employers.
- Employ 53% of private-sector (non-government) workers.
- Represent nearly all the self-employed, which are 7% of our total workforce.
- Provide up to 75% of all new jobs.
- Represent 96% of all exporters of goods to other countries.
- Account for 47% of all sales in the U.S.
- Initiate 55% of innovations.
- Receive 35% of federal contract dollars.
- Account for 38% of jobs in high technology sectors.

Anyone can start a small business, but there are no promises of success. (We discuss how to do this in Chapter W on owning a business.) Each year we have about 500,000 new businesses open, and a similar number close. Studies show that newly opened Asian-owned small businesses survive longer than other newly opened businesses in the U.S., probably because of the owners' dedication to making them succeed. Minorities own nearly 15 percent of American businesses, up from 7 percent in 1982, and 99 percent of these are small businesses. Even though the government fosters the growth of small businesses with their various programs, small-business owners say that complying with government regulations is the most important problem facing them today. Our large businesses have the same complaint. We *are* good at complaining about **red tape** (excessive procedures).

ENTREPRENEURS

Famous 19th century naturalist Charles Darwin said, "It is not the strongest of the species that survive, nor the most intelligent, but the one most responsive to change."

One of our strongest underlying cultural edicts in the U.S. is that we must be responsive to change and move forward. We simply do not know how to **sit still** (accept things as they are); neither did our early settlers 400 years ago. Consequently, our society encourages, assists, and richly rewards individuals and businesses that bring needed changes and improvements.

An **entrepreneur** *[on-trah-prah-NUR]* (another one of our French words, meaning "to undertake") is a person who organizes, manages, and assumes the risks of a business. They are important in the U.S. because they initiate needed change. Our early settlers from Europe were entrepreneurs in a sense. Their belief in striving for change still resides in America. Although small business owners might be viewed as entrepreneurs, in the U.S. we make a further distinction.

Entrepreneurs create substantial wealth and do it relatively rapidly, and in doing so are subject to high risk. Their plan is often based on substantial innovation beyond what small businesses might achieve. Many times these entrepreneurial ventures result in new industries. In the last 20 years or so, such giant U.S. companies as Microsoft, Apple Inc. (that started in the garage of its founder **Steve Jobs**), eBay, Federal Express, and Yahoo!, all started in the minds of a few individuals who envisioned a need for their services or products at a time when others saw no need for change.

Steve Jobs

Money used to set up a new business, regardless of the source, is called **seed money**, just like a seed that starts a plant. The U.S. is the creator and world leader of the **venture capital** industry, something Europe has adopted slowly and progressively. Because banks generally do not initially get involved in financing risky, unproven ventures, venture capitalists often provide private investment dollars to help emerging companies get started. In turn, they may acquire partial ownership—called an **equity position** (stock ownership)—in the venture.

Seed money.

Twenty percent of all U.S. public companies were started with venture capital backing and today account for over 30 percent of the market value of all public firms. Since 1970, they have provided over $340 billion to these then-startup "small businesses" in the U.S. In turn, the new companies have created over 10 million jobs and collected $1.8 trillion in sales. We have about 900 of these venture firms that help plant the seed of what they hope will be the next generation of corporate giants. Sometimes wealthy individuals will do the same. Many of the business schools in our universities now have entrepreneur programs, something that did not exist 25 years ago.

ACCOUNTING SYSTEMS

You may encounter various accounting terms and concepts when dealing with your American counterpart, some of which might differ from your country. **Bookkeeping** refers to the system by which a business keeps track of its financial transactions. Each transaction falls into one of three accounts: **asset** (things owned), **liability** (debt owed), or **equity** (value of ownership). So, if your small business has $10,000 in assets and you have loans of $8,000, your equity position is $2,000.

In the U.S., you will hear the term **double-entry bookkeeping system**, which is based on this mathematical balancing equation: Assets = Liabilities + Equity, or viewed another way, Equity = Assets minus Liabilities. When a financial transaction is posted to one of these three accounts, an offsetting entry is made to another account in order to maintain the equation's balance. One entry will be a **credit** (viewed as a plus), and the other an offsetting **debit** (viewed as a minus).

An accounting system is comprised of accounting records (checkbooks, journals, ledgers, etc.) and a series of processes and procedures. Traditionally, the American accounting system has the following hierarchy of components.

- **Chart of Accounts** – This is merely a listing of all the various accounts and acts like a table of contents to the General Ledger. Accounts are divided into five categories: Assets, Liabilities, Net Assets or Fund Balances, Revenues, and Expenses
- **Journals and Subsidiary Journals** – This is first used to record all detail accounting transactions before they are summarized and then entered into the General Ledger. Journals organize information chronologically and by transaction type. There are four primary journals:
  - Cash Disbursement Journal – Chronological record of checks that are written, categorized using the Chart of Accounts.
  - Cash Receipts Journal – Chronological record of all deposits that are made, categorized using the Chart of Accounts.
  - General Journal – Record of all transactions that do not pass through the checkbook. This includes non-cash transactions such as entries for depreciation and wear and tear of machinery.
  - Subsidiary journals – Such as the Payroll Journal, Accounts Payable Journal, and the Accounts Receivable Journal.
- **General Ledger** – Organizes and groups financial information by specific account. The summary totals from all of the journals are entered into the General Ledger each month. It maintains a year-to-date balance for each account. All balances from the General Ledger are regularly tallied. Once in balance, financial reports can be prepared, including the two discussed below.

The routine aspects of the accounting cycle (recording transactions, posting, etc.) are generally done by **bookkeepers** or data entry clerks. **Accountants** focus on the more analytical aspects of the accounting cycle, such as analyzing transactions and preparing financial statements. Small organizations usually rely on a single individual—sometimes the owner or an outside bookkeeper—to perform all of these functions.

FINANCIAL REPORTS

Two key financial reports are used by U.S. businesses: the **Balance Sheet** and the **Profit and Loss Statement**. Some of their terms or concepts might be used in your business discussions, so understanding them will be to your advantage.

Balance Sheet
XYZ Company
For the period ending _____

	Current Period	Prior Period

ASSETS (anything of value owned by the business)
  Current Assets (can be converted to cash within 12 months)
    Cash (checking and savings accounts)
    Petty Cash (actual cash on hand)
    Accounts Receivable (amounts due from customers)
    Inventory (raw materials, work in process, or finished goods)
    Short Term Investments (stocks, bonds, time-deposits)
  Fixed Assets (also called plant and equipment; not intended for resale)
    Land (original purchase price)
    Buildings
    Equipment
    Furniture
    Automobiles
      Total Assets _____
LIABILITIES (what the company owes)
  Current Liabilities (to be paid in less than 12 months)
    Accounts Payable (owed to suppliers for goods and services)
    Interest Payable (accrued fees due for the period)
    Taxes Payable (tax fees accrued for the period)
  Long Term Liabilities (due beyond 12 months)
    Notes Payable (the balance remaining after all prior payments)
      *Total Liabilities*_____
EQUITY (also called net worth)
  Capital Stock (valuation of stock shares outstanding)
  Retained Earnings (profit/loss accumulation)
    *Total Equity*_____

(Equation: Assets = Total Liabilities + Equity)

Balance Sheet Report – A Balance Sheet is a summary statement of the finances of an organization at a particular date. It shows the assets, liabilities, and equity of a business as of that date. Typically the report will also show the prior period's figures for comparison purposes. It can be viewed as the same report a person fills out to show their credit worthiness if they apply for a loan at a bank. Note the three sections: assets, liabilities, and equity that were discussed above. The assets are separated into current (less than one year) and fixed, while liabilities are separated into current (due in less than one year) and long term. (The word **capitalize** means to record the amount of an item in a balance sheet account statement; an **expensed** item is reflected in the income statement.)

   Profit And Loss Statement – The Profit and Loss Statement, also called the **P&L**, shows the financial operating results for a given period of time. It is usually prepared for a month, a quarter, or a fiscal year, and is of the last day of that period. Simply stated, profits are equal to the difference between revenues and expenses. Notice the different profit calculations made in our sample report below. The profit on sales is first computed as **gross profit** by deducting the cost of the goods sold. Next, by deducting the costs of selling the goods, the **operating profit** is computed. After deducting the other general non-selling expenses, the **net profit** is computed as **earnings before taxes**, and then finally the **net profit after taxes**.

   Hint: A term commonly used in American language is **bottom line**. When used in business discussions, it can refer to net profit. In non-business usage, it might refer to net effect or end result. If someone tells you, **give me the bottom line**, they are telling you to skip over what you have been talking about, finalize your thoughts, and talk about the net result. Another term for this is **cut to the chase** (get to the point). This is exactly what the P&L does for net business results.

Profit and Loss Statement
XYZ Business
For the Period Ending _____

SALES	$1,000,000
(minus) Cost of Goods Sold	-550,000
GROSS PROFIT	450,000
(minus) Selling & Gen. Admin. Expenses	-200,000
OPERATING PROFIT	250,000
(minus) Officer Salaries 50,000	
(minus) Interest 10,000	
(minus) Depreciation 30,000	
(minus) Rent 25,000	
(minus) Other Expenses 15,000	
(minus) *Total Operating Expenses*	-130,000
EARNINGS BEFORE TAXES	120,000
(minus) Taxes on Earnings	-30,000
NET PROFIT AFTER TAXES	90,000

   P&L statements are used for different purposes and can be modified according to serve the needs of the user, such as management or a security analyst who is evaluating a company's stock. The P&L may include all expenses like our sample report above to arrive at a net profit after taxes. One P&L calculation that does not include capital costs is Earnings Before Interest and Taxes (**EBIT**) that refers to all profits, both operating and non-operating, before deducting interest and income taxes. This net result reveals a company's operational ability to make a profit. It also simplifies comparisons of companies that use different capital structures and tax rates.

> **Hint**: Numerous books are available that simplify our accounting basics, including *Accounting for Non-Accountants: The Fast and Easy Way to Learn the Basics* that is available online at amzn.to/accounting4foreigners. Various small business financial software programs are also available to help you get organized, save time, and simplify daily accounting, such as QuickBooks at www.quickbooks.intuit.com and Peachtree at www.peachtree.com.

BUSINESS ORGANIZATION

American businesses are organized in a fashion that best suits their needs. The larger a company becomes, the more formal the organization. In dealing with an American company, you may need to know something about its organization in order to better understand how it operates and how you can determine the right people to deal with if the opportunity arises.

A company that is **vertically integrated** controls many, if not all, of the steps to making its product. Henry Ford vertically integrated the production of his cars by owning iron ore, steel, glass, and other mills involved in producing his cars. A **horizontally integrated** firm seeks to expand the market for its products by offering different products that appeal to different market segments or geographical areas. Ford also achieved horizontal integration by offering different auto brands that appealed to different markets. This is also achieved by buying out competitors. Vertically or horizontally, the company's organization will be diagramed on paper to reflect this integration.

Organization Chart – An organizational chart *[or-gah-nih-ZAY-shun-uhl]* is used to depict the management structure of a business. Some businesses are so small they don't have **org charts**. The charts become helpful when lines of responsibility and communication need to be defined.

> **Hint**: If you are calling on a company, feel free to ask for a copy of their org chart if it will help you understand their needs better. If they don't have one printed, ask your counterpart to sketch one for you. I have sometimes asked secretaries to give me this information before going into a meeting.

The following sample org chart shows one possible organizational structure for an imaginary corporation that makes transistors and light bulbs with national and international sales. Within each of the organizational titles shown below, there might be a lower level structure that could also be diagramed the same way.

The **subsidiary** *[sub-SID-ee-airy]* in our example is another company that is owned by the parent company, sometimes in part, sometimes in whole. It may exist to enhance vertical or horizontal integration. In some companies the president or the chairman might also be called the **Chief Executive Officer (CEO)**. The office of the **Secretary and General Counsel** performs legal and corporate administrative functions. The **Treasurer** keeps tabs on all the assets of the corporation and files government reports. The **Public Relations** Division insures that the public and the industry view the corporation favorably and may advise management on business ethics.

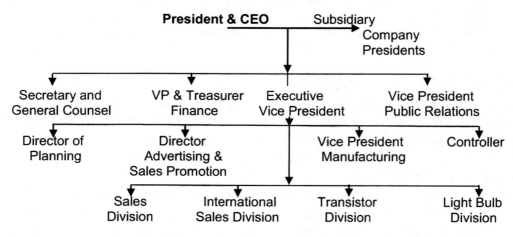

In our example, the Executive Vice President is responsible for the day-to-day operation of the business and has the appropriate divisions reporting to him or her. These include:

- *Director of Planning* – Responsible for analyzing and planning the direction that the company will move in, along with defining new products and markets.
- *Director of Advertising and Promotion* – Promotes the company and its products.
- *Vice President of Manufacturing* – Responsible for procuring materials and producing products.
- *Controller* – Sometimes spelled comptroller, the controller is responsible for day-to-day management of money and accounting systems. People in financial operations are sometimes referred to as **bean counters**.
- *Sales Division* – Consists of sales personnel and managers responsible for selling their products in the U.S.
- *International Division* – Responsible for selling products in foreign countries.
- *Product Divisions* - The two remaining divisions produce their own products and have similar organizations within, such as manufacturing and sales.

In the last 20 years, the term "chief" has become popular in our job titles. The **CEO** (Chief Executive Officer) is often but not always also the president or chairman of a company. The CEO is usually the most important spokesperson and the highest paid member of the company. The **CFO** (Chief Financial Officer) is sometimes the company Treasurer and, in many companies, is the second most important person in the organization. The Chief Operating Officer (**COO**) is responsible for management of day-to-day activities. In some companies he is also the president, but is usually an executive or senior vice president as in our sample organization.

Outsourcing And Organizational Structure – Rather than establishing an organizational department or division to perform a function, a company might employ an outside firm (perhaps yours) to perform it for them. This is called **outsourcing** and might range from manufacturing products or parts, to providing graphic design, computer, or other services. American companies establish customer call centers, for example, in India and other English-speaking nations to slash operating costs. Parts for our Boeing aircrafts are made around the world.

Centralized vs. Decentralized Organization – A company that is centralized requires decisions to be made at the highest level possible; decentralized companies operate in the opposite way. In the U.S., decentralized management is quickly replacing centralized models for managing a business. With global competition, American businesses are seeking more flexible organization structures, especially in high-technology industries that must develop, modify, and even customize products rapidly. As a result, many companies have flattened their organizational structures, reduced the number of managers, and delegated more authority to interdisciplinary teams of workers. This not only allows for decisions to be made faster, it also promotes better employee morale and job growth. Technology encourages this decentralization by providing a line manager or team with information to make the right decisions quickly.

This is exactly what happened to bankrupt General Motors in late 2009 when a new CEO was appointed. His goal was to give people more responsibility and authority deeper in the traditionally over-managed and centralized organization, and then hold them accountable. He quickly changed the management structure and personnel saying they had to move faster, more efficiently, and forget the way GM used to do it because of the **red tape** (excessive control, forms, and reviews) and slow decision making. GM returned to profitability several years later. Our Chrysler motors went through the same thing when Italian automaker Fiat purchased it and **cleaned house** (new personnel and organization) in the same fashion GM did. It, too, returned to profitability in several years.

Hint: If you operate a small business and only have a few employees, you can achieve the benefits of decentralization by empowering your employees to make decisions. It will not only enhance their view of you and your organization, it will make their jobs more interesting. In fact, if an employee asks you how they should do something, reverse it and ask them what *they* would do if *they* owned the business. In this case, they are forced to put on a different **thinking cap** (point of view) and will probably come up with the same answer you would have given them.

Decentralized management also allows upper management executives to concentrate on corporate planning, strategies, and other broader issues because they are not involved in day-to-day decision making. According to surveys, these are the top four activities of top management.

1. Strategic thinking and planning (39%)
2. Plan measurement and monitoring (24%)
3. Internal communication (15%)
4. Crisis management and solving acute problems (11%)

Hint: As you are learning, America is the land of constant change, especially in our competitive businesses environment. As part of his strategic thinking and planning role, an executive friend of mine was concerned about the **changing landscape** (dynamics) of his business. He knew his employees needed to do a better job anticipating and planning change, something his competition was doing better. So he gave his **decision makers** (managers) a copy of the best-selling book, *Who Moved My Cheese?* It provides a simple way to successfully deal with changing times and move ahead effectively. In fact, the title is now used as a slang saying by those familiar with the book. (It is available online from numerous sources including Amazon.com at http://amzn.to/cheeseslang.)

Toyota's Organizational Problem In The U.S. – In 2009, sudden-acceleration problems that had been plaguing Toyota cars in the U.S. finally turned into a public crisis for the world's largest automaker. Over the decade, 2,600 customer complaints were filed with a U.S. government agency with allegations of 34 fatalities due to the problem. Toyota had asserted that many of the complaints were not relevant. Other safety problems were now revealed as well, such as steering and braking that had been suspect in the past. Toyota began recalling several million vehicles in the U.S. for free repair, and 500,000 Prius hybrids worldwide. Shortly after, their Lexus SUV was also found unsafe.

In early 2010, Toyota announced it was stopping production and sales until the problem was fixed. Three U.S. congressional committees and other government regulatory agencies began investigating the company to see if Toyota knowingly ignored these safety issues. A New York grand jury and the Securities and Exchange Commission (SEC) **got on the bandwagon** (joined in) and subpoenaed documents for criminal and securities investigations. Toyota was **in hot water** (very serious trouble).

How did Toyota get into this mess? Investigators say the fractured *organizational structure* of its U.S. subsidiaries impaired Toyota's ability to prevent the safety problems before they reached the crisis stage. Over the prior decade, it had built up a vast complex of engineering centers, test tracks, financial arms, sales offices, and six manufacturing plants from California to New York, from Canada to Mexico.

But Toyota lacked a single U.S. headquarters, so its units here operated independently and reported to Japan in a highly centralized management structure. Records show that Japan let the Americans handle advertising and services and did not interfere. But when it came to money and technical matters, they kept tight control in Japan. So no real decisions were made in the U.S. where the problems were occurring and where managers knew the culture and potential severity of the problems best. Thus there was no coordinated effort to identify, examine, and fix problems.

Documents also show that some of the disjointed U.S. subsidiaries had a strategy to minimize safety recalls, thus saving the company hundreds of millions of dollars even while reports of fatal accidents were increasing. These acceleration safety issues were investigated by a U.S. Toyota operation as far back as 1979 and recorded for U.S. government-required reporting. However, the reports were sent to Japan and ultimately cleansed from the documents submitted by Japan to the U.S. government. Documents further show that Japan had done this for decades.

Toyota headquarters, Japan.

In contrast to Toyota's organization and management structure in the U.S., Honda Motor Co., Japan's second largest automaker, has self-reliant global regions that operate semi-autonomously. Unlike Toyota, its design, engineering, and manufacturing plants in the U.S. report to a single U.S. executive. It has a fine reputation here while Toyota's has been tarnished, perhaps temporarily.

A professor in the U.S. who studied Toyota's quality and safety problems suggests the automaker had a systemic management problem. He had studied 800 cases of corporate and government agency **meltdowns** (rapid collapse or decline) and said the same *cultural* and *organizational* problems affecting Toyota are similar to those that allowed our NASA and Army Corps of Engineers in the U.S. to ignore structural issues leading to the disasters of the Columbia space shuttle (all astronauts were killed because of a mechanical malfunction) and Hurricane Katrina (flooding of New Orleans). He called it arrogance, indolence, and ignorance.

Toyota has since named executives in each of its six regions to watch over quality. It also formed an outside advisory panel led by the former U.S. Secretary of Transportation to give an independent look at future steps to take, and has sped up the pace in which it decides to recall cars. Analysts say this has helped Toyota begin to bridge the gap between the company's inflexible corporate culture and its biggest and most important market, the U.S.

In short, this is a classic example of a foreign company unable to avoid the pitfalls of a centralized management structure, coupled with not understanding the *culture* of another nation and its people who believe **honesty is the best policy**.

LABOR UNIONS

A **labor union** is an association of workers that seeks to improve the economic and social wellbeing of its members through group action. In dealing with a U.S. company, it may be important for you to know if they have unions and what restraints, if any, are placed on the company by that relationship.

In some countries, unions are affiliated with political parties and seek to bring about social change. Korea's unions fought against Japanese colonial rule from 1910 to 1945 and against the South Korean dictatorships of the cold-war era. In the U.S., these formal government ties do not exist, but our unions do try to affect change on issues such as immigrant rights, health care, trade policy, and living wage campaigns. We have thousands of unions, some big, some small. In contrast, the 123 million-member All China Federation of Trade Unions is the sole body permitted to organize workers in China.

Collective bargaining refers to contract negotiations between union and employers. If an agreement is not reached between the two sides, a strike may occur in which the workers do not report to work. Or an employer may conduct a **lockout** in which workers are prohibited from entering the workplace.

Grocery store workers on strike in California.

The U.S. does not impose restrictions on collective bargaining like India and Pakistan where labor legislation and relevant institutions such as the government's labor departments, tribunals, and courts impose major constraints on the process of collective bargaining. Once again, our belief in a **level playing field** comes into play here.

Our labor unions began to form in the 19th century and by the 1950s about 33 percent of nonagricultural workers were union members. Starting in the 1960s their numbers began to decline, and by 2000 only 14 percent were unionized because companies now met most workers' needs on their own. Today it is 12 percent. This drop parallels Korea's where 10 percent of the workforce belongs to unions, down from 20 percent in 1989. The European Union has seen a similar decline over the last 20 years with the four most populated countries having modest levels of unionization: Italy (30%), U.K. (29%), Germany (27%), and France (9%).

Americans' approval of unions has declined as well, from a record-high 75 percent in the 1950s to the lowest approval rating of 48 percent measured in 2009. Unions might bring higher wages and benefits to its members, but this can raise the cost of production for the employer. These increased costs have forced companies to cut back on employment or to transfer their production to foreign countries, notably Asia, where labor costs are considerably lower. This has been particularly true with U.S. textile, electronics, clothing, and other labor-intensive industries.

Hint: If you travel in our state of Hawaii you will learn as I did about the numerous fields that for generations had produced sugar cane and pineapples but now are barren. A native Hawaiian explained to me that with rising living costs there (higher than the continental states), the unions have demanded and got wage increases to the point that their crops can no longer compete with cheaper Caribbean prices. As a result, many of the unskilled field hands are out of work. There are always two sides to these union negotiations.

BANKING AND FINANCE

Banking and finance are important to understanding the overall picture of how our businesses operate. They are also important topics for those foreigners who work here or may wish to invest in America, as many do. Studies show that foreigners generally choose to make U.S. investments to benefit from the highly developed, liquid, and efficient U.S. financial markets, and from our strong corporate governance and institutions.

Our economy relies on banks to provide a vast array of financial services. We have different kinds of banks that differ somewhat in the services they offer, but he term "bank" is generally used to refer to all of them. Commercial banks and savings and loan associations (called **S&L's**) offer these services. Unlike the U.S. where stockholders or private parties own our banks, some countries have both government-owned and private banks.

Ninety percent of the U.S. adult population has a bank account that allows them to write checks. In some economies, cash is mostly used for this purpose. When I traveled in Russia I learned that banks were not trusted by some because a government agency did not insure their deposits. So, when buying a car or apartment, some would take a suitcase full of money to make their purchase. In the U.S., a government agency called the Federal Deposit Insurance Corporation (**FDIC**) (www.fdic.gov).insures deposits in nearly all banks up to $250,000 per customer account.

Americans love to use credit cards, too, allowing us to make one payment monthly to the card issuer, which is normally a bank. Most of our retail establishments, including small businesses, accept credit cards, unlike some countries where they are accepted only in large

cities and hotels. We also refer to credit cards as **plastic**, such as, "Do you take plastic?" Some of our banks also offer **debit cards** that work like a credit card but the money is deducted from the cardholder's checking account at the time of the transaction. The "bank card" in Europe differs from its U.S. counterpart primarily in its concentration on the debit mode, rather than the credit mode.

Credit unions, which function like banks, are formed by people with a common bond, such as belonging to the same church or business. The members pool their savings and earn interest and dividends on them. In turn, they can write checks and borrow when they need a loan, generally at a rate lower than at a bank. A Pew survey reviewed terms for our 12 largest banks issuing credit cards and the 12 largest credit union card issuers and found that credit unions offer more consumer-friendly terms and interest rates. Over a million consumers, fed up with rising fees imposed by banks in 2012, switched to credit unions. And after a public uproar, Bank of America rescinded a $5.00 fee imposed on debit card users. More ways we make our voices heard.

AMERICA'S
CREDIT UNIONS
An association of
8100 credit unions.

The **Federal Reserve System** (www.federalreserve.gov) in the U.S. is the central bank for the government, much like The Reserve Bank of India or the European Central Bank for those nations on the euro currency. The **Fed**, as we call it, performs four functions: influences money and credit conditions in the economy, regulates banks and important financial institutions, maintains the stability of the financial system, and oversees the nation's payments systems. The actions of the Fed directly influence the availability of credit to businesses. It **took its eye off the ball** (not paying attention) in the mid-2000s, contributing to the worst collapse of the economy since 1929.

INVESTMENTS

An **investment** is the use of savings to produce future income. Many foreigners who do well financially have funds available for investments. Others as well throughout the world invest in the U.S. You may hear us refer to four terms when discussing investments.

- **Appreciation** *[ah-pree-shee-AY-shun]* occurs when the market price of an investment you hold is greater than its purchase price. (**Depreciation** is the reverse.)
- When you sell your investment at a profit, this appreciation is called a **capital gain**. If you sell at $20 each the 100 shares of a stock you purchased at $8 each, your capital gain totals $1200. (**Capital loss** is the reverse.)
- **Interest** is money paid to use someone else's money. Banks pay you a fixed rate of interest on your savings accounts so they can loan the funds out at a higher rate.
- **Yield** is a percentage used to reflect how well an investment is paying. If, for example, a stock pays a $1 dividend and the market value of the stock is $10, the yield is an attractive 10% (dividend divided by price). If the stock rises to $20, the yield becomes 5%.

These are five popular types of investments in the U.S.: real estate, savings accounts, bonds, stocks, and mutual funds. Upper-income and college-educated Americans tend to prefer stocks and mutual funds, while Americans with lower incomes and those with no college education favor savings accounts or CDs

Real Estate – People invest in real estate when they buy homes, land, or rental properties. Their value may increase over time and then hopefully sold at a profit. Our retirees sometimes sell the home they have lived in for years at a big profit and buy a smaller house or condominium and live on the difference. The government allows some homeowners an income tax exclusion on the capital gains (profit) resulting from the sale of their home.

Realtors act as intermediaries between sellers and buyers. Some specialize in home sales, others in commercial sales. They handle all the paper work and might assist in arranging financing for the buyer. The seller pays them a pre-defined commission (4-6%) when the transaction is completed. Two nationwide realty firms are Century 21 (www.century21.com) and Coldwell Banker (www.coldwellbanker.com).

A possible investment.

The falling dollar coupled with rising global incomes has made U.S. residential real estate a **hotbed** (intense activity) for international buyers, some of whom use them as vacation homes. Unlike some countries that make it difficult, foreigners can easily purchase real property in the U.S. In fact, they currently account for 8 percent of our total housing market. Canadians are the top foreign purchasers, claiming 17 percent, with the U.K., Mexico, India, and China not far behind. In 2011, the average price paid by foreigners was around $315,000, of which 62 percent were all-cash transactions, and 53 percent were in the sunshine states of Florida, California, Arizona, and Texas.

Savings Accounts – Funds deposited at a bank earn interest at a specified annual rate. There are several different types of savings accounts. **Passbook** savings accounts pay the lowest interest rate and the depositor can withdraw funds at any time with no penalty. Parents might have their young children begin saving their money in a **piggy bank** (small container shaped like a pig or other item) and then graduate to a passbook savings account as they get older, as I did. **Money market accounts** pay a rate of interest that reflects the availability of money in the short term financial markets. Funds in a **certificate of deposit** (**CD**) cannot be withdrawn without penalty for a specified period, such as one or two years, but the fixed interest rates are higher than passbook and money market accounts. CDs are popular savings vehicles for a child's college education. Another vehicle with tax advantages is the **529 education plan** designed to encourage saving by offering state income tax deductions for all or part of the contributions of the donor. Another benefit is the principal grows tax-deferred and distributions for the beneficiary's college costs are also exempt from tax. Brokerage houses and mutual funds can set up a program for you.

Piggy bank.

Bonds – Bonds represent a debt that the issuer of the bond has to repay to the buyer of the bond (bondholder) who is loaning money to the issuer. There are different types of bonds, both government and corporate. The bondholder is entitled to a specified interest payment (rate) and is entitled to full repayment at a specified date (maturity date) for a specified amount (face value). Although some banks sell government-issued bonds to the public, our stock brokerage firms offer a wider selection of bonds to choose from.

U.S. Savings Bond

- **Savings bonds** issued by the federal government are popular among investors because they are sold in small denominations and are safe. A Series EE bond, for example, costs $25 to purchase and can be redeemed (cashed in) in 17 years for $50. They can be redeemed before this date at less than full value. Some parents buy these for a young child's education in later years.

- **Treasury bonds** are issued by the U.S. government. They pay a higher rate of interest than savings bonds. The minimum amount is $1,000. Like stocks, the value of **T-Bonds** fluctuates. Treasury bonds mature over ten years and can be sold on the market before their maturity.

- **Treasury notes** are medium-term debt securities issued by the U.S. government. **T-Notes** generally mature in two, five, and ten years.

- **Treasury bills**, issued by the government in denominations starting at $1,000, mature in one, three, six, or nine months. **T-Bills** do not pay scheduled fixed interest payments to the holder like most bonds do, but are sold at a discount from their face value. If a 180-day T-bill is priced at $9,900, for example, you pay that amount and in 180 days you will receive $10,000.

- **Municipal** *[mew-NISS-ah-pull]* **bonds** are issued by state and local governments. The interest on these is not subject to federal and/or state income tax. These are attractive to individuals in high tax brackets who want to shelter their income from taxes. They generally pay lower interest rates than corporate bonds.

- **Corporate bonds** are issued by business firms usually in units of $1,000 and regular interest payments are made to the holder until the bond matures. Based on interest rate fluctuations, their market value may rise or fall below their redemption value. **Junk bonds** are lower quality bonds (more risk) that usually pay higher interest rates than other types of bonds. The highest security rating for a bond is Aaa; the lowest C.

U.S. Steel bond.

404

To show the wide variety of rates a bond investor can choose from, these are relative rankings—from highest interest rates paid to the lowest—of different bond types: junk bonds, corporate bonds, municipal bonds, 30-year T-Bonds, 10-year T-Notes, 2-year T-Notes, 6-month T-Bills, 3-month T-Bills, and 1-month T-Bills. The rates are affected by risk and length of maturity.

Stocks – Unlike bonds that represent debt to the issuing entity, stocks represent ownership in the entity for those who buy them. Generally, stocks are traded on stock exchanges in units of 100 shares. **Common stocks** provide a means for becoming an owner in a company and sharing in dividend payments. **Preferred stocks** have features of both common stocks and bonds, but like corporate bonds, they also promise a fixed rate of return (interest payment). You will hear the term **short sale**, for which a person borrows stock and sells it, then hopefully buys it back at a cheaper price and returns it to the loaner, typically a brokerage firm. (Not recommended for beginning investors.)

One common yardstick used to judge the relative value of a stock is the popular **price-earnings ratio**, referred to as the **P/E**. Companies report their earnings per share by dividing their quarterly or yearly earnings (net profit) by the number of shares of stock outstanding. In turn, by dividing the market price of a company's stock by its earnings per share, a relative number is arrived at that might give insight as to whether or not the stock appears to be over- or underpriced. For instance, if a company earned $2.00 per share for the past 12 months and the price of the stock is currently $40, it has a P/E of 20. Historically, the overall market has had a P/E average of 15, which implies investors would pay $15 for $1 in earnings.

> **Hint**: Some fast-growing technology shares might have a P/E over 40 while some public utility companies might have a P/E under 10. In general, a high P/E suggests that investors are expecting higher earnings growth in the future compared to companies with a lower P/E. Since it is a relative number, it is useful for comparing the P/E ratios of one company to other companies in the same industry, to the market in general, or against the company's own historical P/E.

You will hear the term **Wall Street** used in conjunction with finance and stock trading in the U.S. Wall Street is the name of an important street in the center of New York City's financial district where brokerages, banks, and stock exchanges are located. (The World Trade Towers were in this district.) You might hear, "What did Wall Street do today?" meaning, what did the stock market do today?

Wall Street, NYC

To answer that question, the **Dow-Jones Industrial Average** is computed at the close of the market each day and reported in the media to indicate how the market performed that day. The stocks of 30 large companies (most are traded on the New York Stock Exchange) are used to compute the relative price movement of the overall market

405

based on these 30 stocks. India's Sensex 30 is that country's version of the U.S. Dow-Jones, as are London's FTSE 100 index, Frankfurt's DAX 30, the Paris CAC 40, Tokyo's Nikkei 225, and Hong Kong's Hang Seng index.

The Dow-Jones average was about 500 in the 1950s and has approached 14,000 in recent years. Over long periods, the **return** on stocks (price appreciation plus dividends) has consistently exceeded the return on bonds and other types of investments. For example, from 1926 to 2001, the stock market returned an average annual gain of 10.7 percent. The next best performing asset class, bonds, returned 5.3 percent.

You might hear of other averages, such as the **Wilshire-5000** that tracks 5,000 different stocks. The Standard & Poor average, referred to as the **S&P 500**, tracks 500 of the largest company stocks based on **market capitalization**, which is the total market value of all outstanding shares of a company's stock. Beginning in 2012, Apple Inc. had the world's largest capitalization at $500 billion (higher than the gross domestic products of Poland, Belgium, Sweden, Saudi Arabia, or Taiwan) followed by oil giant ExonMobil at $400 billion. Microsoft in 1999 was the only company ever to have a valuation of $600 billion; it now sits at $270 billion due to its price per share decline.

A **blue chip** (top quality, outstanding) is a large nationally known company whose stock over the years has been reliable and typically high priced with a low yield. (A blue chip in poker can have the highest value.) The **Fortune 500** list provides a ranking of the 500 largest companies in America based on revenue, the largest of which are blue chips. Published annually by *Fortune* magazine (www.fortune.com), their website has the complete listing and provides a direct link to each company's website.

Fortune 500 companies.

The term "**market**" refers to buying and selling stocks in the stock market. If someone asks if you are "in the market," they are asking, "Are you now buying stocks?" If economic conditions are bad, you might be "out of the market" or **sitting on the sidelines**, a sport term meaning not playing at the moment.

Stocks are generally riskier than bonds, so investors cannot be sure that stocks will always outperform bonds. For this reason, some investors purchase both stocks and bonds for their **portfolio** *[port-FOE-lee-oh]*, which consists of all the investments of an individual. **Diversification** occurs when an investor spreads his or her money around to different investment vehicles and markets in order to minimize concentration in any one area. He or she then has a diversified portfolio. We have a cautionary saying: **Don't put all your eggs in one basket**, because if you do and you drop the basket, all your eggs might be lost.

Bull and bear bookends.

Bears and **bulls** are symbols used to denote how the market is moving. Bears signify a downward stock or market, and bulls signify their going up or people who are optimistic about them. You might be asked if you are "bearish" or "bullish" about the market or a particular stock.

> **Hint**: You will also hear Americans use "**bearish**" and "**bullish**" for things other than the stock market. If you are asked, "Are you bullish about improving trade relations between America and your country?" you are being asked if you think things are going to get better.

An investor buys and sells stocks with firms called **brokerages**. The individual within the brokerage you deal with is called a licensed **stockbroker**. He or she will execute your order upon your instruction. A commission is charged for this service. The U.S. has four primary **stock exchanges** where securities are traded: New York Stock Exchange, NASDAQ *[NAZZ-dak]*, American, and Over the Counter (OTC).

A relatively recent development has been the establishment of online brokerages that provide **online investing**. These firms allow their customers to execute trades using their computers without having to speak to a broker. Their commissions are about $10 per trade, much cheaper than the traditional brokerage house. A

Brokerage firm.

stockbroker in a traditional brokerage firm, however, can offer research and investment advice, something that is not generally offered free by online brokerages. Some of my foreign friends have both types of accounts. One such online firm is www.tdameritrade.com.

Mutual Funds – These are companies that invest professionally in a variety of securities and sell shares in those securities in a bundle to investors. The term mutual fund is less widely used outside of the U.S. Mutual fund companies employ specialists who select specific stocks or bonds based on the nature of a specific fund they manage, such as money market funds, short term bonds, long term bonds, growth stocks, income stocks, technology stocks, small companies, large companies, etc. We have over 10,000 such funds in America to choose from.

Major mutual fund companies may have dozens of different funds to choose from and smaller funds may only have a few. Mutual fund companies have websites that provide insight into their services and funds offered, such as this large fund: www.fidelity.com. Some banks and stockbrokers sell these same mutual funds, too.

Mutual fund listings.

Some of our large daily newspapers provide a quarterly list of various mutual funds by category and how they fared during the quarter. *Money Magazine* (see a list of business publications below) provides frequent mutual fund recommendations for its readers as well as its online site at www.money.cnn.com. *U.S. News and World Report* magazine (www.usnews.com) provides an online yearly summary of the best performing mutual funds in the prior year.

Hint: You can purchase mutual funds directly from a mutual fund company generally without a commission fee, unlike some banks and brokerages that sell them to you for a fee. They are an excellent way to get started investing in the stock market.

RETIREMENT INVESTMENT PLANS

The U.S. has a federal **Social Security Program** (www.socialsecurity.gov) that requires employees to have money deducted from their paychecks and paid into their government-sponsored retirement account. The employer must match the amount contributed by its employees. When we retire, we are paid a monthly amount based on our life's earnings and what we paid into the fund. The day after President Bush was reelected for his second term, he said one of his top legislative priorities would be overhauling the Social Security Program, something that is always being explored. He suggested a modification to the current system that would allow individuals to invest a small portion of their paycheck

Social Security card.

deductions into safe stocks, mutual funds, and other appropriate retirement vehicles in order to achieve higher retirement pay. He failed to convince Congress of the value of his **newfangled** (novel) idea.

In addition to this retirement program, the government allows us to pay money tax-free into voluntary, non-government operated retirement accounts. Some mutual fund companies, brokerages, and banks can assist their customers in setting up these retirement investment accounts. With some plans, the money paid into an account is not taxable as wages in the year it is earned. When we withdraw the funds when we retire, they are taxable, presumably at lower tax rates because our incomes are generally lower when we are not working. These **Individual Retirement Accounts (IRAs)** can be set up by anybody, worker or non-worker. One of our IRAs, the **Roth IRA,** allows the money to be taxable in the year it is earned, rather than when it is withdrawn in retirement years.

Another retirement program you will hear about is called a **401(k) plan**. This is an employer-sponsored savings plan that allows employees to contribute a portion of their gross salary to a savings or profit-sharing retirement plan. These plans, in turn, invest their money in stocks and mutual funds. Employee contributions and income earned on the plan are tax-deferred until withdrawn at age 59.5 or older. Money directed to the plan may be partially matched by the employer. (The 401(k) is named for the section of the federal tax code that authorizes it.)

Hint: If you have the option of signing up for a 401(k), it is one of the best investments you can make. Your employer is giving you money and all the earnings are tax-free until you retire. If you interview for a job with an American company, be sure to inquire about their 401(k) or other retirement plan and factor that in to your overall evaluation of your wages. Learn more about applying for a job in Chapter X - Getting a Job.

We have **financial planners** and **advisors** who for a fee can advise you how to invest your funds. Some financial planners assess every aspect of your financial life—savings, investments, insurance, taxes, retirement, and estate planning—and help you develop a detailed strategy or financial plan for meeting all your financial goals. Like everything else in the U.S., some do a good job, some don't. They generally take a commission on what they sell you, be it an insurance policy or a mutual fund. You can get similar investment advice for free from an insurance broker or from a mutual fund company with no fees. One nationwide advisory firm is Edward Jones Advisors (www.edwardjones.com). This government website provides helpful tips for investing wisely: www.sec.gov/investor/links/toptips.htm.

BUSINESS PUBLICATIONS

America has many excellent finance and business-oriented newspapers and magazines that can help you learn more about managing your money and investing in the U.S. Many also have websites that provide online information.

Try to use the names of these publications and refer to an article if possible if you interact with American business people, even when applying for a job. It might impress them. (It would impress me.)

- The *Wall Street Journal* is a well-respected daily business newspaper. In addition to listing stock and bond prices, it discusses many different American and international business topics. (www.wallstreetjournal.com)

- Most daily U.S. newspapers have a business section that provides stock and bond prices, articles on general business topics, as well as investing. Perhaps the best is *The New York Times*, which also offers information online. (www.newyorktimes.com)
- *Barron's [BEAR-uns]* is a trusted weekly business magazine that deals with investments and business. (www.barrons.com)
- *Business Week* is another. (www.businessweek.com)
- *Fortune* magazine might be found on tables in corporate waiting rooms. It covers broad business issues, similar to those issues that might concern corporate leaders. (www.fortune.com)
- *Forbes* magazine is another good business magazine. (www.forbes.com)
- *Money* magazine is published monthly primarily for the investing public. I refer my friends to this magazine if they want to learn about investing their money. (www.money.cnn.com)

KINGS OF BUSINESS

In the 19th century we had many successful inventor/business leaders who made a major impact on America, the world's economies, and our lifestyle as we know it today. Many were immigrants. In fact, 204 of the Fortune 500 companies today were founded by immigrants or the children of immigrants. The names of these early kings of business are recognized by many in the U.S. Referring to them will show you are **in the know** (knowledgeable). They are listed chronologically.

Eli Whitney (1765-1825) is remembered as the inventor of the cotton gin. In ten days he constructed a crude model that separated fiber from seed that was being done by hand with slaves. This invention made the South prosperous. Whitney also developed the concept of interchangeable machine parts that gave birth to the mass-production concept.

Cotton gin.

The French **DuPont** *[DEW-pont]* family is notable in U.S. chemical history. E.I. Du Pont (1771-1834) opened a gunpowder mill in Delaware in 1802. His grandson developed a cheap and superior blasting powder that made the DuPont Company a leader in the manufacture of explosives. Today, it is one of the largest corporations in the world producing synthetic fibers (it pioneered nylon), cellophane, synthetic rubber, chemicals, paint, and other products.

DuPont

Cornelius Vanderbilt (1794-1877) was an American railroad and shipping pioneer of Dutch heritage. In 1851, at the height of the California gold rush, he opened a shipping line from the East Coast to California, including land transit across Central America in the area where the Panama Canal would eventually be built. By 1873 he connected Chicago with New York City by rail. He amassed a great fortune and founded Vanderbilt University.

Vanderbilt

Andrew Carnegie *[car-NEH-gee]* (1835-1919) was a Scottish-born American. A leading steel manufacturer and one of the wealthiest individuals of his time, Carnegie believed that people could improve their lives through hard work. He used his huge fortune to establish many cultural, educational, and scientific institutions, donating about $10 billion in today's dollars. Carnegie's Endowment for International Peace (www.ceip.org) still seeks to end wars). He said, "People rarely succeed unless they have fun in what they are doing."

Carnegie

J. P. Morgan (1837-1913) became one of the greatest financiers in the U.S. The House of Morgan controlled railroads, shipping, the manufacture of agricultural tools, telephones, telegraphs, electrical power, insurance, and city transportation. After Morgan bought Andrew Carnegie's company, he founded the giant U.S. Steel Corporation that became the nation's first billion-dollar corporation. He was active in financing young companies that are major enterprises today. Morgan made gifts to education, libraries, and museums. Today, JPMorgan Chase & Co. is one of the oldest, largest, and best-known financial institutions in the world.

Morgan

John D. Rockefeller (1839-1937) founded Standard Oil Company that controlled 90 percent of petroleum in the U.S. before the government ended its monopoly in the early 1900s. His ancestors are traced to French Huguenots who fled to Germany in the 17th century. He was one of the wealthiest individuals of his time and a symbol of big business in the U.S. Some, however, have criticized the unfair business methods he used in developing his vast empire. He later became famous for his philanthropy (charity). His grandson donated family property for the construction of the United Nations building in New York City. He said, "Singleness of purpose is one of the chief essentials for success in life, no matter what may be one's aim."

Rockefeller

Hint: When we joke with someone about how **tight** (lack of funds) our finances are, we might say, "Who do you think I am, Rockefeller?"

Thomas Edison (1847-1931), of Dutch and Canadian heritage, is one of the world's greatest inventors and industrial leaders. In his lifetime, he patented 1,093 inventions, the most famous of which was the incandescent light bulb. He also developed the phonograph, the radio tube, the movie camera, a small box for viewing moving films, and made the electrification of cities a reality. He also improved upon the original design of the telegraph and Alexander Graham Bell's telephone. Today, the General Electric Company he founded has extensive international operations. Sometimes working twenty hours a day, he said, "Genius is one percent inspiration and 99 percent perspiration."

Edison

Alexander Graham Bell (1847-1922) invented the telephone in the 1870s. After that, the Scottish-born inventor continued experiments in communication that culminated in the invention of the transmission of sound on a beam of light—a precursor of today's optical fiber systems. He also worked in medical research and invented techniques for teaching speech to the deaf. In 1888, he founded our National Geographic Society

Bell

(www.nationalgeographic.com) that is still dedicated to world exploration and enlightenment. It publishes a monthly magazine and has an educational TV channel. He said, "Before anything else, preparation is the key to success."

George Eastman (1854-1932) started Eastman Kodak Company in 1889 that made photography accessible to amateurs by introducing the low-cost, easy-to-operate Kodak camera and the roll of film. For a century it was a world leader for photographic film products and commanded nearly 90

Eastman

percent of film and camera sales in the U.S. It also invented the core technology used in digital cameras today. Then in the 1980s, Japanese competitor Fujifilm

Kodak Brownie, circa 1910. (Smithsonian)

entered the U.S. market with lower-priced film and supplies, but Kodak refused to believe American consumers would switch from its revered brand. Beginning in the late 1990s, Kodak struggled financially with the decline of photographic film sales and from its slowness in making the transition to digital photography that it invented. Then in 2012, the 123-year old company filed for **Chapter 11 bankruptcy** protection that permits reorganization under our bankruptcy laws. The George Eastman House (www.eastmanhouse.org) is the world's oldest photography museum with a collection of 400,000 photographs by 9,000 photographers.

> **Hint**: There is not a better example of the consequences of complacent corporate culture, especially in today's global economy, than the once proud Eastman Kodak Company. Another example occurred with the introduction of small Japanese cars in the U.S. With the oil embargo of 1973 along with strict pollution controls and safety regulations imposed by the U.S. government, American manufacturers **threw up their hands** (gave up) and began building poor quality, poorly engineered automobiles. (I even had one.) The Japanese saw the opportunity to succeed where American companies had given up. Today, Japanese brands account for nearly 40 percent of new car sales in the U.S., German models 12 percent, and Korean models seven percent.

Henry Ford (1863-1947) was the leading manufacturer of American automobiles in the early 1900s. Of Irish heritage, he developed the assembly line method of production and manufacture of his own parts that reduced the costs of his automobiles. In 1908 when the Ford Motor Company

Ford

introduced the Model T, it sold for $850. By 1924, assembly line innovations helped reduce the price to $290. An automobile was now within reach of the average family and America was never the same. Ford Motor Company today has 90 manufacturing operations worldwide. Paralleling

1915 Model T Ford.

America's culture, Ford once said, "I am looking for a lot of men who have an infinite capacity to not know what can't be done."

The Wright brothers, Wilbur (1867-1912) and Orville (1871-1948) of English heritage, invented and built the first successful airplane. In 1903, they made the world's first flight in a power-driven, heavier-than-air machine in North Carolina. With Orville at the controls, the plane flew 37 meters (120 feet) and was in the air 12 seconds. Thus began the aircraft industry as we know it today.

Man's first powered flight, 1903.

Charles Lindbergh was three years old at the time. Twenty-four years later he was the overnight hero of the world when he became the first to make a nonstop transatlantic flight from the U.S. to France. (The classic film, *The Spirit of St. Louis* (1957), is about Lindbergh.) Amelia Earhart also became world famous in 1932 as the first woman to fly across the Atlantic Ocean alone and later went on to establish speed records. (The 2009 movie, *Amelia*, traces the life of this famed aviatrix who was lost at sea and never heard from again.)

OTHER INNOVATORS

America has always encouraged and rewarded inventors who design and produce new products that improve our lives. For this reason we are protective of intellectual property and patents. The following are additional famous innovators and their products whose names are recognized by the public. Some of our major companies carry the names of these innovators today and their products are sold around the world.

1807 – Robert Fulton opens American rivers to two-way travel with the invention of his steamboat. This leads to further westward expansion and travel throughout the world.

Fulton's steamboat.

1831 – Cyrus McCormick invents a mechanical reaper that cuts standing grain and sweeps it up for collection. It could harvest more grain than five men working with hand tools.

1836 – Samuel Colt invents the first pistol that was equipped with a revolving cylinder containing five or six bullets and an innovative cocking device.

1838 – Samuel Morse invents Morse code and in 1844 the first telegraph message is sent by wire, ushering in the beginning of a new era in communication.

Morse code machine.

1838 – John Deere develops the first American cast steel plow. Today, Deere & Company is a leading manufacturer of agricultural machinery in the world, employing 47,000 people in 27 countries.

1843 – Charles Goodyear perfects his process for vulcanizing rubber to create a soft, pliable substance unaffected by temperature.  Today, Goodyear operates 55 plants in 20 countries.

1846 – Isaac Singer builds the first commercially successful sewing machine.

1853 – Elisha Otis's passenger lift (elevator), rising 40 feet per minute at an exposition in New York City, causes a sensation and contributes to high-rise building.

1858 – George Pullman encourages long distance rail travel by building the first successful railroad sleeping car called the Pullman Railroad Car.

1859 – "Colonel" Edwin Drake drills and strikes oil at a depth of 69 feet at Titusville, Pennsylvania. This ushers in the world's first oil boom that starts oil exploration in the U.S. (The U.S. is the world's third largest producer today behind Russia and Saudi Arabia.)

First oil well.

1869 – George Westinghouse invents the air brake that enables trains to be stopped for the first time by a locomotive engineer. It replaced dangerous, manually applied brakes. His company makes small appliances found in our homes.

1885 – William Burroughs invents the first practical adding and listing machine.

1886 – Ottmar Mergenthaler invents the linotype composing machine. A German immigrant working in a Baltimore machine shop, he worked for ten years to realize his dream. It is regarded as the greatest

Burroughs' machine.

advance in printing since the development of moveable type 400 years earlier. One man operating his machine casts metal letters in one step, doing the work of eight. Newspaper, magazine and book publishing expands rapidly from this point on.

1886 – Coca-Cola is invented by Doctor John Pemberton, a pharmacist from Atlanta, Georgia. A single share of Coca-Cola stock purchased in 1919 when the company went public is worth over $290,000 today.

1890 – Herman Hollerith (1860-1929) invents an electrically-driven tabulator based on a combination of punched cards and electromagnetics. His company eventually becomes IBM (International Business Machines).

1902 – Willis Carrier designs the first system to control room temperature and humidity. Many air conditioning units around the world today carry his name.

1927 – Philo Farnsworth demonstrates the first television.

SUCCESSFUL FOREIGN HERITAGE BUSINESS PERSONS

Proving that the American Dream is open to anyone who wants to work hard, many immigrant business people have succeeded in the U.S. Here is a sampling of a few.

- French-Iranian American entrepreneur Pierre Morad Omidyar came to the U.S. as a youngster. When he was 28 years old he founded the prolific eBay Internet auction site. He is the 145th richest person in the world and 47th in the U.S. "I started eBay as an experiment, as a side hobby, while I had my day job."

Omidyar

- Anthony Rossi (1900–1993) was an Italian immigrant who founded Tropicana Products in 1947, a producer of orange juice in Florida. It grew from 50 employees to over 8,000 in 2004 and became one of the world's largest producers and marketers of citrus juice.

Rossi

- George Soros, who survived Nazi persecution of Jews and later fled communist oppression in his native Hungary, established the most successful investment fund in the U.S. "It's more difficult to bring about positive change than it is to make money." *Forbes* magazine reports his net worth at $22 billion.

Soros

- Born in Taiwan, Jerry Yang created the popular Yahoo! website in 1995 when he was a Stanford engineering graduate student. *Forbes* magazine estimates his net worth at $1.2 billion.

Yang

- Sergey Brin was born in Russia and earned degrees in mathematics and computer science in the U.S. In 1998, along with another Stanford University doctoral student, he launched the Google search engine. Shortly thereafter, it dominated the Web search business. He is the fourth youngest billionaire in the world.

Brin

- Indra Nooyi was born in India and got her master's degree at Yale. After a stint with several U.S. companies including a management consulting firm, she eventually became Chairman and CEO of PepsiCo, the second largest food and beverage business in the world. *Forbes* magazine ranks her as the fifth most powerful woman in the world. She says, "It's a multicultural world out there, and we all have to interact with people who are different." (Another theme of this book.)

Nooyi

- Sidney Taurel was born a Spanish citizen in Casablanca, Morocco, and studied in France and the United States. In 1971, he got a job as a marketing associate at Eli Lilly, the giant pharmaceutical company. As chairman and chief executive of Lilly since the late 1990s, he has also served on several U.S. government advisory bodies. He says,

Taurel

415

"Home has always been wherever I am living at the moment," the same credo of other successful immigrant Americans.

- Charles Wang came to America from Shanghai as a child of eight. He built Computer Associates into a software giant second only to Microsoft. At a dedication speech at a New York university in 2002 when he donated a new building he said, "I've always been proud to say that I'm an immigrant in this great land—proud because immigrants have helped to build this country of ours. Now, like so many of my fellow immigrants, I've been through what they call the **school of hard knocks** [learned from failures]. These challenges and experiences are so central to the character of the United States and its people that it's almost like the air we breathe."

Yang

416

V

BUSINESS CUSTOMS

When you enter a country, find out its customs. – Chinese proverb

As you learned in the prior chapter, American and foreign businesses differ in the way they organize and operate. But they also differ in people-related customs as well, the subject of this chapter. That was a major concern of the international U.S. business executive I met on the plane that I told you about in the beginning of Chapter U.

Business meeting.

When you understand these differences you will feel more comfortable in your relations with Americans and their business organizations. And you might avoid costly mistakes. Many of the general social customs we've been discussing throughout this book apply to business situations, too. One difference, however, is that we tend to be more formal (perhaps more professional is the correct term) in our offices than in our homes or other social situations.

This chapter discusses how to make your business appointment with an American and then how to conduct yourself in the business meeting.

MAKING YOUR BUSINESS APPOINTMENT

Foreign business people might find it relatively easy to locate and set up a meeting with the right person in a U.S. business. This is because many of our businesses have decentralized management that allow for quick decision making. This contrasts with some countries where it can be difficult to understand who will sign a contract to finalize a business deal. Those countries have webs of influence that are more powerful than the actual parties involved in making the deal. In Japan, for example, it may be the *keiretsu*—industrial groups that are linked by a confusing web of business ties, money lending relationships, and cross-ownerships (owning stock in companies that a company does business with), which in some instances are illegal in the U.S.

In some cultures, business people often do business only with those they consider "friends." This requires a great deal of time getting to know a prospective business partner at other social functions before discussing business at all. Americans, on the other hand like to **get down to business** much sooner. If you feel you have a product or a service of value to a U.S. business concern, feel free to arrange a meeting even if you have not yet become a "friend." Profit-oriented American business people value what you have to offer above the short-term social relationship they might have with you. We also prefer people to be **up front** (forthright) about their needs and our friends to be real rather than based on monetary gain.

American Airlines surveyed business people from around the world to see if they would do business with someone they "did not like personally." About 45 percent of American business people said they would do business; only 23 percent of Asians said they would. Again, our business interests take a **front row seat** (prime importance) so to speak.

Business people in some cultures, such as in Asia, are reluctant to say "no" to you out of respect. This even extends to arranging for a business meeting even if they know they have no interest in what you have to offer. The opposite is true in America; if we don't want a meeting we will tell you so. We tend to **tell it like it is**.

A simple telephone call to a *lower-level* person in a U.S. business might be all you need to arrange an appointment. If you are not sure whom you should talk to, sometimes the telephone operator or receptionist can direct you to the correct department.

Introductory Letter - To make an appointment with a *senior* person in a business, it is best to first send them an introductory letter before making a telephone call. Typically the secretary to a senior decision maker will look at your letter and in a few seconds will either read on, send it to another person, pass it to her boss, or discard it. Your letter might be competing with a dozen or more letters daily, so it is important to send an effective one. This is how you do it.

The letter (and your sales presentation later) should follow our popular **AIDA** *[awh-E-duh]* format that we use to create **A**ttention, **I**nterest, **D**esire, and **A**ction. To do this, the letter should be *one page* with short short sentences and contain these elements.

- *Salutation* – Use the correct name of the individual. Speak to the secretary to get the right person and the right spelling. Using their last name, personalize your contact as Dear Mr., Mrs., or Ms. instead of Sir or Madam.
- *Headline* – Start your letter with an opening sentence of about 20 words or less that captures the reader's attention, the same thing newspaper headlines do. Tell them how they will benefit from your product or service. "Our computerized production control system will reduce your production costs at least 20 percent as it has done for 87 of our clients" is a good example.
- *Credibility and Relevance* – Refer to a specific significant benefit your company offers the reader's business. To show your credibility, use a few

418

technical words that the reader at his or her management level would use. Explaining reduced costs creates relevance to most business people.

- *How and Why* – Point out how benefits are derived and how your product or business is unique.
- *Action* – Tell your reader that you will phone him or her in the near future to arrange an exploratory meeting. If the reader is interested, his or her secretary might call you first to make arrangements.
- *Goodbye* – Conclude with "Sincerely," or "Best wishes," followed by your signature.

Remember, you are trying to sell the *appointment*, not the product or service in your letter, a common mistake made by novices that can be a **turnoff** (unappealing) to the busy reader. Years of advertising research suggests these are the five most important elements to getting a favorable response from a mailing.

1. A stated single impressive benefit.
2. It is easy to read.
3. It gets the reader involved.
4. It is something new.
5. It is believably unique or different.

Setting The Time – Let's assume you **land** (are offered) a meeting with an American at his or her office. Consider these points when setting the time.

- You may ask for another time if the one your contact (or his secretary) suggests is inconvenient; we do not consider this rude as it might be overseas.
- Factor in traffic when you make your appointment. In our large cities you might spend one to two hours during rush hours (8-10 a.m. – 4-6 p.m.) to get to your appointment.
- If you are coming from out of town, feel free to ask for hotel references.
- General business hours in the U.S. are from 9 a.m. to 5 p.m. Monday through Friday. I discovered he hard way that some European, South American, and Asian countries take an afternoon break for several hours and their businesses shut down. We have a one-hour lunch break but do not shut down. You might even have to meet with a busy executive on his lunch hour.

PREPARING FOR YOUR APPOINTMENT

Once you have an appointment time set, you need to prepare for your meeting before you **step out the door** (leave for your meeting).

Your Timing – Plan to arrive at your appointment at least 10 to 15 minutes early in case your contact can see you earlier than planned and might spend more time with you. This also provides you with a buffer zone to minimize your chance of being late. American business people tend to be punctual, so if you arrive late it could reflect on you. If you are in traffic and can't make your appointed time, call and tell your counterpart or his secretary what time you think you will be there.

If you arrive late, be sure to apologize, *but not* profusely, as is done in Japan where a late arriver must give a deep, ingratiating apology. Likewise, if you have to wait beyond your appointed time to see your contact, do not consider this rude (as you might in your country) because he probably couldn't end a previous appointment.

Advance Mailing – After you schedule your appointment, it is considered very professional to mail the decision maker a letter to thank him for the appointment, confirm the time and date, along with *brief* information about your company and product/service that he can review before you meet. However, do not assume he has read the material when you meet with him. The Vietnamese like to receive a FAX outlining the meeting's agenda and issues to be discussed prior to the actual meeting. There is nothing wrong with doing this in America, but it is not expected.

Your English – Your English is almost certain to be better than your counterpart's grasp of *your* language. And if English is your second language and your contact doesn't understand something you say, he will probably ask for clarification. Such a response might be considered rude in some cultures, but not in ours. In fact, before you begin your presentation, tell him to let you know when he needs clarification, but *do not* apologize for your English; it will weaken your position.

If you are not sure how to pronounce your contact's name, ask his secretary while you are scheduling your appointment on the phone, or when you see her in person before the meeting. If you forget, it is okay to ask him yourself during your meeting.

To help with your presentation, make a brief outline in advance of what you want to discuss and then rehearse it out loud, pronouncing consonants and elongating vowels, techniques discussed in Chapter Z on speaking better English. You may even take the outline to the meeting with you and refer to it casually.

You might want to look up some appropriate American **buzz words** (action words that grab one's attention), write them down, and study their syllables and pronunciation so you say them correctly. Such words might include *profit, efficiency, payback, cost savings, time savings, patented, unique, rate of payback, guarantee,* or other empowering words or unique phrases that apply to your product or service.

Your Appearance – Dress conservatively as suggested in Chapter P on dress and appearance under the business dress section. Be well groomed. Pay attention to the shine

420

on your shoes. Nice briefcases create a favorable appearance. Cardboard boxes and loose folders with rubber bands are not professional looking.

Your Handouts – If you plan to show pictures or give handouts, make sure they are in proper sequence in your briefcase *before* you go to your meeting so you don't have to search for them during your presentation. Take a list of customers who would give your company a good recommendation. These are your **references**. In short, look and be organized and prepared. The image you create for yourself will be the image your contact has of your company. We have an appropriate "5-P" saying: **Prior Planning Prevents Poor Performance**.

BUSINESS GREETINGS AND INTRODUCTIONS

Now that you have made an appointment, prepared for your meeting, and are now in your contact's office, you need to know how to conduct yourself in business meetings.

The success of your meeting might be influenced by your greeting. These rules are similar to the ones discussed in Chapter H on customs and etiquette. To quickly recap, make a warm impression with a good handshake. Make eye contact. Speak up. Smile. Do not make body contact other than the handshake. And do not take a seat until you are directed to do so.

"Nice to meet you."

Remember, if your contact has dealt with foreigners from your country in the past, he may have found some to be somewhat formal or unfriendly. So, before going to your meeting, stand in front of a mirror and practice your greeting. Did the person in the mirror seem warm and friendly and genuinely happy to meet you? Would you be pleased with his greeting?

Gifts – Do not give a gift at your first meeting; it might appear that you are trying to buy your contact's loyalty. If during your conversation you have a small promotional item such as a **key fob** (key holder) or pen with your company logo on it, you can offer it to him, but expect nothing in return.

Women – Unlike some cultures, our women often hold positions in management so they want to be judged by their performance, not their gender. Do not ask if she is married, where she lives, with whom she lives, flirt with her, ask for a date, or make sexual remarks. If you would like to shake hands with her, go ahead and offer your hand if she doesn't do it first. She will probably appreciate your gesture as a sign of your friendliness, self-confidence, and respect.

Woman manager.

Hierarchy – Introducing people in a business situation is theoretically based on hierarchy, not gender. When you introduce two people, say the name of the person higher in rank first to show respect. However, most will probably not notice if you get the **chain of command** (order of authority) wrong. Still, it is nice to get this right if you can.

Business Cards – Exchanging business cards is not a big ritual for us as it is in some cultures such as Asia's. You might want to immediately hand your contact your card as you first meet so he can refer to it for correct pronunciation of your foreign sounding name. Don't be disturbed if he doesn't read your card as you hand it to him or if he doesn't take it with two hands as you might do in your country. He might put it on his desk while he continues looking at you. This is not disrespectful as it is in some cultures.

Names – Americans like to use first names, and if your counterpart is having trouble pronouncing yours, it might distract him. In fact, as you shake hands you might tell him how to pronounce your name or give him a simple nickname to use. Because some cultures tend to be more formal by using last names and titles, especially the Japanese, do not be offended if you are addressed by your first name. If you don't feel comfortable using his first name, then use his last name. Most likely he will tell you to use his first name as a means of putting you at ease. If he does, try to accommodate him.

Seating – After greeting you, your business contact will ask you to take a seat. Some executives like to sit behind their desks while you sit in front of it. Others might direct you to sit at a conference table in their office where your contact will join you. Your discussion may require a lot of documents be spread out over the table, so it would be a better place to sit than his desk. Or he might ask you to sit in a chair or on a couch next to a table where he will join you. This might be done if he plans to serve coffee. So, do not consider it disrespectful, as some foreigners do, if he doesn't seat you at his desk.

Beverage – If you are offered coffee and you would prefer something else, simply say "Do you have tea" or whatever you would like. You will not be judged by what you drink. Just say "no thank you" if you don't want anything. Sometimes just to be polite, I will say, "I am fine, but if you are having coffee I'll have some, too, thank you," but then I may only sip the coffee as we talk.

BUSINESS MEETING CONDUCT

Because some cultures tend to be group oriented and seek consensus, decisions are probably not made in their first business meetings. This is unlike our businesses with decentralized structures that encourage individuals to make quick, independent decisions regarding their own operation. In Asia, several visits and perhaps some evening entertainment might be required before a deal is completed, but in America a deal might be closed or an agreement made at *one* meeting. So don't come unprepared to discuss something that you assumed would be discussed in a future meeting; there might not be one.

If there are others attending the meeting, there will be cross talk among them *and* you, something that may differ from your country. If they have disagreements they will discuss them openly and perhaps ask for your opinion. You may ask questions directly of anybody there. Unlike some countries like the Ukraine, *individuals* are responsible for the decisions made in U.S. meetings, good or bad; that is why you might face probing questions. Be ready.

Foreigners' Views – Americans often complain that British managers talk too much and are indecisive. British complain that French managers are autocratic and arrogant. French and British complain that Americans **shoot from the hip** (don't think before speaking or acting) and are poor listeners. This is because the role of managers differs in the three cultures.

British managers are expected to work as a team and their interaction is fundamentally collaborative. In French organizations, greater value is put on demonstrable individual competence. American managers have a heightened sense of individual accountability and feel that they must lead from the start. This all derives from our differing concepts of leadership, which in turn, affects the way a staff meeting is run and how negotiations are handled.

Leadership in Meetings – In the U.S. where continual development of individual staff skills is important, some managers might listen to discussions of team members and allow them to come to a resolution themselves, and will only facilitate discussion, resolve issues, or provide information as necessary. This contrasts to Europe where the manager is expected to be the active participant and will direct questions during the entire process.

In some countries like China and Japan, there might be a formal group of people with a leader who acts as the spokesperson. If they have differences of opinion among themselves, they will be resolved elsewhere. The course of the discussion is probably pre-determined. Questions are directed to the team leader. In short, the meeting can be well controlled. The relationship in these meetings is not between individuals, but between organizations. For this reason, and unlike in America, the individuals take little or no personal responsibility.

Situations like these can be uncomfortable for Americans (and Italians) who like group discussions to get at all the details. So you are not alone if you must adjust to different leadership procedures when dealing with Americans, just as when Americans deal with other cultures. Just be alert to our differences.

Informality – Foreigners might find the conduct of meetings with Americans comparatively informal. We might place much less emphasis on protocol. So, do not worry about violating a social rule in your meeting; it might inhibit you.

Over the last ten years, more and more American businesses are offering one day a week where everyone dresses casually. If your host is dressed casually when you arrive at your meeting, do not feel overdressed if you have on a tie. This does not reflect upon you; it merely makes you look professional.

In some Asian, European, and other cultures, lighthearted joking is considered disrespectful during business negotiations. This is generally not true in America where we are more relaxed. You might even hear some swearwords sprinkled in our business conversations. If your counterpart tells some jokes, he might be trying to lighten up the conversation; this is not being disrespectful to you. Feel free to do the same with light-hearted banter, but **steer clear** (avoid) of swearwords or vulgar jokes.

Because Germans smile to indicate affection for the other person, in a business environment smiling and laughter are generally not considered appropriate, the opposite of what they might encounter with a U.S. counterpart. (Do you remember the discussion of Walmart earlier and how they learned about this cultural difference in Germany?) So they need to reconsider this in their meetings with Americans who consider smiling and laughter just a friendly gesture.

Your counterpart might sit in a relaxed position during your conversation in his office or put his feet on his desk or on a table. Do not **follow his lead** (do the same) because it is his office and you are a guest. Do not smoke unless he does. In short, be professional, but not overly formal or informal.

SMALL TALK

We generally chat a bit before we talk business in order to learn more about each other and to establish a bond. We call this "small talk," which is discussed in Chapter H on customs and etiquette. Such conversations are brief. If your counterpart is interested in small talk, be sure to ask some questions of him or make statements, such as: "Have you been to my country?" In some cultures it is acceptable to ask personal questions, such as how much money someone makes or their age. Do not do this in American business meetings because you might be told it is **none of your business** (a private matter).

Japanese business people may ask about your job, your title, your responsibilities, the number of employees that report to you, and so on. Because Japanese is a complex language with many forms of address, they need to ascertain these things in order to decide which form to use when speaking to you. We don't have that in America.

> **Hint**: You might want to take an 8"x10" copy of your nation's map that you can leave with him that has an X to denote your city. Americans know little about the geography of many other countries and it might help you with small talk. Stapled to it might be a photo of your hometown

or even you and your family to personalize it. This will give the impression that you prepare for your meetings. Americans like preparation. We have a saying: **Go the extra mile**.

American business people not only appreciate people who make an extra effort to impress them, but those who are knowledgeable about a variety of things, not just about a product or service they are offering. Because sports are a **big deal** (important) in America and are used for small talk, it is a good idea to use Chapter N on sports to locate the names of the local sports teams so you can refer to them, such as, "Are you a Yankee fan?" (A New York City baseball team.) Check the newspaper before going to your meeting to see the league ranking of the local team and the result of the last game played. Once you gain this knowledge you can use it favorably in your meeting as well as later in your e-mails and letters.

Americans also love to talk about our geography and cities. Refer to Chapter C on geography and Chapter D on history for information on these subjects that you can use. Also, refer to Appendix 9 for information on the state in which your contact is located. Memorize the name of your contact's city mayor or state governor and use it in a sentence, such as, "Mayor Jones seems to be doing a fine job keeping your roads in good repair," or something similar if it relates to your service or product.

Do research before your meeting and make a list of these small talk conversation points with specific names, dates, places, pronunciations, etc. It is okay to take it to your meeting and refer to it casually. Using it will reflect favorably on you as a knowledgeable, prepared person, something American business people like.

TALKING BUSINESS

If your counterpart **gets down to business** (starts talking business matters) immediately, it is your cue that he is busy. He will probably be the first to switch the conversation from light conversation to business talk. If he doesn't and you see time is running out, it is okay to initiate the switch to business talk in order to get your presentation completed (or to your next meeting). After all, that is why you are there.

Because of cultural differences, there are things that foreigners should keep in mind when discussing business matters.

- We deal more with logic; you might deal more with emotions and feelings.
- We are direct in what we say; you might be indirect.
- We like informality in talk; you might like structured formality.
- We like **bottom line** net result talk; you might be broader in scope. We have a saying: "Let's get down to **brass tacks** (the important things)."
- We like yes or no answers; you might avoid giving or asking for them.

Time Consideration – Some Americans consider meetings a waste of time. Time wasted is time lost. On an operational level, they also know that project deadlines are to be strictly adhered to, unlike some cultures that tend to be less time/target oriented and a missed deadline is not a big concern. Here, a missed date might kill your future work with a firm.

We like to be given a big picture first. So be broad in scope in your presentation at first, and then drop down into details in a logical fashion, the same way you read a roadmap. (Some of us don't do this well, which is an example of why you should not always imitate what you see some Americans do.) Once you start your presentation, get to the point quickly. As we say, don't **beat around the bush** (not be specific) and **leave us hanging** (wondering what your point is).

> **Hint**: Sometimes sales people who are strangers call me on the telephone and spend five minutes talking before I understand why they are calling. Out of frustration, most of the time I simply tell them I am not interested and hang up. I prefer not to deal with someone who is this **roundabout**.

Don't be surprised if your contact answers a telephone call in the middle of your conversation. This is not disrespectful as it might be in your culture; your contact may have an important matter that must be taken care of. Again, a timing consideration.

If you agree to do something before a certain time, like sending your contact some papers, adhere to that time schedule. If you have a problem meeting the time, call or send a note stating the problem and offer a new date so your counterpart is not disappointed.

Be Honest – As you have learned, Americans seek the truth first and foremost. Honesty was at the root of our Western culture back in 800 BC when Greek poet Homer said, "I detest the man who hides one thing in the depths of his heart and speaks forth another." So our questions may be blunt and direct in order to get to the **bottom line**, which could also differ from your culture. We have a proverb: **Honesty is the best policy**, so be honest in your meeting to enhance how you are viewed.

Because some foreigners are reluctant to admit they do not understand something or that they made an error, such behavior can have negative consequences. This is especially important for those from cultures like Korea where they might refrain from asking questions if they do not understand something. If you **side step** (avoid) or speak in indirect terms and your contact uncovers the truth about something you are trying to hide or do not understand, you will lose credibility and most likely a business deal. Instead of avoiding a negative question, discuss it and point out the positives about what you have to offer and how its benefits outweigh its negatives.

Profits – Try to ascertain what is important to your contact so you can make your best presentation, including the demands of time, quality, and profit. The primary goal of American businesses is profit, while the primary goal of some foreign businesses is long-term growth. The truth probably lies somewhere in between.

426

The cost of your product or service will be measured against the profit it will reap and the time it will take to recapture the money spent for it. Sometimes short-term profit will be more important than long-term growth, or vice versa. Or, sometimes the time it takes to install your product or service may be more important than a profit motive, particularly if something else in the company is dependent on its installation. This is what you need to ascertain in your meeting, so don't make assumptions as you would in your country.

(asapwi.com)

Provide References – Your counterpart needs to be convinced that what you have to offer is the best choice because he or she alone is responsible. Good references will help your counterpart make his decision. It is our custom to give references (names and telephone numbers of our customers) who will give a favorable report about our products or company. Feel free to talk about some of your successes. Know what your competition is doing and do not be afraid to point out your benefits and their deficiencies. It is okay to point out the negatives about your competition if it is done in a professional way. In some countries, **name dropping** and boasting is considered rude. It is only unprofessional in the U.S. when one brags about himself in a personal way, not about his product or service.

Speed – American business people may appear to be in a hurry and pushy in their business meetings, as contrasted with the slower ways of negotiating in some countries. American business people are often frustrated, for example, with the comparatively slow pace of business in Thailand and the long silence for Japanese executives to respond to a question. Also, in some Indonesian business meetings, it is polite to speak in quiet, gentle tones and to wait 10 to 15 seconds before responding to a statement. In America, this type of behavior might convey the impression you are not sure about yourself or are trying to conceal something.

With this focus on speed, U.S. executives generally consider it logical to resolve items in detail one-by-one, while some cultures like the Japanese look at many issues to be explored and resolved simultaneously. Be prepared to make this shift in your meeting.

Be Direct – The Chinese use the term *mian-zi* to define "face," which implies trust, respect, and influence. This concept of not losing face is very important to Asians, but less important to Americans. For this reason some Asians find it hard to say "no" and choose instead to say they will "think about it" or use other subtle terms that seem like delaying tactics to an American.

Avoid this indirect way because we want a response, even if it is "no." As we say in America, **tell it like it is**. If, however, there is something you need to think about overnight, we have a saying you can use: **Let me sleep on it**. Then get back to your

427

counterpart the next day or so with your response. Do not ignore him because you will lose credibility. Remember what Gandhi, the great India leader, said: "A 'no' uttered from the deepest conviction is better than a 'yes' merely uttered to please, or worse, to avoid trouble."

> **Hint**: I have had numerous exposures to this common problem of indirectness by foreigners and must admit I was offended, as most Americans would be. I met an Asian American university professor and discussed this book I was writing. I asked if he would be interested in reviewing one of my chapters that covered a subject he taught. He said to e-mail him some information about it, which I did. I never received a response. I received polite responses from others who explained why they could not be a reviewer. When in China, I met a publisher and continued to correspond with her about publishing my book when I returned home. After a month I could see that she may have lost interest, and because of interest by other publishers, I needed to know if she was still interested so I wrote her again. I never received a response. Again, I was offended. Foreigners must learn to say yes or no instead of leaving us **up in the air**. I would not deal with these people again under any circumstance or recommend them. If you are noncommittal in a business situation, you lose credibility and most likely will not be dealt with again either.

Part of directness is making eye contact, which can differ in the U.S. from other countries. In Mexico, for example, eye contact is yielded to the person talking, while the listener mainly looks away because intense, constant eye contact is interpreted as aggression. Even subordinates in Mexico do not make extended eye contact with their bosses; out of respect they look at the ground. In America this could be interpreted as disinterest and might have negative consequences.

Wrap It Up – In Vietnam, a visitor is generally expected to initiate or signal the closure of a meeting. In America, your counterpart will probably do it. If he looks at his watch toward the end of your meeting, it may be a signal he is on a **tight schedule** (very busy). Before you end your meeting, ask yourself if you communicated what you wanted to say. Did you ask questions to ascertain whether or not he understood you? Summarize your key points, ask if he has any questions, and thank him for taking time to meet with you.

Make sure you have his business card so you have the correct spelling of his name and company, his job title, and address in case you mail a letter to him. If you plan to send him more information, remind him that it will be coming *shortly*. And keep reminding yourself of the importance of time to an American executive.

Don't expect your host to escort you back to your hotel after your meeting as might be done in Singapore. Your contact may have his secretary call for a taxi. If he doesn't, ask her to do it for you or else use your cell phone. Do remember that many people in car loving-America travel in their own cars so out of habit we often don't think about this consideration.

428

Afterwards – After your meeting, you might send a brief letter thanking your contact for taking the time with you. You can also briefly confirm in writing any specifics such as prices, time schedules, and guarantees that were discussed. Your promptness in sending these communications within the next day or two will make a nice impression. If you are having difficulty acquiring information that your contact is expecting from you, mention that in your letter (or a telephone call) and assure him that it will be forthcoming. Do not delay sending the letter because of your search for this information. Americans like to **keep on top of things** (know how things are going).

BUSINESS ENTERTAINING

Your business meeting might lead to lunch or dinner that day or on another occasion, or even a breakfast meeting with a busy executive. Chapter O on food and dining discusses dining etiquette. Here are a few additional pointers for business entertaining. Unlike some countries where business is not discussed at meals, the opposite is true in America. If you learn about your counterpart's interest in a local sports team, you might ask if he would be interested in going with you to a game at a later time, in which case you would buy the tickets.

Business meal. (BusinessBalance.com)

Luncheon – Lunchtime customs in the U.S. may differ from your country's. If Americans break off a business meeting and go to a good restaurant with Dutch or Danish associates, they may think we are not serious about doing business because they prefer a quick sandwich and a glass of mineral water. On the other hand, if we meet with French or Spanish counterparts and offer them a sandwich instead of going to a restaurant, they might think we are not serious about doing business. So ask your contact what he would prefer to do. If you are from Mexico where lunch is the big meal of the day, don't be surprised if your American counterpart opts for a light luncheon or salad. And don't consider it rude if your business lunch ends abruptly so he can hurry back to work. Also, remember some companies don't like employees to drink alcohol during work hours.

Drinks – You might offer to take your counterpart for a drink after work. Unlike some countries, it is not considered rude if he declines your invitation. In some cultures, forming a personal relationship to enhance business dealings is very important and social drinking is practically essential. You may find quite the opposite in America where drinking is truly optional.

> **Hint**: If an American is attending one of your banquets or parties that has this drinking ceremony, you will create a nice impression if, before it begins, explain that you do not expect him to drink unless he wants to. Ask if he would prefer water or a soft drink. It will put him at ease, just as I

was once overseas. Your host in America should extend this same courtesy to you if you attend his party.

We have **cocktail** (an alcoholic beverage) **parties** for special occasions where many can be invited for food and drinks, perhaps a celebration. If you are invited to one, hold your drink in your left hand to keep your right hand dry and available for handshakes. Hold food in your right hand with a napkin to keep your hand clean.

Etiquette – In a business dining situation, when you are the host (the person who issues the invitation), invite your guest to order first. Even if you are a female host, you can say to the waiter something like, "Please take my guest's order first." This lets the waiter know you are the host and will be given the bill at the end of the meal. At a business dinner, the host pays the bill, regardless of gender. If someone insists on paying the bill, don't make a fuss and risk a scene or hurt feelings. Let the person pay. If someone needs help opening a door, pulling out a chair, carrying a box, or putting on a coat, offer to help regardless of gender.

W

OWNING A BUSINESS

Opportunities multiply as they are
seized. – Sun Tzu, ancient Chinese warrior

Many Americans dream about owning their own business. They want to be their own boss. They want financial independence. They want creative freedom. They want to use their skills and knowledge fully. Foreigners open businesses in the U.S. for the same reasons. Some also start them because their lack of English language skills prevents them from getting jobs. In fact, immigrants own 11 percent of businesses in the U.S. and are 60 percent more likely to start a new business than native-born Americans. They represent 17 percent of all new business owners (in some states more than 30 percent). Foreign-born business owners generate nearly one-quarter of all business income in California and nearly one-fifth in the states of New York, Florida, and New Jersey.

NYC business owner . (NYDailyNews.com)

An official with the federal government's Small Business Administration that helps startups said, "Immigrant entrepreneurs are essential to our nation's growth and economic prosperity…and make our nation more competitive and serve as reminders of the American dream."

Our immigrant-owned businesses tend to be concentrated in both low-skilled and high-skilled ends of the economy. This includes small restaurants at one end and technology and engineering start-ups at the other. In California's **Silicon Valley**, the center of America's high-tech economy, one-quarter of all technology businesses are run by immigrants from China and India.

Even though they are our neighbors, Mexicans and other Latin Americans create fewer businesses and have a lower success rate than immigrants from Asia who are more entrepreneurial. In addition, Asian immigrants have attained higher education levels and

431

tend to benefit from extended families whose members with business experience act as mentors and financers to those starting out.

During the 2007-2010 recession, the values that immigrants had learned about being thrifty, avoiding excessive debt, and relying on family support from their native countries helped them ride out the recession better. As one economist said, "Anyone who invests the time and effort to move to a second country obviously has an entrepreneurial spirit."

Since U.S. citizenship and residency are not requirements, non-U.S. citizens are free to start or expand in the U. S. without wading through any more red tape than a U.S.-born small business owner. Realizing their importance to the economy, our government and some nonprofit groups help foreigners develop businesses. New York City, for example, announced in 2011 three new steps to make it easier for immigrant-owned businesses to start and grow there: a business plan to provide assistance to immigrant entrepreneurs; free courses in Chinese, Korean, Spanish, and Russian to help them develop the skills to launch, operate and expand; and a business exposition to showcase locally-based immigrant food manufacturing businesses and link them to consumers nationwide. The initiatives resulted from a yearlong series of **roundtables** (discussions involving several participants) with community groups as part of the City's agenda to support immigrant communities and empower them to grow and create jobs.

Former U.S. Secretary of Labor Elaine Chao, an immigrant and the first Asian Pacific American woman appointed to a president's cabinet, talked about succeeding in business in the U.S. at a conference for immigrants. She said, "The ability to gain new knowledge is so important—especially for newcomers—because there is not one formula for success in America. It's free and open with many different paths to advancement."

Secretary Chao

She emphasized that the key to success is to know yourself, to know your strengths and weaknesses, to listen, to learn, and to be attentive to what is happening around you. She also advised would-be business owners to use the many assistance programs and resources available in mainstream America. "America is such a dynamic cauldron [kettle] for all sorts of activities…and the possibilities are so much bigger than many newcomers can envision." The former Peace Corps director also said, "Most Americans have a very generous heart. So, if you have a question or a concern, don't be afraid to ask for help."

From my observations, here's **my take** (opinion) on why foreigners are successful in starting up and operating businesses in America.

- Immigrants tend to be risk-takers and have a strong sense of self-reliance.
- Many will work long hours without complaint in order to reach their goals.
- They adapt to new surroundings yet retain some of their cultural traditions.
- Relationship building and strong connections are important to them.

432

- They are creative and artistic.
- They tend to offer quality and good service.
- Attention to detail is important to them.

If you want to own a business in America, here are three different approaches you can use to start one, each of which is discussed below.

- Start a new business on your own.
- Pay another organization to start you up with one of their branch locations.
- Purchase an existing business.

STARTING A BUSINESS ON YOUR OWN

When you mention that you plan to open a business in the U.S., someone may say, "Oh! You are so brave to **start from scratch**," which means doing everything on your own by bringing disparate elements together.

My recommendation to anyone who wishes to start a small business in America is to first contact the federal government's **Small Business Administration** (**SBA**) (www.sba.gov). They provide a wealth of information about everything that has to be done. The SBA has offices in all the states.

Research indicates that many business failures could have been avoided with better planning and research. It is important to first develop a **business plan** that documents all aspects of running the business, including detailed estimates of income and expenses. The SBA website can assist you in preparing this plan. Remember, as a **rule of thumb** (guideline),[*] new businesses generally do not make a profit the first year or two. A bank will want to examine your business plan if you apply for a loan.

There are individuals who can provide you with startup services for a fee. Look in the telephone directory under "consultants" or "business consultants." If you locate vendors from whom you would purchase goods, you might ask them for advice. Some banks, anxious to gain new customers, also provide startup and referral services. You may need an accountant to help set up your new bookkeeping system. Find one in the telephone directory under "accountants" or still better, get a referral. Trade associations can provide you with helpful information about their industry, too.

---

[*]The phrase "rule of thumb" is derived from an old English law, which stated that you couldn't beat your wife with anything wider than your thumb. It is used today to indicate a general guideline.

Hint: Before I started a business, I visited similar businesses and asked their owners and salespeople for their advice. Most were helpful when they learned I would not be a competitor because of geographical distances. I found it an excellent way to learn firsthand about the industry.

Different government agencies require you to fill out forms and apply for permits to operate your business. These government agencies include local (city), county, state, and federal. If you do not plan to hire employees, the process is simpler. Consult the telephone directory and call each agency to inquire about the forms you will need to fill out. The SBA or your local **Chamber of Commerce** (local business people who promote business in their city) can direct you to these offices (www.uschamber.com).

Absentee ownership is a term used to describe the owner of a business who is not involved in running it on a daily basis. In my experience, this generally does not work well for small businesses. You rely on the talents and honesty of another person to operate your business, and their interests may not be the same as yours. Instead, as you nurture your new business, begin to give more responsibility to employees you trust, but still monitor their work.

PURCHASING A BUSINESS OPPORTUNITY

An alternative to starting your own business is purchasing the rights to open a business with the assistance from an organization that will set you up in their business. This is called **franchising**. A franchise is an agreement between you and a company that will assist you in operating one of their locations. McDonald's is an example of one of our most successful franchises. Seventy percent of their 33,500 worldwide restaurant businesses in 119 countries are owned and operated by independent business people. This website provides a wealth of information on franchising: www.franchiseexpo.com. Various magazines and websites such as www.entrepreneur.com advertise franchises for sale.

Successful franchise.

Here's how it works. You pay the franchising company for their service to help you set up the business and train you. In return, you pay for the construction of the facilities and then pay them a percentage of your monthly sales. The advantage, of course, is that you get the use of a well-known brand name with a built-in cliental and the use of their expertise.

The major problem for people who purchase a franchise is the misunderstanding of the obligations of the purchaser (the franchis**ee**) and the seller (the franchis**or**). These agreements are often an 80-page document that can be confusing. So, if you plan to go this route, hire an attorney to review it with you.

Subway franchise.

A financial services firm ranks these franchises as the top 15 based on their financial strength, stability, a strong growth rate, and the size of the parent organization.

Rank	Franchise Name and Description	Start-up Costs ($1,000s)
1.	Subway - Submarine sandwiches, salads	$86-$213
2.	Curves - Women's fitness and weight-loss centers	36-43
3.	Quizno's - Submarine sandwiches, soups, salads	208-244
4.	Jackson Hewitt Tax Service - Tax preparation services	39-85
5.	UPS Store - Postal/business/communications services	146-247
6.	Sonic Drive-In Restaurants - restaurant	710-2,300
7.	Jani-King - Commercial cleaning	11-34
8.	7-Eleven - Convenience store	50-350
9.	Dunkin' Donuts - Donuts and baked goods	256-1,100
10.	RE/MAX Int'l. - Real estate brokerage	20-200
11.	KFC - Chicken fast food restaurant	110-170
12.	ServiceMaster Clean - Commercial/residential cleaning	28-100
13.	McDonald's - Hamburgers, chicken, salads	506-1,600
14.	Jiffy Lube - Fast automobile oil change	214-273
15.	Liberty Tax Service - Income-tax preparation services	38-49

Some businesses that you will frequently see advertised for sale are called **business opportunities**, such as vending machine routes and display rack routes. These are offered by companies looking for individual operators for a certain geographic area. Your "business" would be to keep the vending machines or display racks filled with products. There are a lot of **scams** (illegitimate schemes that take your money) with these and others that let you "work from home." Many promise you will make lots of money, but you probably won't. My advice when purchasing any business is to be careful! We have a saying in America: "If something seems too good to be true, it probably is."

Vending machine.

Different government and nonprofit public agencies exist to protect buyers of franchises and business opportunities. The **Better Business Bureau** (BBB) is a nonprofit agency whose purpose is to promote honest business dealings (www.bbb.com). They have offices throughout the U.S. Call them or use their website to learn if a business or a businessperson has been reported to them for dishonest or unethical dealings. This information is available to the public.

The federal government has laws that must be met by sellers of franchise and business opportunities. The **Federal Trade Commission (FTC)** has a website that discusses different types of business opportunities that should be avoided (www.ftc.gov/bizop). They offer advice to anyone who is interested in purchasing a business opportunity that promotes "be your own boss," "set your own hours," "work from home," and "earn money quickly."

You are entitled to *written* disclosures from business opportunity sellers of vending machines and display racks (such as soda, snack, payphone) that you would

435

restock. These disclosures, required by FTC rules, *must* include the following information to help you validate the opportunity.

- *Prior Purchasers* – The names, addresses, and telephone numbers of at least 10 prior purchasers who are nearest to you so you can arrange to visit them and check out the opportunity *in person*.
- *Proof Of Claims* – The number and percent of prior purchasers who have made as much as the seller claims you can make so you can tell how likely it is that you will do that well. This must also include an explanation of how those profits or earnings were calculated. If they don't do this, they are breaking the law.

Before investing in any business opportunity, here are additional precautions suggested by the FTC.

- *References* – If the business opportunity is a franchise, study the disclosure document. If the document says there are no previous purchasers yet the seller offers a list of references, be careful because the references may be fake.
- *Interviews* – Interview previous purchasers in person where their business operates. This helps reduce the risk of being misled by phony references.
- *Check Government Sources* – Contact the state Attorney General's Office, state or county consumer protection agency, and the Better Business Bureau both where the business opportunity promoter is based and where you live to find out if there are any unresolved complaints. Most have websites.
- *Contact Merchandise Companies* – If the business opportunity involves selling products from well-known companies, call their legal departments and find out if there have been problems with the business opportunity promoter. Ask of they are affiliated with the business opportunity being advertised.
- *Seek Professional Help* – Consult an attorney, accountant, or other business advisor before you **sign on the dotted line** (sign the agreement).
- *Take Your Time* – Promoters of fraudulent business opportunities often use high-pressure sales tactics to get you to sign papers immediately. If the business opportunity is legitimate, it will likely be available when you are ready to decide.

PURCHASING AN EXISTING BUSINESS

A third way to acquire your own business is to purchase an existing one. Locating one is easy. Our daily newspapers have classified ads sections where these are listed under "Business For Sale." We also have magazines devoted to businesses for sale, some of which are free in street corner vending machines or outside

restaurants and super markets. Those that are more professional are sold at magazine stands. Internet sites such as www.bizquest.com offer businesses for sale by geographical location. Owners, business brokers, and franchise operators all use these advertising vehicles.

Before you buy an existing business, consider the advantages and disadvantages of such a purchase. Some of the *advantages* of buying a business are:

- You are in operation immediately and therefore have immediate income.
- The seller can train you and eliminate startup time.
- You may be able to finance the business more easily because of the business' established credit, or the seller may finance it.
- You purchase an existing client/customer base.
- You eliminate a potential competitor.
- The location might be better than if you start anew somewhere else.

The *disadvantages* to consider are:

- You may pay too much for the business if you haven't done your research, or more than if you had started it on your own.
- You may inherit a poor image if customers or employees are dissatisfied.
- You may be unaware of new competition entering the market, or major changes coming to your industry.
- You are left with any previous problems incurred by the seller.

If your search leads you to a business you think you would like to own, you need to take six careful steps before purchasing it.

Step 1: Why Is It For Sale? – The first step is to find the *real* reason the business is for sale. A frequent excuse is, "We are retiring," "We are tired," or "We are moving to another state." Sometimes these excuses are real or are only part of the reason. Other times owners are hiding something. Regardless of what you are told, you must gather as much information to ascertain why it is really for sale. In the process, determine if the business has potential for growth and what shortcomings it might face.

Studies show the primary reason a business is for sale is usually because it is failing in some way. As an example, a seller realizes a retail business is in a bad location and wants to sell and open somewhere else. In ascertaining why it is for sale, ask the owner if he or she will agree to stipulate in the **sales agreement** (see below) that they will not operate a similar business within a certain number of miles that might take business away from you. If they won't, then you know something is wrong.

A talk with the landlord might reveal why it is for sale. Examine the landlord's rental agreement to see if it is expiring. If it is, your rent might be increased if you choose to renew it, or you might have to vacate, more reasons why the business might be for

437

sale. Talk to neighboring businesses; sometimes they know what is going on not only with that business but also in the surrounding area.

Step 2: Due Diligence – If you find a business that matches your strengths and interests, you must then do a thorough examination of the operation. The legal term **due diligence** describes the process of obtaining objective and reliable information on a person or business prior to a purchase. This is a period during which the *buyer* makes sure he or she has all the information needed to proceed with the transaction. From a legal point of view, this responsibility falls on *you*, not the seller. We have a saying: **Do your homework**.

Obtain copies of business documents to substantiate everything the owner tells you, including:

- Financial statements for the past five years with the name of the accountant who prepared them. These are the reports we discussed in the prior chapter.
- Bank account statements to verify that deposits and expenses agree with the business financial statements.
- Documents filed with the government, such as sales taxes paid, worker taxes paid, and the owner's income tax forms. Then, contact the agencies to insure all taxes have been paid.

If the seller refuses to give you any of these documents or says they are not available, walk away, because as we say, **something is rotten in Denmark** (refers to a Shakespeare play set in Denmark where things were not going well), or **something is fishy** (being concealed).

> **Hint**: Most states have laws requiring sellers of *property* to disclose in the sales agreement any known existing problems. However, a wise buyer doesn't rely on them and risk having to initiate a law suit **down the road** (later after the fact) against the seller who withheld the facts.

Step 3: Price – Carefully analyze the asking price of the business, especially if the owner is acting as the broker and selling it himself. To the owner the price might seem reasonable, when in reality the market will not support it. Business brokers, like real estate brokers, are licensed by their state and know the rules and regulations for selling a business. These brokers are good at assessing the fair value of a business based on what other businesses are selling for. Visit similar businesses offered by a broker and gain as much information about them as possible by asking lots of questions. With the knowledge you gain, you will be better able to deal with a seller who is not using a broker, if you so choose.

Prices are negotiable. You can always make an offer less than the asking price, and the owner might accept it or respond with a price somewhere between your offer and the original asking price. This is called a counteroffer. And you can make a counteroffer to the seller's counteroffer. Make a list of considerations that compel you to offer less. Then discuss these with the owner or broker to substantiate your price offering. Remember, this is a negotiating process. Don't be rushed into accepting their offer.

Step 4: Financing – Banks are generally reluctant to loan to individuals buying a business unless they have dealt with them in the past. If the business you are interested in has a good relationship with a bank that is familiar with its operation, it might loan some funds for you to purchase it. Some owners might finance the business with a down payment from the buyer of 20 to 30 percent or more and with monthly payments of the balance due. This will be part of your negotiation. Factor in these payments when projecting the profitability of the business. Will you be able to make the payments?

As a last resort, consider getting financial advice or applying for a loan from a U.S. bank owned or operated by people from your country. For example, we have 72 Asian-owned banks in the U.S., including the 42-branch East West Bank in California that caters to Asian immigrants and descendants. Here are others.

- Bank of the West is owned by France's BNP Paribas and has 660 offices in 19 states. (www.bankofthewest.com)
- Citizens Bank, owned by the Royal Bank of Scotland, has 1,600 branches in the U.S. (www.citizensbank.com)
- HSBC Bank, the U.S. subsidiary of the British banking giant, has 500 offices. (www.us.hsbc.com)
- Spain's Banco Santander owns Sovereign Bank with its 750 branch offices. (www.sovereignbank.com)
- TD Bank is owned by Canada's TD Bank Financial Group with more than 1,000 branches. (www.tdbank.com)
- Union Bank, the fifth-largest bank in California, is owned by Japanese giant Mitsubishi UFJ Financial Group. (www.unionbank.com)

Step 5: Sales Agreement – When price is agreed upon and you have adequate financing lined up, *all* verbal agreements made must then be documented in the written sales agreement to protect you. The agreement should also define in specific terms (hours and days) the amount of time the seller will devote to training and assisting you in the first month or two. If you are buying inventory for a retail operation, you buy it at cost, not retail. Offer less than cost if you think you will have to liquidate it and start anew. Insist on an independent inventory count. Remember, you are buying the assets of the business, not the liabilities unless it is a corporation and these are predefined in the sales agreement. Be sure the sales agreement states that the seller is responsible for all liabilities incurred prior to the date you take over the business.

Hint: Before signing a sales agreement, make sure an attorney and possibly an accountant have read it to insure all aspects of the sale have been examined and your interests are protected. As discussed in the chapter on law, once a contract is signed you cannot go back to renegotiate a price or anything else unless you can prove fraud exists. As discussed in Chapter E on law, lawsuits can be time consuming and expensive.

Step 6: Closing The Deal – The final step is to enter into **escrow**, a process by which an independent trusted third party receives and disburses money and/or documents for the transacting parties. A similar process is used when you buy and sell a house. Banks, escrow companies, and some lawyers perform this administrative function for a fee. The actual escrow agency you use is negotiable between the two of you. You may prefer to choose one that has someone in their office fluent in your native language.

RUNNING YOUR NEW BUSINESS

As a consultant to immigrant business owners, I tell them they are more likely to be successful if they understand much of what is in this book about America, its people, customs, and culture. It is important they understand the differences between how they would operate the business in their native country and how and why we do it here.

For example, I was a customer at a small immigrant-owned business in my city that had a sign in the window stating they accepted credit cards. Like most Americans, I prefer to pay with a credit card. When I purchased something, I was told the credit card machine was broken so I gave them cash. This same thing happened on three other occasions over a two-month period. Finally I realized that they simply did not want to accept credit cards because of fees they had to pay their bank for processing each transaction. I was offended at this dishonesty and never returned.

You have learned that Americans believe **honesty is the best policy** and that we do not like to be taken advantage of. Just because something is done a certain way in your homeland does not mean it will work here, and that includes not taking credit cards. Also, just because a friend from your country does something in his or her business in a certain way here does not mean it is the correct way. Ask your customers how they feel about these things. You might be surprised. In short, be honest in your business dealings and try to understand and adapt to our culture and ethics if you want to succeed here.

Here are more pointers I offer my clients for getting their new businesses off to a good start.

- *Advertising* – This is more successful when done on a regular basis rather than using occasional ads, which we call **hit and miss** (random). Most media have yearly bulk rates that can save you money. Don't overlook new media tools like Facebook, Twitter, and blogs to advertise your business. A good book to learn how to do this is available at www.budurl.com/blogging4retailers.

440

- *Appearance* – I find that displays, smells, and lighting are frequent shortcomings of immigrant-owned businesses. Be on the lookout for clutter and lack of cleanliness in your facility. It can be a turnoff for a customer. Perhaps a consultant or one of your vendors can you help make these improvements.

- *Become Your Own Customer* – Put yourself in the role of your customers. Be honest. If you were your own customer, would you like the way you are greeted and treated? Upon walking into a business, the first indication I have that it is operated by foreigners is by the way I am greeted, if I am greeted at all. Sometimes I am **turned off** (irritated) and leave. So it is important you understand our friendly greetings discussed in Chapter H on customs and etiquette.

- *Competition* – One secret to success is to be aware of what your competitors are doing. Visit their locations and websites. Note their prices. What things do you like that they are doing? What will you avoid doing?

- *Computerized Equipment* – Some computer and software vendors might specialize in certain industries like yours and can offer tips for improving your operation.

- *Customer Lists* – Direct mail is an inexpensive and effective way to advertise to your customers. It has a personal touch to it. Building a good mailing/e-mail/phone list and using it effectively is a good way to build your business.

- *Customers* – Talk with your own customers and ask, "What can we do to improve our service for you." Encourage them to give you an honest reply, not just compliments.

- *Expenses* – These usually turn out to be more than you plan on, so have reserve funds. We have a saying that is attributed to Robert Burns in the 1700s: **The best-laid plans of mice and men often go awry.**

- *Educate Yourself* – Attend seminars at tradeshows. The SBA and Chambers of Commerce frequently hold seminars and provide publications specifically for new businesses. The SBA also offers the free services of retired business professionals who can help you solve problems. SCORE (www.score.org) is a free, nonprofit association dedicated to helping small businesses get off the ground, grow, and achieve their goals through education and mentoring. Their work is supported by the Small Business Administration (SBA) and has a network of 13,000 volunteers.

- *Employees* – To save money, you might initially use part-time employees instead of full time. Good training is important. Offer them a discount on your products/services. Have a friend visit your business as a customer and get their opinion of how your staff treated them. Establish a dress policy and

441

provide a written employee manual for your staff to refer to. Have them help you write it; they will feel part of the business.

- *Landlord Relations* – Establish a good relationship with the management of the property your business in located in. Learn what they can do to help your business, such as participating in special promotions or group advertising. If you need to renegotiate your soon-expiring lease, you might document needed physical improvements you propose they make to the property.

- *Plans* – Be flexible and on the outlook for needed changes so you don't become stagnant. Always have plans for making improvements, big or small. Prioritize them and assign implementation dates over a 12-month period. A ship needs an always-working compass; so does a business.

- *Prices* – Identify who your average customer is and the price ranges that will appeal to him or her. Do you want to sell one item or service at $100 or ten at $10? The answer will affect your selling expenses, business image, products, staffing, and services offered.

- *Promotions* – Special events can help you expand your business if done right. I recommend *A Retailers's Guide to Frugal In-Store Promotions* by Carolyn Howard-Johnson (www.budurl.com/RetailersGuide). It is applicable to different businesses besides retailing. Other books in her series about online promotion of a business are at www.HowTodoItFrugally.com.

- *Trade Publications and Associations* – These are good sources for learning about trends, new developments, and products. Consider joining the Better Business Bureau and the Chamber of Commerce to keep up to date.

- *Vendors and Suppliers* – Treat them with respect. Some may agree not to sell to competitors in your area if your volume makes it profitable for them. Pay your bills on time (30-days billing is common). Some may offer extended bill-paying dating terms for your new venture to help you **get it off the ground** (get started). If you have trouble paying bills, be honest with them rather than not paying. Otherwise, they may cut you off. If you are a manufacturer, a vendor might recommend a larger firm that can produce parts for you cheaper than you can produce them.

Good luck with your new venture!

X

GETTING A JOB

*Choose a job you love, and you will never have to work a day
in your life.* – Confucius, 5th century BC Chinese philosopher

This chapter provides advice on how to get a job with an American employer either in the U.S. or in a foreign country. As you have learned, compared to some countries we are somewhat relaxed with our cultural dos and don'ts. But we do have guidelines to follow when applying for a job, some of which differ from other cultures. Knowing these differences will help you get hired.

Unlike some countries, our government has no direct influence on your job selection. You are free to pursue any education that will prepare you for any job of your choice. When I was in Peru, I learned there were too many students studying at the universities to become teachers. So they decreased the number of openings in the teacher-training program to help fix the problem. In the U.S., we rely on the due diligence of students to make the right selection, so the government does not control our universities. (There's that *independence* thing again.)

This chapter prepares you to properly perform the three steps necessary to get a job with an American business.

1. Find job opportunities.
2. Prepare and submit a **resume** *[REZ-oo-may]* to a prospective employer that summarizes your work experience and training. (We sometimes call this the **curriculum vitae**, a term heard more often in Europe.)
3. Conduct an interview with a prospective employer.

FINDING JOB OPPORTUNITIES

The resources you use to learn about job openings in the U.S. may differ from those in your country. In China, for instance, businesses usually don't recruit white collar personnel using newspaper advertisements or recruitment agencies to the extent we do.

They prefer to use recruitment fairs held two or three times a week at the local labor office. We do have independent job fairs, but so many other resources.

Where To Look – These are places where you can seek job opportunities.

- *Personal Contacts* – Many companies prefer to interview applicants referred to them by someone inside the company. It is estimated that 75 percent do not advertise job openings, but rely on referrals. Contact your family, friends, former colleagues, teachers, and acquaintances and let them know you are looking for a job. This is called **networking**.

- *Help Wanted Ads* – These appear in the classified sections of our newspapers under "Help Wanted" or "Job Offers." The Sunday editions usually have the most listings, just as Italy's Thursday and Friday papers have job supplements. Some newspapers also offer the listings online, such as *The New York Times* at listings.nytimes.com/classifiedsmarketplace.

- *State Employment Offices* – Each state employment office matches employees to employers' needs. They might provide a counselor to assist you in your search. Their offices are listed in the telephone directory or on the Internet. For example, the California Employment Development Department has an online site at www.edd.ca.gov.

State employment office.

- *Private Employment Agencies* – These agencies advertise openings they are trying to fill for clients who hired them to find qualified personnel for them. We call these people **head hunters** because they search about for the best people to be considered for the job. The website for the largest **executive search firm** is www.kornferry.com.

- *Temporary Agencies* – These firms look for workers to fill part-time openings offered by their clients. More and more employers are hiring part-time workers so they can evaluate them for permanent jobs later. The website for a nationwide "temp agency" is www.kellyservices.com.

Job fair.

- *Job Fairs* – Local job seekers meet in a facility that has numerous employers looking for prospective employees. They interact with each other at tables or in booths.

- *Mailing Resumes* – Sending unsolicited resumes to a company is not recommended unless you have first talked to someone there and they requested your resume or they advertised the opening. If interested, they will ask you to come to their office for an interview.

- *Internet* – Individual companies might list job openings on their own websites under "Employment." Microsoft's is at http://careers.microsoft.com/. Firms that list job openings for many different companies operate Internet sites, such as www.job.com. Their resources are especially valuable if you are willing to relocate. Here are a few sites that might help narrow your search.
  - For science jobs: http://aaas.sciencecareers.org/jobseekerx/.
  - By location or employer: www.employmentguide.com.
  - By popular city, state, and category: www.flipdog.com.
  - For U.S. and abroad: www.jobs.com.
  - For Federal government: www.usajobs.gov.
- *School* – Most universities have career centers that help students find jobs. Many, like the one at UCLA (www.career.ucla.edu), even help students learn more about job hunting skills.

Employment Professionals – Employment professionals can not only help you find employment, but for a fee some will counsel you on your career advancement such as this one: www.challengergray.com. The key to success, they say, is to take an active approach and make your own opportunities instead of simply mailing resumes and perusing online job boards. Here is their advice if you are looking for work now or will be in the future.

- *Broaden Your Knowledge* – Explore online courses and local certificate programs to broaden your industry knowledge and talent. That will increase your marketability to a variety of employers.
- *Community Service Groups* – Get involved in these organizations. They are great for building your network and honing your professional skills. Meet 10 new people in your field but outside of your company to help you in your current position and when you enter the job market.
- *Networking Sites* – Join online LinkedIn, Facebook, Twitter, etc. More employers are seeking candidates and advertising positions through these social and professional networking sites. Be sure to create and *maintain* a professional profile on your page because employers may look for updates. Keep your social and professional lives separate on them. Do not post anything that might cause an employer to think twice about hiring you.
- *Professional/Trade Associations* – These groups can provide training and education opportunities, and most hold several networking functions every year. You just might meet a person at an event who can help you find a new job.

- *Remain Positive* – It's easy to get discouraged when much of the job news is negative and the job search itself, even in the best economy, is full of rejection.

PREPARING YOUR COVER LETTER

Okay, now that you have located a job opportunity, the next step is to submit your resume. *Always* use a cover letter to accompany it, be it a hardcopy or e-mail submittal. The letter is always typed or computer-produced as is done in Spain and Italy, but not like France where it is handwritten to reveal something about the applicant. Only use quality white paper, and remember, keep it professional and don't get clever or fancy.

Your cover letter has three purposes.

1. It introduces you and explains why you are sending your resume.
2. It identifies the position(s) for which you want to be considered.
3. You *briefly* sell yourself in a less structured format than the formal resume.

The cover letter has three sections.

- *Introduction* – This states why you are submitting your resume and perhaps how you heard of the job opening. If a friend referred you, give his or her name.
- *Body* – This *briefly* highlights your most important qualifications and may include your degree, honors, experiences, or personal strengths. If you have a particular interest in the job, explain why.
- *Close* – Request an application form or an interview. State that your resume is enclosed. Thank them for considering you.

Here is the proper format for your cover letter (see sample letter below).

- Center it on *one* page, single-spaced, and with one-inch margins.
- If you don't have pre-printed stationery with a letterhead, the typed heading lists your address. This is followed by the date (spell the month in full) and the employer's name and address. If possible, get names so you can address it to a *specific person* rather than a department.
- After the employer's address, type the salutation (greeting) followed by a colon (:). If uncertain about using Mrs. or Miss, then use Ms.
- A complimentary line such as "Sincerely," or "Best wishes" (note: "wishes" is not capitalized) is used to close, followed by four blank lines and your typed name. Sign your name above your typed name. If you enclose your resume, write "Enclosure" two spaces below your name. If you send more than one enclosure, write that quantity in parentheses, such as Enclosures (3).

446

- If your letter is computer printed, use a simple type font, either Times Roman or Ariel like our sample letter below. Use a laser printer because some dot matrix printers do not produce a professional looking product.

Sample Cover Letter

123 Happy Street
Berlin, Germany
123-456-789

January 10, 2012

Mr. Robert Jones, Personnel Mgr.
Acme Media Corp.
123 Busy Street
New York, NY 12345

Dear Mr. Jones:

I am writing in regard to the Graphic Artist–Jr. position that is open in your company. I learned of the opening from your help wanted advertisement in my university's newspaper.

I will graduate with honors this June from Berlin University with a BA degree in art. My grade point average for four years is 3.55. I received certification in 3D animation, which was my specialty. I studied English for twelve years in school. Enclosed is my TOEFL certification with excellent scores.

During the past year, I taught beginning graphic design courses to undergraduate students. I also assisted the faculty in organizing the Spring Open House display of students' work for the public and employers to view. I have also worked part-time for several local media companies in Berlin while I was in school.

I have a particular interest in your company because of the products you produce, especially CDs and magazines, and the Internet services you offer to clients.

My enclosed resume provides further information for your review. I am available to meet with you during your scheduled campus visit in March. I look forward to hearing from you.

Thank you for your consideration.

Sincerely,

Ann Schmidt

Enclosures (3)

WRITING YOUR RESUME

Professionalism is the one quality that most impresses employers when reviewing a resume, whether it is printed or submitted online. It should be well written and visually pleasing. Personnel (or a computer scanner) will scan a stack of resumes, perhaps spending no more than 30 seconds on each resume. For this reason, American resumes are one page and are summary in nature, in contrast to six and seven page resumes used in some cultures. If you send a six-page resume to an American company they will not read it. Type font and paper rules are the same as the cover letter: keep it simple.

If your resume passes this initial screening, it will be sent to the department head where the opening exists. If it passes this second test, you will be called to schedule an interview, first with the personnel department, and if you pass, with the department head.

Your resume should sell your *skills, experience,* and *accomplishments* to the reader with little effort, as shown in the sample resume below. Here's how.

- *Customize* – Tailor each resume to the job for which you are applying. List only skills and qualifications that are *relevant* to that position. General resumes are not effective. People who mail 200 copies of a general resume will be lucky to receive two responses.

- *Accomplishments* – Employ powerful statements, not just a list of job duties and functions. Use action verbs with "ed" added, such as "reduced."

- *Use Bold Print* – Make position *titles* and *places* of employment stand out.

- *Be Brief* – Complete sentences are not necessary because your resume is a listing, not a discussion. Be specific. Instead of saying, "I am good with people," say, "Supervised 10 people and increased department output by 24% in one year." Use numbers, percentages, and dollars.

- *Easy Reading* – Leave sufficient white space (area with no writing) for quick, easy reading. Use of bullets (like you see to the left here) creates nice white space.

- *Be Honest* – If an employer sees you are obviously lying or exaggerating, you won't be considered. And, if after hiring you they find out you lied, that is grounds for firing. Remember our saying? "Tell it like it is."

Things To Avoid – These should not be in your resume.
- Abbreviations and technical terms that may not be understood.
- Eliminate the "I" pronoun by using bullets and incomplete sentences.
- Negative or awkward matters that are hard to write about, including reasons for leaving jobs, problems encountered on jobs, illnesses.
- Availability date to begin the job.
- Miscellaneous details: age, race, weight, sex, height, health status, political affiliation, marital status, number of children, unrelated hobbies, unimportant

test scores (TOEFL is okay if related to the job), sports interests, church affiliations, family background, home ownership, social security number, driver's license, geographic preference, your picture, supervisor's name and title, salary requirements.

• To avoid discrimination, it is illegal to ask interviewees about their age, race, national origin, marital or parental status, or disabilities. Avoid these things, too.

Parts Of The Resume – Okay, so far so good. Let's now get started putting your professional looking resume together. Although there is not one specific format used for all situations, all resumes should at least have four basic parts: *heading, objective, work experience,* and *education* as shown in the sample resume below. Additional parts such as *skills* and *interests* can be used if they are appropriate to the job applied for.

1. **Heading** – Begin a resume with your name, address, and telephone numbers (work, home, cell) and e-mail address centered in the middle of the top of the page. Your name should be bold face so it stands out. If you do not have a telephone, find a phone number where you are confident you will receive all your messages. There are companies that provide this service for a small monthly fee, such as www.answerunited.com.

2. **Objective** – Make your objective specific. Everyone wants a "challenging position that utilizes my skills," which is inappropriate, vague, and one that is commonly used. Stating the *occupation* you are seeking and the *industry* is more effective. If you can't be specific, don't state an objective. Each time you send out a resume you might juggle the objective a tad to make it appropriate for the position you are applying. Here are examples of specific ones.

• To obtain a position as legal secretary in real estate law.
• Seeking managerial position in medium to large size graphic design organization.
• To obtain materials management position in dynamic high-technology manufacturing company.

3. **Experience** – An employer first wants to match your particular skills and experience from your two most recent jobs with the job opening. So list your prior *jobs, skills,* and *accomplishments.* Employers look for the following.

• Are there sufficient years of work at the appropriate level and areas?
• Is the candidate missing any critical experience?
• Does the candidate have sufficient breadth and depth of technical knowledge?
• Does the applicant have the required supervisory, management, or leadership skills required for this position?

- Is there a solid record of accomplishments, such as promotions, awards, certificates, responsibility for increased profitability or decreased costs?
- Are there gaps in the dates of employment, which might suggest something is being withheld?

Sample Resume

THOMAS B. JONES
123 Apple Street
San Francisco, CA 94567
(456) 345-6789
tjones@aol.com

OBJECTIVE:	Manager of Media Services with a progressive international corporation.
SKILLS:	Programming languages: Visual Basic, Java, C, C++ Scripting and markup languages: HTML, XML, JavaScript Internet technologies: ASP, DHTML, Microsoft Transaction Server Database technologies: SQL Server, Oracle

EXPERIENCE: Acme Media Corporation, Boston MA
MEDIA DESIGN MANAGER   1996 to 2011

- Managed a staff of 43 and a portfolio of 17 foodservice, distributor, and government accounts with sales volume of $15,000,000.

- Reduced employee turnover 40% by using decentralized project teams.

- Reduced client billing collection time by 45% and errors by 18% by implementing new invoicing system and related procedures.

- Increased employee productivity 25% and sales dollars 29% by designing and implementing new project management system.

Hollywood Media Corporation, Hollywood CA
MEDIA DESIGN MANAGER   1991 to 1996

- Managed a portfolio comprising an annual sales volume of $9,000,000 in TV, movie, CD, and radio industries.

- Hired, trained, and supervised a staff of 19 full time employees and 20 to 25 diversified accounts. Contracted for freelance media design personnel.

- Reduced overhead 15% with improved project monitoring system and quicker inter-department communication.

EDUCATION:	Boston University – BS, Business Administration; MS, Graphic Design
SPECIAL INTERESTS:	Fluent in Spanish, Japanese, and English
PROFESSIONAL AFFILIATIONS:	International Society of Media Managers. Recipient of 2011 AGDS Award

450

Two basic resume formats are used to list work experience.

- *Chronological* resumes list jobs in order, starting with the most recent job you held and working backwards (as shown in the sample resume).
- *Functional* resumes group jobs under specific areas of skills and abilities.

Most employers prefer a chronological resume. If, however, you are seeking a job in a field in which you have *no prior experience*, use the functional skills format to present your relevant experience and skills up front with your jobs listed under the skills.

In this EXPERIENCE section of your resume, also summarize your *work history*, identify your *accomplishments*, and define your *skills*.

- List your places of employment (or major volunteer work). Include names and cities of each organization with beginning and ending year dates and positions held.
- State your duties and functions by summarizing your major responsibilities. Write the skills you used, knowledge you needed, and equipment utilized. List your biggest accomplishments, projects, and assignments.

Note: If necessary, you may first have a stand-alone section that reads SKILLS and then list them *if they are relevant to the job*, as shown in the sample resume. Employers look for two types of skills: hard skills and soft skills.

- *Hard skills* are acquired such as computer languages, typing speeds, years of management, and tools utilized.
- *Soft skills* are conveyed as a result of your accomplishments. Examples are communication and interpersonal skills, dependability, motivation levels, energy level, and punctuality. To be effective, explain how you acquired them instead of merely listing them.

In describing your EXPERIENCE accomplishments, think in measurable terms: money saved, profits increased, numerical effects, and the impact your action had on people, places, and things in the workplace. Examples:

- Reduced file-searching time 50% by implementing numeric filing system.
- Increased sales 30% with new geographical sales territories and staff.
- Reduced staff turnover 14% by implementing new employee benefit program.
- Saved $61,000 annually by automating payroll department.

4. **Education, Special Interests, Professional Affiliations** – In this last part of your resume, list your education and professional training. Include places attended, dates, certificates and diplomas received. Highlight any specific areas of study or training or organizations and professional affiliations that are relevant to the position you are

applying for. As shown in the sample resume, if you have relevant special interests, such as a language proficiency, you may have a separate section with that name, too.

YOUR INTERVIEW

Our large businesses have **personnel** *[purr-son-ELL]* departments (also called the **human resources (HR) department**). They select prospective employees for an initial job interview. If you appear to meet their requirements, they will schedule an interview appointment with you. If you are interviewing with a small company, you might only talk to the owner.

Once you have landed an interview, it is to your advantage to do more research on that company before you go in. Some companies have an Internet site that provides

Job interview.   (careers.maxupdates.tv)

information about them. While you are in their building, be observant and learn what you can. Read brochures or other information they might have. Notice how people are dressed. Such details may inform you as to whether or not you are a match for the firm and may help improve your interview. Here are more pointers to consider beforehand.

- When scheduling an interview time, studies show that applicants who interview during mid-morning hours have an advantage; probably because the interviewer is not too busy or worn from a long day's work.
- Arrive early because you will probably be asked to fill out an application form. Much of what they ask for on the form will be on your resume, but you still need to fill it out. Be neat and complete all that is asked for.
- You may be asked for references, so take names, addresses, and telephone numbers with you.
- When you send out your resume, do not include transcripts, letters of recommendation, or awards unless you are specifically asked to do so. If required, send copies, never the original. If not sent out, take them with you to the interview.
- A quality brief case adds a professional look.
- Introduce yourself and be courteous to office personnel. (Refer to Chapter H on customs and etiquette to review customs and greetings.) The interviewer might question these people to **get their take** (how they viewed you) on you.
- Have additional copies of your resume ready.

Tip The Scales In Your Favor – A survey of hiring managers was made to determine those factors they use to decide to hire one person over another. Here is what some had to say.

- *Confidence* – "Confidence is important, but there is a fine line between that and arrogance."
- *Creativity* – "We tend to ask oddball questions to gauge a candidate's reaction. I might ask, 'If you were a candy bar, what kind would you be?'"
- *Generalities* – "I hate when I ask a candidate what their favorite thing to work on is and they say 'everything.'"
- *Interest* – "When a candidate displays a true desire to come work for your company, they are often the one you want to hire from the finalist pool."
- *Language* – "If I interview someone who uses lots of **business speak** (non-everyday business terms) and don't give me any impression of what their personality is like, I will usually pass."
- *Positive Attitude* – "Two things can be **deal breakers**: attitude and core values. A positive attitude, strong work ethic, and strong values should **trump** [outweigh] more experience and skill."
- *Preparation* – "I know I have a good candidate for hire when they come in prepared with as many questions about the job and company as I have for the candidate."
- *Sincerity* – "If I'm **on the fence** [undecided] about a candidate but they take the time to e-mail me and thank me for having them come in, it shows me they are motivated, tactful, and professional."

A university study of recent college graduates looking for jobs found:
- Nearly half don't dress appropriately for job interviews.
- Almost 1 out of 3 shows up late for job interviews.
- More than 1 in 4 show up unprepared, failing to adequately research the company to which they were applying.
- Nearly 1 in 4 exhibit poor verbal skills, including mangled grammar.

Your Attire – In order to be taken more seriously, wear neat, clean, appropriate clothing. Refer to Chapter P on dress and appearance. Here are a few quick tips for creating a professional image during your interview.
- *Colors* – Wear subdued colors (like navy blue), styles and patterns. Briefcases, purses, and shoes should also be conservative in color and in good condition.
- *Garments* – Men should wear a suit and tie, even if the company's dress is business casual. Women should dress similarly with a simple suit, dress, or well-tailored pantsuit. Avoid leather jackets and turtlenecks.
- *Hemlines* – Should not be more than three inches above the knee. Don't wear cutoff pants or leggings to the interview.

- *In Style* – Avoid out-of-date suits with lapels that are too wide or too narrow (one inch or less). Men's jackets should be full-body rather than tight.
- *Jewelry* – Should be understated. Don't wear more than two rings per hand or one earring per ear. No face jewelry or ankle bracelets please.
- *Nails* – Nails should be groomed. Flashy nail polish is unacceptable.
- *Purse* – Women might tuck a small wallet or purse inside a briefcase to avoid carrying two bags. Printed or trendy handbags are not desirable
- *Shoes* – Open-toed, backless, or athletic shoes are not acceptable.
- *Smells* – Wear little or no cologne, perfume, or aftershave lotion.
- *Stockings* – Even though it is more fashionable these days for women to go bare legged, this may not be the time for that depending on the company and the geographical location. Wear stockings, even in summer weather. Stockings can be in neutral colors or a fashion color to match your shoes.

Your Demeanor – Be yourself, not someone you think they want to see. Follow these guidelines to help the real *you* shine through the interview.

- *Be Positive* – Phrase your answers in a positive light. If you are asked about an unpleasant previous job or your weakest characteristic, be honest. For example, you might reveal that speaking in front of groups is the area in which you need the most improvement, but that you are taking public speaking classes.
- *Body language* – Body language is a non-verbal communication, so do not squirm, slouch, shift in your chair, swing your feet, fold arms across your chest (it looks defensive), or rub your hands or legs together. These all convey nervousness. Take a deep breath and relax.

- *Enthusiasm* – Try not to let nervousness block your enthusiasm and interest in the job. If you happen to have a telephone interview first, make your voice energetic, warm, and clear. Your interviewer is listening for these signs.

Positive body language.

- *Honesty* – One thousand of the largest firms in the U.S. were asked to define the one quality of an applicant—apart from ability and willingness to do the job—that most impressed interviewers. Honesty was number one. Guarding your answers or answering only what you think they want to hear will make you appear dishonest. Do not exaggerate either.

454

Starting Your Interview – Don't start talking about the job at first. Make small talk initially so the interviewer can judge your ability to socialize (see Chapter V on business customs and small talk). Here are possible topics.

- Comment on something positive you saw while walking in the company or in the interviewer's office.
- Concentrate on getting to know your interviewer as an individual instead of someone who merely interviews people.
- Focus on getting your message across to the interviewer and on how he is responding. If you sense he does not understand you, try again, or ask if he would like more information.
- Try to understand what issues or questions are important to your interviewer based on the types of questions asked of you.

Answering Questions – To get to know you, the interviewer may first pose general questions, then ask about your experience and your reasons for seeking a new position. Then he might inquire about your career plans for the future and your motivation for applying for the job.

When you find yourself **in the spotlight** (attention focused on you), your replies should be clear and relevant. Before going to your interview, have a friend ask you various questions and then the two of you evaluate your responses honestly.

Robert Half International, the personnel firm, asked more than 650 managers in the U.S. and Canada to name the single question they ask that provides the most insight about a job applicant. These were the five most important.

- "Can you tell me a little about yourself?"
- "Why do you want to join our company?"
- "What's your biggest weakness?"

> **Hint**: Employment firms say you should respond to this question by mentioning *one* minor weakness that *does not* directly relate to how well you would perform in the job you are being interviewed for. Also, describe how you are overcoming it.

- "Where do you see yourself in five years?"
- "Why are you looking to leave your current employer?"

To answer these and other questions appropriately, consider these guidelines.

- *Listen Carefully* – If the question is unclear, politely ask for clarification. This is especially important on a telephone interview where you cannot rely on visual clues from the interviewer.
- *Pause* – Consider possibilities before answering a question.

- *Difficulties* – Be truthful, but do not *initiate* subjects that could pose difficulties for you.
- *Get to the Point* – This is a problem my foreign friends who tend to tell a long, unneeded backstory before answering a question. First ask the interviewer if this information is needed.
- *Salary* – When asked for your salary requirements, employers say the best response is to say it will vary, depending on your responsibilities and the financial benefits the company offers (health care, retirement plans, childcare, etc.). If pressed, give a *general* salary range that you would expect. Feel free to ask the salary range for the position. Also, ask about their retirement plan. Refer to Chapter X on business and finance that explains our 401 (k) retirement plan that should be factored in when considering overall compensation.
- *Successes* – Focus on your past successes when answering questions.
- *Subject* – Don't try to change the subject; this is your interviewer's job.

Remember that an interview is a two-way conversation. For the interviewer, he wants to evaluate your *skills*, *capabilities*, and levels of *experience*. For you, the interview is to sell yourself and to evaluate the position. After asking questions, the interviewer usually invites you to ask questions. Employers are impressed by applicants who ask big-picture questions, such as "Where does the company expect to be in a three years?" or "Why is your company successful?"

Concluding Your Interview – At the conclusion of the interview, restate any point you feel merits emphasis. You might summarize a few of your strong skills that you feel would be required for the job now that you know more about the position. If you feel in hindsight that you didn't answer a question as well as you should have, it is okay to address it again. (Actors do this on auditions as they gain more insight into their character after several attempts at it.)

> **Hint**: If you are interested in the job, do not leave before expressing your interest. Otherwise, the interviewer may think you have no interest. Also, you might state that you would appreciate their keeping your resume on file in case you are not selected and another job opening might arise. In other words, show positive interest in the job, the interviewer, and the company.

Thank the interviewer for considering you for the job. Ask for the interviewer's business card before you leave. Be the first to offer a handshake, even if you are a woman.

When you get home, send a brief one-page thank-you letter to the interviewer and restate your interest in the company and the position. If you spoke to more than one, thank each of them individually either by writing separate letters or by mentioning each person's name in one letter. Recap your relevant major strengths that you can now see would lead to your success in the job. Correct any issues that you feel in hindsight might have been misunderstood. Explain why you are still interested in the job.

> **Hint**: Employers say that thank-you letters are surprisingly rare, which is one reason they are so effective. Treat your interviewer as you would a host in a social situation as we discussed in Chapter H on customs and etiquette.

Job interviewing is a lot like acting auditions I have been to. You think beforehand about what you are going to say. You try not to get nervous. You do your "performance." You go home and think of 150 different things you said and did wrong. It is okay to evaluate your performance because you will learn to do better at the next job interview. And remember, just like actors, the things you think you did wrong may not be a **big deal** (important) to the interviewer. So go easy on yourself, something I had to learn the hard way.

Good luck with your job search!

QUITTING YOUR JOB

Career counselors at brazencareerist.com say that if you have serious concerns about your job and leaving, it is best to have conversations with your supervisor early on. Do not wait till you get to a **boiling point** (very angry or upset) and say or do something you might regret later. People will respect you, and if you can't reach an agreement, find a constructive way to leave.

Here are five things they recommend you do *before* leaving your job.

1. Send a mass e-mail to colleagues telling them what you are excited to be doing next, no matter the circumstances. No one wants to hear you are leaving because you hate your job. Have a positive spin so you leave a good impression with coworkers and colleagues who might recommend you for other opportunities.

2. Leave right after you do something quantifiable, such as a successful sales period, so you can walk away with tangible results for your resume. Leaving after a project's successful completion can also distract from any negativity related to your exit.

3. Be a grownup. Instead of blaming the company, admit the job or industry was a bad fit for you and then move on.

4. Offer to help find and train your replacement. Your colleagues will remember that and appreciate it.

5. Provide at least two weeks' notice, but don't assume management will take you up on that. Protect yourself by downloading all the relevant contacts and

information you will need (and are legally entitled to) as soon as you give notice.

JOB MARKET TODAY

The U.S. Department of Labor (www.dol.gov) identifies jobs that are expected to grow rapidly between now and 2018. These occupations are in high demand today and are expected to continue on this trajectory for the next decade. Here are the current 20 fastest growing occupations and their average yearly salaries.

- Biomedical engineers $77,400 (a 72% increase in number of jobs by 2018)
- Network systems and data communications analysts - $71,100
- Home health aides - $20,460
- Personal and home care aides - $19,180
- Financial examiners - $70,930
- Medical scientists - $72,590
- Physician assistants - $81,230
- Skin care specialists - $28,730
- Biochemists and biophysicists - $82,840
- Athletic trainers - $39,640
- Physical therapist aides - $23,760
- Dental hygienists - $66,570
- Veterinary technologists and technicians - $28,900
- Dental assistants - $32,380
- Computer software engineers, applications - $85,430

Top five best-paying jobs in the U.S.
1. Surgeon: $219,770
2. Anesthesiologist: $211,750
3. Oral and Maxillofacial Surgeon: $210,710
4. Orthodontist: $206,190
5. Obstetrician and Gynecologist: $204,470

Top five worst-paying jobs in the U.S.
1. Food Preparation/Serving $18,120
2. Cook, Fast Food: $18,230
3. Dishwasher: $18,330
4. Shampooer $18,890
5. Bartend/Dining Room Attendant $18,900

PAYING YOUR TAXES

Congratulations! You got a job! Guess what? Now, depending on various factors, you may have to pay taxes on the money you are paid. As we say in the U.S., **two things are certain: death and taxes.** To be paid, you must first obtain a **social security number** (SSN) from the federal government (www.socialsecurity.gov). This nine-digit number remains with you all your life. An employer reports your wages to the state and federal government using your SSN. You pay your taxes using this number. This number is used in other ways to identify you. In effect, this is a type of national identification number used by other countries, although we profess not to have one. (There's that *independence* thing again.)

458

Instead of a SSN (depending on your legal status and your visa type), you may need an Individual Taxpayer Identification Number (ITIN). To get one, fill out and send in IRS Form W-7, Application for IRS Individual Taxpayer Identification Number. You can get this and many other forms and information online (www.irs.gov) or by contacting a local **IRS** (Internal Revenue Service) branch office. We have three levels of taxes.

Federal Taxes – The federal government requires each person working in the U.S. to pay taxes on income they receive from U.S. sources, primarily from employment, tips, interest and dividend payments, capital gains, rental property income, and winnings. Certain people have to pay taxes on money they receive from sources outside the U.S.

IRS
Department of the Treasury
Internal Revenue Service

Employers are required to provide you with Form W-2, Wage and Tax Statement by January 31st. It shows how much you earned the prior year and what taxes were deducted. You use this to file your yearly state and federal income tax forms that are due by April 15th. You will be assessed fees if you owe money and are late submitting it.

Keep in mind that your employer has to report to the IRS all money paid to you. If you don't file a tax form, the IRS will know and they will contact you to find out why and might impose a penalty. Tax evasion is grounds for deportation. Appendix 5 provides a sample **Form 1040** used to report your year-end taxes. There are shorter forms (1040EZ) used for simple filings, most likely by students and non-permanent residents.

If you earned money in the U.S. and are here on special visas like an F (student), J (exchange program), or M (vocational school), you *will* have to file an income tax return. Depending on the source and nature of your income, you might *not* have to pay any taxes. If you think your income is non-taxable, **play it safe** (don't take a chance) and consider filing an income tax return anyway. If you do not, you may run into legal trouble.

An **alien** is any person here who is not a U.S. citizen. For taxing purposes, the IRS classifies aliens as either resident or non-resident. Resident aliens generally are taxed on their worldwide income, similar to U.S. citizens. To be classified as a resident alien, you must meet one of two tests.

1. *Green Card* - The Bureau of Citizenship and Immigration Services issued a **green card** that authorizes you to live and work in the U.S. on a permanent basis. (After five years you can apply for citizenship.)
2. *Substantial Presence* – If you were physically present in the U.S. for 31 days during the current year and 183 days during a three-year period that includes the current year and the two years immediately before that.

If neither test is met, you are classified as a non-resident alien. Information on resident/non-resident status is available at www.irs.gov/pub/irs-pdf/p519.pdf.

You may need help filing your income tax forms. More than 80 percent of American taxpayers seek help from a tax preparer or will use tax-preparation software such as Turbo Tax (www.turbotax.com). College students might obtain help from the international student center at school. There are also many organizations and tax accountants that prepare tax returns for a modest fee. H&R Block (www.hrblock.com) has offices throughout the U.S. The IRS website provides assistance (www.irs.gov) and answer questions, or you can telephone (800-829-1040) for information and advice. (State governments also provide these services for their own taxation process.)

State Taxes – These taxes are imposed and collected on residents of states. Like so many other things that vary between the states, there are vast differences here too.

- *Income Tax* - States that tax income generally tax the same sources as the federal government. Seven states have no income tax: Alaska, Florida, Nevada, South Dakota, Texas, Washington, and Wyoming. The highest state tax rate is Hawaii's at 11 percent. Illinois has the lowest at 3 percent. Visit your state's website to see how your income is taxed. If you interview for jobs in these non-taxing states, factor in the tax savings as part of your pay.

- *Sales Tax* - This is paid on the purchase of certain goods at the time of the purchase. In some countries this is called the consumption value-added tax (VAT), but the U.S. has no national sales tax. Sales taxes are assessed by every state except Alaska, Delaware, Montana, New Hampshire, and Oregon. The sales tax is not included in the price marked on the product, so the cashier adds the tax at the register. This generally adds about 6 to 9 percent to the price of an item in those states that have a sales tax. Some cities and counties also add small additional taxes on top of the basic state rates. (In some cases you can use your state sales taxes paid as a deduction on your tax return.)

Local Taxes - Some U.S. localities tax our personal property annually like cars, houses, airplanes, trailers, and boats. The 10 states with the lowest property taxes are all in the South where homeowners average less than $1,000 a year in property taxes, while those in the East can pay more than six times as much. This might seem strange if your country or locality has no such taxes, such as China that is experimenting with them to quell speculative house purchases. In some counties they only tax once when the house is purchased. If you purchase a house in the U.S., the realtor informs you of last year's tax bill or will estimate it if it a new house.

Our final section deals with English grammar and speech, the number one problem area foreigners say they have dealing with American culture. Quick and easy ways are provided to improve your English grammar, speech, writing, and communication skills and to reduce your foreign accent. Tips are provided for enhancing the image you create by avoiding errors commonly made by foreigners.

SECTION IV
AMERICA'S LANGUAGE

To write or even speak English is not a science but an art. There are no reliable words. Whoever writes English is involved in a struggle that never lets up even for a sentence. He is struggling against vagueness, against obscurity, against the lure of the decorative adjective, against the encroachment of Latin and Greek, and, above all, against the worn-out phrases and dead metaphors with which the language is cluttered up.

George Orwell, British author 1903-1950

Y

LET'S USE BETTER ENGLISH GRAMMAR

Order and simplification are the first steps toward the
mastery of a subject. - Thomas Mann, 20th century German novelist

This chapter identifies common grammar problems foreigners have with English and how they can overcome these stumbling blocks. Grammar defines how the various components of a language are used correctly. In Chapter Z on speaking better English, we deal with how you can become a more effective English speaker. These two chapters go **hand in hand** (work together closely). Correct use of grammar will help you communicate with Americans better and put you in a **favorable light** (nice impression).

As you may know, English grammar rules are full of generalities and the generalities are full of exceptions. Even the exceptions have exceptions. This is why English is one of the most difficult languages to master. In fact, a recent European study discovered that most children master the basic elements of their languages within a year or less of starting primary school. However, English speaking children require two to three years of learning to reach the same level. Why? Linguists believe it's the complex syllable structure (a single-sound unit in our words) and the inconsistent spellings, both of which we address in this and the next chapter.

> **Hint**: Advanced English speakers will not find all the exceptions and rules in our crazy language discussed in this chapter. In order to identify, simplify, and explain typical errors made by foreigners, I've focused on *general* rules, not on all possibilities. Those seeking more depth should obtain an advanced English grammar book such as *A Practical English Grammar* that is available from booksellers and Amazon.com at amzn.to/Grammar4Foreigners.

Most of my foreign friends and students who speak English as a second language (ESL) have studied the language in their countries, taken English classes in America, or done both. Most of them have a good *understanding* of our basic grammar rules, but still have problems speaking and writing grammatically correct sentences. I even found this true with the teachers of English I taught in China. Part of the problem is that foreigners do not have the opportunity to apply in real situations what they have learned. They might do well on basic grammar tests as my teacher-students did, but they stumble when they try to put it all together and actually use it.

Even if you think you have sufficient knowledge of our grammar, you *will* become a better writer and speaker after reading this chapter. Please keep an open mind and don't skip over it. Because of the chapter's linear organization, take your time and understand one section before going on to the next.

COMMON FOREIGN ERRORS

In my international travels, I try to read local tourist brochures and signs written in English to learn more about the problems foreigners have with crazy English. I use them as examples in my classes to point out grammatical errors that are common in their country as well as others. Below are two examples from different points on the globe. Yes, they *are* minor errors, but common ones. One purpose of this book is to help you polish your English so you can avoid both little and big grammar **boo-boos** (mistakes).

I was flying on a Hungarian airline from Venice, Italy, to Budapest, Hungary, and read the airline's magazine that had a Hungarian page on one side and a translated English page opposite it. Here are three of several dozen errors that stuck out like a **sore thumb** (very obvious) and are discussed fully in this chapter.

- Foreigners have problems using our three little articles: *a*, *an*, and *the*. The airline president's message was, *"I invite you to concert!"* The correct version should be "…to *a* concert" or "to *the* concert."

- We use matching verb tenses in a sentence. *"…Carpatair has* [present tense] *reached a point where it wanted* [past tense] *to be able…."* So, if you choose the present tense it would read "…*has* reached a point where it *wants* to be able…." If you choose the past tense, it would be "…*had* reached a point where it *wanted* to be…." It may be hard to see sometimes, but there *is* logic to our tenses.

- In a list of two or more items, we generally use "and" or "or" before the last item. *"…in-flight courses cover aspects such as public speaking, facial expression, body language."* It should read "…facial expression, *and* body language."

The second example comes from a bilingual book I purchased in the U.S. written for Asians to improve their business English. Published in Asia, it had several hundred English grammar errors commonly made by Asians. They all could have been avoided if the writer or editor had read this chapter. Here are a few of them.

- Some Asians have problems using "the" correctly. *"We have come to discuss with you about the business.*" This could read "We have come to discuss *the* business [a particular business] with you," or "We have come to discuss business [business in general] with you."

- We match singular/plural verbs with singular/plural nouns. *The other party have the right to cancel the contract.* " This could read "...the other party *has* the right to cancel...." or "...the other *parties have* the right to cancel...."

- Our sentences must have a verb. *What relationship between you?* This could read "What *is the* relationship between you?" or "Are you two related?"

- If a word begins with a vowel sound, we use "an" instead of "a" before it. *"You know how a Americans like to create new words."* This could be "You know how *an* American likes...." or "You know how Americans like...."

- And finally, some of our crazy nouns are both singular and plural so we do not add an "s" to make them plural. *"We need some new equipments."* This could read "We need some new *equipment.*" ("Equipment" is what we call a collective noun that is both singular and plural.)

There were dozens and dozens more in the book, but you get the point: Be careful when reading something in English in your country—it might be a case of the **blind leading the blind** (uninformed people leading others who are similarly incapable). I even find grammar errors in material written by Americans and spoken on TV and in our movies. You will be able to **tune in to** (detect) these errors after you read this chapter.

Numerous websites are available to test your knowledge of grammar errors. This one is particularly helpful—especially for students preparing for our SAT exam. It has sample sentences with errors for you to correct: www.majortests.com/sat/grammar.php.

So, let's begin by examining our alphabet, then our three formal levels of English usage, and the six basic types of words we use. Then we'll put it all together and construct grammatically correct sentences. It's easier than you think if you take your time and progress one step at a time. Ready?

THE ALPHABET

An alphabet *[AL-fuh-bet]* is a set of letters or other symbols that represent distinct sounds in a language. These letters combine to form words. The words combine to form sentences that impart thought. The 6500 languages in the world use about 50 different alphabets. Most languages use between 20 and 30 letters. Our Hawaiian language only uses 12, the fewest of any language. Cambodia's 74-letter alphabet gets the **blue ribbon** (first prize) for the world's longest.

Only a few languages like Japanese and Chinese do not use an alphabet in this traditional sense. In the 1950s, China introduced *pinyin,* a system of writing Chinese using 25 of our Roman alphabet letters, but it has no "V." This explains why some Chinese Americans have problems pronouncing the name of my friend David.

English uses the Roman alphabet that originated in Greece 3,000 years ago. In fact, nearly 30 percent of our *words* are derived from Greek and Latin. Our language has 26 letters from A to Z.* Five of our letters are called **vowels**: **A, E, I, O, U**, which are spoken without friction in the mouth. The remaining 21 letters are **consonants** that are partly obstructed with friction. We discuss these pronunciations in detail in Chapter Z on speaking better English.

LEVELS OF ENGLISH USAGE

We have three levels of English usage: *formal, general,* and *informal.* There are not clear distinctions between these levels, but we do use them in different circumstances.

Formal English – You will find formal English in our academic writings, some textbooks, scientific writings, literary magazines, and formal speeches. It is used primarily by well-educated people and has a somewhat limited use in everyday life. When you know formal English you'll have a better instinct for sprinkling a little of this educated speech into your everyday general speech to add polish to it.

General English – Most of the English we read, hear, and speak is general English. We find it in our newspapers, magazines, books, and on television. It speaks to a general audience but is also the way educated people converse in everyday situations. General English is the level this book is written in and the practical level I teach my students.

Informal English – This lower level is more characteristic of speech than of writing. It is less formal than general English and assumes an intimacy with the person you are communicating with.

> **Hint**: If the above sentence ended with "with the person *to whom* you are communicating," it would fit into the formal classification of English because many Americans do not distinguish between *who* and *whom* when they speak or write. Formal English, however, makes this distinction and does not end a sentence with a preposition like *with*.

When we speak informal English, we are also likely to use slang or colloquial words or phrases that we normally would not use in our writing. These are discussed in the next chapter and are used throughout this book to **bring you up to speed** (inform you) on their use. Yes, that *was* one of our slang phrases you just read and have seen printed in bold since you began reading this book.

---

* This is our alphabet in uppercase and lowercase letters. Vowels are in bold letters.
A,B,C,D,**E**,F,G,H,**I**,J,K,L,M,N,**O**,P,Q,R,S,T,**U**,V,W,X,Y,Z. **a**,b,c,d,**e**,f,g,h,**i**,j,k,l,m,n,**o**,p,q,r,s,t,**u**,v,w,x,y,z.

466

SIX TYPES OF WORDS

Our rules of grammar define how we use words and punctuation to form sentences. Let's first define the six major types of words we use in our sentences: *nouns, pronouns, adjectives, verbs, adverbs,* and *prepositions.* Each has a specific purpose. You need a general understanding of these word types in order to construct proper sentences and to avoid common errors made by foreigners (and Americans!). Let's first learn a little bit about these words and how to identify them. Later, you will learn specific rules for using them correctly in your sentences.

Nouns *[nowns]* – A noun is a word used to name a person, place, thing, or an idea. If you can add an "s" or "ies" to a word to make it plural (more than one), it is a noun, such as "car*s*" or "berr*ies*" We have a few exceptions like "equipment" that we discussed earlier in the Chinese "book of errors." As you can see, the spelling of nouns usually changes in the plural, sometimes causing problems for foreigners because nouns may not change in their language.

Ranking of 25 Most Frequently Used Nouns

time, person, year, way, day, thing, man, world, life, hand, part, child, eye, woman, place, work, week, case, point, government, company, number, group, problem, fact.

Pronouns *[PRO-nowns]* – A pronoun is a word used in place of one or more nouns. You ask someone, "Did you find your book?" and they respond, "Yes, I found *it.*" They use the pronoun *it* in place of the noun *book.*

Ranking of 25 Most Frequently Used Pronouns

it, I, you, he, they, we, she, who, them, me, him, one, her, us, something, nothing, anything, himself, everything, someone, themselves, everyone, itself, anyone, myself.

Both foreigners and Americans have trouble selecting the grammatically correct pronoun. Some foreigners even have a tendency to omit them. It is important that you learn to recognize and correctly use these little but important guys to add sparkle to your grammar.

I, me, mine, myself
you, your, yours, yourself, yourselves
he, him, his, himself
she, her, hers, herself
it, its, itself

467

we, us, our, ours, ourselves
they, them, their, theirs, themselves
this, these, those, that
who, whom, whose
none, someone, anyone, everyone
somebody, anybody, everybody

Notice the *who* and *whom* pronouns above that we discussed earlier? A little later you will learn how to select the proper pronouns in your sentences, including these two **pesky** (troublesome) ones that give us *all* trouble.

Adjectives *[AD-juhk-tivs]* – An adjective is a word used to modify a noun or pronoun. Modify means to make the meaning of a word more definite by telling *what kind, which one,* or *how many*. Our most common adjectives are the little words **a, an,** and **the**, which we call **articles** that indicate if the noun is specific or general. Some languages do not use what we would define as articles in this context. Example: "*The* [specific] *blue* car is parked in *a* [general] garage under *a bright* light." In the above example, *blue* and *bright* adjectives further describe their nouns. (The most frequently used adjective in English is *good*. The top 25 are listed at the end of this chapter.)

> **Ranking of 25 Most Frequently Used Adjectives**
> *good, new, first, last, long, great, little, own, other, old, right, big, high, different,l small, large, next, early, young, important, few, public, bad, same, able.*

Verbs *[verrbz]* – A verb is a word that expresses action, state of being, or helps to make a statement. We have two types. **Action verbs** express action such as *run, play, make, talked*. **Linking verbs** do not express action, but simply act as a helping link (suggest a relationship) between the subject and additional information about the subject, such as "She *is* a lawyer," or "John *seems* tired." Some common linking verbs are *be, become, grow, appear, look, feel, remain, sound,* and *stay*.

> **Ranking of 25 Most Frequently Used Verbs**
> *be, have, do, say, get, make, go, know, take, see, come, think, look, want, give, use, find, tell, ask, work, seem, feel, try, leave, call.*

The most common verb in English (and in most languages) is the verb **to be**. It is a **helping verb** and is usually followed by a noun or adjective to fill out its meaning, such as "I *am* his father," or "Mary *is* pretty." A verb may have one or more helping verbs that work together as a unit with the main verb (especially if it ends in *ly)*. "The girls *had*

468

been playing tennis for an hour before it began to rain." In this sentence, three are used: "They *must have been* running."

We were required to memorize the 23 helping verbs in a 7th grade English class because they affect other words that will be used in a sentence. I have never forgotten them because the teacher grouped them together like lines in a poem so they had rhythm when spoken. They are: *be, is, been, being/am, are, was, were/do, did, done, doing/will, would/shall, should/can, could/may, might, must.*

Besides expressing action and linking, our verbs also indicate **tense**, meaning they tell when something happened (past, present, future). In English, the spelling of some verbs changes with the tense. Notice how the action verb *to run* changes: "I *ran* yesterday and I will *run* tomorrow." In some languages the verb form does not change, which causes problems for foreigners learning English. Also unlike some languages, in English the verb generally (but not always) is positioned *after* the subject (noun) in a sentence.

Later when we discuss how to construct proper sentences, the form of the verb you choose not only determines the tense of your sentence, but also affects the correct selection of other types of words in your sentence.

> **Hint**: Unlike some languages, our verbs can change into nouns and vice versa in our crazy language. For example, the verb "run" can be used both as a verb and as a noun. Here it is used both ways: "The *run* [noun] tired me out, but I will *run* [verb] again in the next race." Use this rule of thumb: If you can put the word "the" in front of a verb and it sounds right, it can be used as a noun; if you can put "to" in front of the noun and it sounds right, it can be used as a verb.

As you can see, because the use of verbs is not uniform throughout our different languages they can **trip up** (cause problems) foreign speakers. Do not feel discouraged if you think you are the only one with a problem trying to understand our crazy verbs. We have trouble with them, too, as well as with those in your language we are trying to learn.

Adverbs *[ADD-verrbs]* – An adverb is a word used to modify a verb, an adjective, or another adverb. Generally, adverbs tell *when, where, how,* and *to what extent* (how long or how much).

Ranking of 25 Most Frequently Used Adverbs

up, so, out, just, now, how, then, more, also, here, well, only, very, even, back, there, down, still, in, as, too, when, never, really, most.

You must learn to distinguish between adjectives and adverbs in order to use proper English. In our flexible language, the adverb will *generally* appear in *front* of an adjective or *after* a verb, but there are exceptions.

469

In these sentences, an adverb modifies a verb (swam):

John swam *then*. [when]
John swam *there*. [where]
John swam *quickly*. [how] ("John quickly swam" is a common error.)
John swam *far*. [where or to what extent]

In this sentence an adverb modifies an adjective: "We walked along a *very* narrow path." *Narrow* is an adjective describing *path,* but *very* is an adverb modifying *narrow,* telling to what degree it is narrow, so it precedes the adjective.

An adverb also modifies another adverb in this sentence: "Mother drove the car *rather slowly*." *Slowly* is an adverb modifying *drove* (it tells how Mother drove, so it follows the verb). *Rather* is an adverb modifying the adverb *slowly,* telling how slowly. Because the adverb generally comes after the verb it is modifying, theoretically we would not write "Mother *slowly drove* the car" but might say it in informal speech.

Mastering this simple act of generally placing an adverb after the verb will add polish to your English. Many of our adverbs are adjectives (like *slow*) that become adverbs when they end in "ly" (like slow*ly*). So when you see one of these "ly" critters, use a dictionary or possibly your computer's spell checker to see if it is an adverb (which I always do). Our best literary writers, including Hemingway (see Chapter K - Literature), avoid using adverbs because they encourage weak verbs. Instead, they use strong verbs to bolster the action of their sentences.

I like *The Frugal Editor* (www.bodurl.com/TheFrugalEditor), a book that goes into detail for advanced editing skills. Here's a list of pesky adverbs taken from it that do not end in "ly": *almost, always, even, far, fast, less, maybe, more, never, not, often, only, perhaps, sometimes, seldom, soon, then, today, tomorrow, too, very, well, yesterday.*

> **Hint**: You may have noticed that I occasionally place an adverb *before* a verb in some sentences in this book. There are situations in our crazy language where this is permissible, such as when adverbs function as intensifiers to convey a greater or lesser emphasis to something. For example: "He *literally* wrecked his car" is better sounding than "He wrecked *literally* his car." And there are other exceptions that are beyond the scope of this book. So if you're not sure, try it both ways. Most English speakers are not aware of all these obscure rules anyway; they would say **don't sweat the small stuff** (they're not important). Here's a rule that advanced writers adhere to: It is okay to break the rules only if you know you are breaking them *and* it will add color and meaning to your prose.

Prepositions *[prep-uh-ZISH-uns]* – A preposition, our sixth and final word type, is used to show the *relation* of a noun or pronoun to some other word in a sentence, such as time, space, objects, or methods. Example: "The rugs *on* the living room floor *over* there are beautiful." The preposition *on* shows the relation of *rugs* to *floor*, while *over* indicates a space relationship. The word *to* is the most frequently occurring preposition in English. Others are ranked at the end of this chapter by their usage.

470

☺ **Here's an assignment for you.** Copy this list of the rankings of the 25 most frequently used prepositions in English; carry it with you and learn to recognize them.

> ### Ranking Of 25 Most Frequently Used Prepositions
> *of, in, to, for, with, on, at, from, by, about, as, into, like, through, after, over, between, out, against, during, without, before, under, around, among.*

A group of words that begins with a preposition and ends with a noun or pronoun is a **prepositional phrase.** Examples: *on* the shelf, *in* the house, *from* the sky, *throughout* history, etc. Learn to recognize these phrases because, as we discuss later, they may need special punctuation (comma) to set them off. They will also influence other correct words to be used in your sentence. They also affect whether or not your sentence is complete if they are not followed up with another thought.

☺ **Here's an assignment for you.** Go through a publication in English and search for simple sentences. Circle five different uses for each of the six different word types we discussed, then put an abbreviation next to the word to identify it: A = adjective, AV = adverb, N = Noun, P = preposition, PN = pronoun, and V = verb.

THE SENTENCE

So far, so good. Now that you know the six basic word types in our crazy language, the next step is to select the correct words to form correct sentences. In English, a sentence is a group of words containing a **subject** and its **verb.** Sometimes it also contains an **object** that expresses a completed thought. Example: "I hit the ball," is a complete sentence in which *I* is the subject of the verb *hit*, and *ball* is the object that completes the thought. "I hit," is not a complete sentence because it is missing an object, and "I hit ball," is incorrect because it is missing the little article that tells it is a specific ball. Besides knowing how to select the correct verbs, subjects and objects, you also need to learn their proper word order sequence in your sentences.

Word Order In Your Sentence – The meaning of a sentence in English is conveyed largely by word order that indicates relationships between the words. The simple order of the main elements is *subject-verb-object.* Because that order differs from some languages, it causes problems for those learning English. This word order *can* be inverted, so sometimes you will see crazy looking sentences that are still considered proper English. But initially it is best to use this simple order and stick to it. Native English speakers write more clearly when they use this simple sentence structure, too.

Let's learn about the correct placement of subjects, verbs, and objects in your sentences.

The Subject Of Your Sentence – The subject is a noun or pronoun (or a phrase) naming the *person, place, thing,* or *idea* about which something is being said. A correct sentence has a subject and you *must* learn to identify it.

A common error some foreigners make is assuming the subject in their sentences instead of providing it. Proper English grammar almost always requires it. The example, "Is beautiful here," does not make sense to us. With the addition of the subject "It," it now makes sense. (Exceptions to this rule include sentences like "Do it," in which the assumed subject is "you." Nonetheless, use a subject to avoid running into trouble.)

> **Hint**: If you use the name of a subject (the noun) in a prior sentence, you may not need to duplicate it in your next sentence. A pronoun such as "it" can be used instead to make the sentence complete: "I love New York. *It* is beautiful here." Either way, you a need a noun or pronoun.

You need to know how to find the subject in your sentence because it determines the correct verb you use with it. In simple sentences, the subject usually comes before the verb and is what the sentence is about. Example: "The *hero* of the expedition *led* his men up the mountain." *Led* is the verb, and you need to know who or what was led to use the correct form of the verb. In this sentence the *hero* led, thus *hero* is the subject, not one of the other nouns (*expedition, men,* or *mountain*).

> **Hint**: Sentences that ask a question can be rephrased into a statement in order to find the subject more easily. "What were you doing?" should be made into "You were doing what?" in which *you* is the subject and *were doing* forms the verb.

The subject of a sentence is never found in a prepositional phrase. Review the list of prepositions above. Learn to recognize them. As we discussed, a prepositional phrase begins with a preposition and ends with a noun or pronoun and is a *secondary* thought that adds dimension to your *main* thought. Prepositional phrases can cause confusion in determining the sentence's correct subject and verb, even for Americans.

Here's an example. "The *building* with large wings on all sides *looks* like one in our city," is a correct sentence. The subject is *building*, not *wings* or *sides* in the prepositional phrase that begins with *with,* and the verb is *looks*.

English speakers, particularly **long-winded** (talking at tedious length) politicians, sometimes error when the object of a prepositional phrase in a long sentence is assumed to be the subject. They then use the wrong verb. In our example, a common mistake would be to incorrectly use the verb *look* (*wings look*) because *wings* was assumed to be the subject.

A subject may consist of two or more words, such as "*Jim and his sister* play ball," in which case *Jim* and *sister* form the plural (compound) subject, and *play* is the correct plural verb. If the connector between the two is "or" we select the singular verb, as in "Jim *or* his sister *plays* ball" because only one of them plays ball.

472

The Verb In Your Sentence – As we discussed above, a verb indicates an action, condition, or process of whatever the subject names. It is important to match the correct verb (both the time-frame tense and singular/plural designation) with the correct subject in a sentence. This is often a problem for foreigners because in their language the verb tense is not expressed in the verb. We discuss these rules for fvtense and singular/plural choices later. For the moment, just be aware that the verb's placement depends on the other components in the sentence, too.

The Object In Your Sentence – We said that a complete sentence must have a subject and a verb that are matched properly, and it must also have a completed thought. A **direct object** is a word that directly receives the action expressed by the verb or names the result of the action. Action verbs must have a receiver of the action, called the direct object. In the example, "Father took us home," *us* is the direct object that follows *took* the action verb. A little later we discuss the problem Americans have selecting the correct pronoun for a direct object such as *me* or *I*, or *he* or *him*, or *she* or *her*.

The object can also be a group of words. Here is what we call a **phrase** that begins with a preposition: *"Before he was in high school,"* in which we have a subject *he* and a verb *was*, but we don't have a completed thought because the preposition "before" alerts us a prepositional phrase follows. We could add *"John walked to school* before he was in high school" to make it complete, or, "Before he was in high school, *John walked to school.*" (Note the comma after the prepositional phrase that begins with "Before.")

Remember, your sentences must have a subject, a verb, and a completed thought, and these must be in proper sequence for good grammar.

☺ **Here's an assignment for you.** Select 20 simple sentences with action verbs in an English publication—perhaps this book—and circle the subject, draw a box around the verb, and underline the object in each of them. Practice this so you can do the same with your own written sentences you compose.

MAKING YOUR SENTENCES CORRECT

Now that you understand the six types of words we use in our sentences (nouns, pronouns, adjectives, verbs, adverbs, prepositions) and the three basic parts of a sentence (subject, verb, object) and their simple word order, you are ready to compose proper English sentences. To do this, you must use *complete sentences*, make your *subject and verb agree*, and use the *correct pronoun* when you need one. Here's how you bring it all together.

Complete Your Sentences – To make your sentence express a completed thought, it must have a subject and a verb and often an object. There is a long list of specific rules for making sentences complete, but in order to keep this simple we won't go into them. You want to get where intuition or common sense tells you when your sentence is complete. Soon you'll be able to tell that something is missing by simply reading or hearing your own incorrect sentences. An incomplete sentence "leaves you up in the air" waiting for something else, doesn't it? After all, that is how you do it in your native language. Here are tips to help you make simple, complete sentences.

Words ending in "ing" can alert you to what might be an incomplete sentence. They cannot be used as a verb unless they are helping verbs. For example, "The girls *making* fudge," is grammatically incorrect and leads to an incomplete sentence. It would be complete by adding the helping verb *were*, as in, "The girls were making fudge." Or it could be rephrased by changing the verb, "The girls *made* fudge."

A sentence beginning with a word that ends in "ing" forms a **dependent clause** and **waves a flag** (alerts) that the clause (group of words) needs something else to complete the sentence. For example, "Learn*ing* to make fudge," needs a verb and object to be complete, such as "Learning to make fudge *was* a fun *experience* for the children." Notice that the whole phrase subject "Learning to make fudge" substitutes for a simple subject consisting of a single noun like "Cooking is fun."

Remember our discussion of prepositions? We stated that a prepositional phrase begins with a preposition and ends with a noun or pronoun. If your sentence begins with a prepositional phrase and ends with a period, it might be an incomplete sentence. In fact, a rule of punctuation states that a comma is placed at the end of a prepositional phrase that *begins* a sentence in order to set it off from the remainder of the sentence. For example, "Before I went to the store," is a prepositional phrase that begins with the preposition *before* and ends with the noun *store*, but it does not complete the thought about what happened before going to the store. Instead, it could be "Before I went to the store, I looked for my shopping list." The prepositional phrase might also come at the end of the sentence: "I looked for my shopping list before I went to the store."

Run-On Sentences – The opposite of an incomplete sentence is a **run-on sentence**. The purpose of a sentence is to communicate your thought. If you get two or more main thoughts in a sentence, you might defeat your purpose. When foreigners ask me to edit their papers, I usually find lots of these run-on sentences. Remember, when you start adding more than one *and* in a sentence between your thoughts, you increase your chance of having run-on. It is best to start out using short sentences. Then as you get better at English you can develop more complex sentences, but even native English speakers try to cram too many ideas into their sentences. Some of our best novelists use short, crisp sentences.

The first step to avoiding run-on sentences is to segregate the different thoughts in your sentence. If you have doubts about whether a sentence is guilty of run-on, read it aloud and your ear might tell you where the complete thoughts begin and end.

Here is an example of a run-on sentence with three thoughts.

> *We sailed out of Hamburg harbor just before sunrise a stiff breeze was blowing black clouds forecast a storm coming from the north.*

Keep your sentences in the simplest form. You could use three in this example.

> *We sailed out of Hamburg harbor just before sunrise. A stiff breeze was blowing. Black clouds forecast a storm coming from the north.*

Here is a more complex form with just one *and*.

> *We sailed out of Hamburg harbor just before sunrise. A stiff breeze was blowing* and *black clouds forecast a storm coming from the north.*

Hint: A foreigner's culture can influence his or her tendency to use run-on sentences. As you have learned in this book, Americans can be more direct in our behavior than some foreigners. The same is true with our writing styles. In English, for example, the structure of a business report is preferably linear in format with a logical flow. It states a topic first, then key ideas, outlines each key idea, summarizes these ideas, and states a final conclusion. In contrast, some cultures use sentences to circle around a topic and avoid explicit judgment or conclusions. This might require more thoughts and sentences that results in run-ons. I once edited the wording of a business website my immigrant American client was setting up and kept telling her to **get to the point** instead of using long, general sentences that said nothing. It was a struggle for her because of her cultural background. This cultural difference is also reflected in how Americans write one-page employment resumes (see Chapter X - Getting a Job) and her culture that typically submits six pages. Remember my admonition: get to the point.

Punctuation – Once you are sure your sentence is complete, you indicate that with a punctuation mark. Our sentences are followed by a period (.) a question mark (?) or an exclamation point (!). A period indicates your sentence is complete. A question mark indicates your sentence is asking a question. An exclamation point indicates you are making a strong statement or, in the case of speech, are yelling. A comma (,) indicates you are separating one thought from another within the same sentence with a pause. I call commas the traffic signals of our language. Periods and exclamation points are used to park our sentences. Numerous punctuation books are available, including *The Blue Book of Grammar and Punctuation* from Amazon.com at www.bit.ly/K8MKS1.

☺ **Here's an assignment.** I was in a Chinese consulate office in the U.S. to register for a visa. To pass the time while I waited, I read an English language brochure that told about China's agricultural reform. I had great difficulty understanding its opening sentence because of its run-on structure. In analyzing it, I underlined at least six main thoughts in that one, complex sentence. Try breaking it into as many simple sentences as you can (or possibly one sentence) to make it easier to read. You may need to figure out the subject, matching verb, and possibly a pronoun for your new sentences.

Among other errors, can you see why "bring" should be "bringing" in order to match all the other "ing" words?*

> "Since <u>embark*ing* on the path of reform and open*ing*-up in 1978</u>, the Chinese government has, <u>tak*ing* an approach of emancipat*ing* the mind</u> and <u>seek*ing* truth from facts</u>, led several hundred million Chinese farmers in <u>carry*ing* out profound and bold rural reform</u>, thus <u>fully releas*ing* rural productivity</u> and ***bring*** <u>about all-round growth in China's agriculture and the rural economy</u>."

☺ **Here's another assignment for you**. Read an English language newspaper, magazine, or book and analyze some simple and complex sentences. Some of our formal publications like professional or scholastic journals use complex sentences, but our newspapers and magazines generally use simpler ones. If a long, complex sentence leaves you guessing what the writer is trying to say, then the writer failed to communicate his thoughts.

> **Hint**: Notice the word *his* in the paragraph above (communicate *his* thoughts). In the past we referred to an unknown person as a male, but did not necessarily mean a male. Today, however, it is politically correct to use "his or her," in which case we would say, "to communicate *his or her* thoughts."

Make Your Subject And Verb Agree – Besides constructing complete sentences and avoiding run-on sentences, it is important that the words in your sentence agree with each other. This is like putting all apples in one basket and all oranges in another one, rather than mixing them. Both foreigners and Americans have problems with this grammatical concept. It is not difficult to figure out if you follow a few basic rules.

Simply stated, your verbs must agree with their subjects. When a word refers to *one* thing, it is *singular* in number. When it refers to *more than one* thing, it is *plural* in number. A verb is like a good friend. It must match its best friend—the subject—that it hangs out with. So, in English, verbs must be changed to agree with their subjects, something not done in some languages.

Some subjects that appear to be plural at first are singular. Words like *group, herd*, and *equipment* are called **collective nouns**. Even though they refer to more than one thing, we think of them as a *single* group, so the noun demands a singular verb. Study these words that are often used as subjects that might cause problems.

---

*Here is just one of many solutions. "The Chinese government instituted bold reforms in 1978 to enhance the productivity of China's 200 million farmers and thus stimulate the rural economy." It puts the whole idea into a relatively simple sentence. However, it does leave out a couple of peripheral ideas that could then be put into several other short sentences depending on the publication for which it is intended.

476

both – plural	somebody – singular	boy – singular
children – plural	child – singular	each – singular
several – plural	someone – singular	neither – singular
many – plural	anyone – singular	anybody – singular
few – plural	everybody – singular	no one – singular
two – plural	nobody – singular	everyone – singular
people – plural	one – singular	either – singular

The names above in bold are singular because they refer to a specific thing or person among their group of things or persons. In the case of *everybody* and *everyone*, the group as a whole is considered singular. You would use the singular verb *is* after the singular nouns, such as "*Everybody is...*" or use *are* with the plural nouns like "They *both are...*"

Here are 12 simple rules to help you make the verb agree with your subject.

- *Verb Rule 1* – The words *some, any, none, all,* and *most* may be either plural or singular. We only know what their intent is by their context in a sentence:

   Some of the pencils *are* [plural] sharp.
   Some of the food *is* [singular] spoiled.
   Have [plural] *any* of the girls been here?
   Has [singular] *any* of the order been shipped? (A portion of order)
   None of his reasons *were* [plural] sound.
   None of his money *was* [singular] taken.
   All of the tires *were* [plural] new
   All of the gas *was* [singular] spilled.

   In the above examples, note that a plural verb is used when the item the subject represents can be *counted*, such as *pencils, girls, reasons, and tires*. *Food, order, money, and gasoline* cannot be counted because they refer to a grouping of something, so the group is considered a single thing.

   When using *fewer* or *less*, the same rule applies. This is another common error. Use *fewer* with something that is countable, and *less* with something uncountable. "Foreigners will have *fewer* problems [can be counted] and *less* trouble [can't be counted] if they learn to use articles correctly."

- *Verb Rule 2* – Don't assume the noun in a prepositional phrase is the subject of your sentence. Prepositional phrases are tricksters that may make it difficult to locate the subject. Find the real subject before selecting a verb. To do this, remove the prepositional phrase for just a moment and you will be able to identify the real subject. Here are examples with subjects and verbs italicized:

   One ~~of the trains~~ *is* late.
   Both ~~of the men in the office~~ *are* courteous.

477

Because *trains* is next to the upcoming verb *is* in the first sentence, you might think *trains* is your subject and use the plural verb *are*. That would be incorrect because *One* is your subject and it is singular. In the second example, *both* is the plural subject, not the *office* or *men*.

- *Verb Rule 3* – Contractions must agree with their subjects. A **contraction** is created when two words are joined to form one. *Don't* and *doesn't* can be grammatical troublemakers. *Don't* stands for *do not*. *Doesn't* stands for *does not*. Generally, formal and academic English frowns upon the use of contractions, but they are acceptable and sometimes preferred in our speech.

Hint: Some foreigners love to use contractions when writing English. I find beginners are more apt to use the wrong verb when they use contractions instead of the two separate words. Also, I tell my students to limit contractions if they want to achieve a more formal tone in their writing.

When the subject is *I* and *you*, you normally use *do not*; hence, you use *don't* with them. Example: "I *do not* want to go," or "I *don't* want to go."
You normally use *does not* for singular subjects; therefore, use *doesn't* for casual speech. Example: "It *does not* work," or "It *doesn't* work." "He *does not* want to go," or "He *doesn't* want to go." If the subject is plural, you would use *do not*; therefore, use *don't*. Example: "They *do not* want to go," or "They *don't* want to go."
The following common errors sound *very, very* uneducated. In each of them, a singular subject is incorrectly matched with a plural verb. Say them out loud so you will learn to recognize them: "he don't," "she don't," "it don't." Now *never* say them again! *It* sounds terrible, *doesn't* it!

- *Verb Rule 4* – Multiple subjects joined by *and* are plural and require a plural verb. *"Betty and he were* arguing." (The subject *Betty and he* is plural.) "The *beginning and the ending* of your story *are* good."
There is an exception to this rule, as there is throughout our crazy language. When the multiple subjects form a *singular idea or one unit,* the verb must be singular. *"Bread and butter is* a poor diet." *"Running and diving* into the pool *is* prohibited." In these examples, the subjects are thought of as units—one food, one action— hence, a singular verb is used.

- *Verb Rule 5* – Singular subjects joined by *or* or *nor* are singular and take a singular verb. "Either John *or* Jerry *is* coming." "Neither my brother *nor* my sister *was* at home." "*Has* either George *or* his mother called yet?"

- *Verb Rule 6* – When two subjects, one of which is singular and the other is plural, are joined by *or* or *nor*, the verb agrees with the nearer word. "Either Senate members or the *president is* to be contacted."

- *Verb Rule 7* – When the subject and the object are of different numbers, the verb agrees with the subject. "The ship's cargo *is* bananas," is correct because *cargo* is the singular subject (*cargo* can't be counted). "Bananas *are* the ship's cargo," is correct because bananas is the subject and is plural because they can be counted.

- *Verb Rule 8* – The use of *together with, in addition to, including,* and *as well as* after the subject does not affect the number of the subject. "Mrs. Jones, *together with* her two daughters, *is* shopping." "John, ~~as well as the other campers,~~ *is* eating." Treat these little add-ons of other people like prepositional phrases, temporarily removing them to discover the true subject. Then pair up your subject and verb as shown above.

- *Verb Rule 9* – Collective nouns may be either singular or plural. Collective nouns are words that name a *group* of persons or objects and often take a singular verb. But they may be used with a plural verb when referring to individual parts of the group. "The class *is* a large one," refers to the entire class as a group, thus singular. "The class *were* not all present," is referring to all those students not present, thus plural. Other frequently used nouns that are usually collective are *jury, herd, club, army, crowd, troop, fleet, flock, equipment,* and *group.*

- *Verb Rule 10* – Words stating amount are usually singular. This includes *money, time, weight, measurement, volume, fractions,* etc. "Two weeks *is* the usual vacation." "Ten dollars *was* more than I wanted to pay." "Three-quarters of our time *has* passed."

- *Verb Rule 11* – The title of a book, even when plural in its form, requires a singular verb. "The book *Vacations in Italy is* worth reading."

- *Verb Rule 12* – By using the words *if* or *wish,* use a plural verb if your sentence introduces the certainty of something never happening or something contrary to fact. *"If* I *were* eight feet tall, I'd be a great basketball player." *"If* I *were* you, I wouldn't do that." "My father would enjoy this restaurant *if* he *were* alive [he is not]." Here's an example where something is not contrary to fact and a singular verb is proper. *"If* my father *was* here [he may have been earlier], I didn't see him." Proper use of this rule will add sparkle to your English because many Americans misuse it.

Use The Correct Pronoun – The third step to making correct sentences is choosing the correct pronoun. Choosing the right one is not only a problem for Americans but for foreigners whose native languages do not differentiate when using pronouns. In our speaking and writing, we are continually deciding whether to use *I* or *me, he* or *him, she* or *her, we* or *us, they* or *them,* and *who* or *whom.* If you select the incorrect one, you sound uneducated to anyone who knows their proper use. In fact, there is probably not a more serious grammatical error that will convey an uneducated quality to others.

To start with, let's look at the two different forms of pronouns called *nominative* (think "noun" or "subject" in a sentence) and *objective* (think "object" in a sentence). To me, the nominative case words—such as *I, he,* and *she*—appear to be more formal sounding (except for *who*) than the corresponding informal objective case words—such as *me, him,* and *her*. Agree? So, I view the formal ones on the *left* side of the verb in a simple sentence as *subjects* and the informal ones on the *right* side as *objects*. That helps me make a decision when I'm in doubt. Here are our commonly used pronouns.

(◀ Subject/left of verb) **NOMINATIVE CASE**	(Object/right of verb▶) **OBJECTIVE CASE**
I	me
he	him
she	her
we	us
they	them
who	whom
whoever	whomever
you	you
it	it

Hint: These are not really formal and informal pronouns. That division is only an aid to help you choose the right one.

Here are five handy rules for selecting the correct pronouns in your sentences.

- *Pronoun Rule 1* – The *subject* of a verb is in the nominative (formal/left) case. Examine this sentence and notice the two people referred to: "*He* and *I* went to the beach today." *He* and *I* are *subjects* of the verb *went*; therefore, we use the nominative case. Sometimes you will hear someone say "*Me* and *him* went…." or "*Him* and *I* went…," both of which sound terrible. Don't you agree? (Think formal/left because the subjects are on the left side of the verb *went*.) Also, it is grammatically correct and a courtesy to put the other person before you: *He and I; John and I; John, Mary, and I; She and I*, etc.

  If there is more than one subject (as in the above sentence), you can determine which pronoun to use by merely dropping one of them and seeing how it sounds. (You did this with prepositional phrases to make sure your subject and verb agreed; this trick works well here, too.)

  If you are not sure about *he* or *him* in this incorrectly worded sentence, "*Me* and *him* went to the beach," merely drop either *me or him* and see how it

480

sounds. You wouldn't say "*Him* went to the beach," so you know you must choose "He.' You wouldn't say "*Me* went to the beach," so you know you must choose "I." And, you want to be polite so you say "He and I went to the beach."

"*Who* played the drums?" *Who* is the subject of the verb *played* (and left of it), thus nominative *who* is used, not *whom*.

"*We* girls believe that John told the secret." *We* is the subject of *believe* (and left of it), thus the nominative case is used.

"Did you and *she* get a promotion?" Earlier we said that when you have a sentence in the form of a question, turn the sentence into a statement: "You and she did get a promotion." *You* and *she* are the subject of the verb *get*. You would *not* say "You and *her* did get a promotion." The correct choice is "Did you and *she* get a promotion?"

- *Pronoun Rule 2* – Earlier we said the object receives the action of the verb. If the object of the verb is a pronoun, then the pronoun takes the *objective* (informal/right) case. Example: "I met *him*." (Think informal right because the pronoun is on the right side of the verb *met*.)

  A problem arises when there are *two objects* for the verb, causing a very common error in English. Example: "I met Andy and *him*." The two objects of the verb *met* are *Andy* and *him*. Very often you will hear people say "I met Andy and *he*," which may *sound* rather formal, but is still incorrect.

  A quick way to avoid this is to drop one of the two objects from the sentence (as we discussed above for Rule 1) and let your ear guide you: "I met *he*" sounds wrong. Another example: "Mr. Smith hired ~~Sam and~~ *me*." By dropping *Sam* you would not say "Mr. Smith hired I," thus you know *Sam and me* is correct and, as noted above, you put yourself last, so *me and Sam* would be incorrect.

  Hint: You might hear teenagers (and some adults) in the U.S. say things like "Me and Tom went to a movie." When I hear this it hurts my ears. But I know these people picked up this bad habit from their peers, some of whom know it is bad grammar. So, once again, do not emulate everything Americans do on the assumption it is right. That includes grammar.

  See how simple it is? If you can master this very common error of using the wrong object pronoun, you are on your way to using excellent English grammar.

- *Pronoun Rule 3* – Forms of the verb *to be* require the nominative (formal/left) pronoun as an object. If your verb is *am, is, are, was, were,* and verbs ending in *be* or *been*, then you use the formal/left instead of informal/right for the

481

object noted in Rule 2. "That *is* she." "I would hate *to be* she." "It might have *been* they."

When answering a phone, say "Yes, this is *he/she*," instead of using *him* or *her* as most people do and you might impress the caller. If someone asks your group who the person was who did something, the respondent should say, "It *was I*," not "It was me." This, too, will add sparkle to your speech, even if it sounds rather formal.

Most people make this error because so many others do and because they don't like to sound too formal. When people say "That is her," it sounds okay to many of us. To say, "That is she" sounds rather formal in speech but would *always* be used in writing. Memorize *am, is, are was, were* that are commonly used in our sentences and use the nominative (formal left) case.

- *Pronoun Rule 4* – The object of a preposition is in the objective (informal/right) case. Earlier we said that a preposition is a word that shows the relationship between a noun or a pronoun and some other word in the sentence. A prepositional phrase begins a preposition, such as "*on* the train," "*in* the house." Look at the prepositions again that we listed earlier and learn to recognize them. Prepositions usually begin phrases that have an object, and when the object is a pronoun you must use the objective form of the pronoun. Think, informal/right. "I am expecting letters *from* Jane and *her*." *From* is the preposition. "The package was intended *for* you and *them*." *For* is the preposition. (You can use the substitution trick discussed for Rule 1 to test your choice here, too.)

- *Pronoun Rule 5* – *Who* and *whom* distinction is disappearing from spoken English. This distinction, however, is still used in educated speech and writing. My recommendation is to use *whom* in your speech when you are *sure* it is correct and you feel comfortable using it. It sounds uneducated when you use *whom* incorrectly, far more so than if you use *who* incorrectly.

Nevertheless, the same rules of nominative and subjective apply here. "It was Bill *who* spoke to me." *Who* is the *subject* of the verb *spoke*. As we stated above, the pronoun takes the nominative case when it is the subject of the verb (think formal/left). "It was Jim whom I saw." *Whom* is the *object* of the verb *saw*, thus the objective case is used, as in "I saw him." (think informal/right).

Hint: Here's a quick trick I use to determine if I should use *whom* or *who*. I substitute *him for whom*, and *he for who*, and then rephrase the sentence and see how it sounds. Example: "She is a girl (*who, whom*) everyone likes." Rephrase it as "Everyone likes (~~he~~, *him*)." Your choice is *him*; therefore, use *whom*. Here's my motto: "If it's *him* it's *whom*; otherwise it's *who*."

VERB TENSES

The final step to good English sentence construction is getting your verb tenses correct. You learned that our verbs express action or just help to make a statement, and they have to agree with their singular or plural subjects.

Verbs also have another function: they allow you to *express time*. This is why we call them **tenses**; they convey *when* an action occurred and sometimes how one action relates to another within the sentence. They point out whether or not the action is *completed* and if other things were or are happening at the same time.

We have a way of thinking and speaking our sentences in a progressive line with three time frames:

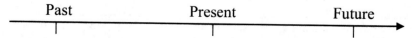

Past   Present   Future

Our sentences have three *basic* tenses: **present, past, future**.

She *swims*. [present tense] (she knows how to swim, or is now swimming)

She *swam* across the river yesterday. [past tense]

She *will swim* across the river tomorrow [future tense]

The *present* time frame refers to anything related to the present moment, or about an action or idea that is always true. The *past* time frame refers to anything that happened in the past and is not connected to the present moment. The *future* time frame is used for something that will happen in the future. As you can see in our swimming example above, a verb can change its basic word form depending on its subject and its time frame. We call the process of defining the different verb forms **conjugation** *[kon-juh-GAY-shun]*.

Regular Verb Tenses – Regular verbs retain their basic spelling and can change their tense by merely adding *ed*, or *d* to the present form or by calling in a helping verb like *will*. Examples:

I walk (present)   I walk*ed* (past)   I will walk (future)

I believe (present)   I believ*ed* (past)   I will believe (future)

Irregular Verb Tenses - An irregular verb is one that does not change its form by merely adding *ed* or *d*. Instead, the spelling of its basic word form (root word) changes. Unfortunately for foreigners, most of our frequently used verbs are irregular and that makes it more difficult to learn them all. Some irregular verbs have two forms, others three. For example, the conjugated forms of the verb *to go* are *go*, *went*, and *gone*.

They *go* (present). They *will go* (future).

They *went* (past). They *have gone* (a form of past).

483

In general, the *present* and *future* tenses are formed from the basic verb, as in *go,* and the *past* tense uses a second form (*went* in our example). Notice how *have gone* (the third form) can also be used to express another past tense in addition to *went* in the example and needs a helping verb such as *had* or *have*. This is a more precise tense we use to add a special timing and relationships to a verb.

☺ **Here's an assignment for you**. Make a copy of these verb conjugations and carry it with you. See how many you can memorize. Say them out loud and develop a rhythm like a poem so they seem to follow each other automatically without thinking, like "do, did, done; swim, swam, swum."

IRREGULAR VERB CONJUGATIONS

awake, awoke, awakened	eat, ate, eaten	ride, rode, ridden
beat, beat, beaten	fall, fell, fallen	run, ran, run
become, became, become	fly, flew, flown	see, saw, seen
begin, began, begun	forget, forgot, forgotten	shake, shook, shaken
bite, bit, bitten	freeze, froze, frozen	shrink, shrank, shrunk
blow, blew, blown	get, got, gotten	sing, sang, sung
break, broke, broken	give, gave, given	sit, sat, sat
bring, brought, brought	grow, grew, grown	slide, slid, slid
choose, chose, chosen	go, went, gone	speak, spoke, spoken
come, came, come	know, knew, known	steal, stole, stolen
do, did, done	lay (to place), laid, laid	swim, swam, swum
drink, drank, drunk	lie (to recline), lay, lain	take, took, taken
draw, drew, drawn	lie (falsehood), lied, lied	throw, threw, thrown
drive, drove, driven	light, lit, lit	tear, tore, torn

Hint: Many websites will conjugate verbs for you, including this one that shows an array of uses for each verb's tenses: www.verb2verbe.com.

To Be Tenses - The form of the *to be* verb is the most frequently used verb in English (and other languages) and it also changes with tense. It doesn't express action, but it helps to make a statement. *To be* has a total of eight forms, three more than any other verb: *am, is, are, was, were, being, been,* and *be*. You *must* learn these *basic* forms and the correct pronouns used with them. Say each of them out loud and memorize them.

Present tense: I *am* – he/she *is* – we/you/they *are*

Past tense: I/he/she *was* – we/you/they *were*

                         I/he/she/*was being* – we/you/they *were being*

                         I/we/you/they/*have been* – he/she *has been*

Future tense: I/he/she/we/you/they *will be*

Aspect - Besides conveying *time*, our verbs also convey an *aspect* about how the verb is related to that time specific frame. In other words, a more exact picture about the general time frame in your sentence. There are four aspects—*simple, progressive, perfect, and perfect progressive.*

ASPECT	MEANING
Simple:	At that time your sentence is referring to.
Progressive:	In progress during that time.
Perfect:	Before that time but already ended.
Perfect Progressive:	In progress before and during that time.

These four aspects can be applied to each of the three basic tenses (past, present, future) for a total of 12 different tenses that specify exactly when and how something happened. Don't worry; we won't discuss all these combinations. If you can master just the *simple* aspect for our three tenses, you will be off to a good start and will be understood.

- *Present Simple Tense* – This tense is used to express an action or condition that that is *always true,* or is *happening right now.* Examples: I *walk* 5 miles a day. The world *is* round. These are all statements of fact that are always true.
- *Past Simple Tense* – This indicates that an action or situation *began and ended* at a particular time in the past. Each of these examples tells the reader that these actions are finished without actually saying so. I *walked* 5 miles today. They used to think the world *was* flat.
- *Future Simple Tense* – This tense is used to describe an event that *will occur* in the future. This takes the form of *will* or *going.* Examples: I *will* walk 5 miles today. I am *going* to write two books this year. These additional five words in your sentence also express a future action: *when, before, until, after,* and *as soon as.* Examples: *As soon as* I finish eating, I *will walk* 5 miles. *Until* John comes, the work *will remain* unfinished.

Hint: I know it is hard to memorize all the tense rules. For now, be aware of the simple past, simple present, and simple future tenses. Eventually, you will learn most of the 12 tenses by sound and will know when they sound right or wrong. Keep your sentences simple and in the subject-verb-object format and you will stay out of trouble. If needed, various books go into these details, including *Practice Makes Perfect: For ESL Learners* available at amzn.to/Practice4Foreigners.

☺ **Here's an assignment for you.** Read an English language publication and see if you can identify the different tenses and observe how they are used to convey time and events. This is a great way to learn. Underline the verbs and identify their tense (past, present, future). It will reassure you that you can function reasonably well with just our three simple tenses.

COMMON VERB ERRORS

We're not quite through with our important friend the verb. Here are six rules for avoiding common verb errors made by both Americans and foreigners. Your English will have luster if you follow these simple rules.

- *Verb Error 1* – Tenses should be consistent in a simple sentence. This is a common error in English. Do not shift unnecessarily from present to past, from past to present, etc., within a sentence (or a paragraph for that matter).

  "He *saw* [past tense] the cause of the trouble, and *decides* [present tense] to take care of it." *Decided* should be used for the past tense. Or, it could be "He *sees* the cause of the trouble and *decides* to take care of it."

- *Verb Error 2* – *Lie* and *lay* are two different verbs and are probably **the most misused verbs** in the English language. Use these two verbs correctly to add luster to your English. The verb **to lie** has an object while the verb **to lay** does not.

  The verb *to lie* means to recline, to rest, or to remain in a lying position. Lie does not use an object. Its forms are *lie, lying, lay, (have) lain.* You *lie* down for a rest. "I love to *lie* in the sun." "The park *lay* in a valley." "I have *lain* in bed for three days with a fever." "The dog was *lying* in the sun."

  The verb *to lay* means *to put* or *to place* something. Lay takes an object. Its forms are *lay, laying, laid, (have) laid.* You *lay* your *book*s on the table. "She *laid* her *purse* on the seat." "I *have laid* my *shoes* in the closet many times." "She is *laying* her *party dress* on the bed." This sentence uses both of these troublesome verbs: I am going to *lay* my *book* on the sand and *lie* down beside it."

- *Verb Error 3* – The verb *to sit* does not take an object but the verb *to set* does. These two verbs are similar to *lie* and *lay* and are misused frequently as well.

  The verb **to sit** (as in a chair) has these forms: *sit, sat, sat.* "I like to *sit*." "Tomorrow I will *sit* in the chair." "I *sat* there yesterday." "*Sitting* in that chair is comfy, so I have *sat* in it for years."

  The verb **to set**—meaning to put something down—obviously requires an object. Its forms are *set, set, set.* "Please *set* the boxes in the hallway." "They *set* the boxes in the hallway yesterday." "Tomorrow I will *set* the boxes outdoors." "I *set* the indoor plants outdoors next to the chair I always *sit* in."

- *Verb Error 4* – *Can* is used for ability to do something; *may* is used for permission. Many Americans use these incorrectly. **Can** is used when *ability* is in question. "I *can* lift 100 pounds." "I *can* walk to the store alone."

  May, on the other hand, is used when *permission* or *possibility* is in question. "*May* I help you?" [Do I have your permission to help you?] "We *may* get there before dark." [It is a possibility.]

486

Hint: **When *may* is used correctly, it sounds so nice, educated, and upper class**, especially when you say, "May I help you?" or respond with "Yes, you may." Someone may *incorrectly* say to you "*Can* I help you?" Your correct response should be "Thank you. Yes you *may*." American children have a game called "Mother May I" in which they ask permission to make movements by asking the group leader, "Mother, may I?" not "Mother, can I?" Unfortunately, as they get older many forget the rules of the game. Remember this sentence to help make the right choice: "You *may* have my permission if you *can* speak English correctly."

- *Verb Error 5* – Some verbs take a preposition after the verb. Koreans and other foreigners may forget to do this in English because they are not required in their languages. For example, "He *runs to* school every day." This applies to other verbs such as *going to, arrived at,* and *engaged to.* However, if you do not intend a coming-or-going meaning, you would not need the preposition as in "He runs every day," which is not about a destination.

- *Verb Error 6* – Match the correct pronoun subject with the correct form of ***to do***. These are the irregular forms of the *to do* verb: *do, does, did, done.* Memorize the pronouns that go with them.

  Present tense: I/you/they/we/*do*   he/she/it/*does*

  Past tense: I/you/he/she/they/we/it/*did*

  Future tense: I/you/he/she/they/we/it/*will do*

  Past perfect: I/you/he/she/they/we/*had done*

Examples: *I do* not understand. *He does* not understand. *I did* not understand it yesterday. *I will do* better to understand it. *I had done* nothing to understand it.

    Don't is the contraction for *do not* (I *do not*, I *don't*), *doesn't* is the contraction for *does not* (he *does not*, he *doesn't*). It sounds terrible when someone says incorrectly, "He *don't*" instead of "He *doesn't*." English speakers will cringe but rarely correct you, even as a favor, because most consider it rude to correct someone's grammar. But we do sometimes give you feedback that indirectly corrects your sentence. For example, if you say "He don't do it," we might say "Oh, I am surprised to hear he *doesn't* do it."

Hint: A common error made by foreigners who don't understand the *to do* verbs is to say, "I no like," instead of "I don't like."

OTHER COMMON ERRORS

    Although Americans are accepting (and grateful) to foreigners who speak our language, poor English habits can limit your ability to communicate clearly, which in turn can keep you from getting the job of your choice and achieving other successes. To avoid this, here are six general grammatical errors frequently made by both Americans and foreigners. Avoiding them will show you know your English grammar.

Common Error 1: Comparisons – Adjectives and adverbs help describe an object. When you make comparisons between two or more objects, the English words you select to show the comparison will change. (Don't worry—this is much simpler than our verb tenses that change!) This can be a problem for those who speak a language where a symbol is used in front of the adjective to show the degree of comparison.

To make a comparison, we have three forms of a given word: the base form of the word, a comparison of *two* subjects, and a comparison of *more than two* subjects. For example, with the basic word *tall*, we use the words *taller* and *tallest* to make these comparisons.

Which building is the *tallest* in the Boston skyline?

To select the correct word, you first have to determine *how many* objects you are comparing. If there are two, use the *comparative* (think "compare two") form of the word. If you are comparing more than two, use the *superlative* (super means the most) form. Examples: The building is *tall* [no comparison]. The brown building is *taller* than the gray building [comparing two buildings]. Of the three buildings, the white one is the *tallest* [more than two buildings].

For short adverbs or adjectives with one syllable, add the ending *er* for the comparative and *est* for the superlative, such as *tall, taller, tallest.* The rule also applies to words with two syllables that end in "y" or "le" such as *pretty, prettier, prettiest* and *clever, cleverer, cleverest.* Generally *the* is used before the superlative form, as in *the tallest, the prettiest,* and *the cleverest.*

With longer adjectives and with adverbs ending in *ly,* form their comparative and superlative degrees by using *more* (two) and *most* (three or more), such as *beautiful, more beautiful, most beautiful,* and *carefully, more carefully, most carefully.*

And last, comparisons to indicate *less* are made using the words *less* and *least* before the adjective, such as *less* satisfactory, and *least* satisfactory. Examples: The car was satisfactory. The blue car was *less* satisfactory than the red one. Of the three cars tested, the white one was the *least* satisfactory.

Study the forms of these common words used to make comparisons. A common error is to confuse the adjective *good* with the adverb *well* that we discussed earlier.

BASE WORD	(2 Objects) COMPARATIVE	(More than 2 Objects) SUPERLATIVE
bad/badly	worse	worst
brilliant	more brilliant	most brilliant
charming	more charming	most charming
expensive	less expensive	least expensive
fast	faster	fastest
good (adjective)	better	best
happy	happier	happiest

helpful	more helpful	most helpful
hot	hotter	hottest
lovely	lovelier	loveliest
much/many	more	most
near	nearer	nearest
often	more often	most often
sincerely	more sincerely	most sincerely
strong	stronger	strongest
well (adverb)	better (*more better* is never used)	best (*bestest* is never used)

Common Error 2: Homonyms *[HAWM-o-nims]* – These are words that are pronounced somewhat the same but have different meanings and different spellings. (The prefix *homo* means "same.") When you speak English you don't have a problem selecting the homonym with the correct spelling because they sound alike. But, if you select the wrong spelling when you are writing, it reflects negatively on your English. Various websites provide extensive listings of our homonyms like www.enchantedlearning.com. Here are a few you should be on the alert for. Watch for "its" and "it's" that are probably the two biggest troublemakers.

a parent: a father or mother　　　*apparent:* evidently so
ad: short for advertisement　　　*add:* short for addition
aisle: walkway　　　*I'll:* contraction of *I will*
allowed: permitted　　　*aloud:* spoken so it can be heard
ant: tiny insect　　　*aunt:* parent's sister
ate: past tense of *eat*　　　*eight:* number that comes after seven
bald: hairless　　　*bawled:* cried aloud (past tense)
blue: a color　　　*blew:* a wind force (verb)
capital: most important, money　　　*capitol:* center of government
dear: beloved; a salutation　　　*deer:* forest animal
forth: forward in time or place　　　*fourth:* the order that follows third
its: shows possession of *it*　　　*it's:* contraction of *it is*
lessen: to reduce　　　*lesson:* a segment of learning
meat: animal flesh　　　*meet:* to connect (verb)
no: the negative　　　*know:* to possess knowledge (verb)
new: opposite of old　　　*knew:* past tense of the verb *know*
patience: willing to wait　　　*patients:* doctor's customers
raise: to elevate (verb)　　　*rays:* thin beams of light
scene: visual location　　　*seen:* past perfect tense of the verb *see*
whose: possession of *who*　　　*who's:* contraction of *who is*
write: make words on paper　　　*right:* the opposite of left; correct

Common Error 3: Misused Words – Using these commonly misused words correctly will add authority to your English grammar.

- *Accept/Except* – *Accept* is a verb that means to receive. *Except* means to leave out or exclude. Examples: I *accept* your apology. Everyone *except* John apologized.

- *Affect/Effect* – *Affect* is always a *verb* and means to influence. *Effect* is a *noun* and the result of something. Examples: The movie *affected* [influenced] us deeply. The *effect* [the result] of the office change was good and *affected* us all emotionally.

- *Bring/Take* – Bring means to move something *to* the person speaking, while *take* means to move something *away*. *Bring* is related to *come*; *take* is related to *go*. Examples: When you *come* to my house, *bring* your hat with you. When you *go* home [from my house], remember to *take* your hat with you.

- *Good/Well* – *Good* is an adjective and modifies a noun. *Well* is an adverb that describes verbs *except* when the meaning is healthy or satisfactory. (Remember, adverbs tell how, when, where, and to what extent.) Examples: The girls played *well* [how they played, thus the adverb *well* is used]. My mother is *well* [she is no longer sick, thus *well* is used to convey health]. My mother is *good* [she is a good, moral person]. He did a *good* job [*good* modifies *job*, thus the adjective is used]. He did the job *well* [an adverb telling how he did the job]. Remember this saying as a guide: "You feel *good* when you do your job *well*."

- *Principal/Principle* – *Principal* refers to first in rank. The head of a school is a *principal*. "The princip*al* is a p*al* [good friend] to the students." *Principle* refers to a main concept or a ru*le* of conduct, such as "The princip*le* concept of his speech was world peace," or "The criminal had no princip*les*."

- *Than/Then* – *Than* is used for comparison, as in "I like blue *better than* red." *Then* is used as an adverb to indicate when in time, such as *at that time*, or *next*. Examples: "It was *then* [referring to a time] that I decided to study English," or "First, learn your nouns, *then* [in that sequence] learn your verbs rather *than* punctuation."

- *Their/There* – *Their* is the possessive form of *they*, as in "They are wearing *their* hats." "The gift is *theirs*." (You would not say the gift is they's.) *There* is a place as in "Go over *there* and sit down." We also use it to introduce a state of being, as in "*There* were six of us," meaning six of us were together. *Their* and *there* are pronounced the same, but never misspell them in your writings.

- *To/Too/Two* – *To* works with a verb, as in "She wants *to go*." It is also a preposition, as in "*Give* the money *to* her." *Too* is an adverb that means *also* or *too much*, as in "I am tall and he is, *too*." *Two* indicates a quantity of 2 as in "There were *two* people in the car." All three are pronounced the same.

  Hint: When writing sentences, we generally spell any number less than 10, and use numerals above them. For example, "Lost in the jungle for nine days, I could not wait to return to my group of 10 explorers." In some **high-brow** (highly cultured or intellectual)

490

works, some publishers spell out numbers up to one-hundred. (There's that *individuality* thing again.)

- *Piece/Peace* – *Piece* refers to a portion of something, such as "May I have a *piece* of cake?" *Peace* refers to calm, or no conflict, as in "After resolving the dispute with my neighbor, we are at *peace*." They are pronounced the same.
- *Stationary/Stationery* – *Stationery* is what you writ*e* on, so if you remember the "e" in the two words you won't get confused. *Stationary* indicates a fixed position. "I writ*e* on my station*e*ry at my st*a*ble writing desk that is station*a*ry" [it won't move]. We pronounce both words the same.
- *Which/That/Who* – The misuse of these three words is very common. Here's a chance to refine your English. *Which* is generally used to introduce clauses (thoughts) that can be removed from a sentence without changing the sentence's basic meaning, so these clauses are set off with a comma. Example: A pony, which was once my father's, is the main character in my story.

  That clauses, on the other hand, are considered part of the sentence's basic meaning and cannot be removed without altering the essential meaning of the sentence. Example: The box *that* fell off the shelf crushed the toy on the floor.

  Who (or *whom*) is used to refer to a human, not a thing. *Which* and *that* refer to things. Example: That is *John whom* I know you will like. This is the *car that* I know you will like.

Refer to writer, editor, and teacher Carolyn Howard-Johnson's helpful booklet on this topic of misused words. It's called *Great Little Last-Minute Editing Tips for Writers* and is available at a nominal cost in paperback and as an e-book at www.budurl.com/WordTrippersPB.

☺ **Here's an assignment for you.** Select a publication in English like a newspaper or a magazine and circle twenty often misused words that we just discussed. Observe how they are used in their sentences. Chances are you might find one of our common errors.

Common Error 4: Double Negatives – Another common error, called a double negative, is a statement in which a second negative needlessly repeats the meaning of the first negative. Examples: "There *isn't* [negative #1] *no* [negative #2] time left." Instead, it should be "There isn't *any* time left," or "There is *no* time left." "She *hasn't* done *nothing* this month," should be "She *has* done nothing this month," or "She hasn't done *anything* this month."

Common Error 5: Apostrophes – The apostrophe *[uh-POS-treh-fee]* (') is used to show that a noun possesses something. If a noun is *singular,* such as one boy, you merely add an apostrophe and an "s" (boy*'s* bike) to show possession. If the noun is *plural* and already ends with "s" you merely add an apostrophe after it (all the boys*'* bikes). If it is plural but has no "s" you add an apostrophe and an "s" (children*'s* bikes) to show possession.

You do not add an apostrophe to possessive pronouns such as *theirs, hers,* and *its* because they already indicate possession. A common error is to add an apostrophe to abbreviations and decades that are merely plurals, *not* possessives. Instead of *SAT's* (our college entrance exams), it should be *SATs.* Instead of *1920's,* it should be *1920s.* (In a few cases, however, it might be confusing to add a small "s," so you might choose to use the apostrophe, as in *T's* instead of *Ts.*)

> **Hint**: Foreigners tend to make English harder than it is when forming simple plurals. I see it all the time on foreign owned business' signs. We don't need anything but an "s", "ies", or "es" to make plurals. Instead, some use apostrophes to do this, as in "We sell shoes' for less" and "We have mechanic's on duty." Obviously the sign was made by a fellow countryman who is equally ignorant of the rules of English grammar. There's that saying again: **the blind leading the blind**.

Common Error 6: Articles – We learned earlier that an adjective modifies a noun or pronoun. By modify, we mean to make the meaning more specific, to tell us *what kind, which one,* or *how many.* The adjectives most used are the little words *a, an,* and *the,* which we call articles. The proper use of articles is one of the biggest problem areas for some foreigners, including Asians, Armenians, and others who fail to use them. This is no surprise since some languages do not use them or use them less often than we do.

Whereas *the* refers to something specific, *a* and *an* indicate *generally,* not specifically. For example, if you find an unattended toy car in the park and no one else is there, you say, "*The* toy [a specific toy] I found must belong to *a* boy [you are not sure which boy]." If you know which boy it belongs to, you would say "The toy belongs to *the* boy in blue over there."

A is used before words beginning with a *consonant sound* (the other 21 letters in our alphabet): *a* car, *a* trip, *a* dollar, *a* G, *a* U, *a* paper. Note that U, even though it is a vowel, when pronounced sounds like *you* which is not a vowel *sound,* whereas **umbrella** is. So, we would say, "Give me *a* U and *an* umbrella." More crazy stuff in our language.

To make pronunciation easier, **an** is used instead of *a* before singular words beginning with a *vowel sound* (a, e, i, o, u). Examples: *an* apple, *an* eagle, *an* hour, *an* umbrella, *an* honor, *an* 8, E, F, H, I, L, M, N, R, S, X. Note that *hour, honor* and *E* thru *X* do not start with vowels, but they *do* start with vowel *sounds* (which we discuss in detail in Chapter Z). Try it. It is hard to say "a eagle" because you must come to a full stop after the "a" to start the next word; "an eagle" flows more easily.

The use of ***the*** refers to a *specific* object. We say "*The* toy belonged to *the* boy sitting on *the* bench in *the* rain." There are times when *the* is not required and, if you include it, it sounds odd to English speakers. My foreign students have trouble knowing when *not* to use *the* when referring to a noun. Remember, when referring to something that is universal, as opposed to something specific, it is not needed. For example, "I often donate money to *women's causes*," refers to women's causes in general, not to a specific one. When you need to be more specific, then use *the* as in "I often give monetary donations to *the* Berlin Women's Benefit for Young Children."

☺ **Here's an assignment for you.** Read a publication in English and circle at minimum 20 articles you find. Study how they are used. You'll soon be able to sense when and how to use them in your own sentences.

UNDERSTANDING ENGLISH WORDS

Did you know that English has more words than any other language, estimated to be one million? Do you know why? No, the answer is not to confuse foreigners who want to learn English. English is a West Germanic language that originated from the dialects taken to Britain by Germanic invaders 1500 years ago from various parts of what is now northwest Germany and the Netherlands. Their native words were the short, simple words we use every day that deal with basic things such as *leg, mouth,* and *father*. About 70 percent of the most frequently used words in English are these native, basic words that our children know by the time they are six years old. These words are usually the easiest for those learning English, too, because many are similar to the ones used in their own languages.

However, of all the words in the English language, 75 percent are borrowed from hundreds of other languages. A large number comes from Latin (spoken by ancient Romans and derived from Greek). We've also borrowed heavily from French, German, and Spanish. If you see the spelling of the American car with the French name, Chevrolet, you might wonder why it is not pronounced *shev-row-let*. The last letter is not pronounced in many of our French words, so the name is pronounced *shev-row-lay* or "Chevy" for short.

All this borrowing makes it easy for English speakers traveling in France, Italy, Spain, Romania, and Portugal to readily figure out the meaning of numerous words in advertisements and road signs. People in these countries speak Romance languages that are also derived from Latin. It facilitates the same way when they come to the U.S. thanks to our Latin heritage and all this word borrowing.

Hint: Just for fun, if you want to quiz an American, here is something most English speakers don't know. Of all the words in the English language, the word "set" (both a noun and verb) has the most definitions (192). As you have learned, we like options and choices in our everyday lives, but this is ridiculous! Agree?

Selecting The Correct Word – In my travels in the Crimea, I asked a Ukrainian tour guide, who was also a teacher of English, to define the most difficult aspect of

English for her and her students to understand. Without pausing she said selecting the correct word because "you have so many to choose from." One day about noon she told our group, "Shortly, we will be going to dinner." I double-checked my watch to see if it was working because in America we use the term "dinner" for our evening meal and "lunch" for a mid-day meal, something she was unaware of.

She said one of the reasons for this selection problem is that in her language (and in Spanish, which she also spoke) they might have, say, two words to generally describe something, whereas in English with all our borrowed words we might have five or more, each with a slightly different meaning, but one right **on target** (the precise meaning).

Does it make a difference if you use an English word that appears to be similar to the word you should use? Yes, because in English it may have a different meaning or might seem awkward to use. Mark Twain, a famous American author discussed in Chapter K on literature, said long ago that "The difference between the right word and the almost-right word is the difference between lightning and the lightning bug."

And to make things difficult for foreigners in selecting the correct English word, we have some odd spellings that can be confusing, even to Americans, as in "Stay *awhile* [adverb]" or "Stay for a *while* [noun]." We also sometimes join two words with a hyphen, as in "on line" and "on-line" or even push them together like the Germans are fond of doing and make it "online." And to further confuse foreigners as well as Americans, there are differences called style choices among our publications. Some papers like *The New York Times* use "Web site," but the *Los Angeles Times* uses "website."

Hint: This university website can help you make the preferred selections for all of our odd words: creativeservices.iu.edu/resources/guide/spelling.shtml.

Parts of Our Words – Even with all this borrowing that formed our odd collection of words, English words still consist of a basic *root* part and they can have additional attached parts either before or after the root. Some languages like Vietnamese use no attachments. Our attachments change the meaning of the root slightly in order to give a more precise meaning, kind of like our adjectives and adverbs do.

For example, an editor at a newspaper *rewrites* articles submitted by less experienced staff writers in order to make them more interesting or grammatically correct. He could describe his job as being a *rewriter* of articles. *Write* is the root word of *rewriter*, *re* is a prefix meaning *again*, and *er* is the suffix that means someone who does something:

Prefix + Root	+ Suffix	= WORD
write	er	*writer* (one who writes)
re write	er	*rewriter* (one who writes something again)

Hint: Because numerous websites discuss these parts of our words, I only list a few samples below. This excellent website helps students **brush up** (renew their skills) for tests they will take to gain acceptance to an American university. They discuss roots, prefixes, and suffixes to help them build their vocabulary: www.southampton.liunet.edu/academic/pau/course/webesl.htm. (Click on vocabulary and then root, prefix, or suffix for alphabetical listings and explanations.)

Roots – English words have a root that can be viewed as the basic part of the word, many derived from Latin and Greek roots. Roots contribute the most meaning to the word, so words that use the same root have a relatively constant meaning. If you know the meaning of one word that has a particular root, but you don't know the meaning of another word with the same root, you might figure it out if you know the meaning of its attached prefix or suffix.

These are the 30 most frequently occurring roots in English words that you should learn to recognize.

ROOT	MEANING	EXAMPLE
ast	star	asteroid, astronomy
audi	hear	audible, audience
auto	self	automatic, autopsy
ben(e)	good	benefit, benign
bio	life	biography, biology
chron	time	chronic, synchronize
dict	say	dictate, diction
duc	lead, make	deduce, produce
gen	give birth	gene, generate
geo	earth	geography, geology
graph	write	autograph, graphic
jur/jus	law	jury, justice
log/logue	thought	logic, travelogue
luc	light	lucid, translucent
man(u)	hand	manual, manufacture
mand/mend	order	demand, recommend
mis/mit	send	missile, transmit
omni	all	omnipresent, omnipotent
path	feel	empathy, pathetic
phil	love	philosophy, bibliophile
phon	sound	phonics, telephone
photo	light	photograph, photon
port	carry	export, portable
qui(t)	quiet, rest	acquit, tranquil
scrib/script	write	ascribe, script
sens/sent	feel	sensitive, resent
tele	far off	telecast, telephone
terr	earth	terrain, territory
vac	empty	evacuate, vacate
vid/vis	see	video, visible,

Prefixes – A prefix comes before the root and specifies a *spatial relationship* or a *quantity* for the root. Some of these spatial relationships can be *together, apart, back, between, away, before,* etc. Did you notice the "pre" in the word "prefix" that means *comes before*?

A few prefixes sometimes, but not always, require a hyphen after them such as *pre-* (pre-Civil War), *anti-* (anti-business), *ex-* (ex-president), *post-* (post-Civil War), *un-* (un-American), and *pro-* (pro-business). (Even I have to consult a dictionary or my computer's spell checker to verify these annoying hyphenated guys.) But most of our prefixes attach directly to the word.

These guys will be helpful to know. Prefixes in bold account for 97 percent of the most frequently used prefixed words in English.

PREFIX	MEANING	EXAMPLE
ab	away from	*ab*sent (not present), *ab*stain (choose not to do something)
ad	near, towards	*ad*jacen t (next to), *ad*jective (describes a close by word)
anti	against	*anti*-business (against businesses), *anti*body (attacks germs)
bi	two	*bi*cycle (two-wheeled cycle), *bi*plane (two sets of wings)
cent	hundred	*cent*ury (100 years), *cent*s (100th of a dollar)
con	with, together	*con*vene (bring members together), *con*verge (become same)
de	not	*de*regulate (not regulated), *de*prive (not allow to have)
dec	ten	*dec*ade (10 years), *dec*imeter (10th of meter)
demo	people	*demo*graphics (people numbers), *demo*cratic (gov. of people)
dis	not, opposite	*dis*agree (do not agree), *dis*suade (persuade not to do)
ex	out of, away	*ex-president* (not president now), *ex*hale (breath out)
im,in,il,ir	not	*im*possible (not possible), *in*justice, *il*logical, *ir*regular
mega	million, super	*mega*flop (failed miserably), *mega*vitamin (high dosage)
milli	thousandth	*milli*second (1000th of a second), *milli*meter (1000th of meter)
mis	not, bad	*mis*understood (not understood), *mis*placed (in a wrong place)
mono	one	*mono*rail (a one-rail train), *mono*tonous (unvaried boring)
non	not	*non*sense (no sense), *non*existent (not existing)
oct	eight	*oct*agon (eight sided figure), *oct*opus (eight-armed sea animal)
per	complete, thorough	*per*fect (done completely), *per*ceive (to understand fully)
pre	in front of, before	*pre*view (view before others do), *pre*text (a reason to do)
pro	for, supportive	*pro*-business (for businesses), *pro*fession (an occupation)
quad	four	*quad*rangle (four-sided figure), *quad*rennial (every four years)
re	back, again	*re*turn (go back again), *re*view (ensure accuracy)
semi	half	*semi*annual (one-half year), *semi*arid (little rainfall)
sub	under, below	*sub*marine (under water), *sub*jected (to undergo something)
super	above, upper	*super*ior (above the others), *super*sonic (faster than sound)
trans	across	*trans*oceanic (across the ocean), *trans*mit (to send across)
tri	three	*tri*angle (angle with three sides), *tri*pod (stand with three legs)
un	not	*un*cooked (not cooked), *un*familiar (no knowledge of)

Suffixes – The suffix comes after the root and indicates *quality*, *relation*, or *action*. They impart meaning to the root word and can convert a word to a verb, a noun, an adjective, or an adverb.

These are some common suffixes you will encounter. Those in bold account for 97 percent of the most frequently used suffixed words in English.

SUFFIX	MEANING	EXAMPLE
ate	to cause, to make	liber*ate* (to make free), deb*ate* (to talk about something)
able/ible	can do, able	ador*able* (can be adored), flex*ible* (able to bend)
dom	state of being	wis*dom* (state of being wise), king*dom* (area of a king)
ence	an act of	promin*ence* (making prominent), exper*ience* (being involved)
er	doer	golf*er* (plays golf), biograph*er* (writes about another person)
ed	past tense verb	hopp*ed* (hop), jump*ed* (jump)
ful	full	wonder*ful* (full of wonder), delight*ful* (full of delight)
ing	indicates ongoing	runn*ing* (run), study*ing* (study)
ize	to make	down*size* (make smaller), romantic*ize* (make romantic)
ia	a medical condition	insomn*ia* (lack of sleep), dement*ia* (decreased brain function)
ism	belief, practice	Mormon*ism* (Mormon religion), rac*ism* (race discrimination)
ist	one who does	pian*ist* (he plays piano), ling*uist* (skilled in languages)
ity	condition, quality of	flexibil*ity* (can be flexible), legal*ity* (in accordance with law)
ly	characteristic of	gent*ly* (gentle like), legal*ly* (allowed under law)
ment	a state of	govern*ment* (is governing), abut*ment* (being adjacent to)
ness	state of being	happi*ness* (filled with being happy), sad*ness* (feeling unhappy)
ory	a place where	dormit*ory* (room for students), laborat*ory* (place for research)
ous	full of	danger*ous* (full of danger), spaci*ous* (full of space)
s, es	more than one	book*s* (book), box*es* (box)

One group of special grammar suffixes adds little meaning to the word. All they do is make the word grammatically correct. In doing so, they indicate if the word is *plural*, is *possessive*, or is *comparing* something; some indicate *tense*. Below is a list of these special word endings. Some are seldom thought of as suffixes, but nonetheless they all come at the end of words and fill a specific function. As noted above, some of these form our most frequently used suffixed words.

WORD TYPE	SUFFIX & MEANING	EXAMPLE
Nouns	*s* (plural)	The boy*s* have a ball.
	's (possessive)	The boy*'s* ball is red.
Verbs	*ed* (a past tense)	He walk*ed* by them.
	s (a present tense)	He walk*s* by himself.
	ing (an ongoing action)	He is eat*ing*.
	en (a past tense)	He has eat*en*.
Adjective	*er* (comparing 2 things)	It is the larg*er* of the two.
	est (comparing over 2)	It is the larg*est* of all three.

☺ **Here's an assignment for you**. Select words in a publication printed in English and circle ten roots, prefixes, and suffixes and see if you can determine the definition of each.

THE MOST COMMONLY USED ENGLISH WORDS

When I'm ask by foreigners which English words are the most important for them to learn initially, I tell them a good starting place is the 100 that are most frequently used. It will be to your advantage to know which of our six word types they are, their correct pronunciations, and how to use them correctly based on the rules discussed in this chapter.

The 100 Most Commonly Used English Words

1. the	11. it	21. this	31. or	41. so	51. when	61. person	71. than	81. back	91. even
2. be	12. for	22. but	32. an	42. up	52. make	62. into	72. then	82. after	92. new
3. to	13. not	23. his	33. will	43. out	53. can	63. year	73. now	83. use	93. want
4. of	14. on	24. by	34. my	44. if	54. like	64. your	74. look	84. two	94. because
5. and	15. with	25. from	35. one	45. about	55. time	65. good	75. Only	85. how	95. any
6. a	16. he	26. they	36. all	46. who	56. no	66. some	76. come	86. our	96. these
7. in	17. as	27. we	37. would	47. get	57. just	67. could	77. its	87. work	97. give
8. that	18. you	28. say	38. there	48. which	58. him	68. them	78. over	88. first	98. day
9. have	19. do	29. her	39. their	49. go	59. know	69. see	79. think	89. well	99. most
10. I	20. at	30. she	40. what	50. me	60. take	70. other	80. also	90. way	100. us

ENGLISH TRIVIA QUIZ

Want to play a trivia game with someone who speaks English? Just for fun…

1. Ask them to say a word that rhymes with month, orange, purple, or silver.
    Answer: There are none.

2. Ask them to give you a sentence with eight different pronunciations of "ough."
    Answer: A r*ough*-coated, d*ough*-faced pl*ough*man strode thr*ough* the streets of Scarbor*ough*, c*ough*ing and hicc*ough*ing th*ough*tfully.

3. Ask them to name the longest English word that does not use any of the vowels a,e,i,o,u.
    Answer: Rhythms.

4. Ask them to name the only letter in the alphabet that does not appear in a U.S. state name.
    Answer: Q. (In case you're wondering, New Mexico and Texas have Xs in their names.)

5. Ask them to explain what these seven verbs have in common speech-wise: bring, buy, catch, fight, seek, teach and think.
    Answer: All their past tenses rhyme: brought, bought, caught, fought, sought, taught, and thought.

498

6. What do these words have in common: about, bring, drag, equality, fox, ground, hill, irate, know, late, and never?

   Answer: Each forms a new word when the first letter is removed, as "about" becomes "bout," and "bring" becomes "ring."

7. Name the shortest English word that contains the letters A, B, C, D, E, and F.

   Answer: Feedback.

8. Name the only four words in the English language that end in "dous."

   Answer: tremendous, horrendous, stupendous, and hazardous.

9. Name the only 15-letter word that can be spelled without repeating a letter.

   Answer: Uncopyrightable.

10. Find the English word that can be formed from all the letters EEEELLNPSSSSS.

    Answer: Sleeplessness.

11. Name the only word in the English language that begins and ends with the letters "und."

    Answer: Underground.

12. What are the ten words contained in the word "therein" without rearranging any of the letters?

    Answer: the, there, he, in, rein, her, here, ere, therein, herein.

13. What is unique about these three words: racecar, kayak, and radar?

    Answer: They are spelled the same whether left to right or right to left. Words like this are called **palindromes**.

CONGRATULATIONS! YOU ARE A WONDER!

You made it through this difficult chapter! I hope you didn't rush through it. If you understand and begin to *apply* the tips given you, you are well on your way to communicating better. In fact, you will probably have a better understanding of fundamental English grammar than some Americans.

Go back on a regular basis—once a day, once a week, or once a month—and review one section in this chapter. Record your progress and how you are improving. If you still don't understand something, make a note in the book and be sure to return to it later. With regular review, the grammar puzzle parts should come together for you.

"Congratulations!"

As a word of caution, if you read or hear an English sentence that doesn't appear to be grammatically correct based on what you learned in this chapter, it probably isn't. You *will* read or see advertisements in the media, or hear actors in movies, that use incorrect grammar. Your fellow countrymen will commit errors, too. Be sure to refer to this chapter or a good English grammar book and look up anything suspicious.

I know we covered a lot of topics. But at minimum, if at first you master just a few of the grammatical problem areas we've discussed, your English grammar *will* improve. When students ask me to identify the simple improvements they might first apply to their English, this is what I tell them.

1. **Plurals** – Don't forget to make your nouns plural as in book*s*, stori*es*.
2. **Articles** – Don't forget to use the little fellows *a*, *an*, and *the* to specify specific or general objects as in *a* toy, *an* umbrella, and *the* boy.
3. **Verbs** – Learn how to conjugate and remember the three *basic* verb tenses: *past, present, future*. Use the correct verb form, as in yesterday I *ran*, tomorrow I will *run*.
4. **Pronouns** – Memorize the correct *to be* verbs that are used with our different pronouns, such as *I am, he does not, she does, they do, he won't*, etc.
5. **Simple Sentences** – Keep your sentences simple and use the easy to understand subject-verb-object sequence. This will help you avoid run-on sentences and will simplify the matching of verbs with your subjects and objects.

Now that you know the basic rules for proper English grammar, your next step is to learn some pointers for speaking better English. This will be fun for you.

Z

LET'S SPEAK BETTER ENGLISH

Talking and eloquence are not the same: to speak and to speak well are two things.
A fool may talk, but a wise man speaks. - Heinrich Heine, 19th century German poet

As an actor, teacher, and world traveler, I am fascinated with the power of speech. I am also intrigued by the many factors that influence how well we speak and are understood. You will learn about some of these important factors in this chapter. By polishing your speech, you will become more effective in your dealings with us and will enhance the image you create.

The aim of this chapter is to address the common problems foreigners have speaking English. In the interest of keeping the chapter simple and focused on these problems, all exceptions and rules of speech are not needed.

Practicing English.

We start with some basics like our vowel and consonant sounds, and then move on to techniques to improve your communication skills. Some foreigners, perhaps like you, know a lot about these introductory soundings. But I still want you to review and *practice* them because, as I have learned in classes I teach, many who *know* these basics do not *use* them properly when they speak; consequently, the quality of their speech suffers. Also, foreign teachers and speakers of English pass on common pronunciation errors, just as grammar errors are passed on. So, do not rush through the chapter. Try to absorb each section before moving on to the next.

I give you three basic tools for improving your English speech: how to make clear individual sounds, how to combine the sounds to pronounce words correctly, and then how to combine the words to achieve good sentence rhythm. Once mastered, these skills will result in accent reduction and better communication.

This is my simple formula for clear speech:

| Individual Sounds | + | Word Pronunciations | + | Sentence Rhythm | = Clear Speech |

On visits to other countries, I always study the English spoken by locals to identify the common problems they have. With a few simple improvements, like those discussed in this chapter, they could speak much better English. For example:

- A guide in Vietnam had an excellent English vocabulary but did not pronounce his consonants well; as a result, I doubt if our group understood more than 20 percent of what he said.

- Our guide in Singapore spoke English well, but she decreased her volume as she completed the second-half of her sentences. Consequently we couldn't understand her.

- A guide in Japan rushed the pronunciation of the last word in her sentences and seldom paused before starting the next sentence. That left us **scratching our heads** (guessing) what she had just said. This same guide knew I was an actor and asked me what I thought of her English "delivery." After I explained her problem and gave her tips for fixing it, she corrected herself for about five minutes and then resumed her bad habit, something we all tend to do when trying to make speech changes.

- I've also had problems understanding Asian Indians and New Zealanders speak English because of their natural tendency to speak fast coupled with an accent that does not emphasize consonants as we do.

In all these cases, the problems are common to many foreign speakers of English. Some exercises like the ones in this chapter will make them all better communicators, even though *they* think they speak English well. Their teachers or friends from whom they picked up bad habits may have thought so, too. But we say **the proof is in the pudding**, meaning in this case the proof is in the understanding of the listener.

> **Hint**: If possible, practice what you learn in this chapter with someone who speaks English well. You can learn golf by reading books on the subject, but you also need an experienced golfer to let you know what you are doing right and wrong. If you can't find someone to help you with sounds, there are websites that perform this function, such as www.fonetiks.org and www.RepeatAfterUs.com.

Learning to speak English is difficult because we have about 50 different sounds, but only 26 alphabet letters to represent these sounds. So, we have to combine some letters to make certain sounds. Each English word (over 50,000 commonly used) has one or more distinctive sounds within the word. Proper pronunciation requires each of these sounds to be spoken correctly. We call this **enunciating**, making sounds crisp and easily understood, something most foreigners must work on because of languages differences.

Here are just a few reasons foreigners have difficulty speaking English properly.

- *New Sounds* – These sounds are not in their native tongue. Some Asians, for example, have trouble with the English L and R sounds because their language does not distinguish between the two. So they have a hard time hearing the difference between English words like *light* and *right* and then saying them correctly.

- *Slightly Different Sounds* – Linguists say the hardest sounds to learn may be those that are similar to, but just a bit different from, the sounds in your native language. It is difficult to overcome the tendency to keep using the sounds you grew up with.

- *Same Letter* – In English (in order to confuse foreigners, I'm sure), unlike some languages we have many different sounds for the same letter. For example, our letter E (the most frequently occurring letter in English words) is pronounced differently in *eagle, red,* and *poorer.*

- *Pronunciation Rules* – Because English has all these irregular sounds, there are a lot of complicated pronunciation rules that—let's face it—are hard to remember.

- *Facial Manipulation* – I had a problem learning French because of the unfamiliar twisting of lip, mouth, and tongue required to enunciate their sounds properly. The same is true with English. To make our sounds, your jaw, tongue, lips, and vocal cords may need to move in ways not required in your native language. But with practice you can do it and no one will notice what feels unnatural to you.

- *Accent Marks* – I quickly discovered in my travels that some languages like Spanish and Slovenian use funny looking accent marks to define a stressed letter in a word, which may influence the meaning of the word. With English, you are on your own. To confuse matters, our spoken stress will sometimes vary for the same word, such as the word "present." Used as a noun ("I was given a **pres**ent,"), the stress comes on the "pres" sound, but if it is used as a verb ("Pre**sent** the facts to me,") the stress comes on the end sound. Luckily we only have a few of these crazy words, so it is a matter of memorizing where the stress comes, which then defines their meaning.

Intonation is the important "music" or lilt of a language. Each language has its own way of "singing," which includes a distinct pitch, melody, and speed. If you use your native language intonation when speaking English, we may not understand you or may **tune out** (not pay attention) to what you are saying because it may not be pleasant to our ear. We discuss intonation later in the chapter.

So, let's get positive and just tackle these little problems one at a time. It will be much easier than you think. Let's first examine the two basic individual sounds in the English language: vowel sounds and consonant sounds.

VOWEL SOUNDS

Remember our vowels are A, E, I, O and U. (Sometimes Y is considered a vowel, but for simplicity we'll ignore this fellow.) Whisper these letters to yourself and notice what happens to your lips, mouth, and tongue when you say them. Even though we have five vowels, for purposes of our discussion we have 14 basic vowel *sounds*. Vowel sounds are made with the vocal cords with no friction of tongue, lip, and mouth. Slight changes in your tongue and mouth changes the vowel sounds made.

Some vowel sounds can be difficult for foreigners to pronounce not only because they may be new sounds, but also because their different spellings may give no clue as to their sound, such as *through* (*ough* rhymes with too), **rough** (*ough* rhymes with *stuff*), and *cough* (*ough* rhymes with *off*).

As an actor, I am constantly aware that *vowel sounds form the melody of our speech,* while the consonants complete the *distinctive sounds* of our words. I learned this from my singing teacher who told me to "fill up the cup on the vowel sounds," meaning, that when emphasis is needed on a word, put it on the vowel sound within the word to get a pleasant sound. As I listen to the recordings of my favorite singers, I notice they do the same thing. If you can master vowel sounds, your speech will have a pleasing melody that makes it easier for us to understand you.

Long And Short Vowel Pronunciations – There are basically two different pronunciations of our vowels: long and short. To achieve good pronunciation, you must be able to distinguish between the two. *Foreigners have a problem doing this, because they tend to produce a sound somewhere in between them.* If you don't make this distinction, Americans might have difficulty understanding some of your words. Actors and famous singers like Frank Sinatra are experts at using them both.

As you might guess, a *long sound* requires you to elongate or string out the time it takes you to make it. Let's pretend the sound of a long vowel is one full beat. *Short sounds* take less time, so let's make them really short, maybe only a one-quarter beat.

Basic Vowel Sounds – These are our basic vowel sounds. Sample words are provided for each one. Notice the differences between the long (elongated) and short, clipped sounds. Say the sample words out loud. For each vowel sound, try to hear the same sound within each of its sample words and notice the different spellings used to achieve that sound. There are many Internet sites that will let you *hear* these sounds. Do a search on each sound, such as "AY sound in English." (Here's one site I came up with: www.rachelsenglish.com/old_diph_ay_say.)

Hint: You will encounter different explanations of our vowel sounds, some of which use international phonetic symbols and others that use alphabet letters that might differ a little from those used below. But most end up with the same 15 or 16 different sounds with similar groupings of sample words for each sound. The same applies to the consonant sounds that follow. In the end, they all achieve the same result of segregating and defining our sounds.

Here are the vowel sounds. Notice the many different spellings of sample words provided for each sound.

- **AY** – Sounds like an elongated letter A is saying its own name: *ate*, *say*, *age*, *H*, *date*, *late*, th*ey*, h*ay*, d*ay*, r*ai*se, gr*ea*t. Press tongue against lower teeth, pull corner of lips back in a big smile, and drop jaw a little as you vocalize.

- **AE** – A short sound: *at*, r*a*n, *an*, *ask*, *act*, l*ack*, s*a*lad. Drop your jaw as you say these. Make sure *hat* doesn't sound like the AH sound in *hot*. Keep the sound short.

- **AH** – A longer sound than AE. It's the sound you make when the doctor puts a tongue depressor in your mouth and tells you to say "ahhhhh" as he examines your throat: *aw*ful, t*au*ght, h*ea*rt, n*o*d, br*oa*d, b*ou*ght, g*ua*rd, *o*n, *a*ll, dr*aw*, c*ou*gh, c*a*lm, g*o*t, w*a*tch, w*a*nt, d*aw*n, D*o*n, sw*a*mp. Make sure *not* doesn't sound like the UH sound in *nut*.

" Ahhhhhhhhhhhhhhh"

- **EE** – Sounds like the long letter E: sh*e*, *ea*t, s*ee*, *ea*ch, *e*vening, ch*ea*p, t*ea*ch, *ea*sy, f*ee*t, p*eo*ple, v*i*sa, b*ea*t, s*ea*t, turk*ey*, w*e*, br*ie*f, sh*ee*t. Say it with your teeth very nearly closed.

- **EH** – A short sound, perhaps like the sound old people make when they don't hear you: *a*ny, s*ai*d, fr*ie*nd, *e*dge, m*e*n, b*e*st, *e*very, s*e*ll. Make sure *pen* does not sound like the I sound in *pin*.

- **I** – A short sound: *i*t, w*i*nter, l*i*ved, *i*s, pos*i*tion, ex*i*st, h*i*t, w*o*men, b*u*sy, s*y*stem. Don't confuse with the long

"Ehhhhhhh"

EE. Make sure *it* doesn't sound like *eat*. Spanish speakers have trouble with this because of the pure way they pronounce the letter I in Spanish, so they pronounce *wish* as *weesh*, and *dish* as *deesh,* and *this* as *thees*. Just fixing this one miss-pronunciation problem will improve their spoken English.

- **AI** – A long-sounding letter I. It says its own name: h*igh*, c*o*yote, g*ui*de, *I*, *eye*, n*igh*t, wh*i*le, Th*ai*land, h*eigh*t, *i*tem, p*ie*.

- **O** – This sound also says its own name. Round your lips like a letter O, push your lips out a bit and don't drop your jaw: s*ew*, hell*o*, *oa*ts, t*oe*, s*ou*l, *o*pen, m*o*st, ph*o*ne, s*o*, *o*ver, n*o*te, yell*ow*, Jell-*O*. Make sure *note* does not sound like the AH sound in *not*.

- **OO** – Not quite as round as O, but your lips are still round and puckered like a kiss, but keep sound short. B*oo*k, w*o*man, p*u*ll, w*ou*ld, l*oo*k, sh*ou*ld, c*ou*ld, sh*oo*k. Make sure *full* does not sound like *fool*, which has a longer U sound.

- **OW** – We make this sound when we bend over to pick up something and yell "ouch." Begin briefly with the AH sound and end with a tight W with lips rounded: *ou*t, fl*o*wer, cr*ow*d, m*ou*se, n*ow*, all*ow*. Make sure *down* does not sound like the AH sound in *Don*.

"Owwwwww!"

- **OY** – Starts with O sound and rolls into and ends with EE: *oi*l, n*oi*sy, b*oy*, j*oi*n, enj*oy*. Make sure *soy* doesn't sound like *so* that has a long O sound.

- **U** – Round your lips and elongate. Think the admiring sound as in *"ooouu, nice dress!"*: gr*ew*, int*o*, can*oe*, f*oo*d, gr*ou*p, thr*ough*, d*u*ty, s*ue*, f*oo*l, t*o*, tw*o*, t*oo*, kn*ew*. Make sure *pool* does not sound like the UH sound in *pull*.

- **UH** – When someone asks you a question for which you don't have an answer, in English you might say "uhhhh." It is an easy short sound: *a*bout, b*a*rgain, for*ei*gn, reg*io*n, c*o*lor, fam*ou*s, b*u*t, *o*f, h*u*sband, b*u*d, c*o*ver.

"Uhhhhhh"

- **UR** – This is the sound a dog might make to warn you not to approach: "grrrrr." Pronounce the R and put dimples at the corners of your mouth and give a slight smile: doll*ar*, h*er*, mot*or*, s*ir*, f*ur*, *ear*ly, acr*e*, jo*ur*nal, *ur*gent, w*er*e, yest*er*day, c*ur*l, occ*ur*, h*ear*d, b*ir*d. Make sure *bird* doesn't sound like the UH sound in *bud*. Note all the crazy spellings for this sound.

"Grrrrrrr"

Problem Sounds – Here are several examples that show how just a *slight* difference in a vowel pronunciation is important. Can you tell the difference between them and their long and short sounds?

- *Heed* (pay attention to) versus *hid* (to conceal).

   "Heed" (EE vowel sound) is a *long sound* as in *she, eat, see*. Spread your lips tightly with a little smile, and extend the vowel EE sound a little longer than normal. Say this sentence, "Don't fr*ee*ze the ch*ee*se, pl*ea*se, Lou*i*se," to see if you elongate the EE sound in the words.

   "H*i*d" (I vowel sound) is a *short sound* that foreigners confuse with the EE long sound. Your lips should be very relaxed and the pronunciation is much quicker, like a quick drum beat. Notice how *hid* is pronounced much quicker than *see*? Say this sentence, "*It i*s w*i*nter and the w*o*men are b*u*sy w*i*th the s*y*stem."

506

- *Bat* (a flying animal) versus *bet* (a gambler's wager).

    "B*a*t" (AE vowel sound) is a *long sound* made by relaxing the muscles in your mouth and slightly dropping your jaw. Say this sentence out loud, "I r*a*n *a*fter my h*a*t while chasing a b*a*t," and elongate the AE sounds for more clarity.

Bat

    "B*e*t" (EH vowel sound) is a *short sound* made by relaxing the muscles in your mouth and placing your tongue high in your mouth. Make sure it does not sound like the letter A. Say this sentence, "I s*ai*d to the m*e*n it's b*e*st to have a fr*ie*nd attend."

Bet

☺ **Here's an assignment for you**. Practice each of the 14 vowel sounds by standing in front of a mirror and watching your mouth as you pronounce the sample words. Exaggerate your mouth's movements and the long and short sounds. Use a tape recorder. Hopefully the vowel sounds match in all the sample words for each given vowel sound.

CONSONANT SOUNDS

Consonant sounds are the other sounds in English, the non-vowel sounds. Most of these sounds are found in other languages, so only a few may be new to you. Our consonant sounds, however, like vowels, can be confusing because of their odd spellings and inconsistencies. For example, if you learned to read English before you learned to speak it, you might pronounce the letter *d* in "e*d*ucation" as a D sound rather than a combined D + J sound that many of us do.

In English, P, M, N, H, and W are among the first consonant sounds acquired by children while Z, J, V, and the TH sound (as in *th*ink and *th*ought) are among the last to be mastered. This is why people I encounter in Turkey, Spain, and South America pronounce *mother* as mudder and ***this*** as diss.

To reduce your accent and add clarity to your words, you need to distinguish between our long and short consonant sounds. Put your hand on your throat and gently pronounce P-P-P. Notice how P causes no vibration in your throat because you are using air and your lips for the vibration. P is a short, soft **voiceless consonant** because it does not use your voice box. On the other hand, say Z-Z-Z and notice how you have strong throat vibration when saying it. This is a long, hard **voiced consonant**.

The Internet has numerous sites where you can hear the correct pronunciation of our consonant sounds. For example, do a search on "English B sound." (I found this one: www.pronunciationtips.com/consonant_b.htm.)

These are our consonant sounds.

- **B** – (Voiced) Press your lips together, pop them open to let out a puff of air while using your voice, and start to say "buh." Say bo*a*t, *Bob*, ra*b*bit, kno*b*. Don't forget to pronounce Bs at the ends of the words, too. For *Bob*, say *buh-obb*, making sure to lightly pronounce the last B. When at the end of a word, clip off the end of the B, making sure you do not add another sound, such as Bob-*ah*, another common problem for foreigners, especially for Italians whose many words end in vowels.

- **CH** – (Voiceless) This is the sound a choo-choo train makes as it chugs along. It combines the very beginning of a T sound along with a slight "sh" sound. Press your tongue tip on the gum behind your upper teeth as if you are beginning to say T. Move your lips forward and smile. Remove your tongue quickly and let out a puff of breath as you change from the T to the "ch" placement. Say *ch*air, wat*ch*, *c*ello,

"Choo choo, chug chug"

  *ch*ose, *ch*osen, signa*t*ure, *ch*eck, wat*ch*, su*ch*, kit*ch*en. Don't confuse this with the "sh" sound in *sh*ares, or the S sound in *s*ink.

- **D** – (Voiced) Press your tongue tip on the gum behind your upper teeth and keep your lips parted. Pull the corner of your lips back in a slight smile, lower your whole tongue quickly and let out a puff of air using your voice. Say *d*o, *d*id, *d*one, *d*oing, buil*d*, bal*d*, and ba*d*. Be sure to pronounce the final D, clip it (make it a short beat), and do not add an *extra* vowel sound at the end of the word.

- **F** – (Voiceless) Put your upper teeth toward the inside of your lower lip and smile slightly. Force the air out between your lip and teeth and drop your lower lip. The upper lip is not used. This is a hard sound for Vietnamese, Koreans, and Filipinos because they confuse it with the P sound that uses both lips. Say *f*ound, *f*ew, *f*our, *f*or, *ph*one, *ph*ony, sta*ff*, gru*ff*, rou*gh*, fi*f*ty, thri*f*ty.

- **G** – (Voiced) Lift the back of your tongue to the roof of your mouth. Drop your tongue and jaw quickly and let out a breath using your voice. Don't lose the G sound at the end of the word, but don't over pronounce it either. Say girl, *g*ap, wa*g*on, ba*g*, ta*g*, *g*a*g* and don't add another "ah" or "eh" or "ink" type of sound at the end. In my travels in the Ukraine and Romania, a common error I spotted was adding a "guh" sound to words ending in G, so *king* sounded like *king-guh*, and *ring* like *ring-guh*. Some even pronounced *going* as *go-ink*. Remember this tip: pronounce *going* so it rhymes with *coin*.

- **H** – (Voiceless) Open your mouth and let the air come out as if you were panting like a dog. Say *h*and, *h*air, *h*ot, *h*eavy,

"Huh, huh, huh"

508

*h*ad, *wh*o. The French have trouble forcing this sound, thus "help" sounds like "elp" and "hunter" like "unter."

- **J** – (Voiced) This sound combines parts of the D and J sounds. Press your tongue tip to the roof of your mouth and move your lips forward. Remove your tongue quickly as you drop your jaw and let out a puff of breath as you change from the D to the J placement using your voice. Say *J*ohn, *J*ill, *j*ump, an*ge*l, brid*ge*, *j*ury. In some words, the letter D in conjunction with a vowel creates this sound as in e*du*cate, sol*di*er, and proce*du*re.

- **K** – (Voiceless) Lift the back of your tongue to the roof of your mouth slightly forward. Drop your tongue and jaw quickly as you let out a breath. The letter C can make this sound, too. Say *c*ar, *c*an, *c*ould, *k*ite, bas*k*et, *c*andy, *c*rooked. Be sure to pronounce final K sounds but clip them so you don't add an extra sound: boo*k*, hoo*k*, too*k*, shoo*k*.

- **L** – (Voiced) Place your tongue slightly behind your upper front teeth and pull the corners of your lips back as you smile. Exhale as you push your tongue against the back of your upper front teeth. Half way through the sound, pull your tongue back as you finish the sound. The bottom lip does not move and the lips are not rounded. Say *l*ate, *l*ow, *l*ake, do*ll*ars, he*l*p, to*l*d, te*ll*, be*ll*, b*l*ack, g*l*ass, c*l*imb. The L is silent in some words such as ta*l*k and wa*l*k.

An Asian student had trouble pronouncing the L at the beginning of a word, as in *lots*; she pronounced it as *rots*. However, she could easily pronounce the L in the middle of a word like *pilot*. To fix the problem, before she pronounced the first L in a word, I had her first focus on the L sound in *pilot*, which would put her tongue in its proper position for the L sound at the beginning of a word. She would then say la-la-la as in *pilot* and then form her beginning L sound in *lots*. You can learn little tricks to suit your needs, too.

Asians also have difficulty when the L is next to another consonant sound. You pronounce **glass** correctly as *guhl-ass* by combining the G sound with the L sound and inserting a slight vowel sound between them to form a *gull* sound. The word **please** can become *pull–eeze* to get that L sound correct. Take your time and don't rush these combined sounds, another common problem for foreign speakers of English that leaves us guessing as to what they just said.

- **M** – (Voiced) This is what we (and our president shown here) say when we eat something tasty and say "mmmmm, good." Place your lips together and hum through your nose to produce a nasal sound. Say *m*ay, *m*ight, *m*ust, *m*oon, le*m*on, dru*mm*er, hu*m*, du*mb* (the *b* is silent), cru*mb* (also a silent *b*).

"Mmmmmm good."

509

- **N** – (Voiced) Press your tongue tip on the gum behind your upper teeth as you start to hum through your nose and make a nasal sound. Say *n*ight, *n*ever, *n*ow, ope*n*, *n*urse, su*n*, pia*n*o, fu*nn*y, *kn*ife (it's a silent *k*). Colum*n* and hym*n* have silent N's, so you only pronounce the M at the end of these words.

- **NG** – (Voiced) This sound occurs only at the end of a word or at the end of a syllable within a word. Lift the back of your tongue up to the roof of your mouth as if you are trying to block air from entering the back of your throat, and then hum through your nose making a nasal sound. Clip off the end of the sound so you don't make a "guh" sound at the end. Say si*ng*, lo*ng*, bri*ng*, bri*ng*ing, fi*ng*er, ki*ng*. (This clipping is especially important for Spanish, Korean, and German speakers.)

- **P** – (Voiceless) Press both your lips together and bring a little air forward to them in your mouth. Pop them open and let out a quick puff of air. To practice this, stand in front of a mirror, lick your upper lip, then let out a strong puff of air trying to spray your saliva on the mirror. Obviously you won't do this when speaking to people, but the exercise will help you develop that P sound. Say *p*lay, *p*lease, *p*en, *p*ick, *p*um*p*, ha*pp*y, *p*erha*p*s, *p*robably, dum*p*, to*p*. The P is silent in *p*sychology, recei*p*t, and *p*neumonia. Vietnamese use the P only at the end of their words, so they need to work on this sound when it begins a word.

- **R** – (Voiced) This is a difficult sound for Asians, particularly those who have a hard time distinguishing between R and L sounds.

> **Hint**: My Asian American friend and I had a good laugh when she handed me a bar of sweet rice and said, "Here is some sweet lice for you." Lice are tiny insects that nest in people's hair.

Lift your tongue tip and curl it slightly back toward the top of your mouth. In fact, put a pencil across your tongue and let it push your tongue back and down a little as you make dimples at the corners of your mouth. Now curve the sides of your tongue upward and touch the rear of your tongue to the rear of your mouth and use your voice. Do not substitute the L sound as in *late* for *rate*, which will happen if you move your tongue forward and touch your front teeth. (The pencil method keeps your tongue from coming forward and making the L sound.)We have some crazy spellings for the R sound, such as wo*rr*y, *rh*yme, *wr*eck (that's a silent *w*), and co*l*onel[1]* that is pronounced *ker-nel*! Say *r*an, *r*un, *r*ound, *r*apid, a*rr*ow, ca*r*, ou*r*, fathe*r*, fa*r*the*r*, a*rr*ive.

---

*Colonel comes from the Old Italian word colonello, a commander of a column of troops, which in turn derives from colonna, the word for a column. English usage followed Spanish practice that spelled it "coronel," pronounced the way it looks with the R sound.

Like the letter L, the R can be difficult to pronounce when it is next to another consonant sound, but *it has to be pronounced* or you lose the meaning of the word. The word *present* has the P consonant sound before the R sound, and combined you would say "*prez-ent.*" (You can use the same trick we used for the L sound. It may be easier if you say *pur-ez-ent*, making the "pur" go very quickly as soon as you have the position of the mouth figured out.)

Don't make the mistake of dropping the R in *present* and coming up with the word *peasant*. (A present is a gift; a peasant is a poor person from the countryside.) To help you practice your important R sound, say this sentence until you are sure all your **R**'s are pronounced properly. Here is what we call a tongue twister like the ones accent-reduction and acting coaches use to help their clients:

> **R**epeat your **R**'s **r**esponsibly, **R**obert, as you prope**r**ly **r**un **r**apidly through their **r**igid p**r**onunciations and lea**r**n **r**ight f**r**om w**r**ong **r**easonably well.

- **S** – (Voiceless) This is the sound a snake makes when it hisses. In fact, say *hiss* and you have the same sound an S makes. (At last we found one logical sounding word in English!) Lift the tip of your tongue near the gum behind your upper teeth but not on them. Widen your tongue so the sides gently touch the inside of your upper teeth to the sides. Open your teeth slightly and spread your lips in a little smile. Gently blow air down a groove in

  "Hisssssssssssssssss"

  the center of your tongue through the space between your tongue's tip and gum ridge. Be careful not to make the Z sound, or you will turn the word *hiss* into *his*, *sue* into *zoo*, and *sip* into *zip*. (When we discuss the Z sound below, you will see that sometimes an S does make the Z sound in i*s*, wa*s*, doe*s*, way*s*, rea*s*on.)

  Say *s*ip, *s*ong, *s*ing, *s*ting, *s*ay, pa*ss*, mi*ss*, *s*cience, *p*sychology (silent *p*), ye*s*, *y*esterday, hi*s*tory, *c*ircu*s*. Sometimes a C makes an S sound, as in the first C in *circus*, while the second C does not. Crazy, huh? Vietnamese do not use S at the ends of their words, which causes them problems with this sound.

- **SH** – (Voiceless) This is the sound we make when we signal someone to be quiet. We put our index finger vertically in front of our lips and say, "Shhhh." To make this consonant sound, lift your tongue tip near the gum behind your upper teeth but farther back than when you make an S sound. Then move your tongue back so the sides firmly touch the insides of your

  "Shhhhhhhhhhh"

  upper teeth, then move your lips forward as you do when you give a kiss. Blow the air down the middle of your tongue. Notice how it has a slightly lower tone than the hissing S sound noted above? Say *sure*, *tissue*, *shoe*, *dishes*, *fish*, *sugar*, *information*, *racial*, *chef*, *conscious*, *short*, *nation*, *rush*. This is an amazing array of spellings for the same sound! Agree?

> **Hint**: It is very important to distinguish between the S sound and the SH sound, as my immigrant American friend learned. She told me about the time she invited a customer in her business to "Please *sit* here," but said it as "Please *shit* here," which (crudely) means please go to the bathroom here.

- **T** – (Voiceless) Press your tongue tip on the gum behind your upper teeth with your lips parted. Lower your tongue and jaw quickly and let out a puff of air. Say *toy*, *Tom*, *tinker*, *boat*, *hat*, *lit*, *sit*. Make sure you pronounce these strongly, especially on the ends of words. If you don't, you may blend your words together so "*sit down*" sounds like "*sidown.*" In fact, the T sometimes sounds like D when we say them quickly or carelessly in such words as *ninety*, *quarter*, *water*, *letter*, *little*, and *later*. Remember, your English will be much more distinctive and pleasing if you are careful with your T's. In fact we have a saying when we want people to pay attention to detail: **don't forget to cross your Ts**. Asian Indians who speak English are sometimes careful to make this sound correctly.

- **TH** – (Voiced) In all my travels from South America to the Middle East to Asia, *this is probably one of the hardest sounds for foreigners to learn.* Instead of using the TH sound, they use the D, F, S, or T sounds. Spanish and Italian speakers, for example, substitute the D for the TH sound when they say "dis" instead of *this*, "dair" instead of *their*, and "den" for *then*. For many, just this one simple change will greatly enhance their English pronunciation.

  Place the tip of your tongue lightly against your upper front teeth so it protrudes out just slightly beyond (or flush with) the bottom of your teeth. Blow air between your upper teeth and your tongue, forcing your upper lip to move outward slightly while your tongue remains against the teeth. (Be careful not to use the S sound from the bottom of your mouth with your tongue against your lower teeth.) Say *mouth*, *theme*, *thick*, *with*, *south*, *month*, *thump*, *theatre*, *theirs*, *then*, and make this sound heard, don't hide it. Just to confuse you, we *do* have a few words in which the TH is pronounced as T: **Th**omas, **Th**ailand, **th**yme (pronounced as *time*), and **Th**ames (a river in

England where all these crazy pronunciations originated and where it is pronounced as *tems*).[*]

- **V** – (Voiced) Put your upper front teeth lightly on your lower lip. After you begin your voice sound, immediately create a little space between the upper teeth and the lower lip and pretend you are showing a little bit of your upper front teeth as you lightly raise the area between the upper lip and the nose. Do not round your lips; the corners of the bottom lips will pull back slightly. Do not use the W sound for a V sound. Say sto*v*e, *v*isa, tele*v*ision, *v*ote, a*v*ailable, moti*v*e, fa*v*orite, *v*ery, *v*owel, and *v*ictory. Notice how vowels follow the Vs? For good pronunciation, be sure to make the V sound heard. (This sound is difficult for some Chinese, Germans, Armenians, and others who tend to get it wrong as well.)

- **W** – (Voiceless) Round your lips to form a small opening and push them forward as if you are going to blow out a candle. Let the air come through as you pull back the corners of your mouth as if to begin a smile. Say *wh*en, *wh*y, *wh*ere, *wh*at, bet*w*een, *wh*ite, *w*ith. We have some words where the W is silent, such as t*w*o, *w*rite, ans*w*er, and s*w*ord. Don't confuse W with the V sound. I was in Austria where they tend to confuse the two, and a tour guide, who was trying hard to use correct English, wanted to say, "The *v*iolin is *w*onderful," but instead said, "The *w*iolin is *v*onderful." Surprisingly, the same occured in Turkey, even though a number of their words are derived from French that also uses the V sound.

- **X** – (Voiced) This strange fellow makes two different sounds when used with two different consonants: the K+S sound in some words, and the G+Z sound in others. Place your tongue down in your mouth with its tip against the bottom front teeth. Say the word si*x* to get the slight K+S sound (rhymes with kic*ks*), and e*x*ist to get the G+S sound that sounds like egg*s*-ist. Say fi*x*, chec*ks*, si*x*teen, e*x*actly, e*x*ample, economi*cs*, wal*ks*, and e*x*cept. (This sound is foreign to some Asians.)

---

[*]The modern sounding of the word Thames illustrates a phenomenon in the English language. The river is first mentioned in English in 893 when it was called the "Temese," which is how it is still pronounced today *[tems]*. The spelling "Thames" first appeared in 1649 when respelling occurred in English during the late Renaissance. At this time the prestige of Latin and Greek prompted scholars to correct the form of many English words, and in many cases the pronunciations of these words also changed. However, the pronunciation of Thames remained unchanged and provides an example of the well-known discrepancy between English spelling and pronunciation that causes problems for foreigners (and our youngsters) learning our crazy language.

- **Y** – (Voiced) This is the beginning sound of the word *yuck* that we shout when we taste or observe something terrible. Raise the middle of your tongue and lower the tip behind your bottom front teeth as if you are going to yawn. Press the tongue forward with the tip remaining where it is, moving the middle of the tongue forward without touching the roof of your mouth. Say *yarn*, m*u*sic, *y*es, *y*ear, and *y*ellow. *Union* has two Y sounds. Even though it begins with the U vowel, it has a consonant Y sound. Then at the ending of the word we pronounce "ion" that sounds like "yun." Some weird spellings with the Y sound are sen*i*or and *u*nited.

"Yuck!!"

- **Z** – (Voiced) Place your tongue behind your lower front teeth. Widen your tongue so the sides gently touch the inside of your lower teeth. Open your teeth slightly and spread your lips in a small smile. Blow the air down the top of your tongue as you tighten the area between your lower lip and your chin and show a little of your lower teeth. Say *z*one, *z*ebra, no*s*e, pre*s*ent, *z*ipper, ea*s*y, hi*s*, do*es*, *X*erox *[ZEE-roks]*, Brazi*l*. Note the crazy spellings for this Z sound. (This sound is foreign to some Asians, too.)

ENDING SOUNDS

As we say, **so far, so good**, we're making progress. Now that you know the different sounds in our crazy language, you are ready to put them together to pronounce words. **Are you game** (willing to do it)? First, let's examine our sounds that *end* a word. These ending sounds can be a problem for foreigners and add to their foreign accent. Dropping the final consonant sound in a word is a common problem for some foreigners, particularly Asians.

In your language, you might end your words with a vowel or an open sound and are not accustomed to placing any emphasis at the end of your words as we do. Koreans, for example, may not pronounce consonants unless they are followed by a vowel in the same syllable. So when they speak English they tend to add a vowel at the end of their words that end with a consonant, such as h*at*(uh) and Frenc*h*(uh).

You may remember in the previous chapter on grammar that the ending of a word in English may define it as being possessive, plural, or past tense. If you don't pronounce the ending sound *clearly,* your listener may have to guess what you are trying to say. We discuss more of these good speaking practices a little later.

Let's examine four word-ending sounds and the rules for pronouncing them. They are plural endings, past tense endings, consonant cluster endings, and suffix endings. Admittedly, the rules are hard to remember (even I had to research them!). It might be easier if you grasp the concept and remember the sounds associated with the word types and the examples given as you build your vocabulary. Soon it will come naturally to you as you hear the words pronounced correctly and remember their endings.

Plural Endings – As you have learned, when a noun refers to more than one, we call it plural and usually add an "s" to indicate more than one, such as "book*s*." Some languages do not have plural nouns, while others form them differently. Consequently, some foreigners have a hard time remembering to make nouns plural when speaking. *You must pronounce the ending of your plural words.* We have three rules for pronouncing plural nouns.

- Use an **S sound** if the word ends in one of these *unvoiced* sounds by merely adding an S to make it plural: F, K, P, T, TH. Give a puffed S sound (a hiss) at the end of these words. Say bluff**s**, wreck**s**, top**s**, bat**s**, and birth**s**. (Some collective words, such as equipment, are already plural.)
- Use a **Z sound** if the word ends in one of these *voiced* sounds: B, D, G, L, M, N, NG, R, and all vowel sounds. Say com**b**(Z) = combs; car**d**(Z), gong**s**(Z), bal**l**(Z), ra**m**(Z), he**n**(Z), comi**ng**(Z), runne**r**(Z), pie**s**(Z)["e" is a vowel sound]. You will notice that your mouth is almost forced to make a Z sound rather than an S sound.
- Use an **EZ sound** if the word ends in one of these sounds by adding *es*: CH, H, S, SH, Z. Say chur**ch(EZ)** = churches; plu**s(EZ)**, bu**sh(EZ)**, bu**zz(EZ)**, and wi**sh(EZ)**.

As a tool to help you, record below your most frequently used plural words (or problem words) and practice saying them with the correct ending sound, such as the example "bats – S." In time you won't need to think about the ending rules and you will just do it automatically.

Word + Sound	Word + Sound	Word + Sound	Word + Sound
bats - S			

Past Tense Endings – As with plural endings, some languages do not have the past tense forms of verbs, or if they do, they do not add consonant sounds at the end of them. *It is important you learn to pronounce these endings clearly.* Here are three rules.

- Use the **T sound** to pronounce the past tense when a word ends in these *unvoiced* sounds: CH, F, K, P, S, SH and TH. Say wat**ch**(T) = watched; buf**f**(T) = buffed; wal**k**(T) = walked; dri**p**(T) = dripped; mis**s**(T) = missed; wa**sh**(T) = washed: unear**th**(D) = unearthed.

- Use the **D sound** to pronounce the past tense when a word ends in these *voiced* sounds: B, G, L, M, N, NG, R, Z, and all vowel sounds. Say rob(D) = robbed; jog(D) = jogged; fill(D) = filled; storm(D) = stormed; gun(D) = gunned; wing(D) = winged; tar(D) = tarred; blitz(D) = blitzed; stone(D) = stoned; zero(D) = zeroed.

- Use the **ID sound** to pronounce the past tense when a word ends with a T or D sound. Say dent(ID) = dented; post(ID) = posted; roast(ID) = roasted; need(ID) = needed; add(ID) = added.

Again, record your most frequently used or problem verbs with their correct past tense endings.

Word + Sound	Word + Sound	Word + Sound	Word + Sound
watched - T			

Consonant Cluster Endings – English has words that end with two consonant sounds. A problem arises for foreigners when they do not pronounce the *final* consonant in them because the speaker is focused on the previous one. If this happens, the word *start* is pronounced as *star* and can really confuse the person you are stalking to. Practice saying these words with emphasis on the last *two* consonants in each word: wor*k*, mus*t*, des*k*, wor*ds*, star*t*, consonan*t*, and car*d*. It will help if you practice taking your time to elongate the next-to-the-last sound, as in *desssk* for *desk*, and star*rrr*t for *start*. Also, be sure to clip the final sound so you do not add an "uh" sound to it, such as start-*uh*.

Suffix Endings – Earlier you learned that suffixes are endings that give added meaning to the root word, and can change a word to a verb, adverb, noun, or adjective. If the word ends in *ee* or *eer* (which means a doer of something), you need to stress it. Here are examples with the stress shown in capital letters.

engin**eer** - en-gin-EER car**eer** - ca-REER trust*ee* - trust-EE
a**gree** - a-GREE de**cree** - de-CREE

On the other hand, if the word ends in *ic*, *ical*, *ity*, or *tion*, the stress comes somewhere before the final ending but we still need to hear that final sound.

luna**tic** - LUN-a-tic poli**tical** - po-LIT-i-cal
flexibi**lity** - flex-i-BIL-i-ty pronuncia**tion** - pro-nun-ci-A-tion

Congratulations! You can now pronounce all the basic sounds in our crazy assortment of 50,000 words that we use the most.

SYLLABLES

Now that your vowel and consonant sounds are nice and clear, you can group the sounds together to pronounce a word correctly. To do this, you must first learn to find the **syllables** *[SILL-ah-bulls]* in a word, which is another problem for foreigners. When you know how to do this, you will not only pronounce your words correctly, but will find that spelling them is easier, too.

A syllable is merely the beat of a distinctive sound in a word wrapped around a vowel. Each is sounded as if you were hitting a drum with one beat per syllable. Short words such as *high*, *no*, *it*, and *yes* have one beat, or one syllable. With vowels noted in bold, some words have two beats such as my last name *Johnson* (**john**-s**o**n), *hello* (hel-**lo**), and *goodbye* (g**oo**d-b**ye**). Some words have three syllables: *avenue* (**av**-e-n**ue**) and *discounted* (dis-**count**-ed). Some have four beats: *America* (a-m**er**-i-ca), *necessary* (nec-es-s**ar**-y). Some words have five: *representation* (rep-re-sen-ta-tion). Some syllables may have more than one vowel in it, such as *discounted* above.

Your dictionary is a very good friend if you want to learn to identify the syllables in our crazy words. Use yours (or the Internet) to look up the word *mechanical* and you will see it listed as "me-chan-i-cal" in which it is divided into its four syllables. After you have done this for a while, identifying and pronouncing syllables will come to you naturally.

Once you have finished learning about syllables, you will be able to locate the syllables in this long word below that originated in a song from our popular movie, *Mary Poppins*. It has become part of our vocabulary, though no one knows its meaning and you probably won't find it in a dictionary: *supercalifragilisticexpialidocious*.

When you can identify syllables, you will also know when to split a word at the end of one written line and continue on to the next line. This is a common problem in some countries where I've seen public signs written in English for tourists, especially in China, with incorrect hyphenations or none at all. A **hyphen** ("-") is added between syllables when a word must be divided at the end of one line and continued on to the next line. For example, if *encyclopedia* [en-cy-clo-pe-di-a] is too long to fit on one line, you could write "encyclo-" on one line and "pedia" on the next or any variation thereof (except before the last syllable). It is important, though, that the hyphen is used between syllables and does not break one up.

Syllable Rules – A new syllable is formed around each new *vowel sound* in a word, and it stands by itself in pronunciation, as in *goodbye* (good-bye), where *good* has the OO vowel sound and *bye* has the AI vowel sound that we discussed earlier.

When two vowels are separated by a consonant, the consonant is usually pronounced with the *second* vowel. *Pronounce* is an example, where the two O vowels are separated by the consonant N. Thus, the syllables would be *pro-nounce*, not *pron-ounce*. There is an exception (naturally!). The consonant *is* pronounced with the *first* vowel when the vowel is short and stressed, as in *wagon*, where the consonant G comes between the two vowels. We say *wag-un* instead of *wa-gun*. Also, if two consonants come together in a word, they are pronounced separately and each forms its own syllable, such as goodbye (*good-bye*) and discounted (*dis-count-ed*). This gives clarity to your spoken words.

☺ **Here's an assignment for you.** Please attempt to locate the syllables in this word that we talked about above by putting slash marks "/" between the syllables. Go ahead, **roll the dice** (take a chance) and see what you come up with.

S U P E R C A L I F R A G I L I S T I C E X P I A L I D O C I O U S

Pay attention to where the vowels are that are noted in bold. Then refer to the **footnote** (a note printed at the bottom of a page) for what I come up with.[*] When I try to spell this long word, I need to first locate the syllables to come close to the correct spelling, even if it *is* a made-up word. You can use this same technique to aid your spelling of everything you write.

Syllable Pronunciation – In terms of pronunciation, words with two or more syllables will have only *one* syllable within that is *stressed*, meaning that it will be pronounced *louder* and/or *longer* and often at a *higher pitch* than the other syllables. This correct stress is important when speaking English; if not done correctly your word might not be understood.

Your English dictionary shows you the syllables in a word, but it also indicates which one receives the stress with this symbol "'" placed after the syllable that is to receive the stress. Some use CAPS to designate the stressed syllable, as I do below.

Look up the word *decorate* and you will see "dec'-o-rate" that shows the three syllables and indicates that the first one receives the stress as in *DEC-o-rate*. Say these words with stress on the syllables in capital letters:

   arithmetic (a-RITH-me-tic)   contribute (con-TRIB-ute)   prevent (pre-VENT)
   advertisement (ad-ver-TISE-ment)   vocabulary (vo-CAB-u-lar-y)
   automobile (AU-to-mo-bile)   simplify (SIM-pli-fy)   prefix (PRE-fix).

Finland doesn't have this selection problem because they emphasize the first syllable in their words. Other languages like Spanish sometimes use accent marks to alert speakers to the stress.

---

[*]su/per/cal/i/frag/i/lis/tic/ex/pe/al/i/do/cious.

518

To show the importance of stressing the correct syllables in our words, my well-versed English speaking tour guide in Barcelona, Spain, kept using three words on our two-hour bus drive to Montserrat and I had no idea what they were. So I could not decipher the meaning of those sentences in which he used them. After **scratching my head** (puzzled) for a half hour, it dawned on me he was putting the emphasis on the wrong syllables in those three words, or sometimes combined them to make one sound, or even omitted some sounds.

We pronounce "monastery" *[MON-as-ter-y]* with emphasis on "mon" but he put it on "as" and combined the last two syllables as "tree" so it sounded like "monASStree." The second word, "cemetery" *[SEM-ih-tair-ee]*, has emphasis on "cem" but he put it on "et" and again combined the last two syllables and made a "tree" sound and it came up sounding like "cemENTtree." (I couldn't see any cement trees about!) And finally, "punctuality" *[punk-choo-AL-i-ty]* has emphasis on "al" but he put it on "tual," and omitted some syllables and combined others to say "punkTULi." I thought he was referring to a punk rock band named The Tulies.

My guide was most grateful when I helped him with these words during a bus stop. He was surprised to learn that mispronouncing just one key word in a sentence might make the sentence unintelligible. He admitted he will always have isolated problems with his English but will learn from native English speakers if he invites them to help. I hope you will have the opportunity to get help, too.

Hint: Many foreigners, like my tour guide who have an extensive English vocabulary, have learned much of their English from reading, so they have never *heard* many of the words that they use. It's great that they are reading extensively, but they also need to hear the words pronounced. For that reason this book lists websites where you can hear them spoken, including www.howjsay.com and www.fonetiks.org.

SENTENCE STRESS

If you grasp the concept of all the different pronunciations of our strange English words up to this point, celebrate to your heart's content. Go buy yourself a triple-decker ice cream cone to reward yourself. If not, **keep the faith** (believe you can do it). With practice and experience, much of what we have discussed *will* become more apparent to you. Don't despair if you can't remember all the rules. With practice, you will come to recognize when something sounds right or wrong in your speech, just as you do in your native tongue.

We talked about syllable stress within our words. Let's now look at stress within our sentences. The purpose of speech is to communicate your thoughts. As an actor, I am aware of how a sentence can be spoken with stress on different words to impart a slightly different meaning each time. To show you the importance of this, the **shot** (picture) of me

to the right is from a stage production in which I played a former president of the U.S.[*]
For some reason I wasn't getting a laugh from a sentence that was
supposed to be funny. After several performances in which I
experimented, I finally found the proper stress within the sentence that
produced a laugh each time I spoke it. Little adjustments like this can
bring big results to your speech, too. Thus our goal is to make your
speech pleasant and intelligible to the American ear.

"Mr. President"

To begin with, English is a *stressed* language in which we vary
the stress in our words *and* within sentences. Many other languages are
syllabic, meaning each syllable receives equal importance. Because of this, they might
pronounce each word in an English sentence with equal emphasis and don't know where
to speed up, slow down, or stress or de-stress words. This adds to their foreign accent.

Two simple factors affect the way you speak an English sentence: **volume**
(loud/soft) and **pitch** (high/low frequency, such as a man's low voice or a woman's
higher voice). We vary the volume and pitch throughout our sentences to give them a
pleasing rhythm that may be *very* different from how you speak in your language. This is
called the overall *sentence tone*. If a speaker does not vary the tone of his sentence, his
speech will be monotone (single tone). Even changing the tone of an English word will
change emphasis and help make the overall sentence more easily understood.

In English, our pronunciation focuses on specific stressed words in a sentence
while we glide over non-stressed words. When I studied Shakespearean acting in
England, this concept became apparent to me. Not only was I trying to learn words that
Shakespeare wrote 500 years ago (some of which I had no idea what they meant), but I
was also trying to speak clearly *each and every one of them* in sentences while attempting
to use a British accent. It became much easier when the teacher told me to speak the
sentences the way I would normally in America; that is, decrease the importance of some
words to get a more fluid, pleasing sound.

> **Hint**: If you listen to beginning actors or children who are learning to read out loud, you will
> notice that their sentences sound monotone because they place equal stress on each word. As their
> reading skills advance they develop a rhythm and learn to put stress on key words and minimize
> emphasis on less important words. This nice beat and clarity is what I want you to learn to do
> while still pronouncing *all* your words clearly. Listen to an English broadcaster and notice how
> they glide through their sentences while combining all these essentials in their delivery.

---

[*]In case you have an interest, you can rent a video of the movie *The Best Man*, which was based on the
stage play of the same name. It is about the presidential election process in the U.S. Or better, you can
purchase the written play at http://amzn.to/VidalPlay. Note playwright/screenwriter Gore Vidal's
wonderful command of English and the absence of wasted words. This is the only play I ever acted in that I
did not change one word, something actors do frequently.

First, let's compare the stressed and non-stressed words in our spoken sentences and then we'll move on to overall sentence tone.

Stressed Words – Words that you want to stress in your sentences are those words that define the *content* of your sentence. These are nouns, verbs, adverbs, and adjectives that were discussed in the previous chapter on grammar. To review:

- **Nouns** name a *person*, *place*, *thing*, or an *idea*.
- **Verbs** express action or help to make a statement. Action verbs (not linking verbs) that express action are stressed.
- **Adverbs** modify a *verb*, an *adjective*, or another *adverb*. Generally, adverbs tell *when*, *where*, *how*, and to *what extent* (how long or how much).
- **Adjectives** modify a *noun* or *pronoun* to make the meaning of a word more definite by telling *what kind* it is, *which one* it is, or *how many*.

Your listener will interpret the meaning of your sentence differently when you change the stress on one or more of these words. You can do this with **horizontal** (elongating it) or **vertical** (adjusting volume or pitch) word stress.

You can change a word's stress *horizontally* by elongating it, making the sound last longer. Try this aloud with the sentences below. Use the same volume and pitch for each word in the first sentence. Then take more time pronouncing the vowel in the stress words, making them longer than the others. When you elongate certain words, you give nice rhythm to your sentence. Notice how the meaning of this sentence with the word you choose to elongate.

"Look, that's John."	- No particular feeling imparted.
"Looooook, that's John."	- You want to get their attention.
"Look, th*aaaaa*t's John.	- You want to specify a specific person.
"Look, that's J*ooooo*hn."	- You are amazed to see John.

Vertically change the emphasis of your sentence by increasing or decreasing the volume or pitch. Say out loud and do that on the words in capital letters to achieve similar effects spoken above.

"LOOK, that's John."	- You want to get their attention.
"Look, THAT'S John."	- You want to specify a specific person.
"Look, that's JOHN."	- You are amazed to see John.

You can also combine horizontal and vertical stress on the same word for maximum effect. Stage actors do this to overcome long distances separating them from the audience.

Non-Stressed Words – Non-stressed words are generally not stressed in a sentence because they perform housekeeping or grammatical functions. (You could stress them, however, if you wanted to emphasize a particular point.) They consist of pronouns, prepositions, articles, and linking verbs as we discussed in the grammar chapter. To review, here's a quick **rundown** (summary).

- **Pronouns** are used in place of one or more nouns, such as *you, he, she, it, we, they, none, somebody*, etc.
- **Prepositions** show the relation of a noun or pronoun to some other word in a sentence, such as *of, for, past, from, across*.
- **Articles** are the little connective words *a, an*, and *the*.
- **Linking Verbs** are not used for stress because they do not express action, such as *be, is, been, being; am, are, was, were; do, did, done, doing; will, would; shall, should; can, could; may, might, must*.

Combining Stressed and Non-stressed Words – By combining stressed and non-stressed words correctly in your sentence, you create a spoken melody that makes it easier for the listener to understand you. I had a difficult time understanding the English of a Spanish speaking guide in Ecuador because she put equal emphasis on each word. Consequently, she was both boring to listen to and unintelligible. I kept **nodding off** (falling asleep.) Sometimes this emphasis problem happens when people learn a language from a book and have no sound to imitate.

Let's compare two different ways of speaking the same sentence. First, say this sentence out loud and pronounce each word clearly and with equal stress and no rhythm, just as my tour guide did.

> "I went for a walk in the park and watched people walk around
> with their children and dogs as rain fell from a gray sky and
> music played in the distant village."

Now say the sentence below again, but put stress only on the **bold** stress words and see how you can say it more quickly and how the words seem to flow more smoothly. Give your sentence some rhythm as if you are reading a musical score with gentle ups and downs, and with elongation of some of the stressed words. Also notice how the non-stressed words in italic are gently kept together in a little phrase of their own.

> "I **went** *for a* **walk** *in the* **park** and **watched people walk around** *with their* **children** and **dogs** as **rain fell** *from a* **gray sky** and **music played** *in the* **distant village**."

This is an exaggeration, of course, but it conveys the point. You still must pronounce the consonants of the unstressed words or they will not be discernible to your listener. This example will help you develop a gentle rhythm, a lilt, and help eliminate monotone. If possible, record this little exercise on a tape recorder and compare the two

522

different approaches with and without emphasis. Keep working at it until all the words are understandable and you have an easy flow. If possible, have an American do the same exercise and listen to their rhythm.

☺ **Here's an assignment for you.** Get an English language newspaper, book, or magazine and pick out six fairly long sentences. Read them aloud into a tape recorder with all words having equal stress and volume. Next, underline the stress words in each sentence. Re-read them with emphasis on the stress words. Do you notice the difference? Did it take less time to speak the sentences the second time? Did you have a noticeable rhythm as opposed to a monotone sound? Did you elongate a vowel in some of the words to give stress? Good! You even may have had an easier time pronouncing some of the words. Please practice this each day. Caution: Do not develop the

Practice reading a newspaper.

bad habit that many foreigners do. They think that once they have good rhythm they do not need to pronounce the consonants or the unstressed words clearly…try to hit a good balance.

☺ **Here's another assignment.** Search the Internet for "Sinatra – All My Tomorrows." Listen to how this famous American singer elongated his words—especially vowel sounds—to give added importance, rhythm, and clarity. Sing or speak along with him to practice the same effect. Nice, huh? He mined for gold in his words. In music circles, Sinatra was known for what they call his "phrasing," which is really what we've been talking about in this section.

Frank Sinatra

SENTENCE TONE

Actors, radio, and TV announcers must create interesting sounding sentences for their listeners. Besides stressing individual words in their sentences, as we discussed above, they also view the spoken sentence as if it were written on a sheet of music and they give groups of words gentle overall ups and downs. You can do the same. By doing this, you add overall tone and rhythm to your sentences. They all send important signals to your listener that makes you easier to understand.

Here are some tips for adding pleasing overall tone to your sentences.

Tip #1: Statements – A sentence that is merely making a statement can end with a *slight* overall drop in stress and volume. This may signal that you are through speaking and the listener may then respond. It also might signal that you are finishing one thought and are getting ready to switch to another thought. This helps your listener anticipate what you are going to say. For example:

I was sitting in the park   Luckily,
▼ and it started to rain. ▲   ▼ I had my umbrella.

By varying just *slightly* the tone of these two sentences as shown above, you make it more interesting to your listener. You could also choose to use stressed words as we discussed earlier. For instance, you might elongate *park* or *rain* and *luckily* or *umbrella* to give added emphasis.

If a prepositional phrase or a dependent clause comes at the beginning of a sentence, it can sometimes take the most stress, and the phrase that ends the sentence will then be spoken with a slight decline. You might want to do the opposite or even make the entire sentence rise in tone depending of the intent of your sentence. For example:

▲ Being of sound mind, ▼ I decided not to get involved.
▲ When you are in doubt, ▼ consult a dictionary.
▼ Just across the road from me, ▲ I spotted a deer!
▲ Wanting to impress my boss, ▼ I took English classes every evening.

Tip #2: Questions – By stressing or de-stressing the last word in a sentence, you can change a statement into a question, or vice versa. Read these sentences aloud and listen how the meaning of the sentence changes with no stress, decreased stress, and increased stress.

(No stress)   It's wrong. (Sentence is monotone, a statement.)
(Decreased stress on *wrong*) It's ▼ wrong. (Decreased importance of being wrong.)
(Stress on *wrong*)   It's ▲ wrong? (Sentence becomes a question.)

Tip #3: A Series Of Items – When you are talking in sequence about three or more things, your tone may increase with each one until you reach the last item and you drop the tone. This drop signals your listener that you have reached the end of your list. Say aloud:

"In my English class, we learned about nouns, verbs, adverbs, adjectives, and [slight drop] prepositions. We learned the vowels are A, E, I, O, and [slight drop] U."

Notice how, after you drop your voice on the ending of each group of words, you get a small, natural pause before you continue. This helps you to be better understood, offers your listener a chance to respond, and even gives you a little time to consider what you might say next.

Tip #4: Linking Words – Another method to alert your listener to what is coming in your spoken sentence is to link together the *words within the phrases* in a sentence by using a similar stress for them. This is like putting an assortment of 24 different colored jewels on a table and sorting them out by color, then stringing them together by groups of colors to form a necklace. An acting teacher once told me this is the job of an actor, to string together one thought after another while making an overall pretty necklace of thoughts. Your listeners will be better able to follow your groups of words in their minds as you say them because you have organized them into associated groups.

Let's pretend an inexperienced actor delivers these lines in a monotone voice with no stress. When done this way you have no idea where he is going with his sentence until he has finished it.

"I will meet you under the apple tree with a surprise for you
about the time you return from your trip out of town."

Now, let's analyze the phrases or thoughts in this sentence and see how you can string them together using pauses and intonation to aid your listener in better understanding what you are saying.

▼ I will meet you under the apple tree	(8 pink jewels)	(lower tone)
▲ with a surprise for you	(5 bright red jewels)	(higher tone)
▲ about the time you return	(5 bright yellow jewels)	(higher tone)
▼ from your trip out of town.	(6 light blue jewels)	(lower tone)

Notice how the last three phrases or thoughts happen to start with a preposition. A prepositional phrase is a collection of associated words all its own. In terms of sentence tone and rhythm, it is important that you gently tie the words together within these phrases so your listener knows they are connected. Notice how at the same time some words might be stressed gently as we discussed earlier, like *meet*, *apple tree*, *surprise*, *time*, *return*, and *trip*. If you can do this, you are on your way to being better understood.

ABBREVIATIONS

An abbreviation is any shortened form of a word or phrase. You will encounter different types of abbreviations in the U.S., the most common being acronyms and initialisms. They are used most often to abbreviate names of organizations and long or frequently referenced terms.

We love to use these in our informal writings and to take short cuts in our speech. You might also see or hear them in our advertisements. Generally, when used in speech, they are so common most everyone understands them. However, a **rule of thumb** (general rule) is they must be explained if not commonly understood. We have thousands of these fellows. If you don't understand one in your conversations, feel free to ask its meaning. There are numerous websites you can use to look them up, such as www.acronymfinder.com or www.acronymslist.com.

An **acronym** *[AK-row-nim]* is a *pronounceable word* formed from each of the first letters of a descriptive phrase or series of words. The word "acronym" is from Greek: *acro* (head) and *nym* (word). For example:

AIDS: acquired immune deficiency syndrome, pronounced as "aids."
ASAP: as soon as possible, pronounced as "a-sap."
AWOL: absent without leave, pronounced as "a-wall."
IRA: individual retirement account, pronounced as "eye-ruh."
KISS: keep it simple stupid, pronounced as "kiss."
NATO: North Atlantic Treaty Organization, pronounced "nay-toe."
PIN: personal identification number, pronounced as "pin."
WASP: white Anglo-Saxon Protestant, pronounced like the bee: "wosp."

Initialism is a group of initial letters for a name or expression with *each letter* pronounced separately. For example, the shortcut pronunciation of the British Broadcasting Corporation (BBC) is "b-b-c."

Here are a few of our widely used ones.

AA - Alcoholics Anonymous organization. **AC** - Air conditioning. **AKA** - Also known as. **ATM** - Automated teller machine. **BYOB** - Bring your own bottle (of liquor for a party). **DBA** - Doing business as (if a business' name differs from the owner's). **FAQ** - Frequently asked questions. **FBI** – Federal Bureau of Investigation. **FYI** - For your information. **GM** - General manager and General Motors. **ID** - Identification. **INS** - Immigration and Naturalization Service. **IQ** - Intelligence quotient. **IRS** - Internal Revenue Service (federal government's tax collector). **MC** - Master of ceremonies. **NFL** - National Football League. **OJ** - Orange juice. **PDQ** - Pretty darn quick. **Q&A** - Question and answer. **R&R** - Rest and relaxation. **SOP** - Standard operating procedure. **TBA** - To be announced. **TGIF** - Thank God it's Friday. **TLC** - Tender loving care. **VIP** - Very important person. **VP** - Vice president. **YTD** - Year to date.

SLANG SAYINGS

When Americans try to explain something to a foreigner, they might say, "We have a slang saying (or word) for that," and then quote one to emphasize a point. Most use the catchall term "slang" to refer to all of our unique sayings that might not be easily understood by foreigners. There is not universal agreement on their definitions, let alone how they should be grouped together. For ease of understanding, I group them into slang, idioms, and proverbs based on how they differ in cultural tone, whom they are addressing, and their ease of understanding.

If someone uses one of these "slang" words or sayings that you don't understand, be sure to ask for clarification. Also, do not use one unless you are sure of its meaning. English speaking Australians use strange slang that is not understood by Americans and we have to ask for clarification, especially when they sing "Waltzing Maltida," their unofficial national anthem. They probably have the same problem with our culturally unique slang.

Numerous books and websites are available to learn more about our "slang" words and phrases. One website to explore is www.manythings.com, a site for those learning English as a Second Language (ESL). It has lots of information on slang as well as puzzles and quizzes to test your English knowledge.

Slang – Slang in the narrow sense is jargon that consists of words or phrases that have their very own meaning to a certain group of people such as teenagers or those who have the same jobs, backgrounds, or interests. Each generation and social class also has its own slang and one may have trouble understanding the slang of the other. Because it lowers the dignity of speech or writing, slang is used in casual or playful speech or writing, or in creative writing as dialogue.

For example, we could use the word "can" to refer to a bathroom (not a metal container) in this sentence: "Where is the can?" This slang usage conveys a lower-class speaker. We are no longer using slang when we say "Where is the restroom?" which sounds better. Be careful not to use too much slang in your speech because it can convey an uneducated tone if overdone.

> **Hint**: When I hear foreigners use a lot of slang in their English sentences, I know they have been associating with lower class or uneducated people in America. For some reason it sounds even worse than if an American had said it. It **sticks out like a sore thumb** (is obvious).

Here are some slang words you might hear us use.
argh – an exclamation of disappointment.
awesome – very good, excellent, fun, appealing.
beat – exhausted (not hit).
boo-boo — a mistake.
bread – money (not a loaf).
bro – a male in the same kinship group; someone treated like a brother.
buck – a dollar (not a male dear).
bust – failure (not a bosom).
can of worms – nothing but problems (no can or worms).
chick – attractive girl (not a chicken).
cool – likeable, in style (not a temperature).
deep pockets – someone who has lots of money.
geek – a nerd, introvert, overly intellectual, somewhat dislikable person.
hip – in the know, current (not the body part).
hot – hip, attractive, sexy; a stolen item (not a body temperature).
no worries – not a problem.
pad – my house, apartment (not a cushion).
smooth – very good, cool, excellent.
the misses – one's wife.
the old man – one's father.

whatever – you don't care, as in "Yeah right!" said with sarcasm.

yeah right – a terse expression of doubt or disbelief meaning the opposite of what the words say.

Idioms – We have a word for a broader grouping of these "slang" sayings that we call idioms. They are very particular to our English language but have a more general audience than slang. An idiom is a phrase where the words together have a different from the dictionary definitions of the individual words. They do not make sense when you try to understand them verbatim, which makes them hard for foreigners to understand.

One such phrase is **sticks out like a sore thumb**. In this phrase, something is not really "sticking out," but means it draws attention. Literally translating the sentences will not help you understand them any better. So, you simply must learn what these phrases mean as a whole so you don't feel lost when someone uses one.

Because they both may be hard to interpret, slang and idioms used in this book are listed together in the Index under "slang/idiom." Here are a few popular idiom expressions you might encounter.

- *Don't beat around the bush.* This has nothing to do with bushes. It means that you are not being straight forward. You give unnecessary details or talk a lot and avoid getting to the point.
- *Don't count your chickens before they hatch.* This has nothing to do with chickens. It means don't make assumptions and don't plan on getting something before you get it, such as a gift or inheritance.
- *Don't look a gift horse in the mouth.* Accept gifts graciously. Don't complain about what you are given as a gift, even if you don't like it.
- *Don't put all your eggs in one basket.* If you put all your eggs in one basket and you drop it, *all* your eggs will break instead of a few. The saying has nothing to do with eggs. It means don't necessarily rely on just one option. We often use it to advise investors not to put all their money in one stock.
- *Give me a hand.* This says you want help from somebody, not necessarily their physical hand.
- *Six of one, half-dozen of the other.* This has nothing to do with six of something. A half-dozen is a quantity of six, so it doesn't matter which option or item is chosen, they are both the same.
- *Take it easy.* This means to relax or calm down. It is not referring to taking the easy way out of a situation
- *That's just the tip of the iceberg.* This has nothing to do with icebergs other than the fact we only see 10 percent of their body above water. The saying means you are only seeing a small portion of the big picture and more is hidden or may soon be apparent.

- *The ball is in your court.* It is your turn to make a move or decision; you now have the power.

- *There's more than one way to skin a cat.* This has nothing to do with cats. It means you should think about all the different ways to do something, not just the most popular or obvious. It suggests my way differs from yours.

- *They are like two peas in a pod.* We use this when two people, usually friends, co-workers, or relatives have a lot in common, have great chemistry, or share interests or other characteristics.

- *We will cross that bridge when we get to it.* This has nothing to do with bridges. It means don't worry about that right now; let's deal with it when the right time comes. Let's take things one-step at a time.

- *Which came first, the chicken or the egg?* This has nothing to do with chickens or eggs. It means you are not sure which one was the cause, which one was the effect, or what the sequence of events was or will be.

- *You are barking up the wrong tree.* A dog may bark at a tree, assuming a hunted animal is in the tree when it isn't. It means you are making the wrong assumption or not looking in the right place. You should look at another alternative, change your approach, or rethink your position.

- *You are skating on thin ice.* This has nothing to do with ice. It suggests you should be careful, you are close to making a wrong assumption, or will do the wrong thing. Also, it can be a warning you are close to making someone angry so proceed with caution.

- *You get more bees with honey than vinegar.* This suggests *you* will get better results dealing with people if you are nice to them instead of being sour like vinegar.

Proverbs and Sayings – Our third group of sayings consists of easily understood proverbs (basic truths or practicalities), aphorisms (embody a general truth), and other sayings to impart advice or knowledge. Foreigners have no problems with these because they are more direct than slang and idioms. They, too, are used to clarify a point, such as this popular one: An apple a day keeps the doctor away. That saying indeed deals with apples and doctors, so it is straightforward and easily understood. All of these sayings found throughout this book are listed in the Index as "saying/proverb." So are the sayings of famous people that you might hear us use, such as those discussed later in this chapter.

GOOD SPEAKING TIPS

In Chapter H on customs and etiquette, you learned how to be a better conversationalist, that is, how to carry on a conversation with an American, how to greet people, how to discuss things, and other personal pointers. In Chapter V on business customs, you learned how to talk business. Here are tips for further improving your spoken words during these and other occasions.

Tip #1: Do Not Be Afraid To Try – As I travel the world and come into contact with people who know English, I can sense when they want to speak to me but are reluctant to do so. As part of their culture, some foreigners believe that if they do not speak well it might reflect on their family or education and they will lose face. You need to remember, most Americans do not speak a foreign language, so we respect foreigners who are learning ours, regardless of how well they speak it. Though we do not pass judgment, we may wish for clearer communication, one of the objectives of this chapter.

Time after time I talk to foreigners who learned English from native teachers in their countries and have picked up common errors passed on to them. In order polish your English, try to speak to someone who speaks it as a native language. When you have the opportunity, take advantage of it with no fear of trying. Fear is a powerful force that directs how we do things.

Ralph Waldo Emerson, a 19th century American writer, advised, "Do the thing you fear, and death of fear is certain." I know as an actor that until I was able to conquer the fear of being on stage in front of hundreds of people with the possibility of forgetting my lines I could not improve my delivery. When I conquered most of this fear, I felt much more comfortable and it showed in my delivery. You can do the same with your English delivery.

> **Hint**: It is said of actors that if they are afraid, they are thinking about the audience instead of the character they are supposed to be portraying. The same is true for you and your English. Do not focus on what you think the other person is thinking about your English. Instead, focus on your English and your fear will diminish, something my students affirm is true.

I visited a museum in Nagasaki, Japan, where my large group of visiting Americans was allowed to proceed to the front of the line inside the museum. We passed hundreds of high school students lined up waiting their turn to enter. As I walked by them, I made eye contact with each student hoping one of them would speak to me. It was obvious they wanted to, but I could see that most were afraid to try. About every 50th student said "Hello" to initiate a conversation. I would stop, smile, and say, "Hello, do you speak English?" They would say "A little," and I would say "Me, too," which made them laugh and gave them confidence to begin a conversation. This humor seemed to **break the ice** (remove tension) and they sensed I would not be critical if they made an error. I then asked them questions that I knew would be easy to answer. It was obvious that those who spoke to me were glad they had the rare opportunity to do so. We have an American saying: **practice makes perfect**.

> **Hint**: Most Americans visiting a foreign country will be pleased if you want to practice your English with them. Just say, "Hello, where are you from?" Be sure to smile and make eye contact

before you speak so they know you are not a threat, not begging for money, or not trying to sell something, all common occurrences for tourists. You might then say, "Do you mind if I practice my English with you?" Oh, and don't forget our imaginary circle that we discussed in Chapter H on customs and etiquette.

Tip #2: Ask If You Don't Understand – I find some foreigners think it is rude to ask us questions about English words they don't understand. Maybe they think it will reflect on their intelligence, as is common in some countries, so they want to save face. If you are involved in a conversation where you are expected to respond and you do not understand something, let the speaker know. The purpose of speaking is to communicate thoughts. I have one foreign-born friend who is not afraid to say to me "Please repeat," or "Say again, please." She claims that if she asks, she remembers; otherwise, it just **passes her by** (is forgotten). Other friends do not let me know, so by the lack of their response or the look on their face I sometimes ask them what they don't understand.

When English speakers talk to foreigners, we may pause briefly after a sentence or phrase to measure their reaction to what we just said. Most people do the same thing with young children when explaining something that might be complicated. Sometimes when we talk, it might take multiple sentences to build up to the final sentence, and if you don't understand one of the preliminary sentences, you won't comprehend the final one. So, take advantage of these pauses to ask for clarification.

Tip #3: Learn To Speak Up – When foreigners have self-doubts about their English speaking ability, they tend to speak softly. The same is true of new actors who have not conquered their fear of being in front of an audience. In both cases, their ability to communicate suffers. This decline in volume, coupled with your accent, makes it hard for your American listener to understand you. So on the first day of the classes I teach to foreigners I have each student stand at the rear of my classroom with his or her back to me, and I stand at the front with my back to them. I then ask them questions. They quickly learn that they need to speak up to be heard to carry on a conversation. They can do it, but they need encouragement and practice. This is particularly true for women from cultures that encourage them to speak in soft tones.

Michael Wong, who teaches English in downtown Beijing, defines developing courage as the first step to speaking English well. "Then it goes to the *pronunciation,* then the *sentence structure,* then finally trying to think the same way [culturally] as foreigners do." This mirrors the same approach of this book.

Hint: Speaking up is especially important in business dealings. Each month I receive a telephone call from an Asian owned health clinic to remind me of an upcoming appointment. The callers are young first generation Asian women whose cultural belief is they must be soft in voice and action. The firm's name has three words in its title, but they rapidly blend them together into one sound. That, coupled with their soft voices, on several occasions has led me to think they were selling something and I hung up not knowing who they really were because I couldn't understand them.

531

Tip #4: Be A Good Listener And Observer – Ernest Hemingway, one of our famous 20th century writers (see Chapter K - Literature), once revealed, "I like to listen. I have learned a great deal from listening carefully. Most people never listen."

Acting teachers will tell you that in order to be a good actor you must be a good listener because acting is nothing more than observing and reacting. If you want to speak English well, you must learn to be a good listener and observer.

In high school, we were taught to not write down each and every detail our teacher told us, but instead to listen to the overall concept and write that down. Similarly, if you become too involved with all the small details in a sentence spoken to you, you will miss the overall message. Teachers of English as a Second Language (ESL) also say it is best not to take the time to immediately translate a spoken word you don't understand into your native language. If you do, you will probably miss the essence of what is being said.

Keep in mind that Americans tend to repeat themselves when speaking. If you missed something, it might be reworded differently in a moment or two. Because our stress words convey the real meaning of our thoughts, the other words are less important anyway. Have you ever watched a movie in your native language and found you didn't hear 100 percent of what was said, yet you were still able to understand what was going on? Similarly, advertisers say the average person only hears every fourth word in a radio advertisement yet they still grasp the overall message.

Psychologists say that a person's impact on another person depends seven percent on what is actually said, 38 percent on how it is said and 55 percent on body language. Body language consists of posture, facial expressions, gestures, and eye contact. Unlike some countries where the use of hands when speaking might annoy the listener, it is readily accepted in the U.S. (We joke that Americans of Italian heritage would be unable talk if they didn't use their hands.) So try to *anticipate* what an American is going to say based on their body language.

President Bush's body language says "I'm bored."

Good listeners do not interrupt the speaker. I had a telephone conversation with a foreign businessman and every time I attempted to ask clarification on a particular point, he interrupted me before I finished my sentence. This has happened to me frequently by others from his country where this is acceptable. He probably thought he knew what I was going to ask or say, and perhaps felt he could save me the time of asking questions. In most cases he was wrong, so I had to repeat myself several times by interrupting him in order to get my answer. Interrupting unnecessarily puts you in a **bad light** (unfavorable view).

Tip #5: Sing A Song, Watch A Movie, Repeat – When traveling overseas, I often hear American songs sung in perfect English by foreigners who can't speak English. They are able to do this by listening to the American recorded version of the songs and then mimicking what they hear. You can do the same thing to practice your English pronunciation and give rhythm to your sentences. Rent an American movie and memorize some lines just as they are spoken in the film. If possible, record both your spoken lines and the lines from the film on a tape recorder and play them back for comparison.

> **Hint**: My favorite movie for using this technique is *My Fair Lady*, which I discuss in Chapter L on film. Try to pronounce the famous "Rain in Spain" lines from the movie. In fact, if you want to show off your newly acquired talent, speak these lines correctly to an American and you might receive applause and you can take a bow. I use recorded music by American singer Nat King Cole in my classes for students to sing along with him. His diction is distinct and the songs are slow. I have seen his CDs in shops overseas, so I know they are available. If not, listen on the Internet or purchase an audio CD or MP3 download from Amazon.com at http://amzn.to/KingCole.

Nat King Cole

Imitating our radio and TV broadcasters and commercial announcers also helps internalize a more natural speech pattern and makes it more receptive to the American ear. Use a tape recorder for this learning process, too.

Tip #6: Silence Can Be Uncomfortable – Some Americans feel awkward in a conversation if there are long pauses. This is particularly true if you are talking on the telephone. Certain Asian business people will wait 15 seconds before responding to a question. To us it conveys the impression they are bored or distracted. We may even think we've been disconnected and hang up. Conversely, we feel awkward if you speak too much and we don't have an opportunity to respond. Try to reach a happy medium try to detect if your counterpart is comfortable.

Tip #7: Make Eye Contact – If you look away from the person you are speaking to, you convey the impression that you are bored with them, you feel superior to them, or you are embarrassed. You don't have to stare at them, but make sure you are talking *to* them, not away from them. Unlike some cultures, eye contact—even by children—is not rude but is a sign of confidence and respect.

Tip #8: Slow Down – Most of us speak rapidly to each other in our native language and we are understood. However, for foreigners, speed may be their enemy when speaking to an American. You do not have to talk fast just because your American counterpart does. You would probably tell us to slow down (or wish we would!) if we were in your country speaking your language.

Make sure the first five words in your sentence are spoken distinctly and do not run together. Otherwise, your listener might be trying to figure out what you started to say and will miss some of your remaining words. Also, by slowing down, it makes it easier to pronounce ending consonants and elongate some vowels as we discussed earlier.

I experienced this problem firsthand with a tour guide in Alexandria, Egypt, who had studied English in the U.S., had an excellent vocabulary, and spoke up with confidence. However, she spoke so fast that I doubt if any of us understood more than 30 percent of what she said. Her speed was the same as when she spoke to her countrymen in her native language.

The next day a tour guide in Cairo, Egypt, with an equally impressive knowledge of English spoke slower and we understood 80 percent of what she said. We also appreciated it when she asked us if we understood something she said because she wasn't sure she phrased it correctly. So, remember, even if you feel confident with your command of English, it does not **give you license** (permission) to speak fast until you lose most of your unique native speech rhythm. This is especially true for Asian Indians who have grown up speaking English.

If you are speaking a word that you have difficulty pronouncing, slow down and elongate some of its vowels, or pause slightly between syllables. I find some foreigners are reluctant to do this because they think that if they stumble on a word we won't notice it if they hurriedly say it, which of course is not true. If you listen to advertisements on American TV, you will note that speakers often slow down on a word or elongate it to emphasize it, such as, "This is a wooooooonderful [wonderful] price." You can do the same to add clarity to your speech.

Tip #9: Contractions Are Okay – When we combine two or more words to form one word, we call the new word a contraction *[kon-TRACK-shun]*. As you learned in the grammar chapter, contractions *aren't* (are not) used in some writing because they are considered informal. I find my foreign students make more grammatical errors by selecting the incorrect verb when they do use them.

Once mastered, however, in speech *they're* (they are) your friend. They can add rhythm and flow to your speech, something President Obama and his speech writers are aware of and why is is a good orator. Here are some of our commonly used contractions.

won't – from *will not*	*I'd* – from *I would*
can't – from *cannot*	*I'll* – from *I will*
doesn't – from *does not*	*aren't* – from *are not*
we'd – from *we would*	*we'll* – from *we will*
wouldn't – from *would not*	*would've* – from *would have*
don't – from *do not*	*isn't* – from *is not*
it's – from *it is*	*shouldn't* – from *should not*
we're – from *we are*	*we've* – from *we have*

534

won't – from *will not*   *they'd* – from *they would*
haven't – from *have not*   *they'll* – from *they will*
he'll – from *he will*   *weren't* – from *were not*

A trick that actors use to make a strong statement is to separate the two words. For example, say these two sentences out loud and determine which one makes the stronger statement.

"No, I *will not* do that job."   "No, I *won't* do that job."

If you place emphasis on *will not* when speaking this sentence, you give your sentence more emphasis than if you place stress on *won't*. You sound firmer, perhaps even angry. Several of my tour guides have used this technique when telling us, "*Do not* be late returning to the bus or we will leave you."

Foreigners must be careful to pronounce the ending of a contraction clearly. If you don't, "doesn't" sounds like "does" and "wouldn't" like "would," another common problem I encounter around the world. If you have trouble pronouncing these ending sounds clearly, then don't use contractions until you can. Practice enunciating and elongating the ending T, D, S, and L sounds in the examples above.

Tip #10: Respectful And Educated Speech Is Nice – Here are a few tips to add a little sparkle to your English speech and enhance the cultural image you convey.

- *Ain't* – You will hear "*ain't*" (rhymes with *paint*) spoken to mean "is not." Don't ever use this word! Instead of saying, "I ain't going to work today," say "I'm not going to work today." "Ain't" is extremely low class. You will, however, sometimes hear it used by an educated person in a joking manner to give playful emphasis to a thought, like "You ain't seen nothin' yet."

- *Either/Neither* – You can add a touch of sophistication to your persona by the way you pronounce *either* and *neither*. Most people pronounce them as "eether" and "neether." Some highly cultured and intellectual people might pronounce them as "eye-ther" and "n-eye-ther." However, none of these pronunciations is wrong.

- *Filler Words* – You will hear some Americans inject filler words like "*you know,*" "*like,*" "*man,*" and "*umm*" throughout their sentences as filler for a pause or hesitation." Don't do it because, you know, man, it sounds like, umm, uneducated, y'know. I had a tour guide in Casablanca, Morocco, who used "you know" in nearly all of his sentences, sometimes three or four times in the same sentence. It was annoying and distracting so I was focused on this instead of the historical information he was trying to impart. I noticed he did it each time he had a little trouble coming up with the correct English word or phrase but wanted to keep his speech rhythm going. This is unnecessary, you know, because, you know, like man, there is nothing wrong with, umm, pausing to gather your thoughts, you know. It helps to say the filler word in your mind but not speak it. The same applies to long "uuuhhhhhs" some foreign speakers (and Americans) use to avoid silent spots. Some Germans have an annoying habit of making a nasal clicking noise as filler. The proverb **silence is golden** dates back to ancient Egypt and 5000 years later still implies that often the best choice is to say nothing.

- *Like I Said* – You will hear someone say, "*Like I said...*" when referring back to something they said earlier. An educated person will say, "*As I said...*" or "*As I say....*"

- *No Subject* – As you learned, our sentences must have a subject. But sometimes in our casual speech we might drop the subject. For example, if you and a friend are parting, he or she might say, "See ya later," instead of "I will see you later." Or, "Long time no see" instead of "It has been a long time since I saw you." This can have a cute, warm feeling about it.

- *Not Understanding* – If you have a problem communicating with an American, do not say, "You don't understand." This implies that they, not you, are having a problem, when in fact it may be you. Instead, say "Let me rephrase it," or "I'm probably not explaining it clearly." That way you don't put the other person on the defensive and play the **blame game** (refusing to accept responsibility). They will appreciate your consideration. Hopefully English speakers will extend the same courtesy to you.

- *One* – Some people (especially professors) use the word "*one*" in place of "you" when referring to people in general. For example, *you* might say, "*You could say that going to the dentist is not fun,*" or, "*One could say that going to the dentist is not fun.*" Use of "one" sounds more educated if not overdone.

- *Sir Or Ma'am* – If you want to show respect to another person, you can sometimes use the words "*ma'am*" [mam] (short for madam) for a female, and "*sir*" for a male. Ordinarily, sir and ma'am apply to a person of high respect or position. But you can say them to ordinary people in special circumstances and it might reflect favorably on you if done with respect and sincerity. You could say "Yes, sir," or "Sir, may I help you with that." I might say "Thank you, sir," to a man who arrives at a door before me, but holds it open for me to proceed first. (This is somewhat akin to the Chinese use of *shifu* in which respect is given to another person.)

- *Got Versus Have* – When I hear foreigners use the word *got* excessively instead of *have,* I know they have been around lower educated Americans or fellow foreigners. *Got* is the past tense of *get* and means to receive: *I got the present from Mary. Have* means to possess: *I have the present Mary gave me,* not *I've got the present Mary gave me.*

536

Tip #11: Different Words But Similar Meaning – English speakers use a variety of words, all of which have the same general meaning. And each English speaking country has a few of their own. As a result, you might have a problem trying to discern the exact meanings of our spoken words. If this arises, ask for clarification. As an example, when describing a quantity of more than one, we can say: *some, a few, several, a little, a lot, a bunch, a group, numerous, many, a truckload, a ton, not many, quite a few, quite a lot, a handful, a fistful,* etc. If you are in a situation where you need to know the exact amount, feel free to ask for it. We also use lots of different words for money: *buck* (one dollar), *mullah, grand* (thousand dollars), *clams, loot, dough, greenbacks, and two bits* (25 cents). Most of these are considered slang and would be used in informal speech with friends in America, though some may be used in other countries, too.

Tip #12: Numbers Require Clear Pronunciation – Some foreigners have a problem figuring out and pronouncing the names of numbers in English. Our numbering system, like our money system, is based on tens (10s). For clarity, we place a comma "," to the left of each set of three numbers. Each comma indicates a new group—thousand, hundred thousand, million, etc. Some non-English speaking cultures use the comma as a decimal point and the decimal point as a comma. In Chile I saw a billboard advertising a 3.5 percent home interest rate as "3,50". The taxi meter in Madrid, Spain, said my fare was "23,15 Euros."

This is how we pronounce our basic numbers from 1 to 20 both as numerals and the sequencial order they come in. Remember to pronounce strongly the ending sounds of each, especially the TH and EN sounds that we discussed earlier in this chapter.

1 = one or first	11 = eleven or eleventh
2 = two or second	12 = twelve or twelfth
3 = three or third	13 = thirteen or thirteenth
4 = four or fourth	14 = fourteen or fourteenth
5 = five or fifth	15 = fifteen or fifteenth
6 = six or sixth	16 = sixteen or sixteenth
7 = seven or seventh	17 = seventeen or seventeenth
8 = eight or eighth	18 = eighteen or eighteenth
9 = nine or ninth	19 = nineteen or nineteenth
10 = ten or tenth	20 = twenty or twentieth

This is how we pronounce our decade (10s) numbers. The ending *ty* (TEE sound) *must* be pronounced strongly.

20 = twenty	30 = thirty	40 = forty	50 = fifty
60 = sixty	70 = seventy	80 = eighty	90 = ninety

Here are some sample numbers and their pronunciation:

1 = one	5 = five
10 = ten	15 = fifteen
100 = one hundred	105 = one hundred and five
1,000 = one thousand	1,005 = one thousand and five
10,000 = ten thousand	10,500 = ten thousand five hundred
100,000 = one hundred thousand	150,000 = one hundred and fifty thousand
1,000,000 = one million	1,500,000 = one million five hundred thousand
10,000,000 = ten million	10,500,000 = ten million five hundred thousand
100,000,000 = one hundred million	150,000,000 = one hundred and fifty million
1,000,000,000 = one billion	1,500,000,000 = one billion five hundred million

The simplest way to figure out our numbers is to first determine the term for the left-most unit and then work right. Pay attention to the number of commas (groups of three numbers) to the right of the number in question.

In early 2010, the media reported the U.S. had spent a total of $963,423,129,921 to finance the wars in Iraq and Afghanistan. How would you pronounce this number?

"Nine hundred and sixty three *billion* (notice three commas to the right),
four hundred and twenty three *million* (two commas to the right),
one hundred and twenty nine *thousand* (one comma to the right),
nine *hundred* and twenty-one."

Whew! That's a lot of **dough**. That word rhymes with "row" and refers to money, not the stuff bread is made of. Note that "twenty-one" is hyphenated. We only do that with numbers twenty-one through ninety-nine. 105 is written as "one hundred and five" as shown above.

Foreigners must be *very* careful to pronounce their ending sounds, such as the ending N sound in fifteen, or the ending Y sound in fifty. If you don't say them clearly and with stress, they sound alike and your listener and you might be in for a big case of misunderstanding, as has happened to me.

Also, you might try to pronounce the individual numerals after saying an important number. For instance, if you use the number 150 in your sentence, first pronounce it as "one hundred and fifty" followed by "one, five, zero." We don't normally do this because we understand each other, but you might try it if you are struggling with your accent or if you are asked to repeat the number. Also, slow down your pronunciation and put emphasis on the consonants. Your listener will appreciate your extra effort. The best tour guides I've had around the world all use these tricks with numbers.

Other number pronunciations:

- *Zero* – On occasion, some people pronounce zero as the letter O ("oh"). This isn't correct and will be understood only when speaking an all-numeric number, such as a telephone number or a dollar amount.
- *Dates* – Unlike some countries, when we express dates we put the month first, as in "November 6, 2012" or 11/06/12. (Military people write or say it as 6 November 2012.) "**9/11**" (nine-eleven) defines the infamous date of the terrorist attack on the U.S. on September 11, 2001. "**24/7**" (twenty-four-seven) indicates something operates 24 hours a day, seven days a week, or "**24/7/365**" (twenty-four-seven-three-sixty-five) for every day of the year.
- *Decimal Point* – When there is a decimal point, we say **point**. For example, 97.5 would be pronounced "ninety-seven-point-five."
- *Money* – When talking about dollars and cents, $97.50 is pronounced as either "ninety-seven-fifty" or "ninety-seven dollars and fifty cents."
- *Million* – We sometimes use "million dollar" to describe something big or important, like "She has a million-dollar smile," or "Why Princess Di's car crashed is the million-dollar question."

Tip #13: *Alliteration Is Alluring To All* – Alliteration *[ah-lit-er-AY-shun]* occurs when the first sound of associated words repeats, as in the three "A" words in the heading of this section. It can be graceful, as when Shakespeare's Macbeth says, "So *foul* and *fair* a day I have not seen." Language scholars have long known that people are more likely to remember expressions that employ alliteration. Presidential candidate John Kerry claimed in a speech that the Bush administration's legacy would be "**d**eficits, **d**ebt, and **d**oubt." If you are delivering a speech or writing something and want to give your audience a powerful expression, consider alliteration.

To show how powerful alliteration can be, Spiro Agnew, President Nixon's vice president, delivered an address in 1971 in which he criticized those who were attacking the Nixon administration. If he had said, "America has more than its share of people who are critical about everything," his line would have been forgotten in minutes. Instead, he said, "America has more than its share of the *nattering* [chattering] *nabobs* [self-important people] of *negativism*." Four decades later he is still remembered for his famous line.

Tip #14: Metaphors Are The Colorful Paint Brushes Of Speech – Fourth century BC Greek philosopher Aristotle wrote, "The greatest thing by far is to be a master of metaphor. It is a sign of genius." Powerful speakers today still use metaphors to add luster and give depth to their thoughts. You can, too.

The term **metaphor** *[MET-uh-for]* in Greek means to "transfer." A metaphor is a figure of speech that is used to paint one concept with the attributes normally associated with another. A metaphor is distinguished from a **simile** *[SIM-uh-lee]*. Both compare two seemingly unrelated objects, but a simile makes the comparison more explicit, usually connecting the concepts with the words "like" or "as." "You are *like* sunshine" is a simile. On the other hand, the metaphor "You are the sunshine of my life" more gently equates someone's loved one with warm, bright sunshine.

Princess Di

The expression "Candle in the Wind," the name of the popular song Elton John sang at Princess Di's funeral in 1997, is a metaphor that equates life's fragility to the flame of a candle in the wind. The song's first line is metaphorical, too: "Goodbye England's rose."

Tip #15: Use Famous Sayings – Americans like to use popular sayings by famous people to make a point. You will make a nice impression if you use them occasionally and refer to the name of the person who made them famous. Here are some popular ones. (More are listed in the Index under "sayings/proverbs.")

- *Harry Truman* – This U.S. president (1945-1953) was known for saying "**The buck stops here**." Buck is slang for a dollar. When we "pass the buck," we shift responsibility to someone else. You could say, "As Truman said, the buck stops here," meaning that you accept final responsibility for something negative that happened or for a decision that must be made.

Truman

- *Bill Clinton* – This U.S. president (1993-2001) was known for saying "**I didn't inhale**" when asked if he had ever smoked marijuana. This term is used jokingly as a **tongue-in-cheek** (kidding) response when it is obvious you did something but you playfully want to deny it.

Clinton

- *Clint Eastwood* – This famous actor said, "**Go ahead, make my day**" in the movie *Sudden Impact*. He played a hardened **cop** (policeman) who was **fed up** (tired of) with crime and pointed his gun at a robber: He was sarcastically telling the robber to try to reach for his gun, in which case Eastwood would shoot him, thus making his day more eventful.

Eastwood

- *General MacArthur* – When he evacuated from the Philippines, our WWII hero told the people "**I will return**." He did return toward the end of the war to the island nation that he so loved. When you want to impress upon someone that you will return with something important, like a signed contract, you could say, "As MacArthur said, I will return." They will know you intend to accomplish what you set out to do and return with the results.

MacArthur

- *Richard Nixon* – This U.S. president (1969-1974) defended himself during the Watergate Affair (and later resigned) when he said "**I am not a crook.**" It was laughable because everyone knew he was being dishonest about his involvement. We use this line jokingly when we are accused of doing something that we obviously didn't do by saying "As Nixon said, I am not a crook."

Nixon

- *Franklin D. Roosevelt* – This U.S. president (1933-1945) is famous for saying "**The only thing we have to fear is fear itself**" during the hard times of the Great Depression and WWII. You might say, "As FDR said, we have nothing to fear but fear itself," when giving encouragement to others.

FDR

- *Bugs Bunny* – This loveable cartoon rabbit character is famous for saying "**What's up, Doc?**" which means, what is happening or what's going on?

Bugs Bunny

- *Arnold Schwarzenegger* – The actor had some choice movie lines that are remembered by Americans. In *Terminator* (1984), he said with his Austrian accent, "**I'll be back.**" You might hear an American mimic him when they have to leave a bad situation but will return someday to fix it. And in *Terminator 2* (1991), he said, "**Hasta la vista, Baby!**" just before he shoots his enemy. It is Spanish and English mixed (some call that Spanglish) and means "See you later, Baby." It is one way you can say goodbye to something or someone you never want to see again.

Schwarzenegger

Tip #16: Language Translator Machines – Some foreigners carry language translators. They can be helpful in your conversations, but asking a person to define or clarify a word instead of immediately using the translator is better. One of my friends always writes down the word and its meaning on paper she carries in her purse and has developed a wonderful vocabulary doing this. If you still have trouble with the word, then use the translator when the speaker has finished a sentence, but not in the middle of it. You might even say, as she does, "Excuse me while I look up this word."

I taught a class overseas and at first allowed my students to use their translators in the classroom during writing exercises. Beginning the third week, I did not allow them and was amazed at how much their writing improved. They began to think and write in English, instead of translating their thoughts from English to their native language and then back to English. Their confidence soared as did their English skills.

PRACTICAL ADVICE FOR ENGLISH LEARNERS

Here are a few more tips that TEFL teachers (Teaching English as a Foreign Language) tell their students to help them become better English speakers.

1. *Mistakes* – You will make mistakes, so be patient with yourself.

2. *English Clubs* – Join English clubs or conversation groups such as this one: www.learnenglish.de/Level1/TasteOf/tasteclubs.htm.

3. *Games* – Many game consoles today have English speaking karaoke games like SingStar on PlayStation (www.singstar.com/en_US/). SingStar is a competitive singing game that allows you to sing to your favorite music artists and their original videos. The game judges your performance and gives you a score at the end of the song.

4. *Rules* – Do not feel frustrated by the crazy rules of the English language. Most native English speakers cannot explain all the rules. Instead, try to immerse yourself in the new language and pick up the bits and pieces at stores, restaurants and other places where English is spoken. Programs like www.Neopets.com have fun, free games to practice your English.

5. *Vocabulary* – The better your vocabulary, the better your conversational English. Numerous websites are available that present you with a new word each day, such as www.wordsmith.org.

6. *Learning Programs* – Many English-learning programs are available online or from mail order such as Rosetta Stone (www.RosettaStone.com). Another one available from Amazon.com is *Improve Your English: English in Everyday Life (DVD w/ Book)* that lets you hear and see how English is actually spoken from real-life speakers (http://amzn.to/DailyEnglish). It also has a transcript and workbook designed to refine your listening and speaking skills.

7. *Thesaurus* – A **thesaurus** *[the-SAW-rus]* provides lists of words that have similar meanings. "Happy," for example, might have synonyms like "glad," "content," or "jovial." It can help you find the right words for every occasion. A dictionary is a valuable tool, but it won't do as much to help you learn a broad range of words that have similar meanings as a thesaurus will. Microsoft Word also has a built-in thesaurus that you can click on. (Amazon.com has one available in print at http://amzn.to/GreatThesaurus.)

8. *Children's Books* – Children's books provide an easy approach to learning English for both adults and children, especially the books of Dr. Seuss. Visit his website for fun and games at www.seussville.com/#/home. An excellent book for foreigners is *Dr. Seuss's ABC: An Amazing Alphabet Book!* that can be purchased from most booksellers including Amazon.com's website at http://amzn.to/SeussABCs.

9. *Literature* – Once you have mastered the basics of English, reading our literature will **broaden your horizons** (provide further insight) further. These recommended authors and books are discussed in Chapter K on literature.

- Start with the works of Ernest Hemingway, noted for his simple words and mastery of the English language. A favorite of many new English students is his *The Old Man and the Sea*. It can be purchased online at numerous book sellers, including Amazon.com at http://amzn.to/HemingOldMan in print or Kindle format.

- James Herriot's easy reading book collection known as *All Creatures Great and Small* portrays a mid-twentieth century veterinarian in the English countryside. It is available in print or audio from Amazon.com at http://amzn.to/CreaturesGreat.

- *Where the Red Fern Grows* is written in simple language and centers on a boy and his dog. It comes in print, audio, and Kindle format from Amazon.com at http://amzn.to/RedFern.

- *Travels with Charley* is a travelogue by John Steinbeck, an American master of 20th century literature who, like Hemingway, makes simple but powerful vocabulary choices. It is available from Amazon.com as print, audio, and Kindle at http://amzn.to/SteinbecksCharley.

- Carolyn Harper Lee's *To Kill a Mockingbird* is a classic that will give you a good introduction to great literature and enhance your English comprehension. Amazon.com offers it in print or audio format at http://amzn.to/KillMockingbird.

IMPRESSIVE WORDS

A Chinese Proverb says, "If you wish to know the mind of a man, listen to his words." Certain English words reflect an educated or cultural tone and allow you to express yourself more accurately than more commonly used words. They also help you understand more of what you hear. There are many books and websites you can use to expand your English vocabulary such as www.increasevocabulary.net or www.m-w.com. This Kindle book, *Build Your Vocabulary Skills*, will help expand your vocabulary using a mnemonic memory technique: http://amzn.to/VocabularyBuild.

Many of our high schools and colleges provide lists of advanced words that students are expected to know before graduating. Being familiar with them will aid foreign students taking tests to enter college in the U.S. This website lists words that are on the college SAT vocabulary tests: www.majortests.com/sat/wordlist.php.

To get you started, I am giving you a few words that educated Americans might use in place of more commonly used words. If you use them, it is important you pronounce them correctly with emphasis on the correct syllables. Look them up in a good dictionary for further clarification or in a thesaurus for similar words.

Ambivalent *[am-BIV-a-lent]* – Simultaneous opposing feelings; unable to decide between two choices. Instead of using "uncertain," you might use ambivalent in this sentence: "I was ambivalent about staying in the U.S. or going home to Japan."

Ameliorate *[ah-ME-leo-rate]* – Make or become better, improve. Instead of using "lessen," you could use ameliorate: "All my fears about learning verb conjugations were ameliorated when I got an A on the first test."

Arcane *[are-KANE]* – Mysterious, secret, unfathomable. Instead of using "hard to understand" you might use arcane: "At first, the process of learning English tenses was totally arcane to me. It had no logic. I couldn't remember all the crazy rules."

Arduous *[ARD-you-us]* – Hard, grueling, tiring. Instead of using "difficult" you might use arduous: "Memorizing ten new English words each day for one month was an arduous task."

Assuage *[ah-SWAYGE]* – Calm, sooth, appease. Instead of using "lessened" you might use assuage: "It was an *arduous* task, but her fear of skydiving was assuaged after she did it the first time."

Capricious *[kah-PRE-shus]* – Erratic, unpredictable, unreliable, fickle. Instead of using "wavering" you might use capricious: "He is too capricious for this job because it requires a lot of focus and dedication."

Circuitous *[sir-KEW-it-us]* – Indirect, roundabout, meandering. Instead of using "the long way" you might use circuitous: "Because he took a circuitous path to class, he was five minutes late."

Cogent *[KO-gent]* – Convincing, logical, compelling argument. Instead of using "good," you might use cogent. "I must admit my advisor made a cogent argument why I should study English at night school instead of watching TV."

Cognizant *[KOG-nih-zant]* – Awareness, perception of. Instead of using "knew" you might use cognizant: "I was cognizant of the risks of doing it by myself. Nonetheless, it was the *efficacious* [see below] thing to do considering the limited time we had to do it in."

Convoluted *[kon-vo-LOOT-ed]* – Complex, twisted, drawn-out. Instead of using "complicated" you might use convoluted: "Her convoluted explanation of English language verb tenses was confusing and hard to follow."

Copious *[KOPE-e-us]* – Abundant, plentiful, many. Instead of using "a lot" you might use copious: "Because I took copious notes in my English literature class, I got an A on the test."

Cursory *[KUR-sir-ee]* – Hasty, hurried, superficial, passing. Instead of using "quick" you might use cursory: "A cursory examination of 19th century American history reveals the importance of immigrants in the building of the early West."

Deleterious *[dell-eh-TER-ee-us]* – Harmful effect. Instead of using "bad" you might use deleterious: "The low grade he received on his mid-term American geography paper had a deleterious effect on his final class grade."

Ebullient *[e-BULL-yent]* – Overjoyed, exuberant, fun, jovial. Instead of using "happy" you might use ebullient: "Upon learning that she got the job promotion, she was ebullient and shouted for joy."

Efficacious *[eff-eh-KAY-shus]* – Producing the desired effect, effective, efficient. Instead of using "good" you might use efficacious: "The teacher's thought-out, efficacious approach to teaching English verb tenses made learning easy for all of us."

Empathy *[EM-pah-thee]* – Capacity to identify with another person, sympathy, compassion. Instead of using "understood" you might use empathy: "Because she was an immigrant American English teacher, she had empathy for those students who had trouble learning adverbs."

Emulate *[EM-you-late]* – Try to be like, imitate. Instead of using "copy" you might use emulate: "Young actors try to emulate his acting style because he is so famous."

Epiphany *[ee-PIFF-ah-nee]* – A sudden realization of the essence or meaning of something. Instead of using "vision" you might use epiphany: "Suddenly, I had an epiphany that I needed to study verb tenses in order to improve my English."

Epitomize *[ee-PIT-oh-mize]* – A perfect example, exemplify, symbolize. Instead of using "symbol of" you might use epitomize: "He epitomizes the typical immigrant American student who works hard to get good grades in college and then lands a good job."

Facetious *[fah-SEE-shus]* – Teasing, playful, tongue-in-cheek, not serious. Instead of using "kidding" you might use facetious: "I told my manager facetiously that I wanted a four month vacation. His playful response was, 'Make a choice: your job or your vacation.'"

Fallacious *[fah-LAY-shus]* – Faulty reasoning, mistaken belief, erroneous. Instead of using "false" you might use fallacious: "His argument that trade barriers benefit all countries is fallacious."

Gargantuan *[gar-GAN-choo-en]* – Gigantic, enormous, vast. Instead of using "huge" you might use gargantuan: "When I enrolled in the English vocabulary class, I knew I had a gargantuan task ahead of me."

Innocuous *[in-NAWK-you-us]* – Harmless, innoffensive. Instead of using "innocent" you might use innocuous to impart that it hurt no one: "Her comment was misunderstood by most of us, but I knew it was innocuous. She did not mean to be critical of us.

Mitigate *[MIT-ih-gate]* – Make less intense or severe, alleviate. Instead of using "lessen" you might use mitigate: "My fears were mitigated when the teacher told us that in the past all of her Arab American students had passed her speech class."

Penchant *[PEN-chent]* – Inclination toward doing. Instead of using "liking" you might use penchant: "She obviously has a penchant for putting people at ease in tense situations. She can *ameliorate* tense times so people can speak with candor."

Perfunctory *[purr-FUNK-toe-re]* – Superficial, done merely out of duty. Instead of using "routine" the word perfunctory might fit your need better: "The waiter gave me a perfunctory greeting. He was expressionless and didn't make eye contact."

Recapitulate *[ree-kah-PIT-you-late]* – To repeat in concise form, summarize. Instead of using "went through again" you might use recapitulate: "At the end of the two-hour class, the teacher recapitulated the five basic rules for speaking English well."

Reciprocate *[ree-SIP-roe-kate]* – Performed, experienced, or felt by both sides. Instead of using "payback" you might use reciprocate: "I loaned her my class notes; she reciprocated by letting me use her laptop for the day."

Sagacious *[seh-GAY-shus]* – Showing insight or good judgement. Instead of using "smart" you might use sagacious: "She made a sagacious decision to enroll in the English pronunciation class.

Salient *[SAY-lee-ent]* – Prominent, conspicuous. Instead of using "key" you might use salient: "The salient points of his argument were that we need to work together and understand each other's views."

Vehement *[VEE-eh-ment]* – Forceful or intense in expression, emotion, or conviction. Instead of using "strong" you might use vehement: "My English teacher was vehement when he told me for the fourth time that I must learn to use articles in my sentences!"

BRITISH ENGLISH vs. AMERICAN ENGLISH

The British colonization of America in the 17th century brought the English language to North America. The language has since evolved so we sound different and have different words and spellings. George Bernard Shaw, the famous early 20th century English playwright, said "England and America are two countries separated by the same language." This is an overstatement because, if you can communicate with Brits, you will be able to do so with us Yanks and vice versa. Don't worry if you use the "wrong" word; **it's no big deal** (unimportant).

In British English, collective nouns (*group, crowd,* etc.) can take either singular or plural verb forms, while our collective nouns are used in the singular verb form (*crowd is…*) for agreement.

In British English, the irregular form of a verb is commonly used, as in the words *learnt, spoilt,* and *spelt* while in American English we use *learned, spoiled, and spelled.*

546

And foreigners who have had more exposure to British or Europeans than to Americans use *whilst* and *favourite* while we use *while* and *favorite*. Again, no big deal.

Many of our spelling differences are in the suffixes of words that are otherwise ~~spelt~~ (sorry about that) spelled the same:

British	American	Example
-ise	-ize	minim*ise* vs. minim*ize*
-our	-or	behavi*our* vs. behav*ior*
-re	-er	cent*re* vs. cent*er*
-ce	-se	defen*ce* vs. defen*se*

Here are some of our word-meaning differences to chuckle at, just as we do.

BRITISH	AMERICAN	BRITISH	AMERICAN
bellpush	doorbell	gear box	transmission
bin liner	trash bag	grammar school	high school
blower	telephone	ground floor	first floor
bundle	package	hooter	horn
call box	telephone booth	lift	elevator
chemist shop	drug store	lorry	truck
chips	french fries*	mean	stingy
chit	memo	nappies	diapers
cinema	movies	notecase	wallet

You will find differences between the English spoken in other English speaking countries as well. I find people from Scotland, Ireland, and New Zealand more difficult to **tune in to** (understand) than our cousins in Jolly Old England.

═══════════════

---

*In case you're wondering, we don't capitalize french fries because it refers to the cut of the potato, not the country of origin. The same with brussels sprouts. However, like so many other variations in our crazy language, some will capitalize them and they will be correct, too. As I say, Americans like options and variety.

APPENDIX

APPENDIX *[ah-PEN-dix]:* supplementary material that is documentary or explanatory and included at the back of a book for added insight.

Appendix 1

Lincoln's Gettysburg Address

President Abraham Lincoln's Gettysburg Address is considered one of the most famous speeches in American history. He delivered it during the American Civil War at the dedication of the Soldiers' National Cemetery in Gettysburg, Pennsylvania, after the Union armies (Northerners) defeated those of the Confederacy (Southerners). The battle had the largest number of casualties in the four-year American Civil War. ("Four score and seven years ago" refers to the American Revolution of 1776.) This is the website for the national park: www.nps.gov/gett/index.htm.

Gettysburg, Pennsylvania

November 19, 1863

Four score and seven years ago our fathers brought forth upon this continent, a new nation, conceived in liberty, and dedicated to the proposition that all men are created equal.

Now we are engaged in a great civil war, testing whether that nation, or any nation so conceived and so dedicated, can long endure. We are met on a great battlefield of that war. We have come to dedicate a portion of that field, as a final resting place for those who here gave their lives that that nation might live. It is altogether fitting and proper that we should do this.

But, in a larger sense, we cannot dedicate—we cannot consecrate—we cannot hallow—this ground. The brave men, living and dead, who struggled here have consecrated it, far above our poor power to add or detract. The world will little note, nor long remember what we say here, but it can never forget what they did here. It is for us the living, rather, to be dedicated here to the unfinished work which they who fought here have thus far so nobly advanced. It is rather for us to be

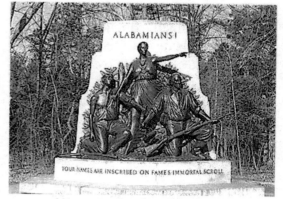

Monument at Gettysburg, Pennsylvania.

here dedicated to the great task remaining before us—that from these honored dead we take increased devotion to that cause for which they gave the last full measure of devotion—that we here highly resolve that these dead shall not have died in vain—that this nation, under God, shall have a new birth of freedom—and that government of the people, by the people, and for the people, shall not perish from the earth.

551

Appendix 2
Top 50 Liberal Arts Colleges in America

Published by US News & World Report for 2012 (state codes in parentheses)[*]

1. Williams College (MA)	25. Bryn Mawr College (PA)
2. Amherst College (MA)	27. Colorado College (CO)
3. Swarthmore College (PA)	27. University of Richmond (VA)
4. Pomona College (CA)	29. Mount Holyoke College (MA)
5. Middlebury College (VT)	29. College of the Holy Cross (MA)
6. Wellesley College (MA)	29. Scripps College (CA)
6. Bowdoin College (ME)	29. Bucknell University (PA)
6. Carleton College (MN)	33. Barnard College (NY)
9. Claremont McKenna College (CA)	33. Kenyon College (OH)
10. Haverford College (PA)	33. Sewanee-U. of the South (TN)
11. Davidson College (NC)	33. US Air Force Academy (CO)
12. Wesleyan University (CT)	37. Occidental College (CA)
12. Washington and Lee U. (VA)	37. Trinity College (CT)
14. Vassar College (NY)	37. Connecticut College (CT)
14. US Military Academy (NY)	40. Lafayette College (PA)
14. US Naval Academy (MD)	40. Union College (NY)
17. Hamilton College (NY)	42. Whitman College (WA)
18. Harvey Mudd College (CA)	42. Furman University (SC)
19. Smith College (MA)	42. Pitzer College (CA)
19. Grinnell College (IA)	42. Center College (KY)
21. Colgate University (NY)	42. Franklin & Marshall (PA)
21. Bates College (ME)	47. Dickinson College (PA)
21. Colby College (ME)	47. Gettysburg College (PA)
24. Oberlin College (OH)	49. Skidmore College (NY)
25. Macalester College (MN)	49. Denison College (OH)

[*]©US News & World Report, L.P. Data is gathered each year on up to 16 indicators of academic excellence from each college. Each factor is assigned a weight that reflects judgment about how much a measure matters. Finally, the schools in each category are ranked against their peers based on their composite weighted score. This magazine's website at www.usnews.com/education offers information about 1400 schools in America. It also provides information on tuition, acceptance rates, scholarships, and a host of other valuable data.

Appendix 3
Top 50 Universities in America
(Published by US News & World Report 2012)

1. Harvard University (MA)	25. University of Virginia *
1. Princeton University (NJ)	25. Wake Forest University (NC)
3. Yale University (CT)	28. Univ. of Michigan-Ann Arbor *
4. Columbia University (NY)	29. U. of North Carolina-Chapel Hill *
5. Stanford University (CA)	29. Tufts University (MA)
5. University of Pennsylvania	31. Boston College (MA)
5. Massachusetts Inst. of Technology	31. Brandeis University (MA)
5. California Institute of Technology	33. New York University (NY)
5. University of Chicago (IL)	33. College of William and Mary (VA) *
10. Duke University (NC)	35. University of Rochester (NY)
11. Dartmouth College (NH)	36. Georgia Institute of Technology *
12. Northwestern University (IL)	37. Univ. of California-San Diego *
13. Johns Hopkins University (MD)	38. Lehigh University (PA)
14. Washington U. in St. Louis (MO)	38. Case Western Reserve Univ. (OH)
15. Cornell University (NY)	38. University of Miami (FL)
15. Brown University (RI)	38. University of California-Davis *
17. Rice University (TX)	42. Univ. of California-Santa Barbara *
17. Vanderbilt University (TN)	42. University of Washington (WA)*
19. University of Notre Dame (IN)	42. Univ. of Wisconsin-Madison *
20. Emory University (GA)	45. University of Texas-Austin *
21. Univ. of California-Berkeley *	45. University of California-Irvine *
22. Georgetown University (DC)	45. Pennsylvania State U.-Univ. Park *
23. Carnegie Mellon University (PA)	45. U. of Illinois-Urbana-Champaign *
23. Univ. of Southern California	45. Yeshiva University (NY)
25. Univ. of California-Los Angeles *	50. George Washington (Wash. D.C.)

* Public School

Appendix 4
Colleges with Largest Percentage of International Students
(Published by US News & World Report 2012)

The policy of many universities is to strive for cultural diversity, which contributes to the betterment of education for all students. But some are better at it than others.

1. New School (NY) 25%
2. Illinois Institute of Technology (IL) 20%
3. New Jersey Institute of Technology (NJ) 19%
4. Lynn University (FL) 17%
5. University of Tulsa (OK) 16%
6. Carnegie Mellon University (PA) 16%
7. University at Buffalo—State University of New York (NY) 15%
8. Florida Institute of Technology (FL) 13%
9. California Institute of Technology (CA) 12%
10. Andrews University (MI) 12%
11. Brandeis University (MA) 12%
12. Polytechnic Institute of New York University (NY) 11%
13. Columbia University (NY) 11%
14. Purdue University—West Lafayette (IN) 11%
15. University of Pennsylvania (PA) 11%
16. University of San Francisco (CA) 11%
17. University of Southern California (CA) 11%
18. Northeastern University (MA) 11%
19. Princeton University (NJ) 11%
20. Emory University (GA) 10%
21. University of Illinois—Urbana-Champaign (IL) 10%
22. Binghamton University—State University of New York (NY) 10%
23. Harvard University (MA) 10%
24. Worcester Polytechnic Institute (MA) 10%
25. Yale University (CT) 10%

Appendix 5
Sample Income Tax Form 1040 – Page 1 of 2

Form **1040**	Department of the Treasury—Internal Revenue Service (99) **U.S. Individual Income Tax Return**	20**11**	OMB No. 1545-0074	IRS Use Only—Do not write or staple in this space.

For the year Jan. 1–Dec. 31, 2011, or other tax year beginning , 2011, ending , 20 | See separate instructions.

Your first name and initial	Last name	Your social security number
If a joint return, spouse's first name and initial	Last name	Spouse's social security number

Home address (number and street). If you have a P.O. box, see instructions. | Apt. no.

▲ Make sure the SSN(s) above and on line 6c are correct.

City, town or post office, state, and ZIP code. If you have a foreign address, also complete spaces below (see instructions).

Presidential Election Campaign
Check here if you, or your spouse if filing jointly, want $3 to go to this fund. Checking a box below will not change your tax or refund. ☐ You ☐ Spouse

Foreign country name	Foreign province/county	Foreign postal code

Filing Status

Check only one box.

1 ☐ Single
2 ☐ Married filing jointly (even if only one had income)
3 ☐ Married filing separately. Enter spouse's SSN above and full name here. ▶
4 ☐ Head of household (with qualifying person). (See instructions.) If the qualifying person is a child but not your dependent, enter this child's name here. ▶
5 ☐ Qualifying widow(er) with dependent child

Exemptions

| 6a ☐ Yourself. If someone can claim you as a dependent, do not check box 6a | | | | | Boxes checked on 6a and 6b |
| b ☐ Spouse | | | | | |

c Dependents:

(1) First name Last name	(2) Dependent's social security number	(3) Dependent's relationship to you	(4) ✓ if child under age 17 qualifying for child tax credit (see instructions)
			☐
			☐
			☐
			☐

If more than four dependents, see instructions and check here ▶ ☐

No. of children on 6c who:
• lived with you
• did not live with you due to divorce or separation (see instructions)

Dependents on 6c not entered above

d Total number of exemptions claimed

Add numbers on lines above ▶

Income

Attach Form(s) W-2 here. Also attach Forms W-2G and 1099-R if tax was withheld.

If you did not get a W-2, see instructions.

Enclose, but do not attach, any payment. Also, please use Form 1040-V.

7	Wages, salaries, tips, etc. Attach Form(s) W-2		7	
8a	Taxable interest. Attach Schedule B if required		8a	
b	Tax-exempt interest. Do not include on line 8a	8b		
9a	Ordinary dividends. Attach Schedule B if required		9a	
b	Qualified dividends	9b		
10	Taxable refunds, credits, or offsets of state and local income taxes		10	
11	Alimony received		11	
12	Business income or (loss). Attach Schedule C or C-EZ		12	
13	Capital gain or (loss). Attach Schedule D if required. If not required, check here ▶ ☐		13	
14	Other gains or (losses). Attach Form 4797		14	
15a	IRA distributions	15a	b Taxable amount	15b	
16a	Pensions and annuities	16a	b Taxable amount	16b	
17	Rental real estate, royalties, partnerships, S corporations, trusts, etc. Attach Schedule E		17	
18	Farm income or (loss). Attach Schedule F		18	
19	Unemployment compensation		19	
20a	Social security benefits	20a	b Taxable amount	20b	
21	Other income. List type and amount		21	
22	Combine the amounts in the far right column for lines 7 through 21. This is your total income ▶		22	

Adjusted Gross Income

23	Educator expenses	23		
24	Certain business expenses of reservists, performing artists, and fee-basis government officials. Attach Form 2106 or 2106-EZ	24		
25	Health savings account deduction. Attach Form 8889	25		
26	Moving expenses. Attach Form 3903	26		
27	Deductible part of self-employment tax. Attach Schedule SE	27		
28	Self-employed SEP, SIMPLE, and qualified plans	28		
29	Self-employed health insurance deduction	29		
30	Penalty on early withdrawal of savings	30		
31a	Alimony paid b Recipient's SSN ▶	31a		
32	IRA deduction	32		
33	Student loan interest deduction	33		
34	Tuition and fees. Attach Form 8917	34		
35	Domestic production activities deduction. Attach Form 8903	35		
36	Add lines 23 through 35		36	
37	Subtract line 36 from line 22. This is your adjusted gross income ▶		37	

For Disclosure, Privacy Act, and Paperwork Reduction Act Notice, see separate instructions. | Cat. No. 11320B | Form **1040** (2011)

Appendix 5
Sample Income Tax Form 1040 — Page 2 of 2

Page **2**

Form 1040 (2011)

Tax and Credits	38	Amount from line 37 (adjusted gross income)			38	
	39a	Check { You were born before January 2, 1947, ☐ Blind. } Total boxes			
		if: { ☐ Spouse was born before January 2, 1947, ☐ Blind. } checked ▶ 39a			
Standard Deduction for —	b	If your spouse itemizes on a separate return or you were a dual-status alien, check here ▶ 39b ☐			
• People who check any box on line 39a or 39b or who can be claimed as a dependent, see instructions.	40	**Itemized deductions** (from Schedule A) **or your standard deduction** (see left margin)			40	
	41	Subtract line 40 from line 38			41	
	42	**Exemptions.** Multiply $3,700 by the number on line 6d			42	
	43	**Taxable income.** Subtract line 42 from line 41. If line 42 is more than line 41, enter -0-			43	
	44	Tax (see instructions). Check if any from: a ☐ Form(s) 8814 b ☐ Form 4972 c ☐ 962 election			44	
	45	**Alternative minimum tax** (see instructions). Attach Form 6251			45	
• All others: Single or Married filing separately, $5,800	46	Add lines 44 and 45 . . . . ▶			46	
	47	Foreign tax credit. Attach Form 1116 if required . . .	47		
	48	Credit for child and dependent care expenses. Attach Form 2441	48		
Married filing jointly or Qualifying widow(er), $11,600	49	Education credits from Form 8863, line 23	49		
	50	Retirement savings contributions credit. Attach Form 8880	50		
	51	Child tax credit (see instructions)	51		
Head of household, $8,500	52	Residential energy credits. Attach Form 5695 . . .	52		
	53	Other credits from Form: a ☐ 3800 b ☐ 8801 c ☐	53		
	54	Add lines 47 through 53. These are your **total credits**			54	
	55	Subtract line 54 from line 46. If line 54 is more than line 46, enter -0- . . . ▶			55	
Other Taxes	56	Self-employment tax. Attach Schedule SE			56	
	57	Unreported social security and Medicare tax from Form: a ☐ 4137 b ☐ 8919			57	
	58	Additional tax on IRAs, other qualified retirement plans, etc. Attach Form 5329 if required			58	
	59a	Household employment taxes from Schedule H			59a	
	b	First-time homebuyer credit repayment. Attach Form 5405 if required			59b	
	60	Other taxes. Enter code(s) from instructions _____			60	
	61	Add lines 55 through 60. This is your **total tax** . . . . ▶			61	
Payments	62	Federal income tax withheld from Forms W-2 and 1099	62		
	63	2011 estimated tax payments and amount applied from 2010 return	63		
If you have a qualifying child, attach Schedule EIC.	64a	**Earned income credit (EIC)**	64a		
	b	Nontaxable combat pay election	64b			
	65	Additional child tax credit. Attach Form 8812 . . .	65		
	66	American opportunity credit from Form 8863, line 14 . .	66		
	67	First-time homebuyer credit from Form 5405, line 10 . .	67		
	68	Amount paid with request for extension to file . . .	68		
	69	Excess social security and tier 1 RRTA tax withheld . .	69		
	70	Credit for federal tax on fuels. Attach Form 4136 . .	70		
	71	Credits from Form: a ☐ 2439 b ☐ 8839 c ☐ 8801 d ☐ 8885	71		
	72	Add lines 62, 63, 64a, and 65 through 71. These are your **total payments** . . . . . ▶			72	
Refund	73	If line 72 is more than line 61, subtract line 61 from line 72. This is the amount you **overpaid**			73	
	74a	Amount of line 73 you want **refunded to you.** If Form 8888 is attached, check here . ▶ ☐			74a	
Direct deposit? ▶ See instructions.	b	Routing number		▶ c Type: ☐ Checking ☐ Savings	
	d	Account number			
	75	Amount of line 73 you want applied to your 2012 estimated tax ▶	75		
Amount You Owe	76	**Amount you owe.** Subtract line 72 from line 61. For details on how to pay, see instructions ▶			76	
	77	Estimated tax penalty (see instructions)	77		

Third Party Designee

Do you want to allow another person to discuss this return with the IRS (see instructions)? ☐ **Yes. Complete below.** ☐ **No**

Designee's name ▶	Phone no. ▶	Personal identification number (PIN) ▶	

Sign Here

Under penalties of perjury, I declare that I have examined this return and accompanying schedules and statements, and to the best of my knowledge and belief, they are true, correct, and complete. Declaration of preparer (other than taxpayer) is based on all information of which preparer has any knowledge.

Joint return? See instructions. Keep a copy for your records.

Your signature	Date	Your occupation	Daytime phone number
Spouse's signature. If a joint return, **both** must sign.	Date	Spouse's occupation	If the IRS sent you an Identity Protection PIN, enter it here (see inst.)

Paid Preparer Use Only

Print/Type preparer's name	Preparer's signature	Date	Check ☐ if self-employed	PTIN
Firm's name ▶			Firm's EIN ▶	
Firm's address ▶			Phone no.	

Form **1040** (2011)

Appendix 6
The Pulitzer Prize for Literature

The Pulitzer Prize for literature is an annual award given to fiction in book form by an American author, preferably dealing with American life. Joseph Pulitzer, publisher of the *New York Globe* newspaper, established the Pulitzer Prize through an endowment to Columbia University in 1917. The winners comprise a fine reading list for foreigners because the plots or themes of these books do not necessarily paint a positive picture of American life, though they often do of American character.

Here is a selection of popular authors and books that Americans might recognize if you use their names. Many have been made into movies as well.

1937: Margaret Mitchell – *Gone With the Wind*
1939: Marjorie Kinnan Rawlings – *The Yearling*
1940: John Steinbeck – *The Grapes of Wrath*
1943: Upton Sinclair – *Dragon's Teeth*
1945: John Hersey – A *Bell for Adano*
1947: Robert Penn Warren – *All the King's Men*
1948: James A. Michener – *Tales of the South Pacific*
1952: Herman Wouk – *The Caine Mutiny*
1953: Ernest Hemingway – *The Old Man and the Sea*
1955: William Faulkner – *A Fable*
1956: Mackinlay Kantor – *Andersonville*
1960: Allen Drury – *Advise and Consent*
1961: Harper Lee – *To Kill a Mockingbird*
1963: William Faulkner – *The Reivers*
1968: William Styron – *The Confessions of Nat Turner*
1976: Saul Bellow – *Humboldt's Gift*
1979: John Cheever – *The Stories of John Cheever*
1980: Norman Mailer – *The Executioner's Song*
1982: John Updike – *Rabbit is Rich*
1984: William Kennedy – *Ironweed*
1988: Toni Morrison – *Beloved*
1998: Philip Roth – *American Pastoral*
1999: Michael Cunningham – *The Hours*
2001: Michael Chabon – *The Amazing Adventures of Kavalier & Clay*
2002: Richard Russo – *Empire Falls*
2003: Jeffrey Eugenides – *Middlesex*
2005: Marilynne Robinson – *Gilead*
2006: Geraldine Brooks – *March*
2007: Cormac McCarthy – *The Road* (Extremely violent.)
2008: Junot Díaz – *The Brief Wondrous Life of Oscar Wao*
2009: Elizabeth Strout – *Olive Kitteridge*
2010: Paul Harding – *Tinkers*
2011: Jennifer Egan – *A Visit from the Goon Squad*

Pulitzer Prize for literature medallion.

Appendix 7
Academy Awards – Best Picture

These are the winners of the best film category since the award was first bestowed in 1927. Some were foreign made. For information on a film, to go this website and enter the film's name: www.imdb.com.

1927-28: Wings	1970: Patton
1928-29: Broadway Melody	1971: The French Connection
1929-30: All Quiet On the Western Front	1972: The Godfather
1930-31: Cimarron	1973: The Sting
1931-32: Grand Hotel	1974: The Godfather II
1932-33: Cavalcade	1975: One Flew Over the Cuckoo's Nest
1934: It Happened One Night	1976: Rocky
1935: Mutiny On the Bounty	1977: Annie Hall
1936: The Great Ziegfeld	1978: The Deer Hunter
1937: The Life Of Emile Zola	1979: Kramer vs. Kramer
1938: You Can't Take It With You	1980: Ordinary People
1939: Gone With the Wind	1981: Chariots of Fire
1940: Rebecca	1982: Gandhi
1941: How Green Was My Valley	1983: Terms of Endearment
1942: Mrs. Miniver	1984: Amadeus
1943: Casablanca	1985: Out of Africa
1944: Going My Way	1986: Platoon
1945: The Lost Weekend	1987: The Last Emperor
1946: The Best Years Of Our Lives	1988: Rain Man
1947: Gentlemen's Agreement	1989: Driving Miss Daisy
1948: Hamlet	1990: Dances With Wolves
1949: All The Kings Men	1991: Silence of the Lambs
1950: All About Eve	1992: Unforgiven
1951: An American In Paris	1993: Schindler's List
1952: The Greatest Show On Earth	1994: Forest Gump
1953: From Here to Eternity	1995: Braveheart
1954: On The Waterfront	1996: The English Patient
1955: Marty	1997: Titanic
1956: Around the World In 80 Days	1998: Shakespeare In Love
1957: The Bridge On the River Kwai	1999: American Beauty
1958: Gigi	2000: Gladiator
1959: Ben Hur	2001: A Beautiful Mind
1960: The Apartment	2002: Chicago
1961: West Side Story	2003: Lord of The Rings, Return of King
1962: Lawrence of Arabia	2004: Million Dollar Baby
1963: Tom Jones	2005: Brokeback Mountain
1964: My Fair Lady	2006: Babel
1965: The Sound of Music	2007: No Country for Old Men
1966: A Man for All Seasons	2008: Slumdog Millionaire
1967: In the Heat of the Night	2009: The Hurt Locker
1968: Oliver!	2010: The King's Speech
1969: Midnight Cowboy	2011: The Artist

Oscar statuette.

Appendix 8
Yes, Virginia, There Is a Santa Claus

In 1897, eight-year old Virginia sent a letter to the *New York Sun* newspaper asking if there was a real Santa Claus. The response is history's most reprinted newspaper editorial, appearing in part or whole in dozens of languages in books, movies, and other editorials, and on posters and stamps. This is a copy of the *Sun's* editorial.

Is There a Santa Claus?

We take pleasure in answering at once and thus prominently the communication below, expressing at the same time our great gratification that its faithful author is numbered among the friends of THE SUN:

"DEAR EDITOR: I am 8 years old.

"Some of my little friends say there is no Santa Claus.

"Papa says 'If you see it in THE SUN it's so.'

"Please tell me the truth; is there a Santa Claus?

"VIRGINIA O'HANLON.

"115 WEST NINETY-FIFTH STREET."

VIRGINIA, your little friends are wrong. They have been affected by the skepticism of a skeptical age. They do not believe except they see. They think that nothing can be which is not comprehensible by their little minds. All minds, VIRGINIA, whether they be men's or children's, are little. In this great universe of ours man is a mere insect, an ant, in his intellect, as compared with the boundless world about him, as measured by the intelligence capable of grasping the whole of truth and knowledge.

Yes, VIRGINIA, there is a Santa Claus. He exists as certainly as love and generosity and devotion exist, and you know that they abound and give to your life its highest beauty and joy. Alas! how dreary would be the world if there were no Santa Claus. It would be as dreary as if there were no VIRGINIAS. There would be no childlike faith then, no poetry, no romance to make tolerable this existence. We should have no enjoyment, except in sense and sight. The eternal light with which childhood fills the world would be extinguished.

The Sun.

TUESDAY, SEPTEMBER 21, 1897.

Not believe in Santa Claus! You might as well not believe in fairies! You might get your papa to hire men to watch in all the chimneys on Christmas Eve to catch Santa Claus, but even if they did not see Santa Claus coming down, what would that prove? Nobody sees Santa Claus, but that is no sign that there is no Santa Claus. The most real things in the world are those that neither children nor men can see. Did you ever see fairies dancing on the lawn? Of course not, but that's no proof that they are not there. Nobody can conceive or imagine all the wonders there are unseen and unseeable in the world.

You may tear apart the baby's rattle and see what makes the noise inside, but there is a veil covering the unseen world which not the strongest man, nor even the united strength of all the strongest men that ever lived, could tear apart. Only faith, fancy, poetry, love, romance, can push aside that curtain and view and picture the supernal beauty and glory beyond. Is it all real? Ah, VIRGINIA, in all this world there is nothing else real and abiding.

No Santa Claus! Thank GOD! he lives, and he lives forever. A thousand years from now, VIRGINIA, nay, ten times ten thousand years from now, he will continue to make glad the heart of childhood.

Hint: The "Yes, Virginia, there is a Santa Claus" phrase is sometimes used ironically to indicate the impossible will not happen when someone is being overly positive. If, for example, you say teasingly to your boss, "May I have a raise and an extra two weeks' vacation?" your boss might smile and say, "Yes, Virginia, there is a Santa Claus." He might even say playfully, "Sure, is there anything else you would like?" On the other hand, it is also used to affirm that miracles can happen. One discerns the difference only by the context and the tone of voice used when saying it.

Appendix 9
The 50 U.S. States

Americans are very state oriented. So it is to the advantage of foreigners to refer to relevant facts, names, and places in the states of their American counterpart to enrich their discussions. Refer to each state's website for up up-to-date information by typing the state's official abbreviation (postal code) after "www.state." and before ".us" as in this sample address for the state of Alabama: www.state.al.us. These are our state codes.

AK – Alaska	IL – Illinois	NC – North Carolina	RI – Rhode Island
AL – Alabama	IN – Indiana	ND – North Dakota.	SC – South Carolina
AR – Arkansas.	KS – Kansas	NE – Nebraska	SD – South Dakota
AZ – Arizona	KY – Kentucky	NH – New Hampshire.	TN – Tennessee
CA – California	LA – Louisiana	NJ – New Jersey	TX – Texas
CO – Colorado	MA – Massachusetts	NM – New Mexico.	UT – Utah
CT – Connecticut	ME – Maine	NV – Nevada	VT – Vermont
DC – Dist. of Col.	MD – Maryland	NY – New York	VA – Virginia
DE – Delaware	MI – Michigan.	OH – Ohio	WA – Washington
FL – Florida	MN – Minnesota	OK – Oklahoma	WI – Wisconsin
GA – Georgia	MO – Missouri	OR – Oregon	WV – West Virginia
HI – Hawaii	MS – Mississippi	PA – Pennsylvania	WY – Wyoming
ID – Idaho	MT – Montana		

✓ For additional general information on states: www.netstate.com.
✓ For information on each state's senators: www.senate.gov.
✓ For a wealth of information on each state: www.infoplease.com/states.

U.S. states and their capital city locations.   (Courtesy of www.worldatlas.com)

Appendix 10
U.S. History Government Quiz

How well do you think you know America? I am surprised at how much foreigners who have never lived or visited here know about the U.S., and by my students who like to be tested on their general knowledge of America.

So I give them the test below that the government uses to test applicants for U.S. citizenship. The two main subjects tested on the naturalization test are English and civics. Applicants are expected to demonstrate strong skills in basic English communication, such as reading, writing, and speaking. In addition, an understanding of  fundamental rights and freedoms that characterize the American culture is also tested. Upon passing the naturalization test and taking a naturalization oath, applicants are sworn in as U.S. citizens.

The applicant is asked up to 10 of the 100 questions about the U.S. The interviewer reads the questions in English and the applicant must answer in English. In order to pass, at least six of the 10 questions asked must be answered correctly.

This government website offers more information on the testing process and how one can achieve citizenship: www.uscis.gov. Another website offers a free test that will prepare you for your interview with the INS agent at your naturalization hearing: www.immigrationquiz.com. With these tests you will be better prepared to pass your citizenship interview. Or, in the case of others, just to expand their knowledge of the U.S.

Most high school students in the U.S. should be able to answer the questions. You should be able, too, after reading this book that is current as of 2012. If you do, you will have a good overall understanding of the U.S.

1. What are the colors of the American flag?
  A - Red, white, and blue
2. How many stars are there in the American flag?
  A - Fifty (50)
3. What color are the stars on our flag?
  A - White
4. What do the stars on our flag mean?
  A - One for each state in the Union (United States)
5. How many stripes are there in the flag?
  A - Thirteen (13)
6. What color are the stripes?
  A - Red and white
7. What do the stripes on the flag mean?
  A - They represent the original thirteen (13) states
8. How many states are there in the Union (United States)?
  A - Fifty (50)

9. What is the fourth of July called?
   A - Independence Day
10. What day do we celebrate Independence Day?
   A - The Fourth of July
11. Independence from whom?
   A - England
12. Who were we at war with during the Revolutionary War?
   A - England
13. Who was the first president of the United States?
   A - George Washington
14. Who is the president of the United States today?
   A - Barack Obama
15. Who is the Vice-President of the United States today?
   A - Joseph Biden
16. Who elects the President of the United States?
   A - The Electoral College (for explanation see www.archives.gov/federal-register/electoral-college/about.html)
17. Who becomes president of the United States if the president should die?
   A - Vice-president
18. For how long do we elect the president?
   A - Four (4) years
19. What is the Constitution?
   A - The supreme law of the land
20. Can the Constitution be changed?
   A - Yes
21. What do we call a change to the Constitution?
   A - An amendment
22. How many changes or amendments are there to the Constitution?
   A - Twenty-seven (27)
23. How many branches are there in our federal government?
   A - Three (3)
24. What are the three branches of our government?
   A - Legislative, executive, and judicial
25. What is the legislative branch of our government?
   A - Congress
26. Who makes the laws of the United States?
   A - Congress
27. What is the composition of the Congress?
   A - The Senate and the House of Representatives
28. What are the duties of Congress?
   A - To make laws
29. Who elects the members of Congress?
   A - The people
30. How many senators are there in Congress?
   A - One-hundred (100) – 2 per state.
31. Can you name the two senators from your state?
   A - (fill in) _____

32. For how long do we elect each senator?
    A - Six (6) years
33. How many representatives are there in the House of Representatives?
    A - For hundred and thirty- five (435)
34. For how long do we elect the representatives?
    A - Two (2) years
35. Who comprises the executive branch of our government?
    A - The president, the cabinet, and departments under the cabinet members
36. What is the judicial branch of our government?
    A - The Supreme Court
37. What are duties of the Supreme Court?
    A - To interpret laws
38. What is the supreme law of the United States?
    A - The Constitution
39. What is the Bill of Rights?
    A - The first ten amendments to the Constitution
40. What is the capital city of your state?
    A - (fill in) _____   (see Appendix 9)
41. Who is the current governor of your state?
    A - (fill in) _____   (see Appendix 9)
42. Who becomes president of the U.S. if the president and the vice-president should die?
    A - Speaker of the House of Representatives
43. Who is the Chief Justice of the Supreme Court?
    A - John Roberts, Jr. (for information on the Supreme Court go to
        www.supremecourt.gov/)
44. Can you name the thirteen original states?
    A - Connecticut, Delaware, Georgia, Maryland, Massachusetts, New Hampshire, New
        Jersey, New York, North Carolina, Pennsylvania, Rhode Island, South Carolina,
        and Virginia.
45. Who said, "Give me liberty or give me death"?
    A - Patrick Henry
46. Which countries were our principal allies (friends) during World War II?
    A - United Kingdom (Great Britain), Canada, Australia, New Zealand, France,
        Russia (U.S.S.R.), and China.
47. What is our 49th state?
    A - Alaska
48. How many terms can a president serve?
    A - Two (2)
49. Who was Martin Luther King, Jr.?
    A - A civil rights leader
50. Who is the mayor of your local government?
    A - (fill in)_____.
51. According to the Constitution, a person must meet certain requirements in order to be eligible
    to become president. Name one of these requirements.
    A - Must be a natural born citizen of the United States; must be at least 35 years old by
        the time he/she will serve, must have lived in the United States for at least 14 years.

52. Why are there exactly 100 senators in the Senate?
    A - Two (2) from each of the 50 states
53. Who selects the Supreme Court justices?
    A - They are appointed by the president and confirmed by Congress
54. How many Supreme Court justices are there?
    A - Nine (9)
55. Why did the Pilgrims primarily come to America?
    A - For religious freedom
56. What is the head executive of a state government called?
    A - Governor
57. What is the head executive of a city government called?
    A - Mayor
58. What holiday was celebrated for the first time by the American colonists?
    A - Thanksgiving
59. Who was the main writer of the Declaration of Independence?
    A - Thomas Jefferson
60. When was the Declaration of Independence adopted?
    A - July 4, 1776
61. What is the fundamental belief of the Declaration of Independence?
    A - That all men are created equal
62. What is the national anthem (song) of the United States?
    A - The Star-Spangled Banner (see americanhistory.si.edu/starspangledbanner/)
63. Who wrote the Star-Spangled Banner?
    A - Francis Scott Key
64. Where does our freedom of speech come from?
    A - The Bill of Rights
65. What is the minimum voting age in the United States?
    A - Eighteen (18)
66. Who signs bills into laws?
    A - The president
67. What is the highest court in the United States?
    A - The Supreme Court
68. Who was the president during the Civil War?
    A - Abraham Lincoln
69. What did the Emancipation Proclamation do?
    A - Freed the slaves
70. What special group advises the president?
    A - The cabinet
71. Which president is called the "Father of our country?"
    A - George Washington
72. What is the 50th state of the Union (United States)?
    A - Hawaii
73. Who helped the Pilgrims in America?
    A - The American Indians (Native Americans)
74. What is the name of the ship that brought the first Pilgrims to America?
    A - The Mayflower

75. What were the 13 original states of the U.S. called because of British control?

    A - Colonies

76. Name 3 rights or freedoms guaranteed by the Bill of Rights.

    A - 1. The right of freedom of speech, press, religion, peaceable assembly.

        2. The right to bear arms (the right to have weapons or own a gun, though subject to certain regulations).

        3. The government may not quarter or house soldiers in peoples' homes during peacetime without peoples' consent.

        4. The government may not search or take a person's property without a warrant.

        5. A person may not be tried twice for the same crime and does not have to bear witness against himself.

        6. A person charged with a crime still has some rights, such as the right to a trial and to have a lawyer.

        7. The right to trial by jury in most cases.

        8. Protects people against excessive or unreasonable fines or cruel and unusual punishment.

        9. The people have rights other than those mentioned in the Constitution.

        10. Any power not given to the federal government by the Constitution is a power of either the state or the people.

77. Who has the power to declare war?

    A - The Congress

78. Name one amendment that guarantees or addresses voting rights.

    A - 15th, 19th, 24th, 26th (see www.usconstitution.net/const.html)

79. Which president freed the slaves?

    A - Abraham Lincoln

80. In what year was the Constitution written?

    A - 1787

81. What are the first amendments to the Constitution called?

    A - The Bill of Rights

82. Name one purpose of the United Nations.

    A - For countries to discuss and try to resolve world problems; to provide economic aid to many countries

83. Where does Congress meet?

    A - In the Capitol building in Washington, D.C.

84. Whose rights are guaranteed by the Constitution and the Bill of Rights?

    A - Everyone's (citizens and non-citizens living in the U.S.)

85. What is the introduction to the Constitution called?

    A - The Preamble

86. Name one benefit of being a citizen of the United of States.

    A - Obtaining a federal government job, traveling with a U.S. passport, petitioning for close relatives to come to the U.S. to live

87. What is the most important right granted to U.S. citizens?

    A - The right to vote

88. What is the United States Capitol building?

    A - The place where Congress meets

89. What is the White House?

    A - The president's official home and office

90. Where is the White House located?
   A - Washington, D.C. (1600 Pennsylvania Avenue, N.W.)
91. What is the name of the president's official home?
   A - The White House
92. Name one right guaranteed by the first amendment.
   A - Freedom of: speech, press, religion, peaceable assembly, and requesting a change of government
93. Who is the Commander in Chief of the U.S. military?
   A - The president
94. Which president was the first Commander in Chief of the U.S. military?
   A - George Washington
95. In what month do we vote for the president?
   A - November
96. In what month is the new president inaugurated (sworn in and takes office)?
   A - January
97. How many times may a senator be reelected?
   A - There is no limit
98. How many times may a congressman or woman be reelected?
   A - There is no limit
99. What are the two major political parties in the U.S. today?
   A - Democratic and Republican
100. How many states are in the United States?
   A - 50

INDEX

B

C

F

G

Index

Hurricane Katrina, 333, 399
hygiene, 180

I

IBM, 27, 373, 380, 414
ice breakers (conversation), 131
Iceland, 22
idioms, xiv, 176, 178, 528, *See* slang/idioms
illegal search, 25
illicit drugs, 97
imaginary circle, 126, 140, 147, 268, 531
immigrants, 5, 9, 15, 16, 17, 19, 53, 55, 65, 80, 125, 312
    artists, 231
    assimilation, 30
    children, 27
    illegal, 9, 24, 25, 68, 81, 86, 343, 349
    media, 291
immigration, 1, 80, 81, 349
Immigration and Naturalization Service (INS), 92
imports, 378
income, 27, 338
independence, 9, 36, 37, 45, 65, 66, 71, 123, 142, 181, 308, 339, 431, 443
Independence Day, 308, 562
India, 22, 36, 78, 127, 183, 197, 274
    business ethics, 383
    culture, 212, 295
    economy, 20, 375, 376, 406
    government, 34
    holidays, 308
    labor, 400
    law, 86
    people. *See* Asian Indians
    school, 164
    standard of living, 19
    students in U.S., 170, 359
    teachers, 157
    viewed by Americans, 343, 354
    workforce, 377
Indianapolis 500, 307
Indians (American). *See* Native Americans
Indians (Asia). *See* Asian Indians
indirectness, 427
individual freedoms, 65, 344, 354
Individual Retirement Account (IRA), 408
individual rights, 86, 121, 181, 288
individualism, 8, 9, 109, 121, 123, 125, 200, 223, 282, 306
Indonesia, 32, 274, 344, 383, 427
industries, 33, 332
inflation, 374
informality, 175, 180
infrastructure, 14
initialism (abbreviation), 526
innovators, famous, 413
insider trading, 97
institutions, 155, 341
insurance, 143
intellectual property, 78, 373, 383, 384, 413

Intermountain West, 54
International Herald Tribune, 293
international issues, 343, 349
International Monetary Fund (IMF), 328, 376
international relations, 341
International Space Station, 347
international trade, 342, 378, 386
Internet, 166, 172, 178, 291, 298, 301, 302, 330, 331, 437, 445
internment camps, 24, 82, 233
interstate highways, 328
introductions, 127
investments, 402
invitations, 133
IRA (Individual Retirement Account), 408
Iran, 88, 183, 295, 349, 415
    viewed by Americans, 343
Iraq, 88, 360
    viewed by Americans, 349
Iraq War, 2, 40, 79, 288, 310, 351, 538
Ireland, 344, 376
Irish, 28, 55, 129, 208, 220, 253, 320, 412
    heritage in U.S., 16, 247
    immigrants, 25
IRS (Internal Revenue Service), 459, 526
Islam, 5, 100, 101, 106, 107, 318, 359, 361
isolationism, 310, 311
Israel, 106, 301, 344
    viewed by Americans, 343
Istanbul, Turkey, 87, 144
Italians, 29, 146, 221, 309, 423
    business, 286, 415
    heritage in U.S., 16
    immigrants, 25
    religion, 100
    speech, 508, 512, 532
    sports, 248, 253
    values, 344
    view of Americans, 355
Italy, 18, 205, 270, 301, 446
    business, 375, 390
    economy, 376
    holidays, 318
    language, 493
    legal, 86
    schools Americans attend, 170
    unions, 400

J

Jackson, Michael (singer), 97
Jamestown, Virginia, 64

Japan, 17, 21, 56, 60, 82, 135, 237, 310, 323, 330, 337, 353, 375
    business, 6, 375, 380, 399, 417, 420, 423, 439
    business ethics, 383
    cars, 412

N

"Cries she with silent lips, 'Give me your tired, your poor your huddled masses yearning to breathe free, the wretched refuse of your teeming shore. Send these, the homeless, tempest-tost to me, I lift my lamp beside the golden door!'"

Individual Books in *A to Z* Series

Individual books are also available for the four major sections in this all-in-one *A to Z* book.

Book 1 – AMERICA'S HERITAGE

A – WE THE PEOPLE
B – GOVERNMENT
C – GEOGRAPHY
D – HISTORY
E – LAW
F – RELIGION
G – MEASUREMENTS

Book 2 – AMERICA'S CULTURE

H – CUSTOMS AND ETIQUETTE
I – EDUCATION
J – RELATIONSHIPS
K – LITERATURE
L – FILM
M – ART
N – SPORTS
O – FOOD AND DINING
P – DRESS AND APPEARANCE
Q – MEDIA
R – HOLIDAYS AND TRADITIONS
S – WHAT AMERICANS THINK
T – WHAT FOREIGNERS THINK ABOUT AMERICA

Book 3 – AMERICA'S BUSINESS

U – BUSINESS AND FINANCE
V – BUSINESS CUSTOMS
W – OWNING A BUSINESS
X – GETTING A JOB

Book 4 – AMERICA'S LANGUAGE

Y – LET'S USE BETTER ENGLISH GRAMMAR
Z – LET'S SPEAK BETTER ENGLISH

CPSIA information can be obtained at www.ICGtesting.com
Printed in the USA
LVOW05s1404110614

389599LV00006B/82/P